THE
SUMMA
DOMESTICA

Order and Wonder in Family Life

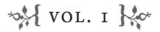 VOL. I

Home Culture

LEILA M. LAWLER

Illustrations by Deirdre M. Folley

SOPHIA INSTITUTE PRESS
Manchester, New Hampshire

Sophia Institute Press
Box 5284, Manchester, NH 03108
1-800-888-9344

www.SophiaInstitute.com

Sophia Institute Press® is a registered trademark of Sophia Institute.

paperback ISBN 978-1-64413-392-7

ebook ISBN 978-1-64413-393-4

Library of Congress Control Number: 2021940523

First printing

THE SUMMA DOMESTICA

**To Elizabeth Day Edwards and Salah Eldin Elmaghraby,
my mother and my father.**

*Death has now mended the separation
that took its path through my heart.
My memories begin in you; may your memory be eternal.
Reader, in your charity, pray for them and for me.*

For this cause I bow my knees unto the Father of our Lord Jesus Christ, of whom the whole family in heaven and earth is named, that he would grant you, according to the riches of his glory, to be strengthened with might by his Spirit in the inner man; that Christ may dwell in your hearts by faith; that ye, being rooted and grounded in love, may be able to comprehend with all saints what is the breadth, and length, and depth, and height; and to know the love of Christ, which passeth knowledge, that ye might be filled with all the fulness of God.

EPHESIANS 3:14–19, KJV

CONTENTS

A PREFACE

in Which I Explain What to Expect in This Book; Please Don't Skip

More than a decade ago, I thought of posting enough material on a blog to trick myself into working up a draft of a book the aim of which would be to "maintain the collective memory," in the words of my daughter Rosie, "because," she said, "it's *important*." Without the collective memory, we are doomed to one of two fates: forgetting what those before us have learned, to our own impoverishment and that of any children we might have; or being forced to reinvent it all in every family. Such a project by its nature cannot succeed, for memory, and especially the memory of a culture, must, by definition, transcend any merely personal scope and reach across the generations.

At first, I thought the task was futile because (naturally) everything was as yet unwritten, but at least the process would be amusing while it lasted, for blogging was a natural fit for me, that much was clear. I can be counted on for an opinion or advice, no matter how unsuited I may be to offer it or how great the topic. But I was not sure how one short post at a time could lead to anything worth saving.

But then the question became how to wrestle it all—the more than fifteen hundred posts written over more than ten years—into book form. I can only say that I tried to do it, and with the indispensable encouragement of our readers, here it is!

The title, *Summa Domestica*, simply means "a compendium of domestic things"; my tongue-in-cheek reference is to the *Summa Theologica* of St. Thomas Aquinas, in which he treats in a systematic way all matters pertaining to faith, philosophy, creation, and reason. In your hands you have a compendium, all right! As to pretensions to completeness or precise systematization, I have none.

My daughter Suzanne (Suki) once blogged about my birthday, resulting in many greetings from regular readers of our blog,[1] even those who rarely, if ever, left comments. Her message and the comments were lovely, and what I said in response to those comments, I think, makes a good overview of this book as well: my purpose in writing at all, my hopes, and my vision.

I offer that response here (in revised form, of course, as the tone that seems somehow so suitable to the blog suffers a lot when printed!) as a preface to what you are about to read and as a model (or warning!) of the form the book takes, which is to say, an attempt to capture that decade-long conversation in these three volumes:

> I'm happy about Suzanne's post, because it brought out so many readers, however embarrassing it might have been for me to be praised in this way. The comments were most enjoyable. Some of the readers visited the comments for the first time on that occasion, which was so gratifying!
>
> Not everyone realizes that on a blog with a fairly large readership, we do notice the regulars and keep an eye out for them. We love *visiting* this way with you.
>
> I must say that some of the comments betrayed an overly uncritical view, as when it's assumed that my house is incredibly tidy or organized or that my children or marriage are perfect.
>
> You know that simply can't *be*. As to the people in my life, they are absolutely wonderful, and I love them. They unload the dishwasher, placing one more cake pan in the precariously loaded cupboard up above the stove, teasing me with "Someday we will

---

[1] Like Mother, Like Daughter (www.likemotherlikedaughter.org).

post a picture of all this to show the world the crazy mess in here that threatens to brain us as we slave away for you!"

The point of what I try to do here can be found in what a friend with her own craft-and-project-ridden old house says: that people have a spectrum they operate on, where they imagine someone less skilled than themselves at one end and someone quite fabulous at the other, with themselves smack in the middle. The less perfect end of that scale serves an *essential* purpose for our well-being: "If that person can do it [whatever "it" is for you at that moment], so can I," we console ourselves.

That's truly what got me motivated to write. I am that person on that end of the scale. If I can do it, so can you. I really don't have it together, but I do know how to function with a measure of peace, or at least a strong sense of what I'm doing it all for. That is very different from having it all together but maybe no peace and no clue where it all ends up.

I clicked from blog to blog back in those days just before I started writing, seeing the appeal of the form that was just taking off. However, I noticed one genre: those who had small children and could not express how they managed to accomplish what they depicted or how they would avoid disaster if they had more children. And then there was the other genre: the sort of site that was just so fabulous that I, a more experienced reader than the younger set at whom the content was targeted, could see that what the site presented was impossible without a paid staff to do the *actual* childcare, housekeeping, and even homeschooling that was supposedly going on while the author was posting.

I began to think that it might be helpful to share what I've learned in the real world of a family trying to make it on one income, just in case you are thinking of reinventing my particular wheel; I thought this offering of mine could possibly be more helpful in its own way than the ones telling you to refold your linens or power-wash your siding on a schedule. Call it the education of a girl who *didn't know how to sweep a floor.* Don't get me wrong! Those style mavens really have amazing taste. They are the other end of the spectrum, and we probably need them too.

A lot of the sites I would visit made me think that if I were young, I'd find it hard to shake the idea that if I didn't restyle my house all the time, live in a certain place with a certain cachet, or otherwise be the person I was reading about, I wasn't much. But I also didn't find advice to accept disorder as inevitable for one who pursues creativity to ring true to my experience.

I found these advice givers not helpful to those of us with novels to read and people to feed.

Yes, God has blessed me with a somewhat photogenic, if repair-needy, house (I mean, it's basically in the condition you'd expect from wildly impractical dreamers with a minuscule, nay, nonexistent, remodeling budget) and a truly lively, smart, and loving family (and yes, I admit it, they're photogenic too). All that made it easier for me to get my message out. But remember, those things are perfect for *me*, not least because they make me look good and make it look as if I sort of know what I'm doing. They'd probably drive *you* crazy.

But what I want to say is this: Do you believe that God has sent you the perfect people and situation for you? Because He has.

And as I wandered around the Internet, I thought you—other dedicated but perhaps frustrated moms—might want to discover this fact about your own lives, rather than be made strangely discontent by all the supposed fabulousness or frustrated by protestations that order doesn't matter. I found that I didn't like reading a post that consisted of a long list of things I could do to get "it" right (whatever "it" is—cleaning, homeschooling, cooking, organizing, being a good Christian). Too much information at once makes me anxious.

I thought that perhaps there was a place for a voice—mine—that tried to explain just one thing at a time, as gently as she could (given her rather sharp personality). I thought that there might be a place for an examination of the beauties of an orderly way of living, even amid the undeniable chaos of family life; being realistic about how uncontrolled and unpredictable life really is while acknowledging the struggle in doing things well.

Beyond encouragement for putting some order into daily life with family, I have always wanted to communicate to struggling friends the sense of wonder that comes in silence; sometimes it is the only way to pass on the most valuable gifts; the assurance that we don't always have to be actively teaching, talking, instructing. In short, to let you know that in a family, you don't have to be always producing evidence that something is getting done!

When Rosie started our blog *Like Mother, Like Daughter*, I soon found the means of getting my thoughts down on virtual paper, if only to have something to leave my children about the journey they were on with their mother.

The fact that *our readers* responded to Suki's post makes me happy, especially because I've visited some of *their* musings, and I know that where I dabble, they excel. Where I try to plant a few tomatoes, they have a farm; where I store some jars of pickles, they put up food for a year. Where I try to smile, they are extraordinarily cheerful in adverse situations. In this project, it has been the *readers* who have been the best reward.

Thank you!

That is something like what I wrote then, and it still stands, and makes a good apologia for this volume you hold in your hands.

My original idea was to tell you what I know, such as it is, *incrementally*. Thus, you may find here some repetition, backtracking, overlap, and idiosyncratic organization in general, but my conviction is that I certainly need such a method for truths to sink in. Thus, I've tried to preserve the "online journaling" format, but also give you a book. For the shortcomings of this method, I ask forgiveness, for they are all mine.

If I couldn't be sure you would understand how it happened, I would never have the courage to undertake the task of telling you how to keep a home.

ACKNOWLEDGMENTS

he Holy Trinity be praised!

And, without further ado, let me mention with great gratitude, some mortals:

To Charlie McKinney, publisher of Sophia Institute Press; a man of discernment, clearly, but also of what, in retrospect, looks like superhuman patience combined with the ability to see beyond a raft of distracted messages that offer little hint of what the author has in mind, to this *Summa* that you hold in your hands. To Nora Malone, an editor whose touch is sure, and without whom the twin authorial challenges of prolixity and blog-post diction would not have been overcome; any lapses are not attributable to her. To Carolyn McKinney, graphic designer, intuitive capacitator, and aesthetic enabler.

To my beloved children. To my daughters: Rosie Turner, who initiated the whole project that has emerged as this compendium, starting the *Like Mother, Like Daughter* blog an Internet-eon ago, naming it, allowing me to highjack it, and supporting it and me in innumerable ways with great patience and love; and her sisters, Suzanne (Suki) Saur, Deirdre Folley, and Bridget Lawler. They are my unfailing advisers, contributors, and guides to the right way to say something (and warnings about the wrong way, since they are all more perspicacious than I). A further debt of gratitude to Deirdre for her drawings, which bridge the gap from inarticulacy (mine) to understanding (yours) with deft beauty. To my sons, Nick, Joseph, and Will, who, along with their manly affection and support, offer the benefaction of good humor.

To my daughter-in-law, Natasha, whose sweet encouragement has often buoyed me, especially in the past year, when my mother was sick and then dying. And to my sons-in-law, Philip, John, and John, respectively, whose cheer extends from accepting that much of their food will be photographed preparatory to their eating it, all the way to humoring their mother-in-law and making me feel that, far from being mocked in the usual manner, I am appreciated. This speaks more of their temperaments than of mine but is nevertheless a joy.

To my grandchildren, who fulfill the blessing we received at our wedding, to see our children's children. They are gift and delight.

To my friends in my community, women of faith, who have taught me so much and listen to me opine with wonderful equanimity. There are too many to name, but without them, many of my ideas would not exist, let alone have reached verbal expression. To Annie Triolo (Rosie's sister-in-law), honorary daughter, and neighbor, who always nods firmly when asked whether some arcane piece of advice or book recommendation should be included in the final manuscript. If I left anything out, it's not her fault!

An unexpected reward in these years of writing and speaking has been the blessing of new friends. To Mary Eileen Gaudette and Emily Barton, for intelligent and timely commentary on this manuscript. To Giulietta Bockhorn; God's Providence sent her family off camping without her, so that she *just happened* to have time to answer my urgent pleas for help in making my way through the overlapping themes I've compiled here. She showed me the forest when I was slogging through the trees; rare and above rubies is the reader who tells one what one's project is all about.

To all of those dear readers of *Like Mother, Like Daughter* who encouraged, nay, *insisted* that I write a book, whose comments over the years have provided the necessary fuel to power the engine that is me, telling you what to do.

Most of all, to my husband, Phil. "Don't get it right, get it written" is his professional advice; many authors credit their family members with unnecessarily prolonging their work—or, more likely, blame them. I have no such excuse, having a journalist as a spouse. To him my full gratitude is owed and freely given. Every wife should have a man who smilingly accepts and even encourages all her schemes and plans and goes beyond, to indulge her in all her whims. I always say that in the end I get what I want, and that is because of Phil, and is Phil.

THE SUMMA DOMESTICA

PART 1
Order and Wonder, She Blurted

I think all the moms who waited while our children were in Irish step-dancing class knew that my friend Nancy and I were the homeschoolers—we chitchatted with them, but we got into deep conversations with each other about our respective daughters' schooling. One day, when Nancy happened not to be there, I talked more with another mom who had already shown every indication of being committed to the normal suburban school-and-activity model. She asked me (as they always do), "What curriculum do you use?"

Now, I knew very well from previous interactions that she wasn't interested in any "I want to do this" sort of way, but only in the "I'm bored, might as well ask" sort of way, so I wasn't too much in the mood to elaborate. On the other hand, every child of God deserves an honest answer, if one can be found that meets the occasion.

I have been asked this question many times in the past almost twenty-five years, and I have discovered that even the most sincerely attentive parent, infused with a lively willingness to absorb any shred of helpful guidance, will find himself drowning in the abundance of detail that I am willing to impart. One is tempted to offer a gentle and noncommittal shake of the head and leave it there, but I'm not self-controlled enough for that response.

So that day, waiting for the girls to finish up their class, I found myself saying something to this small-talk-making, politely inquiring mom that I believe distills what I really think about the home environment, regardless of the choices made for schooling.

"Well, curriculum is neither here nor there, really. Education is much more about life itself in the home; and home ought to provide two things for the development of the child. Really, the home has to try to provide ..."

I looked at her rather blank face and just plowed ahead, blurting out, "It has to provide ... Order and Wonder."

That's what I told her. And then I was so impressed, because, for the first time, I had put into words what I was slowly, ever so slowly, figuring out myself, as I neared the end of my adventure in educating my children.

I told her what I try to tell you here, that the home is where the child learns Order and Wonder, and the parents too, even if they don't educate their children at home.

Out of the corner of my eye, I could see the other moms perking up as we chatted; there was definitely a sort of stricken air in the room. I would be stricken too if I overheard such a thing! Suddenly a whole world of things I am not doing, and ways I am failing, opens up.

But fear not. I will try to make what I mean clear. Or rather, I will try to show you how to stumble along just the way everyone does, even if they seem not to. At least having some goals gives some focus to the struggle.

I give the dance-class mom credit for a sense of humor that I hadn't suspected. As we spoke a little more, she laughed and said, "There's order and wonder at my house—we *order* food at McDonald's because we don't know what's for supper; we *wonder* where our clean clothes are!"

The almost mechanical details of home management, "order" with a lowercase *o*, are absolutely necessary for harmonious living. Without these details, there is constant anxiety and stress; all the energy that could go to higher things gets expended on the lower.

But, while necessary (yet so strangely difficult for so many of us to achieve!), this sort of order is not sufficient. I think that we can all intuit that having a smoothly managed household would turn out to be stultifying if there weren't some other kind of order, Order with a capital O, that it pointed to.

This other, not unconnected Order has to do with the rhythms of the day, the week, the seasons, and the year; there is the rhythm of memory, of history and its commemoration. As soon as we begin speaking of it, we immediately see how much we want to be able to anticipate this order and make room for it in our lives and the lives of our children.

Then there is another (yet not separate!) Order, even higher, and that is the liturgical year, in which we meet Christ Himself.[2] We express our faith by living this holy rhythm; without it, we can neither know nor pass on what we believe. This sacred time is the foundation of all theology, no matter how rarefied it may seem, and, theology being the queen of sciences, this other sort of Order can be seen as the foundation of all knowledge, of all delight. Therefore, yes, our comparatively smaller mission to educate our children—our curriculum, you might say—depends on it!

Suddenly we are talking not about order, but about Wonder. How connected these two ideas are, although they are so often thought of as modes that oppose each other!

What is wonder? Scripture and the ancient philosophers agree that to be in awe of what we do not know is the first step not only to knowing but also to the love of knowledge and of wisdom. Wisdom differs from knowledge in that it is knowledge *rightly ordered*—you might say, in God's light. Further, wise men agree that wonder, this sense of delight at the greatness of creation and our place in it, doesn't end; the more we learn, the more we wonder.

We see this delight in the eyes of children. We also see the light go out when we make the mistake Dickens describes in *Hard Times*: "not to encourage a child's mind to develop and expand itself like a young flower, but to open it by force like an oyster."

We want our children to look up at the stars, to marvel at a new little batch of minnows in the sparkling water, to listen to the geese flying away on a mid-September morning. When we think ahead to their education, we want it to be full of wonder. How closely this wonder aligns with the order of the cosmos—the rhythms of the universe—and with the beauties of the unfolding of each liturgical season. Why, the image of the family on Christmas morning, kneeling at the crèche, practically defines the wonder we hope they experience.

The order of the home, too, facilitates a sense of well-being that opens up the heart to gratitude for being alive. The child who hears the little

---

[2] Pius XII, encyclical *Mediator Dei* (November 20, 1947), no. 165.

noises of supper being prepared in the kitchen as, curled up on the sofa, he reads a book, knows that he is loved. There's a sense of peace in rooms that are tidy and clean. Waking up to the knowledge that one will be taken care of gives a freedom to explore and to be carefree. Having the sense of contributing to the running of a household inspires a young person to stretch his horizons.

Order and wonder turn out to be united to each other, most deeply in the life of the Christian and united to the liturgy, doing all things in God's time. It's a mistake to think that marvelous moments of awe will redeem chronic chaos. Routine on its own won't make us happy; we must look up at the stars.

Order and wonder: too much of one or the other, and we are out of balance, burning out, and convinced we can't do any of it!

But don't be daunted. Know that marriage, your marriage, brings with it grace; a very specific grace aimed like a true arrow at a particular challenge: raising and educating your children. In this volume I try to offer details of the remote preparation, one might call it, necessary to accomplish the task of education, which is the question that motivated me to begin writing.

Escaping Modernism's Fatal Doubt

Modernity, or the paralyzing state of Disorder and Doubt, somewhat oxymoronically began long ago. Although it's about casting off ancient ways and, specifically, certainties that the ancients knew, it's getting old. Even though we might personally not wish to sever our ties completely with tradition, we have lived so long breathing modern air that we hardly know how to help ourselves. We modern people can't escape applying modern remedies to problems, especially when the problems are modern ones to start with.

We can identify a lack of centeredness in our world, a certain anxiety created by doubt; but our response is to try to convince ourselves and others of the importance of centeredness by that most modern of solutions, *more work and more explanations*; we default to plans and programs—our faith in which is rock solid—against experience. The more we exert our will, the more anxious we become; even as the programs we institute increase our tension, the more we seem to have recourse to them. We have checklists for our checklists! We don't notice that our precious plans drive people away.

Really, what we need to know is what the British essayist Walter Bagehot advised: the way to keep old customs is to enjoy old customs. That's a
laconic British way of packing a lot of wisdom into a little sentence.

We have to stop and ask what is meant by "enjoyment." If we are surprised by the word "customs" in the quotation by Bagehot, surprised into
questioning whether we are correct in assuming that we mean "entertainment," we'll be closer to finding the answer. We'll be forced to admit that
the concept of entertainment presupposes a dichotomy that consists only
of "work" and "nonwork," or "inactivity"—and that "inactivity" for us,
we have to admit, has a utilitarian flavor: we seek entertainment in our
"nonwork" periods so that we can rest up for another go at work.

But enjoyment has to do with something for its own sake. Perhaps we
can intuit that, and our intuition is confirmed by the sense I started with,
that we lack a center in our lives. No amount of work fills up the void; no
amount of entertainment does either.

Enjoyment means gratitude for things as they are; it means accepting the
whole of life and creation as a gift. God Himself, on viewing His creation
on the seventh day, said, "It is very good." He rested, and we might say He
simply enjoyed what He had made.

Josef Pieper writes about this attitude of receptivity that must be expressed in joy, calling it "festivity" and locating it in the experience when
we step away from our normal, "default" condition of work (which is good
and necessary) and offer to God the sacrifice of "doing nothing." Pieper
calls this "the universal assent to the world as a whole."[3]

Even though we know that things are not as they ought to be, that there
is suffering and deformation and toil—even slavery and horror—we have
"the conviction that the prime festive occasion, which alone can ultimately
justify all celebration, really exists; that, to reduce it to the most concise
phrase, at bottom *everything that is, is good, and it is good to exist.*"[4] As C. S.

---

[3]   Josef Pieper, *In Tune with the World: A Theory of Festivity* (South Bend, IN:
      St. Augustine's Press, 1999), 30.
[4]   Ibid., 26.

Lewis notes, we would not even know that the bad things *are* bad unless we had the Good to compare them with.

Realizing this goodness of creation, we naturally praise the Creator. And it follows, Pieper asserts, that "there can be no deadlier, more ruthless destruction of festivity [or enjoyment] than refusal of ritual praise. Any such Nay tramples out the spark from which the flickering flame of festivity might have been kindled anew."[5]

The "old customs" we might relearn in order to enjoy them again are many. Most are quite simple. The oldest of all are the ones that relate to family life and to liturgy, to worship (Pieper's "ritual praise"). Begin with Sunday, that least modern of days. Worship, celebration (enjoyment), rest. These are what will restore our spirits and bring the world back to its senses, with nary a program to explain it all. If you begin with Sunday, you will find that your whole week has a new meaning.

[5] Ibid., 32.

The Gift of Womanhood

As I see it, there are two obstacles in the way of homemaking.

First, some of us—many, I'd dare say—just don't know how to do it. When I started my adult life as wife and mother, I didn't even know what I didn't know. I had a classic case of what economists call "the unknown unknowns." You can see how such a situation represents an almost insurmountable problem; who can rescue herself from this state, I ask you.

But time goes on. When you become responsible for other people, you begin to get a glimmer, somehow, that you are going to have to cope. You will have to learn some things—or flee.

I've called our situation a loss of collective memory, a breach in the normal cultural handing down of basic information from generation to generation. That sort of teaching is done by unconscious modeling, by doing, and by observation, not by explanation. At the moment, the information we need is found only in books, if it's found at all; yet books are not the best way to convey it. I definitely reinvented the wheel as a young wife and mother, and when I looked up after a couple of decades, I was horrified to find that young women in what had been my position were compelled by the same lapses to reinvent all over again.

Now, of course, extreme social media consumption presents a challenge to competence—namely, perfectionism. We are subjected to a vast number of images and exhortations to achieve an unrealistic level of not life but lifestyle—far beyond what was in the monthly magazines our foremothers sometimes perused. Although we can still not quite manage to make lunch every day, these images make us believe we can attain domestic perfection—or ought to.

All of this, our fate, I will address; but for me, the issue is one of competence, not perfection. If you need these answers right now, skip the rest of this overview (you can come back later) and head on to the chapters on Motherhood in the Field.

The Second Obstacle

The second obstacle to homemaking is the question that gnaws at the entrails of the post-feminist person: Why the woman? *Why me?*

The two obstacles are bound up with each other. Even that woman who is convinced that making a home is her glory wakes up in the morning with no idea how to go about doing it; this daunts her and throws her into questioning mode. Almost every particular aspect, after all, can be done by a servant or a machine, which makes the venture seem pointless or worthless, especially when contrasted with the glamour of a career (leaving aside the reality that even women with a career still need to know how to keep a home).

She can become competent, but because she receives no honor, her competence doesn't fulfill; it leaves her feeling sad.

So this book must of necessity have these two aspects—one, abstract and even philosophical, anthropological, and theological (however amateurly pursued, because I assure you, I have no credentials, academically speaking); the other, almost unbelievably practical. "You ladies talk only about the price of potatoes," a (male) friend once accused. Well, potatoes we must buy, and on only the one income of our husbands. But we can talk about other things as well. And so we will.

I found myself trying to answer the "why the woman" question because of that kind of party conversation I find myself engaging in quite a lot, perhaps because most strangers are surprised at the size of my family (I have seven children, all grown now), and their surprise leads them to begin probing, if only in that frivolous way some have (perhaps as the result of having had a few drinks), asking questions mainly for entertainment value.

Or so they think—that is, I cannot help but believe, quixotically, that there is at some level a true spirit of inquiry. Thus, no matter how noisy the situation, no matter how difficult it is to hear one another or to convey a response or to have that response be taken seriously or soberly, I take what my husband lovingly (and with exasperation) refers to as the bait.

More often than you would think, the conversation turns to the question of why I maintain that it is the woman who makes the home. Can't a man do this thing just as well?

I think this is because the position of housewife holds no social status, especially for one, like me, who attended an elite college after a lifetime of intensive indoctrination in the value of education, professional work, and equality with men out in the world and then was launched into a world of those whose background is the same.

That first bit of party chitchat—"What do you do?"—is always going to be a bit awkward. Even if the interlocutor is well versed in the appearance of judgment-free valuation, you feel the sheer effort in the sincere, self-conscious attempt to remain interested in speaking with you when you answer, "I stay home" or "I'm a housewife" (as I like to put it, being no stranger to the delights of *épater la bourgeoisie* myself).

Contrary to perceived wisdom, things in this awkwardness department were sharper when I was a very young woman than they are now. People today are well versed in the necessity of not judging; yet their eyes continue to glaze over.

If I'm speaking to a professional woman, there will be a variety of responses that I won't go into here. Women are on guard with each other at parties and wary of appearing to judge. But if it's a man I'm speaking to, things are often a bit different. Sometimes I think a man is more interested in having me refute the position he's advancing, however convinced he appears.

I know what's coming, and I have the advantage of the formidable aspect—mainly of disapproving eyebrows. If I were retiring rather than spirited in temperament, the next stop would be a lonely one at the hors d'oeuvres table. But because I can't help my "I dare you" look, very often this man will counter with a "That's wonderful and very important to society"-ish style of response. If he's a bit older, there may be a tinge of longing, a brief dropping of the veil, for something I hope will be clearer later on in this book, but for which he certainly has no name. But if he's feeling the effects of a couple of drinks on a stomach bolstered only by a few dainty canapés, and if he's the provocative sort, he might start picking a fight.

I won't disappoint, of course.

He asks why I stay at home. To take care of the children, the home . . .

Did you never have the desire for a career?

Not really.

But you seem intelligent. Isn't it a waste?

No, but thanks. I'm contributing to society in my own way.

Doesn't it bother you that it's because you're a woman that you have done this?

No.

Why can't a man be the one to stay home?

Well, a man doesn't give birth to the child.

But I mean after the child is born?

But a man doesn't have breasts to feed the child.

[Impatiently] *So six months and then, why can't the man stay home?*

Well, a baby needs to be nurtured for more than six months and even nurses for more than six months, and then there are more babies, God willing. But even if there weren't, a man wouldn't want to stay home—not for that long. You wouldn't!

[Can't be seen admitting to this, because men and women are not only equal but exactly the same, other than the breasts, but a flicker of assent does cross his eyes, and also a flicker of fear for daring to assent.] *It just seems so unfair that the woman is expected to give everything up.*

Aren't children worth it?

Then they should be worth it to the man! [Ah, a little mistake there—what have you admitted, my friend?]

Well, isn't there more to it than the children? Even if I hadn't had children, I would want to make the home, among other things, because I don't think a man can really do it, and also because ... because ...

But by now the music has gotten so loud that we can't hear each other, and others have elbowed in to ply him with more alcohol, and he's too sure that his way of engaging with the world is the best way, being a man; or at least, he's too invested in his way, because he and his wife depend on her income, so we can never really have this conversation. Not like this.

As the years go by in this feminist world of ours, what was urged on us as girls (and my girlhood coincided with the feminist ascendency, which was as abrupt as it is complete) has, over my lifetime, become so unassailable that society has no qualms using every means to impose it. Technology seems to have rendered moot any claims by biology. As I write, large and important corporations offer women the employment benefit of freezing their ova for future use, to "level the playing field" with men—to take their reproductive years and transpose them to a more opportune time. Whether the promise will be kept—whether the woman's body will cooperate with this experiment—can be discovered only with the passage of time. That many other such promises have been nullified by reality won't stop the attempt.

Meaningful human activity has been reduced to the one mode—production, work, and participation in life as an economic unit. My male friend's argument crystallizes into the one point that fertility in a woman is contrary to her interests and *therefore* a burden, something whose effects may be borne for a few years and then put behind one; in a pinch, it can be put on ice until an undefined "later." Womanhood is a hindrance to the real important stuff of life.

Perhaps you, dear reader, don't accept this characterization either.

But how to answer? What is the satisfying response?

What is it that makes the woman the one to make the home and nurture those in it (broadly speaking), rather than provide for and protect it (also broadly speaking)?

In fact, is it better to be a man?

To some women, these questions are absurd. There are some who instinctively find their peaceful place in the world as wives and mothers—and never give a thought to the conflict going on around them. These women have never given devotion to a family a conscious thought: they simply *are* devoted, never questioning the reasoning that leads to their choice. They are few and far between in our day, but they do exist; I have met them.

Then there are some, equally peaceful, who may indicate by their speech that they are feminists, or they may seem tacitly to agree with the feminist outlook—they may even have a career and have followed the path of the modern woman to a certain level of honor in the world—and yet they also raise a family, remaining unperturbed by the conflict that seems brewing in the bosoms of some of their sisters. The case of these women is a bit difficult for the ones who struggle, because they seem to have what the others can't manage.

Perhaps it's a question of luck, temperament, more resources, or just things' working out. They can hardly be the pattern for all women, though, because of those very factors, however hard they are to pin down, and because the unrest still exists in the others.

These—these for whom I write—feel the conflict and have heard the arguments for having it all (that rallying cry of feminists) and even gone down the path, sometimes very far—and then, with great purpose and dedication, commit themselves to homemaking. Or they have a strange thought inside that they would like to but are afraid to listen to it.

If you are wondering where I fall, it's obvious and intuitive to me that God made me a certain way that goes right down to the very depths of my being, that the way He made me is good and even *the best*, and that even with my shortcomings, nurturing is what I do because I am a woman. And even more, taking care of this sphere, the inner one, the hidden one, is not a sacrifice but a glory.

The world needs the home. If there are only workers and no homes, then man will become nothing more than a piece of machinery; children will certainly be trampled. Beauty will be drained out of life. The home needs a maker; my conviction is that God made women to make the home and to guard beauty from utilitarianism.

I speak of the reasons here because I believe the challenge of our day is to put them into words. When a fellow at a party asks me *why*, I have to answer with the deepest answer I can find, even if he never hears it. Like you, if not like him, I am not at peace with conventions; I want explanations rooted in causes. (Later in this book, we will revisit these themes. It takes time, and I'm hoping you'll come along with me, if only because of the novelty of it all.)

Part of what makes our party friend so sure he knows that equality—in the sense of sameness—is an axiom turns on the rather uncomfortable implication that its opposite, a complementary vision of the sexes, requires him to protect his family and provide for it. Perhaps unconsciously he senses the corollary to my proposition that the woman by nature makes the home, and it fills him with a certain dread.

If so, he's right: men are made, by virtue of their manhood, to rise to the role of protection and provision, but they are also devastatingly taught in our culture that they won't be asked to; further, that if they try, women will mock them. Manhood can stand a lot of things, but mockery is not one of them.

So, yes, men are afraid. Everyone is in a state of high anxiety, simply because people can't find a place in life to settle and be at peace when equality is their main criterion. I propose that there are not stereotypes (a category devised to allow generalization) but *givens*, real ones. Just as geometry can't proceed without givens, life without givens will be endlessly questioned rather than lived.

"Male and female He made them," and "in His image." These are givens. To refuse to accept them not only as given but as *a gift* is to invite madness.

To answer my own question, posed at the end of the last chapter (*viz.*, "Is it better for a woman to be a man?"—a question coming to a sharp point in these days of gender ideology), I believe it's *not* better for a woman to be a man, and I think that the healing of culture depends on her being herself, that is, possessing womanliness, in search of the complement of manliness that provides a shelter for her.

At that party, the questions continue:

Why must it be the woman who is taken care of by the man?

Because she is the one who has the babies and nurtures them and continues to find reasons to nurture them and to make her home.

Why must it be the man who protects?

Because without this challenge, his manhood is corrupted. His energy is outward-directed, no matter what! It's intended to be outward-directed for a positive purpose, the building of society.

So you're saying the woman doesn't contribute to society?

What follows in this volume is an attempt to answer that question.

On Womanhood: Receiving in Order to Give

But which of you having a servant ploughing, or feeding cattle, will say to him, when he is come from the field: Immediately go, sit down to meat: And will not rather say to him: Make ready my supper, and gird thyself, and serve me, whilst I eat and drink, and afterwards thou shalt eat and drink? Doth he thank that servant, for doing the things which he commanded him? I think not.

So you also, when you shall have done all these things that are commanded you, say: We are unprofitable servants; we have done that which we ought to do.

LUKE 17:7–10, DR

---

his book on keeping a home is largely addressed to women. If you are a man, I am happy you are reading. But I suppose, in my imagination, I am speaking to other women.

I hear them asking, "Why should *I* have to do all this? Why is all this a woman's lot to preside over? Am I not good enough for the world to recognize my work with something tangible, like a paycheck? How can I explain my home—what it is, why I would devote myself to it—to someone else? To myself? What about someone who isn't Christian?"

A lot depends on the answer. Some women know the answer in their hearts. Some women are just drawn to becoming wives and mothers, even if it takes us a long time to figure out the practical aspects (and some just do it all, effortlessly, right from the start, which hardly seems fair to us struggling ones!).

Some are a little bitter, maybe, thinking about what might have been. Some are not at all bitter, but scared—wondering about the risk of it all and whether, at the end of the time of making choices, the sense of having chosen wrongly will be crushing.

Some are joyful and are open to finding out more of what making the home entails. In my writing all these years, nothing has edified me more than to know that such people exist. They are very eager, despite the negative culture we live in, and it's a marvelous thing to be able to function without being tripped up by constant doubts.

But to answer the question in an orderly, satisfying way, we have to do some reading, I find.

For the record (for those who are skeptical that the busy yet inquiring mother could read to discover the answer), it was when I had many children underfoot that I read almost all the books that formed me. I might have had a few lapses in concentration on other fronts, I admit. But nursing a baby is a great excuse to pick up some light philosophy! (By "light" I mean that the physical book can be held with one hand!)

One such (conveniently small) book that opened up my thinking on the womanhood question is *Mulieris Dignitatem* (*On the Dignity and Vocation of Women*), a letter of Pope John Paul II. This letter condenses his vast teaching on Christian anthropology (often called the Theology of the Body) as it applies to women and our vocation in particular.

There are two things to keep in mind regarding *Mulieris Dignitatem*. First, and many overlook this fact, John Paul II wrote this letter *primarily* to offer women a deep reflection on what, for us, is the most important reason the priesthood is not open to our sex. God has a vocation in mind for us already. Insisting on the priesthood as a sort of "last frontier" in "tearing down power structures" makes us miss what this vocation is. Second, whatever you have heard about what this letter means to women, you have likely been misled by people who have not read it. An honest reading simply cannot extract from it any sort of feminist affirmation. It is a paean to motherhood and virginity (in the image of Mary, Virgin and Mother), from first to last.

The feminist mentality is fixated on equality to the extent that it is almost impossible to speak of reality in any other terms with a feminist. In order to understand anything about womanhood apart from the rigid category of equality, we will have to confront it.

"Equality Is Not the Deepest Thing"

My copy of C. S. Lewis's *That Hideous Strength* is mightily well worn. I have read it many times, and if I open it anywhere—for instance, to try to locate a quote for a post I am writing—I am immediately immersed in a world completely imagined and full of prophecy in both senses of the word: prescient vision and universal truth telling.

It's a story about the end times, in one way. In another way, it's a little love story: a conflicted young woman is newly married to a man who is neither particularly good nor particularly bad. Jane, the wife, is a perfect type of today's woman (giving the lie to those who would like us to think that our struggles are so very post-1970—the book was written in 1943). She is working on her doctoral thesis on John Donne, determined to continue her scholarly career even after her marriage: "That was one of the reasons why they were to have no children, at any rate for a long time yet."

Despite working on the poet's "triumphant vindication of the body" (she was "not perhaps a very original thinker"), she has no clue of what the vindication of her own body might be. She is pouty and a tad bitter toward her new husband. She feels vaguely as if he has abandoned her. She doesn't much like sex.

As Jane is revealed to be at the epicenter of apocalyptic events in the novel, she has an unsettling conversation, for our purpose (which, you will remember, is to discover the answer to the question "Why the woman?"), with Mr. Fisher-King. He is the Christlike figure of the book and the director of the battle they find themselves in.

> "I thought love meant equality," [Jane] said, "and free companionship."
>
> "Ah, Equality!" said the Director.... "Equality is not the deepest thing, you know."
>
> "I always thought that was just what it was. I thought it was in their souls that people were equal."
>
> He replies, "Equality guards life, it doesn't make it. It is medicine, not food."

The irony is that Jane married Mark because of love, not because of equality, and found that love eluded her with its consummation, leaving her thinking only of how she could escape.

When I was young, going to liberal public schools and living in university towns, equality was (as it remains) the main obsession; its achievement at that time took place in an atmosphere of upheaval. Not only was my life unstable because of my parents' divorce, but I lived on the edge of societal unrest, quite literally: in the late sixties, the New Haven racial riots threw the city into panic and chaos. Later the trial of the Black Panthers and Bobby Seale caused a political crisis, left and right, with talk of race, murder, and torture bandied about. The Winchester gun factory, a few blocks away from where I lived, seemed to be a potential flash point of mob violence, although it never occurred, thank goodness. Of course, as a seven-to-ten-year-old, I understood nothing of the details or even of the broad picture. To me, "riot" meant "adults were not in control," which I in my short life already had reason to know to be the case.

The conversations floating above my head were intense ones, often centering on power and anarchy, personal and political. Most people I knew claimed to embrace some sort of revolution, and most of them were also experiencing a disintegration of their personal lives. They spoke of sacrifice, but it always seemed that they wanted the sacrifice of others. Their comfortable lives belied their self-interest—this was apparent to me: that their talk was revolution by proxy only.

As I girl, I wasn't terribly interested in equality, being quite sure not so much of my equality to others but rather—and I say this with a keen sense now of having lived long enough to know better—of my superiority. If the essence of girlhood is to envy boys, as Dr. Freud has taught, no one had informed *me*. Such a thing never entered my mind.

I always felt privileged, even while, as an only child of divorced parents, I was somewhat neglected. I didn't attribute any shortcomings in my life to anyone's usurpation of my rights. I believed utterly in my teachers' creed, which my free-thinking father subscribed to as well: that education was the path to true aristocracy, that of the mind; the corollary, religion, was superstition.

But I lacked emotional stability. I sought solace in books. I lived more in the world of stories than in the real one, which was, to me, a frightening and chaotic place. I hear people my age talk about their calm, peaceful childhoods. I have no idea what they can be speaking of. To me, the world of the sixties and seventies was a tumult—within and outside my own little head, within and outside the walls of my home.

The fairy tales I took refuge in had in common the idea of a personal quest or task or test that one had to perform or pass, and what was being overcome was the self. (This literary struggle over self was probably my salvation, humanly speaking.)

I desperately loved these tales—not Disney fairy tales, but old stories from Grimm and Lang. "The Enchanted Pig," for instance, was one of my favorites, and still, I believe, one of the better insights that the collective consciousness, if there be such a thing, has provided concerning the truth of the relationship between men and women: that it is one of love through sacrifice. The heroine must sacrifice herself to find happiness: cutting off her little finger to provide the top rung of the ladder that she must use to reach her husband, who had been removed to the highest peak, going up seven mountains, fighting seven dragons with seven heads.

In these stories, I found and was drawn to the idea of *hierarchy*, the true hierarchy in which the princes and peasants alike must find their interior nobility or sink to the lowest depths of creation.

This world made sense and seemed fitting, and it satisfied a very deep longing that had nothing to do with being equal to anyone else, but in being better—more sensitive, more responsible, more singled out. It had to do with being a princess who nevertheless accepts life as a goose girl as the prerequisite for her final reward.

The real world, on the other hand, was constantly leaving me cold and anxious. It was deeply unsatisfying. It's hard now to remember or to have an accurate rendering of how colorless things were in the sixties—how literally drab the colors were, at least to a pair of sad eyes looking out on a run-down city. I don't think the popular TV series *Mad Men* is the reference work people make it out to be at all, but rather, a twenty-first-century gloss on what was, in truth, a vitiated landscape. Where there were colors, as the sixites wore on, they were the harsh psychedelic colors of a palette wielded by designers wanting to shock. A child instinctively knows whether those around him have his well-being at heart; I knew that the world was abruptly being remade by people who were thinking about themselves.

From my vantage as a child, there was the old worn-out way of doing things, which certainly had no magic in it. And there was the frightening, shocking, demanding way that was becoming quite normal, as the riots morphed into war protests and people purposely abandoned basic hygiene or interacting in civilized (they would have said "conventional") ways.

Simultaneously, as prosperity rose, a mode of life emerged that was as soulless and sterile as the hippie revolution was dirty and chaotic. I remember visiting people in the new, quite large apartment complexes—among the first I had ever seen—with central air conditioning and many amenities hitherto unknown in the lower echelons. Maybe because I lived in old cities, I had never seen anything like this comfortable anti-aesthetic before, all beige carpeting and concrete walls, climate controlled and bland, an antidote to the decrepit, passing age. But it didn't seem much like an improvement. I always had an extreme sensitivity to smells, and climate control instantly felt damp and, in its own way, worn out.

It all left me sad, since my New England sensibilities called for improvement back to the past, toward hand-finished wood, screen doors, porches, and old lawns, if change there must be. Yet, at the same time, who doesn't get caught up in the idea of getting rid of the dust, metaphorically?

I couldn't help admiring the clear bright colors of the newly stripped and remodeled houses of my friends' well-to-do parents, who were pioneering the "do-it-yourself" movement. Their hip take on everything from vegetarianism to architecture excited me. *They* weren't bourgeois, and they weren't hippies—their excitement at the opportunity of a self-made, self-imagined life resonated with me. I listened carefully to their views and tried to understand their theories, especially about equality.

Often they were really quite incredibly impractical, as when a friend's father opined that the world would be a better place if people took turns doing each other's work. Could he really mean, my teenage mind wondered, that a man should collect trash for two years and then be a lawyer for the next two? Didn't seem realistic.

My memory still doesn't turn up any irony in his words. He must have known that the trash man could never do his job; it was obvious that he couldn't do the trash man's. Nevertheless, in many ways, all these confident, knowing people attracted me, and I tried to embrace their worldview.

In the seventies (I think I was fourteen) I subscribed to *Ms.* magazine. I devoured it. Amusingly, from my point of view now, I seem to remember the strongest pull coming from one issue with a feminist retelling of a fairy tale, supposedly with an updated, liberated princess. I had such high hopes, but it wasn't a good story. Anyone who knew good stories knew that this one was fatally flawed on its own premise, which in itself planted the seed of doubt for me.

I was a kid, on my way to growing up. In the normal course of development, one seeks to put away childhood things, and it crept into my consciousness that although the arguments and narratives I read in *Ms.* were, of course, imbued with the one theme of power politics, they had something else in common: adolescent self-absorption.

Have you ever heard of the feminist "click!"? Gloria Steinem—and *Ms.*—invented and brought into the lexicon the click!: that moment at which a woman achieves consciousness and awareness of herself apart from the roles thrust on her by society. The magazine featured these individual stories prominently.

But they didn't move me. They often seemed like whining. Occasionally they were stories of injustice, but no more so than any of the myriad injustices that people eternally perpetrate against each other and suffer in their turn, with no particular reference to sexual roles other than as a handy stick in the general beating that is the all-against-all of life at its worst. And often these authors were disturbingly childish, in the sense of an immature exploration of their own orifices, too bored to bother looking up from playing in the muck, using their adult position to make it sound as if this wallowing was somehow artistic, creative, or revealing.

The magazine was a forum for expressing and indulging in all the unproductive thoughts and urges that I was trying to leave behind, just in the simple act of growing up. Most of the self-referential content repelled me, and the political rants were irrelevant. Hadn't I been encouraged by my parents, including my Egyptian (Muslim) father, to excel in everything academic? But aren't men from other cultures the very first in the ranks of the oppressors, according to the gospel of Gloria Steinem? Didn't I have every opportunity available to me in any field? There was no oppression that I could see. I knew many professional women—if anything, my world lacked happy homemakers! It certainly lacked devoted mothers. Instead, if I was honest, what I was witnessing was an increasingly dreary landscape of strident people of both sexes, scrabbling for position and increasingly engaged in an opportunistic rush to identify with some sort of victim class.

Equality to me was an irrelevant, because unfulfilling, assumption. But what did I base that conviction on? Some today want to claim that the women's movement gave the level playing field to those who—now—feel no gratitude. But I was there at the beginning, and all I saw was a lot of unseemly behavior that ended more in the destruction of family life than in any utopia of parity. I was one of many unhappy children in that world, that progressive, leading-edge world.

Meanwhile, I began to think and read about the education of children. It made sense to me, above all, that the nurture of small children depends greatly on the attention of their mother—her presence and her intimate knowledge of their needs. The development of the mature, adult person depends on the foundation laid in early childhood—an observation that was being made simultaneously with the agitation for liberating women precisely from their role as mothers. But isn't the development of a more just society dependent on the maturity and virtue of each adult person? So, it seemed to me, it all goes back to whether the woman, the mother, is willing to provide the nurture that underlies it all. (I hadn't yet begun to think about the indispensability of the father.) Yet these proponents of equality were not willing to reconcile these two ideas. While women were demanding liberation, the strong claim that others have on them was becoming more apparent, even in popular culture.

The male-oriented and industrialized society interfered with the closeness of the mother and child and thereby with the fulfillment of womanhood. It was the abandonment of tradition that gave men the power to push women and their gifts aside.

Medicalized childbirth, bottle-feeding and the subsequent stress of yearly childbirth, maternal coldness due to lack of bonding in breast-feeding, isolation of children away from home: Weren't all these things the result of male ascendance, of a harsh male ethic of uniformity and a mechanized outlook? But the feminists only wanted to talk about equal pay and a place in the workforce, or if they did talk about babies (who, after all, are the new generation, presumably important in the scheme of transforming things for justice's sake), it was in the context of what the world owed the woman to be free of them, not any sacrifice one person makes for another, for a loved one.

Tellingly, those "click!" tales seemed to be more about parental neglect and selfishness than any other factor. There's no question that many women had grown up seeing their mothers treated poorly and resenting it. But did they question the factors that gave rise to that state of affairs? It's amazing how the seeds of radicalism are planted in the deterioration of the parents' marriages, with the inevitable neglect of the children coming in its wake! But how to reconcile the dire necessity, precisely from a social point of view, of devoting oneself to one's children and their proper nurture, with the power struggle enunciated by feminists?

What *about* equality?

Womanhood: In the Beginning

In the Gospel of Matthew, when the Pharisees approach Jesus with a question about divorce (really an intense question about men, women, and marriage [Matt. 19:3–8]), Jesus responds twice by making reference to "the beginning." In *Mulieris Dignitatem* (as in his larger work on the Theology of the Body), John Paul II follows Jesus' example, and it's a good thing, too, because it never really works to accept the terms of a discussion where there is not goodwill or where terms are hopelessly confused. It's better to go back "to "the beginning."

Looking at evils (such as divorce and inequality), even if one acknowledges that those things are occasionally necessary ("because of the hardness of your hearts") or clearly a fact in history (such as the undoubted mistreatment of women at various times and in various places), doesn't get you any closer to discovering God's original intent or uncovering true goodness and meaning. It doesn't get you to the bottom of things.

So John Paul II, trying to explain to the late-twentieth-century feminist universe how it could be that man and woman have a vocation to a sincere gift of self (no power politics allowed), starts "in the beginning," with Genesis. Christians immediately see that starting here gets at God's original intent for man, before the Fall, before our waywardness starts clouding the picture.

We (as do many others) believe that God is good and what He intends for us is good. We just have to uncover what that might be. But even simply from an anthropological point of view, the Bible presents one of the oldest and most coherent accounts. There might be older stories of creation, but the biblical one seems the most complete.

Even if you don't believe in God, or accept Scripture or the authority of the pope, or have ever thought of Genesis as anything other than a childish story or perhaps even one derogatory to the female sex, you may be surprised by the depth of what John Paul II has to say about women in his study of Genesis.

So let's dwell on it a bit. (This part is in chapter 3 of *Mulieris Dignitatem*.)

God deftly (and I really am filled with wonder at the economy of motion) creates the world, the sun, the stars, the waters, the land, the animals, the fish, and the plants. Don't skip lightly over this part just because you've heard or read it before. When you read it slowly, it is revealed as not only marvelous but also quite unlike any way we would think of expressing the things we think we know. And He saw that it was all good.

What we have to stop and contemplate for a moment is this: as much as we appreciate the beauty of every lark and mountain and droplet of water, it's probably impossible for us to grasp, with our present limitations, the true perfection they had before the Fall, fresh from God's hand.

And yet we really should try, because we are aware that if only we can somehow erase from our consciousness the lurking suspicion that if we *could* commune with the tiger, it might maul us, or that the killer whale almost certainly would kill—in other words, if we could enter, at least imaginatively, the world as it first was—we could start to appreciate the delight God has in what He has made, at that moment when He first made it.

And then we might get a glimpse into what might be behind His next step, which is to create man in His own image. Man, "the high point of the whole order of the visible world": a person who is (unlike any of the other things He made, however mighty, gorgeous, whimsical, or precious) rooted in matter, but with an immaterial and immortal soul.

The angels are persons, but they are pure spirits. It's nothing to them if God chooses to express Himself in this physical way, except insofar as they are disposed to love whatever God does. The rest of creation is material, made of matter with no spiritual aspect. Only man is both.

After that one act of will at their creation when some fell away, the angels simply do what God wants done, all admiringly, without really entering into the spirit—or rather, matter—of the thing; that is, of creation. Or if they enter (as in Scripture we see that they do), it is by only appearing to have bodies.

It's clear from the account in Genesis that God wanted a creature made in His image (for what God does is by necessity what He wants). Someone who could freely agree that yes, this creation of Yours is all truly magnificent, and what's more, I see what You have in mind here! I see the possibilities! I can cooperate with this in going out to be fruitful and have dominion over all the earth (Gen. 1:28). In his nature, man participates in the immaterial world and in the material world.

Man is a person. Woman is a person. They were thought up in the same instant in this particular, unique way. Although the angels are in the image of God in that they have pure intellect, it is only man whom God creates male and female. To me, this suggests that in some incredibly unfathomably deep fashion, both—male and female—express something about God's image that nothing else in creation does. (What that is, I do not pretend to know; I believe it is contained in the first part of the Gospel of John, and hinted at in Paul's Epistle to the Hebrews. All I want to say here is that there is something glorious in being created in God's image, and our material nature is part of that glory.)

This account in Genesis, on its own, is fulfillment enough for anyone who questions just what the balance of power is between man and woman; that is, it answers that there is no "balance" (in the sense of a stasis brought about by opposing forces) because their relationship is not meant to be one of power at all. Man and woman are equal in dignity and are meant to cooperate, not conflict. The rest of the creation account reveals a lot about the question that really bothers everyone, which is that if man and woman are equal, why are they not the same?

My Awakening

The last time I went to my beloved camp deep in the North Carolina mountain wilderness, I was about thirteen.

I didn't go there as a camper—it's a boys' camp (very posh now, it seems to me; it was quite humble back then, or maybe I didn't know about such things). I begged and pleaded until my dad took me for the yearly family camping weekend at the end of their season; we hadn't gone there for so long, but it was a place that moved me with the love that only a child has for the places of childhood.

The deep woods, the cabins, the beautiful lake with the rope swing off the second story of the dock, the icy plunge into the clear waters—canoeing, kayaking, even hiking, which I was in no way suited for, being too scrawny to handle climbing and carrying a pack—I loved it all. Most of all the horses. The girls' camp down the road had many horses, but this one had a few, and if you could find someone to take you, you could go riding on a trail with a lunch basket. That was just bliss for this city girl—pure joy.

Even though the counselors were too detached to notice me (and, truth to tell, probably too preoccupied and tired at the end of summer to think much about these pesky people who weren't real campers), I revered them. They were so rugged, so knowing, so youthfully old.

The first night, as always, we were greeted with a hayride to the top of the mountain for a fried-chicken picnic. I don't remember the meal or very much else. I remember only one thing. A woman was there with her six children. I think I had never met such a large family in person. When I became aware of their presence at the family camp, I instantly gravitated toward them, and once I had gotten a clear look at them all in their vastness, I promptly fell passionately in love.

The mother seemed to me to be lovely: slender, pretty, with a very kind expression. Her children were all a blur as far as I was concerned, but they were shyly cheerful. They flocked around her like little chicks. On the hayride, they nestled together, her arms around several of them.

They might have made friends with other campers, but they talked only to each other. They completely and utterly ignored me and even the other little girl who was my age. I could have been invisible, for all the notice they took of me, despite my best efforts to materialize in their consciousness somehow. Yet, probably for the first and possibly only time ever, someone's inattention to me didn't make me feel rejected or sullenly hateful. I felt that they were perfect—just perfect—in themselves, regardless of how much they failed to notice me. I felt—again, most unusually—that they were indeed justified in acting as if I simply wasn't in their world, because I was truly not worthy to be one of them, however much I longed to be.

I think they left after the first day; I didn't see them again. I'm not sure what makes me remember them, except for the vision I had been left with.

Here I was, a little bundle of contradictions, all tied up in knots inside, no fun to myself or anyone else. I had a strong attachment to my mother and to my father, who were divorced; things were complicated. I was getting stuffed to the gills with the kind of anger you encountered back then in the places I inhabited: protests, zero population growth, women's rights, abortion, contraception, free love, "God is dead," relativism, on and on and on. They were vibrations that penetrated me all the time. I was too young to evaluate. I simply absorbed.

At the same time, I read constantly, almost obsessively, perhaps as a defense against this barrage of destruction. Unlike today, the destroyers of culture had not yet realized that it damages their efforts to leave old books around for a child to find (now they simply remove them). So I read old books. There wasn't much else to read!

In those books I encountered one particular doctrine that helped me along my path to finding God, and that is the irrefutable notion that good and evil exist and can be known, often through the wonder inspired by beauty—including beauty in nature.

It's through contact with (I won't say understanding of) this reality and its effects that I experienced an uncovering of faith, which took place after a certain point in my development when my mind was awakened to logic; and every step of the reasoning out of the existence of good—the Good God—was like a new layer of truth exposed for me.

And the vision that I had on that evening by a mountain lake, climbing into a truck full of hay, was of motherhood in all its tender glory. That vision fed a secret desire that I would never admit to all the career-demanding, family-scorning folks around me in those days: a desire to become that person.

So, many years later, when somehow I was a wife and mother and unfit follower of God, it was with a sense of quiet recognition that I read John Paul II's explanation of the second chapter of Genesis. Not that I had had this knowledge before, but the gaining of it was a confirmation and a fulfillment.

Did you ever wonder why there are two accounts of creation? As we saw, the first account reveals the goodness of creation and the forming of man and woman in the image of God—a truth that bears much contemplation. So much so that, as John Paul II says (starting in the third paragraph of chapter 3 of *Mulieris Dignitatem*), the second account (Gen. 2:18–25) seems to provide an extended meditation on what exactly this means.

There we read that man was alone. He had all the uncorrupted beauty of the unspoiled, fresh, lovely world at his disposal to do with what he would (and remember, he had no bad thoughts as yet, so any idea that came to him would be a fitting, wonderful, and delightful one), but he was alone, and God saw this.

Almost to drive the *aloneness* point home, God brings each and every creature to Adam for naming. Just think! Any account you've ever heard of the bond between man and beast pales before this opportunity for Adam to commune with nature, to embrace even a lion, never mind a dog or a cat, as a bosom friend. To name, to give each thing its own identity—I think from our vantage point of disappointment and shame in the weariness of the world, this represents an astounding opportunity.

"But for Adam there was not found a help meet for him" (Gen. 2:20, KJV). Something is missing in all this perfection. Something ... something ... What could it be? Adam wants to give of himself, and there is no one to give this gift to!

So God takes Adam back to a state of pre-Creation. John Paul II goes into much more depth on this passage in his writings. He explains that by "God caused a deep sleep to fall upon Adam, and he slept," Scripture intends for us to know that Adam, generic man (for Hebrew has such a word, whereas English has "man" for both the generic and the specific), is called into existence anew, as *ish* and *isha*—male and female, man and woman.

From all eternity, God knew that there would come a day—our day —when people would get confused about what it means to be a man and a woman. So (among other reasons; I'm not so silly as to think this is the *only* reason) He put this other account in the Bible to express this deep meaning about how it came to be that the human being would have two essential (as opposed to contextual, conditioned, arbitrary, imposed, or cultural) forms: male and female.

When Adam emerges from this state, in which God forms Eve out of his rib, he makes a significant statement in the form of his cry: "This is now bone of my bones and flesh of my flesh" (Gen. 2:23, KJV)—in other words, he says, "At last, I am not alone. Here is one like me, also made in the image of God."

We observe the loneliness of man in a perfect world that does not contain another who is like him and yet—other. By himself he experiences aloneness. With the beasts he experiences aloneness. But with woman he experiences "a fit helper"—a soul mate, if you will. And notice further what others have pointed out, that she comes from his side, to be at his side. Not his foot, to be beneath him, or his head, to rule over him, but under his arm, to share in his task and to be protected by him.

And they shall be one flesh. Here, at the beginning, we have the whole program of marriage. We know it's what God wanted, since it's before the Fall, as opposed to just a mixed-up result of many bad choices after the Fall: a man will leave his father and mother and become a unity of the two with his wife, and this is how they will make love manifest—being fruitful and multiplying and filling the earth—with another person, the child, the only possible fulfillment of this solution to the problem of loneliness.

Other and Greater Powers

Are you a secret footnote fanatic? I love footnotes.

As a sometimes wildly nonlinear person (whose thoughts and conversations consist mainly of digressions and barely intelligible metaphors, parallels, and connections, parenthetically expressed, the origins of which are known usually only to me and then dimly so, as you can see), nothing delights me as much as being able to follow the subterranean (or subtextual) workings of the author's thought process. As dry as the skeleton of a reference can be (e.g., *Paradiso* XXXIII, 140–145),[6] it sometimes leads to delight.

---

[6]   Do you recognize this citation? It's a reference to the last lines of Dante's *Paradiso*, just for footnote fun:

> Except that then my mind was struck by lightning
> Through which my longing was at last fulfilled.
> Here powers failed my high imagination:
> But by now my desire and will were turned,
> Like a balanced wheel rotated evenly,
> By the Love that moves the sun and the other stars.

How much more so when the footnote is chatty, don't you agree? Instant gratification for the geeky, convoluted, or merely curious. And this habit of perusing footnotes proved most fruitful for yours truly!

Pope John Paul II wrote *Mulieris Dignitatem* to address the issue of why women can never be priests. It's not a question that ever bothered *me*. I had and have no desire to be a priest, none whatsoever. I wanted to be a wife and mother. To me, it was always clear that the priesthood exists to offer a fitting sacrifice to God and to mediate the sacramental grace that saves. I look to priests to provide what I need for my adventure of bringing souls into the world to receive grace.

I'd no sooner second-guess the ultimate meaning of this adventure *for me* than I'd expect a priest to want to be a mother!

However, I've come to see that people really do have different fundamental approaches to deep questions. Realizing this has motivated me, over the years, to try to get to the bottom of equality and priesthood and just what it is that women are contributing, on an ontological level, to the overall picture of the meaning of life. Not everyone is satisfied with "it's just the way it is, now get on with things" (though, truth to tell, I often am).

Anyway, there are thoughtful, convincing, tradition- and Scripture-based arguments on the topic of the male priesthood: see Pope Paul VI's *Declaration on the Question of Admission of Women to the Priesthood* (1976) and Pope John Paul II's *Ordinatio Sacerdotalis* (1994). Yet somehow, for those who are determined to see things in terms of male power structures, it's just always too easy to say that men keep the priesthood for themselves because they want to run things and are stronger, so they will.

John Paul II decided on a different approach with this letter (after writing the above-mentioned one defining the male priesthood *de fide*, a matter of assent in faith). He sought to offer a persuasive picture to show that women have their own calling, which is rooted in the very beginnings of creation. His message is that love brings forth the world—love of God for His creatures and creation—and that love defines the relationship between man and woman. As we've seen, this love takes a particular form for each. The love of the man takes the form of a gift—the desire of Adam to give himself to another just like himself, except with a unique capacity for receiving that love.

The vocation of the woman is to receive the gift offered by the man for the purpose of returning it, and the gift and the response are so great that they find expression as another human being, also made in the image and likeness of God.

Now, in the course of explaining the spousal relationship between Christ (the Bridegroom, and hence too the priest) and His Church (the Bride, a vocation perfectly expressed in the Blessed Virgin, who is the new Eve, the Mother of the living and of the Church), John Paul II makes an interesting point that adds another layer to the discussion on marriage and the sexes. He speaks of the Church as twofold (in section 7, 27); the Church can be thought of as "both 'Marian' and 'Apostolic-Petrine.'" In other words, yes, there's the doing, saving, and Christ-manifesting Church, represented by Peter and the Apostles (hence, Petrine), which is always bringing the people of God toward the heavenly vision of the spotless Bride, represented by Mary (hence, Marian).

This all brings me to footnote 55, which is a bit long, for a footnote, and speaks of how Mary precedes Peter:

> A contemporary theologian has rightly stated that Mary is "Queen of the Apostles without any pretensions to apostolic powers: she has other and greater powers."

She is the queen of priests (her title "Queen of the Apostles," by the way, can be traced to the fourteenth century and has its origin in Acts 1:13–14, where we are told she appears in the midst of the apostles as they prayed on Pentecost). She doesn't have priestly powers herself. "She has other and *greater* powers."

What could that mean? Greater than being an apostle? That would have to be pretty great, whichever way you look at it, whether you think of the priest as *serving* the world or as *having power over it*.

These words led me to so many reflections about womanhood, the leisure necessary for being contemplative, Sunday as the day of leisure and contemplation, family life, the current crisis in political philosophy (in which we have abandoned leisure and Sunday rest and find ourselves reaping the whirlwind in our disordered civic life), and how being a woman is at the heart of the restoration of culture. So there is a lot to accomplish quite apart from being called (as a man) to the very specific role of priest; so much that it seems to involve a realm that ought not to be dismissed because it happens *not* to be the visible one at the altar or in the confessional.

In the hierarchy of things, men have a position of authority, and it's undoubtedly true that the priesthood (which, by the way, is not open to any man but only to those called) is a special kind of authority. I am arguing that this hierarchy is real and must be respected.

In affirming the place of woman as helpmeet and the man as authority—in short, the hierarchical reality—those who oppose feminism seem to create a problem for the woman, who is still a person (often a spirited person, because those who are not spirited don't worry themselves over any of this). This person naturally chafes at being "relegated" or not allowed to pursue excellence as she sees it through a male lens.

Part of the reaction is pride. Part of it is a healthy resistance to a pagan idea of authority as power, and hierarchy as a power and quality structure. After all, Christianity has given us this resistance, because Christ's authority is ratified by His Crucifixion—a fate that is the antithesis of power.

The man's inclination not to see that there is something more, something higher, than *action, doing, striving*, and *conquering* intensifies the confusion, compounded by his (very male) propensity to convince others that what he, a man, does is best, that the male perfection is the highest, noblest, and most worthy.

Most men secretly believe that men are superior and by dint of this confidence are very able to convince most women that they are too. They can't help themselves, and neither can we women, in whom men find a ready audience. We too have a nature, and this nature tends towards doubt and readiness to listen to another voice. We women tend to be ready to be convinced against our own interests. This is how the serpent overcame Eve, by leveraging her womanhood against her. (And where was Adam, and why did he not protect her? His failure is why we call it the sin of Adam and not the sin of Eve. That outcome is also a consequence of hierarchy.)

But what is left out of the argument between men and women is that Our Lady is both the most perfect exemplar of acceptance of reality (reality of patriarchy, hierarchy, "lowliness") and the most perfect achievement of the entire human race, male or female. The paradox of Christianity is that equality is revealed as empty ("he did not think equality something to be grasped at" [see Phil. 2:6]) *and* that patriarchy coexists with another final word. Even Our Lord allowed His Queen to command Him. And that is how she becomes "Queen of the Apostles"—by an interior submission to her own lowliness ("do whatever He tells you" [see John 2:5]—not "do what I tell you"). To serve is to reign!

In writing his more fatherly letter to women, that is to say, in a more positive and loving way (suited to women), John Paul II sought to express what the woman's gift is, rather than leaving it as a negative "you can never achieve this level of excellence or have the power that men have," which is the false paradigm the world uses. The woman's gift is to preserve and to serve the realm of being, of seeing, of active receptivity—of motherhood. John Paul II is saying that "Why can't a woman be a priest?" is the wrong question; the correct one is "why priests can't be mothers" or really, to say that we must stop comparing by *setting against*; woman has her own calling.

Karl Stern, in his book *Flight from Woman*, expresses very well what is meant by "other and greater powers" ("powers" in this context meaning virtues). He says that true creativity is lost when there is a flight from woman, as has occurred in the modern era (literally, he argues, in the cases of its philosophers). "Woman as real or potential mother possesses the sense of creativeness by which one lets something grow, nurtures it, allows it to follow its own mysterious law of becoming. Man's sense of creativeness is that of making things work." Later, "a woman gives birth, with that immediate sense of certainty that the whole world has been created for this particular new human being." He points out that this is true for Our Lady par excellence.

The liturgy proclaims (sometimes in so many words) that Mary is the "highest honor of our race." But she cannot be that without also accepting her place in the patriarchy: she cannot turn Ephesians upside down because to do so would be to contradict her status as "lowly handmaiden," which is her entire claim to her throne. To be the Queen of the Apostles means to accept precisely that she is not an apostle and has nothing to do with the mechanism of apostolic function if I can put it that way—yet it all flows through her and is mediated by her.

Most men today seem not quite to understand Mary's exalted place (in large part because the modern Church has retreated from emphasizing it), speaking of her more sentimentally than realistically. Do they ever ask, with the Song of Songs, "Who is she that cometh forth as the morning rising, fair as the moon, bright as the sun, terrible as an army set in array?" (6:9, DR).

Sometimes men who speak in defense of patriarchy do so with a spirit of both triumph and pity. They forget that Christ's crown signifying His Kingship and indicating the type of rule the Father had in store for Him from all eternity is made of thorns driven into His skull. They perhaps have not understood the consequences of accepting Mary as their queen, to understand that they are not the best (as a sex, and neither is woman as a sex: they complement each other). They don't quite understand what it means to them to be a Christian man—just as most women don't understand the hidden world they could lay claim to, if only they weren't convinced by women who listen to the wrong men, to be like men!

Does this mean that I think that women are better than men, because the Blessed Virgin is exalted above all other creatures? Some Catholic feminists argue that woman is superior to man. Could it be that the Pauline exhortation to be submissive to the man's authority is in error, once we realize the exalted stature of Mary? Could those who argue for a goddess figure in the Mother of God be right?

To hold such a position would be idolatry and contrary to everything observable in human nature. The energy needed to resist it is proof enough that hierarchy in general—the ordering of everything in the universe—is a given, and so is patriarchy in particular. Knowing that the Christian patriarchy holds Mary in her place of highest honor does hold a secret for the feminine soul. The secret is that hiddenness is glorious, that the lowliest shall be raised, and that to serve is to reign.

The Truth about Woman as Bride

Continuing the reading of *Mulieris Dignitatem* after that little diversion into the greater powers of Mary, we call to mind that the origins of marriage are "in the beginning."

Despite being under the pain of the effects of the Fall, which (through the sin of Adam) render a lot of the first ideas God had for us null and void, we do have access to this original idea of God's about marriage. It's those words of Christ's in the nineteenth chapter of Matthew that give us the guarantee, the sort of password to get back through the checkpoint at the gates of the Garden of Eden: "In the beginning it was not so."

There at the beginning we find Christ (the tree of life, the new Adam) and Mary (the new Eve, the one through whom *enmity* to sin will come).

> The *Redemption restores* ... the *good* that was essentially "diminished" by sin and its heritage in human history....
>
> Mary is "the new beginning" of the dignity and vocation of women, of each and every woman. (*Mulieris Dignitatem* [MD] 11)

The second thing, and this is really important (this will be on the test): *The truth about woman as bride*: "The Bridegroom is the one who loves. The Bride is loved: it is she who receives love, in order to love in return" (*MD* 29). That is, the essence of marriage reveals the nature of man and woman: the man gives the gift of himself to the woman, who receives it *in order to return it*—and this relationship also forms an image of the spousal meaning of Christ's union with the Church. We must understand these words with their multivalences. The Bridegroom is the man and also Christ. The Bride is the woman and also the Church. And furthermore, if in His image God made man, male and female, and God's reality is trinitarian, then the image of the human relationship is trinitarian also. The persons don't share identity—equal plus equal, congruent, the same—but have complementarity: giving, receiving in order to return the gift, and the gift, which in the Godhead is the Holy Spirit and in marriage is the child.

Although man and woman are equal in the dignity of nature, it's not a sameness of each giving a gift to the other. It's a bit more complex than that. The man is made by God to want to give himself to someone *like him* (bone of my bones), and the woman is made by God, completing His creation, to be the person who receives the gift. When she receives the gift, and precisely by means of her receptivity, she is able to give the gift in return: the child, the embodiment of the love of the two, united in one flesh.

We often think of "two becoming one flesh" as meaning the physical union of the two in the act of love, but it has this other dimension, also physical but more than physical: the expression of the love of the gift and the reception of the gift in the form of another human being, another flesh of my flesh, another image of God: the new *person* who also has a soul and a desire to give the gift of himself.

This receptivity of woman, John Paul II makes clear, isn't just in the context of marriage: it defines her universally, in how she, as a woman, approaches everything, "representing a particular value" — femininity, which *means* "receiving in order to give in return."

You can see how this extra, seemingly little insight must be true — *if* you can get over our almost visceral resistance to having femininity defined in any way as distinct from masculinity. That resistance is a result of the ascendency of the antithesis of love — power — which automatically relegates anything "not male" to an inferior category. Often we women ourselves do this relegating, because we take men seriously when they thump their chests, instead of quietly feeling our own worth where it truly lies.

You can see that if there is only *giving* of gifts, there will be only clashing, clanging, violence even — as at a restaurant, when everyone at the table is insisting on paying the check, to give a mild example. It can quickly get loud and even unpleasant. No, there must be receiving also.

This receptivity is not passive; it has the active quality of interiority that allows gestation. In order to return the gift with transformation, it must first be received. Only in the impatience of time do we take a snapshot before the whole story is told. We must be patient to see things as they are.

My heart jumped to see John Paul II reveal in this letter on women what the difference between man and woman is and to locate it precisely in the very essence of each, defining their complementarity without destroying the equality of their dignity. His insight resolves the seemingly intractable battle of the sexes, bringing great peace.

PART 2

On the Woman in the Home

When I started my married life—you will laugh at me—I literally didn't know how to sweep a floor. No matter how unskilled you may think you are, I was much, much worse. Fortunately, I didn't get the idea that it didn't matter; instead, because books such as *Kitchen Gardens* and others came my way, and because of many factors I'm sure I know nothing about, I intuited that trying to learn even simple things and become good at them, even if they frustrated me greatly and seemed both beyond my ability and beneath my notice, would be fruitful for my life with these others who are given to me. Somehow, I did start to see that it was going to be worthwhile to grapple with the work around me, even if it seemed like drudgery.

We reasonably assume that anyone taking an outside job would be given a manual, a mentor, or some instructions. We assume that a woman in this position would need time to master her task. Yet in the realm of *homemaking*, our assumption seems to be not only that we needn't try to be good at the job, but that just as we are figuring things out (say, when our children get to school age), everyone will expect us to quit and move on to something more fulfilling.

How frustrating! Are these just years to be muddled through, or is there a real reward *in the field*, awaiting us?

I maintain the latter! I have a vision of *home*, a refuge and a radiating light, that comprises many small doings, some perhaps a bit of a slog (but what job doesn't have aspects of drudgery?), some amazingly creative, all simply *needing to be mastered at some level*.

I submit that only when a woman seeks good judgment in these matters will she experience what she thinks is lacking—the joy of devotion.

Good Judgment and "Living Differently"

he following astute quotation caught my eye, not least because it unexpectedly appears in an older, humble gardening book:[7]

> A wise lady once said, "If you haven't good judgment you'll never make a good cook or anything else."

What does this mean? How can we get this good judgment this wise lady speaks of? Isn't good judgment something you have or don't have? Doesn't it seem unfair to say that if you don't have this mysterious quality, you'll never be good at cooking or *anything else*?

Is good judgment a virtue? Can it be learned? I had never thought of virtue at all when I was younger. When I became a Christian, I suppose I had a vague idea that God makes the person better. We have a grace of virtue granted in Baptism through which we have Christ's life (and

---

[7] Mary Mason Campbell, *Kitchen Gardens*, illustrated by Tasha Tudor—a little gem of a book.

thus, goodness or virtue) infused in us. We cooperate with that grace by wishing to grow in goodness and by trying to! Josef Pieper, in his book *The Four Cardinal Virtues*, tells us that St. Thomas Aquinas speaks of "the pre-eminence of that 'fuller' prudence ["good judgment"]) in which the natural *and* the supernatural, the acquired *and* the given, are combined in a felicitous, in a literally 'graced' unity."[8]

Good judgment, also known as prudence, the *queen* of virtues, comes primarily from experience and memory. We have to do things, or try to do them; we have to make mistakes, remember how things came about, and try again. Prudence can't be developed without reflecting on our actions after we do them and our experiences after we experience them.

Pieper tells us: "Trueness-to-being of memory, open-mindedness, clear-sighted objectivity in unexpected circumstances: these are qualities of mind of the prudent man. All three are focused upon what is 'already' real, upon things past and present."[9]

To paraphrase Pieper (who is paraphrasing St. Thomas Aquinas) on this point: a less-prudent plan *carried out* is, in fact, more prudent than a more-prudent plan that is never acted upon. The main thing to understand is that good judgment is about present action, not great plans (and certainly not abandonment of action).

Paradoxically, then, we won't have good judgment until we make up our minds to try to "be good at" cooking or "anything else"—that is, the task at hand. This becomes obvious when we observe our children as they stumble about or stammer or try to draw pictures—we see that they have to *begin* by doing things, however imperfect their efforts may be. Same with us, and perhaps the humility of the process is one of the things Our Lord had in mind when He urged us to be more childlike.

I'm convinced that one reason we aren't "good cooks" or good at "anything else" in the realm of keeping the home, specifically, is that we simply aren't willing to learn (and to find ourselves "incompetent" for that learning

---

[8]   Josef Pieper, *The Four Cardinal Virtues: Prudence, Justice, Fortitude, Temperance* (New York: Harcourt, Brace, and World, 1955), 14.

[9]   Ibid., 17.

period, most likely), *even though the tasks really are things we ought to do.* Simply put, if the wife and mother doesn't do them, they remain undone. I'm not talking about individual tasks, most of which can be outsourced to some extent, if (and it is a big if) the financial means are there. I am talking more about the whole domain of creating and tending the home as the work of one's life.

We will finally understand the virtue of prudence if we think of it (along with the ancients) as conscience—as knowing what we ought to do, in the "here and now; in short, knowing" the demands of goodness for us, in whatever circumstances we find ourselves.

If this state of unwillingness persists, we are then trapped in not *liking* the work that goes into making a home. We make excuses about not being good at it, or we compare ourselves with another woman and conclude that for her, these things just come naturally or that she even has a special gift, but that the whole enterprise doesn't happen to give us joy, so maybe we should go on to something else.

Because we are not good at these things, we sort of despise them—or at least dismiss them.

A Meditation on Simple Convictions

What are the simple convictions that a woman might hold fast? The conviction that children need their mother; that it's ultimately enjoyable, important, and spiritually healthy for a woman, even a woman who could be successful in the world, to devote herself to her family; that when a family does not have the wife and mother (same person) devoted to it, everyone from the baby to society suffers.

I have noticed that even so-called conservatives, impressively credentialed movers of public opinion, by and large, have wives who have separate careers or who themselves work (if they are the wives) and that this fact bears on the ability of the rest of us to hold on to our convictions and to have confidence in them.

Because of this state of affairs, this conflict of interest or convictions, if you will, I'm not sure that even my little meditation can be received at face value. But I will make the attempt.

We are addicted to wanting to find new ways to do things: when thinking of all the ways we must "subdue the earth," human nature tries to do things better, to be innovative, and to improve technique. As the daughter of an engineering professor, I loved reading in *Cheaper by the Dozen* how the young Frank Gilbreth challenged veteran bricklayers to a masonry contest. Just through observation, he had noticed inefficiencies that slowed them down. His way really was better, new, and improved—and that's the way it should be.

But not everything is subject to this kind of improvement; forcing the issue can lead to vast and unintended consequences. Yet our nature, which is also our fatal flaw, drives us to it. This fatal flaw is to expand on our propensity to be active and to achieve, by means of our own will, all the greatness we can encompass and to call it all ours. You can find a little discourse on this flaw in the First Letter of John: "For all that is in the world, the lust of the flesh, and the lust of the eyes, and *the pride of life*, is not of the Father, but is of the world" (2:16, KJV, emphasis added).

So naturally, those who *do* and *achieve* attract our attention. And we start to listen, in spite of ourselves, to those who (perhaps on account of a need to rationalize choices they didn't quite think through) claim to have found a new way to do fundamental things—not necessarily bricklaying but, for instance, raising children or living as a family.

Over time we find that we are tempted to affirm, against our innermost longings and even fundamental principles, something that we never intended to, or that we simply forget important but hidden things. We aren't aware that it can be a kind of false humility to let go of what we've identified as worthy, simply because others insist. There is nothing praiseworthy in being open to doubt when we know the good.

For women, especially in our time, this is the constant battle. It's hard not to be worn down. We will always be unsure that we are right when we've committed to devotion to the family. We don't see or hear any affirmation for what we have chosen; on the contrary, we find only congratulation for worldly honors, even from those who ostensibly value what we value.

Social media have increased the volume of the voices telling us that we are good enough only when we have exhibited the right degree of achievement and what the world calls excellence (it's not the ancient philosophers' definition, though—sometimes I wonder if these intellectuals have read their

Boethius). It makes sense, doesn't it, that in an age of individualism lived in public, individual success, well documented online, will be most prized.

We won't hear a general outcry praising the hidden life of devotion that in this journey of ours brings lasting satisfaction. Ultimately that is probably better for the soul, don't you think? But in the short term, it is obviously more difficult; thus, we'll have to cultivate fortitude, and for a very good reason, apart from our own sense of worth: Who will love children from day to day with a love of service, if not their mother? Who will make the home, if not the wife? Who would forgo financial security, public honors, and prosperity for a happy home, if not the wife and mother? Even the most highly educated and smartest women have realized that all the honor in the world doesn't make up for a neglected family. Believe me, I have an e-mail folder full of messages from ladies who turned away from the expectations of the world in order to find peace.

Some read "devotion" as "not working" and when they do, they go on to apply to my words a meaning they do not have. As I've said elsewhere, I've known women in demanding careers who are devoted to their homes in the way I'm speaking about, putting their responsibility to make the home first. I've also known women whose worth lies in their work; they regard home as a landing place for which they have no particular responsibility.

I'm doing my best, little as it is, to help anyone who wants to "live differently" (in the words of Pope Benedict), on account of the hope we are given, especially when it comes to the practical details. I will always maintain that the family is God's plan for life in this world of ours, and that any sacrifice we make to fulfill His plan is worth the pain we might suffer.

Some Thoughts on the Woman's Role

 ere is a response one might make to what I have said: "Working is a matter of choice. We should support each other, not create conflicts." You may be thinking this yourself.

People make choices, and their choices are based on their priorities, spoken or unspoken: where to live, what job to have, how far to commute, what house to own or if to own at all, whether to welcome children. Everyone always has a choice. It's the criteria with which you make your choices that are worth examining—for the way they serve or don't serve your goals and responsibilities.

Further, these choices ought to be based on principles, which, in turn, have to correspond to *the way things are* or, to put it in philosophical terms, to the natural law. Men and women are made a certain way, each sex with its own perfections and defects.

The objection here raises the specter of "judging" another's choices, with the hidden premise that to do so is wrong. It's true that we cannot judge in the sense of condemning, but beware of dismissing valid observations with the seemingly unassailable admonition not to judge. We judge all the time, and rightly so. If we did not judge bad conduct, we could not function as a society.

Without condemning anyone, my aim here is to point out differences known to everyone and previously understood divisions in the spheres of life that lead to flourishing. What I'd like to bring to the fore is a healthy examination of whether we are right, as a society under the ideology of feminism, to dismiss care of the home as an inferior undertaking.

Another point that someone might bring up to counter what I have said: "We are experiencing financial difficulties. For me, the wife, to work seems like the only answer."

For most of our married life and the lives of our friends (and we are blessed to have friends just as committed as we are), my husband's and my priorities have meant living in what others would call poverty (which I hasten to say is not a word I would use), with few amenities, relying on God's providence. One family close to us is expecting their eighth child and still rents, with no ownership in sight, as they live on a modest public servant's salary. Their priority is to welcome children, and their home is clean and happy. Another family with ten children (one of whom has a serious illness) lives in what would be described in a real-estate ad as a two-bedroom house (they've reclaimed the tiny attic) in a very high-cost area. They love each other and are a great example to their community. I know many people who admire them and seek their wisdom.

Another family with five children bought a house that their friends feared would fall down the hill! But they put in the requisite elbow grease. The father's job is far from secure. At age fifty-eight, he's in the same place most men of his educational background reach in their twenties, career-security-wise. It takes its toll on him, I'm sure. But the most important thing for him was that his children grow up in a certain place surrounded by certain people. Everything else is secondary to him. He readily and enthusiastically admits that it's the knowledge that his wife is content and happy, that she is the heart of their home, that keeps him going.

I purposely excluded high-income, extended-family-supported situations from my discussion because I wanted to point out that the decision for a mother to stay at home is worth it, despite a loss of income. I know this from personal experience, from when *my* husband was unemployed for eighteen months and we barely cleared $20,000 that year, with six children. I am not glamorizing the choice to live on one income.

But in all my years of marriage, I notice that the people who are the most financially well off are the ones with the highest anxiety levels, such as the investment banker I met at a soccer game, who lived in a million-dollar home and worried to the point of illness about his ability to support his two children.

Now, having said that, let me note that I rarely use the term "stay-at-home mom" because history shows that women have worked hard alongside their husbands in the fields and have done their share to keep the bacon on the table. Yet even those hardy pioneer women relied on their husbands to protect them as they bore and nurtured the children.

Most people, men and women, in most places and times in history, have worked extremely hard simply to subsist. The mark of a good civilization is that the woman, the wife and mother, is able to fulfill her nurturing role, protected by her husband.

The term "stay-at-home mom" is poor shorthand for what I prefer to express with more fullness: to make the point that devotion to home is more important than young parents today realize, not for the wife's work at the laundry or even the food, but for how she can spend time and energy on providing the love and shelter of the *persons* who take refuge there. It's worth moving for, it's worth taking a different job for, it's worth finding a different house for, it's worth doing without for. And if your thought is "poor me!" take a moment to thank your husband for being a good provider.

One last thought: Feminists seek to put women on an equal footing with men in the world. Because equality is the paramount value in the modern mind, certain inconsistencies in the rhetoric are never examined.

One such inconsistency is that feminists insist that we women unshackle ourselves from the limits of hearth and home and seek the exhilarating freedom afforded to men in the professional world. For decades, we were exhorted to have it all and do it all, to excel and to conquer, blasting through the glass ceiling and claiming our place in the boardroom and any other place of power. Yet when anyone points out that the great majority of women seem not to want to do this, their argument pivots to *need*, that women *must* work simply to hold things together; that anyone who thinks women should stay home is operating out of an unexamined position of privilege, not realizing the pressure put on women to work.

Further unexamined is the situation created by the feminist agenda itself, where the entire educational system, geared toward pushing girls away from home life and into careers, creates one concrete, decisive factor in their lives: debt. The *need* to work as adults stems directly from the situation created by the *desire* to be a liberated woman in control of her own destiny in a career. Never does the feminist ideology grapple with the reality that the person in this situation will marry and have children *whom she will want to care for*.

Thus, the burden of a willfully self-contradictory ideology is borne by its victims, as is always the case with ideologies. The difference with this one is how thoroughly indoctrinated the victims are; they themselves parrot the talking points, confronting neither the contradiction nor its unhappy results in the lives around us.

We have labored under this debilitating conflict long enough. It's time to expose its destructiveness. Underlying the insistence on women working and the duplicitous switch between lofty ideal and dire need is the assumption that as a life pursuit, home is not worthy and work is. The truth that men tend to hide (manlike) is that work exists to support the home.

> I think I can understand that feeling about a housewife's work being like that of Sisyphus.... But it is surely, in reality, the most important work in the world. What do ships, railways, mines, cars, government etc exist for except that people may be fed, warmed, and safe in their own homes?... We wage war in order to have peace, we work in order to have leisure, we produce food in order to eat it. So your job is the one for which all others exist. (C. S. Lewis, letter to Mrs. Johnson)

ASK AUNTIE LEILA
"I Feel Guilty Not Working"

Dear Auntie Leila,

I had part-time job. I liked it. When my baby got a bit older and my husband started traveling, that little job was the greatest source of anxiety and worry. It took away my peace and made me into the kind of mother I never wanted to be: frantic, weary (in all the wrong ways), and disorganized. So I resigned. And now I feel guilty! It's all self-imposed guilt, as my husband is completely supportive. But I feel guilty spending money I no longer contribute to, putting all the financial burden on my husband's shoulders, and not being out in the community.

Thank you,

A Young Mom

ear Young Mom,

We all need encouragement. We discover wonderful things about the meaning of life and then lose our insights, usually because it turns out to be hard to put them into practice. The need for an infant to have close contact with his mother; the irreplaceable value of an intact family; the beauty of home life; the possibility of living simply—these are all things that have been written about eloquently but perhaps embraced by few. It quickly seems too hard to nurse a baby, give up a job that gets you out of the house and the chaos, understand the person your spouse is developing into, or live within a budget.

It's just all very hard! The going gets tough, and the weak fold. What makes us weak? Not having encouragement from friends. When you have a friend, you can get through a lot.

> Ointment and perfumes rejoice the heart: and the good counsels
> of a friend are sweet to the soul. (Prov. 27:9, DR)

Let's make our homes places of peace and love, order and wonder. Making a family requires a sense of responsibility—to find a way (and your way doesn't have to be the same as another family's way) to put it first. I happen to think that a family can't be a family without the wife and mother making the home. Yes, many women work, but the stresses they experience at *having to do it all* testify to my statement. Even when the mother dies, the home receives a special grace of preservation in her memory. But when she runs away, either physically or mentally, the insufficiency is felt.

Let's notice that if the woman is nursing the baby, and another baby comes along (which is how it *usually* works, when left to itself, and why shouldn't it be?), and the babies start to need to learn things in their own way and at their own pace, and not be rushed, and then they get older and need more learning and guiding, and there probably are more babies, this woman is uniquely qualified to be the manager of the home, and more than manager, its loving maker. It takes a great upheaval, in fact, to shake her *out of* this role.

For her to leave her home to get money in paycheck form represents a hardship or at minimum a stress (*even when her outside work is fulfilling*); but it is a challenge and a joy for her to figure out how to use the money that there is, be it ever so little.

And for the husband, it's a privilege to earn the money, even when it doesn't seem to be enough, even though he might have to work two jobs to do it; because in return he gets a loving home, which is something he can't make on his own.

I don't reject the idea that a woman can contribute with a salary. There are lots of different people in the world and many different circumstances. Sometimes babies don't come at the tremendous pace expected; sometimes there are other family members who do a lot of the tasks in the home. Even so, the wife makes her home in the sense of giving the whole its form. It's her glory.

When the family is young, it seems like a doable thing for both husband and wife to work at jobs. If there is a lot of support and many extra hands, I think it can be doable, although there is an opportunity cost in the form of energy directed outward when interior growth needs to happen. Many of the formative ideas I talk about in this book are most easily and organically incorporated in those early years. If there isn't that support, I think it's *not doable*. Not by me, anyway! A lot is lost. I've now seen enough to know that many women end up regretting having thought of those early years as expendable from the home.

Maybe you can do it, my dear reader who might be balking. I just want to say this: you might not notice the strain for a long time, and by then it might be too late, because the early years are when you're honing your skills and thinking your thoughts.

What are those skills? Among other things, and since this question specifies *monetary* contributions to family life: *skills* in managing the home!

Money is pretty practical. It's so practical, it hurts sometimes! In a world where houses, college, food, clothing, fuel, and so on are all are priced based on one person without any dependents or on two people working full-time, where does devoting yourself to home fit in? How do you make it work financially?

A family can live on *one* modest income. I've done it, and I've seen many do it—yes, today. I know you can do it too, and I want to give you some thoughts on how.

Dear Young Mom, I think it might help you if you could see the whole scope of the undertaking!

Know that by not working at a job you are freeing your husband to *earn* the money and *to rest* in the knowledge that it will be well spent. Now, you say you feel that you have it easy and are getting away with something by not earning. It's hard to describe to you what the family is like ten, fifteen, and twenty years after its beginnings. It's hard to explain the *investment* that you and your husband are making right now. So it's a case of making up your mind, even if you can't see how it will work out.

What can you do?

Spend time reading: about money management, about the education of children, about taking care of the home—not to mention forming your own mind by reading the great literature you may have missed in school.

Learn to garden. Growing some of your own food pays off. A lot of grocery trips are for fresh items, and if you have them in your garden (or freezer or pantry), you cut down on other expenses, because staying out of stores is key to not spending money!

Learn to make things. Put up a shelf, sew a skirt, knit a sweater.

Learn to get a bargain. Make up your mind that you will not pay full price for anything unless you know for a fact you can't get it cheaper, whether it's meat, furniture, cars, or clothing. Say no to paying full price. There are a few exceptions, but don't worry about it. Train yourself to resist the markup.

Learn to "thrift." When you stay home, you have time. Time is on the side of the bargain hunter. You might not have brand-spanking-new whatever it is right away, but you will have it, eventually, because someone will sell theirs on Craigslist or at a yard sale. You just have to wait. There is almost nothing you can't find if you are patient.

Learn to find treasures in the trash. Keep your eye on the side of the road. People put out stuff they want to get rid of because they know someone will pick it up. They usually don't really want their grill or bed or shelves to end up in the trash; they just don't have the motivation to sell the item and are happy that you are picking it up. Ask if you aren't sure.

Learn to plan your menus. My experience was that I saved *one-third* of my grocery bill simply by planning my menus, even without the added step of shopping sales and stockpiling pantry items. That's when I was already staying home. The savings will be even greater if you compare menu planning to tired-working-mom meals, the most expensive kind! I have a whole system mapped out for you here in volume 3, and my system is better than any other I've seen because you won't be making *my* menus: you'll be making your own.

Don't compare yourself with big spenders who indulge in consumer goods and have a high lifestyle. They have their priorities, and you don't know what kind of debt they are in. Truly, in our age, the tricky part of the switch to one income is simply relinquishing the habit of buying everything new. Compare yourself, if compare you must, with committed pioneers of all ages who wanted freedom and faith for their families.

Consider yourself in training.

Sometimes you have to rise above "what everyone thinks" and choose for yourself. Sometimes you know that what you are doing doesn't carry a dollar sign but has real value, even real monetary value. Sometimes you have to take the long view. Isn't that what women are all about? What we do is gestational in nature. We know that it takes nine months of hidden life to produce that squirming newborn.

We ought to know that in ten years our lives will be very different from the way they are now, different in a way that will demand so much from us that our husbands will be grateful that we are home to deal with it all. We also can't predict the economic future. Many a family ended up being grateful that they already had the habits of thrift and economy *before* hard times hit, when the learning curve is painful.

Dear Young Mom, the thrifty, managing wife *does* contribute to her husband's earnings! And the wise woman's contribution to the community can't be measured! The gift of bright-eyed, happy children to the world is literally incalculable! The community itself is sustained by devoted marriages lived out in a complementary way.

As you embark on this different way of life, another hidden benefit will reveal itself to you. Contrary to what we women think, men desire their wives to appreciate their provision, even if it is lowly in the eyes of the world. The subtle message of the woman who thinks her family can't survive on the one income brought in by her able-bodied husband is that he is not man enough to take care of them. (I have noticed that this danger is avoided in circumstances where the man is disabled when his wife frames her going out into the workplace as a necessary evil, not as a fulfillment of a vision of their prosperity.)

Once you see how you, the woman, have your gifts, you will come to appreciate that the man's gift is to be free to be the provider, and that even if he isn't a rich man in the eyes of the world (even if he's a "failure"), in the eyes of his family—his wife—he's a hero and a good man. The world sees one way; we must have the courage to see another way.

The contribution in the home that I have described (made by the manager and creative genius) will take a lifetime to assess. Be patient and know that you have friends to support you, even if you can't see them!

When I put this post on the blog, it was, as usual, accompanied by photos of my home. Most of my mail is positive, but once I got a message that chastised me for what the writer referred to as visual boasting of my beautiful, privileged, perfect life. She was convinced that I am a huge hypocrite, exhorting others to live on a small income when I have a luxurious environment. So here I wanted to make a point: every picture I have posted (and there are a lot, of all the rooms in my house) features things I've "thrifted," found for free in the trash or on the side of the road, been given, or, if new, found on clearance (in the case of pretty bowls and such that I can't resist). Yes, I found a lovely sofa at a yard sale and had it reupholstered after many years of wearing out the original upholstery! And on and on. The things I speak of are doable.

Deciding to Be Home

Within the bosom of the woman is a deep desire to be home. The problem is that, as a result of having a nurturing nature, women are good at doing what other people think they should do. The tendency to doubt that the woman has an irreplaceable role in the home means that sometimes women find it difficult to admit that what other people expect is not what they truly desire.

Most women today bravely and against self-interest (but really, against the interest of feminine nature) accept that they cannot remain home, according to society's expectations. But a little something is ripped away whenever a woman finds herself more away than not, less with her children than she had dreamed, often not the one to make the little domestic choices and find solutions.

Even the woman who works from home feels a stress at being beholden to someone else's schedule that a man doesn't experience; that outside pull means that her body is there but her mind is on her commitments. Often there is a screen she's tethered to, and ordinary interactions with family members become interruptions and vexations. Working at home means there are no boundaries at all; hardly the pat solution many seem to think it is.

This situation, of a woman feeling the need to work in order to be fulfilled, feeds her sense of not being competent in the area of homemaking. If she stays home and gives up outside work commitments, she worries that she won't know how to make up for the income she loses. Does she know how to shop frugally? To manage housework on her own?

I understand. My goal is to offer help for women to learn how to stay at home and to live on one income. As with many an endeavor, more than half the battle is starting, even without knowing all the answers. In so many things, I find that, once I start, each step presents itself in a binary way: up or down, right or left. All I have to do is decide at the time, provided my goal is clear, and the path reveals itself. Prayer together, husband and wife, and conversations, *and simply doing* lead to the answers.

Over the years, I have had readers tell me of the rather dramatic ways in which they have reorganized their lives, including selling their "dream-home McMansion" for a rental in the city, so that they can stay home. Some have told me of walking away from high-powered careers, and of disappointing parents and in-laws, to resolve the inner conviction that they are needed at home.

Living on one (small) income means resetting expectations, especially about spending. I discuss this aspect in volume 3, but here I will confine myself to the observation that the biggest expenses for most families are housing payments and health insurance. Ideally, the latter will be covered by the husband's job, but if not, I recommend looking into a health cost-sharing plan (such as Samaritan Ministries).

I believe that mothers are happier at home. The home needs a center, a heart. Paradoxically, we may feel this most strongly when we have been away from our home, and the atmosphere that greets us upon our return is not what we would want; we know it would be different if we had been there.

It seems to me that some women and their families have learned to live with a certain tension, borne of the need on all sides to assure one another that everything is fine. Maybe the children are longing to be relieved of this burden.

One fear that lurks in the background for many women is that their children won't respond to them the way they do to the people they hire, and that they themselves won't find their children's company enjoyable.

Often, and here I think we come to the real anxiety, a woman who looks longingly at the possibility of staying home with her children doubts her ability to care for them. One reader put it to me this way: "The woman who takes care of my children does this professionally. Would I just be surviving every day with little ones? Would their days be worse with me than with her? . . . Still, they're mine . . . and I want them."

The trouble is that outsourcing, and thus objectifying, the care of children will always tend to make the already doubtful mother feel that she is indeed inadequate. Think of the helpless mothers in British literature who cower before their competent nannies!

Well, certainly no one wants to spend money to get the sort of shenanigans that children normally dish out (including injuries, illnesses, and naughtiness!). And no wonder British households had nurseries, where Nanny could relax from parental assessment of her performance but was at least a part of the household. Professionalizing childcare creates the sense that mothering means supervising the children's every waking moment (with the fear of lawsuits lurking somewhere in the background), interacting constantly with them, and above all, getting "results" from them to affirm that money is well spent and one's position has been well earned.

Gone is the un-self-conscious relationship so necessary to real family life.

The best way to recover it is to consider that in stepping away from paid work outside the home, the woman is not turning toward devotion to children per se, even though this is the way most women express what they are doing. Believe me when I tell you that even childless women sense the need to leave the workplace (or never enter it). You see, the devotion I'm speaking of is to the home. Ultimately, the children will grow up and leave. The husband and wife's *marriage* is what creates the sacred space of the home, and the home is the fitting object of devotion.

The home offers a culture of the family and hospitality for friends and strangers. The home is the place from which the children venture forth, having been formed, in order to take their gifts to make new homes of their own. And they will go. A home remains, when it has a heart, and reveals a new phase—one we are missing today, now that we are several generations into the experiment of abandoning this intimate and sacred space.

Committing to serving the home frees the woman from expectations about how the children will fare when professional support is removed. She can discover her task of eliciting from them an ever increasing sense of responsibility to life together in the home, and to help them not to be "happy" or to be "fulfilled" or to "reach their highest potential" but to find their vocation for the time when they leave home to make their own.

Ironically, now that enough time has passed since the feminist movement took hold, many women who resisted, seeing their devotion as child-oriented rather than work-oriented, express bitterness when the children leave. Having spent their time totally involved in their children's every need and wish, husband and wife find they have neglected their own friendship. The woman hardly knows who she is apart from the children's activities on which she has spent so much energy, and their father is almost a stranger. These women feel robbed and regret not going along with the feminist idea of seeking worth in a career. Thus, the phenomenon of divorces when the children go off to college, otherwise so incomprehensible.

And yet, we know that there is significant bitterness in knowing that the children came and went and their mother wasn't there, having been absorbed in her career! Is the woman's lot bitterness, regardless of her choices? Is there peace to be found? Understanding the commitment as being to the home (however humble it may be) helps the woman avoid disappointment when the inevitable occurs.

Having a home with a wife and mother in it is what matters to your children and to your husband and, most likely unbeknownst to you, to the neighborhood and the world. Seeing herself as devoted to the home allows a woman to have many interests and creative outlets (all of which, in turn, enrich her family). As to making it work on one income, G. K. Chesterton said in his brilliant essay "What's Wrong with the World": "Thrift is the really romantic thing; economy is more romantic than extravagance.... Thrift is poetic because it is creative; waste is unpoetic because it is waste.... If a man could undertake to make use of all the things in his dustbin, he would be a broader genius than Shakespeare."

Discontent

Sometimes when I wander around the Internet, I get anxious, and that feeling that *I'm doing it all wrong* starts to creep up the back of my neck. My hands get sweaty, and I experience palpitations. My eyes start to spin. Most of all, everything seems drab and wrong and dirty and unfortunate. I can see Walker Percy looking at me with his knowing, slightly sad eyes, watching me spiral off into the ether.

I experience *discontent*.

My discontent arises because I'm comparing myself with everyone else and finding myself wanting. But the truth is, today, here, now, there is nothing for it but *this*. I can make things better, I can make things different, but if I don't embrace the here and now and the "this," I will have literally *nothing*.

When I was young, I wanted to be like the heroine in each book I read. Gradually it occurred to me that the girl in book A was spunky and loud and made people laugh with a toss of her dark hair, and the girl in book B was quiet and understanding, and people took note of her once she had died. Even to me it eventually became clear that you couldn't be both. These girls were mutually exclusive! They canceled each other out!

You would appear to be insane if you tried to be both! Besides, you can't make yourself die—not while being spunky!

In a moment of unusual objectivity, for a child and for me, I surmised that it was the particularity of each girl, even if contrasting with that of the other, that made her endearing, *not any one attribute*. More: it is the author's loving gaze at the particularity that renders the person so lovable. When you stepped away from the story, you could even imagine not finding the laugh or the soft eyes annoying. Maybe that much-admired spunky gal in the book is someone we know who makes us a little crazy in real life! Maybe that's why some people don't enjoy some of those books.

Never mind that. It's this particularity that we need to find in our own place. These people who make us happy, these pretty things, these funny animals, and especially our very own real realities: let's find them and learn to look at them in a way that makes them part of our contentment, part of our way of loving and being devoted to the here and now, which comes directly from the hand of God.

Suffering is part of the bargain—the big sufferings that we dread and even the little ones. When we speak to one another about the piles of laundry, or a cranky child, or a shoelace caught in the vacuum's beater bar, we are acknowledging to each other that things can get to us, but it's that wink in the falling dusk; we'll keep on!

Affirmation in the Thick of Things

 e women have a hard time because we often alternate between agonizing over staying home with the kids and needing affirmation from the world.

I would never have made it this far without reminding myself not to seek affirmation in "how things are going." You know, in that calculus we subscribe to (probably just by dint of being women): *things going well* means *I'm good* and can feel affirmed.

"Going well" tends to mean such circumstances as: everything handmade, children looking adorable in photo shoot, house clean by 9:00 a.m. and renovated by Christmas, husband feeling well cared for, weight down, waist wasp-like, mani-pedi scheduled, carpets spotless, dog winning trials, credit cards paid up ... I'm good.

The paradox is that getting good at what we do does help us to be happy and find contentment, but only if it's in the context of a hearty acceptance of the predictable awfulness of things, and I mean that in the most cheerful way possible—especially when "what we do" involves children, who necessarily are not going to be as tractable as, say, machines. Or even geese.

Clever men, focusing on machines! Sure, run your factory! "Oh, the machines broke down at the factory today!" Boo hoo! I bet they *stood still* while you tried to fix them and didn't start crying because you forgot their special bear or gave them the wrong-colored cup. Sure, manage your accounts! (Those are kinds of machines, if you think about it a certain way—well, they're not toddlers, now, are they?) I bet your accounts don't stuff their toys into the toilet.

Sometimes we ladies don't want to get out of bed, ever, and our possibly misguided thought in those bad moments is that maybe we need to get affirmation outside the home. We start listening to the voices that tell us that we need acclaim—we need the world!

Of course, this only subjects us to the craziness of leaving what we have already identified as our calling, as we know by all the women in the workplace who are longing to be home (and possibly get back into bed if that is what the day calls for!).

Either way, it seems that the real issue is that a lot of women think that children are extensions of themselves. They love their children (or their idea of children). And then reality hits, and they spend a lot of time wanting to get away from those very children. These women thought, maybe, that the children would cooperate with the whole affirmation project. And they end up not liking their children all that much because children aren't great at affirmation, most of the time.

Not liking one's children is due to the surprise at finding out that children are their own little persons, whose rationality doesn't check in for quite a while—long enough for you seriously to lose your way if you don't have some perspective.

The rational thing for children to do would be to be grateful to you for giving so much up for their little sakes—and thus behave in a picture-perfect, wholly affirming way. But they don't do that; in fact, they often behave in precisely the opposite manner, tempting the unwary mother to think that she has received a sign that she is in the wrong business. But of course, if this were the case, the human race would have given up on family life a long time ago.

Women (and anyone doing a hard job) are better off resolving not to try to prove to everyone, even to themselves, that things are going smoothly, since they won't be, most likely, because kids are involved, with their irrationality and ingratitude and all. We want instant results, but in this case (like many other important works), time must be allowed to pass.

Meanwhile, commitment shouldn't mean that I will need to *be* committed—to the loony bin, that is. Seek affirmation from the knowledge that you are doing what is right and you are doing all you can. Be affirmed in realizing that you are building something, and your children are just a part of that bigger thing, not an end unto themselves (although they are very important!), so it's not devastating if they don't look picture perfect. You need to work on getting them to behave, of course, *not* for your affirmation but for this reason: that you will like them more *now*, and *later* they will have the freedom that only self-control offers.

Leave the outcome—the results—to God. Making mistakes is part of the process. God doesn't require more than the effort.

Understanding this truth, you will like it all better: being with the children, taking care of the home, supporting your husband as he supports you.

I hate to see women give up and think the world will give relief from the stress; I hate to see them give in to detachment from home life as a sort of defense mechanism. The solution, insofar as we can say that life has a solution, is neither to make peace with mediocrity nor to double down on perfection.

Contentment, true peace, lies in letting go of the idea that instant affirmation and success are the measure of goodness, while striving always to be better, with God's help. We women must be brave.

Housewifely

Stay, stay at home, my heart, and rest;
Home-keeping hearts are happiest,
For those that wander they know not where
Are full of trouble and full of care;
To stay at home is best.

— LONGFELLOW

When you smell the top of your newborn's head, a bond grows between you. It starts as a little thing, but the depth of it is true. When you drink in the smell of your home, you bond with it. Yes, it's messy and slippery and maybe, I will make bold to say, even a bit bloody (like a newborn!), but there is the potential for love there, if you press it to you and don't hold it at arm's length.

Long ago, some women rejected the word "housewife" because it seemed demeaning to them: "I'm not married to a house." So this worthwhile thought, that a woman has much to do and love in her home, nearly faded from memory.

Well, here are a few housewifely activities you may have thought it necessary to scorn (like using certain old words) but that might restore a sense of "woman of the house" where it is lacking; small gestures, but redolent of satisfaction and contentment.

1. *Put on an apron.* Not exactly an activity, but a housewifely thing to do.

There is a "girly-girl" resurgence in sweet, frilly, adorable vintage-style aprons, and who am I to repudiate something fabulous, with ruffles and possibly polka dots, that you can put on over your party frock just before your guests arrive? That little number with the lacy pocket and the big bow is where it's at.

However, try a sturdy twill number for your everyday tasks. It won't need to be starched and ironed, but it will protect the shirt that *does* need to be ironed (more on that below). And you can wipe your hands and even the occasional nose on it. Then toss it in the wash.

I remember once complaining to an older friend, a very elegant, soft-spoken, old-school lady with a passel of children, then nearly grown, none of whom betrayed evidence of ever having given her any trouble, that my pregnant belly attracted every manner of stain as I went about my daily business in the kitchen. I'm sure it cost her, because she never gave a hint of wanting to offer correction (unlike some people I could name), but she mildly and gently murmured, "You might find an apron helpful."

Astounding advice.

Lo! The discovery! When you put on an apron, you do not merely protect the garments. You announce your commitment to the task at hand,

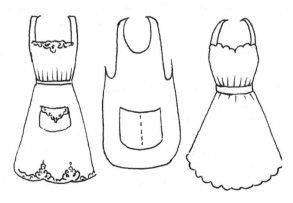

your willingness to suffer the slings and sputterings of the pots and pans, your resolve to see the work to the end. Cutting up raw poultry is not outside the realm of possibility when you wear an apron. You can carry potatoes from the pantry to the sink in it, when you realize that in your haste you forgot a bowl. You can stow your clothespins in its capacious pockets. You can grab a hot handle with its edge and also dry a pot with its clean underside.

When you put on a work apron, you put on your work attitude.

And when you take it off, your clothes will be clean.

2. *Make the beds.* I know, making beds is only a teensy-weensy step up from cleaning toilets on the drudgery scale. It seems quite pointless. Yet, when you make your bed, your room looks amazingly better. You may even first change the sheets. Think what that will do for you when evening comes!

Children should make their own beds. Still, you make your rounds to each bed, pulling up a cover here, tucking in a corner there, placing the favorite stuffed animal just so on this pillow,[10] moving the metal trucks

---

[10] Wait—am I serious? Placing the stuffed animals on the pillows? Before you give up on me as hopelessly out of touch, just consider. When our bigs were little and we were moving into our own home, the house we were renting was on the market. I was conflicted because of the desperate difficulty, to my mind, of having a show-ready, neat house when I had to contend with four young children *and* being pregnant! It seemed impossible.

I felt that it was the height of sacrifice for me even to vacuum. My mother would help me out with the clutter and bed-making a bit, and she would arrange the stuffed animals (of which, like you, we had an inexplicable profusion) on the children's pillows. I noticed that it took her literally five seconds to pick them up off the floor and place them attractively on the pillows!

And then—this is the discovery—you know what, *they are not on the floor anymore!* And—*they are cute instead of annoying!*

Someone had to show me.

Eventually, we all came to think of this as how the room looks when it's straightened up, and they did it themselves, or willingly allowed the clutter to be properly disposed of. That's another benefit: five seconds' effort by you, a sense of stewardship for them.

off that one. Some people suggest that you should never remake a child's bed, lest you damage his self-esteem. I contend that a child's self-esteem is in no way tied to the result, *the made bed*, which he, in fact, takes no notice of at all, this particular task being a whim of yours that is utterly and completely irrelevant to his concept of the universe and its workings. There is nothing you can do to the bed that will affect his perception of having humored you (and escaped punishment) by a wholly perfunctory rearrangement (for neither better nor worse, in his estimation) of the accouterments on the mattress and his subsequent erasure of the process from his memory.

Thus, you may pretty it up to your heart's content, resting assured that the most likely result will be complete oblivion as regards maternal tampering. It's possible that, when the children enter the room, they will have a subconscious sense that "things are as they should be" and are possibly even "nice"—without in any way registering that a change has taken place, much less sending any affirmation your way. They certainly will not be said to *suffer*. As long as you are cheerful and have expressed, at some point, pleasure with their efforts (if efforts there were; I mean, don't make things up), that is all they know. Do as you will.

The act of making or remaking their beds will quite naturally, in resistance to the laws of thermodynamics, propel you into a quick Blitz of the rooms. No fear. Nothing more will likely happen. You won't be caught in the snares of a Deep Clean, in all probability. (The Blitz and the Deep Clean will be explained in volume 3.) You have too much to do at the moment. But a quick tidy sets to rights, satisfies your housewifely sensibilities, and gives you some interesting reflections on possible future topics of conversation with your offspring regarding Shoving Blocks under Beds, Piling Clothes in Corners, and Storing Legos under Dressers.

3. *Hang the laundry outside on the line.* Maybe it's just me, but simply going outside—stepping out of the kitchen, to be precise—instantly refreshes my interior atmosphere. It gives me perspective. It grounds me (I do think there is something to "grounding"—the idea that touching the ground helps your body recalibrate—I often hang the laundry barefoot).

When the dryer is *right there*, it can seem utterly absurd to hang the laundry outside on the line. I have no objection to using the dryer, in winter, and especially for the myriad little undies and onesies and socks, although of course, even such sundries can be hung out if you are so minded. The dryer is the most expensive appliance you likely run in your household, so perhaps that thought might be the impetus for discovering the added benefits of this admittedly time-consuming task.

You *will* save money. It's silly to complain about high costs if you aren't willing to do a few things to cut back. The little things add up.

But even more, the sunshine is good for you *and* the sheets and towels. It might take longer to get used to the stiffness of these things, when we've all been made to value "downy-soft linens." But once you do, that very stiffness represents a job well tackled. And you know what? It doesn't take that long to hang out even two loads of laundry. I always think, "I really don't have time for this!" and *nearly* give in to the dryer. Yet suddenly I'm done.

You can combine hanging out clothes with giving the baby an airing —another old-fashioned idea sadly out of practice. Even the youngest baby benefits from the twenty minutes it takes you to get the washing on the line. He sits in his pram or on a blanket and watches you. He could even have a nap out there in the fresh air.

As soon as I'm out by the clothesline, my mood changes. The very pressure on my ears is different. My head expands. I hear the birds singing (or fighting, as was the case the last time I was out there; the blackbirds were attacking a large hawk in a tall oak, until he flew away in defeat).

And, as happens in the bedrooms, I notice other things. I see not a few weeds that can be pulled, I remember the mowing, I catch the cucumbers growing too big, I tear out the peas. I have often staggered into the house with an oversized basket of dried clothing *and* some beans in my apron pocket *and* slightly dirty hands. No harm done.

Get a good big laundry clothesline that can hold at least two loads if you have the room. The pins can be found at any dollar or hardware store, if not at the grocery store. But, if nothing else, get a rack for the kitchen corner. Or how about the type of drying rack, well known in other countries for apartment dwellers, that hangs out the window? Could you make use of it where you are? You won't be outside, but you will experience the rhythm of hanging at least some clothes to dry.

4. *Iron some clothes.* Apart from the serious frustration of finding a good iron that is not too heavy, ironing is an incredibly rewarding housewifely task and also the least tackled.

But why? Like other things, if you have it set up (or ready to be set up), you may do it. If you do it, you will find out something staggering: you can wear something other than yoga pants! The reason you wear yoga pants (or jeans, or jeans skirts) and T-shirts exclusively is that you haven't discovered the joys of ironing, or at least the joys of having ironed clothes!

Yes, it's dangerous to iron with a crawling eight-month-old. So, once a week, during the baby's nap or playpen time, schedule an hour to iron a few things that you have set apart in a laundry basket. And then you will see.

The reason you think you need new clothes is (well, aside from the fact that you may need them) that new clothes come ironed and your old clothes need to be ironed by you. So iron them. Suddenly, especially if you also employ that magical substance *spray starch*, something that seemed rather tired and not worth taking the T-shirt off for becomes a valuable part of your wardrobe. And if you also *wear an apron* (see number 1), you may possibly be able to hang it up at the end of the day and wear it again.

If your husband and boys have some ironed dress shirts hanging in their closets, Sundays will be much happier. Your girls' pretty frocks look special (and not as if they were dragged out of the hamper) if they are pressed.

One trick for housewives is to have a clean place for your freshly ironed items. Hangers are nice, but not necessary for most things. Try hanging the items neatly over a chair or folding them and placing them back in the basket. Your ironing standard can't be the one used for a servant who has no other task than to press your garments. Don't strive for perfection. Just get the clothes to the point where they would look fine if you immediately put them on and went out to sit in your car, which will likely be the case.

But ironing goes beyond all this.

You stand there, just … thinking … and restoring order. Crumpled rumpledness becomes smooth crispness. It's quiet. The scent of the ironing soothes you. Even in summer, the warmth isn't objectionable (and I've been known to enjoy the fan blowing right on me while I iron). You can listen to a podcast if you've had the foresight to set the children up with a quiet game of their own. It's the ideal rest-time activity if you don't need a nap.

If these things seem impossible because you feel you truly don't have enough time, it might be worthwhile to see if you can slow down a bit. Maybe you are trying to do too much. These tasks, unlike the running around that we often feel forms the core of our main work, restore order, and it's liberating to accomplish what could have been last on the list. Competence has its rewards. Housewives know this secret.

Enjoyment

You know (or you will know once you've finished these volumes) that I'm a person who makes rules. Long ago, maybe when I was first married, I made a rule for myself: no making big life-changing decisions in February—because of course you aren't going to feel that great about anything until March, when the sun reminds you that there is still hope.

I don't know about you, but I find myself spiraling into a real sense of doom in certain seasons, feeling that help does not seem to be on the way. Some belittle this sense, pointing out that it's just a common occurrence, and a little ridiculous, to start thinking things are really just much worse than they have ever been, and I'm sure there's something in that.

On the other hand, history shows that some eras are pretty bad, and it's just as well to face hard times bravely and try to tell the truth about the good.

But, regardless of whether there is a certain level of badness and the aging process simply makes one more aware of it, or there really is an increase of badness, I think it's important—even a duty—to try to spend some portion of every day, even a few minutes, in simple enjoyment.

Knitting is a craft that I enjoy, not least of all because it involves *sitting down*, especially after a winter day of hauling logs and sap when we are maple syruping and getting thoroughly smoky (which I also enjoy). The feel of the wool yarn, the pleasure of thinking of the recipient, the satisfaction of ordering my movements and the material into an aesthetic creation—these elements add up to enjoyment!

Enjoyment is a good to set against all the bad, even if there is no commensurability at all, laughably none. Since Adam's fall, however, there has been evil in the world, and there always will be, until the end of time. If we want the world to be better, we must live some good in it, not only doing good (which is important, don't get me wrong) and telling about the good (also important), but also enjoying … something. If we wait until everything is perfect, we will die not having appreciated anything. Only God is perfect.

So if there's something that you enjoy—simply laughing at the children's antics, conversing with a friend, listening to or playing music, making something beautiful, enjoying your spouse's companionship, gardening, watching the sun rise earlier every day—that is very good; be sure to do it.

Competence Frees You from Drudgery

Competence: you need it to escape the feminist's dream-turned-nightmare of life seeking a paycheck—a life apart from her family; away from the husband she wants to encourage, the children whom she longs to nurture, and the home she longs to make, the society she wishes to serve.

This woman is tired of pitting herself against men rather than working alongside them toward a common goal; she is tired of the war of all against all. She did achieve, or she knows she could achieve, something in the rat race, but she has come to see that there's something she's missing.

But if you are that woman, you are also just tired. So many days you wonder about the joy or pleasure in the actual daily round of life. You love your children. You understand that whatever your outside commitments are, those commitments in the home have the value of *devotion*, which can't be quantified. Among other things, you also see the importance of someone whose job it is to maximize carefully the money that's made, rather than necessarily making any herself. You see the important role you have of managing the home and its resources.

In theory, you think that homemaking and even homeschooling are good ideas, and you love your husband (although you have your doubts about him when he ventures to wonder what exactly you do all day that is so tiring!). You've read books that encourage you in this way and you have felt motivated.

It's just *the practice* of this new (old!) way of life that's getting you down. And, maybe, just maybe, a wee touch of the sense that affirmation is lacking.

Let's name our demons. In the back of your mind, there's that fear that if you ever give in to, say, getting good at cleaning toilets on a schedule, why, there would be no turning back. You would probably find yourself muttering "Garn!" and start peddling old bones and rags. You'd have to sip gin toothlessly out of a small, dirty flask. Your children would pity you, and your husband would run away with a svelte blonde whose degree in art history was actually paid for in full. Darn those college loans, anyway.

But honestly, the day I discovered I just really enjoy putting on my apron, folding my kitchen towel just so on the oven-door handle, getting supper ready, and then sitting to read to my kids with things humming along around me—that was a good day, even if I did yell a little along the way. No one clapped; I know no one else was impressed, but still, it was good.

My ability to read nonfiction remained undimmed. I continued to be able to carry on conversations with grown persons. I did not lose my ability to understand how molecules combine. I retained an interest in current events (more or less; I won't pretend there weren't some years I became vague on world topics!).

My college French is at least no worse than it was. No, that's not really true, but I brush up every few years, as one child or another enters high school. Which brings up the real satisfaction, which is knowing that I did my best to provide an environment in which education could occur. I could have worked at a career and earned enough to provide for fancy private schools, but I do believe that something would have been lost.

Later we will delve into all the particulars. For now, I am hoping to inspire in you the desire to become competent at what you may have previously scorned.

This Part of the Island Is Where You Are Now

O nce, thanks to the generosity of friends, we had a vacation on a small island off the coast of Maine. It was lovely. There were two stores and one hotel. There was beach on every side. We stayed in a cute house and thoroughly enjoyed everything about it.

The little general store that was open for a few hours every day was a longish walk from the house; everything cost so much because everything had to be brought in on the ferry. The other place was a gas station you had to drive to in the old clunker left by the owner—everyone on the island has an old clunker to drive, as well as at least one dead one in their yard, because of the high surcharge to ferry the dead cars back to the mainland. Other than the dead cars, it's very pretty there.

We were getting gas and took it into our heads to need to know whether this gas station was further from the mainland than the store. Was it east or west? We were not sure what we were getting at. Neither was the geography-free teenager pumping the gas. She was completely flummoxed by the question (and I don't remember exactly what we asked her; it was probably dumb).

After a few awkward moments, she extricated herself by saying, "This part of the island is where you are now."

This has entered into the collective family memory because it's so true!

You overhear a conversation about curriculum between two home-schooling moms.

A friend tells you about a fabulous school two hours away that meets a child's every need.

You search for ideas for a playroom on Pinterest and spend an hour drooling.

Each one of these things is anxiety-attack material. You can spend your whole day focusing on what you don't have and didn't do!

But to be a woman on a mission or a man with a plan, you have to identify your goals and stick to them. Don't lose your focus! If it gives you an anxiety attack, it's a distraction. It's not helping.

If it makes you say, "Yes! That's what I've been looking for (or thinking of or knowing I could do)!" then pursue it, but on your own terms, at your own pace.

If you will never be able to afford it, that's a sign it's not for you (although it's always worth wondering if you can find a way to hack it!).

If you know that pulling weeds is what you should be doing, then pull weeds.

If you have little children to run after, then you probably aren't going to be driving two hours to a prep school. And that's a sign that it's not for you.

If you have a train to catch, catch it.

If you know that not taking a shower is more of an issue for you than not putting silver leaf on the edges of an occasional table, then get off your phone and take a shower!

If you can make something pretty, even if it has nothing to do with putting silver leaf on anything, do it.

That's my pep talk for today. You are doing fine, just don't lose your focus.

This part of the island is where you are now.

On Your Own Spiritual Life, the Source of Your Strength

The interior life is a kingdom. Without going deep within my own secret heart, I can never truly discover God's will or speak to Him in friendship. I must pray. St. Teresa of Ávila noted that the person who spends a half hour in prayer in the morning "has already traveled half his journey." But without prayer, Dom Jean-Baptiste Chautard warned, "the day will almost unavoidably be tepid."[11]

Without prayer I cannot have peace, the peace that surpasses all understanding, yet my life as a wife, mother, and grandmother is a busy one, not easily susceptible to a rule, or so it would seem (a rule being a pattern of prayer that one commits to, regardless of whether one feels like praying at the time). We women in particular hear a lot of voices telling us what to do about our spiritual lives; we need solid criteria for choosing what and whom to listen to.

Each liturgical season brings with it the call to renew and refresh, to deepen our relationship with God. A troubling development in the proliferation of so-called devotionals marketed on social media specifically

[11] Dom Jean-Baptiste Chautard, O.C.S.O., *The Soul of the Apostolate* 5, 1.

targets women, so busy and laden with cares and anxieties as we try to balance the many voices, valid and less so, clamoring for our attention and, frankly, our dollars.

My best advice is to go to the treasury of the Church for tested spiritual direction. In his book *Christ and His Mysteries*, Bl. Columba Marmion offers a valuable guide on *how* to discern the order of our rule:

> We see how important it is in this matter to distrust our own judgment, our own lights; how important it is not to base our holiness upon such or such a practice of devotion, however excellent, which we choose for ourselves, nor upon such or such an observance of our religious rule.
>
> Such an observance may be suspended by a higher law, as is, for example, the law of charity towards our neighbor. Holiness for us must be based before and above all upon the fulfillment of the divine law, the natural law, the precepts of the Decalogue, the commandments of the Church, and the duties of our state.
>
> A piety that does not respect this hierarchy of duties ought to be held suspect: all asceticism that is not governed by the precepts and doctrine of the Gospel cannot come from the Holy Spirit who inspired the Gospel. "Whosoever are led by the Spirit of God," says Saint Paul, "they are the sons of God."

Although Marmion speaks here about Phariseeism, which emphasizes rules and adherence to form above God's law, what he says can also be applied in particular to spiritual reading (or other media) that manipulates our emotional state, causing us to make a false and ultimately counterproductive connection between our actual spiritual progress as God sees it and *how we feel about it.*

It's this sort of Phariseeism that concerns me now, because in our time sentimentalism, motivationalism (if I may coin a word for a particular genre), and the therapeutic dominate.

Let's go through that passage again, line by line, and see how Dom Marmion can help us discern the helpful from the unhelpful.

"We see how important it is in this matter to distrust our own judgment, our own lights; how important it is not to base our holiness upon such or such a practice of

devotion, however excellent, which we choose for ourselves": On some level, all devotions are ones we choose for *ourselves.* Even if they are suggested by a spiritual director, well, we chose the spiritual director and chose to take his suggestions. Only the Liturgy is outside of this movement of our will toward or away from a particular devotion.

It's not wrong to take practices (prayers, readings, penitential acts) upon ourselves, but we have to be aware that they *are* chosen by us, and for our own sake, we need to have a healthy suspicion *of ourselves,* because the self is not God. We must take great care of what we consume spiritually because it can either feed our souls or lead to spiritual sickness.

"Nor upon such or such an observance of our religious rule": If you are a member of a religious order or, as a lay person, have taken upon yourself some rule (such as becoming a Third Order Carmelite or even imposing upon yourself something like "a mother's rule of life" suggested by a layperson), you need to remember something: *that rule does not supersede God's law.* Religious life requires many little and big sacrifices of one's will under obedience, for perfection's sake; nevertheless, charity and truth are always paramount:

"Such an observance may be suspended by a higher law, as is, for example, the law of charity towards our neighbor": For the wife and mother, husband and child are "neighbor" before all others. If your children are sick, for instance, it's the better part of devotion to tend to them, not rigidly to adhere to your prayers before the Blessed Sacrament. The mother of a family has the duty to see to it that they get supper. If their supper is scanty and cold, it doesn't excuse her that she was praying.

But let's be realistic: I don't think that most of us suffer from excessive adherence to our preplanned schedule of spiritual development! The danger to our spiritual well-being doesn't lie there, I venture to say.

Most women today, reading this, are trying to get some prayer, any prayer, into a life filled with unexpected circumstances and distractions and all-around busyness. And most of us aren't overschooled in self-discipline, either. We can't help it, poor us. We are really quite comfortable and likely to remain so.

Here is Dom Marmion's prescription: *"Holiness for us must be based before and above all upon the fulfillment of the divine law ..."* The divine law was summed up by Our Lord in the Great Commandment:

> Thou shalt love the Lord thy God with thy whole heart, and with thy whole soul, and with thy whole mind. This is the greatest and the first commandment. And the second is like to this: Thou shalt love thy neighbour as thyself. On these two commandments dependeth the whole law and the prophets. (Matt. 22:36–40)

"The natural law": The natural law can be looked at, briefly, in two ways. The first way is simply to acknowledge and respect the causes of things, meaning, above all, their ends or goals. For instance, the end or goal of eating is nutrition, and pleasure is a gift that goes along with that goal. If we make pleasure the first goal in eating, we go against the natural law. Children have to develop according to their natures; if we try to rush them or fail to help them in the way they require at the proper times, we go against the natural law.

The second way to look at the natural law is expressed in the cardinal virtues, or virtues that can be approached and understood by reason, making them accessible to all. These virtues are prudence, or right judgment; justice, or giving each his due (including God and ourselves); temperance, or self-control and achieving the right order of things interiorly; and fortitude, or the courage to *do* the good.

You can see, even with this little explanation, how vast a field of devotion is open to us simply by naming these things! Reality itself is cause for joy; contemplating all these good things brings us far along in the spiritual life.

"The precepts of the Decalogue, the commandments of the Church": Having already mentioned the divine law, Marmion reinforces its importance with another reference to the Ten Commandments (the Decalogue's precepts, so frequently extolled in the Liturgy; pay attention to the Mass and the Divine Office, and you will quickly realize how often we are exhorted to

love the Lord's precepts, to walk in His ways, to learn His commandments, to keep them, never to forsake them).

How often do we take to prayer the commandments of God as taught to us by Holy Mother Church? When do we ponder her teachings regarding the different kinds of prayer and their importance for us, her expositions of the natural and divine laws, her exhortations to piety?

Do the devotional aids coming into our inboxes or tempting us from catalogs emphasize this vital core of the spiritual life?

"And the duties of our state": The "state" of a woman with a husband and a family is the state of matrimony. Do we think of that state as involving duties *that it is in our spiritual interests to fulfill,* or do we see it as a sort of *self-*fulfillment exercise or even a burden; something we have to be talked into all the time, something we can't confront or fulfill without constant pep talks and assurances that we will be left with a reasonable amount of freedom, that some part of our inner self will remain untouched? Sometimes I think that women enter into this state freely and then spend the rest of their lives trying to escape!

We should ask ourselves whether this devotional aid that we're signing up for will help us go deeper into our duties (which convey God's will, remember!), deeper into the details of Holy Scripture, and deeper into life's hierarchies, or whether it pulls us away by enticing us with visions of emotional fulfillment. Is this prettily designed spiritual guide in reality a "prosperity gospel" in that sense, creating in us an expectation of a transcendent realization in the *now,* discernible in our *feelings?*

The reality of a state of life (marriage is one, religious life is another) cannot be escaped: it curtails our scope of action *for the purpose* of a greater good; it is precisely *service* to our fellow man (and child!). There is no other way to do anything of value other than to exclude some possibilities.

As long as every choice is open to us, we *have not chosen.* When we choose, by definition we limit the scope of what we can do; yet, paradoxically, we find our true creativity. If we seek creativity up front, we get personal destruction. Artists know this: form bestows freedom.

G. K. Chesterton pointed out:

Every act of will is an act of self-limitation. To desire action is to desire limitation. In that sense, every act is an act of self-sacrifice. When you choose anything, you reject everything else.... Every act is an irrevocable selection and exclusion.... The artist loves his limitations: they constitute the thing he is doing.[12]

I think we could also say, "Every *lover* loves his limitations: they constitute the possibility of love."

The difference between spurious and real spirituality is that the latter reminds us that suffering and self-denial are the essence of the Christian's life, in the pattern set by the Savior. Our suffering joined with Our Lord's suffering brings us along the road of purgation—the only road that leads to understanding (what the saints call illumination) and, finally, to union with God. Purgation is a necessary step; there is no avoiding it.

One's state of life brings with it things that must be attended to. When we do so with love, this disposition *in itself* constitutes a devotion. Here is the heart of the mystery, to be accepted or rejected. If we allow ourselves to be led *away* from total self-giving to God's plan for us (that is to say, to God), we allow ourselves to be led away from the offering of love. And that would negate devotion.

But attending to the things that pertain to one's state in life frees one to love.

"*A piety that does not respect this hierarchy of duties ought to be held suspect*": This observation is the tool of discernment, moving forward into a new season, liturgical or personal (when the Spirit gives us that moment when we may choose to go deeper in our spiritual lives). Piety, the expression of devotion and worship, submits to the hierarchy, or ordering, of duties and, indeed, of life itself.

No doubt whoever is offering us a spiritual practice is motivated by a desire to bring us closer to God; but *will* we end up closer if we fail to

---

[12] G. K. Chesterton, *Orthodoxy*, chap. 3.

consider God's claims on us before embarking? Instead of being led by feelings and emotions, let's be tough-minded; we should hold suspect anything that doesn't move us closer to accepting our responsibilities with love.

"All asceticism that is not governed by the precepts and doctrine of the Gospel cannot come from the Holy Spirit who inspired the Gospel": "Asceticism" isn't a word that appears in most of the popular spiritual offerings on the market. Sadly, the Christian woman of today is not guided in the traditional wisdom of denial of self; she is not encouraged to identify the cross, take it up, and be heartened in knowing that in Christ, the burden is light. In short, the person searching for spiritual guidance does not find what Marmion urges, an asceticism founded on the Gospel. She finds no spiritual help at all.

We *should* be able to lean on trustworthy authority in the Church, on bishops who protect the well-being of the faithful, guarding the flock against false shepherds and opportunists. Sadly, most of our protectors have fled the fold. Their indifference to the monetization of devotion, the rise of a spiritual marketplace teeming with self-proclaimed experts, seems even to be part of their plan. Our pastors seem happy to outsource their duties, to engage surrogates for that which ought to be accessible directly from them. They have succumbed to the marketing principle that the buyer needs something new all the time, when really, they are the custodians of the treasury that is the Church's ancient wisdom for the soul.

The Church is constituted, by virtue of being the Body of Christ, to offer each person what he needs to be holy, in a practical manner. But in our confused time, it might not be easy to figure this all out. And let's be clear: "results" might not be discernible right away or even for quite a long time—to this the martyrs testify. Spiritual direction isn't a commodity. All the more reason to make sure the source is trustworthy and *time*-tested. As St. Paul says, "But to me it is a very small thing to be judged by you, or by man's day; but neither do I judge my own self" (1 Cor. 4:3, DR).

Being a Christian means grasping this hiddenness, accepting it, being willing to follow Him even in the darkness, *with a trustworthy guide.*

We can do hard things, my friends! Armed with knowledge (such as this truly helpful passage from Dom Marmion), we can fight this battle and win!

"Whosoever are led by the Spirit of God," says Saint Paul, "they are the sons of God."

The Spirit of God is not a vague, formless penumbra of an enabling and manageable deity. He is the Third Person of the Trinity. If we want to be one with God, we have to submit to His Spirit and not go our own way to seek affirmation apart from Him.

What do I recommend, then?

I don't have any quick, downloadable, prettily scripted ways to get spiritual enlightenment, nor have I done an in-depth survey of what's available. It might take some work to find what is really good for you, in *your* present situation. Ideally you'd have a wise spiritual director, but I know how rare those are.

St. Teresa of Ávila tells us that St. Joseph is an admirable spiritual director when we can't find a here-and-now one.

Keeping in mind that Blessed Columba Marmion himself taught that prayer, *conversation with God*, is at the core of the spiritual life, I have a few suggestions:

- *Magnificat* magazine: As of this writing, the spiritual readings in this guide are generally sound and venerable. If a particular reading from a saint from the past calls out to you, look up the book that it comes from and read it. Truly, these ancient texts are worth seeking out. (In fact, *Magnificat* is where I found the Dom Marmion quote I based this chapter on.)
- *The Soul of the Apostolate* by Dom Jean-Baptiste Chautard: a spiritual classic that convinces the reader that without prayer, works are dead.
- If you're looking for a book about the cardinal virtues and how to grow in them, I recommend Christopher Blum and Joshua Hochschild's *A Mind at Peace*. It is based on the teachings of St. Thomas Aquinas.
- For the busy woman who wants a direct infusion of grace, maybe this is the season to delve into the Divine Office. You can download the Universalis app and have the daily Hours at your fingertip. What about choosing one Hour (say, the Office of Readings; it takes twelve to fifteen minutes at the longest) and making a

commitment to pray it at a certain time each day, or before you head to other destinations on the Web?

• In our book *The Little Oratory*, David Clayton and I explain how to pray along with the universal Church by means of your home altar. Honestly, if you haven't made your own little oratory in your home, now is the time. Living along with the liturgical year of the Church is the key to prayer.

I leave you with Cardinal Désiré-Joseph Mercier's "secret to sanctity" and happiness:

Every day for five minutes control your imagination and close your eyes to all the noises of the world in order to enter into yourself. Then, in the sanctuary of your baptized soul (which is the temple of the Holy Spirit) speak to that Divine Spirit, saying to Him:

O Holy Spirit, beloved of my soul, I adore You. Enlighten me, guide me, strengthen me, console me. Tell me what I should do; give me Your orders. I promise to submit myself to all that You desire of me and to accept all that You permit to happen to me. Let me only know Your Will.

If you do this, your life will flow along happily, serenely, and full of consolation, even in the midst of trials. Grace will be proportioned to the trial, giving you the strength to carry it, and you will arrive at the Gate of Paradise, laden with merit. This submission to the Holy Spirit is the secret of sanctity.

PART 3

Destruction-Proofing Your Family

Your marriage and your family are precious and irreplaceable. You don't want to watch them being destroyed (or worse, be the cause of their destruction), but unfortunately the collective memory on the subject is almost completely lost. In this section, I hope to offer you some thoughts from the other side; these are insights I wish someone had given me early on. Some seem mundane; some seem hopelessly idealistic. All, however, are tried and true.

The Long View in Family Life

ost parents (most? who knows, I don't have statistics or anything; this is what I see and have experienced) approach the first decade of their life as a family in one of two ways, and I will describe them to you, but one thing to notice is that both err because they think that things will be this way forever, with life ahead of them, little kids running around. Because the first years together represent such a drastic change, they think life will always remain in that stage.

The first sort of parents think their choices, big and small, don't really matter, whether they strengthen the important roles they each play in family life or weaken them. No doubt they are very young, and I say this even though people get married later and later these days: maturity comes with experience and not necessarily with age. This sort lets their somewhat undefined desires or even whims dictate where they are going and how they will get there.

They don't realize how necessary forming habits in their children is to the future happiness of all. They let them grow willy-nilly, pacifying rather than disciplining, leaving family culture to the four winds and then wondering why things are so unpleasant. "Later, when we're older, we'll think about how we want our family to be." I call these the Slacker Families.

The second way for parents to approach their first decade of family life is to try so hard to control every detail that their quest for instant results wears everyone out. They seek constant affirmation from their children in the form of perfect behavior. They are relentless in their demands, tireless in their productions. There is no room for real life or for rest. "Later, when we've gotten this thing down and polished up for the photos, we'll think about how we want our family to be." I call these the Perfectionist Families.

Slacker Families and Perfectionist Families are both completely unconscious of the coming second decade of family life. No one foresees their *young* family turning into an *older* family—not really. It's a failure of imagination! No one can *imagine* a time when the children don't climb the walls but do interact with others; when the older kids in the family are emerging from their sweet (to them—for us it's another matter!) unconsciousness, either with or without self-control.

So, sadly, families wander around daily life rather cluelessly, or else they push things to the breaking point with their desire to compress a lifetime of development into a few years; in both cases, after a time, each sort loses family unity—the one from feeling overwhelmed by the chaos and the other from exhaustion—and generally lets things fall apart.

Slackers who thought misbehavior was cute or, at a minimum, not susceptible to remedy, simply give up when those same kids grow to be rather frightening roving teenagers. Those who didn't make an effort when their children were young find that their older children don't make an effort with them.

Perfectionists who wouldn't dream of letting their three-year-old have a cookie hardly notice that they never eat a home-cooked meal with their sixteen-year-old. Those who carefully planned every moment of their young kids' lives have no idea what their older children are up to because they themselves are too busy and, to tell the truth, are defeated by the sheer demandingness of it all; thinking that raising children is just a matter of imposing superficial order, they are stunned into retreat when personalities emerge.

The couples who began with good intentions of date nights and scheduled interactions, even when their first child was newly born, hardly speak to each other (often out of the necessity imposed by their choices of two jobs and intense activities) when their children are adolescents.

You really see what that next stage is only when it's over. There is no one to tell you this, though, because when everyone has only a few children, there's a lack of continuity. If the survivors are gone before they can tell you about what they've learned, it can be too late. And the so-called experts are all dealing with their own crashing lives.

Who will encourage you? Where is the support? What could family life further down the road look like if the news about it wasn't completely conditioned by parents whose own development is arrested, and who hide the fact that their own children's characters are formed by default?

Four Secrets to
Protecting Your Unity

All this being the case, I'm going to give you my four secrets of divorce-proofing and destruction-proofing your home.

Disclaimer: Nothing evil in this fallen world is impossible. Destruction happens. People have free will. The best intentions and execution are no guarantee, and for that matter, we don't know what God's plan for our salvation is or what suffering is necessary before it's accomplished. I'm not saying that I have all the answers, and I've made my share of mistakes. All I really have to offer are the things I learned on the way.

Fortunately for both of us, I'm just grabbing you by the shoulders in order to turn you toward the real source of wisdom, the Holy Spirit. Your fighting chance comes from being able to hear the voice that speaks to you within yourself, from God. My suggestions are for exactly this: to let the Holy Spirit to guide you. A few principles found in something greater than my opinion will help you arrive at that point.

Keep Sunday for Worship and Rest

If there were one thing I would tell a young family, especially one that was having trouble (even on the brink of splitting up), or a family that was worried about the teen years, or really anything at all, it would be this: make Sundays a true day of rest.

I believe that only the mother can really make this happen, week in and week out. Only the mother can make it possible for the crazy activities to stop, for the family to worship together and to sit down together for a meal. The father, if he hasn't already done so, soon comes to see that his marking of this day changes his family's life. He can want all these things, call for them, and facilitate them, but if the mother doesn't make the practical effort, they won't happen. And if the mother isn't resting and, even more, enjoying, no one is.

Yes, it's another thing the mother has to do. But it's the best thing, and when she comes to view the rest of the week as preparation for this day, it will not be too hard.

Somehow, early in our marriage, without his saying much about it, I became aware that my husband simply did not work at his job on Sundays. He would read and (I suppose!) think, but he never specifically worked on office matters on that day. It took me a long time to figure out that I, too, could manage things a bit better, even as our family grew.

I came to realize that the bigger our family got, the more important it was not to leave things undone with the thought that "I can do it Sunday." I still had to process laundry, I still had to make dinner, but I began to see that thinking of Sunday as another day to get things done was making our lives hectic, and it was *I* who was creating this tone by not ordering my work to Sunday rest.

Work expands to fill the time available, according to Parkinson's law. If you have in mind that you have seven days to do your work, then seven days it will take—and you probably still won't be done (that's part of the law too). The terrible thing about working every single day is that, without rest, a person can never see things except from a sort of grindstone, even Sisyphean, perspective. We'll never have time to think or to ponder things peacefully if we never stop working.

The way to begin is to commit. Even if Dad has to work a shift on Sunday, even if the kids have soccer in the afternoon, even if there is so much laundry that if you missed this day you would never be found again under a mountain of dirty clothes, start by doing *something* to make the day one of worship and rest. Make it so that at some point it is a real day of the Lord.

Now, some Sundays, that might mean a real old-fashioned Sunday dinner after church with plenty of relaxation in the form of reading the paper, visiting with extended family, and playing games. Some Sundays it might mean an early Mass with the day spent burning brush and enjoying the sunshine after a long winter or a ride to the beach in the summer for a whole day of waves. You might spend the afternoon visiting Grandma at the assisted-living home or helping neighbors with a fallen tree in their driveway.

You might have roast beef; you might have soup. You might have friends over; you might be "just us." It might be brunch; it might be a late supper. But you all sit down together, light a candle or two, and take a deep breath. You might sit down on a blanket after a hike and have a picnic!

Correct your children's manners during the week; try not to do too much correcting during the Sunday meal! Try to *enjoy*—the day, each other, God's enjoyment of His creation.

The point is to make this day different from the others. If you prayerfully do this, however modestly and humbly (by which I mean that you do it for its own sake, not for any benefits, although benefits you will receive), you will see God's blessings showered on you and your family.

Life where Sunday worship and some sort of rest are paramount is very different from life where those goals are optional and Sunday is viewed as another working day. There's no way to explain how the Spirit will calm you and set you on your way with the commitment to set Sunday aside. You just have to make it and then experience the result.

Setting Sunday rest and worship as a priority orders the week. You shop on the other days because you have resolved not to shop on Sunday (barring a real emergency). You prepare your meals so that Sunday's meals are tranquil. You do your washing throughout the week so that Sunday's wardrobe is ready and there isn't a mad rush for those very articles that help us sense its importance: good clothes, dress shoes.

On Sunday the family puts God first. Then comes true rest and relaxation, a time to set busyness aside and experience ourselves as children of God. Josef Pieper likens this time of worship and rest to the removal of a dome that presses down upon us in our normal workaday world, preventing us from seeing the stars. For one day, it is lifted and we know ourselves as creatures who owe gratitude to our Creator. We see things as they are.

In this way, grace comes into our lives, when previously we were only at best haunted by the idea that we should pray, without knowing how. We begin to understand prayer and how it fits into every day and every moment; we finally bond in prayer for each other; we embark on a life with Christ.

"The ultimate meaning of the active life is to make possible the happiness of contemplation," Pieper tells us,[13] and indeed the reverse is true as well; if we do not experience the happiness of a state of enjoyment for its own sake, we will not find meaning in life, no matter how actively we pursue it.

Eat Dinner Together as a Family

Make it a goal to have dinner together on Sundays as the high point of the week, the unshakable ground of your life together as a family. I think we can all conjure up a vision of the happy family sitting around the nicely set table, satisfied after a delectable meal, enjoying a gentle, edifying conversation. As soon as you begin working toward this goal, you'll quickly notice that it is not easily achievable—but I will tell you how to do it: you simply must eat together as a family on days that are *not* Sundays, because paradoxically, doing things easily and naturally *comes with practice*.

I use the word "dinner," but you have to think creatively if you have a tricky schedule or some issue I don't know about. Breakfast together? Main meal during the day? Just try to figure it out and pray about it.

Eating together as a family ... how can I express this ...

If there were a natural sacrament, this would be it. If there is a model for problem solving, this is it. Loved ones gathering, talking things over,

---

[13] *Josef Pieper: An Anthology* (San Francisco: Ignatius Press, 2011), chap. 44.

enjoying silliness and good stories, appreciating food lovingly prepared (however simple): this is our communion!

Earlier, I contrasted the first decade of family life with the second, the one that people so often can't imagine. Well, this ideal family life at the dinner table happens in that second decade. The first decade—it seems like a far-off dream.

Those Slacker Families I talked about will never get to the peaceful family dinner because they won't like one another very much. Having never set any standards or created any order, having never cultivated manners, civility, pleasant speaking voices, sitting still, and listening, they can hardly expect to enjoy their time together.

The Perfectionist Families, having nagged, yelled, despaired, and demanded nothing less than, well, perfection, can hardly be surprised that after about ten years, they are tired out; the husband can't please the wife, who is a mere shadow of herself; and their kids want to sneak off. And it's then that the seeds of destruction of the marriage, for both kinds of families, begin to sprout.

So my plea, as we go into this discussion, has two parts: that you, with your *young* family, aim for that paradoxical state of mind that consists in setting standards and expecting them to be met *and* simultaneously, without any relaxation of your glorious vision, that you not despair over meltdowns, naughtiness, wiggling, squabbling, and general chaos.

If you can keep this balancing act as your objective, and if you can, above all, keep your sense of humor, you will make it into that second decade when it really all comes together and you will truly enjoy each other, reaping all the fruits of your hard work and studied refusal to despair.

I have lots of practical advice on all this later in this book. For now, simply resolve that dinner together at least four times a week (especially on Sunday) will be your goal.

Let the Babies Come to You

I grew up in a time and place where a great number of bad ideas collided, bursting into uncounted shards and splinters of poisonous yet undetectable debris lodging in the hearts of innocent victims and rendering them deeply suspicious of everything that was hitherto regarded as simply normal. I assumed from a very young age that responsible people use birth control; only irresponsible, sex-crazed, yet also repressed—and mainly Catholic—people do not.

I took this position for granted—and as far as I could tell, everyone around me did too—the way people assume such super-obvious things as that more money is better than less money, or being appreciated for your accomplishments is simply your due, or that pursuing higher education is better than not pursuing it and automatically makes you a better person.

It wasn't a matter of making an effort to believe this. I knew nothing else. I knew no large families or even any happy families that I could see (fortunately I did encounter some in books). I accepted the birth-control axiom the way everyone accepts that we are all progressing to a loftier state than the one allotted to our predecessors, those sad downtrodden unwashed who remain in the Dark Ages while the rest of us sail into the Age of Aquarius (also unwashed, but for indefinably higher reasons) without the burden of progeny.

Then, after my conversion to Christianity, I read something that changed my mind. What I read was simply a statement that the Catholic Church teaches otherwise. It's a good thing to question authority, as I had been raised to do (by every means from ubiquitous bumper stickers to assigned reading), unless the authority in question is absolutely trustworthy—in which case you only harm yourself by questioning it.

I studied the arguments from nature and from Scripture that went along with this stunning development (the development in my mind, not in the universe), although they weren't as important to me as the knowledge that the authority that Jesus established is the source.

It may not come as a surprise to you that although my mind was willing, my flesh—or, let's say, my instincts and practical ability—were not up to the task. You might even say that my mind tottered to think that I, a bride of nineteen, could certainly end up with a couple of dozen children! To say I was afraid would be vastly to understate the nature of my panic, which was rather comprehensive. Yet, decades later, here I am with merely seven children, and what forethought could not encompass, experience has.

So allow me to try to sum it all up in the form of my third secret to destruction-proofing your family.

Husband and wife, embrace your mission as the king and queen of your little kingdom, your family. Enjoy, when you want to, what we may quaintly and not without relief from the pressure of modern freedom from constraint refer to as the marital embrace, simply accepting the children God sends you as the gift that they are.

I realize that to most, this advice sounds extreme.

But I had to tell you just in case you, like me, had never thought it was an option. I had to tell you in case you had never heard about this possibility anywhere else. I had to bring it up at least, so that you would know that it can be done.

This approach shouldn't be yet is—in this day when there is a sad lack of collective memory—a hard saying. So, if indeed you are still with me after the shock, let me point out a few points you might not have thought of.

1. Things haven't worked out the way the contraception boosters predicted. Even a quick survey would take volumes and be far outside the scope of this chapter, but suffice it to say that I wouldn't need to tell you secrets to protect your family's very existence if circumstances weren't bad. We can't shake the sense of looming and indeed present disaster, even with the brazen promises of modern science.

Everyone spends a lot of time trying to assure us that our society is not that bad and is about to be truly wonderful, but if we look at one simple metric, a child's security growing up in an intact family (the strongest predictor of health and success and happiness that there is), there is no question that things are spiraling downward without much hope of rescue. When I was five years old in 1965, the illegitimacy rate in our country was 8 percent. Today in some urban areas it's as high as 70 percent.

Families are mostly either destroyed or never formed, and the ones that are intact are under siege. The result of all this strife is all around us, but we act as if it is not, because our experts keep calling for more of what got us here, which is the decisive separation of the marital act from its inherent goal, children.

2. Contraception isn't magic, although we always talk as if it is.

There are two kinds of contraception: the kind that doesn't really work at all to prevent pregnancy, and the kind that works at a tremendous cost.

Of the latter, there are two kinds: the kind that works (only not always; certainly not always over time) because it chemically alters the woman's body in frightening ways, rendering it inhospitable to the child; and the kind that mutilates the body (and still doesn't always work!). And then there is abortion, evil mop-up squad of failed contraception.

No, not magic.

We are making ourselves stupider, because the more time goes on, the more we know that contraception is either dangerous or useless, the more we still act as if contraception works and having babies is a disaster. So that way is going to be inherently bitter. It will take its toll. It is a bargain with the enemy.

3. Even though most of us see the reality of point 1 all around us and wrestle with point 2, I hear the inevitable and reflexive response: "Auntie Leila, what about the need to limit family size?"

I have two words for this response: Child Resistance.

Maybe the words of a wise priest I know will help put this into perspective. He told me that in his (long) experience, most couples sought his help (with Natural Family Planning)[14] due to their *inability* to have children.

---

[14] I am not really discussing Natural Family Planning here. I'm certainly not anti-NFP, which I think is very helpful when a couple wants to conceive. I'm against "Child Resistance" as a way of life for married people. I'm trying to step outside the societal clutch in the stomach over this issue. Therefore, I'm not particularly interested in parsing the guidelines for using NFP or attempting precision on the topic. I feel that once Child Resistance as a way of life is abandoned, this all takes care of itself. I have noticed that not much good comes of delving into NFP for the sake of using it better to avoid children. The conversation quickly becomes prurient and unchaste.

I would simply ask a couple trying to understand all this what I asked myself in a life-threatening situation: If NFP "failed" (as all methods of avoiding conception can, including sterilization), would I have an abortion to save my life? For any clear-thinking person, the answer must be no. Therefore, the obvious conclusion is that if I must not risk my life by getting pregnant,

In other words, if we removed the near-universal use of birth control, we would not see every couple having the maximum number of children posited by a biology textbook and popular imagination. That is what the purveyors of contraceptives would like us to think (because after all, they are selling something), but the reality is otherwise.

As with everything else, there's a curve to it if you put it on a graph. Some couples, yes, would have a lot of children. Some would have none. And the majority would fall somewhere along the curve, having maybe

---

we should abstain completely. This seems the only truly protective option for the husband to make, since it is not right for one person to risk the life of another for the sake of his pleasure. Indeed, complete abstinence is what those of the past did when faced with this difficulty. It can and has been done, for love will overcome the greatest difficulty.

I realize that to our modern minds such thinking seems impossible. I only ask that we consider what we expect of a couple who have encountered a physical difficulty that doesn't allow them to enjoy the marital embrace, such as a decisive injury. Would we counsel despair in that case? Of course not. We should realize that the possibility exists that the couple would have the physical ability to have intercourse but not to welcome a baby (in the case of a life-threatening illness).

My own experience is that God sent me confidence that all would be well, despite what I was told was the risk (and that is how we got our dear Bridget!). But when prayer and research yield no confidence, then how can NFP be justified, as accurate as it is? My reasoning applies to contraception too, so often urged as the only rational response to a dire reason for avoiding pregnancy: Every form of contraception has a failure rate, including sterilization. If it fails, would the woman seek abortion? This is the question that has to be asked but is always avoided.

And for those who are on the part of the curve where having children is difficult, NFP holds the surest help, which is unsurprising, since it's the only inquiry into fertility that doesn't try to bludgeon it. By all means, do learn more.

Let's not get sidetracked from the main point, which is that most married people are perfectly able to accept whatever children God sends but simply have not considered nor been encouraged in what actually ought to be the normal state of loving each other when they want to and accepting the babies that come.

This secret is how the family stays intact, for God will not be outdone in generosity.

two to five children. I don't know; I'm certainly not intimating that I have any hard data here. *But neither does anyone else*, so maybe we should just think about it.

Just think of all the variables, even without counting the fertility of each of the spouses (which also have to combine the right way): their age when they get started, illness, separation (such as work and deployments, to say nothing of getting mad at each other), accidents, and the almost completely forgotten natural, built-in mechanism of breastfeeding that spaces babies—not to mention babies themselves, whose demanding existence seems designed to keep parents from procreating, at least in the first couple of years!

I've gotten many e-mails from readers asking me what I think about having another child, or how you know if you are ready for another child. I always reply, "How do you know that you *will* have another child?"

What if you could see your life from God's perspective and could know that He would send you only one more child? Or none? Would you act differently? Yet all the medical advice we get, all the advice from relatives and friends, is premised on the opposite assumption, based on Child Resistance: you will get pregnant if you don't take steps to prevent it. Well, real life (even conditioned as it is today) says otherwise. There are folks on that other end of the curve; what if you are one of them?

4. Is a child something to be resisted? If we are going to be questioning things, can we start here? I think that when we collectively agreed that marriage can be taken or left, we made the child the scapegoat, the locus of all our anxiety. But in the context of the family, of marriage, the child is always pure gift. If you are struggling, get rid of something else—solve the *actual problem*—before you put up a defense against the child. You were a child.

When you step away from that little matrix of assumptions, that you *will* get pregnant without constant "protection" and that a baby is somehow, on some fundamental level, *something to be resisted*, you might catch a glimpse of the consequences of not implementing my secret (which, after all, is God's plan for marriage):

- The constant pressure of worrying that a child will derail your plans or make you poorer or sicker
- The constant anxiety of worrying that your method of preventing conception will fail; we pray "lead us not into temptation" but then put ourselves in the position of being tempted to "solve the problem" with abortion
- The wear and tear on your relationship with your husband—not, perhaps, quite noticeable when you are in your twenties, but in that second decade, starting to show—as you approach each and every encounter with an underlying sense of repelling the inner meaning of your actions

It's this last element that I think no one really discusses. Unless you've lived through it—the days and years of running past each other to get to soccer practices and dance recitals and meetings of the planning board, shift changes and overtimes and bosses' unreasonable requests, the flu going through the house and operations and a bout with cancer—it's hard to explain that marriage isn't the simple cost-benefit calculation between sex and babies it looks like when you are very young.

Most people assume that you'll have your two-point-zero children and then you will only have to cope with the stresses brought on by procreation for a few years, and then it's Easy Street for the two of you. But is that how it works out in reality? Reality is what I care about.

When you are near forty and the biggest thing on your mind is mortgage payments or your slowing body, you might find that the fight against babies that may or may not come is not only exhausting; it's also pointless and has drained your married life of meaning. You will not have predicted that a baby, should one be granted to you, multiplies love, even as it complicates things (of course, because good things are complicated in this fallen world of ours).

You certainly won't have the mental energy to fend off those who simply say nay. From where you are now, relatively early in your marriage, perhaps, you can't anticipate any of that or even predict that it will be your struggle.

What I see is that Child Resistance makes you and your husband suspicious of each other. It divides you. It prevents friendship (which I will discuss in the next chapter). It also makes any advice targeted at your relationship useless, because who can be less nagging, kinder, more loving, and more generous when the very purpose of your life together has been frustrated by ... yourselves?

What good is there in knowing your temperament or love language or any number of habits for success if, at the most fundamental level, your communication is compromised? When the language of your body is at odds with the language of your intentions, how can you find a way out?

I really get impatient with marital advice when it doesn't address the main point of marriage, which is to build a family—that is, a unit of glory—by means of your bond. God may or may not send children, but if you've closed off His very intention at the source, how can you hope to catch any other graces?

If you think about it, there is no other area in life in which we just assume that God got it all wrong and made us (especially women) wrong. That man fell at the beginning and now we deal with the consequences, yes, fine; that much is clear. That the way we're made is wrong in its original form as God's plan for all humanity for all time—why would we think this? And aren't we leaving something important out if we do think it? Can't we trust that He would get this right? What if your real protection from destruction is not controlling the number of children but living according to God's plan?

When you remove all this frustration and distrust by committing to enjoying each other in the marital embrace when you want to, accepting with an attitude of trust the children who come, you align your married life with its purpose. You will find peace.

It won't be peaceful peace, because, in a stunning revelation, life is not easy. What if, in fact, you are one of those couples on the other end of the curve? With lots and lots of children? You will still be frustrated—like everyone else, of course—and you will probably suffer terrible things—ditto.

I myself almost died in childbirth with my sixth child, and my husband promptly lost his job for the ensuing eighteen months. We've seen that side of suffering. Our family (like every family) has endured many things I can't go into, but just don't think I am naively dismissing the pain that comes with what the world calls living dangerously (and so it is, *no matter what*). And I know about the other things—the ones you might face, the ones I haven't lived through.

Don't be fooled, especially where there is a time limit to your "awareness potential"—the point beyond which all this will be moot, and you'll merely be living with the consequences of whatever your stance has been. But there's suffering and there's suffering. I would rather not have the kind of suffering that comes from trying *to avoid suffering* by refusing a treasure.

Children are a treasure. They are the expression in living flesh and immortal soul of the unity of the husband and wife. Every child God gives the couple is a chance for them to give Him the fulfillment of His promises, beside which all human works and art pale; children are *His* direct works and art, His image. Removing the worldly lens, we can see that children are truly the prosperity of the family. Rejecting this gift makes no sense unless we have been deceived.

If you've ever read any good stories, you will recognize the deep truth that happiness comes from choosing the path that aligns with the destination, come what may, not the path that avoids suffering. Destruction-proofing is a paradoxical undertaking: it is more about taking holy risks than staying safe.

What if we did the unheard-of? What if we took a look at the Baby Question and just said something like, "God in His word tells us that children are a gift. We'll do all we can to work hard and live simply, enjoying each other and accepting the children who come, trusting that He has a plan for us"?

I suggest that there will be peace and joy!

The Final Secret: Be Friends

Well, of course there are many secrets. Who am I[15] to say that I've identified the four most important things? I've thought of four, and I'm sticking to that! So far we have the first, that *Sundays are for rest*. Keeping Sunday a

---

[15] Who am I to come up with secrets? These are thoughts from more than forty years of marriage and from many conversations with friends whose marriages have also weathered many storms.

holy day creates a connection within your family and a connection between the family (and each person in it) to the vast beyond.

Then, *eat dinner together*, especially *after* you've given up on ever getting anyone to behave: in other words, don't give up. Among the many blessings of eating dinner together is one that is relevant to my final secret, and that is that you really get to know and love each other. You *enjoy* each other's company.

Indispensably, love when you want, *and accept the children God sends.* I wasn't able to go on to what I have to say in this chapter without first pointing out that in our deeply child-resistant culture, it's unheard of to suggest that this is the way to live; it seems foolish even to dream of opening yourself up to a way of life that *trusts.* But this way is the least stressful way, as hard as it is to believe that, and the one that will protect your family from attack.

But God hath chosen the foolish things of the world to confound the wise; and God hath chosen the weak things of the world to confound the things which are mighty (1 Cor. 1:27, KJV).

There is also something else: "Those who have hope live differently," Pope Benedict XVI tells us.

Trying to live out the fourth secret while resisting children will not work. *Husbands and wives are meant to be friends with each other*, but how can they, if, in their intimate life together, they treat the most precious gift of self as a *threat and something to be resisted?*

The fourth secret, now, can be divulged: be friends. Friends admire each other. Friends choose to be together. And friends are polite to and considerate of each other. The husband and the wife should be friends.

When you are first married, you are lovers and expect to *feel*, as well as be, so forever. Then the fires subside, and all the books tell you to be sure to try to fuel the flames with certain methods. Surely you don't need advice from me on that score. Open any magazine (except ... don't; they are not helpful, because they miss the point, which is that you have stopped being friends).

My thoughts are more about when you are dealing with every day—how you react to each other, how you speak to each other, what your ordinary attitude is. Friends treat every time they make contact with a certain eagerness.

Their voices naturally animate upon meeting, expressing their anticipation. They smile with shared adventure. They make sure the other knows that the encounter is appreciated, though they rarely discuss their mutual affection.

Now think about husbands and wives. Think about how your voice sounded over the phone. Was it flat and merely informative? Did you convey a smile with your voice? Did you sign off warmly?

How do you walk through the room where your spouse is busy? Do you interrupt heedlessly? Do you make eye contact in a friendly way?

Think about how friends laugh at each other's quips. I notice that men laugh uproariously at each and every lame joke the other makes, fanning themselves into a veritable bonfire of hilarity at the endless, less than freshly minted puns. For guys, there is no pun that should be left unsaid. There is no exhaustion in punning.

I think that's great. They are having a great time! So just imagine if every one of those men went home and just managed a gentle chuckle at something his wife said in passing. Think how it would make her day to be appreciated for her sense of humor.

It's not that he doesn't think she's witty. He certainly thought so when they first met! It's just that now, he's in the habit of not laughing when she talks. Sad for her; he makes her feel as if he's not really friends with her.

Being a woman, I am intimately acquainted with the way women relate to each other. Having good friends is a joy. You really prepare for getting together with your friends. You dress carefully; you're cheerful; in general, you bring a great attitude to meetings with friends. Just imagine if you acted this way for your husband?

I wonder how much the enjoyment we get out of being with friends is proportional to the effort we put into it? You can object that it's different, since you don't spend all your time with your friends; at least, not as much as with your spouse. You don't live with them!

Well then, bring *just a little* of that energy into your interaction with your husband. Give him a little admiration; at least a *proportional* amount of sparkly eyes and peppy conversation. Offer him one fraction of the consideration you give your girlfriends. When I put it that way, doesn't it seem a bit silly to stint him?

Here's the thing. It's really hard to be with someone for years and years and not see all his flaws, exclusively. Only an *effort* at admiration will overcome the tendency to devolve into a flaw-noticing machine. Want to survive with your marriage intact? This is it! This is the secret, I tell you: cultivate admiration. Admiration is a balm; it is the very oil of grace that keeps life humming along.

For some reason, with our friends we are aware of how our own flaws must seem very evident to them. Yet with our loved ones, we do the opposite: we assume that only our spouses' shortcomings are noticeable, and *our* behavior is the gold standard!

C. S. Lewis said, "In a perfect Friendship this Appreciative love is, I think, often so great and so firmly based that each … feels, in his secret heart, humbled before the rest."[16] (As an aside, I will say that this is a good way to judge whether any person should be a friend.)

A marriage counselor was heard to say that the habit of despising a person is nearly impossible to recover from. Couples who are in "despise mode" get divorced. A couple can survive anger, but contempt is poison. What is the antidote? Maybe there is none, humanly speaking.

Don't get to that point.

Keep "despise mode" far away by making a resolution to work at its opposite: admiration and respect. Feed admiration and respect with *gratitude*. Can't think of anything to be grateful for? At the minimum, this vexing person you are married to accepts *you* and remains married to *you*. Who else would? I don't kid myself that there is anyone else. (Of course, the Chief is far from vexing—he is amazing and treats me like a queen! This makes it all the more astounding that he puts up with me.)

Now here is the practical part that I hope you will attend: men and women need to be admired in different ways. Sure, there is a basic human level of appreciation that everyone likes to receive. There are many books out there that will tell you what those are (for instance, don't criticize, don't nag, try to understand the other's point of view).

---

[16] C. S. Lewis, *The Four Loves*, chap. 2.

But to you husbands, I say that your wife needs to be admired for her beauty, for her character, and for her devotion. It doesn't hurt to let on that you appreciate all that in specific ways.

Let her finish what she is saying; give her the impression that listening to her is worthwhile; in this way, she will feel loved. And the truth is that most men married their wives because they *do* appreciate them and care about their thoughts. But they fall into the habit of acting as if they don't.

Let a beat go by before you respond to show you're giving some thought to what she said. Don't just wait impatiently to throw in your own stellar comment. Laugh at her jokes.

I've sometimes noticed that a man will listen to any random person *except* his wife when they are in a group, all but ignoring her. You've heard it before, you say? Try treating what she says at least as respectfully as your buddies' possibly less-than-daisy-fresh remarks, and watch her blossom. Take her insights seriously. She knows you, and God put her there to tell you some things you need to know.

To you wives, I'm warning you, we have no idea that a man must be loved *as a man*. Does your husband know you admire him? Can he be ad-mirable if his one true love won't gaze on him with approbation? And do you further know that he wants to be admired for being strong (*physically* strong) and protective? For taking care of you and your (possibly numerous, if you follow secret number 3) family? Why do we withhold this blessing from our men? Why do we refrain from openly admiring them?

Is it because we feel a strong sense of responsibility to rid him of his faults? I think this is true in the sense that spouses are given to each other to help each other to Heaven. But it's false to think that through contempt we can change another human being. Husband and wife are one flesh in their marital union, but they are separate persons and ultimately that has to be respected.

Take a break from trying to fix him (after all, you liked him well enough when you chose him), and try a little admiration. Try giving him that look—that look that says, "*You* are my man."

Once, I observed an acquaintance roll her eyes in exaggerated disgust at her husband's clumsiness—something trivial, I assure you; something that she would have bent over backward to cover up if a friend of hers had committed the gaffe. At that moment I knew their union was doomed, and so it proved to be. That's the test, isn't it? What does it profit you to treat your friends with patience if your own husband can't make a mistake without the whole world knowing it?

Has there been bitterness between you? I'd be surprised if not. But try admiration first, and then work your way up to forgiveness, rather than thinking that admiration and friendship will come later, when you've sorted things out.

Wives, when he comes in from wrestling with bears (or getting sand off the driveway or removing the guts of a mouse that the cat left on the mat—whatever the case might be), tell him how much you appreciate it.

Husbands, when she starts to tell you about something she read or wants to discuss with you an issue with a neighbor, listen with a smile.

Both of you, don't let the children prevent you from listening to each other. They can wait their turn.

When you fail, forgive each other readily. When there is a problem, address it in a friendly way rather than as a criticism. If there is something you need to address, tease lovingly or exaggerate wildly—anything rather than that exasperation that dwindles to simple nagging.

The sad fact is that most people with marriage issues don't realize that they are in a dull state of entitlement combined with a good amount of rudeness. We expect a self-help book or a date night to rescue us, when really, all those remedies will work only if we've grappled with some of what seem to be ordinary moments and put some spunk into them.

Are you friends? Do you laugh together? That's the key. That's the secret!

PART 4
Motherhood in the Field

I n this part of the book, I will try to give you all the details of how to live life at home. I am mainly addressing the woman; I hope men can learn something too, but it's easier this way.

The details of establishing home life have been all but forgotten. Over the years, I have had enough questions along the lines of "But *how* do you do this thing" that I wrote all the answers out, or at least all I could. My hope, though, is that, through these examples and instructions, you receive the understanding that you, too, can reach back to the way things used to be done and, with a little exertion, obtain for yourself and those in your home a measure of peace, of order and wonder.

Waking Up in the Morning

How much do you hate waking up in the morning? I'm the same way.

If you live for jumping out of bed and are an amazing morning person, I love you, but please go read another book.

If you drag yourself out from under the covers every day, late, can't function until the second cup of tea, feel paralyzed by the nursing baby and overwhelmed by the messy beds, and never even get dressed until noon, read on, because I will help you. You can't possibly be as averse to the morning as I am.

Everyone else will tell you to get up on time and take a shower, but I will tell you *how* to do that!

Begin by deciding what is *on time* for you.

Never mind your neighbor who wakes up in an hour that begins with a "five" and works out, prays, and cleans her house before her family even stirs. We will never be like her, and we are just going to try to maintain charity toward her.

Instead, change your thinking about yourself. Figure out what is the *latest* possible time *you* can get up in order to be ready for the fixed point in your schedule.

What would that fixed point be? Hubby leaves for work at 7:15, and you'd like to kiss him goodbye? (Did you know that men who kiss their wives goodbye in the morning have a lower rate of heart disease than men who don't? Fact. And perhaps motivation.)

Kids have to catch a bus at 6:50? Mass starts at 7:00? For me, it was the latter that finally made me figure out what to do with my sorry sleeping-in self. I wanted to get to daily Mass.

Let's say, for the sake of argument, that you've been getting up at around 8:00 (or so you tell yourself because it's actually later due to the baby nursing so comfortably in bed with you), and your kids often get up earlier than you and sort of run amok, spilling various liquids while getting their breakfast, playing dinosaurs in the living room, maybe even (gasp) watching TV. You never even get to schooling until after lunch, when you've dug out of the mess.

So, even when you do get up, there's sort of a mountain of chaos created, as it were, while you were sleeping, as if the one from the day before weren't enough. You feel grubby, milk-stained, bleary, and disoriented. There is a vague sense of guilt tinged with defiance as you face, day after day, the knowledge that your husband's last look at the house has been ... this, with an admixture of relief that at least it wasn't you, in your present state.

What to do?

You've tried setting alarms. You've tried not caring. But now you know that you need to get up at a certain time—for the sake of argument, let's say 7:00. And you just can't do it!

And note that I'm not saying that each and every one of us should get up at 7:00. I get up at 6:15, an unthinkably early time, for me. Your "on time" might be 9:00 or noon (maybe you are a nurse with a night shift)—or 6:00 or 4:30 a.m. Maybe you just had a baby. Don't stress out about getting up at someone else's "on time." Please use your common sense.

Here's the secret: stop thinking of your target time as *early* or even *on time*. Try thinking of it as actually a *little late*. But you have to work up to that. So in the next week, start trying to get up at, for example, 7:45 instead of 8:00, and think of 7:30 as pretty darn early, so that you can begin to consider a little before 8:00 as late.

The first day will be terrible, because likely you aren't going to bed at a good time either. Struggle through and do what you have to in order to get to bed earlier, probably an hour earlier than you have been (I'm basing this all on me, you realize, so adjust accordingly). If you have trouble falling asleep, I have a few suggestions:

- Cut out all caffeine (including coffee ice cream) after 10:00 a.m. (If you see this new rule as permission to eat coffee ice cream *before* 10 a.m., who am I to stop you? By the way, it recently dawned on me that perhaps my nursing babies' trouble with sleeping was all the caffeine they were getting from me. Sigh.)
- Don't take a nap during this adjustment period.
- Work yourself up to your target time in fifteen-minute increments rather than going cold-turkey. Sleep cycles are hormonal—chemical—and you have to work with yours.
- Relax your jaw as you fall asleep. Make an effort to open your mouth with your lips together, if that makes sense! Take note if you are pushing your tongue against your teeth and relax it.
- Try to take twenty slow, deep breaths in a row. This is prodigiously hard to do. Relax your jaw and breathe slowly. After about five breaths, you will realize that you are as tense as an adder and breathing like a stressed terrier. Start again! Keep trying, and soon it will be morning!
- Make sure you take your iron and vitamin D or cod liver oil. Also try a bath or a foot bath or even soaking your hands in warm water in which you've dissolved Epsom salts. Magnesium helps you sleep, and most of us are deficient in it. Magnesium is much better absorbed through the skin than taken as a supplement!

After a few days, start thinking of 7:30 as a little late and 7:15 is quite early, nearly hopelessly so. You can set your alarm for 7:20 and enjoy sleeping a bit late.

You get the idea? The following week, start thinking of 7:00 a.m. as a little late; it's 6:30 that's so early. Thank goodness you don't have to wake up at that outrageous time! See? Two weeks ago, you thought you'd never get up before 8:00. Now you're in the sixes!

As you do this, start pondering the issue of the shower. If you can find a way to get yourself in the shower first thing, do it! Do you need a hook for your towel? Do you need a good bathrobe? Don't make taking a shower an adventure, a daily safari! Don't force yourself to make a brand-new decision every day to take a shower—do you know what I mean?

"Okay, well, it's ten o'clock, the plumber is coming, maybe I'd better get in the shower, although he might get here before I'm done. Gee, what should I do?"

Be showered without undergoing this kind of decision-making process, which is exhausting, daunting, and paralyzing! Figure out what you need, make it handy, and take a shower before anything else happens. Make it a habit, not a decision. That way, you are ready for the plumber as well as the unexpected visitor, not to mention your husband and kids!

It's all very well to be a disheveled mess every morning when your kids are little. But you kind of want standards as your kids grow. You want them to know that you like to look good around them; that you are not *fine* with being a disheveled mess in their presence, just because you are close to them. The most important thing you can do to be a more loving mom, a happier wife, a more efficient housekeeper, and a more intelligent mother is to be rested, clean, and dressed! (Well, don't forget meals and laundry, as I said.)

Now, that's not so much to ask, is it?

You know, I'm all for talking about the ideal of the vocation of the wife and mother, but at some level, it's sort of a job. It is at least a responsibility. What would you think of a worker who was never really groomed and was consistently late for her job? Ouch.

Is your hair a problem? Does this seem like a random question? When my kids were little, my hair was long, thick, and curly. It took all day to dry and made me so cold in the winter that I became somewhat immobilized.

Could a perky, easy haircut make things run more smoothly? If so, the expense is incredibly worth it. A trip to the hairdresser in this case is the equivalent of a new vacuum cleaner, a running car, a deep freezer. While you are at it, buy a blow-dryer and some good products. Wouldn't everyone be happier if you didn't have the same tight ponytail every day?

Do what has to be done so you won't hate looking in the mirror every morning.

Are clothes a problem? Sometimes stay-at-home moms don't get up because they dread looking in the closet. Think about what you wish were there and get it! Maybe you need a few more very practical items. Maybe you need some inspiring cute items. Maybe you have only one outfit to nurse in! Go get a few good, attractive things to put on already!

Buy yourself some nice foundation makeup, very sheer; eye liner that is appropriate for your coloring; a little blush; a nice lip gloss. You already have a whole extra half-hour to work with! Get dressed, gel your hair, put on a smidgen of makeup, and voilà!

What about the baby? Can I suggest a playpen? You need a safe spot to put the baby while you're in the bathroom. Playpens seem last century, but it's a shame they went out of fashion. Oh well. If you can stick the baby in bed with an older kid while you shower, do it. If your husband can take the baby out of bed so you can get up, let him.

Eventually you will get to the point when you consider your target "on time" time a little on the late side. You will not mind getting up because you will feel more in control of your fate and less as if you are battling a rogue force from the jungle, complete with strangling vines. You might even make your bed before you leave the room.

You will never really like getting up, but you can do it! If I can, so can you!

More on Showering

I have to talk more about showering. It seems to be an issue with some moms who find themselves at home with small children—a state that strikes them as something akin to finding oneself in the outback facing a herd of kangaroos, or maybe going to Mars without the flight manual.

Now, I realize that many, many people are good at doing certain normal things that are or ought to be part of every normal person's life.

Other people—idealistic, romantic, well read, intelligent people—can't seem to manage these things, partly because they are thinking so hard, and partly because they can't, and this will sound very strange to the others, buy themselves what they need to get started.

Well, at least you will be amused by this little glimpse into my sadly impaired past.

Among other impractical things, and being very young (nineteen, though my husband is older than I) when I got married, I took a shower when I noticed I was dirty. Usually this was every day, as with other folks. But other times, if I was involved in something else, I didn't take a shower. (I don't think I'm completely alone in this—it has something to do with only having to take care of oneself, I think.)

Truly, I just didn't have a routine. It was something I had to think about in order to accomplish it; sometimes I showered because I didn't have anything else to do. Since often I was prevented from showering by something I hadn't planned on, had forgotten about, or suddenly wanted to do, I was often not as fresh as I would have liked to have been at any given moment.

I was cute and not oppressive to others, don't worry. But sometimes I was less showered than other times, in a way that made me not feel ... cheerful.

And I had a vague seventies hippie idea that it was a bourgeois vanity to indulge in new towels, blow-dryers, and sundry items necessary for efficient grooming. (You kind of had to be there to understand those days.)

In due course, we had a baby, and that was a bit of a shock. I wanted a family more than anything, but the reality of a little person to take care of all by myself stunned me, to the point where even something as mundane as going to the bathroom seemed a bit beyond my capabilities.

Little by little, by dint of simply being forced to make do, I found out that you can bring the baby in with you to lie on the rug while you take care of yourself; you can leave him in his crib for twenty minutes; you can leave the four-year-old with a ten-month-old in a playpen, while the two-year-old naps.

And somewhere along the line, I realized something else: that I felt wonderful, elated in fact, under two circumstances, and it might be that revealing this will expose me dreadfully, but here goes: I felt positively renewed after I mopped the kitchen floor and after I washed my hair.

This led me to tell my husband in so many words: if you see that I'm feeling depressed, please remind me to wash either the floor or my hair, or both.

And he did. Many, *many* times he (a very hard-working young man) would gently say, "Hon, do you need to wash your hair?"

And I would think, yes, I do. Or I'd sigh and reply, "No, but I should wash the floor."

One day it came to me. If I just washed my hair every other day (it was very long and very thick), come hell or high water, I would ensure that I would not experience a sense of the futility of life on account of my hair.

The heavens just parted and dropped that information right down into my brain.

I also started washing the floor on a regular schedule, but we're not really talking about that right now.

Skipping to where I really worked this out—and really, many of you might want to find something else to read—I am now going to tell you what you need to do and what you need to buy to avoid the pitfall of not having showered: to eliminate this cause of mental distress from your life completely, unless the power should go out or there is some other act of God.

First, and dear friends, I really don't care what time of day you deem best for this: pick a time. Night? Morning? Kids' naptime? After the gym? (But do bookish, impractical, pregnant or nursing moms go to the gym? I didn't and don't.)

Now, you need the following:

- *Your very own towel*, and maybe even two towels. I have one large towel for my body and one smaller one for my hair. It's okay. You rate two towels. You have my permission. Give some thought to a hook right by the shower for said towels.

- *A bathrobe.* This is an old-fashioned garment that you may not have heard of or may not have considered anything you would ever in a million years want. But it is useful—let me explain it to you.

  - First, it enables you to go from point A to point B without being either fully clothed or completely naked or even wrapped in one of your towels. It's truly a great invention.

  - It goes over undergarments in case of forgetting that the clothing you wanted is in the dryer.

  - It goes over nightclothes in case of wanting to start the coffee when your husband's college roommate is visiting and could appear at any moment.

  - If you get one with a terry lining (or that's terry all the way through), it completes the drying process while remaining firmly secured to your person, should you have to receive a box from a delivery man's arms, get the dog out of the driveway suddenly, or even run out of the house in case of fire.

- ◆ It's not wet, unlike your towel, and it's not clothing, unlike your clothing, although some are quite pretty.
- ◆ You might even find you can remain robed long enough to pluck your eyebrows, clip your toenails, and attend to other grooming necessities. I'm not saying you have to have a bathrobe. I'm just saying, consider it.
- *Slippers.* The floor can be cold. Slippers can be nice. Why not get pretty ones or very warm shearling ones if you live in an icebox, as I do? Throw away the ratty Mickey Mouse scuffs your roommate gave you in your freshman year.
- *Shampoo and conditioner.* Stock up on what you like. You don't have to spend a lot, but do get yourself something you like.
- *Soap.* And by soap, I mean soap, body wash, whatever makes you feel clean and leaves your skin healthy. Stock up on soap, because it would be silly to say to yourself, "I can't take a shower because there isn't any soap."
- A *razor.* Paralyzed by your hairy legs? Just stick the razor (any double-bladed disposable razor will do; just change it often) in the shower, and while your hair is conditioning, give your legs and underarms a quick pass, using plenty of soap.

If you shave on a regular basis, you don't have to do it very carefully, not in the sense that you don't have to be careful with the razor, but in the sense that you needn't worry about a surprise occasion for which the choice to have bare legs would be nice.

Think of frequent shower-shaving as having one of those robotic vacuums—just randomly doing some of the job all of the time.

- *Moisturizer and antiperspirant.* Use after you dry off.
- A *blow-dryer.* If it's less than 90 degrees outside, you really want to dry your hair before going somewhere. It just looks better.
- *Product.* Don't you love that word? Something very specific with the most generic name possible. Why don't they call it "thing" or "stuff"?

One reason you might not wash your hair often enough is that it might have the tendency to frizz, like mine. If so, you worry that the first part of your day, at least, will be spent with the sure knowledge that you look like something out of an eighties yearbook.

But *product* (and a good haircut) will solve this for you. After you blow-dry your hair, work through your locks a dab of something described something like "crunch curl anti-frizz hard curl supermega hold gel" — basically, nice-smelling glue. It will change your life, and you owe it to yourself to try a few until you find the one you like.

Now, if you can't shower for some reason, I'm going to go further with some really old-fashioned advice, as well as a collective-memory item if there ever was one.

How to Sponge Bathe

Why, Auntie Leila, do you have to go there?

Because I seem to specialize in detailed instructions about stuff everyone knows how to do.

But *do* people know how to sponge bathe in this day and age of instant hot water, endless clean towels, and a bathroom for every family member? Hmph. What if there are twenty people staying at your house and you have only four minutes in the bathroom? What if you are camping? What if you are in the African bush?

Brush your teeth.

Fill a basin or sink with very warm water.

Get a washcloth and some soap or body wash.

Wash your body in sanitary order, rinsing the cloth and resoaping as needed: face (rinse after washing, then use just a bit of soap), back of the ears, neck, underarms, euphemistic areas (front, then back), feet. If you have the luxury of replacing the water at any point, do so. Place the washcloth in hamper in such a way that it can dry and not sit there in a damp lump.

Freshen your hair with a bit of clean water on your hands (if your hair tends to be frizzy, start the ablutions by running the dampish washcloth over your head). Apply scent. You are as good to go as you can reasonably be expected to be under the circumstances!

Teach your children to sponge bathe. Auntie Leila fears that the younger generation believes that if there is no shower, there is no way to get clean, which isn't true.

My dear friend, you will do the others in your life a good deed if, rather than unwittingly projecting via your exterior the sense of cluelessness you feel inside, you offer them the hopeful sign of your fresh, cheerful presence every day that you are able. I know that it isn't always possible. We all have our bad patches, even in the most well regulated households! Try your best, though, and you will see results in your everyday life.

Having a Baby in the Culture of Freaking Out

here's a funny combination of a lack of stability in people's personal lives and extreme consumerism that makes some women quite anxious.

If you grew up with some fundamental uncertainties (decades-old entrenched habits of divorce, self-medication, scarcity of babies in everyday life, and some other societal upheavals that you might be familiar with) and if, on top of that, you were exposed to the relentless practice, from a young age, of using shopping as a drug or control mechanism, you are going to be seriously off balance when you are faced with something as elementally challenging as bringing forth new life from your body.

Even if you are in an emotionally and physically healthy place but are surrounded by (i.e., went to college with, roomed with, or are friends with) such people, you are going to feel the panic creeping in. You are not immune to freaking out.

It's depressing to see someone *worrying*, to the point of making herself sick, about what she will buy for the baby. I'm wondering at the energy used to identify the hippest stroller, which, naturally, is shockingly expensive.

I'm all for getting a good stroller, but let's keep some perspective (and start honing some thrifting skills).

But I'm more concerned about two other freak-outs. First, today's girl is frantic that she won't be thin after her baby is born, and she's probably right that her body will change.

If you find yourself feeling this way, give yourself some mental room, because you have a new mission: nurturing your baby and your new family. Narcissism (or fear) will just slow you down. You will be a different shape and full of various fluids. It takes time to understand the physical processes, so give yourself time. Know that despite the occasional naturally thin person, most ladies wear maternity clothes directly after giving birth.

Assume that for six weeks your body will have to work back to equilibrium after being asked to provide life support for "two persons in one" and then launch right into providing life support for "two persons in two."

One reason modern mothers worry about their weight after pregnancy is that they are panicking about fitting into their work or office clothes again in a mere six weeks—another good reason to plan to be home with Baby.

Fortunately, nursing the baby uses a vast amount of calories. Your only task will be to make sure that you eat enough high-quality food: simple, wholesome meats, grains, vegetables, and fruits, with enough fats to supply all the nutrients you need. Please eat some real butter! Eat real meals, three times a day. Drink a lot of water, iced tea, and cranberry juice (with no high-fructose corn syrup). And you *may* be pleasantly surprised at how quickly the weight drops off and you are ready to get back to life as usual. I don't guarantee that, but for those who feel that nursing doesn't do the trick, imagine how your body would have responded had you not had this demand on the calories.

Instead of dieting and worrying about perfectly normal and probably hereditary weight gain, start thinking about what the right way to feed a family is, because soon you won't *be* the baby: you'll *have* a baby.

Another body-related panic centers on labor and delivery. One reason C-section rates are so high is the medicalization of obstetrics—the attitude that childbirth is best controlled by medicine instead of assisted by it. But let's be honest. If there weren't a demand, there wouldn't be such a supply.

I'm shocked to know that there are women who consider a C-section the "easy way out," because it's not. Educate yourself. I had one C-section (with Bridget), necessitated by my ruptured uterus with my sixth child, William. The C-section recovery was miserable for me, far worse than recovery from natural delivery. Yes, labor and delivery can be hard (and most of mine were hard). They can also be not that bad or even ridiculously easy, particularly if you are reasonably fit—not *obsessive* about going to the gym, but just limber and strong.

The college-girl's panacea, working out at the gym to offset binge eating or exhaustion is no way to live. It buys into a dualistic and mechanistic view of the body. And it will lead to poor health. You simply must sleep!

Believe that your body was made by God to bear and nurture babies. It's not a disease to be pregnant and give birth, and chances are, things will be fine. If there is a problem, we are very blessed to have modern science to step in, but we have to keep it within the bounds of common sense.

Be the person with common sense. Become a mother.

Every Woman Can Nurse Her Baby

After the postwar era, when bottle-feeding was the norm, some writers began to stress research showing that a baby suffered the worst kind of failure to thrive, not from lack of nutrition necessarily, but from a lack of loving contact. Certain studies were invoked involving deprived monkeys and poor orphans whose physical needs were met, but whose skin was never touched more than was absolutely necessary; whose eyes were never met with a sweet gaze.

When I was born, in 1960, my mother nursed me. Yes, she breastfed me, but she also carried me, cooed at me, held me in her lap while she read, and when she wasn't holding me, she laid me on a blanket on the beach or put me in the pram under a leafy tree, where, one day, the goat that lived on the farm my parents were renting was found with his hoofs on either side of my head, using the carriage to get a purchase on the higher branches! Popular and medical opinion was very much against my mother—it was the heyday of rigid bottle-feeding schedules and sterile, remote handling of infants. The supposedly scientific way was pushed as the best way.

Despite all the loss of memory that came afterward (related to those common practices, I have no doubt), both personal and in the world, I kept her way of raising babies tucked in my heart. She would tell me about when I was little (the goat story was a favorite for conveying both the shock of the terrible unforeseen risk and the laughing confidence that everything would turn out fine, as, obviously, it did), and, of course, there are pictures, too. But do I remember looking up at those green-black leaves rustling with the sunshine behind them? It seems unlikely, because I was so young. And yet ...

Before bottle-feeding, every baby was breastfed. Bottles were invented for those few poor infants who, lacking a wet-nurse in an emergency, would otherwise be given bread mushed in cow's milk. Bottles were a technological response to a problem, not a replacement for a natural process. Ever since their invention, public health officials have known that disease follows their widespread use.

Today's experts have to reconcile the implacable drive to return women to their former unfettered life, to the status quo ante (whether work or slim figure or both) with the indisputable benefits of nursing. So they reduce breastfeeding to its nutritional benefit alone. No one talks any more about the fundamental emotional attachment between mother and child, unless it's in the context of a "movement," which is counterproductive. The whole dimension of nursing a baby is just a human need.

Preparing for my own children, of course I read many books, because reading is what I do to get ready. Over the years, I have noted a change in the type of advice a mother gets.

Today, we have lost common sense: babies are imprisoned in their car seats, going from vehicle to stroller to swing to crib, rarely allowed to be in any position other than on their backs, suffering from "bucket syndrome" — compressed brains and flattened heads — and fed as if the only thing that matters is getting a certain amount of nutrients into their bodies. One gets the impression that if this could be done more efficiently than the bottle — by IV, perhaps — it would be. I'm dismayed even by the advice given on supposedly pro-breastfeeding sites and in books that offer "natural" encouragement.

So here's my two cents, what I would tell you if we were sitting at the kitchen table together: Virtually every mom can breastfeed her babies. With the proper patience and encouragement, a vast number of women can feed their babies milk from their very own breasts. It makes sense that if your body can have a baby, it can also nourish the baby.

Bottles come in when you find yourself on the margin, in the small percentage who can't feed their babies from the breast. Not to mention that if you've adopted a baby, you will be mighty glad about bottles, and also if you are very ill after giving birth, as I was once.

Nursing means holding, comforting, caring for. It means achieving that level of intimate communication with a nonverbal person such that you know whether his cries mean his tummy is uncomfortable or he is hungry. It means rocking and singing to and cradling and knowing each other's special smell.

Every mother can *nurse* her baby.

Every mother needs to take care, in our ridiculous running-around world, that she is on *baby-time*. You have a lot of obligations and a lot of places to be. When you breastfeed, the logistics of it all pretty much demand that you stop what you are doing to hold the baby. You can't very well prop your breast! If you bottle feed, you are sorely tempted to prop and hand off and otherwise just mainstream that baby into the wild river of life.

I do use the words "nursing" and "breastfeeding" interchangeably sometimes, but "nursing" means more than "breastfeeding."

No matter what, the most important thing is that the baby be held and loved. Some professionals might give you the idea that while you might need to hold a baby to feed him, for the most part they prefer that the baby lie on his back in some safe receptacle. Nurses hurry the baby away if they are allowed to, and most certainly don't like the idea that a sleeping baby is somewhere other than in the bassinet (to be fair, a lot of this is hospital regulations that become internalized).

But it's vital for the baby and for your development as a mother that you spend a lot of time *holding* your baby, whether to feed him or simply to enjoy the feeling of that tiny body in your arms.

Fathers, too, need to hold babies, and a secret is that a fussy baby often settles down only when he hears that deep voice and feels those strong arms.

As much as I think breastfeeding is the perfect way to feed a baby in every possible respect, without hesitation I would say to you that it's better to bottle-feed a baby you're cuddling in your arms than to breastfeed coldly as a repugnant duty. I have seen women offer the breast exactly as they would offer a bottle, not holding the baby close, not relaxing, sitting bolt upright. It's far better to bottle-feed with my definition of nursing the baby—holding, cuddling, relaxing—than to offer breast milk in a propped bottle, withholding the warmth of your body and spirit from your little one.

Obstacles

Many mothers are made anxious and convinced to abandon breastfeeding by experts who officiously declare that the newborn is not getting milk. I have seen this again and again. Nature's way is for mother's milk to come in slowly and in the meantime to provide baby with vital colostrum. Obviously, formula from a bottle given right away will result in weight gain; that proves nothing, and the more important finding would be long-term health and development. Babies are designed by the good God to be able to wait for their mothers to recover from their birth and build a milk supply. They can wait for days.

In order for the milk to come, the mother must be given time without stress. A new mother will likely feel awkward. After giving birth, she's on the spot, often having to ask professionals to please give her the baby—the baby they are so competently handling. She has already been subjected to exposing private parts of her body, and now she has to coax this sleepy little stranger to do something he has never done either! This task is made more difficult the longer she has to wait to try. If those around her insist on weighing and cleaning the baby directly after birth, the window for baby's interest tends to close, and he just wants to sleep.

Don't be afraid. Embrace the awkwardness. Ask your husband beforehand to maneuver his body so that you have some privacy. Ask him to help you to become what you want to be but, in your vulnerability, may not be able to insist on at the moment.

As I say, babies are normally alert right after they are born and there is a short window of interest, with good latching and vigorous sucking, before he lapses into sleep. Later, when he wakes up, he will know what to do. Thus, it's important to tell the person helping you that you want the baby's cord to stop pulsing on its own before it's cut and for the baby to be brought right up to you as soon as possible.

Even if the baby shows no signs of wanting to nurse (imagine! the baby can't stay awake after a little thing like getting born!), keep his tender new skin against yours, covering both of you with a light blanket. (Beforehand, see if you can work it out that the powers that be do all their fussing—weighing, measuring, and whatever else—a little later. See if you can sign something waiving the terrible eye drops or at least postponing them.)

When the baby wakes up, try again. Even a little sucking or a little funny activity that might or might not be latching on will start up the milk production. The more he tries, the more milk you will have, but not for a while. Be patient and don't worry. It's not like putting in an order at McDonald's, you know. It's a delicate system, part chemical, part physical, and part emotional, and at first it takes days to get into gear.

Giving yourself permission to learn is the first step on the journey of motherhood, which is a *lifelong* exercise in patiently nurturing the development of this other person, in lovingly exerting effort now for future rewards, in accepting the work of the present to prepare the banquet for later. Don't give up on this first challenge too easily; it has great implications for every other step of the way.

I talked before about our culture of freaking out. It's not only girls who freak out. It's people who have studied all this, in theory, but who have no faith in it. They want instant results, and woe to the poor girl who, never even having seen this done, most likely, has to stand up to them.

Sore nipples? Trouble latching on? Fussiness? Breast too empty? Breast too full? Of course! All these things happen to everyone. Remember that anything physical seems clumsy at first. Everything has a learning curve.

Remember learning to ride a bike? At least you get to be comfortably resting for the challenge of learning to breastfeed. And that brings me to another point. For some reason, it's important to the experts that you sit up to nurse a baby, and yet sitting up is not always an option, either at the start or later on.

You can nurse a baby lying down. Even when you sit up, you should be relaxed and comfortable. Prop your arm with a pillow. Cuddle your baby close. Don't mind at first what he does: get to know him! Smell his sweet head, stroke his tiny arm, kiss his little fingers, and before you know it, you'll be on your way.

The concern at the hospital is that you will fall asleep, because what's worrying everyone is a potential lawsuit. However, in the light of the history of the human race, our time seems strange in its insistence that mother and baby not be comfortable together.

Sharing Feedings

Many women today have come through their lives up until their first baby without ever being solely responsible for anything. Even assignments at school are often given in groups. Nothing ever completely depends on *you*.

It's tempting (and nurses in particular seem quite taken with the idea) to think that if you bottle-feed, your husband will be able share the "chore" of feeding with you, particularly getting up at night.

Resist this line of thinking. Breastfeeding is the right thing to do, and persevering will help you resolve whatever issues you ever had with taking responsibility. It's the expert-level course for your certification.

Even if you have to use the bottle, the poor man needs to sleep so he can go to work and earn some money so that you can be free to stay home and be the queen of your little universe. Proper nurturing (see above) is not going to happen if you go back to the office, and Baby wants Mommy, not Daddy, at 2:00 a.m. Knowing you can snuggle in bed together removes the misery. Your husband will have his chance later if the issue is the necessity of a good burp, but for feeding, no, it's all you.

If you embrace your fate, running to meet it with joy, you will be rewarded with your cup overflowing. If you trust your body and summon up a little patience with it, you will have a happy, contented, responsive baby. Things won't be perfect; they never are. But they will be as they should be.

There are physical conditions that I'm not qualified to address (and sometimes even doctors miss). I understand that and am confident that the blessing of the Internet means that you will almost certainly find a remedy.

It's important to me that this message, that all mothers can nurse (in the sense of cuddle and hold) their babies, is uttered without qualification.

On Getting to Know
Your Newborn

Here's how to give yourself the best shot at being peaceful and relaxed with your brand-new baby, the baby you don't know yet. For problems and issues about breastfeeding, see the chapter "Every Woman Can Nurse Her Baby" (which is not meant to be comprehensive) and go on the Internet to find the really helpful sites that have all the answers. I'm not giving medical advice here; I'm just talking to you in a cozy way.

If you don't come from a culture of being surrounded by women who easily and in a relaxed manner breastfeed their babies, you are simply not going to know certain things! Who will tell you? It isn't even a "telling" thing, but alas, that's what I have to do here. Please bear with me and know that if you had trouble when you tried breastfeeding your baby, I have the utmost sympathy for you and would only like to make things a little better for the next time.

Here is the little point I want to make here: assume that the new baby needs to be nursed, held, breastfed (or fed from the bottle). Make your default position be "I will nurse him." For some reason, many nurses, grandmothers, and other "helpful" people, including most authors of books out there, set themselves one task: to figure out what the baby needs *other* than nursing. Speaking as a grandmother myself, I will admit that *one* reason is that they want you to rest. But it's puzzling how committed they can be, even when it's so clear that the baby needs Mama.

There are one or two things the baby might need other than nursing, I'll admit. He could be chilly. Often mama is a bit overheated and doesn't quite realize that baby needs a blanket. (Sometimes he's overheated and needs a layer removed.) And of course, it may be that his diaper is dirty. You can change it before nursing him. Sometimes he needs to burp, it's true.

Other than that, *your* default in these first days and weeks must be that the baby needs to be nursed.

During the first week (can we just hold off the "helpful" advice for one week?), he probably does not need a pacifier, a swing, a burping longer than a few minutes, "time away from you so he doesn't smell the milk," a bottle, or whatever else they cook up.

Is he looking around? Wonderful. Enjoy! Have something to eat and drink. Is he sleeping? Wonderful. Close your eyes and sleep too. Is he fussing, or does he seem to need something? *Try nursing him.*

There are, of course, times when it becomes obvious that something else is needed. Again, he may indeed need to burp or even poop. (Do check the diaper first.) He may even need to stretch out. Very soon you will become proficient in identifying these times. Stunningly, you will get to know your very own baby and his needs.

Hold him in your arms in any case, these first days and weeks. The few instances when you won't be holding him will be obvious: you are in the bathroom, Daddy's holding him, he has been put down somewhere cozy near you and went to sleep and you are eating something (but then Daddy picks him up), you went to sleep (but come to think of it, you are still holding him).

And there are times when you may be so exhausted that you do need someone to take the baby so that you can sleep or you may die. With each of my babies, there would be at least one time when I was so at the end of my rope that if I drifted off, a noise like a stick of dynamite would go off inside my head (this is a known syndrome—I'm not making it up). So at that point, yes, they (husband, mother, kind neighbor) can bounce and pacify and pace and swing, just long enough for you to recover. I'm not talking here about those instances, which do pass. I'm talking about normal, everyday (albeit new and yes, tiring) existence with your infant, about the *default*.

Here are some things that people will say to you, getting inside your head by making you think that nursing is the *last* thing to try, confusing you, and making you anxious (and this list is very general—believe me, I know that people say some crazy things):

"He's not crying!" Well, let's not purposely make the baby cry in order to get what he needs. Goodness knows there will be enough crying without that. But if at any moment he is making that little "eh, eh" noise, or, of course, crying, or bobbing his little head up and down, or sucking his little fist, go ahead and nurse him. Yes, nurse him before he starts crying, even.

"He has already nursed." So? He really may need to nurse again. Any number for feedings per day that anyone throws at you is an *average*. It's of limited usefulness. The only way to tell if the baby doesn't want to nurse again is to try nursing him. Any experienced nursing mom will tell you that there are many occasions when baby will indeed nurse again, even having just nursed!

Infants often nurse pretty much continuously all day and all night, for that matter. Guess what! They have to *survive*. Where are you going? You're not going to a road race! (See the chapter "Reasonable Postpartum Time.")

Just think, "Ah, I will go ahead and nurse the baby again. It's okay."

"He has been nursing for a long time." Well, babies nurse for more than just hunger. Ask yourself why we feel the need to disturb a peacefully nursing baby? Why?

There are technical reasons why babies should nurse for long periods and even on empty breasts. I discuss these elsewhere, and of course the Internet is full of experts who address this issue. But mainly I want to say, why do you want to disturb a nursing baby? Very soon there will be many disturbances without our creating them.

"He'll get used to nursing all day, every day and all night too, and you'll have no time to yourself!" Clearly, that is not true. Please look around at all the

older people you know, some of whom *must* have been nursed, and see that they are indeed not nursing at all times.

First, you just had this baby. He really does need to eat a lot. And it's a bit much to subject you to anxiety gridlock by warning you against feeding him all the time *and* that he isn't regaining his birth weight.

Interestingly, if you just got a job at a big investment bank, you'd be expected to be there all day and mostly all night. They literally send a car for you early in the morning and deliver you back late at night, and your food is catered there so that you *can't even leave to have dinner elsewhere*. People would be praising you for having such a prestigious job, but it would be even more demanding than having a newborn, and you would not get to lie down, ever. If that's what you really wanted to do—be an investment banker—you'd put in the hours, knowing that eventually you'd have some free time and a summer house in a swanky resort.

But somehow, when it comes to nurturing a little person, no one can give you even two weeks to figure things out!

Second, the baby will develop a rhythm, and eventually there will be time to do other things. It's a process of elimination; you have to eliminate that he needs to nurse, and to do *that*, you need to nurse him by default.

"You should get a pump and use it." Big disclaimer alert here: if you are committed to some sort of thing where you are pumping because you have to be away from your baby, I am really not the person to consult. Plenty of advice out there. I do hope that you will take the first few weeks and not pump.

For you others, I want you to know that pumping isn't something you have to do to breastfeed. Many, many mothers—indeed, the vast number of mothers—have nursed their babies and never pumped! Somewhere along the way, it seems to have been deemed a necessity. Does that really make sense? Think about it—anatomically.

To you I want to say:

Maybe you acquired a pump without really knowing much about it. You know that cupboard above your fridge? The one you never open because you have to teeter on a chair after first having moved the stuff off the top of the fridge, which you don't want to do because it has that sticky dust on it? Put the pump up there.

If you ever, God forbid, have to go to the hospital for some reason, there it will be, and your husband can get it down. Otherwise, get it out of your sight. Because babies actually need so little, people are enamored by anything they can grasp onto as a "necessity," especially if it involves a machine of some sort. But in fact, you don't need it in the normal course of things. Nursing isn't about getting milk A into Baby B and *nothing else*. But if it were, a pump would just be adding a step.

"What if you have to nurse the baby out in public? You need a bottle, so you need the pump." No. Just nurse the baby by holding him somewhere in the vicinity of your chest.

If you give yourself lots of time to nurse the baby in those first days (see the chapter "Reasonable Postpartum Time"), you will figure out the mechanics and the seeming awkwardness of it all in the privacy of your own home. By the time you are ready to go out, you'll be beautifully able to do it. I myself nursed babies in every conceivable place: restaurants, lecture halls, churches, airports, museums, parks, movies, airplanes, parties. Certain of my babies couldn't settle down to nursing with noise or hubbub (too interested, even at a young and tender age), so I would excuse myself to a quiet place (all the while exuding "it's not for your sake I'm leaving, but for hers" vibes), or I'd just stay home (and that never seemed like a burden at all; somehow making the decision to do what's needed for Baby makes it fairly easy to give up things that would otherwise seem hard).

Again, if you were that new recruit at that investment bank, you'd never see the inside of a museum, and you'd be the pride of your alma mater. They'd give you an award for not ever going anywhere.

So take the first two weeks to put all that out of your mind. Your job is to rest and to nurse the baby. Wonderfully, if you can possibly not fret about "nursing too much," you will automatically be more rested, because you will be sitting or lying down so much to feed the baby.

You will be on your way to having a peaceful experience, or, for that matter, to finding out that you have a little barracuda on your hands who keeps you hopping, because some babies are tough nursers, that's a fact. It's not that everything will be perfect. Auntie Leila never promises that!

"*His night and day will get switched.*" This just happens. Early on, the baby will be quite awake all night. It has nothing to do with nursing him. It has to do with his having conked out during the day because you were resting and the hum of life in general soothed him. Suddenly it's quiet in the world, and he finds his ability to keep awake, so he does.

Just do a few extra things with and to him during the day: a washcloth washing if his cord hasn't fallen off, a bath if it has, getting him nicely clean and changed; a little fresh air with Daddy while you nap; being picked up more during the day. At night, after a long feeding, give him a good burping (Daddy is so good at this), change him, and think positive thoughts about how the night is for sleeping. Do not panic.

As you get stronger and more able to move about during the day, he'll get the idea that it *is* day, while still staying close to you and nursing plenty at night. After two weeks, try not to change his diaper in the middle of the night if you can help it. Soon he will give you at least one (maybe more!) four-hour stretch of sleep at a time during the night with only a little rousing to nurse.

The most dreadful comment of all:

"*You will spoil him.*" Even if it could be true that by meeting your infant's needs, you would spoil him (and it's not true), the good news is that you can always rectify anything later.

Right now your mantra should be "I'll worry about that [spoiling, being out of shape, not wearing high heels for the photo shoot, getting back to work—all of it] later." You need to understand how breastfeeding works —that it's a demand-and-supply system.

Success for most really does depend on having the baby near and being willing to nurse him rather than put him off with strategies. By "success" I don't mean every moment will be a glowing symphony of angels' voices, but simply that you'll get to know your baby (whether he's easy or hard) and have enough good milk for him. And you won't be anxious.

You need confidence that your new baby can't be spoiled by getting love, affection, and milk from you. Hold him in your arms, relax, and don't worry.

Let nursing him (even when bottle-feeding—that is, picking him up, cuddling him, holding him in your arms) be your default position rather than a last resort.

When the two weeks are up, give yourself until Baby is six weeks old. "At six weeks I'll consider myself back to normal." By six months you won't even remember what all the nervousness was about.

Postpartum means one week, and then six weeks, and then six months. Keep moving the goal line.

Random Nursing Tips

I'm no expert on nursing, but I'm not sure who is, because there are so many variables—you, your body, your baby, his body ... So much is just a matter of learning as you go. You could read a hundred explanations and still be frustrated. Then someone mentions something, and you wonder why you never thought of that!

The books and sites want to be comprehensive, both in scope of material and audience appeal. Yet there are some things they never seem to say!

If we were talking it over in my kitchen, here are a few things I would tell you, things I heard only once or didn't hear at all, but just figured out for myself. These tips apply not just to the new baby but to any stage of nursing. So here, I'm not being comprehensive—I'm just telling you some random things, a few little ideas that helped me a lot, because, truth is, it wasn't a piece of cake for me either. And if I could do it, so can you!

1. *Drink plenty of fluids.* My very first OB told me that when the baby came, I needed to concentrate on *drinking three quarts of fluids a day* in order to have enough supply. I took him very seriously and got into the habit of making sure I had a drink of something while I nursed: ice water, diluted cranberry juice, or, preferably, iced tea (although you have to get decaf tea

or the baby will not sleep; this is something that honestly didn't occur to me until just recently—way too late, needless to say). Not one other person—doctor, nurse, or midwife—ever told me about proper hydration for nursing; I do think it saved my nursing career.

Now, lots of mamas have no trouble. They don't think about drinking until they are thirsty; they never have trouble with supply; they never have a breast infection. I had a good supply but was very prone to infections. Drinking enough (and especially the cranberry juice when I felt things going downhill) really helped.

Your loved ones (even your four-year-old) can feel useful knowing that they can help with the baby's feedings by bringing you a drink as soon as they see you sit down to nurse.

Try to find drinks that don't have high-fructose corn syrup or aspartame ("natural flavor"). This eliminates almost all sodas (unless you get some pricey ones at the specialty markets or make your own) and cheap cranberry juice.

If you have yellow urine in the morning, *you aren't drinking enough*. It should be almost clear. A doctor told me that one time when my urine sample was dark enough for him to comment. This goes for your kids too. Some people just forget to drink when they are thirsty, resulting in a lot of health problems. Some crankiness problems, too.

2. *Understand the relationship between sucking and production.* The breastfeeding books will help with this. It's amazing how long it takes to wrap your mind around the fact that your body is not only calibrated to respond to demands for milk but also has a built-in fail-safe mechanism to prevent seesawing back and forth between too much and too little.

That means that it takes a few days to build up supply and a few days to let it diminish. You see why, don't you? Otherwise a baby who, for some reason, just randomly wants more one day would call up a too abundant supply the next day (it works by days and *time of day*), and then the following day, after baby can't eat all that, too little. So you have to be patient. You have to accept that a baby in a growth spurt will be a bit fussy for a few days until your supply catches up. Yes, you have to sit more, nurse more, lie down more, drink more, eat more, realize that you have a baby! Everyone else needs to realize this too and not pester you with fears of failure.

A baby in a steady state (not experiencing a growth spurt) will leave you feeling full in your breasts for a few days until things equalize.

Why do we think that growth is a smooth curve? It's more like a sudden bump after you thought you had it all figured out. Also, being a baby means constant growth spurts.

3. *Calling up more milk (or just getting started) requires Baby's sucking on an empty breast for a while as well as just all-around nursing more—nursing longer.* So you do need to nurse especially a new baby beyond the point where you feel you have no milk. Don't go until it hurts—switch to the other side. Yes, there is that long-term process for building milk, but your body will also produce a little more if Baby asks for it *right then*. It will satisfy Baby briefly and get you through until your body gets the message: more milk!

If you don't do this—nurse until you're empty, switch sides even if you feel that you're empty on the other side—you may consistently have a low supply, eventually drying up. And of course, you need to make sure that your own fluid levels are high (see the first tip).

Remember that your newborn baby is getting valuable colostrum and can wait, is designed to wait, for your milk.

4. *Learn how to switch sides.* Along with getting adequate fluids, how to switch sides is the number-one thing to learn when you're having a little difficulty. In theory, baby should nurse on one side, get half the feeding, and then be willing to go to the other side and get the rest. Obviously your two breasts will produce more milk at a feeding, if asked to do so on the previous days, than just one by itself. And you will alleviate the unpleasant lopsided feeling (and look).

The problem—and please read carefully, because I am not advocating *not* finishing a feeding—the problem that I found is that my poor hungry newborn and infant would nurse frantically on one side (and some prefer one side, making this all the more tricky), get a good amount, and fall asleep!

Then I'd try switching, but he'd be fast asleep, and no amount of coaxing would get him to be interested in the other side! The books say that when a baby falls asleep in the middle of a feeding, apply a cool washcloth, rub his feet, blow on his face, et cetera, et cetera. These techniques had no effect on my babies. That baby was asleep and that's it.

That really wasn't a good amount of milk, however, so in an hour he'd be hungry again, only to repeat the process. Also, maybe his poor tummy was too small yet. Meanwhile, breast number two would become hard as a rock, leading to a breast infection or awkward pumping methods to reduce pressure.

Here's my solution. Once, and I don't know where, I read that a baby gets a good proportion (I can't remember the percent, but it was high) of milk during the first five minutes of nursing. Enough to convince that breast that it has, indeed, been called upon and should produce a good amount at that time the next day.

I learned to offer the first breast (which, as you know, should be the one not offered last, because that evens out the production, but don't stress about it) for only those five minutes (after letdown) or *whatever time is one minute less than the time before the baby falls asleep*, then switch to the second and let him drain that one until he is full or falls asleep.

If this is your problem, that once he detaches while asleep, the boat has left the harbor, try my solution. As long as he isn't actually asleep with the first breast, he'll latch on to the second breast and keep sucking.

5. *Unless your baby is really frantic for food, try to get into the habit of anticipating a feeding by a few minutes and changing him before you nurse him, if you know he needs a change (i.e., is at all wet).*

It helps to change him when he is seemingly just so fussy and wanting to nurse a lot yet not really paying attention to his job. It's easier than realizing halfway through the feeding that he has something else on his mind and having to get up. It also helps you remember to wash your hands and get yourself a drink and a pillow for under your nursing arm.

(Parenthetical plea: Do *not* rely on baby wipes for getting your hands clean. Wash them with soap and warm water! How grossed out I have been seeing people change a messy diaper, wrap it up, and feel as if they're done! This goes for dads, too.)

Babies really don't like having wet or dirty diapers. The feeling of well-being enables them to nurse better and more comfortably. This, in turn, is better for your supply, because Baby is concentrating and sending the right messages. Finally, when he has nursed himself to sleep, he is more likely to sleep more comfortably and not wake up too soon.

Besides, it's good to know that you'll get to everything in the proper order. It's good to have a rhythm in all the things you do.

6. *Figure out the baby's rhythm.* "Responding to the baby's need to be fed ("nursing on demand," which sounds peremptory but let's just go with it) doesn't mean not having any idea of what's going on. The more you know about what is likely to happen on a given day, the better off your family will be. It's just silly to face each day without a clue about how many times you are likely to have to sit down to nurse or, for that matter, do anything else. You don't want to be always reacting (a little too late) to your baby. You want to be ahead of the curve if at all possible. (And I readily admit that with babies, very often, who even knows?)

Your job is to find out what the baby needs from you without any worries about the implications for the future. A newborn who nurses every hour is implying nothing whatsoever about what he will do in two weeks or two months. Why waste a second of anxiety over it? Give him what he needs now.

Once you are getting the hang of things, and you feel better and know the baby better, you start to notice that, yes, it's just about every two hours that he needs you, or perhaps every hour during the day and every four hours at night. (Just as an example! It might be quite different!) The point is, you notice his rhythm, and it helps you to know more about him, to be ready for him before he's beside himself with screaming (because you know you have other things to do), and not to be surprised that you have to stop what you are doing and attend to him. You will notice when he is more likely to sleep in Daddy's arms and you can get a shower. You will notice when he's more awake and lively, and you will appreciate that time more.

Just start thinking of it as his rhythm, and you will be less frustrated when he doesn't quite stick to it! The little stinker won't, and it's no use letting it get you down.

7. *If you know your baby's rhythm, you can solve the "day-night" problem.* First, know that babies everywhere, nursed or bottle-fed, do this mischievous thing right at the start. But you can fix it.

You see, your baby is going to nurse a certain amount in a twenty-four-hour period. Some babies get mixed up because a busy or overtired Mom is stretching the times in between nursings during the day, unbeknownst to herself, and this applies to "total on-demand nursers" much more than they realize. Even babies nursed on demand settle down to a rhythm of about once every two hours and then once every three to four hours, in the space of a day.

But, being so "on demand" that we aren't paying attention, we fail to see that we are putting him in the car seat (where he falls asleep) and taking older siblings hither and yon; we are handing Baby off to be rocked by someone while we get dinner ready for eight people; we are bouncing him through the checkout at the supermarket; and each time we are stretching him beyond the point he really is ready to eat—maybe, let's say, half an hour here, twenty minutes there.

In a day, that adds up to maybe one-and-a-half to two hours, which is an extra feeding! So, again without our noticing, he makes up for it at night, when he nurses constantly.

Fix this by making a point of *not* putting him into the car seat until you've sat down and nursed him, even if it means that the older kids have to load the dishwasher before you leave (or whatever other thing you would be running around doing). Say no to an outing if you know your baby conks out in the car and can't be convinced to nurse at his usual time; you can go when he's older. Shop more frequently with shorter times in the store for a while, or schedule the trip for early in the morning when you know he'll sleep. Plan simple menus so you aren't caught in a complicated pre-dinner frenzy, because nursing him at 4:45 instead of 5:15 might make the difference between his waking up once or twice before midnight.

In short, let his rhythm clue you in to ways to put more nursing in during the day so that he'll stretch out the nights more. You won't have changed the total amount of nursing—*just when it occurs.*

8. *Get proper nursing bras.* I know some people say they would rather pull their regular bra up. If it works for you, fine. I found it pressed down on my breast uncomfortably to do that, sometimes leading to a blocked duct, and I preferred flapping down. I like the suggestion of cutting off the fronts of camisoles to go along with your bra and provide a little coverage on your sides when you lift your blouse or T-shirt.

9. *Use nursing pads.* It really helps make you feel better about life when you aren't afraid of leaking all over. Get a lot of them and toss used ones in the wash in a mesh bag for lingerie. (Mesh bags are well worth finding, by the way, for little baby socks and your bras and all sorts of other little, long—such as bathrobe belts—hooked, or delicate things that will otherwise make laundry a nightmare.) Keep the nursing pads really clean (wash in at least warm water with the towels).

More on Baby's Falling Asleep While Nursing

I'm a big advocate of just relaxing and letting the baby nurse until he falls asleep. Of course, as the experts point out (and I'm *not* an expert, but I do know about this), the hindmilk, the milk that the baby gets when the breast seems empty to you, contains the marvelously nutritious fats he needs for good health. On top of that, it's just a joy to experience your baby's contentment, feel his total relaxation, and also be off your feet yourself. If you bottle-feed, you need to figure out how to get this aspect of life with baby into his feedings.

Taking care of a baby isn't about mechanically meeting his needs, doing the minimum possible so as to get on to other tasks. It's about establishing a rhythm that includes some of the things distinctly not valued outside the home, such as a good dose, every few hours, of inefficiency. Maybe I'm the only person this ever happened to, and it wouldn't be the first time, since I sometimes think I walk in a haze of complications that don't exist for others,[17]

---

[17] For instance, I also had a baby who couldn't be allowed to fall completely asleep on the breast. He was what the doctor called, on the very first day,

but as I mentioned in the last chapter, sometimes the baby would frantically latch on, nurse like a fiend for however long on that breast, and then fall deeply asleep after about twenty minutes, when he should have been ready to get going on the other side. I think that one factor is that I usually did have a good supply, which might not be the case with you.

If I let him fall asleep that way, he'd be done, period. Maybe an *hour* later he would be interested in the other breast, but even I can't sit in one place for two hours most of the time (well, I certainly did with my first child, but after that, inefficiency has its limits, as does discomfort; I never was any good at pumping or hand expressing).

If left on the breast, he'd continue sucking in an unconvincing way. If taken off to switch, his little jaw would clamp shut and it was as if Morpheus had kidnapped him for good. Nothing, and I mean nothing, would stir him. (The irony, right? If I had *wanted* him to stay asleep, he'd be crying.)

Of course, he'd then wake up in an hour needing to be fed. Meanwhile, I was working on two things for this little one:

1. Getting him to have a good rhythm for nursing. I'm not talking here about the first week or so, when anything goes, as far as I'm concerned, but later on, when you need some sense of order in your day; order, to be sure, established by an infant, but order nonetheless. Maybe that doesn't make sense to you, but this order is not the imposition of a schedule but the discernment and yes, encouragement of a pattern.

2. Keeping things balanced in my body, since I was prone to breast infections and wanted to minimize engorgement. I did nurse a couple of babies sort of thoughtlessly, doing one breast at a time, but after some traumatic bouts of mastitis, I came to feel that there must be a better way.

---

using a medical term, "a barfy baby": a baby with a highly developed gag reflex. If he nursed until the breast was completely empty, the nipple elongated, and his throat relaxed, he'd gag and throw up the whole feeding! Talk about not getting the benefits of the hindmilk! So I had to find the very last safe moment and detach him, poor thing.

I started thinking: the baby gets most of the milk from the breast (although not that hindmilk, true) within the first five minutes of nursing —after letdown. It can take some minutes to let down, but I think that a hungry baby isn't going to be in danger of falling asleep until he's gotten *something*!

What I did was to switch him *before* that moment when he starts to change gears from all business to drifting off to la-la land.

If I waited, say, ten minutes to unlatch him, it was no good. He'd fall asleep off the breast, having gotten no benefit from that second part of the feeding on the first breast, and indeed it is a grave mistake to restrict a baby that way. If that is the case, it would be better to nurse only on one side and let him go on sucking.

Don't think you are doing something wrong if you let the baby fall asleep at the breast! Quite the opposite. He needs the end of the feeding and the bliss of drifting off in your arms.

Anyway, at that magic point before complete insensibility, there'd be a yell of frustration at being interrupted as I detached him, and I'd have to have that second breast ready and waiting, all fumbling with snaps and closures having already been achieved. Then he'd latch on satisfactorily for the second round and everything would proceed as usual: getting all the foremilk of the second breast *and* sucking in his sleep to get the important hindmilk.

So the question of hindmilk is moot. In the case of nursing only on one side, there's hindmilk from that one side. My way, there's hindmilk from the one side, *the second side*. It's a wash.

I'm not saying give *only* that first five minutes or that it is undesirable for the baby to fall asleep while nursing. I'm saying that you can increase your supply, even it out, and get in both sides while still offering the benefit of getting that hindmilk if you switch earlier than the twenty minutes usually recommended—*in the case* of a little stinker who falls asleep *too soon* and won't wake up!

If your supply is low, or you *can* wake the baby up, it's likely that you will not have these issues. You probably can do just what the books say and go the twenty minutes on one side and be fine on the other. So do that! It's obviously better! Use your common sense. This tip is for those babies who are committed sleepers (when they want to be). Maybe I just have intense kids. (And why would they be that way? Hmm?)

As they grow, the goal is to get a good feeding, including hindmilk, out of both breasts, and it did work that way for my babies. When they were older and more alert, they did a good job at nursing on both sides completely.

As an aside, I think that some babies nurse on only one breast and it becomes a habit. Later, when they need much more milk, this habit leads to nursing more often, one side per feeding, which can be exhausting (some mothers are fine). When a baby nurses on both sides from the get-go, I think it might be easier to keep up with demand without spending all day, literally, nursing.

I think we can all agree that two doses are better than one, but that takes time in some cases, and a net overall increase in milk consumed, with the second side for the hindmilk, is better than nursing on only one side.

More Thoughts on Breastfeeding

A lot of mothers simply give up on breastfeeding their babies, not because they don't desire it but because they don't have the energy to solve all the problems they might encounter on their own. Over the years I've gotten a certain knowledge base from my own experiences and those of my many friends with numerous children. In writing the blog, I've learned even more from our readers. I pass these experiences on to you here.

Tongue-tie. I think we assume that the pediatrician will be on top of abnormalities of the baby's tongue, but the truth is that breastfeeding success is not at the top of the pediatrician's priority list. If things are not going well, there could be a problem. Keep in mind that the tongue-tie can be on the side, near the back. It is not normal for a child to have difficulty nursing to the point of not getting nourishment (and gaining weight) or for the mother to be black and blue from trying to feed him.

Times between feedings. Beware of professionals who tell you that baby should be nursing only every three or four hours. I would say that a five-month-old can certainly go three or four hours between a couple of his feedings in a day but will still need a few that are closely spaced. Learn your child's rhythm and help him along by trying to nurse on both sides for each feeding. Just make sure that he is completely draining the second breast so that he gets that important hindmilk. In a few days, the fore- and hindmilk issue should sort itself out.

Your comfort. It's not necessary to have a picture-perfect rocking chair in a nursery; in fact, most of the time you will be plunking yourself down wherever you happen to be, because life goes on while baby needs to be fed! Be comfortable. Lean back, lie down. I found I needed a pillow under my arm. Odd aches and pains and even tendonitis ("baby elbow") can be avoided by making sure your muscles aren't tense when you're holding your baby. Getting a glass of something to drink ready before you sit down with baby is a must. You can train older persons to bring you one. And of course, prepare just the right reading: the ideal book can be held with one hand and isn't too heavy (literally doesn't weigh too much). Having your "nursing reading" (Jane Austen novel or what have you) ready at hand keeps you from endlessly checking your phone. You can get a lot read this way, and nursing becomes a real break for you. Of course, the older children will often take nursing time to request a read-aloud, which is perfect.

When you are feeding the baby lying down, put a pillow behind your back and make sure your neck is supported. Don't twist your arm into a weird position or you will wake up with baby elbow (like tennis elbow but from babies, not tennis).

Modesty. Renaissance painters depicted the Blessed Virgin with her breast exposed, feeding her Son. I'm not prudish about nursing, but a few little measures can keep you feeling put-together. Camisoles help to keep the tummy and sides covered when you lift up your blouse or shirt; get some nursing camisoles that flip down, or cut away the bra portion of cheaper ones.

Latching. Nipples can be too flat for effective latching. Try milk cups, also known as breastfeeding cups. These are not nipple shields, but plastic cups that you place in your bra that not only force nipples out but catch the letdown on the breast that Baby is not nursing on (and if you sterilize those cups you can save the let-down milk, sometimes more than an ounce!). Try lanolin and Medela Hydrogel pads for sore nipples.

Undersupply. For more milk, eat oatmeal in any form, including cookies. Beer is excellent for increasing milk supply, and back in the day, the doctor prescribed a Guinness a day for my own mother. Fenugreek helps, but slowly. Continue your prenatal vitamins:—low milk supply can be due to low iron. Warning: Reglan taken to increase breast milk is known to have a side effect of severe panic attacks. It works to increase milk production for some mothers, but for others, especially those with a history of depression, anxiety, postpartum depression, and so on, it can cause trouble.

Oversupply. Switch to block feeding: nurse on demand but only on the one side, in three-hour blocks. Stay away from oatmeal!

Mastitis. Do not let your breasts get cold (and wet), or you'll be susceptible to mastitis. Wear cardigans or big scarves or shawls. Change your nursing pads promptly if you leak. Use pads made of natural fibers; felted wool pads (they can be made from the softest old wool sweaters), if you can stand wool next to your skin, or nice smooth cotton ones are better. You can make your own by cutting large circles about the size of a salad plate and zigzag them together at the edges on your machine. They are easy to wash with the rest of your laundry.

If you get mastitis, a cold cabbage leaf over each breast will reduce the swelling and cool the breasts down. Hot compresses on the hot, hard duct can work wonders. Marshmallow root helps a great deal with milk supply; take three to six capsules a day plus lots of water.

For any bottle-fed baby, as your child's mother, commit to doing all the feedings if possible. The nursing I speak of consists of holding, fondling, and making eye contact, most of which occurs during a feeding. This goes for the bottle too! This is how that deep bonding occurs. Feeding the baby is not simply a matter of getting Nourishment A into Baby B.

As perfect as mother's milk is for baby, mother's arms and mother's presence are more so. The premier advantage to breastfeeding is that it facilitates nursing, by the fact that the milk is in the mother's breast! Putting the milk into a bottle and then being away defeats this built-in advantage, even if it technically counts as breastfeeding.

Hold the baby in the nursing position, and of course, hold, don't prop, the bottle (even if the baby can hold the bottle, you hold it too). Skin to skin, singing lullabies, holding comfortably, making eye contact, offering loving touches. The important thing is that Baby is loved and held by Mama!

Weight gain. Breastfeeding babies are programmed to wait for mother's milk to come in. Of course, bottle-fed babies gain right away, but that doesn't mean that the breastfed baby is not doing well. Stick to your guns and insist that if the diapers are normal, you just need time.

High bilirubin count. Consult the La Leche League site to understand jaundice in babies and to know what questions to ask. Nursing babies often do have elevated bilirubin counts, but at the same time, feeding well is an important factor for flushing the blood. Often you can lower the counts on your own, without a hospital stay—and traumatic separation from your infant. The blood tests will show if you are succeeding.

Phototherapy helps break down bilirubin in the blood. Take Baby's clothes off and put him near a sunny window (he can lie on a sheepskin or another warm surface, for instance, a heating pad safely tucked under layers of blankets), if it's chilly. You can rig up fluorescent lights (like grow lights for your seedlings!) over a bed; sleep with the baby there so that as much feeding as possible can take place under the lights.

A phototherapy wrap is also available; it's a blanket with lights imbedded in it!

From the La Leche League site:

> If a doctor suggests that you stop breastfeeding and give your baby formula, ask about using phototherapy to treat the jaundice while you continue to breastfeed. In most babies, jaundice is short-lived and harmless. For sure, there may be times when it is necessary to treat the jaundice, but in these situations, parents and health professionals should remember that frequent breastfeeding in the first days of life helps ensure successful breastfeeding in the weeks and months to come. The goal is a healthy baby who continues to breastfeed.

Bilirubin levels can go down in a day when the baby is treated with frequent nursings and exposure to light, so be confident when you suggest an alternative to separation.

A mother's instincts. Every mother nurses every baby differently and in her own (and her baby's own) way. Trust your instincts; take advice that seems to help; leave aside advice that doesn't.

Practical Tips for Avoiding and Solving Thrush and Mastitis

Thrush is a painful fungal infection that can discourage breast-feeding, but you can overcome it. If you are feeling a pain like dozens of tiny needles stabbing your nipples or experiencing painful breasts (without any hard lumps indicating blocked ducts), or noticing shiny or flaking skin, take the following measures (and do your own research on your favorite breastfeeding site):

- Practice good hygiene. You should anyway, because children are sort of a breeding ground for disease, sorry to tell you. You don't need antibacterial detergents and sprays. You need old-fashioned hand washing with warm water and soap.
- Wash your hands after diapering. With warm water and soap. Babies come with yeast and it can get out of control. Diaper rashes are often caused by yeast. I had one baby whose rash was misdiagnosed by the doctor, and I kept putting cortisone cream on his poor behind, which only makes it worse. Fortunately, the nice lady at the diaper service told me to use a different cream and to air out his diaper area, since yeast thrives on dampness.

- Keep bras (cotton), nursing pads (don't use anything but cotton pads), nighties, and towels clean and dry. Wash them in hot water. Wash your hands before you nurse the baby.

- Eat less sugar and carbs. Eat more protein, yogurt, and salt. Yeast thrives on sugar.

- Often with thrush, the baby will have white spots in his mouth. If so, use the remedy the doctor prescribes on your breasts too, whether or not you think you have thrush.

- Try doing your washing with a vinegar solution, as vinegar kills yeast. Let your breasts air dry after a shower. If you can be discreet, allow some sun to get on your skin.

- Gentian violet works. Sometimes doctors go for the pharmaceutical remedy, but the old-fashioned ones work better. You will have purple nipples, and your baby will have beautiful purple lips for a while! But it does the job. You will find the protocol for using it on a good nursing site online.

- And above all, keep nursing. You don't want a plugged duct on top of everything. I found that the pain was intense for a few minutes but subsided if I just plunged in. Offer your pain to God for your child and all children and mothers! If you follow these tips and the ones you find online, it will be over soon.

If what you have is cracked and sore nipples but not a hot pain like you are sending knives, not milk, through your nipples, it could be eczema, which needs a different treatment.

Mastitis

When you get a sore spot on your breast, before it turns into mastitis, get in the shower and massage the spot with your hand and the hottest water you can stand. Then, if possible, get into bed or lie on the sofa, and nurse the baby on the sore side first. Position him so that he sucks the strongest on the side with the blockage. A cabbage leaf placed over the sore area can help a lot.

Mastitis is sure sign that you are doing too much. Rest and rest some more. And wash your hands.

ASK AUNTIE LEILA
Difficulties in Nursing a Toddler

Dear Auntie Leila,

I would love to hear thoughts on what nursing is like beyond twelve months. My daughter is almost thirteen months and still a very avid nurser. I am on board with continuing to nurse, but when does it end? That sounds ungrateful, but I have dysphoric milk-ejection reflexes (DMER: a surge of anxiety and other bad feelings for a couple of minutes with every letdown) and along with it very mixed feelings about nursing. I love the closeness but hate the anxiety and the exhaustion that feeding another person from your body brings. How does one stay mellow and accept the sacrifices of motherhood, especially the physical ones (nursing, exhaustion), in this "culture of freaking out"?

Love,

Dixie

Dear Dixie,

Some babies are really babies at thirteen months. Others are little toddlers, racing around. My first two were walking at seven to eight months! By a year, they were on the go for sure.

As to the DMER, I can't relate, but I will say this: sometimes in life there are things we know are good to do, but they hurt. If you can offer up the suffering of those few minutes, do join it to Our Lord's suffering, in order to "make up what is lacking the suffering of the cross for the salvation of souls," as St. Paul reminds us to do (see Col. 1:24).

Meanwhile, let's think about how to lessen the demands of this baby. Read the chapter "Ask Auntie Leila: Weaning and Solid Foods for the Healthy Nursing Baby," below. Work peacefully toward helping your daughter start to get more calories from table food.

Maybe think about how animals handle their ... well, irritation with their babies. They just push them away or even swat them! I'm not advocating being as mean as a cat! But I think that redirecting a demanding child's attention is valid. When my babies started crawling away while nursing, nipple still attached, because they were so darned interested in all that was going on around them, I just did away with those feedings. I am not opposed to offering a bottle instead—to a toddler who is wearing you out, not to an infant.

Think of it this way. You've given your child your all. Now she's on the go. She still needs to suck. With toddlers you need some strategies. I think giving her a bottle now that she is well into the table-foods stage is just fine if it helps her relax and feel the calm that sucking gives. Later, she can wean onto a cup, as all mine did with no trouble.

I don't agree with the pediatrician on bottles after a year. They always discourage bottles, but why? Why be so ready with them for infants (who should not have them—see above) and so stingy for toddlers? We know that sucking helps with jaw development, and yet some toddlers are just too active to nurse without wearing Mama out, as I say. It won't hurt their teeth (that bugaboo) if you don't let them take it to bed. Yes, it would be ideal for the toddler to continue nursing, but for some, it's just not in the cards. If they will go to a cup, that's fine, but if a bottle increases peace, go for it.

A Note on "Date Night"

Since all the pressure is going to be on you to go out soon, resuming "normal" life as quickly as you can, along with perhaps a bit of anxiety "not to let the baby change anything," I will give you a different view. As always, be peaceful.

It's fun to go out, and you should take your infant with you. He wants you and needs you. My personal view is that it's only going to make you cry to leave your tiny baby home. I know I would not have enjoyed it, and that's why I rarely did it. My friends who have big, happy families really never did it either, as far as I can tell; not as a scheduled necessity, anyway.

But the more important fact is that when the baby is little, you have a window for concentrating your energy on him. It doesn't last very long and has no implications at all for future demands. Everything has its time, and it's a little premature to be putting romance front and center in your lives right now. The strained quality of your time out shows that.

Your love, your relationship, will change from what it was before the baby came, and that is something our society and its experts know very little about. They don't understand that it will become much deeper and better and won't suffer from the short time when Baby is taking Mom's attention.

If you have fun going out, great. I'm not trying to impose a guilt trip. But don't be surprised if date night isn't all it's cracked up to be in the first few months of your baby's new life. And don't feel pressured to have a date night if it seems more tragic than exciting. When you're ready for date night, when that tiny baby is so big that he's jumping into Grandma's arms and waving goodbye, you'll find you don't have to yank yourself away from him to go.

Reasonable Postpartum Time

Let's start by putting far from us the thought of that friend we all have who ran a road-race the week after her baby arrived. She shouldn't have done it. Not that she *couldn't* (she obviously could), but it wasn't good for all the rest of the ladies that she *did*. Like a professional driver who observes speed limits, her aim should have been to serve the common good. And that means not running that race just then.

In order to get off right with this baby, you need to assume that you won't be running any races and that you will be wearing your maternity clothes for at least six weeks. And that each and every thing you wear will be nursing-friendly. Everything. Yes, even the pretty outfit you wear to the baptism.

As to clothing postpartum: assume your wardrobe will go in reverse order from your pregnancy. You won't have to look at those things you wore in the last four weeks, thankfully, until the next time you procreate.

Isn't it terrible how little fits at the end there? When you are seven months pregnant, you think "This will be okay; I've got this; my belly isn't crazy big." But, unless you are unusually tall, by thirty-six weeks, your belly will be outrageous and your clothes will be somewhat absurd.

But you *will* need your maternity things from just before the extreme belly days for the time *after* the baby comes. And, if you are just pregnant now, it's worth it to try to find loose clothing *that opens in front*. Because you will need loose things to nurse in.

What I want to tell you here, across from you at the kitchen table, is this:

Postpartum does not mean "the day after you have the baby." It means "one week after," "six weeks after," and also "six months after." Those are your milestones. When you are in sight of one, readjust and think of the next. Keep moving that target out.

At twenty-four years postpartum, I'm willing to let go of some of my expectations.

Well before you hit that six-week mark with baby (still postpartum, remember), you will find that you can dip into your looser things that you wore earlier in pregnancy, and then one day (not soon) you will be wearing normal clothing again.

Two points: You will almost certainly never wear your skinniest things again—not because you are fat, but because your bones have moved further apart, as we like to put it, and second, if the season has changed, this all becomes more complicated; but still, think maternity and loose, not skinny and tight, for sanity's sake.

Far better to discover that your maternity pants are falling down— yay!—than that your skinny jeans are still too skinny—boo!

In general, make it easy on yourself to postpone any reckoning of bodily changes by what you are wearing and what you choose to do, physically speaking.

So now you are coming home from the hospital in your fairly attractive, loose clothing, with easy access for nursing. You can sit up for a bit if you want, but what Auntie Leila really wants you to do is to go right to bed or at least lie down on the sofa. Later you can sit up. You will know it's time when you really want to sit up! And likewise, you will know it's time to move around when you can't stay put any longer. I am hoping that some of your lovely friends have set up a meal train for you—because of all those meal trains you set up for them.

If they haven't, struggle through as best you can and resolve to be the one who makes dinners for your postpartum friends. You will see, your turn will come. Until then, muddle through somehow, and do accept any help you are offered.

Does it make you anxious to think this way? I suggest you examine the reasons for your unease. Do you not like the thought of needing and accepting help, of resting, of letting things go? Does it help to realize that it's for a good reason—that is, getting a good start with the baby (which we will cover)?

A little note for your husband: Make sure your wife is rested. Tell her she's beautiful. Figure out what is for dinner and give it to her on a tray in bed. Very soon she'll be up and about. For now, help her let go of her anxieties.

Keep in mind that in this time your goal is to *nurse* your baby. You should *breastfeed* your baby if you can, and you almost certainly can. Maybe you really can't breastfeed. But every mother can *nurse* her baby: cuddle, hold, and in general understand that nursing the baby isn't *reducible* to a delivery system for nutrition. Rather, the milk is a vehicle, if you will, for getting to know and love your baby. It also happens to make him grow.

You can go read or reread the section on nursing for some nitty-gritty details. But the key here is this: Hold your baby and nurse (cuddle, coo too, love) him. If you are feeding with a bottle, make up your mind that you—and only you as much as is humanly possible—will feed your baby in your very own arms. All the tips above are to this end: that you are rested and able to take care of your new baby!

ASK AUNTIE LEILA

Feeling Pretty after Baby

Dear Auntie Leila,

Can you share some wisdom about body image and marital intimacy? Since having my (first) baby over two years ago (it was a complicated birth and took a long time to heal from physically, and I think perhaps longer mentally), I am constantly revisiting how I feel about my body.

I am gradually trying to let go of the weird notion that I need to look like a supermodel, without the personal makeup artist, thousands of dollars, and starvation!

I wonder how you (or others) maintained (and maintain) your idea of remaining attractive while pregnant or breastfeeding, at different stages of life, and so on. How do you hold the two "selves" together? (I guess it's telling that I think of myself as two people—the mother and the pre-mother who had her own life and felt attractive. Ideally I'm sure I should be one person!)

Ellie

Dear Ellie,

I'm going to be practical in my answer, and we will also get input from my husband, Suki, and Rosie.

Motherliness and maintaining your sense of attractiveness as you go through various stages ... ah, yes.

You see, you are not alone in feeling like the post-headlights deer after you have a baby. Not *everyone* feels this way, and I have nothing but wonder for those who do not. As a nineteen-year-old, thin and not very strong, undergoing an extremely difficult labor and delivery, my own devastation would have been complete had I not been too numb to contemplate it.

What had happened to my body was only part of the larger question of what had happened to me. Even though, six weeks later, I fit into my teensy clothes, I felt so strange. It's not so much that the physical changes affected my sense of attractiveness—they did, though I'm sure others hardly noticed anything different. It's just that I didn't feel like myself, and the change in my body was a small part of the overall upheaval. So I know what you mean.

It's true that the majority of images we see are of women who look girlish even after multiple births. It stands to reason that some will, according to the ever-handy 10-80-10 rule: that 10 percent of average women will balloon, 80 percent will be a little different but not much, and 10 percent will be thin or thinner than ever. Breastfeeding helps most women get back into shape (and most don't realize that), but a lot of it is just the luck of the draw, inheritance-wise.

The market, which uncannily detects anxiety and ambivalence, naturally caters to the way we, at the moment, wish we looked, by ever so helpfully waving under our noses images of only the 10 percent who are endowed by genetics, hard and possibly destructive work, and computer manipulation to look as if they are freshmen in high school, despite their reproductive activities.

Let's never mind all that, on the grounds that it's just not helpful to getting us to our goal, which is really enjoying the process of figuring out how integral this motherhood journey is to our womanhood.

Even when a woman isn't a physical mother—if she is a religious sister, or not given the gift of physical children in her marriage—she's called to motherhood as the fulfillment of God's plan for her.

Let's do some practical things to be happy with how we look right now, and possibly learn some deep truths about womanhood along the way. Before we get started, take a shower and wash your hair (see "More on Showering"). You will already feel better. The goal here is getting in touch with the prettiness of the new you. Let's start from the inside out.

1. *Grooming.* Trim your nails and shave your legs. Treat your feet and do what you can to smell fantastic.

Get a nice haircut. One's hair is important, and the cut and style have to be fabulous but not fussy, so that you can run around with your child without giving your hair a lot of intensive care. Use the proper products (I discuss this the chapter "More on Showering," a true treasure-trove of too much information). A woman's hair is her glory. Make it the best it can be. If it's long, don't just pull it into a tight ponytail. Try a messy bun if you like it back, or a loose French braid. If it's short, make sure it's feminine and not utilitarian. A little more volume flatters. Nothing will look right on you if your hair is not becoming, and everything will suddenly look better if it is. If we wore a head covering (and every mother of a toddler has to wonder why we don't), we would just have to choose a pretty one. But this isn't medieval Norway, and we probably don't. So style your hair.

Rosie says, "Make sure you hold the baby in front of you for photos. And a couple of pins keeping the hair in front a bit styled makes a ponytail more put together." In other words, your hair should frame your face, not pull it tight.

Use a little makeup if you want to. If you do, use it every day, first thing in the morning. I'm not telling you that you have to wear makeup. I'm saying that it's better to use none than to plaster it on only to go out, never putting in the effort "just" for your husband at home. As I tend to be a little ruddy, I use a little foundation, a dab of blush, eyeliner (my eyelashes are skimpy), and a smidgen of lip gloss. Could you manage that much? Pluck only stray hairs on your brows and do give them a little lift with the liner, being sure to make little strokes and not draw anything like a line. Brows are the accent marks of the face.

Once groomed, you can head outside in the fresh air and do some moving around, especially when you are practically, comfortably, and attractively attired as suggested below.

2. *Have the right underwear.* It needs to fit and not be an embarrassment in case of ambulance rides. Once you are over thirteen, and I am assuming you are, you need more than just a bra—you need camisoles and slips and the right kind of spandex for certain outfits. Only recently having recovered from the 1970s myself, with all that implies in the lingerie department, I have come to see the value in these items. You don't have to spend a lot (you can frequent those nice discount stores), but you should consider every penny you spend as well worth it.

In the same vein, have some cute nightwear. This is definitely a G-rated book. With the overwhelmingness of having to replace everything when your size changes, Hubby's discarded sweats are likely to have become your new PJs. I really mean just have nice things to wear to bed.

Nevertheless, cuteness is a priority, and I say that as someone who wears flannel from October to May. It's cute flannel!

3. *Analyze your favorites.* Every woman has at least a few items of clothing that she feels just work for her—so much so that it's hard to let them go when they get a little . . . antique. We need to make a mental list of what the exact characteristics of those items are so we can replace and amplify them.

For instance—does the pair of jeans you really love have a waist that hits you just so? Is that old shirt you reach for just the right amount of blousy at the hips? Do you wish you had that pleated skirt from your aunt's closet again? Did you think that a jacket nipped you in at the waist just so?

Make some rules for yourself. Here are mine (I'm average height, thick through the waist, small hips, nice legs, short neck, bad posture, and not ready to consign myself to the dustbin of fashion, but not able to wear just any old T-shirt either):

No crew necks, ever (as distinct from a flattering scoop neck that doesn't chop you at the thorax). Nothing fussy at the shoulders, but a ruffle on a v-neck is fabulous, as is anything to soften the neck area, such as a portrait collar or any little detail. But "poufy" sleeves make me feel stuffed.

No sweat pants. Nothing short at the waist, like a short cardi or a cropped shirt. A longer look is better for me. Nothing above the knee—the only exception is just-above-the-knee skirts for hot weather because I will never, ever wear shorts again, and that's fine by me, and my knees aren't dumpy yet.

Nothing with a dropped waist if it doesn't also flare out, because something A-line makes me look fine, but anything that nips in under the belly just looks horrible. But a pencil skirt is good if it is cut right.

Nothing that bulges at the waist or abdomen, such as a bow or a zipper-button combo. But I don't like low-slung jeans. Mom jeans (high waist, wide seat) are obviously out, but it helps to have something pulling you in right there if you're like me.

Notice when a garment in an ad is unfitted and cropped and the model is doing that odd leaning-forward-with-a-pout thing that models do. The truth is, she's so thin that she'd look great in a paper bag (although even she might not feel comfortable in one!). Or the picture is Photoshopped. But the *garment* is not a good one.

Start making your list and sticking to it. Get only clothes that make you feel at least confident and comfortable. When you meet someone who seems comfortable, cute, and put together, ask yourself why. Is it that she has a nice cardigan? Always wears earrings? A necklace? A nice scarf? I'm sure one thing you'll notice is that she works with her figure, not against it.

Try skirts, especially ones described as "fit and flare." A skirt with a bit of swing and going at least just below the knee can work wonders with a less-than-perfect figure.

Some of the sites that are often recommended as offering more feminine clothing still fail to please me in that their skirts are too stinking short. Also, let's have some sleeves. Sleeveless just doesn't look great on most people (don't get me started on strapless!), and it makes me angry that they are eliminating the most time-consuming aspect of dressmaking but still charging a lot for the dresses.

Invest in a good pair of jeans (try the kind with the stretch panel that includes a fake zipper placket and button—very forgiving while still stylish, because your top will go down over that area anyway). Tops that have a bit of gathering at the neckline and come down almost like tunics also help.

Becoming a mother made me realize that I had to have a practical wardrobe, and that took me years to achieve. For one thing, it was the eighties, and clothes didn't fit *on purpose*. I'm really sort of bitter that I spent my most attractive years wearing "man-tailored" type clothes and shoulder pads. I wish I had thought this all through then and supplied myself with exactly those items that I reach for but aren't there.

Rosie says, "Watch *What Not to Wear*. It helps you see that each woman can look her best right now, and emphasizes the feminine. Just get clothes that fit, and don't worry about the size." The genius of that show is that it does something paradoxical: it teaches us that changing the superficial leads to deep results. A lot of the women they work with seem as if they could use a psychiatrist, honestly. Yet after their transformation, which is completely cosmetic, they seem to be able to grapple with a lot of problems that were overwhelming them. I wholeheartedly subscribe to this approach, which goes against what we usually assume, that we can't do anything about superficial issues until we root out the deep ones. But we might as well try this way! It's cheaper than therapy, even with the shopping.

Rosie also says, "I ran into a friend who has lots of kids. I'm sure she felt a little ungainly, because she had just had a baby, but she exuded joy and kindness and looked radiant. She was truly, physically, beautiful. That's how I want to be."

Suki remembers how, even before she was married but had a job teaching young children, she hit upon a formula that still works for her: "I'd rather know that I look nice and put together than have a lot of outfits. I don't want to be uncomfortable or spend time thinking about what to wear. I have to know I can do anything in my work clothes. I can sit on the floor, pull down a map, and so forth. Nothing low-cut for me. I don't like high-waisted things, as they make me feel short. If I feel unattractive, I find it's best to concentrate on looking put together."

4. *Colors.* Back in the day there was a book called *Color Me Beautiful*. (Once again Auntie Leila reaches into the mists of time for a how-to book that really worked, although you will laugh at the styles because they are truly pricelessly bad—but maybe all styles in our ungainly age will seem so?)

The main idea is to ascertain where you fall in a grid that has two variations on two main ideas: warm skin tones, cool or muted tones, or clear tones. I think that now they've changed it to be about hair and eye color, but the author, Carol Jackson, specifically said that hair and eye color aren't the main factor for all but a few people; it's *skin tone* (specifically undertone, warm or cool) that determines the hues and shades of colors that flatter you.

You discover your undertone by looking at yourself, by having others look at you and give their opinion, and by thinking about what you love to wear already—what makes you feel like *you*. Every woman can wear just about every color, but the question is whether the warm or cool version of the color flatters you. Another question is whether the muted or clear version is more attractive *on you*. For instance, we can all wear green, but should it be a green that is clear and cool (with lots of blue in it) or a heathered one with a good dash of yellow? The answer lies in your skin tones, whether they have an underlying cool or warm, yellow or blue cast. Training your eye to detect the "temperature" (warm or cool) of a color by means of studying a simple color wheel pays dividends in your wardrobe.

Trust me, this method works so well to help you zero in on what makes you feel wonderful and attractive. It also helps you decide when to spend money on something important when you're on a budget and sick of making mistakes. If it's not in your colors, skip it. Don't quite believe me? Think back on shopping mistakes. You will find that you, a "winter," just never wore that camel coat even though it was so elegant; or you, a "summer," never wanted to put on that red blouse, not even once. There's a reason, and it has to do with those things not being the right color *for you*.

5. *Retrain yourself to see things in their proper light.* Analyze photos for their reality content—both as to whether a style could work for you and if it's being presented realistically.

The fact that styles favor the emaciated and immature doesn't help. After all, it can only be a truly warped and perverted fashion mind that offers only horizontal stripes, short skirts, and stretchy fabrics that hug the body. Seeing is so related to reality. We pervert our ability to see when we constantly subject ourselves to unreal images as if they are real! We have to make a conscious effort not to look at those images and compare ourselves.

At least you are young! Try searching for mother-of-the-bride attire and have a good laugh at what image is being projected there. Apparently mothers of the bride are meant, in popular imagination, to be a cross between a Barbie beauty queen and a particularly immodest mermaid. But enough about my problems.

Detach from images that force you into false comparisons. When you look at other (real) women, find the beautiful in them, no matter how "imperfect" they look. I guarantee that when you cultivate this habit of being less critical of others, you will be more accepting of your own body.

I just want to remind you of what dear St. Augustine says: "Do thou serve Him who made thee, so that that which was made for thee [your body, for instance] may serve thee."[18] Putting the body in the proper perspective helps us reconcile the changes we undergo.

To step away from the exceedingly practical for one moment and address your question, involving as it does the sense of division in your person and the uncertainty about the ends for which you were made: it turns on this need that the Incarnation remedies. Our dear Lord came to resolve the need to reunite Earth and Heaven. God gave us our bodies with a nuptial meaning—which just means that a woman, loved by her husband, becomes a mother, and that makes her more beautiful in every way.

We always struggle with this problem, with feeling out of sorts and somehow not quite prepared for whatever stage we are in. Perhaps it seems unfair to have to readjust life as a wife just as you are adjusting to life as a mother! Yet this struggle will bring you to a new maturity and something even better.

Here is what my husband says: "The husband wants his wife. He knows who you are. Yes, you want to look good for him, but he understands you and what makes you the way you are and the way you look—it's you he

---

[18] St. Augustine, Exposition on Psalm 143, quoted in Pius XI, encyclical *Casti Connubii* (December 31, 1930), no 98.

wants. You should realize that with each passing year (and each new baby), you become more distinctively you: the flesh-and-blood woman he loves. The good part of him wants only the real you, not some Hollywood (or worse) false image. He has to feed that good part and deny any bad part that would take him away from reality, and you have to help him by being open and honest as well as trusting. You have to help him a lot, because he's always battling with those false images."

Your husband is meant to help you through this time of change, with his loving protection. And he is proud of you for what you've done, loving you exactly how you look, especially after the baby comes and while you are nursing.

You know, a lot of husbands go through trauma of their own when the baby comes and don't dare say a word about it because clearly, what their wife has experienced trumps everything. But this event merits a conversation or two. The husband has to be encouraged to affirm his wife's value and to overcome the fear he has that he will be able to take care of what has been entrusted to him.

Wives, don't underestimate that fear. *Your* fear is assuaged by the undeniable, immediate gift of the baby. But his fear is only fed by everything he encounters, since the manly virtue of providing for his family is not worth much to those he deals with, most likely, and doesn't bear fruit for a long time.

You can make him want to be brave by your appreciation and admiration of his provision, and he will be emboldened to express how much he loves you in your new, more womanly mode—because what he really wants out of this life is a loving home, a devoted wife, children who will honor him, and the hope that he will not die alone. Try being cheerful and not complaining! All this, and more, he will get, if he, too, keeps his eyes on what is real.

For us, the lust of the eyes is really this longing to look like someone else, and we have to resist it. For him, the lust of the eyes really is lust in its specific sense, and the only remedy is to love someone truly beautiful.

Husband and wife are like Adam and Eve in the garden (they really are, as marriage leaps right over the divide of the Fall and takes us back to the original plan God had in mind). Those two didn't need any pictures. They were writing their own marriage manual when it came to intimacy, and each married couple does the same, all over again. Each husband and wife are the new Adam and Eve.

There is no comparing *in love.*

ASK AUNTIE LEILA

Postpartum and the Perfectionist Mom

Dear Auntie Leila,

What tips do you have for the new mother, when it comes to keeping house and getting sufficient rest and still making sure to enjoy the cuddly baby, particularly when there are other children? My baby breastfeeds, and I want to be sure I can really care for her well while also keeping our three-year-old happy. I am usually very good at staying on top of meals, laundry, and housekeeping, but I know we have to figure out a new normal, at least for a few months. My amazing husband helps with cooking and cleaning, but he has to go back to work soon. I really don't know anyone in a similar situation; my friends' older children are in daycare or preschool.

Thank you!

Polly

Dear Polly,

A big congratulations to you on your new baby! You seem (unlike me!) to have a pretty high standard for your housekeeping and things in general. People like me have to be constantly exhorted to do a little more, to keep going a little bit further and not to be okay with disorder.

Then I worry that those who are a little more perfectionist are getting from me that I think they should do more, but actually perfectionists have to ease up on themselves a little. That is the trouble with giving and getting advice. So much depends on context!

New baby time is a time for letting go of perfection. Know what your duties really are. For you, your duty is to feed your baby and get her settled. To do that, you *must* be rested!

During this time, limit your duties to your family (when your help leaves and you're on your own) to making sure they have food and clean clothes. If you can get in a tiny bit of tidying, say, one room every couple of days—not deep cleaning, just putting a few things away, dealing with papers, and maybe getting a room ready for a vacuuming, but not vacuuming it yourself—that is enough.

In a short enough time, you will be going out of your mind and ready to get back to a more normal routine.

In the book *Lark Rise to Candleford* (not the movie, which has more characterization), we find a sort of fictionalized anthropology of a community's doings. It's a great book to read while nursing, truly a "collective memory" book that tells of the work these people did, with few resources and in relative poverty.

The women helped each other give birth, and they insisted that the new mother stay in bed for ten days. Of course, each mother, having taken her turn, was aware that the other women were shouldering her work as well as their own. The author tells about how the new mother would be docile for a while, maybe two to four days, because she knew her baby's survival depended on it. But before the ten days were up, as long as she was healthy, she was eager to resume her work.

Note, by the way, how kind this approach is to the weak or the sick, making a *long* rest the norm for the healthy; in our society, we have to impose that on ourselves. Our norm is to assume the ideal, leaving a woman to count herself a failure for not meeting it.

By the way, when you are back on your feet, try to bring a meal to every new mom you know, or do her laundry or dishes, and carpool. Then, with the next baby, you'll get some help. Not that Auntie Leila is mercenary that way. But we have to help each other, sometimes by showing how it could be done. Also, ask God to send you friends who don't send their children to daycare.

You are now one week into your life with baby. You must give yourself one whole week more. Your husband won't mind vacuuming one room when he gets home. He won't mind serving the food, simple meals that can be made with a minimum of fuss. He won't mind processing the laundry or stepping over laundry baskets.

In the third week, you can start adding a little more. By then, you can dust and vacuum one room a day, but that's all! Keep in mind that you can do a lot in an hour, so don't stress or feel that if you aren't cleaning all day, you are being lazy. Also keep in mind that, while it's normally easier on everyone to maintain a cleaner house, a dirty one can be brought back to its clean state quickly. All in good time.

From three to six weeks, remind yourself that you are still postpartum and give yourself permission to have a down day after a busy one, a day that you do nothing but lie on the sofa with the baby and read books to the toddler. This rest is vital for your body as it rises to the demand of producing more milk for the growing baby.

Think of ways your little boy can burn off excess energy. In cold weather, you can let bath time stretch to an hour: give him a can of shaving cream and let him enjoy it! If a friend wants to help you, let her take him somewhere where he can just run.

Even if you are normally restrictive about videos, the postpartum time is when you can indulge in a few for the toddler so that you can rest—just make sure they are simple ones that don't involve much drama, lest you create more problems than you solve.

Maybe you could make playdough one day (better, allow that person who's asking what she can do for you to bring you some), and let your child really have a ball with it, if he likes things like that. But that should be the one thing you do all day! My husband always told me (after some big crashes when I did too much): do only *one* thing each day.

Ask Daddy to forgo the vacuuming one evening in favor of a walk around the neighborhood with your son; he could take him to the store for diapers and a run in the aisles — or whatever it takes to get his energy out before bed.

Pray about how God asks perfectionist mothers to let go of their expectations for themselves. You have the satisfaction of knowing that no matter how bad it seems at your house, it's nowhere near as bad as it has been at my house!

You are doing so well!

Lots of love,

Leila

Dear Auntie Leila,

I cannot say how many times since you sent me that e-mail I have thought that I should reply to you to let you know we survived. And we thrived!

Really, it was the best thing to receive, and I cannot say how many times I read it with gratitude. The best part of all was your reassurance that it will never be as bad here as it was at your house. It made me laugh, and it made me remember that with little ones, we are all in it together. So true!

I did totally forgo vacuuming for six weeks. I swept the wood floors (we didn't have any rugs at the time). When my dad came to visit, *he* vacuumed for me — it needed it by then! And by that point, I felt well enough to start to clean a bit here and there. Soups and crockpots were my friend. And I started baking a lot again by the time the baby got a bit older.

One of your readers commented about how one's imperfect home can be a grace to a friend, freeing her from the need to have a perfect home! I have actually had a conversion of sorts since I sent you my plea for advice and wisdom. Suddenly I am doing crazy things like inviting new friends over even in the midst of a pretty major home renovation, hosting Complete Stranger Overnight Guests for a night (friends' parents who needed a place to stay … dear people!), cooking supper for a huge group, and not fretting about whether the windows are all clean (which is truly what I used to freak out about before people came over, that and many other things). And the world is still spinning on its axis; our lives our greatly enriched.

I've also taken your advice on offering meals to new mothers. I had so little support after my second child was born that it is still hard to look back at my sense of sad surprise when no one from church, two women's groups, or community offered meals. (That was not the case with our first child. They came out of the wood-work to help; not so much from church, but other community members—but somehow I think by the second child, the novelty had worn off and people sort of thought I could do it. And I did! But a casserole would have been received with great gratitude!) I think we as a culture are losing this collective sense of what we can do for new mothers.

I love all the wisdom in your post, Leila; it was a balm to me and really helped me through those early days when it all seemed so overwhelming. And I will save this and the useful comments because, Lord willing, we may be in new-baby mode again come wintertime!

We are also now part of a homeschool group, so now I have some buddies who have had several children; and their older children are at home, so we can commiserate. That's a blessing, too. Anyhow, thank you for the encouragement. It was then and it is now so reassuring. You are the best, dear Leila.

32

ASK AUNTIE LEILA

Preparing for a Second Baby

Dearest Auntie Leila,

In about six weeks, our second baby will arrive. I'm over-the-moon excited to hold him or her and in awed disbelief that I get to be someone else's mother, too.

So, yes, I'm thrilled! And I'm not really all that nervous or stressed out. I've learned a great deal about trusting in God since becoming a mother! But, while I think I've tried to, for lack of a better word, mentally "prepare" myself for what the transition from one to two might be like, I'm betting I don't know the half of it!

People have no problem telling you that you'd better make freezer meals ahead of time, but I'm guessing you have more eternal secrets, such as helping a young girl to *think* about things so she may keep a happy heart, even through all the possibly rough adjustments and sleep deprivation to come.

I stay home full-time, and I have about three weeks of help lined up for when the baby comes, so that I may nurse and snuggle and not get up to do too much too soon. We also have friends and neighbors who will bring meals for two to three weeks. Oh, and I have a huge old-fashioned playpen, and I'm not afraid to use it; Big Sister is quite accustomed to spending time there when Mama needs to mop or what have you.

Sincerely,

Mandy

Dear Mandy,

Congratulations!

You have the most important piece, the help, lined up. Take advantage of it! With a little toddler, it's just as important for you to stay in your nightgown and rest, lying down, as much as possible as it was when you had your first, but after a day or so, try doing so for a few hours at least on the sofa, so that you aren't in the position of being in your room, a ready target for your older child to burst in and jump up on you and what suddenly seems like (and, to be fair, is) a very fragile infant in comparison.

If you can manage to rest where things are going on, even for a little while, Big Sister can do her normal motoring around but have you there to check in with. Then you can retire to your bedroom for a long nap while someone takes her on a walk or otherwise occupies her. Even an hour a day spent on the sofa in that first week will be helpful to get your daughter used to the baby's being part of her life.

Still, let her clamber on the bed with you and don't worry: even an "accidental" kick or shove to the baby won't be too fatal! (Hopefully someone will have taken her shoes off first!) She isn't being naughty, and soon she will learn to be gentle. It's better to say, "Let's be gentle" and to show and demonstrate gentle strokes and pats than to get angry and say, "Don't be rough"; a child that age really doesn't get it. Demonstrate what you want to see from her. Give her a dolly to practice on!

I will tell you one thing: when the baby is born, your little girl will seem positively enormous to you—sort of horrifyingly so! Your husband too. You will wonder how you ever coped with those giants before! So be ready for that and just laugh. Soon enough you will regain your equilibrium!

When you are first alone with the two babies, you may feel overwhelmed. And there will be those panicky moments. My husband used to remind me to try to do only one thing each day. It was helpful, coming from him, and given that he was willing to come home and do the three or ten things I couldn't get to.

Chores will have to wait. It's true that once I brought a meal to a new mother whose laundry was neatly folded in a basket (granted, the basket was on the kitchen table) and whose house was astoundingly neat and tidy. I repressed the urge to ask *her* to bring *me* a meal, because I can assure you that things were not that orderly at my house! Some people are naturally tidier than others! But for most of us, the chores will have to be done one at a time for a while, if that. Remember that if you have managed meals and laundry (even if that means you've gotten someone else to do them), you are doing what you can.

Grocery shopping will be the hardest of the outings to get used to, I think. Try to put it off as long as you can, and I realize that might not be long enough. I definitely went first with the newborn, leaving the toddler at home; the early evening can work. Once you figure out once again how to wear the baby or maneuver with the car seat, you can add the other piece of the equation, the wiggly toddler. Teach her to touch the side of the car or the cart while she is waiting for you, once you are convinced she won't just run away. Get the baby settled and then get your toddler out, talking her through the process so that it gets imprinted on her mind.

What seems impossible now will be very possible sooner than you dreamed. Just take your time. Find the parking space near the shopping cart that someone left out in the parking lot. Put baby in the carrier, then get the toddler in the cart; or put the car seat in the cart and then get the toddler out. Resist thinking about anyone watching you. (Am I the only one who continually visualizes hordes and droves of judging onlookers?)

Once in the store, I used to go first to grab a bag of pretzel rods, deploying one straight away. I find a pretzel rod will last a toddler for most of a grocery trip, won't spoil an appetite, and doesn't disintegrate into a paste the way a treacherous graham cracker does.

Keep the outings to one, and plan your escape route. Do little practice runs that you can ditch. Soon you will get the hang of it! There's nothing like *doing*, you know? You really do have to try it without too much of a mental picture. It's like knitting something or kneading dough: there's only so much you can visualize beforehand.

One other thing: remember that your toddler can be best motivated to behave by being a helper and a worker. Give her something to carry for you. Ask her to throw away a diaper. Have her fetch the wipes. Everyone likes to be thought of as contributing and capable, and she will be just that!

All will be well. Even the tiredness and the tears—every one of us has gone through that, so don't let it get you too upset. All the best to you!

God bless and a big hug,

Leila

33

ASK AUNTIE LEILA

How Do I Tell People We're Having Another Baby?

Dear Auntie Leila,

We are expecting our fourth child. I'm not sure I can conceal it anymore, at least not with any measure of comfort. We will be attending a wedding. Somehow the fourth child seems to be the dividing line between a "normal" family size and an "absurdly large" family size in the minds of many Americans. We are not Catholic, so we can't rely on religion to explain it for us either. Suggestions? Words of encouragement? We know this is what we want and that our friends and family will get used to it eventually, but I'm not looking forward to breaking the news. Was this ever an issue for you?

Thanks,

Maria

People, do you not realize it's the saving of civilization we're working on here?

Maria, if you are looking for words of encouragement, you've come to the right place! No one will encourage you more than Auntie Leila! Unless it's your other children—yes, come to think of it, they will be your biggest cheerleaders. Their joy will astonish you. Nothing can prepare you for the ecstatic love that the children will have for this unseen baby.

Gradually you widen your circle of trust. There is a reason why in the past, women waited a little longer to tell; not that they were ashamed; but they were discreet and knew the value of intimacy, safeguarding the vulnerability of this tender stage.

The likelihood is that all is well, and in due time, you will want to tell others. And then, yes, the frowning relatives must know. This task is so much easier to do if you have your happy brood and proud hubby at your back. You put on your bold face, and you announce, or better, he announces, *with* champagne and *no* hint of concession (such as, "this is the end for us" or "one last child" or any other such foolishness, because you're not God and neither are they), that you are expecting!

What can they do but say, "Congratulations!"

Oh, well do I know that they can do plenty more than that. Even others who share our faith can loose cutting remarks; the temptation is to lash out with bitterness or retreat in pain. No doubt part of what prompts unkindness is a genuine, if misplaced, concern for your well-being. Having subscribed, however unconsciously, to the world's view of autonomy, their own growing sense of powerlessness in old age, and detachment in their own families, they feel helpless to do anything for you. They may even have had negative experiences themselves. So concern manifests itself as querulousness.

Never mind all that. Get your priorities straight. Astounding to have to say, stunning as this news is, a man and a woman commit themselves to each other in marriage for the purpose of mutual encouragement and the raising of a family! Nothing is more fitting, reasonable, and natural than the arrival of children. Anyone who offers anything other than congratulations is the one with the problem, not you.

What *is* our problem? The saints called it *human respect*: the putting of others' opinions, which can be formed by all sorts of conditions, including matters we know nothing about (and if we did, we'd probably pity them from the bottoms of our hearts), before what we know is right.

The world has made a trade-off between persons and things, coming down firmly in the camp of the latter, which includes intangibles such as *health, security,* and *wealth*. I'm all for those things and would like plenty more of them. But ... priorities.

You're not in perfect health and you got pregnant? Your body was made to have a baby, and you would be amazed at what women overcome. You don't have a lot of money? Children don't care; they love you.

Proper ordering of goods may very well inspire you (I hope it does) to lessen the amount of running around you do: to stay home and schedule a rest period every day instead of racing the other children to many activities. Yes, even asking the other children to sacrifice good things is acceptable in God's eyes, if not the eyes of college admissions boosters. It's worth a lot of sacrifice to have another child. A child is the greatest gift God can give a family. Will we wish we had done things differently? Of course! We're all full of regrets. Let's just make sure we don't have to regret being ashamed of our children!

I know you're not ashamed, Maria—you just need encouragement, because your life is changing from one of mild engagement to extreme commitment. You're on a mission, only you didn't know you had left base camp.

You ask if I've had this experience. Oh yes. Where I live, the dividing line between "careless" and "committed whacko" falls between four and five children (vestiges of the old times when the people looking askance are themselves from large families, so they've at least heard of that kind of behavior, though they'd never engage in it themselves).

We happened to be perched at that time in a place where people were very outspoken due to their ethnicity (most towns in the Boston area, if they are not Yankee, are Irish, where the disapproval is just as strong but the utterance will be limited to a "God bless you!"—meaning He clearly has work to do with a nut like you). These neighbors told me, when I was expecting Deirdre, our number five, in no uncertain terms, that I was crazy and there was no way I would survive. Being almost completely alone and new in town, I started almost to believe them. I was panicky when she arrived. But you know, I was also by that time an experienced mom with a gaggle of lively and helpful children, all of whom were over the moon with this new baby, and a husband who thought that everything was just dandy, including how I handled things.

I don't know what you picture yourself taking a stand for. I know that many of us can imagine that when Jesus said, "Blessed are you when men revile you," He had in mind a great gesture of faith where we defend His Resurrection or something. Little do we suspect that *truth itself* needs a defense, and little do we suspect that the truth we will be asked to stand for may seem self-evident, basic, even, to our mind, trivial.

If the world is so lost that it doesn't realize that the natural function of human bodies, given at the very dawn of creation, sanctified by the unbreakable commitment of two hearts, is a truth, then *that is the truth we must be reviled for.*

What if we won't even really be reviled, but only be made to endure some unpleasant conversations? Well, that's what we have to offer, and may it do some folks some good.

This brave stand will obtain for us not martyrdom but a big happy Thanksgiving table with lots of loving faces and grandchildren and someone to call us every day. The other misguided ones will be alone in a nursing home unless *our children* take pity on them and visit them. Not to mention be their doctors and pay taxes so that they have roads to drive on. So we will endure them patiently.

Remember the four cardinal virtues? *Fortitude* is just this, the strength to stand up to suffering. If our battle is in the land of impertinent, even rude, comments about the size of our families, then we had better fight it there bravely. *Prudence* is knowing the right order of things: that babies come before whatever these people think we should put first. *Temperance* is self-control: not allowing ourselves to be overwhelmed by the desire to hide, not seeking comfort, and responding with restraint and charity. *Justice* is giving others their due: God first! His due is that His truths be acknowledged in the order He gives them.

Finally, I just have to react to the comment: "I can't rely on being Catholic to explain it." Or, "We're not Catholic, but we're expecting more kids."

Of course we can all see that even Catholics aren't having lots of kids, sadly, so why this thought?

Well, it's because the Church teaches and has always taught this: that children are a very great gift from God. I, a Catholic, have children for the same reason you do: because I love my husband and am united to him in a holy project (same as you)—namely, building a family. The Catholic Church gives me all I need to be "ready always to satisfy every one that asketh you a reason of that hope which is in you" (1 Pet. 3:15, DR), by having really stood fast on this truth; and besides, by being the channel for the grace to carry it out, to the best of my ability. "Be not conformed to this world: but be ye transformed by the renewing of your mind, that ye may prove what is that good, and acceptable, and perfect, will of God" (Rom. 12:2, KJV).

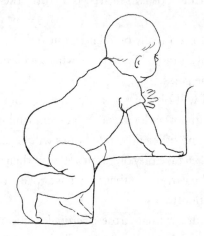

ASK AUNTIE LEILA

Weaning and Solid Foods for the Healthy Nursing Baby

Dear Auntie Leila,

How does one transition from the little-baby stage—nursing often at night—to the next stage, introducing solids? Can one go too far on the breastfeeding side, to the neglect of this transition?

Love,

Emily

D ear Emily,

The transitions of life (such as a baby going from nursing to sitting up and eating solid food) are more easily navigated when we rise to the challenge of keeping things orderly.

Ah, order. What makes it hard to be Auntie Leila (who has only one qualification: having gotten seven persons beyond this stage) is knowing where you, dear reader, are on the order-disorder scale.

I happen to be equally ordered *and* disordered, I think. The result is that my house is *sort of* clean and neat, my day *sort of* has a schedule, and I am *often* up for chucking it all to do something unplanned.

But some people are very disorderly. And some disorderly people nurse the baby (talking about an older, sitting-up baby) *whenever*, without any clear idea of the baby's rhythms and expectations, and get frustrated with how much *more* disordered having a baby makes them than they already were. So they get impatient and stop nursing altogether.

Some people are overly orderly. It drives them crazy that babies need to nurse whenever, and they are so motivated by their vision of a perfect house and life that they can't abide any uncertainty, so they stop nursing altogether.

As you read this, you have to know where you fall on that scale, take what helps, and ignore what doesn't. The books by the experts are helpful to a point, because they do provide a lot of information about a baby's needs, but not so much about the whole project of running a household along that fine line between rigid, cold perfection (fortunately an unattainable goal) and chaos (all too attainable, alas).

I do like the older baby books, by the way. There have been babies for a long time, so the newer books aren't necessarily better than the older ones. New baby books always assume that you are racing out the door to work, without acknowledging that they have thus abandoned their stated premise, which is to tell you what is best for *Baby*.

Anyway, we're going to try to get a little different perspective here, because well do I know that if you are there with a little baby (not to mention a few toddlers strewn around and, just to addle your brain thoroughly, a pre-adolescent or two), you aren't just meeting this little one's calorie requirements; you are integrating him into family life and helping him grow up. You are starting the project of being surrounded by wonderfully interactive friends (your children), who enjoy eating with you and who love the family table for all the entertainment and wisdom it provides them with.

Can one "go too far" in nursing the baby? It can hardly be done. Oh yes, there are some fat sedentary nursing babies, even though nursing advocates will tell you it's not possible. Temperament will out, even in the very young.

However, I'm not talking about that small percent of babies who need to be convinced somehow that there is more to life than nursing. Nor am I talking about that small percent who are allergic or underweight or have medical or psychological issues that require you to consult with a real expert and, above all, to use your God-given smarts to do what is required, which may involve exclusively nursing quite a bit longer.

I'm just talking about your run-of-the-mill fabulous, pudgy, sweet baby who has started crawling, sitting up, looking around, and chattering. You have figured out that he will nurse at more or less predictable intervals of *an average* of two hours. You have noticed that because he goes three hours without nursing during his nap, the feedings are more like every hour and a half in the morning. It's a rhythm, and you've got it down.

At three or four months, the doctor may have suggested solid foods. I hope you just ignored him! The reason he has said that is that he suspects you will try anyway, he figures you are working, and he wants to get his two cents in. After all, very few women continue nursing after three months, sadly. But you don't need his permission to keep breastfeeding the baby.

There is a very simple test: Is the baby contented, happy, thriving, developing, growing on a satisfactory curve *for him*? (In other words, you compare the baby's growth to his very own personal curve, not to the curve of that elusive creature, the Average Baby.)

Now, some babies start getting teeth at three months! And some don't sit up until they are quite old. Babies develop very differently, and that is something you have to internalize. When the day comes that your baby has some teeth, sits up very well, and shows signs of being very interested in what you are eating, that is when you can start giving him food.

Some call this weaning, but he is still going to nurse, hopefully for a long time. However, approaching this transition the way I'm going to tell you will help you when the day comes and it's time to stop nursing.

He needs to nurse when he's a big baby. It's just that he has other needs too. For instance, a baby who is getting teeth develops a need to bite on things. And a baby who sits up gets very frustrated when everyone is at the table having a wonderful time and he can't do that too! At least, that's how it was with my children. That baby just wanted to be part of the action.

Also, for me, it was very tiring and disruptive to hold a large, squirmy, grabby baby at mealtime. No matter how committed I am to nursing the baby, I have to take others' needs into account too. I have to be able to eat. My husband has to be able to eat. The older children can't be annoyed by a baby crawling across the table. It isn't fair, and it creates this atmosphere of craziness that doesn't help teach them to be calm at dinner, does it?

It's not fair to anyone simply to resign yourself to many months with that one baby—or years if you count up all the months with all the babies (maybe a decade!) of unpleasant disorder at the table. It isn't just about the baby. It's about the whole tone of your day changing, more or less permanently, because of the "temporary" behavior of the baby. You can see how this really is about order.

I remember once, long ago, visiting a friend who had a one-year-old who literally crawled on the table, messed in the butter, cried to get down, cried to get up, and generally created chaos. Finally I realized what was missing: a high chair! A high chair is a wonderful piece of furniture.

Now I'm going to tell you a secret that is going to panic you at first, but when you wrap your mind around it, you will discover how liberating it is. Ready? It's this: you may have to do more than one thing in advance to make mealtime peaceful!

Are you surprised every day that the baby wants to nurse just as you sit down to eat? Or that when you are making supper, the baby wants to nurse? Or that you can't seem to get supper ready because you are often nursing the baby?

What about this: What if you got supper ready in the morning (or ready to be ready), rested during naptime (I really have to insist on that), and then made time to nurse the baby an hour before you were ready to serve supper, or within the hour? Then, when you are ready to eat, put the baby in the high chair. If he shows signs of wanting a bite of your food, give him some on his tray. If he shows signs of wanting a bowl and spoon of his own, give him some applesauce or mashed potatoes in a bowl with a spoon, and let him go for it. The main thing is that Baby is sitting up with the family, talking, and laughing along with everyone else—and staying put in his own spot, even if for a short time.

It's not so much the food as the sociability. Before you know it, the food takes care of itself. Little by little, he tells you he wants more. Without even thinking about it, you make the change from nursing to eating at mealtimes, over a period of months.

At first, the time in the chair is short. He gets tired and fussy. If you aren't really caring about the amount of food, but rather just enjoying the interaction, you will be fine with quickly cleaning him off with a warm washcloth you have handy and getting him out.

Now, having had his big-boy time at the table, during which, note, you have not stressed about what he has eaten because he nursed before and is just fine, he will be done with the boring old table and want to get back on the floor with his toys. Maybe he will sit nicely in your nap or nurse again, having been worn out by the effort of acting big. Maybe your three-year-old would be willing to make a tower of blocks for him to knock down while you finish up (because three-year-olds aren't good for more than fifteen minutes at the table either).

Once you notice that he does, indeed, eat a good amount during a high-chair session—and that might not be until he's more than a year old—then you have to plan ahead for him to have food that's appropriate for him so he doesn't go hungry. I say this because the idea that he will eat whatever you are eating doesn't always work out, and you have to have a backup.

Don't believe me? I have two words for you: steak salad. Steak salad is not going to be something a small child with only a few front teeth can eat!

So have some baby-friendly food at hand. Make this part of your meal planning, *to be sure you have something the baby can eat.* It doesn't have to be mush. It shouldn't be mush (unless you are having mush yourself). But it can't be steak salad. You may even spoon-feed him on occasion, once this meal is part of his caloric intake (as opposed to just a fun interlude between nursing times). I realize that makes me old-fashioned, but there it is, and I came by it honestly, because I started out with a very "liberated parenting" view of baby food and came to see that sometimes you have to spoon-feed.

Some young children just can't concentrate because they have gotten so hungry. You can give them something to hold on to while you get them going with a serving of yams mashed with butter or some chicken potpie.

Or maybe this whole operation goes better at breakfast than at dinner. You could spoon-feed your child some yogurt while he eats scrambled eggs with his fingers.

Or maybe at times it works to get him in the high chair *while* you are making dinner, so that he can chomp on things and chatter to you. Then you clean him up, and he'll be content to play nearby while you eat with the rest of the family.

Don't stress about it or think that a certain amount has to be eaten or all will be lost. Know your own child, and trust his body to know him too. Start with one meal at a time, and don't give up on nursing *before* the "meal" until he's ready; rather, do the grown-up foods along with nursing, and put the emphasis on enjoying his presence at the table or with you in the kitchen and not on the quantity he eats.

If you see this next step more as a sociability issue than an eating issue, you will have a smoother time with this transition to eating solid foods.

Feeding Baby Cereal,
Natural Child Spacing

If we were sitting at my kitchen table and peaceably knitting together and talking about whether to give the baby solid foods, there is something else I would tell you, something that I didn't find out myself for a few anxious years, but it made my life so much calmer and gave me such wonder for the beauty of God's plan for our lives, despite old Adam and Eve's best efforts to mess things up, that I am very sorry for those who don't know about it.

Doctors don't know about it, or they scoff at it because they were taught to scoff.

Other mothers don't know about it, because they listen to doctors at funny times, and because our collective memory received a body blow when suddenly bottles and pills and devices became unavoidable, and a general feeling took hold that babies are *not* a gift from Heaven but something to be planned, avoided, and feared.

But little by little, this knowledge is coming back to us, and I would like to offer it to you.

You see, besides the fact that the timing of the baby's development is your cue to start giving him little things to eat in his very own chair, and besides the fact that breast milk really is the very best food for a little one who is just starting to move around, and besides the suspicion that maybe cereal isn't so great if your child turns out to have sensitivity to certain foods—besides all that, there is something else.

Remember when I told you before that nursing an infant requires you to discover his rhythm and to make certain conscious efforts to meet his needs, even though it will be a little trying at times? A baby seems to settle in and then, suddenly, because of a growth spurt, he will dismay you with what seems like a setback. He's nursing so much more often because, at about three to four months, he is growing like crazy. Not only is his body getting bigger and stronger, but he's learning all sorts of skills that take an amazing amount of energy, all of which he's getting from you.

So of course, just as you think to yourself, "Whew! Now I can get back to running around, making cookies for the meetings, shopping, losing some weight, vacuuming, and all sorts of fun stuff," you find yourself sitting down yet again to nurse the baby!

Well, as I always say, embrace the "setback" and do what's necessary in the way of drinking more fluids, resting more, eating well, and yes, maybe vacuuming a bit less, in order to make enough milk.

You see, not only is the baby's body changing, but your body is changing at this moment as well. Before modern medicine, many babies died at this age, sad to say. And in order for our species to survive, the woman's body is made to ask the question, "Well, is there a baby or not?"

If you give in to the doctor's directives on solid foods, you will essentially be telling your body, "There isn't a baby." The doctor, who really just wants to be sure the baby gets fed one way or another, certainly doesn't feel justified in telling you, "My dear sweet lady, make a few sacrifices in the short term to reap all sorts of benefits later." But if he did, you would find, if you were patient with yourself and with the baby, you (via your hormones) will be telling your body, "There is still a baby."

You can read about this in depth in a book I recommend: *Breastfeeding and Natural Child Spacing* by Sheila Kippley. The idea is that your body will go on to provide you with a period of no ovulation—natural child-spacing. In God's providence, the body is designed to keep another pregnancy at bay for just the right amount of time, as long as you convince it that you are, indeed, still taking care of a little baby.

When the baby, at six months or nine months or one year, is sitting up, asking for a bite of beef stew or baked apple, and nursing less overall, then your body will start preparing for another child. Eighteen months or two years or thirty months is a fine interval between siblings until you get old and tired, and then, amazingly, things slow down on their own.

Now, look. As with everything else, biological things work for most people, let's say 80 percent (I don't know the figure and *neither do you*, because hardly anyone has more than two children and even then, with all sorts of interference). So, of course, there are those at one end of the spectrum who are going to conceive right away if they do nothing else (and, what no one tells you, even if they use contraception, very often), and those at the other who have difficulty conceiving, no matter what they do (and you may not realize that there are more of these than you think). But the chances are that you are one of those for whom this will be just fine, and you should give God's plan a chance. You will have faith and trust if you can overcome your fear of a child, and you can do that if you realize that a child is a gift from Heaven, welcome no matter what.

Also, the time is short, when all this is going on. It's worth putting in a few months of dedicated nursing (besides all the other benefits, of course) to pull this off. Just give yourself and the baby a couple more months of sweet, snuggly (sometimes annoyingly demanding, I know) nursing time. You will be so peaceful in the end.

Everyone has her story, but in general what I've said is scientific fact and has worked for all the generations of women up until the twentieth century and was *known by them* to work. Nothing in this life works perfectly, but even so, God has a plan for each of us.

Taking Commonsense Care
of Your Sick Child at Home

Women naturally wish to nurture. The occupation of nursing arises from the woman's nurturing capacity, and even if it is now a profession, nursing is an important skill to have in family life. Practical knowledge about taking care of others isn't optional! Stop what you are doing, and mother your sick child. I will tell you how.

The greatest obstacle to caring for your sick child, besides being cut off from the basic knowledge of remedies and methods, is all the outside commitments we've become accustomed to, combined with the sense that if one is not "doing something productive" one is somehow a failure. Women's being expected to work outside the home—or being extraproductive at home to show that they are not somehow dependent—has resulted in sick children not being cared for properly. A lot of homemaking consists of *being ready* for those times when someone needs you—and it's hard to justify this way of using time to a world that measures productivity in equal units and output. Thus, the collective memory has failed us when it comes to the ordinary, commonsense care of sick people.

I've seen too many impractical (and simultaneously stressed) moms *not* taking care of their sick children. Not that they are neglectful on purpose: they simply don't know what to do. They seem surprised that their normally active one is flopping about, cranky, and lacking energy to do anything for himself. These moms go about their business in what seems to me an oddly detached way, watching the pitiful thing from afar. I think the detachment, while it looks really callous, is born of helplessness and a vague reliance on "experts" and "professionals" to step in.

Their approach is simply to continue along with whatever they had planned, treating the illness as something on the margins, to be dealt with only when absolutely necessary. Only if they themselves succumb do they stop what they are doing.

These are the parents who rush to the ER or the doctor at a sign of illness (when they do begin to notice). In addition, schools require notes from doctors to verify the flu (and employers are doing so as well). Of all the stupid ideas, this one is high on the scale. People get sick—the last thing we need is for them to be out and about getting notes and infecting everyone else!

So let's learn how to take care of our own children, and let's be in a position to do so.

Necessary warnings:

Anyone who is suddenly very sick with severe vomiting, diarrhea, and fever needs to go to the emergency room right away.

Anyone who has trouble breathing and whose tissues become bluish needs to go to the ER.

Anyone whose pulse is faint, who loses consciousness, or who shows signs of dehydration, such as extreme thirst, little urination, or sunken eyes, needs to go to the ER.

If a person is vomiting and not getting relief, press the tummy on the lower right—pain there could be appendix trouble.

In what follows, I am not talking about this kind of severe illness. It's worth it to read up on what constitutes an emergency. Call the doctor if you need help figuring things out. You have to use good judgment, or it will be impossible to be a good parent!

You know, when our children experience the normal illnesses of life (colds, flu, and so on), even though it's sad and pathetic, we have a wonderful opportunity to serve them in a completely different way from the way they are used to. We can take a break from all the demands of daily life and just take care of them. Rather than viewing this part of motherhood as a stressful chore that reveals our incompetence, we can see it as a real blessing, when we know what to do.

Mothers do so many things, including being nurses; nursing is an extension of motherhood, really. But we have to learn how to do the right thing, and even professional nurses don't give us a clue. Some might assume we already know the tricks of the trade and don't bother mentioning them. Others might not know themselves, as it seems to me that this very practical, day-to-day side of nursing is being lost.[19]

For instance, a few years back, Bridget had what turned out to be Lyme disease. She was achy, feverish, and miserable. I took her to the doctor's office, suspecting something more serious than a flu, and they ran tests. As we were getting ready to leave, the nurse asked me, "Is she going back to school today?"

That question, delivered with utmost neutrality and even with the expectation of a positive answer—about a child with a temperature the nurse herself had measured at 103—encapsulates an attitude that frustrates me so.

---

[19] I love my nurse friends. I know that many of our readers are nurses and wonderful ones at that. But nurses are so overworked with the process demanded of them in the modern hospital (or doctor's office) that they just don't have time for certain things. In our stay at Children's Hospital, I was the one who had to bathe my Bridget's face, help her brush her teeth, and make her comfortable in so many ways. Her dear nurses spent a hefty chunk of their time in the room on the computer, filing notes. Her roommates didn't have those things done for them either, nor did I hear anyone encourage the parents to do these important yet utterly basic elements of care. When you don't have time for something, you don't do it, and then soon you forget how to do it or that it's important at all—and so does everyone else. I doubt that those things are considered nursing care at all anymore. So forgive me for pointing this out. I'm sure there are exceptions.

Sickness isn't an irritating interruption at which you throw magical pills, hoping for a quick cure. You don't ask the sick person to bear the brunt of your plans, your schedule, your routine. This, my friends, is why a child needs a mother: so that he doesn't spend the day in the nurse's office at school, huddled feverishly in a chair—not to mention potentially infecting large numbers of people!

So what are these procedures that put you in control of the situation, rather than leaving you at its mercy, helpless and without a guide?

I will tell you. As always, adapt the information to your situation. I'll try to give you the big picture with the little details. It's up to you to change what you need to for your circumstances.

1. *Establish a place near you for the sick one. I suggest the sofa* during the day and a mattress on your floor next to your bed at night for a very young child.

The *best remedy* for anything that ails anyone—regardless of severity, and even when drastic measures must be taken by trained personnel—is rest and good nourishment. The body needs to take a break from working to keep itself going at high speed, maintaining warmth, and supplying energy for bursts of activity.

Children (and plenty of adults as well), however, do not usually know to stop their activity. They will just keep running around until they collapse—we call this *dying-fly syndrome* (DFS). Have you ever noticed a dying fly? Unlike flies in the prime of their lives, the dying fly buzzes loudly, hurls itself off windows and walls, and generally makes its presence known until it suddenly expires in the onion dip.

DFS is often seen even in healthy times as the rising level of frantic energy right before bedtime. Some parents wait for the child to hit his head on something so he will cry and they can put him to bed! Better to just have a bedtime.

Likewise, with sickness, DFS manifests itself in increased activity. But the wise parent steps in. You, the mom, need to be the alpha—the implementer of the *standard operating procedure* (SOP)—when it dawns on you that your child is not himself in one way or another.

Put him on the sofa so he is handy for that best remedy (rest and nourishment if he can take it). I say sofa, not bed (during the day). Bed is too far away when you

- aren't sure what is wrong with him and need to keep an eye on him while you figure it out
- are pregnant, nursing a baby, or otherwise need to jump up a thousand times for other things (if he's way off in his bedroom, that's too tiring for you)
- have a sickie who's so little that you have to check him all the time; and bed is too lonely for him (even an eighteen-month-old can get tucked in on the sofa)
- can't quite convince him that he's sick (bed then becomes too much of a commitment on everyone's part—better to just stop there on the sofa)

If he's not sick, not much will keep them there. Being on the sofa for more than thirty minutes just isn't going to work unless he's really sick! So it's a good and loving way to filter the mere complainers from the actually ailing. "Oh, you say you don't feel well? Poor thing! Here, let me get you comfy on the sofa." Take his temp. Far better than forcing a sick child to prove himself so with a breakdown.

Needless to say, this phase of the SOP—applying the best remedy and seeing how it goes—must be undertaken with no electronic stimulation of any kind. No TV shows, movies, games. Just the kid on the sofa. (Deploy the show only if it's necessary to glue him there at first when you are positive he's sick. But try to do without.)

If he is truly ill, not much will get him up. Your dynamo will suddenly wind down, pathetically submitting to treatment. It's like turning off a switch to have him there. And you will know that you were right.

2. *Cancel your plans*—yes, even if it means losing the deposit on the reservation for the birthday-party venue. Maybe you can freeze the cake for later. But it is not acceptable to power on through when your child is sick.

The best remedy is *rest in a nest.* On the sofa you will make a nest. Get a blanket or two, a pillow, a pile of books. Make sure your child is warm (if he's hot from a fever, he won't tolerate the blankets and you will know—even so, keep him out of drafts). Insist he stay in the nest.

Once this SOP is normal—indeed, standard—in your home, the children will submit without a murmur. Just keep at it. Insist on that thirty minutes. Yes, the under-two will need you most of the time—you too will be immobilized there—so bring books. But the sofa usually means that you can at least get up to do a few things when he conks and still have him right there, propped with pillows and safe as a bug in a rug, or transferred to an equally comfy nest on the actual rug, if you think he'll roll off the sofa.

You will find that as your family grows, you'll need multiple sofas! We once had a flu that had two persons, one at either end, on each of four sofas. We were darned sick. The advantage was that it was a kind of ward. The one healthy person (Suki!) could efficiently administer ginger ale to all.

3. *Know the kinds of sicknesses:*
  a. Barfing or diarrhea, or both
  b. Far, far better: non-barfing

For just normal (even awful) sicknesses, here's my take.

You will get to know the *warning signs* of each.

For the barfing kind, your child will, best-case scenario, tell you his tummy hurts. Worst case, he will give you no warning, but look you at you blankly and then hurl. Sorry about that.

My grandson says, "My sides hurt."

My kids would say, "My mouth tastes funny."

Or the child will not seem interested in food. (Here is a good reason not to insist that a child eat everything on his plate, but only one bite of each item, and to be alert for the times he really just miserably can't eat even one bite! That, my friends, is not a discipline issue.)

Or he will be all too interested in food (a sad but known side effect of a weird feeling in your stomach is to want to throw food down your throat, the results of which are not pleasant when the real cause makes itself known).

Or *something*—something that you will learn to recognize, hopefully in time. Rosie calls it "the tell." For Pippo, it's that he wants to snuggle—which he really doesn't, ever, unless he needs to barf, apparently! Yikes.

If it's a barfing sickness, get a basin handy. Dump the contents of the basin in the toilet, and wash the basin out with hot water and cleanser—you can use the tub for the final cleaning if your sink isn't big enough. Dry with a rag towel. (I explain all the things below.) If the child is old enough and can make it to the bathroom, help him and clean him and it up afterward. Everyone needs a sympathetic cooling hand on the brow when they are barfing.

If your kid is throwing up, roll up the rugs in front of the sofa or next to the bed, if possible. It is much easier to do this than to clean barf out of a rug. In general, it really pays to take a few minutes to figure out your hierarchy of barf locations and how to maximize your chances of an easy cleanup.

My sister-in-law would tell her kids to "get down low," in an effort to minimize the collateral damage if they couldn't make it to a basin or the bathroom. One time, her son called her from upstairs: "I feel sick!" "Get down low!" He ran to the top of the stairs, the better to communicate with her, and, stooping low, barfed down the entire flight.

So yes, that's life.

Do not feed a barfing person. The stomach has to rest completely! Some illnesses allow for the occasional saltine and sips of ginger ale. But sometimes it becomes clear that nothing will be tolerated; this could take hours. As long as the child isn't getting dehydrated to the extent outlined above, it's better to let him be until the stomach stops seizing, even if he can't drink for a while. Then, once the barfing has stopped, give twenty minutes in between spoonfuls to make sure it's all staying down.

Then introduce the bland diet, little by little. Go slowly, or you will regret it!

By the way, there is a certain kind of vomit that results not from a stomach bug but from having swallowed too much nasal mucus. It's worthwhile to learn the difference—it has to do with how the contents look (very "mucusy" or not) and how the person feels other than the one or occasional episode. Teach your child to blow his nose, not sniff down the mucus. You can put a little dab of eucalyptus ointment under his nose—it helps clear the passages and loosen things up. A child who vomits for this reason will often be hungry afterward and doesn't need a bland diet.

If it's a non-barfing sickness, you will know by the hot hands of feverishness, glittery eyes, papery, flushed cheeks or else too-pale complexion, congestion, and clear fluid coming out of the nose. For these sufferers, it will be days with tissues, a wastebasket, and their food on a tray. They can eat what they want, what everyone else is eating—right there on the sofa. (Sometimes we would join the sickie to keep him company or send a delegation.) Ice cream helps and is, indeed, medicinal.

Someone who is sick for a long time will probably want to watch some shows or otherwise have what we call "mindless entertainment." But if you allow this, keep it within limits. What we call "the buzziness" of the TV can make headaches worse and strain sick eyes. Insist that screens be turned off for a good bit of the day so that peace and quiet reigns and real rest occurs. It's quite normal for sick people to spend a good part of the day asleep! It's good for them.

4. *Have on hand the things you need.* Time will teach you. My suggestions:

Blankets. Every family room needs a few quilts and lap blankets for normal comfort. These get a good workout when sickness strikes! But children also appreciate their own baby blanket or quilt to be brought to them when they are sick. The SOP initiates when they are tucked in on the sofa with their blanket. A sick person needs to be kept warm, because the body can't do its normal thing when it's sick. Often the worst thing about being sick is how chilled you feel ... until you get so hot, and then the blanket can just be set aside.

Have the child wear *pajamas or other comfy clothing.* Take off buckles and belts and other poky items. The best thing is to have two layers: an underwear T-shirt and another cotton top. Give a girl a loose braid so her hair stays out of her face and feels comfortable.

Pillows. After you determine that a child is really sick, get his own bed pillow for him. That way, he can be really comfortable and even go to sleep, which will be the best thing for him.

Paper towels and tissues—seriously. This is a note for my dedicated old-fashioned, thrifty friends. I love you but these disposable things are here for a reason and this is it: germs.

Old towels. Towels wear out. Keep a stash of these (not near your newer ones, because for some reason, everyone reaches for the unpresentable ones—so embarrassing) for a sick person (also for drying the dog after a bath and wiping up the quart of apple juice that gets spilled in the kitchen). If it's a barfing sickness, a rag bath towel can go under the child in case of uncontained nighttime vomiting. You will save many a sheet change by popping an old towel (or even multiple layers of them, to be peeled back one by one as needed) under a kid.

A *basin, or barfer,* as we call it. I use those pink plastic basins that you take home from the hospital after you have a baby. They are not cute, and I'm sure you could rustle up something cuter, but besides just being free and there and stackable, they are rectangular. Somehow there's more coverage with something that goes right across the body, versus a bowl, which curves dangerously outward from the zone of horror. Get it out at the first sign of distress, and put it away after having washed it out with hot soapy water when things are better. Some advise keeping a basin under kids' beds; certainly be prepared in the car with plastic bags and wipes.

Disposable plastic cups. There is a stage in the stomach bug where all that's coming up is just a little bile—not much volume. It's so worth it to supply plastic cups and just throw them away as needed. I hear from Rosie that the Duggars do this. "I imagine if you had, say, nineteen barfing kids, it would be especially clutch."

Washcloths and more basins. A person who is too feverish to spend time in the bathroom needs to be wiped down with a nice, warm soapy washcloth at least twice a day and rinsed off. If the fever is high, the water should be cool. You need a basin (not the same as the barfing one) to do this job properly.

Old sheets. These are also helpful for lining the sofa or bed, folded over. If the worst happens and everyone is sick at once, you can spare yourself bed changes by placing a folded sheet over the results—usually quite minimal—of the millionth barf. Yes, of course, no one should lie in a dirty bed. But if you can't stand upright because you yourself are sick, this will get you through the night. Also helpful: plastic tablecloths if your offspring turn out to be prolific barfers—pile layers on top; old comforters; changing pads with something absorbent on one side and something waterproof on the other (these can be easily sewn up ahead of time); folding camp cots for when you need to be in their room or when you need them to be in your room.

Basic medicines. Have on hand children's ibuprofen, acetaminophen, an antihistamine, eucalyptus ointment, and cough drops. Get those zinc cough drops and deploy them, along with a dose of ibuprofen, at the first sign of sore throat of the kind that comes from a postnasal drip and an inflamed uvula. You can often stave off an illness this way. I've tried it many times, and it works.

Humidifier. Get a hot-mist humidifier for coughs. The cold-mist kind is fairly useless. When someone has a respiratory illness, the nighttime room needs to be steamy. Hot-mist humidifiers sometimes get buildup from mineral deposits; they may look unsanitary, but by definition, the steam is sterile (making it safer than the cold-mist kind).

A tray. A folding tray helps for meals. When a person is achy and feverish, he is hungry but just can't sit up at the table.

Pull-Ups for little ones, even those who are potty trained.

Ginger ale and bland-diet items. Have a supply of the things you will need (see my bland-diet appendix in volume 3) in the pantry and freezer. Regular ginger ale doesn't have ginger in it, but it does have high-fructose corn syrup—which is not healthy! If you can find it, get the natural kind that isn't too spicy. Then hide it from the cocktail makers. *Keep nursing babies* as much as they need to nurse.

5. *Let the default be to stay there on the sofa*—even for days (going to bed at night, of course), until proven better. What is proof? See number 1: not much can keep the child there! And the fever is gone. Give the child a stash of beloved books and little toys to keep him company if he gets restless.

Many times, sheer boredom leads the person to think he is improved. If so, time to clean up—give him a bath, have him take a shower—but take a wait-and-see attitude. Be wary of holding the birthday party. Many people feel better during the day but then toward evening demonstrate that they are not better, not at all. After the bath, have the child head back to the sofa so you can see how things are going if you are at all in doubt. It's terrible to resume activity too soon and end up sick again!

If, after another spell on the sofa, he's not better, at least he's clean. If he is better, at least he's clean.

Use the opportunity to change bedding, do a load of towels in hot water, vacuum the room, and generally get things back to normal. Sometimes there's a relapse, but even so, it's nice to have things spruced up, because being on the sofa can feel grubby after a while (and, in fact, is grubby).

Finally, a few more practical tips:

- Siblings can take care of each other, play quiet games, and rest together.
- Be sure to wash your hands often, to eat well, and to stay hydrated.
- Do the laundry as soon as you can. Don't let barfy things pile up! But scrape away any solids into the toilet: the washer can't handle *any* solids, and the last thing you need is a busted washer! Use at least warm water, hot for those old towels, sheets, and comforters.
- Use a good cleanser on doorknobs and all surfaces. Change the bathroom hand towel daily! Stash paper towels and spray in there for the faucet handles and so on. Enzyme cleaner works for the places where bodily fluids have left their mark.
- Chart medicines. When you have more than one person on antibiotics or asthma medication and are trying to keep straight who got ibuprofen when, you need a chart. It's much easier to overdose someone than you might think!
- Put a small trash bag near a sick person for tissues and so on, to keep the area tidy. In a pinch, it's another barf bucket!
- Disinfect or replace toothbrushes.

Final Thoughts on This Important Work

When you implement my Standard Operating Procedure, you will start to see ways to make things easier on yourself when there is sickness. Having everyone in the same room, comfy and cozy; lining up your simple sick meals; saving your steps where possible.

Streamlining sick care and having a plan becomes even more important when Mama also falls ill. Not running ragged trying to find basins, towels, and so on, but having thought it all out beforehand enables others to take over or at least be helpful (including even young children).

A word about how men often seem to take getting sick, offered by my own husband: sometimes the wife doesn't realize that because Dad gets sick last (or next to last), he has actually been doing a lot of things around the house—so, when his turn comes, he is that much more exhausted. Perhaps he has been thinking, "She's run ragged; I'll just lie low and not be an additional burden." This is a noble thought—what he may not realize is that his wife needs active help and feels burdened by what she thinks is selfishness.

In this case, the wife just has to say, "Please, I need you to do such-and-such—I can't!" Over the years we found that when everyone is sick, one person can rally just enough to change a diaper and then collapse; the other one then takes over for just long enough to allow him a rest before she collapses. But you have to speak up.

I turn now to the naughty child who recovers just before bedtime—there used to be an adorable book we found in the library called *The Bad Baby*. I haven't been able to find it, and I don't remember the illustrator, but it charmingly depicted just this scenario. There were no words, just adorable drawings of a pathetically sick baby whose mother is full of pity and loving care all through the day. Naturally, just as he recovers at night, she is totally worn out and looks on, bedraggled and exhausted, as he swings from the chandelier! But in the end, she loves him, of course! It's just life. Babies *are* bad that way!

Taking care of a sick person is work. You have to give up on your plans. Things pretty much come to a standstill. Acknowledging that this state of affairs is rather more likely than not offers affirmation for the decision to limit outside responsibilities as a general decision. Being sick is part of life, and we have to know how to handle it.

We don't often think of illness this way, but it has its benefits. Many a child has learned to love reading or discovered a new interest as a result of being sick on the sofa for a long time. More importantly, the details of being cared for stay with a person forever. The mother is in this sense a missionary of love, and her field is her home!

PART 5
Discipline

When we help a child gain control over himself and become aware of the world around him, we prepare the ground for his formal education.

Joseph W. McPherson, veteran educator and headmaster of The Heights, an esteemed boys' school in Washington, D.C., defined education as a "leading out":

> Leading from what? While most people would say leading from ignorance, I think that the more important state from which education leads is self-absorption, the idea that one is the center of the universe and that one's own self and one's desires are the criteria for living one's life.
>
> Leading to what? I would say an ability to engage the world in a noble, generous, creative way.

I never conversed with McPherson, but I am sure he would agree that this leading from self-absorption begins in the child's earliest years, before the school ever sees him. In the same essay, McPherson goes on to say:

> Adults who, self-contented, take the path of least resistance in their lives and who avoid self-examination and the struggle for improvement of their characters cannot possess ... authority.

He is speaking of the authority to teach, which is based on the trust the child feels in the teacher's evident mastery of his own self, or lack of it.

Thus, being able to discipline children presupposes being able to discipline ourselves. This conclusion is woven into everything I suggest in this section. Self-control is the key to a child's liberty—"the glorious liberty of the children of God" (Rom. 8:21, KJV)—and can usually be elicited only when the adults in his life possess it. This paradox is resolved in the gracious plan of the family, that with our children, we too are able grow, sometimes staying only a step ahead of them, if the truth be told. No matter. What is important is that we are learning together in the family the place of life and love.

Two Rules of Discipline

hen I give talks about discipline, I want to tell parents how much I hope that they learn, if it doesn't come naturally, to show their affection for their children: to cuddle them, to hold them in their motherly or fatherly embrace, to tell them often how much they are loved.

And then I want to say two important things to them:

1. Stop reacting to their children.

2. Stop seeking affirmation from their children.

I want to tell women especially to commit themselves to realistic discipline starting now (whenever "now" is in the parental journey—it's not too late), making sure to have conversations with their husbands for wholehearted unity in this project.

But I have to admit that in my enthusiasm to give advice, I had to ask myself the question: What exactly do I base my ideas on?

Of course, there is experience and study. I could submit a bibliography, for sure. But what is an acceptable objective authority for deciding how to discipline one's children, as opposed to seeking advice from random moms, suspect individuals with Ph.D.s, and self-made experts—of which, for all you know, I may be one?

I realized that I would have to show that my ideas are more than just my opinion; I would have to show that while each family is different, with astonishingly different temperaments, problems, backgrounds, challenges, and methods, the basic principle that children must be disciplined comes from God, the ultimate source of objectivity.

This is the question I had to answer for myself: Does God discipline *us*? He is the Father; we are His children. What *means* of discipline does God use?

Does He give time-outs, cajole, bribe, threaten, shower with affection, think we should just know that He wants us to be good and leave it at that?

Is He permissive, hoping for the best?

Well, I have to say that experience and study show that He does indeed do all of these things, except hope for the best, as hope is a virtue not needed by Divine Persons and "hoping for the best" is a foolish policy when it comes to forming children.

But the other things, yes! Surprisingly, He uses all those methods, as we can read for ourselves in Sacred Scripture.

But I really wanted to know what He says about discipline, as a principle. So I looked it up, and here is what I found:

> For whom the Lord loveth, he chastiseth; and he scourgeth every son he receiveth. (Heb. 12:6, DR)

> But if you be without chastisement ... then you are bastards, and not sons. (Heb. 12:8, DR)

> Now all chastisement for the present indeed seemeth not to bring with it joy, but sorrow; but afterwards it will yield, to them that are exercised by it, the most peaceable fruit of justice. (Heb. 12:11, DR)

The most peaceable fruit of justice.

So the first step, it seems to me, if a parent is wondering how to raise healthy, happy children, is to pray about these passages, preferably with your spouse. Read the whole section (Heb. 12), not just these passages.

Here are some thoughts to get you started:

- Search for what "discipline" and "chastisement" and "scourgeth" mean in the context of this passage. What is the Greek? Where else is it used in Scripture?
- If these words make you uncomfortable, ask yourself if your doubt or uncertainty is due to misleading principles that we ourselves have been raised with, in an age that does not value family, God, or following any goals other than self-fulfillment.
- Note that this passage ("Whom God loves He chastiseth") is taken from the Old Testament. What does it tell you that the teaching here in the Letter to the Hebrews reaches back so far, to the beginnings of the collective memory, to shed light on how we become real sons of God, the New Testament promise?
- What about this bit: that all discipline (as it is often translated) brings sorrow at first? How do we incorporate the truth of this observation as parents? Are we realistic about it? Where is our affirmation coming from at that moment that our child displays sorrow when we have validly chastised him?
- And finally, how much do we desire the "most peaceable fruit of justice" for us and our whole family, and what are we willing to do, as parents, to get it?

Act, Don't React

Remember my first golden rule of parenting: act, don't react.

Aren't we all at some point dazedly wondering, "Who are these children, and how did they get to be so ill behaved? I'm going to try to give you a little crash course in energetic, active parenting, in which you just have to decide that no one else will do it if you don't.

I think you will agree with me that we have to learn all this basically by reading books, because there are few examples of good parenting around, especially of larger families.

But we can't read the *new* books, because they are written by people who clearly don't know how to raise a family, who seem not to think you *can* raise a family, or who think wonderful goals are enough (e.g., "have a godly family by being a great person") but offer little advice that helps you when you are sitting in a dirty kitchen and your children are throwing "gross, disgusting" food at you.

So I'm going to try to tell you something practical.

You need to read the Bible, because God shows us how people were quite unable to handle life in the world. They knew the difference between right and wrong from the very beginning, but He ended up having to make some specific rules.

In the Liturgy of the Church, we are always given passages from Scripture that are all about how beautiful God's law is; and how Jesus Christ came to affirm, not do away with, God's law; and what peace God's precepts impart to the soul who embraces them. We are told, in fact, of the beauty of meditating on this law (see Psalm 119,[20] for instance).

With this background in mind, read all the Little House books and also all the Little Britches books. (Read *Little Britches* on your own first; the father dies, and it's *so* sad that your eight-year-old boy might be too young for it; see what you think. But the series is pure gold.) *Mama's Bank Account* is another one.

In fact, get all the old books for children you can find.[21] As you are reading them (out loud to the kids or just to yourself), try to pick up the subtext, the part aimed at *you*, of how the parents are oriented. It will slowly dawn on you that they are united, strict, and understanding, and where they are not understanding, the kids just have to handle it.

Your kids also just have to handle it. This is my second rule of parenting: don't seek affirmation from your kids. Remember: you are doing what is best for them—the best you *can* do, given your weaknesses, frailties, shortcomings, and proclivity for making mistakes. We are all going to make mistakes all the time, and we can't let that fact, which will be brought home to us every day, stop us from *acting* and *doing what we think is best*.

Let me give you an example. Jane, a reader of mine, wondered what to do about her daughter, who had told her that the breakfast she served was "disgusting."

Why would you let someone treat you this way? Ask yourself: Is there a culture in the home of not saying "thank you" in your family? Of being unkind?

---

[20] Psalm 118 in the Douay-Rheims version.

[21] You are only making your life harder if your children read books featuring bratty children and weak parents, and I hope that I don't have to mention that the Disney channel is not your friend. Children all too easily imitate bratty behavior, so give yourself a break and don't go there.

Maybe there is. Spend a week thanking your husband for being such an excellent provider, because if you are reading this, you have a book in your hands and time to read it.

I'm sorry that our copy of Laura Ingalls Wilder's *The Long Winter* was long ago read into shreds, because I would like to quote for you the part where Ma serves a supper of yet more potatoes, and Pa says something like, "Caroline, you really know how to make a meal out of nothing," and Ma (who had a beautiful home back east, with china and real furniture and silk dresses, but who gave herself wholeheartedly to her life with Pa, even though, I think we can admit, it took its toll on her) says, "Oh, Charles, you are such a wonderful provider." Keep in mind that they were one loaf of brown bread away from starvation.

After a week of being truly grateful for what you have and letting everyone know it, Ingalls style, you should talk with your husband about the dire lack of manners exhibited by your offspring. Ask him what he thinks. Perhaps you need to let him know, if this is the case, that the children speak to you the way he speaks to them, and it's not kind. Listen if he tells you that they are just reflecting your own tone.

Begin again. Obtain his backing and his promise to give the children a stern talking-to about how you both made a mistake in allowing the decline and fall, but things are changing, so be warned! Yes, admit that you were wrong!

If your husband is willing (it's better coming from him, but you can say it if you need to), *he* should tell the little darlings that they shouldn't be surprised if they get into trouble for being rude, because you realize it's a bad *habit*, but it needs to be broken.

And maybe he will realize that he himself hasn't been respectful enough of you or has forgotten to thank you. Maybe he's not Pa and doesn't get it just yet. Just keep thanking him and asking him to help with the children's manners, and you will see improvement, believe me. After the talk, you must spend a week following through, or, as I like to put it, *acting, not reacting.*

Let's say that after all this, your princess comes down and says, "This breakfast is disgusting."

It's up to you. Some options:

Take the contents of the plate and calmly throw them away. Auntie Leila would totally back you up on this.

Ask her to leave the room and come back in and thank you for breakfast before even tasting it. She may then say the following:

- Thank you for making me breakfast! I'm sorry, I don't feel hungry right now. May I wait for a while to eat it? I don't mind if it's cold.
- Thanks for breakfast, Mom! I'll do my best to eat this, but you know, Mom, eggs aren't my favorite. Tomorrow I'd be happy to make myself a bagel if that's all right with you.

You see? She simply is not allowed to say that the food is disgusting! What if she said that in front of guests? What if she said that to someone she was staying with? You would be mortified! But the real cause of your mortification should really be that you allowed a child of yours to behave so poorly! Your shame should be for yourself.[22]

If things are so bad, if all this happens at breakfast because she knows you are trapped with her all day and are afraid she will cry and fight, and she doesn't respond well to this treatment, surprise her by walking away, saying, "I'm not talking about this until Dad gets home," because he has already agreed to back you up.

Starting now, there's a *rule* about the food: we don't say nasty things about the food.

---

[22] You may be enabling bad manners in your child. For instance, your child doesn't like a certain food—say, yogurt. You are at a friend's house, and she offers him cake that she makes the mistake of describing as "blueberry yogurt cake." You immediately say, "Oh, he doesn't like yogurt."

Instead, give him a chance to decide for himself. He may want cake so much (and it might look so appealing) that he might be willing to try it! And then maybe he will like yogurt, or at least realize that yogurt cake doesn't taste like a bowl of yogurt.

You can suggest: "How about a little piece to see if you like it, and then I'm sure Mrs. Smith will give you the rest later if you do"—if you are worried that he will just waste it. On the other hand, you could finish it, and then you'd have extra!

I learned to love ham and cheese sandwiches spread with butter this way. The world becomes a more delightful place when our whims aren't indulged.

This rule has many sub-rules:
- We don't say "hate" about the food.
- We don't say "gross" about the food.
- We don't make faces about the food.
- We are grateful and are certainly allowed to express preferences in a way that wouldn't offend the queen, were *she* to be making dinner at *our* house.
- Anyone who says anything bad about the food can go hungry or be forced to listen to the story of when Laura and her siblings ate nothing but corn and wheat they ground up in the coffee grinder during the long winter, and how they were so happy when they got salt cod for dinner one night.

Here are other examples of ways in which you can act to avoid bad behavior rather than reacting to it:

You dread going anywhere because the children will fight over where to sit in the car. Solution: Make a rule about the seating—biggest to littlest, boys and girls, whatever you want. Maybe your kids have a solution (ours came from our kids)! But then, it's law—for the common good! Or, if you have car seats for certain children, figure out where *you* want each older child to sit, based on how helpful it will be to you. And then, that's that. Don't react by arguing about who sat where last time; don't complain about how bad you feel when they argue.

You keep stepping over coats, mittens, boots, and other paraphernalia. Solution: Make a row of hooks and get a couple of shelves. Insist that everyone take the time to hang things up and put things away. Make them line up their boots, and put someone in charge of neatening them; this is a great chore for a five-year-old who has nothing better to do with his life. Yes, this takes energy on your part. Did you think that raising children doesn't take energy?

You can't face breakfast because your kids don't eat and then they leave a mess. Solution: resolve *not* to serve your kids all the time. They need a plan and encouragement for arriving at breakfast in some semblance of readiness to eat, having taken care of basic hygiene needs and possibly made their beds; afterwards they can clear their places by tidily putting their dishes directly in the dishwasher or tub of soapy water.

Take a shower before breakfast even starts, and stay off your device until you've supervised cleanup. Yes, you have to postpone doing what you want to do, but of course, this is what you are asking them to do. Demonstrating self-control contributes to a household where the members have self-control.

Get the idea? It's your life, your home, your children. If things aren't basically fun, orderly, and happy, then change them! You have a mind: use it! Act, don't react!

Dear Aristotle, He's So Clever

Adults who feel overwhelmed by their children's misbehavior could ask themselves if they themselves are disciplined, if they have self-control. Do parents have a strong, loving relationship with each other?

If you, the parents, always bicker and speak rudely or snappishly to each other, let me tell you, your kids will be brats. (Although, truthfully, there are many ways to get bratty children. Some of the most loving people have bratty children! That's because they are sweet but sort of wimpy, and children will take advantage of just about everything.)

Parents have to shed their immaturity and begin pondering child development—what to expect of a six-year-old, of a twelve-year-old. So much goes into family relationships, even down to the physical and emotional bond between mother and child and the less obvious but also crucial interaction between father and child.

Can we distinguish between a behavioral problem and one of low blood sugar or lack of sleep? Are the children bored into mischief?

Also, consider the differences between children. Some are too tender-hearted for a spanking; others practically need to be spanked on a regular schedule! (Just kidding about the schedule. I write about spanking in another chapter.)

We need to be clear on the goal, which is twofold: to enjoy a bit of peace at home and to be able to tell God that you took seriously the obligation to train your child to be virtuous—which, as dear Aristotle reminds us, is the ability to do the right thing *for its own sake.*

And, as that wise teacher also says, this is all a matter of habit—not only for children, but for anyone. Thank goodness, because there is no way to instill in someone the desire to do right for its own sake. You can only lead this horse to water. Habits must be formed; we're not born with them! Yet we all do all sorts of things for all sorts of reasons.

All human actions have one or more of these seven causes, says Aristotle: chance, nature, compulsions, habit, reason, passion, desire.

So you know, your kids might be nice by chance (or something we commonly call chance) or by an accident of genes. Lucky you. Will they always be so, under the myriad circumstances life will throw at them? Will they have other virtues as well, some of which may seem less than nice?

Of the things in that list you can control, you might get some human action out of the children because you are always yelling, because you are always convincing them (begging, pleading with, bribing, "reasoning with," or possibly "motivating by passion"), because you are always angry with them and threatening them ("compulsion"), or because they crave the ability to be good ("desire"). But, in my experience, desire for the good that carries over to action doesn't happen until later, when they are so old that it does you no good in the matter of *enjoying your family now,* which we would all like to do; and for them, the grown children, the problem will still remain that even with desire, they face the difficulty of acquiring habits!

Better to give them the habits pronto. (Don't get me wrong. You will also yell, beg, threaten, plead, and bribe, but you will do so on a much reduced scale.)

The very first habit a child must learn is prompt obedience.

Even a very young child can learn to obey the first time. Because most parents don't really believe this, they don't even try!

They never tell an eighteen-month-old to pick something up please and bring it to Mommy. They never tell a one-year-old to stop the dangerous squirming on the changing table. They never tell a seven-month-old not to pull Mommy's hair. They don't understand that it's well worth putting the baby down to get up and get the toddler off the table with a spanking. If you make up your mind to do this for one week, you will nurse the baby in peace for a year, with the toddler playing happily nearby.

In the laundry section in volume 3, I tell you that a two-year-old can put laundry in the proper hamper. Now, you have to be patient and walk along with him and help him do it. Maybe you have to coax, cajole, and sing laundry songs for a month! You might have to administer a rebuke and then put it in yourself if he defies you (don't make a big deal of it; just act as if you expect him to obey, and realize he's two and probably won't). You may have to ignore his not doing it half the time. But if you have the expectation that he help (eventually), if you are convinced that it's the *habit* of obedience that will make your life easier in the end, you will regard it as a worthwhile investment.

Foolish parents constantly *react to* (or ignore) their children's misbehavior, instead of taking the time to instill good behavior.

They constantly seek affirmation from their children, and so fall into various errors. They don't have the confidence to drop a certain conflict, they are afraid of administering the punishment necessary, or they retreat after administering discipline, out of surprise that their children show them *attitude*.

Attitude is that reaction you'd rather not have. Obviously, we would love for everyone we correct to respond with an immediate "You're so right; I will change my ways forthwith!" But if you think about it, that's just not realistic. You will find that you can safely ignore attitude or call it out ("Young lady, enough!"); just don't take it all that seriously; certainly never let attitude affect your will to discipline.

A child who's told no in a firm, calm voice — and you do try that first, right? — may sass. Are you surprised? Just ignore, wait, and insist.

A child who's spanked will seem devastated, crying loudly! Are you grown-up enough for this? Are you mature enough to acknowledge that it's unlikely that your three-year-old will thank you for a punishment? You will not spoil the good effect of discipline by letting a moment go by and then giving him a hug. Just look at him from way on high and know that someday he actually will thank you for loving him. Not now. But someday.

Remember our passage from Scripture? Whom God loves, He disciplines (or, more strongly, chastises)—so that they will be sons and not slaves (or bastards), remember?

And all discipline, at the time, seems to bring not joy but pain!

We just have to understand and use the understanding to overcome our laziness or other issues. Discipline at first seems hard, not only to the person being disciplined, but also to the person disciplining. So often we shy away from the reality that, of those choices in Aristotle's list of what motivates actions, we have to choose the hard ones.

Do you back down or never begin? Your retreat from clear duty does two things:

1. It gives the child power over you, which, in turn, creates anxiety, since even he feels on some level that such a state of things is disordered. You plunge into a vicious vortex of testing on his part, backing down on yours, and ever increasing, ever controlling anxiety.

2. It deprives him of the rest of the promise of that passage from Hebrews, that in the end discipline brings the peaceable fruit of justice!

The promise meets the two parts of our goal. First, there will be peace in the home. Second, as wise Aristotle says, all virtue can be expressed as this: doing what is just!

So the peaceable fruit of justice is . . . virtue, the habit of doing the good.

Self-Control and Where to Get It

ave you seen what has come to be called the "Marshmallow Study"? By observing young children's ability to resist consuming a marshmallow and then following up on their outcomes later in life, the study shows, rather persuasively (and unsurprisingly to those with any common sense at all), that children with self-control grow up more likely to be wealthy, successful, and healthy than those without. Not that those worldly aims are what we are ultimately aiming for. That would be unworthy, and besides, that's not the point.

The point is self-control in order to achieve a meaningful life. I think it might be harder to design a study that tracked less-concrete goals than the ones mentioned. I'm not sure how you would ascertain if people had restrained their marshmallow desires and grown up to love truth, serve the good, and appreciate beauty, so we'll use the metric given.

Anyway, we all know that we *prefer* to be around people who have self-control. That's so obvious that it might surprise you that I even say it that way, but honestly, it has implications for whether we wish to enjoy the company of our children.

Whom do you enjoy the most? The people you know whose spontaneity and sense of humor sparkle, but not at the expense of their responsibilities? Or the ones who are needy, never know where their keys are, and tend to get food on themselves while they eat?

Would you rather be around someone who will bring you a meal if you are sick or someone who seems always to be taking advantage of your generosity? Do you want your children to grow up to think of others or to be rioters? I mean, the rioters are people's children, after all.

Most of the frustration parents feel at their children's lack of self-control is firmly rooted in *their own lack of self-control!* Further, I can see that the reason I lost my center of gravity when my kids were young was that I often felt incompetent, and that feeling in turn left me without the ability to temper my reactions.

When a reader writes to me about her sad lack of patience with her children—not the ordinary impatience that comes with just being human, but that crazy "I can't be with them all day because I might explode" kind—I always suspect that what's at the bottom of it is that *she* doesn't know how to do the simplest things in her day.

In this section, we're trying to work on developing the virtue of self-control in your children, focusing on chores and discipline.

But I wanted to be sure that you understood about your duties and your ability to accomplish your tasks, such as waking up on time, showering, making meals, doing the laundry, and cleaning.

Accomplishing these daily goals can be difficult for anyone who wasn't trained in good habits as a child, and we do want to break the cycle of not having good habits; so it's a good time to discuss my true devotion to, if incomplete acquisition of, the old-fashioned cardinal virtues: prudence, temperance, justice, fortitude.

To be fully human, we need each of these qualities, and they work together to make us able to acquire and fruitfully use the greater theological virtues, which are gifts of grace: faith, hope, and charity.

Prudence means seeing things as they really are and being able to act accordingly. This virtue requires a love of reality. Prudence can also be more or less equated with conscience, God's voice within guiding us not only to know right from wrong, but to know it in a particular case on which we must act.

Justice is giving each one (including ourselves) his due and is the closest in the natural law to charity, St. Thomas Aquinas tells us; without it, we won't truly love our neighbor, for who can be said to love someone from whom he withholds what he owes?

Fortitude means having the power of acting for the good, despite opposition or obstacle. It doesn't mean fearlessness but the will to act whether we are afraid or not. It's not enough to know the good. We must do it.

To describe the virtue of temperance, the ancients used the image of the charioteer (the will) keeping horses (the appetites) in check as they pull the chariot (the self). We want the powerful and beautiful animal part of our nature—doing away with it would be fatal—but it must be controlled by our intellect (prudence). We are not fully human if we are at the mercy of our senses. When we are temperate, we don't go overboard one way or another. Another word for temperance is self-control.

You can hardly have one of these virtues without the other. Fortunately, God gave us the perfect setting in which to develop them all at once, with a minimum of danger and vexation. That setting is the family. Children are God's way of teaching us virtue as we teach them; that's the secret.

In our time, unlike any other, technology has made it possible for individuals to survive for quite a while without depending on one another. We've lost the knack for knowing what a family really is. We seem to think a family is a sort of vehicle for mutual entertainment or shallow fulfillment. Having never worked on anything concrete (knitting? gardening? furniture making? brewing? spackling? car repair?), many latter-day would-be adults, in our prosperity, think of life as the process of acquiring things.

Immature people, tricked by detachment from the true purpose of marriage, which is *building a family*, think that children are an interruption of life rather than life itself. The interruption seems intense but limited, after all; the unsuspecting parents figure that they can endure some painful moments until, they hope *soon*, they can pass on the irritation of the day-to-day child-related drudgery to others.

Even when parents wish to enjoy their children, their imagination is limited by this idea of entertainment. To most people, life is *work*—but not work at home or on the home—and *play*—but not the play that comes as a joyful outcome of celebration. Instead, the only functioning category left is fun (entertainment)—something that distracts from the tedium of work. Yet how disappointed they are after an expensive vacation or carefully planned outing. How unpleasant the children seem and, above all, how ungrateful.

The reason for this disappointment is that fun is just not fun when no one has self-control! But when would anyone have developed this virtue? How is this virtue acquired?

Not running out the door! Not by being frantic! Not by trying to escape from *home*.

Today's parents miss the most rewarding and fulfilling aspect of the family, which is the actual, sometimes mundane, sometimes all too exciting, life together of those entrusted to your care. Love strives to build something lasting together, each person overcoming his selfishness and unbridled needs—controlling them, in fact—for the sake of the others, by means of the work done together and the times of real rest, the kind of rest that restores the soul.

When a child becomes aware of what's going on around him, he just wants to imitate and help. Children really do love to work alongside the adults who love them. Some people don't see this, because they are too busy with outside activities. The focus of each day becomes getting from one place to another efficiently, and efficiency, so important to us grown-ups, is the bane of the child's existence. Frustration ensues when we try to wrestle a child into our adult world. That frustration is nothing compared with what he feels when he can't help you because you are rushing somewhere!

The frantic activity of our lives causes us to miss the real charm of his little efforts, which are nothing compared with the charm he feels when he knows he has done something to help the bigs in his life. We must wisely see the course his interest will take over the years, when we *prudently* allow him time to develop his funny and possibly destructive attempts with a broom or carrying logs, into the competence of a real contributor to the life of the household. Charm builds on charm if you let it.

The family is where this development takes place with unique security. The family is where everyone loves everyone else, where the papa is strong and a little fearsome, the mama is soft and a little demanding, and the brothers and sisters can have a wonderful time together if they are worn out enough by chores not to fight too much. Little by little, because of pitching in and relying on each other, everyone in the family grows in virtue.

ASK AUNTIE LEILA

A Control Freak Mama
Wants to Know

Dear Auntie Leila,

I'm a first-time mother, and my son is nearing is first birthday. Although this has been a fascinating year, it has also been incredibly challenging. I am what some may call a bit of a "control freak" and find assurance in routine and planning events.

Can you recommend a book for the control freak—for a mother who desperately wants to relax and be a little more willing to go with the flow?

Thank you very much,

Your faithful, frazzled reader Evelyn

---

ear Evelyn,

I'm trying to remember how it is that I learned to relax a bit (not much; I'm a control freak of the very highest order, not with any particular result, other than driving everyone crazy), and it was much harder for me, I'll bet, because I'm a control freak *and* I didn't have any skills in housekeeping, planning, or life in general (really! I didn't know how to approach basic things such as getting to the doctor or what have you). So I was both knocked off balance by the unforeseen consequences of having children and frustrated with my poor skill set in coping.

I do think you need some role models somewhere. Nothing like some real life to set you straight.

Are there mothers nearby with a bunch of kids? Could you spend time with them? Do you know families who have older kids as well as toddlers? If you know a mother who has recently had another baby (not her first), could you bring her supper and maybe observe how she does things?

Make it a priority to establish a little pocket of friends (see the St. Gregory Pocket section). Be open to ladies even needier than yourself, but keep an eye out for those who can mentor you just a little, even if they don't realize they are doing so.

To have a realistic idea of what a child does at each stage, I recommend *Child Behavior: The Classic Child Care Manual from the Gesell Institute of Human Development*. I think that it's really important to know what a child can do and wants to do. Much of the panicked need to control a toddler comes about because we are flashing forward to our child as a 6-foot, 190-pound un-potty-trained grabber of oatmeal and puller down and destroyer of random yet moderately precious objects. It's a nightmare, but mostly of our own imagination, as you will discover both from your encounter with families and from this book.

Armed with knowledge, you will be confident to proceed on this plan, that even moderate application of modest standards will *eventually*—note the emphasis—yield a tolerably civilized person.

That a certain, shall we say, *interim period* of chaos must be undergone is a reality we must adjust to. This adjustment may or may not be assisted by the occasional application of a favorite cocktail or, if the earliness of the hour demands abstinence from alcohol, simple rest periods on the sofa with a warm compress on the forehead. Hence the importance of afternoon quiet time (and morning and afternoon naps for a one-year-old), mama's real solace.

Your reading also includes all the old-fashioned *children's* books that teach us so much in their depiction of adult responses to children. We can glean the fallen tidbits that restore collective memory where we find them. E. Nesbit and Laura Ingalls Wilder come to mind. Even reading about the practical British nanny in the nursery was helpful to me: "Oh, I can give him some bread and milk and put him to bed! Good to know!"

Simply asking the question demonstrates goodwill. Only good mamas fret. Pat yourself on the back and take the rest of the day off. Seriously, schedule in some enjoyment. Once you realize that this child and your day are perfectly normal for what they are, you can relax a bit and take joy in your present situation, in all its glorious disarray.

The One Method of So-Called Discipline That Doesn't Work

 truly happy home is one in which the people love each other and enjoy each other's company, even when not everything is perfect (which, of course, is all the time).

So you know what is the one "technique" I witness the most for getting a kid to behave? The one most moms rely on, as far as I can see?

The one that does not work?

It goes like this: Mom is shopping, sitting in the dentist's office trying to read a magazine, or chatting with other moms at Princess's dance class.

Eventually, she notices that her darlings, who are, let's say, between the ages of three and eight, are not behaving.

They are whining.

They are bickering.

They are hungry.

The are bored.

They are brats.

And at that moment she whips it out: The Weapon of Mass Destruction of All That Is Meaningful to Her.

She actively engages in tearing down her own house and sowing her fields with the salt of discontent. She says, without a flicker of thought: "If you don't stop, you won't watch a movie tonight [get ice cream, go to Disney on Ice tonight with Grandma, get a toy, go to Six Flags next week, play a video game ..."

Now, let's take a look at all the reasons this is a terrible thing to say to a child.

1. Has the mom ever been a child? Does she not know how deadly boring it is to be dragged to the grocery store or to be made to wait for eons while some pointless activity, such as waiting, is being carried out?

Did she plan for this inevitable boredom? Did she bring a coloring book, a book, a toy she keeps just for this type of moment? Could she take a walk with her child, look out the window with him, produce a snack, make up a game about naming the things on the grocery-store shelves?

Does she show any humanity whatsoever in acknowledging to this child, this fruit of her womb and suffering, this hope of her future, that she has indeed put him in a wretched situation over which he has no control and is developmentally unable to see beyond?

Does she really think that a six-year-old has the whole picture of his day in mind? Has motherhood really taught her so little?

Does she make any effort to express to him her intention to get him out of the mess she's gotten him into, to go so far as to cut short her own enjoyment (if such is what she is experiencing at the moment in a conversation or a perusal of goods) in order to make his suffering less, if he will just stick with her a little longer?

2. Does she take a look to see if he is still bundled up in his winter coat, hat, mittens, scarf, and boots while being dragged through some overheated godforsaken temple of doom that sucks up all her attention? Does she even realize that he's burning up and can't tell her, because he's only four, and developmentally unable to separate his desperate boredom from his physical distress?

Does she look at her watch to notice that it's lunchtime and then remember that he had only a bowl of cereal for breakfast, and that while she's pawing through the clearance rack, he's reacting to a dip in blood sugar that would make even an adult run for the coffee shop?

Has she packed a protein snack—a few nuts and a half an apple, a piece of cheese and a dried apricot or two, a granola bar—to tide him over?

Does she seriously have so little mercy that she would go so far as to say to him, "You should have eaten your lunch," when it's now 5:30, with no end in sight to this nightmare they are in?

3. Does she notice that the warning signs of this full-blown whiny, crabby state began about fifteen minutes ago and that, up until then, her child behaved remarkably well for a prisoner with no recourse to due process? Trust me, the rest of us in the waiting room, grocery aisles, or dressing room noticed.

Does this mom take any steps to ward off this terrible behavior with remedies for his physical state, sympathy for his plight, or distractions for his mind? Or does she react to him only out of habit, when she notices strangers or persons wholly indifferent to her ultimate happiness (the other ladies at baseball practice or the doctor's office) casting disapproving glances her way? Does she have no insight into the injustice of such lopsided values?

Had she told her child before they arrived exactly what she expected of him? Had she warned him of likely consequences before the meltdown began?

4. Speaking of injustice, does the mom know that her threats can produce only bitterness in one too young truly to understand all the consequences of his behavior?

If she has been so foolish as to promise a far-off good (for what can he know of those? and what if uncontrollable circumstances render them moot?), what can withholding it teach a person whose horizon is at the maximum ten minutes?

Does she know that he will only taste the bitterness of the dawning realization that this person who should know and love him best is willing to take away things that seem impossibly good—for no reason that he can see?

Small children are naughty. They are naughty for a variety of reasons, only a very few of which stem directly from their will. If the reasons come rather from externalities (boredom, discomfort, hunger, helplessness), what control do they have over them? If they stem from their own will, what does revoking distant rewards accomplish?

Better to give a spanking then and there, risking censure from the authorities, than to engage in such futile efforts as threatening to take something distant and wonderful away.

But better still to have known that such behavior was at least a possibility and to have taken steps to prevent it, if only out of self-preservation!

5. What are the mom's motives, anyway?

Either it really pains her to have to deprive her child of a good—and I guess we would all like to think that we are so very selfless when we have recourse to this method—or there is some calculation going on here that doesn't reflect well on this lady's purity of character.

Is there a tiny bit of her—and I've been here too—that wakes from a stupor of laziness and just wants some control and a little revenge? Is there a part of her wonderful crystalline soul that wants to get back at this creature who is preventing her from shopping in peace or reading a magazine during the twenty minutes before an appointment?

And does she really think that the child of her bosom doesn't sense this weakness and won't exploit it to its fullest?

Because he will. Because, most of all …

6. It doesn't work.

As I have tried to stress, small children can't think that far ahead, so they are responding (if they do respond) to the fact of the threat, not the meaning. It's a little dance they've danced before.

If they cry piteously, they appease this ignorant parent for a second, and nothing gets solved. They are still bored, hot, hungry, and crabby; they are also fairly confident that Mom will forget the threat.

If, instead, they are defiant, she doubles down with a whole host of threatening gestures that make her look very dumb; of course, this is *their* revenge. They are completely in control!

If she threatens something silly, they don't really care, and anyway, whining really works on her, as they know: they can get her to give in on the ice cream. I've seen moms who threatened to withhold desserts later hand them over *before* the meal—after being worked on by a skilled operator.

If she threatens something huge, they know they can work it around. No way is she ruining Grandma's evening out, so they know that's bluster. No way will she cancel vacation—they know Dad will bail them out of that one.

A young child doesn't have the long view, so none of this crosses his mind at the time, but habit will give him the assurance that things will work out in his favor, even if he can't figure it out right away. So anyone who uses this "technique" is *training her children to outwit her.*

And the final proof that it doesn't work is that there she is, the next time, in the same rut with them—not planning, not thinking ahead, ignoring, and then threatening (and not, incidentally, demonstrating to them that consideration for the comfort of others is of no consequence).

I sit with her at every game. I see her every week at the store. I have seen all of this and done a little of it myself.

And, saddest of all, I see that this mom doesn't enjoy being with her kids, because they are always misbehaving and never listening.

It's possible that occasions will arise when you need to take a treat away from your child. Keep counsel with yourself and wait and see. If justice demands that you do so, show your children that you are sorry that they can't enjoy something they had looked forward to.

And please, for the love of all that is peaceful and holy, think of something else to do to get them to behave! I will help you.

How My Husband
Convinced Me That Spankings
Are Good Discipline

The effectively spanking parent has to spank only rarely.

My husband convinced me, and I think our children were pretty well behaved. The following is meant to be a jumping-off point for husband and wife to find out whether they are correct in the way they discipline—that is, whether the discipline they are using is effective; that is, whether their children are reasonably obedient according to their stages of development. That is all that really matters: the outcome. Our argument is that spanking is a healthy way to achieve this outcome, but every family is different, and husband and wife need to be on the same page to get to the goal of a happy home where the members have self-control. There are some handy questions for discussion at the end of this chapter. Why not get a couple of glasses of wine and talk things over?

I hope you appreciate how hard it is to know where to begin to present a rational discussion on the topic of spanking. Few issues are as instantaneously productive of insanely overheated debate.

There are so few children in our disordered society that there is little support for discipline of any kind, as the experts have taken over; this has gone on for so long that some people are scarred by the way they were disciplined, or the children they are dealing with are either similarly damaged or incredibly sensitive. Another issue is that seldom does anyone define the term or limit the scope of its application.

I admit that it *seems* wildly inappropriate to insist on spanking as an effective tool. I beg only for common sense—and a hearing.

If your child is hypersensitive, then by all means find another form of discipline that works. I myself had one child for whom spanking was counterproductive. It simply produced a reaction all out of proportion to the event without any corresponding improvement of behavior. I found that the lightest swat was the most he could stand, and usually it was better simply to put him in a corner or otherwise separate him.

If you can say that your child is well behaved without spanking, then all the best to you. You are doing a great job, and why fix something that isn't broken? But be honest. The people who advocate the soft, gentle, "Christ-centered," or otherwise spank-free approach very often have no children, have children who are brats, or have extremely compliant children, few in number and female in sex. (I feel bound to say, for the sake of warning you, that one so-called expert I know of who deplores strict discipline as unchristian is not trained in child psychology, nor, tellingly, according to a source who knew his family, did he have well behaved children.)

Also, please be aware that when I speak of spanking, I am speaking of training young children, no older than six. By the time the age of reason has dawned (usually around seven), the mother has failed if she must use corporal punishment to get results, and her failure will be that her children will laugh at her. A father can administer a spank for another year or so but should be wary of doing so. (My husband would never spank our girls once they got to be about three, sometimes to my chagrin, but later I saw his point.)

By spanking, I mean the force necessary, applied to the child's rear end, to make him pay attention. Honestly, for the most part, this is minimal. My husband often would demonstrate the truth of his assertion that the same swat offered in jest produced shrieks of laughter!

In his words:

Many people think of spanking in terms of causing real pain and even maybe injury. Not right. With all our kids, I played the game where I'd chase them and, when I caught them, whap them on the (diapered) bottom, harder actually than when I spanked them for disciplinary purposes. They thought this was great fun! The physical pain of spanking is not going to cause trauma (unless the parent loses control); it's the rebuke that hurts.

If the infraction is serious and the point isn't being made, sometimes it's worth it to administer the blow to a bare bottom. You are aiming for the stinging reality check! Never, in all our years of child raising, did I or my husband ever produce a mark of anything more serious than redness.

But really, most children are sturdy little imps bent on making mischief and behaving most uncivilly. No amount of cajoling or pleading will have the least effect, whereas spanking is a ready wake-up call to the person whose sense of the dimension of time and place are very limited.

A spank is a coming up against the wall of reality to the disassociated, limit-free creature whose capacity to take in information delivered verbally is very low. And it is also the liberation of the word-bound; the way out of the maze of the enabling, whining-prone, and hardly effective flow of words that a child quickly learns to harness to his own ends.

The parent who is tempted to talk a child into behavior should really try to enter his world. If you can, try to remember what things looked like to you in your earliest memories. You were desperately trying to figure out relationships and facts of the most elementary kind! Even the shapes of things seemed dim.

To a little child trying to assimilate all the information the world is hurling at him, the additional burden of a heap of explanations poured onto his head is quite unjust. Viewed from the point of view of a toddler, even being put in time out can seem pointless, and it certainly is pointless to be struggling with him over *staying put* in time out, with the reason for his being there in the first place long forgotten.

Far better to have the firm grasp of a hard fact—"I really shouldn't push the baby"—incontrovertibly presented—"or I'll get a spanking." Words are joined to this reality, but as a conclusion, not as a proposition. To him, this is freedom! Of course he cries; it hurts to be rebuked. But he gets it. And usually he's not the little shrinking flower you think he is. No, he's quite resilient and happier than otherwise to be given a positive direction to take his life in from now on.

A little older, and you see open defiance set in. Here, if swift retribution is not made, life will become hellish, because, just as it's easier to cut down a sapling than a full-grown oak, so it's easier to spank a sassy five-year-old than to convince a thirteen-year-old to have respect. The first time, you explain that while that snappy answer may be something he has overheard, it is disrespectful. The second time, he gets *reality feedback*. When a child is choosing his own will over your fairly and clearly expressed direction, he needs to learn obedience.

Here is when the argument from the opposition comes in, that one must explain and convince, not spank. As verbal as I am, and as important as I think words are, I must warn the unsuspecting parent against the trap of becoming an *enabler* of bad behavior.

This syndrome occurs when, through a reluctance to drive home one's point with a smack on the bottom, one endlessly explains. (Or one endlessly tries to impose time out.) But you do realize, don't you, that endless explanations don't hurt? They bore, they exasperate, they incite further misbehavior, but they do not represent a move on your part that is costly enough to the child to make him prefer to change his behavior rather than risk it again. In fact, he can keep you going for a good long while just by making you talk! And that puts him in control. And that means you are not disciplining.

A spank transcends all the talk. It also tends to be self-eliminating, once committed to; in other words, the effectively spanking parent spanks rarely.

Let's say, for instance, that you have told your five-year-old that you don't like a particular form of footwear popular with young people because you think it inhibits their free movement and could lead to fungal infections. You might be wrong (you don't say that), but that's your standard. There; now you, the authority in the matter, have explained it.

Once I overheard the following conversation at a yard sale.

FIVE-YEAR-OLD. "Daddy, can I get these jellies?" [Jellies were plastic
shoes that came in exciting colors and cute shapes. I didn't let
my kids wear them either.]
DAD. "No, I don't allow jellies. You know that. You know I think
they aren't good for growing feet and could give you bad
infections."
FIVE-YEAR-OLD. But, Daddy, they are pretty."
DAD. "No, you know I don't allow jellies."
FIVE-YEAR-OLD. Daddy, they are so cheap! They are only a dollar!
Please can I have them?"

At this point Daddy, truth to tell, is absorbed in all the bargains and
is hardly listening. Yet, he can continue to enable, with a patience that
would surprise a saint.

DAD. "No, honey, I don't allow jellies; they aren't good for your feet."
FIVE-YEAR-OLD (voice rises and becomes quite whiny). "But Daddy,
all the other girls have them, and these are so pretty, and they
are so cheap!"
DAD. "No, honey."

I followed them around, surreptitiously, in amazement, to see how
long they could keep it up. It was a long time. It hardly ended even as they
were leaving. They could still be at it, twenty-five years later, for all I know.

Now, on the one hand, he didn't give in. So, a point for him. And he
gave his reasons, so there's another point. But do you see that the devil got
about a thousand points for this exchange, because the dad arranged things
so that his daughter wasn't convinced that she should stop asking? He must
also have given in to her in the past, because she seemed to think she had
a chance! And his words weren't meaningful to her; they were like a boring, annoying game that you can't help playing but wish you didn't have to.

What should he have done? Well, he should have, at the second query,
looked at her squarely and said, "I've told you my reasons. You might not
understand them, but that's okay. Stop asking me, or you will get a spanking."

And then, if she continued, he should have taken her home and spanked her! Yes, he would have missed the sale!

That way, the next time, she would stop bugging him with the knowledge that not only did he have a good reason for what he said, but he would insist that she accept it, even at a cost to himself. He would probably never have to spank her for that kind of infraction again. He probably would not have had to spank her at that moment, but the availability of the disciplinary tool would have made him cut things short.

When she was fifteen and wanting to go to a bad concert with sketchy friends, the two of them would have her lifetime's worth of these episodes to fall back on. She would already trust him enough to take care of her. His work would be easy by then. With his way, the endlessly talking way, he has only trouble ahead with the bad habits he has given this child.

Please use common sense and your bond with your child to understand how to discipline him. A child who is tired beyond caring can't be spanked. A child who has gotten into a lot of trouble recently might just need some quiet time next to you on the sofa with a book. A child who really isn't aware of his actions can't be spanked!

Once, as a small child, my husband was surprised when his parents came down the basement stairs to see what the noise was. There he stood, a broken ketchup bottle at his feet.

"Why did you break that bottle?" they asked.

"I wanted to see if it bounced!" came the reply. Well, they did what should be done: they laughed!

But you know when your child is facing off with you, when he's testing you, when he has pushed the limits. You know when you are choosing his good — his safety, his well-being, his need for a good habit, his pressing need to learn obedience — over his self-will. And at that moment, a good spanking can make a world of difference.

So here are some areas of free and frank discussion for spouses, keeping in mind the ages of the children:

1. *Are our children brats?* I must say that I have observed people who seem unshakably convinced that the answer is yes, when their children are only

behaving according to their age. It's normal for a three-year-old not to remember to say "thank you," for instance. Be patient. However, you must ask yourselves: Do others seem to enjoy having them around? Do they routinely destroy property, ours and others'? Are their voices routinely not suited to the occasion or venue? Do they have situational awareness appropriate to their age? When we are not present, can we be confident that they have been pleasant company?

2. *Do our children promptly obey us and other figures of authority?* Do we project calm authority, or are we often frantic or oblivious? How does someone project calm authority? If we thought of our family as a sort of pack, what would it mean to be the alpha pair in that pack? Who is, currently, the alpha in *our* pack?

3. *What in our past prevents us from addressing these problems realistically?* Is it fair to handicap our children (for lacking the virtue of self-control is the worst handicap a child can have) because of our problems? How can we become objective about our children's needs and detached from our own reactions?

4. *What will be the most effective form of discipline with the particular child under discussion?* How does it differ from another child's? What have we observed to be the most effective? What doesn't seem to work? Why?

5. *Are we willing to devote, say, one week to forming or reforming this child's attitude regarding obedience?* That is, can we block off time to concentrate on this and avoid a lack of follow-through? What further study will we need to do this?

Read Hebrews 12:6–11 together and lovingly discuss it. Call to mind that each person has a guardian angel to whom we have recourse. Pray for wisdom!

More on Threatening

By the way, I have nothing against threatening per se. The threat has to be immediate, though. "Do that again and I'll have to feed you to the goldfish" or "That toy is going on a high shelf not to be seen for a week if you don't cut out the throwing," *not* "You won't be able to go to the drive-in with your cousins next week." The former are the threats of a person in control. The latter is the threat of a lazy weakling who will live to regret her words if she should remember them, which she won't.

I once had to apologize to my neighbor when I realized that she could hear me saying stuff like the former (only for me it was "I will tear off your arms and feed them to you"). One evening, I heard my neighbors' car pull into their driveway, which was right outside my window. It was pretty late, the night was still, and I was suddenly aware of the amazingly silent way they shut their car doors instead of slamming them, and the low voices with which they said the kinds of things you say to one another as you are going into the house; only if you are we, you shout them.

Suddenly I became conscious—with that acute consciousness that comes only with a shifting point of view—of just how noisy we all were (and how inconsiderate that really is). I hadn't known only because she was so quiet and never said anything to her kids above a whisper in her air-conditioned house, while our windows were wide open with me yelling juicy threats at the top of my lungs.

I had to tell her that if she heard me saying anything like "One more word out of you and I'll knock you into next week" (a favorite saying passed down from my grandmother), she wasn't to think that any violence was actually transpiring.

"Oh, no," she lied. "We never hear anything!" Now you can understand why I had to move to a house in the country.

Are we all clear? Adapt according to your style and the child's age. Try to use your common sense.

ASK AUNTIE LEILA

The Cranky Two-Year-Old

Dear Auntie Leila,

I asked my almost-three-year-old to take her shoes off (easy, slip-on, no-hands-required shoes). Her response: "I don't want to."

"I didn't ask if you wanted to. I asked you to please take your shoes off."

She then wandered around, very pointedly *not* taking shoes off. I knew she was tired and getting cranky. We were one Hail Mary away from her nap.

What do I do here? Do I just give her a pass because the reason for her obstinacy is so clear (she's tired!) and because she's usually such a well behaved girl? Do I push it, knowing she'll end in tears because she's tired and cranky?

Obviously, at some point, she's going to have to learn to overcome her personal discomfort (sleepiness, crankiness, or what have you) for limited amounts of time in order to keep the train on the tracks, especially when those tracks are leading *straight to the solution* to the discomfort.

Or we're setting the table for supper. Hands are washed, plates are dished up, the baby's in the high chair, and the twins are doing their before-dinner chore of helping Mama set the table (napkins, utensils, salt and pepper). One of the girls appears at the door to the kitchen and refuses to take the napkin from my hand to walk five feet over to the table to put it at Daddy's place.

I am usually good about keeping meals on the early side, and before-nap times on the low-key side. But sometimes the fates just conspire against me and give me one cranky, petulant two-year-old who acts as if she needs a spanking—only, she's usually so good, so well behaved, so sweet, so compliant, so willing to help out, so willing to sing sweetly and play with her sisters.

How would you handle this?

Catharina

Dear Catharina,

First, let me commend you on having what certainly sounds like an orderly, happy household, which is no mean feat with this number of littles. My hat is off to you.

Your situation will be *even better* by being able to say yes to the question, "Do you know what to expect of a two-year-old?"

You are immersed in their world, and they are responsive and good; this can cause your perspective to be a tiny bit off, even though you are doing a great job—a job so good that most moms would envy you!

I remember feeling this way. At every stage of his life, I felt that my eldest was just as old as he could be! I look back and wish I had been a bit ... kinder.

You are expecting a lot. And usually getting it. But you may be forgetting that children are made to be naughty. They will never be good all the time, and if they are, something is awry, really. Although it makes life a bit difficult, we do want them to stretch their behavioral muscles.

So I would hope to handle it by trying not to get myself into a losing situation with a two-year-old and often, of course, failing. It takes practice to do while not letting them sense that they have a certain power over you because you want to avoid conflict. You have to be smart and use your common sense.

It's not good to give in out of laziness or weakness, but it's okay to be wiser than a two-year-old—to know when a power struggle will not help anything.

You are building good habits with your children, little by little. It takes time. You are nowhere near the stage where this child can have reliable self-control to overcome physical and developmental realities to obey you. It's when something seems so reasonable to you and she just won't do it that you become frustrated!

But as we know in a theoretical way, reason is not a two-year-old thing.

So in the shoe situation, either just move on because it probably doesn't matter, or scoop her up, take the shoes off, and say, "Oh, yes, Mommy, those shoes go here!" and put them where you want them to be (direct her attention to the next step in the process, not the one you are both stuck on).

When you find yourself saying to yourself, "Oops, that was asking too much," be as gracious as you would to your husband or your best friend and try to help her out of the situation. You could even say, "Oops, that was too much, right?"

Next time when it's getting toward nap time, do a lot for her, because independent toddlers can use being babied a little more (just as babyish toddlers can use a little intentional detachment).

In the napkin scenario, you could do one of a bunch of things. Don't make a big thing of every little issue.

1. You could make a joke (if you are sure it won't frustrate)—"Oh, too hungry to carry a heavy napkin!"—not in a mocking way, but in a light and humorous way.
2. Just say "take it" with a little warning swat on the diaper and then get your attention off her.
3. You could get the baby to do it.
4. You could scoop her *and* the napkin up and carry both over to Daddy (or his place).
5. You could wink at your husband (if he's there) to ask for the napkin in a quiet, deep voice. (This is actually the best, because

Mom gets tired of always disciplining. Develop the code with your husband at some point so that a wink or nod alerts him.)

6. You could ignore her for a bit and see what happens. Sometimes a little child knows he can push a button, and if nothing happens, he sees what would happen if he did it after all. And then you can be quietly approving.

7. You could just skip it. In a few minutes you could just put the napkin in its place yourself and carry on.

Of course, you wouldn't be giving in. You would be choosing not to enter into the two-year-old world. You become a bit remote, very high up—not down there at her level, battling it out.

Not everything is a confrontation, and you are not raising an automaton. There will be other opportunities. And a little naughtiness is to be expected. I'm glad you have a sense of humor! It will serve you well.

It doesn't matter, I think, because if she's obeying most of the time, you are on the right track. I wouldn't say this for a five-year-old necessarily, but two is very young.

ASK AUNTIE LEILA

"I Don't Want to Be 'Yelling, Screaming, Crazy Mom'"

Sadly, it seems that the people who just won't discipline their children aren't going to be the ones to ask advice. Too bad, because when I see them at the store, I'd really like to give them a piece of my mind. Or hand them a parenting book. Or make them read my blog!

Instead, we seem to be having an epidemic of lovely, earnest book- and blog-reading moms who are maybe a wee bit ... serious ... when it comes to their children. They need a heavy dose of SOH (sense of humor) and perhaps a dash of POV (point of view), not to mention a bit of SWIM-KIPYNPE (so what if my kid isn't perfect; you're not perfect either).

My heart truly goes out to you, my friends, because you are such over-thinkers that you are putting a mountain of cares on your little children's shoulders! Relax! Enjoy! It's all so good ...

Following is a note from dear Anne.

My three-and-a-half-year-old and I are in a power battle currently. He is my only gift from God (and it looks as if he will always be my only), and I feel as if I am "doing it wrong." He told me the other night when I asked him why he was being naughty that he was just "an evil, evil boy."

My husband and I were older when we had him, and I don't know what I'm doing in the mothering department. I feel over-whelmed. He's a very smart, verbal little guy. He's surrounded by adults, and I feel as if I expect him to entertain himself too much while we do the necessary stuff of running the house. I think I expect too much of him, that I yell too much, and that he and I are both missing his childhood. I read your post on threatening, and that is me. I do take away stuff or threaten to take stuff away (unfortunately I usually do end up removing privileges), and I hate it. I hate being "mean mom." I want to be "loving, nurturing mom," not "yelling, screaming, crazy mom." Help!

Dear Anne,

Do not fear. All will be well — not because I'm such a font of wisdom (I'm not, and I don't know you, and I haven't seen you in action) but because God is good, and He will not fail to help you if you ask Him.

1. *Start praying to your boy's guardian angel every day to help you know how to love him in just the right way.* When you pray for your child, first, you gain the peace that even your mistakes will be made into something beautiful by God. Second, little by little, you will find the answers you need for him. It might take a while, but you will find them.

Angels are very practical. They are not the airy-fairy beings we think of. They are God's messengers to us to help us with the nitty-gritty of our interactions with each other and with the physical and spiritual world. Learn to depend on your child's angel. Ask your own angel to help you remember this.

Also, if you are Catholic, make good use of the sacrament of Reconciliation in this matter. The priest, in the person of Our Lord, will help you see that you must just be patient, because a little child will always be naughty. This is normal.

2. *Stop threatening.* Don't put things in overtly moral terms. Just say "naughty," not "bad"; and say "cut it out" or "stop that obnoxious noise," not "that is evil" or even "nasty." If you must say no, mean it, wait, get a result, and move on.

3. *Realize that your son needs a lot of physical activity.* Many mothers forget that their toddlers should be running around in the fields all day chasing the dogs and each other.

When one is older and more tired and there aren't siblings to keep each other busy, this becomes the mother's task, sadly for her need to rest. When my eldest son was this age (and only had his baby sister, and I was pregnant), we went to the playground every single day!

Swimming lessons, getting together with friends with little boys who are active, even long walks—schedule your week so that your priority is that he has at least two hours of physical activity a day. Yes, one way or another! Shove him outdoors in the rain with a bucket, set him to digging a hole, get him to move wood from one pile to another.

One of the very best things I've seen was a sandbox one father made for his boys. It was a veritable shallow pit in his yard the size of about four of what most of us think of as sandboxes. There were a ton of trucks out there, and army men, and all sorts of things. I wished I had seen it about fifteen years earlier!

Do not let your son be bored. A kid with five siblings can be bored—it's good for him—but an only child has too many opportunities to zone out, and it's not healthy.

4. *Observe your son, and try to find out what makes him feel loved—what makes his face relax, what makes you both feel relaxed.* How about reading out loud with your arm around him? Make sure you read old and traditional books. Nursery rhymes and simple fairy tales are best, because they help a child make sense of the puzzling adult world they are forced to deal with.

Does he need to wake up with a cuddle? Does he need a hug at bedtime? Does he like walking in between you and your husband, swinging arms? How about telling him what a precious gift he is, how happy he makes you? How about cutting his sandwich in a sailboat shape? How about just diagonally? Could you do that? It's amazing how happy a three-year-old can be made just by having his sandwich cut diagonally. Somehow it just says "I love you" to him.

My dear mother-in-law once confessed to me that all my husband ever wanted was to have his sandwich cut diagonally, but "I was just too busy to do it!" She didn't really say that with any irony. I certainly don't blame her, as I too did not give my children their heart's desire.

I remember my father telling me over and over, "You are the apple of my eye, you are the whole world and everything in it!" It's like a song; you just keep singing it! You don't have to be sentimental as you sing it … you don't have to be able to picture the stars as God's daisy chain, if you Wodehouse fans know what I mean. You don't even have to be a particularly good parent to say it. You just have to say it in a moderately nice voice every once in a while.

5. *Find a person who has a reasonable relationship with her little boy and try to imitate her.* Watch your friend pat her son as he runs by or give him a quick smack with no words if he is doing something he knows he shouldn't but isn't a big deal. Make friends with people who are good parents and learn from them. Use your hands to get him to where you want him to be; don't verbalize every thought you have about your child's behavior. Smile at him with your eyes. Enjoy him! All will be well.

Less Exasperated, or Two Rules That Might Help

Want to be a little less exasperated with your gaggle of small children? Two little rules that might help, given in the spirit of "Do what you want, but notice that feeling of sinking under it all, and do something about it."

I know that you don't ever want to squash your darlings' creativity, their sense of control over their lives, and their general expressiveness. (Or you might not have thought about it and simply received this child-rearing philosophy without examining it.)

And I myself endorse all sorts of methods of child-rearing that encourage independence and a can-do attitude. But if you want a tiny bit more sanity and think that you yourself might benefit from not, in fact, spending your every day mopping up apple juice, finding out you have no blueberries for that cake, wondering what the goo is on the condiment shelf, extricating your kids from their eleventieth game of Angry Birds, wondering why they don't read, and generally feeling like a martyr, may I suggest two little rules that proved invaluable for my life with many children?

1. The refrigerator must not be opened without your permission.
2. No electronic device may be turned on without your permission. (This rule used to read: No turning on the TV without permission, but I recognize that things have gotten way, way more complicated, with months-old infants more tech-savvy than many adults. Make the rule as universal as possible.)

Whom do these rules apply to?

As a default, until proven otherwise, anyone under the age of sixteen.

No, but seriously, it is madness, utter madness, to have your five young children given free range over the foodstuffs. No wonder you are a crazy woman.

Some day (hopefully soon), when everyone has internalized the reality of the forbidden zone that is the fridge, you will find yourself with a helpful child who can pour liquids without spilling them.

It's not necessary, contrary to what you may think, to spill liquids every single day, sometimes multiple times a day, to get to the competent stage. (They are welcome to do most of their spilling at the sand table, in the pool, and with the bean game.)

Things spill. That we know. You will handle spills with much less exasperation if they aren't built into your day because the children are viewing the fridge as their own personal playground.

Likewise those things with buttons. It is simply much, much easier, though perhaps painful at the time, to put in the week that it will take you to undo a bad habit, or the day to instill a new good one, than to spend all day, every day, yelling "Turn that [computer, phone, iPad, TV, what have you] off! Read something!"

Here's how it works—how it worked for me, someone who would probably be okay with your doing whatever you like as long as I can finish the chapter of the book I'm reading. The toddler turns the thing on, no doubt because you failed to park it or its remote in the designated, inaccessible place, so also think about that.

You gasp and say, "Oh, no, Mommy has to say if you may do this. Say 'Please may I turn it on?'" Then, when this has been said, respond with "No, not now. Mommy will tell you when."

If something goes on without your permission, instantly pounce and administer the punishment (whatever is warranted to the degree of intent, foreknowledge, disobedience, and outright defiance). It may be that you simply put it on a shelf they can't reach. It may be that they get a spank. Depends. Use your God-given smarts and authority.

Be consistent. Make sure that everyone knows that these things don't just go on or open for no reason.

After, as I say, a week (if this is already a problem), you will experience the peaceable fruit of justice. Your children will have tested your resolve; you will have stood firm. They will have explored your weakness, your tiredness, your laziness, your lack of willingness to set the nursing baby down for a second, and your softness, and they will have reached the limits; this is good for them.

Do not give in. It's worth taking the baby off the breast for the time it takes to sort things out. This part will last only a day or two, and then you will never have to revisit. Baby will nurse blissfully forever after.

At that point, the turning on of an entertainment device becomes an act, rather than something *against which you react*. See?

This is how you teach self-control to little ones. First you impose it with great firmness and determination, due to your conviction that the greater common good will be served. Then you all enjoy the fruits, and then you find that it's their habit too—one that they teach to the younger children!

You have to do it only once!

All this applies to food as well. Where the electronics issue results in mental fallout, the food issue results in material fallout, and having a tidier kitchen and cleaner furniture is going to be its own reward. In addition, you will find that the children are hungrier at mealtimes and designated snack times, which is healthier for them.

But, Auntie Leila, can they never do those things for themselves?

Of course they can! They will ask you!

"Mom," your five-year-old politely requests, "can we have some of those yummy snacks on the plate in the fridge?" (Because she saw you put them there and indeed probably helped you make them.)

"Yes, my precious darling child, in a few minutes you can get them out for your sister and brother. Put them on the table for us when it's time—I'll let you know."

"Mom, can we eat that chicken for lunch?"

"No, my delightful offspring, I'm saving that for our Caesar chicken salad tonight. We'll have that tuna instead."

You will progress to *requesting* that they open the fridge! "Young one, fetch us the watermelon. We'll have it on the porch."

See? Civilized.

You may even find yourself graduating from jam all over the vegetable drawers to shelves with designated foodstuff categories—ones that bring joy to all who behold them. (I kid, but you know when the fridge is organized versus rummaged in and grubby? It's quite nice.)

You will notice your children reading, working on their schoolwork, and making up their own sweet games (often, sadly, Angry Bird–style games, but at least using actual three-dimensional objects that they hold in their hands). Things will run more smoothly.

Toilet-Training Observations

Children who are developmentally ready or preparing to toilet train often delve deep into tactile play—for instance, running their hands through a bin of dry beans and pouring them from jar to jar, enjoying using a funnel, entranced by a small pitcher and a bowl. You will also find that they begin to show interest in lining up their toys—you may come upon nice rows of Matchbox cars or dominoes laid out just so.

Certain folk tales help them with the toilet-training stage as well. Maybe someday I'll write a dissertation on the hidden meaning of "The Three Little Pigs" and its importance in the child's subconscious.

Think about it: The house is a classic symbol for the body, and the pigs must exert an ever-greater effort (represented by the three attempts to build an "un-blow-downable" house) to master the control necessary over the bowels.

Once you see it this way, every time you read the tale you will understand the appeal—not only the big bad wolf going down the "chimney" (narrow passage) into the "pot" (need I say more?) but even the necessity of each pig dying before the last one lives triumphantly in his new-found state of self-control. He doesn't mourn his "brothers" because the subconscious recognizes them as symbols of his past selves, the incompetent ones whose demise is welcome so that his new, better self can emerge with mastery.

Let this be a lesson to you in meddling with time-tested stories. We take for granted the skills we have used for years; we have simply forgotten how difficult it was to attain them. But we're robbing our children of valuable tools in the fight when we abandon the collective memory in favor of some bland doctrine of niceness or anti-violence that is utterly irrelevant to the situation.

Even whimsical riffs on "The Three Little Pigs" might be amusing to adults, but they simply aren't satisfying to that three-year-old struggling with his baby self. Save them for the five-year-olds who know the original well!

Our three-year-olds need this traditional story read to them over and over (and it's so simple that you can memorize it and tell it as you are driving or holding hands while walking).

And break out the red lentils and funnel.

ASK AUNTIE LEILA

My Three-Year-Old Won't Nap

Dear Auntie Leila,

I have a very difficult time getting my almost-three-year-old to nap, despite routines and schedules.

I've tried giving up the nap for her. She cannot keep herself together, though, and usually starts falling apart around 4:00 p.m. By that point, she is rubbing her eyes, falling over things, and just crying and screaming for me to hold her (even if she is in my arms). She even starts nodding off if we are doing an activity or during dinner. It feels so stressful for me.

I have tried "quiet time" without the pressure of sleeping.

She screams loud enough to wake up the baby—even when I am lying down with her. My husband tells me to just go with the flow. I want to have routine for my family. I think that it is evident that she needs the midday rest. On the days when she naps, life goes smoother—we are able to make it through the day mostly happy and productively. We can have some family time in the evenings with

Dad upon his return from work. Without the nap, dinner becomes a stressful event, and we rush through our meal to get her to bed.

My husband and I have been talking at length about our parenting. It is difficult to balance mercy with teaching obedience. I think we probably gave my daughter too much "authority" in the beginning based on a parenting philosophy we were following at the time. We are now trying to make decisions together, as husband and wife. I just wonder if that is what is making our current situation difficult.

I would be grateful for any insights!

Lauren

Dear Lauren,

I have two practical thoughts for you, but first a quick word about the larger issues of child development and how we approach, in general, life's little problems.

Developmental Phases

When the eldest child turns three, it's a new phase for the whole family. Different folks come to this realization at different points, but basically, it's a little scary to realize that here is a person with definite likes and dislikes as well as the power—let's not kid ourselves—to turn life upside down.

Why did we let ourselves in for this?

Did you know that just as children enter new stages of development, so do parents? Why doesn't anyone give us a heads-up, instead of making it sound as if we should know everything already?

Why don't they refer to "The terrible parents of twos" or "Meltdown when the kids get into college" or "Stop spitting when you say, 'What? What? *Where* are you going?'"

Who says we know what's coming next or how to deal with it? Even on the front page of the *New York Times* there is utter cluelessness about who is responsible when your kids get mean texts (hint: you and the other parents—not the school, and not the government; and further hint: a twelve-year-old doesn't need to be able to receive or send texts—no, not even from the coach—but I digress).

It's like mass amnesia—people haven't the faintest idea what to do next because they don't know who they are or how they got here! We're learning as we're going. Somehow the older generation lost its will to pass on wisdom, and in fact, things get more complicated as time goes on, not less.

Have you ever heard mothers wishing aloud for the time when they could solve their child's problems by changing a diaper? Well, listen to me and my friends. "I wish I could just change a diaper." There you have it.

And just as a child often responds negatively to the various physical and emotional stresses brought on by having to grow, so parents have to struggle to widen their experience; and that growth process is often difficult, alas. The reason, of course, is that we have fallen natures—we don't unfold in our development like a puppy or a vine!

Even the growth of a child, whom we think of as so innocent and untouched by the shadow of the world, is fraught with frustration and pain. How much more do we tainted adults have challenges that are met with tears rather than the smooth perfection we seem to expect (against all experience)!

Expect Imperfection

The sooner you learn that frustration is part of the process, the happier you will be. You'll come to *expect* that sinking-drowning-choking feeling of not knowing what to do (and needing a nap), rather than falling into the steel-toothed, razor-edged, double-whammy trap of wondering why things can't be perfect.

Do you want to know what your own worst enemy (and mine) is?

Thinking things should be perfect.

Being upset when things are not perfect, because momentarily we lost sight of the fact that we are human beings who got kicked out of Eden long ago. We're on our journey home. We are not there yet!

All this to say that little human beings between the ages of two and three, four if you're lucky, do give up the afternoon nap.

What it took me a long time to realize (about this and other things) is that it's not as if one day they nap and the next day they've given it up for good. No, there is a transition where maybe four days (not in a row) they need a nap and then the other three they don't, and this lasts for weeks or months. They want to be little on some days and big on other days. Some days are tiring, others, less so.

Little babies need naps every day, and so do moms! So what to do when the toddler is off and on?

Oh, it can be very tiring!

As I read your question, I see that you have been trying the things I would suggest. And of course I can't tell what kind of personality your child has. Is she generally compliant? Is she strong-willed? You have to take what I say with *what she's like* in mind.

There are two main areas to look at. Physically, she may be ready for less napping, even though it results in a "tired day," and there are remedies for that. Emotionally, she is trying to establish independence from you, and this is a very good thing, although it can feel like disobedience or that you are losing control.

Physically

A child who doesn't take a nap must go to bed much earlier and must eat much earlier. I found it helpful to have a 3:00 or 4:00 p.m. "tea" (cheese, crackers, fruit, and milk; a bowl of oatmeal; a small plate of yesterday's leftovers; grilled cheese … something easy for you but filling for her). Let her help you put it on her own little table on a little plate.

Active toddlers and small children generally eat more for breakfast and lunch and less toward the end of the day, which is the opposite of how adults (in our country) eat, and they are happier that way. Try it. (Look at the total number of calories a day, rather than eating a certain amount at a certain meal. Some young children — I have had a couple — eat two breakfasts, a big lunch, and no supper! That just feels wrong! But it works for them.)

Then comes a little playing while you get supper ready for Dad, story time, a walk with the baby in a stroller, or whatever you want to do from, let's say, 4:00 to 5:00, then a nice long bath with plenty of play time, clean pajamas, and in bed by 6:30 or whatever is around an hour or so earlier than her normal bedtime. (You will have to be on top of what's for dinner, and that information is in volume 3 of this work.)

Your daughter can sit with you for the meal but probably won't eat much, if anything, and that's fine. Let her eat a piece of bread or whatever she wants, or nothing, and just enjoy your own time. Don't stress through dinner with a tired toddler! Someday she'll be more able to appreciate family time.

You can try the bath first and then the small meal. The only thing is that if she gets a second wind, she'll probably need another bath!

If she takes a nap on a certain day, you can follow your old regular schedule and keep her up a little later. As you do with the food, taking into account the total amount eaten all day, look at the total number of hours of sleep in a given day. If there is nothing in the afternoon, you make it up with an early bedtime. But don't make the mistake of missing her sleepy time—it's all more about when the sleepy times are than what the clock says, and the horrifying fact is that if you miss the sleepy time, you are in for another three hours of misery until another sleepy time comes around.

If lying down with your toddler at naptime works for both of you, that's fine.

Emotionally

But maybe for this toddler, *not lying down with you* is her way of expressing her desire to be a bit more on her own, which is the emotional side of the problem, and this is the goal, you know, though it seems difficult as you go through the process. The goal is that she do what she needs to do, for herself.

Yes, there is no way she should be screaming and waking up the baby. That is so naughty. But in her own way, she is saying, "Mommy, I'm not a baby. I want to do my own thing. I have figured out how to disrupt everything, and I would rather you didn't let me do that, but I can't let go of needing not to be a baby."

The solution is to affirm the bigness while clearly not allowing the naughtiness. In other words, giving her an "out" by arranging things so that it's not a power struggle—so that you both get what you need.

How to do this requires thought and prayer.

The simplest way (but I think in your question, you are saying this doesn't work) is to say, "Baby's sleeping, Mommy desperately needs to put her head down for a few minutes. You listen to this story CD [twenty or thirty minutes], color in this book, play with this playdough, look at these books on your quilt spread out on the floor, play with your dollies . . . and when rest time is over, we'll do some other things."

Do not—do not—say, "If you are quiet for twenty minutes, I'll buy you a toy" or "if you are not quiet for twenty minutes, I won't buy you a toy" or any other if-then bribe or threat statement.

It's different to say, "Here's a fun thing you can do," such as playing with playdough, "and as long as you're quiet, you can have it."

Don't say (as I so often hear), "See, you're so tired and bad, you're going to have a nap."

I wouldn't take a nap if someone said that to me.

Just do what you need to do to distract her for half an hour; make naps or rest sound like the reward, not a punishment; or at a bare minimum, make the nap sound as if it's part of the system with no particular value judgment attached.

The thing is, if she doesn't nap when you've made it sound like the consequence of bad behavior, she'll feel as if she beat you, rather than that she missed out on a quiet peaceful time. You—not she—will have made it into a power struggle rather than what it is, a part of your day.

I highly recommend adopting a little "naptime song" that follows the "it's naptime" announcement so that the mood stays happy and not punishing. "Time to have a little nap; it's nap time, my little lamb," sung in a peaceful lullaby tone as you gently head away from the living area and toward the bed, creates a conditioned response of sleepiness. It's important to start the song before you pull away from whatever activity is going on.

Also, enlist her in the care of the baby. Have fun whispering and tiptoeing. Enjoy big-girl time. The two of you are a great baby-care team. You're on the same side. She loves the baby; she just doesn't want to *be* a baby. Except when she does.

Even if you think she needs a nap, by removing the power struggle, you leave it up to her. If she can relax enough, she will fall asleep, but if it's about controlling the time, she won't, and you will make up for it later (not without some little bumps on the road, but that's okay). Honestly, most three-year-olds do not nap! (It's a terrible prospect, I know!)

If the situation is beyond this, put the baby to bed and then do some work: making supper early, folding laundry, anything!—just powering on through for about an hour.

I'm assuming that the baby naps for at least two hours. Maybe in the second hour you can see how the rhythm and energy is going and take advantage of a quieter pace that the toddler is setting to be able to put your head down for a few minutes.

I don't know how you rest, but I strongly encourage you to develop the ability to nap sitting up with your head back on a pillow or just partially lying down on the sofa! Somehow going to bed is repugnant to most older children, even if it's you and not they who are going, but they can tolerate a nap—in this case, yours!—if you can just get it done on the sofa. And for you, the fifteen- to twenty-minute nap is far more productive than the two-hour under-the-covers marathon that leaves you groggy.

Stop the Screaming

The screaming thing has to be circumvented, and maybe it will take a week of no nap for you at all before the conditioning or habit is worked out. However, if she screams just to push your buttons and a week of trying different habits doesn't change that, you could tell her—*well before the episode begins*—"If you're going to scream for no reason, you will get a spanking. Or, if you feel like screaming, you can come give me a hug instead, and we'll be happy." You could even tell her to go outside and scream if you think a spank won't help. But then you have to deal with the neighbors.

Give her a chance to control herself (kindly, as if you know it's hard). If she doesn't, give her the spanking and then either let her alone or give her the hug, whichever calms her down. Certain children of my acquaintance had to be left alone for five or ten minutes before emerging from the emotional bind to accept the hug and snuggle. It didn't work to try it before the spanking worked itself out.

It seems as if it would help to talk to the child, but it won't. Have the insight to understand that she is indeed a person, not a machine with a reset button that's talk-activated.

Don't forget to take your iron so you can make it through this readjustment period without your nap!

Dear, dear Lauren, don't blame your previous parenting. This struggle happens to everyone. We are all on a developmental curve—until we die! It's part of the normal process of the change from baby to child—and from inexperienced parent to more experienced.

This child has places to go and things to do that you cannot imagine, and she has to have some say over her basic needs. You do know best, but you have to work *with* her on it, not against her. *Things' going smoothly* is not what gives us peace. Just doing what we should be doing with love is what gives us peace!

You are doing a wonderful job, being a committed mom to your little ones!

Lauren wrote back to me (Auntie Leila loves to know how it works out!):

Thank you, thank you!

This is the absolute best advice I have been given. You really "get it," and now I have some tangible ideas to try out. My Bella is so strong-willed—gets it from her Mama, which is probably why we are constantly at odds lately. I think I could stand to respect her as her own person more often (within reason, of course) and realize her need for "bigness."

This reason that you suggested—"emotionally, she is trying to establish independence from you, and this is a very good thing, although it can feel like disobedience or that you are losing control"—seems very accurate to our situation. In fact, this is exactly what it feels like for me: loss of control and disobedience. However, now I am realizing that this is not necessarily what this phase is about.

I am definitely going to try the early supper or snack idea; I think that this will help immensely. And I will set her up with some material on a soft quilt with pillows downstairs (away from the napping baby) while I lie on the couch with my feet up to rest and say my Rosary.

And, I feel validated now that you wrote that mommies needs naps too: I do hit a tired point during the day. My baby nurses every two to three hours during the night, and my daughter usually wakes once (sometimes twice), needing me to put her back. The morning seems to come so quickly. I can't help but feel tired around midday.

Leila, thank you so much for taking the time to respond and encourage me. I feel as though you truly understood my difficulty and gave me some practical ideas to work with. Thank you.

Thanks, Lauren! Oh yes, moms need naps!

ASK AUNTIE LEILA

The Difficult Five-Year-Old Boy

This chapter was written in response to what seems to be a veritable epidemic of boys out in the world who are misbehaving in a major way. The basic question I am receiving is as follows (I'm going to compress them into one, as this topic does seem to be of general interest):

Dear Auntie Leila,

My oldest child, a boy, is turning five. (Alternately, "My third child and first boy is almost five." Once in a while, "my daughter," but not usually.) My husband and I have been really frustrated with his behavior lately. I will try not to exaggerate, since he really is a sweet boy when he wants to be, but most of the time he is disobedient, disrespectful, untruthful, and getting into mischief that he should have been beyond getting into a long time ago. For example, I can't trust him to go to the bathroom on his own without getting into the toothpaste or unrolling all the toilet paper. The other day, left alone for ten minutes, he got into my makeup, drenched himself in my perfume, and used my eyeliner for war paint. These are the sorts of things his two younger brothers do when unsupervised, but I thought he was past that stage. He seems to be reverting.

When he misbehaves, we send him to his room or spank him.

The other day, he bit his baby sister, then argued with me about it, and then got a swat for the biting and arguing. Then he threw a temper tantrum because he got a swat, so he was sent to his room, and then he had the nerve to sneak around the corner and throw little rocks at me because he was mad about being punished for biting! Things will just keep escalating like this until he gets to a point where he's a sobbing little mess who needs to be picked up and cuddled because he has reached the pit of despair. Then he gets the talk about why what he did was wrong, and about making good decisions, et cetera, et cetera. He will sincerely apologize, and yet somehow, this never seems to deter him the next time. Next time means in five minutes!

I want to put him in front of the TV just to get a break. I am at my wits' end. I am worried about the effect of all this misbehavior on my other children!

Help!

Concerned, Desperate, et cetera, et cetera

Dear Concerned and Desperate,

Some little boys are naughty as a matter of course, and it all reaches a peak between the ages of four and five! As much as this is a developmental stage for the little blighter, it's one for you as well. You are leaving the stage of your life where you basically move toddlers through their day (or, if your older children are girls, have enjoyed a time of rather inward-directed energy) and into a somewhat frightening realm where the subjects are discovering that they are autonomous and they are going to make the most of it.

What worries you is that this child will be a delinquent, reports of whom will be passed among your friends on social media. You are sure you won't be around to read them, having expired from the effort required to manage him. You are beat.

But don't worry. Things will be all right! Your heedless five-year-old will be your strong and considerate seventeen-year-old. I realize it's a long row to hoe, but hopefully it helps to know that things get better! At any stage, always apply the first line of defense. No matter what the age (mothers of teens, take note!), no matter who the difficult person in question might be (mothers, it might be you!), make sure that they are getting enough sleep and enough food! Make sure the day is structured and has plenty of outdoor time and little or no screen time. Give him more breakfasts (two breakfasts for one kid is quite normal) and more rocks to break (meaning swimming lessons, moving wood, digging holes, and anything that tires him out!). He needs to reach maximum energy expenditure at least once every single day.

Give him lots of affection before the trouble starts. He's still a little kid! Give him a hug long enough to let him smell your mommy smell, kiss his naughty cheeks, hold his hand.

What I really want to talk to you about, though, is to make sure that you have the alpha roles well in hand in your family. When a child becomes demanding, it's all too easy to let him become the lynchpin of all activity, finding yourself referring everything to him and always checking to see that his reactions are okay. Even just making sure he behaves can cause all the energy in the family to revolve around him. You react, rather than act. Particularly act for his good, not out of distress over his naughtiness. Children are naughty! Take it more in stride.

Think of dogs. They are pack animals. The pups and every animal in the pack know who the alpha pair are—information that is conveyed by means of a complicated series of actions and signals. One important one: the alpha pair indicate their status above all by ignoring the non-alphas!

For instance, the other dogs run up to them and jump around—the alpha pair will make a big point of looking off into the distance or even just turning around. Dogs indicate their superior status by putting their heads on the necks of the "under" dogs. Those who work with pack animals observe that the underdogs immediately become calm once they know who the alphas are; they become anxious that *they* might be the alpha until they receive the information that they're not.

Since only certain animals are capable of being the alphas (or animals of a certain maturity), keeping things straight makes the others feel secure, and that security is reflected in their subsequent behavior, which becomes much more peaceful, once the ranks are established. How does this translate to human behavior in a family? It's important that you and your husband talk to each other without paying too much attention to the children—at least sometimes! It's important that you, the alpha pair, are taking care of business and not having things revolve around the children in the sense that you look at them as you do something, let them interrupt you, take care of them first, and so forth.

And certain children, more than others, need this structure to be clear.

Take care of the foundation—you and your husband. Sometimes (it isn't possible all the time, of course—all the more reason to make the effort at least once in a while), put him first, answer him first, ask him what he'd like, and so forth. And your husband should try, at least a good portion of the time, to show you the same deference.

Once that is cleared up, you can go on to the actual transgressions.

If your boy says something rude, you can just ignore him. Little by little, you can let him know that he has to speak appropriately. It's not necessary to react to every infraction! Whatever you do, do it swiftly. Don't let him wear you down. Either set him straight or let it go.

If he does something truly naughty, such as biting his sister, he should get a swift punishment that he knows he deserves because you have told him beforehand about it. There is no arguing. He bites; you say, "That was very naughty." He gets a spanking and goes to sit on the stairs. Let him cry and rant. Then when you decide, he comes down, and you have a hug and a very limited bit of soft conversation about how you know he is sorry and he must not be naughty like that again. If he won't sit on the stairs, then just a spanking is enough.

Five is on the older side to be biting. It might not be possible for you to deliver a strong enough message that the family is done with this behavior, so you can also just say, "Daddy is going to take care of this." Discuss it beforehand with your husband, and make sure that he's on board, that he will come home on the early side if you ask him, and, in general, that he will be the heavy. He should take it very seriously and very calmly—no ranting and very little talking. He can just say, "Son, I am disappointed that you did something so naughty. A big boy doesn't bite his little sister; it's dirty fighting. You are your sister's protector. Now come get your punishment." After the punishment, he should leave the little miscreant alone for about twenty minutes, after which he can give him a hug and go on without dwelling on it. Later, and completely unrelatedly, his father should tell him that he is proud of him for some good act toward his sister (perhaps somehow prompted for the occasion).

Growing up is, from the very first moments of birth, a process of separation and the realization that there are other people who have "selves" that must be taken care of.

Start cultivating a spirit of service in his little heart. He should do things for his sister, carry bags for you, open doors, help unload the dishwasher, and in general be your "big boy" who is so strong and does so much for you! Even if you have bigger boys, well, every boy needs to start working on being a big boy.

It isn't so much naughtiness that you should be working on as helping him to gain awareness of others and how he is affecting them. Wait before you react. If he says something disrespectful, wait. Let it sink in. Then calmly say, "That was disrespectful. Speak more respectfully."

Speak in a low voice and don't overreact. Be the alpha. Be far above him and look on him from your lofty height. Don't let him get under your skin! Don't argue, don't plead, don't get into dramas. Expect good behavior and quietly point out what is not good. (However, do not lose patience with yourself if you yell or otherwise feel that you have lost control. You are human, and it's fine for children to know the limits.)

I think that standing in a corner is a good punishment for this age. It can be in the room where you are. Just put him there and make him face the corner until you say he can get out. Let him know—let him hear—that life goes on without him. It's a good lesson.

Before you get together with others or go to the store or what have you, tell him simply and clearly how you expect him to behave. "I expect you to say hello Mrs. Smith, look her in the eye, and shake hands. Don't ask for food; only take out one toy at a time. I'm not going to correct you there, so I'm relying on you to do a good job and hold up the honor of our family." If necessary, practice shaking hands and so on.

Then, do *not* correct him there if at all possible.

Afterward, tell him that he did well with x or y or else that you were disappointed that he didn't shake hands or thank Mrs. Smith. The next time, let him know what to do beforehand the same way. Let him figure it out. Be ready to leave quickly if necessary. Don't always be correcting at the time—or even prompting. If you can, assume that he did say hello and thank you while you were otherwise occupied, because it can be demoralizing for him to be corrected for things he took care of.

Let him have some activities with other boys. They will provide healthy "reality feedback." Let them!

Also, be very sure that you are not speaking about him when he can hear. I have noticed moms commenting on their child's behavior—"John is behaving so badly today, and I don't know what to do with him! He's my challenging child." Saying this in the child's presence is highly destructive. I'm sure you don't do this.

Instead, give him hugs and cuddles—on your own terms. I like to say, be strict *and* warm!

If you hang in there, don't look to your child for affirmation, keep your standards, and don't get upset when things go wrong (at least most of the time—Auntie Leila knows that mistakes happen even in the best-regulated families), you will find that all will be well. Children go through stages, and your son is at the stage where he needs to start interacting with others and getting his rough edges rubbed off.

He is growing up, and that is a good thing; consider the alternative! The challenge is to guide him to a better place with all that energy!

51

ASK AUNTIE LEILA

Should I Use Affection as a Discipline Tool?

When you are reading parenting advice, advice not given to you by Auntie Leila, you need to ask yourself if you would like to be treated the way the expert is telling you to treat your child (or for that matter, your husband, but that's a different chapter).

Me, I'd rather be spanked (I mean, if I were a child), and get it over with, than be lectured incessantly. I'd rather be yelled at than handled with exasperated, barely controlled "patience" accompanied by a real sense that my company doesn't bring any joy, ever.

I don't like being manipulated. Do you?

Once I received a message from a lovely reader, obviously well inten-tioned, pleading for help with a messy slob of a husband who leaves his dirty socks everywhere and never puts anything away. She wrote, "I have cajoled and kissed when he remembers, I have left Post-it Note reminders, and, finally, I have had tantrums."

Another lovely reader, clearly as sweet as can be, was tearing her hair out with her unruly young (under-seven) brood. She told me, "I'm working on giving the older ones appropriate punishments and lots of extra affection when they behave. When they are being good, I hug them and tell them I love them. When they are not being good, I tell them why they are breaking the rules and ask them to repeat the rules to me; but it's not working. They just never listen to me at all."

Here is what I answered them:

You have your issues, and Auntie Leila understands that. These people, big and little, are truly driving you crazy.

However, the real issue is the sheer amount of nonsense that goes around in the guise of discipline (acquiring habits of virtue), when really, what is happening is the attempt to *control* behavior! Behavioral modification is one thing; maybe it's got its uses in psychology for such problems as fear of elevators or flying. But somehow, the ideas out there have been filtered into family life to the point of danger. Withholding affection? Bestowing affection as a reward?

Would we want to be treated this way?

Affection is a human need along the lines of shelter and food (well, actually, more important than those things); affection just can't be made a matter of negotiation or manipulation.

What parent doesn't give affection freely, just as he gives food and clothing? What wife or husband controls behavior with kisses?

So let's just give kisses and hugs all the time. Put your four-year-old on your lap if she's having trouble getting over that fallout over her eggs. If she can't pull it together, she might need to lie down on her bed.

I'm telling you this because I think some people don't know that a four-year-old needs to sit on your lap. And when you're frustrated with her, you are even less likely than ever to pick her up. Yet, it's what she needs! Your little boy too! More picking up!

Dads need this reminder too!

Give your six-year-old a snuggle when he's passing by, whether he's behaving or not.

Use your arms and hands and your cheeks more. If you have to give a punishment, let a little time go by so that the chemicals in the body can resettle and the mind can calm down, and then give a real, heartfelt hug and some kisses.

If events make you feel less than huggy or kissy, just explain the case. "I'm mad because you left a wet washcloth on the bed! What is this, a fraternity?" With a child, just be stern or strict or even angry ("You seriously left your bike out all night again?"), dole out whatever punishment is necessary, preferably not a vague and meaningless threat, and then as soon as you can, go back to being warm and affectionate.

Honestly, the problem is that the powers that be (those "experts") have removed all the truly effective tools. They have robbed you of the simple knowledge that you *are* the parent and that your authority matters.

They've deprived families of the disciplinary tools of spanking; letting Dad take care of it, whatever it is, when he gets home; yelling, which, although it's not ideal, has the merit of being real and locating you in that universe where you are human too (things won't crash to bits if you yell once in a while—you can work on your anger, but your kids can understand that they provoked you). Our experts make you feel like a failure if you yell! But any child would rather have a parent who yells occasionally (trying, of course, to avoid such displays of anger) than one whose hugs are conditional.

The experts have left us nothing but the psychologically damaging techniques. The tedious time-out dance of futility, the laughable reliance on reason (because we all know that a toddler wants nothing more than to hear your reasons and explanations and will surely heed them), isolation (not to a bedroom but to a small closet—this technique is used in schools *routinely* these days), and finally, most sadly, the use of feelings to manipulate. The idea of using affection as behavior modification is couched in positive terms: "Smile and say 'good job' or 'I love you' when your child meets your expectation," and that is bad enough; naturally this will devolve into failing to be affectionate, affirming, loving when the child has been naughty.

It is a cold way.

It's making the expression of your love contingent on the child's performance, which pretty much will always mean he won't get any love, because, in breaking news, children are often naughty (and husbands often forget to use the hamper).

Discipline and punishments and (in the case of husbands) serious communication are necessary parts of love! And affection is too. "God loves you, and I love you too. Nothing could make me stop loving you." Unconditional love means acting forthrightly for the person's good.

But after all, a naughty child is still your child. You just want behavior, but you don't realize a family expresses itself by means of affection! I personally prefer to be loved unconditionally! When *you* have been naughty, don't *you* still need a hug?

Warm and strict, when necessary, with the children, warm and angry with your husband. We all get mad, and that's just life. It's preferable, of course, to have a calm conversation to avoid misunderstandings and unpleasantness; it's not always realistic.

Let's just not weaponize affection.

Instead of Saying "Because I Said So"

There are so many things you say to your kids every day (and here again I'm talking about kids older than two or three):

"Please give the dog water."
"Why do I have to be the one to give him water? It's not my turn! Why me?"

"Please pick up your blankety-blank socks."
"Can you hand me that cup, please?"
"Why? Why do I have to get it for you? Why don't you ever ask anyone else to do anything, ever?"

"Get your sister out of the sandbox."
"Why? Why do I have to?"

"Let's eat."
"Why do I have to come in now? Everyone else is staying out! Why?"

On and on ... and you just can't explain each and every thing! Life would be perfect if everyone just did what you said (actually, it would be perfect if they did the stuff on their own without being told, since I really don't think anyone needs to be told that a dirty pair of socks doesn't belong in the den, for the love of all that is good and holy, but never mind that right now).

However, the fact is that these are human beings with a will. The goal is not to raise automatons or robots or martinets or soldiers or well trained pets. The goal is to raise thinking, kind, active human persons.

So here's a secret:

> Instead of endlessly explaining (and making that fatal mistake of allowing the argument to take over) ... *or* ...
>
> Instead of saying "Because I said so," which, though a phrase that gets tossed out sometimes, might give you that twinge of regret at (1) having conceded tacitly that it is a power struggle after all and (2) having committed a rudeness ...
>
> How about looking them in the eye and firmly saying,
>
> "Please go do what I said with prompt obedience, cheerfully, *and I'll tell you why when you get back.*"

It's frankly stunning how well this works.

Usually they go off and do the thing and completely forget they ever had an objection!

They don't bother coming back (after all, you did explain, with the patience of a whole legion of saints, ten times at least, why a dog will get sick and die if it doesn't have water, a fact that is nevertheless perfectly obvious to the meanest intelligence and doesn't need to be stated). Or, they cheerfully return to get a kiss! We aren't even a particularly kissy family, and I've been so surprised at this show of affection when I've insisted on prompt obedience! It turns their heart amazingly.

Occasionally the bitterness and sheer unfairness of being made to do something lingers. A child may come back and say, "Okay, I did it. Now tell me why!" That's the moment to give a hug and a kiss and the explanation (*one more time*) and then the much-needed morsel of food or that nap to sustain life in this dire form that presents itself to you.

In any case, you will have accomplished the goal, which is prompt obedience without endless questioning. A few times of saying, "Do it, and then I'll give you the reason," and the habit of prompt obedience will be instilled; you won't have to say it again. The goal will have been achieved in a way that affirms that it's not hearts of stone you want in your little ones, but hearts of flesh.

A note: sometimes "why" is a bid for interaction. You may also ask the child: "Why do you think so?" or just a cheerful, encouraging: "Go do it and then come tell *me* why!" Often, the child knows the answer, but he just wants to talk to you about it.

My Secret to Consistency in Discipline

We've talked a lot about discipline here, and one thing I have not addressed is consistency.

Believe me, I am very aware that it's hard to be consistent when you don't know what each day will bring, and besides, you never know how you are going to feel. Pregnant, nursing, hormonal—it's not easy to remember or be able to follow up with the predetermined punishments or even to know whether the punishment fits the crime.

Long ago, my husband and I figured out a simple way to ensure that we always maintain consistency in our approach with our children, and I think it has really paid off. The kids are grown now, and they are healthy and happy. Above all, they have self-control and rarely step out of line. There's no doubt that our method works, and now you are going to benefit from our vast experience.

It's simple. Here's what you do: every day at a predetermined time, just line the kids up and spank them all.

If you think about it, this is the way to go! Don't agree? Let's go over the benefits.

1. *No more wondering if they are doing anything wrong.* Okay, is this what's holding you back from adopting my elegant secret? Please. Obviously they will all have done, at minimum, one thing wrong at some point during the day. Can we just think about your kids for a minute? Or if you are in denial about your little darlings, just think about yourself at their age. Right. They will have done at least one naughty thing every day—enough to deserve a spanking. So just line them up and spank them.

2. *As I said, consistency.* Experts agree that it almost doesn't matter what standards parents apply, as long as the children know where they stand and can predict their behavior. So clearly, the more consistent you are, the better. What is more consistent than doling out a beating at 8:00 p.m. on the dot?

3. *Fairness.* A great thing here is that you won't have to inquire about who has done what. Just spank them all.

    What is the number-one issue on every kid's mind?

    How unfair you are.

    Do you see that this just takes care of that little problem completely?

4. *Conservation of energy.* Do you realize how much energy and sheer force of will it takes to sort out all the "he did this" and "she took that" claims that bombard you all day long? What are you, a judge? No. You are a tired-out shadow of your former self. If I were you, I wouldn't even spank them all myself. Do what I did, and wait for your husband to come home and handle it.

5. *Managing expectations.* When children know you will inquire into their every movement and action, they just come up with more movements and actions! They are naughtiness machines! This way, their incentive to keep you busy is low. They know they'll be spanked no matter what, so they will probably just leave it at one naughty thing and go about their business. It could be argued that careful sorting out of who did what actually increases naughtiness! So don't fall into that trap!

6. *Spanking reduction.* Yes! It's true! This method results in fewer punishments for most children! They will thank you because this way they only get one spank every day! Win-win!

NB: If you are against spanking, don't get your knickers into a twist! Just make them all sit on the stairs for thirty minutes, or send them to their rooms. A side benefit to this method is that it takes approximately thirty minutes to enjoy a nice cocktail before you have to put them to bed, so that works out well.

A further NB: The *preemptive spank* also has been shown to work. They always act up at church? Find it difficult to handle suppertime? Line them up for the preventative spank, and enjoy some peace!

The important thing is to punish them all at once and at the same time every day!

Okay, there you have it. Simple, effective, consistent!

(In case you have not yet caught on, I want you to know that this is all a joke; I wrote it on April Fool's Day one year. And yet ... No, just kidding!)

Dinner Together: The First Phase, with Young Children

You will remember that one of my rules for keeping your family together is to be sure to eat your meals together. Children at the table can seem like a challenging discipline problem. You need strategies to make your time together enjoyable. The following sections are aimed to give you the perspective you need.

Preparing for the Future Now

Let's get down to business with this dinner plan. We all know it's a good idea. Why is it so very hard?

I'm not necessarily the ideal person to give advice; I'd say I'm just the handiest, and that is all. For instance, once our first child (who shall remain nameless, as this is an embarrassing story, even if he was only one) was cutely wandering around the living room as we entertained a newly married couple. It was a hot Washington, D.C., night, and I thought it would be refreshing to serve a nice watermelon (neatly cut into bite-size pieces) as a starter while we waited for our leg of lamb to grill.

The lamb was taking a long time to cook, and the evening was wearing on. The couple gamely sat, with little other than watermelon to sustain them, chatting with us. The baby (who loved fruit) kept toddling up and eating watermelon. The lamb kept on not really cooking, even though I switched it to the oven, and kept cranking up the heat, and man, it was getting hotter in the kitchen.

I remember that we were maybe on a bit of a mission to convince this couple that having a baby was a wonderful, life-affirming thing to do, and not a way to cramp your style at all. When we finally sat down to eat, and it was really late by that time, I put the baby in his highchair at the table. Still talking brightly, I began to carve into the lamb (which was quite rare), when the baby coughed and, I think, started to choke a little on his millionth piece of watermelon. Really, he was amazingly good, for a toddler—very patient and not fussing at all. He had been happy with his fruit! Until, quite surfeited, he—yes, the worst happened. That little choke caused a mighty, projectile, and definitely *pink* upheaval, all over the table.

I can't remember how the evening ended. I'm sure that this couple went on to embrace a large family ... or else they remain childless to this day, and it's all my fault!

So early on, a vividly hued vomit warned me that I'm in no position to give advice.

We're just so eager to start, aren't we? We want to be a family! Eating dinner together! It just seems as if there is a lot to overcome while we're waiting for that moment when we seem to have arrived.

I remember seriously questioning the sanity of trying to eat with my husband in the presence of children whose sole aim in life seemed to be to discover the maximum amount of nagging I could do in the space of one meal. The dear man would beg me not to correct them. I would beg him to correct them. Obviously, you can't *not* correct them! They are sliding off the chairs—exclusive of ever actually sitting in them! They are literally under the table! They are deliberately making me insane! Do something!

But what *can* you do?

Conjure up a mental picture. In ten years—in the *next* decade, which I realize seems very far away—these same little unruly beggars will sit around this table and actually speak with you, if only for a few minutes. True, we can't really make out their faces right now in this mental picture; it's a little blurry. True, there are other little beggars sliding off their chairs. I think one of them might be wriggling out of his five-point harness and making his way up Mount Tray. But *some* conversation is taking place.

In a mere *fifteen* years, the number of upright bodies forms the majority. You hardly notice the giggling under the table when you aren't correcting it, and occasionally one of the gigglers comes and sits on your lap and just listens. In this mental picture, you have the ability to hear what some of the beggars are thinking. The little giggler on your lap is full of wonder at the amazing people, her siblings, who can capture the attention of Mama and Papa. She secretly thinks in her toddler way, "Someday, I'll talk to them too."

This picture can keep us going for a while. I alone have survived to tell you (well, there are some others!) that it will happen if you are persistent and patient. *It takes time.* Meanwhile, here are some things you can do today to make this picture come true.

Before the Meal

1. *Know what is for dinner, and get started on it twenty minutes earlier than you think you need to,* so that you can clean up a little beforehand, so that you can sit and eat somewhat peacefully, without the sense that the kitchen will explode. Work backward with me for a second: If what dismays you (other than jumping, sliding children) is facing an exploding kitchen after supper, you need to have cleaned up the cooking mess before you eat. To do that, you need to start cooking a little earlier, so that you have time to whisk things away. To do that, you have to have known what was for dinner in time. (This issue is covered in volume 3.)

2. *Have dinner a little earlier than you think you might ordinarily have it.* Not quite the same as my first point: this is moving the whole shebang earlier, so that infant meltdowns don't coincide with adult meltdowns.

3. *Light a candle at the table tonight.* (Perhaps a pillar or votive candle is the best choice at the moment, for the sake of not setting the house on fire.) It's your beacon of culture. It's your promise that someday, that mental picture, above, will become real for you. It's your promise to yourself to be patient. If you don't have a candle, put it on your grocery list and then later, order a good quantity of them. Request pretty (and durable) candle holders for Christmas.

During the Meal

If your children are very young now, what I say here will sound like the opposite of "eat dinner with your kids," but bear with me. Here are some steps once the meal has begun:

1. *Focus on having dinner with your husband, and try to enjoy it and him.* You have many, many years to get this thing down. What is important is that you and he have a conversation at dinner. You can talk, among other topics, about how, gradually, to make dinnertime family time.

If your husband tends to come home late during the workweek, why not get the babies fed, bathed, and in their pajamas? You know, tender young bodies can take being buckled and strapped and shod for only so many hours! Get them clean and into their soft nightclothes. If they go to bed before your husband gets home, that's okay. You can always aim for breakfast together; usually it's a less stressful meal. Maybe some days the babies' naps will allow them a later night, or the weekends can be for hanging out together. Soon, they'll be older and more able to stay up with Dad.

If they (or some of them) stay up for dinner, don't try too hard to feed them at the table when you are trying to eat as well. Play it by ear, every day if necessary. Some days, it might be helpful for Daddy to try his hand at "shoving the oatmeal into him." (Not how Auntie Leila would say it, as you know, but one's husband has been known to express it this way. He is a professional writer, after all.) Some days, it is not helpful to attempt it.

Better to give them an early supper or nursing and have up to twelve relatively peaceful adult minutes at the table. Not alone, probably, but not stressed out, either.

What would this look like?

- The toddler sitting up at the table as if to join you, but with a token plate of something appealing to him (dessert, perhaps), since he has already eaten. After a few minutes (or maybe longer! Who knows? Toddlers are so hard to figure out!), he wriggles down and goes to play, and that's fine.
- The toddler and the baby on a blanket on the floor or in the baby's playpen, playing with the baby's toys.
- Do you have a little table and chair in the dining room or nearby where you eat? Maybe now is a nice time for special coloring.
- The toddler on Dad's lap, the baby on Mom's.
- A very small infant asleep in a bassinet, having been bathed and nursed before suppertime, near the table while you enjoy dinner with Daddy.
- Papa enjoying holding his infant, giving Mama a break so she can eat, and the toddler playing with his toys nearby.
- Mama nursing the baby at the table. I think, in fact, that's what I mostly did, since I personally have a little trouble being on time with dinner. (Shhh! Don't tell Auntie Leila's secrets!) If you feed the toddler beforehand, it works out. What won't work out is not feeding the toddler until it's too late. (Did you know that children sometimes get too hungry to eat?)

2. *Very young children do not need to eat an adult's idea of a balanced meal.* (Elsewhere I'll go into what young children should be expected to eat.) This is where your own childhood reading comes in very handy. Remember *The Secret Garden*? Remember your E. Nesbit? Those children ate nursery food, and it did not include salads.

Whenever I worried that my children weren't getting all the food groups, eating plenty of fruits and vegetables, et cetera et cetera, I remembered that for most of history, children were just fed simple diets and nursed for a good long while. If it was good enough for Laura Ingalls, I think our kids can survive. After all, the reality is that we in the United States have the most varied diet imaginable! So stop worrying about that spinach salad (which, by the way, is a leading cause of E. coli poisoning), and give the eighteen-month-old another helping of whatever homecooked simple food he seems to like this week. I promise that, as he gets older, we'll change our strategy a bit.

As much as I'm trying to convince you that dinner with the family is your goal, for now, try to wrap your mind around the paradox of how enjoying dinner with your husband every evening will get you there.

I warn you—if the two of you focus all your energy on your two little barbarians, making them the center of every moment of your day, in a few years you will not have much to say that isn't in baby talk.

Young children take their cue from you. When our bigs were little, I was very blessed to have my husband sometimes say to me, in so many words, "Look at me! Talk to me!" And we would talk right over the din, right through it, sometimes even running away from it. (Yes, he once took me by the shoulders very gently and maneuvered me right into the bathroom and closed the door on the both of us, so he could finish his sentence!)

Here is a test for tonight. When you say grace, which, of course, you are trying to teach your dear little ones, are you looking at them when you say it? Nodding and smiling as your toddler blesses his little heart? Chuckling?

Don't get me wrong. I'm as delighted and smitten with the cuteness of it all as the next person when it comes to lisping tots learning their prayers. *But*, if night after night, year after year, you look right at your children when you pray, well, it's no wonder they rule the roost.

Bow your head and say grace, and I guarantee you nothing terrible (well, nothing that can't be undone eventually) will happen for that thirty seconds. You can peek if you need to. The point is, it's good for even a small child to experience the shocking, yet ultimately liberating, experience of not being scrutinized for a bit—of not being the center of everyone's attention, even if it's just for the time it takes to say grace.

Three Things You Need for Dinner Together

Remember, we're talking about dinner together through the years. This near-daily occurrence has so many implications for family life, child development, marriage ...

Now that the children are getting a little bigger, things are getting busy for you!

I remember when Suzanne was born; Nick was four, Rosie was two. The pressure of the children outnumbering us made me suddenly realized that I was a "real" mom and had to make dinner at a certain time. I hadn't yet developed my system for menus (which we're getting to), and my friend hadn't yet told me that I had to know what was for dinner by 10:00 a.m., but at least I was getting a clue that "dinner prep" meant more than "Oh dear, it's 5:30! Maybe we should eat!"

Dinner started to be fun, if zoo-like. When another child (Joseph) came, and then another (Deirdre, and let me tell you, that child had to be watched every second, or she'd be in the dishwasher or somewhere up in the rafters), well, all I can say is that I hope that no one who knows me from back then thinks that I think that I had it all together and my kids behaved perfectly.

Because I *know* I didn't and they didn't! But you learn a few things along the way, and here they are. I realize that I haven't addressed *behavior* here directly, and in a lot of ways, that's what you're desperate to know. I like to go into the practical details that I think alleviate the pressure. Dinnertime is important—yes, for behavior too.

1. *Understand that everything you do with your children is practice for other things you do with them.* Don't let this knowledge overwhelm or paralyze you, but also don't fall into the trap of thinking that if you let them crawl on the table and eat with their hands for breakfast and lunch, they will magically know their lobster fork from their strawberry spoon when they are invited to dine with the queen or be able to remain upright when your neighbors visit, for that matter.

You have to strike that balance between convenience, efficiency, and yes, relaxation during the day when they are "alone" with you, and manners, behavior, and a sense of respect in the evening when Dad gets home. So I do frown on paper plates, your nose in a book (different from everyone reading something at breakfast, for instance), the radio on (well, how can you stand the din?), and most counterproductively, everyone sort of grabbing his food—on all but the rarest occasions (by which I mean *never* for grabbing, *as needed* for paper plates, such as during a power outage or when you sprain your ankle or something).

It's not all that difficult to gather, say grace, and pay attention to what you are doing for the fifteen minutes you eat lunch—only a little preparation is required on your part. Visit with each other, enjoy the food, and be polite: "Thank you, Mama, for this nice lunch." "Thank you, darling, for helping me with the drinks." Read them a chapter of a book for the duration if you like.

These practices will pay off when you're at Grandma's on Sunday and the children are just in the habit of glancing at you to see where you are in the process of whatever it is you are doing, rather than just intent on getting nourishment as quickly as possible—which, as you know, is rude.

2. *Have a place for eating dinner.* If you are used to eating in the kitchen but your family is getting bigger, it might be time to understand the function of the dining room.

It might be that your kitchen is quite suitable for busy meals to be eaten in it. Just consider, though, that when you have a lot of children, the kitchen is an *overwhelmed* environment. When you are committed to baking bread, braising chickens for healthy meat and broth, washing your garden produce, and keeping everyone well supplied in the cookie department, you will end up racking up the miles in that room. By the end of the day, despite your best efforts, it might not be the tidiest venue in the house. Besides, you may just really need to *get out of there.*

So, if your kitchen table isn't well out of the traffic pattern of the work, consider getting that dining room up and ready for daily use. Most houses are set up this way, with a small (if any) eat-in area in the kitchen and a dining room, although many newer homes have dining rooms that are also, sadly, too small. If you have this problem, I feel for you and hope that your kitchen is a legitimate eat-in one, away from the messy work stations.

I know that, when we have company especially, it's almost impossible for my kitchen to be as neat as I would like, since we have few counters. I am grateful for my dining room, and from the time our eldest kids hit puberty, we ate in the dining room pretty much every night. You see, as the children get older, their bodies take up more room! Maybe the size table you need just won't fit in your kitchen! I know this was the case for me at one point.

The Shakers kept a tabletop propped against the wall until mealtime, setting it on "legs" that doubled as workbenches at other times, and in this way, they used their one space wisely. If there is some sort of barrier, even visual, between you and the place where you've been working, that will help.

Think about church. It's a special place set aside for worship. As you enter, you ready yourself for what is about to occur. You notice the altar boys lighting the candles in the same pattern that they use every week. The polished chalice and filled cruets are on the preparation table. The lace cloth is on the altar, having been lovingly washed and ironed well before the day. There is no rush, no slap-dashedness.

We need to bring something of that sense of time, place, and preparation to our dinner, with all that is proper to the family setting, of course. It's up to you, as the mother, to think through where, when, and how you will eat (and then the others can help you make it happen).

Is the table sturdy? Are the chairs or benches adequate? Do I have the right cloths for the table? Napkins? Candles? Forks? Knives? Serving dishes or cooking pots that can go to the table?

Seriously, for want of enough clean forks, many a mother has sunk beneath the weight of family togetherness. Go to the thrift store and get enough cutlery to last the entire day. That place setting for four that you got for your first apartment *is not enough*.

3. *Enlist the troops.* Start preparing the dining area well before you need to, especially if you use the table for crafts or schooling. There is no rule against setting the table at four o'clock, even if you are eating at six! Even if

you aren't putting out vulnerable dishes, you can get the children to clear things off and start the process.

Everyone has a job to do. On the day that the iron enters your soul about this area of life, make a list of each and every job if you need to, and divide them up. Even a two-year-old can distribute the napkins. Make sure someone has the job of unloading the dishwasher, because *an empty dishwasher is the key to sanity.* (If you do dishes by hand, then the dish drainer needs to be clear and the first able person to rise from the table should fill the *empty* sink with hot, soapy water.)

Preparation of the environment prepares the mind and heart. The children experience the rhythm of the day as its ritual. To them, all things can be holy, as indeed they are. They feel excitement when they are responsible for making things both orderly and wonderful. Maybe Daddy is coming home! Maybe he is already home (as he is here), but he will now turn his full attention to his family! They love that with all their hearts. Give them something to do to make it happen. As long as you are not always rushed (and of course, no one can help sometimes needing to rush), they will respond to your lead.

Now you are ready to sit down. You made your food. You have your habits. You have your table. You have your minions, or rather, children, who take pride in their work. The candles are lit. Grace is said.

Now, some thoughts on how to quell the ensuing uprisings, riots, and unrests.

Seven Strategies for Dinner with the Barbarians

Sometimes I get into arguments with people about whether housewifery is drudgery. It's funny to me, because it seems obvious that just about every job has a drudge aspect. I suppose that even a top executive sometimes does nothing more exciting than rearrange the paper clips.

Once, in a gathering of friends, someone was really badgering me about this. He kept saying, "Your life is cleaning bathrooms—just drudgery! There is nothing redeeming about that job!"

Since the bathrooms need to be cleaned, I don't find it a big deal. But I was interested to know what he thought would be a job free of drudgery or boredom of some kind.

"For instance, what do you do for a living?" I asked.

"I'm an accountant."

After the laughter in the room died down, it was generally acknowledged that I had won that round.

No offense to any accountants reading this, but drudgery is a matter of opinion.

My point here is that everything we do has a goal, and if we keep that goal in mind, difficult chores and even drudgery, rather than looming large and overtaking our consciousness to the point at which we can't function, resume their true proportions.

Preparing food, cleaning the house, folding laundry, getting to appointments—all these things can be handled if we're moderately competent (because nothing is worse than boring stuff we have to do but are not good at) and if we're doing them for a greater purpose.

A day is our portion of time. In a day, we have our goal and we have our working toward the goal. The "working" sometimes is drudgery, I admit that. The goal, well, the goal is being together, and that means—dinner!

If you are starting to understand why I harp on the idea of competence, but you are a little afraid about dinner because the little rascals outnumber you around the table, here are some strategies to help you. This section is intended for when the children are babies on up to about fourteen or so.

I call them strategies, but don't get the wrong idea. It's not that they are techniques. We're not trying to manipulate anyone. Calm authority is the key. Be confident in your God-given authority, and remember that it is something you are developing right along with your growing family. Together, you can guide and form your family to be what you want it to be, taking into consideration, of course, the personalities of everyone involved. That last part—about personalities—is where all the surprises come in, but fortunately they are good surprises, ones that make us grow!

The following strategies, then, are tools for competence in forming interpersonal relationship skills and managing interactions—also known as making a family. Investing in these strategies now, when you seem so very helpless against that combination of their sheer numbers and your lack of experience, will pay off great dividends in the future. You must trust that your children really don't know anything different from what you tell them and demand of them (which is why you have to be careful of the shows they watch, lest they sense that there is another way other than yours). Always remember: for a long time, you have them where you want them. If you served them a dinner of beans in a trough, they would think that was normal.

See how much better you feel already? Okay, on to the ways of doing this thing.

1. *They don't have to sit with you for very long.* Don't get too complicated. If the children help get the table ready, say grace with you, and are expected to sit for just ten or fifteen minutes, it will be easier to get them to behave. Remember, eating dinner together is about you and your husband sharing your meal and your conversation with each other. Joining you is a privilege. It's not about the children being there for every second of it, with the focus on them exclusively. If you're enjoying them, fine. If not, dismiss them before they make you cry.

Teach them to ask to be excused if they are getting wiggly; ask them if they would like to be excused if you are about to lose your mind. The usual expectation is that the youngest will not last as long as the eldest, but sometimes the latter can be called upon to watch the former while you just relax over your meal with Dad. Or you can use your wily tactics to clear the room of all but the one child you really want to talk to or correct or question in order to get to the bottom of something that needs attention.

When a child is excused, he can take his own place setting away and return for another item. At the minimum, he knows that he is on call for clearing and cleaning up later on if needed. (We will talk about cleaning up the kitchen in volume 3.)

It doesn't hurt to give everyone a pep talk before dinner about behavior. Be clear on what you want. "We're going to sit quietly, eat quietly, and enjoy each other. Or else."

If you know that you don't have to endure the littles' energy for long, you can refrain from too much correction during the meal. Remember, the *other* meals are the time to practice manners and behavior. At dinner, let your husband correct the children and be sure to back him up. You can always discuss your approach (and differences therein) another time. If he's too tired for discipline, then you do it, but he has to back you up.

2. *Everyone has to be polite.* Most of your problems over the food will disappear if you demand courtesy. If Dad is willing to give swift justice in the form of banishment or a spank when rudeness rears its ugly head, there

will be no issues on this score. For instance, who would ever say, "This looks gross"? At our table, we talk quite a bit about the food, and I would say that the excellence of my homemade pizza is due entirely to decades of intensive critiques of my efforts. But the norm is to be grateful to and supportive of the cook. For years, my husband raved over each and every meal I served. That really set the tone, and I am grateful.

Parents, be polite to each other. Never talk to each other as if you are one of the kids. Fathers, talk to your wife with a loving tone. Mothers, don't continually interrupt your husband to attend to, correct or admonish a child. Make the child wait until your husband has finished his sentence. Too many mothers interrupt those they are talking to in order to attend to a child but are somehow able to finish a point themselves! If you make the child wait for *the other person*, no harm will come. In this way, you demonstrate respect for your husband. Fathers, notice that she is trying to concentrate on you and deal with the little troublemaker yourself.

Politeness extends to other manners, especially those related to the consumption of the food—the use of a napkin, the importance of not smacking the lips, the holding of utensils, and so on. All of these things are practiced at other times intensively, and parental discretion will be the arbiter of whether they are noticed at dinner.

Occasionally a massive reboot needs to occur, and a whole dinnertime can be devoted to remediation. Sometimes a word put in at another moment does the trick: "Hortense, I'm going to remind you now to work hard at chewing quietly at the table so I don't have to say anything at dinnertime, but I may glance at you! So be watchful." Generally, it's wise to model refined behavior (at dinner!) and hope for time to do its work.

If your children are over the age of reason and still not eating with finesse, then you must do something about it quick. It's not a matter of correcting them at the dinner table; it's about their habits at all times, and their general situational awareness! Get them to think about how their mouth feels with food on it, about the noises, about having to get up to clean up a mess. And provide them with a good video of the correct manners. Bet you can find one online!

3. *One conversation.* This is *the most important one.* I cannot overemphasize the long-term benefits of this strategy for a culture of courtesy in the home.

My husband had a boss at a Washington, D.C., institution whose leadership he still extols. This boss knew how to build up around him a group of loyal, intelligent people who were willing to work energetically. One thing he would do in a meeting that Phil particularly appreciated was to remind everyone to pay attention with this phrase: "One meeting!" That man did not suffer side conversations lightly.

At the table, my husband would often pull everyone together by saying, "One conversation!" By "one conversation," I mean that only one person is speaking at a time and the others are listening, as far as is practicable. I don't mean that you choose a topic beforehand and discuss only that.

Let me tell you why this is on my top-ten list of great things my husband does to make our family ... well, *my* kind of family.

First, it's just survival. The din would be too much without this rule.

Second, it makes it possible for conversation to occur in a reasonable, civilized way. If you allow multiple conversations, things quickly descend into multiple fights—with hitting (speaking here of families, not think tanks, but you never know).

Third, it develops the skill of listening; a skill more in demand than supply. Listening is a habit. Habits are formed in the home, usually at the dinner table.

Fourth, where there is a conversational free-for-all, the dominant personalities end up only talking to or vying with each other. Less assertive family members stay mute or, in a truly terrible development, pick off other non-alphas for side discussions, leading to that worst of social offenders, the picker-offer—you know, that person at a party who can't join a general discussion, but insists on engaging you, *sotto voce*, one-on-one, often using body language to turn you away from the main group. These party poopers are bred in families who don't have the one-conversation rule. They are compensating, not very well, for never having been trained in the art of discussion with multiple people, and very often they are from larger families—but ones without a strong orchestrator of the conversation.

Fifth, the good leader has good awareness about the less dominant types and includes them, giving them a chance to speak. (Your little sign or motion to him can facilitate awareness: "So-and-so has something to say.")

Often, dominance correlates with age. With Mr. Lawler's technique, the youngest (or somehow quietest) child, having indicated a desire to say something, can't be drowned out or shouted down. He has his say. He has the floor, even if he is only three! Sometimes he doesn't indicate that he wants to join in or, in fact, shows reluctance to do so. All the more reason for the alert parent to draw him out. The unpleasant trait of dominance through passivity is thus arrested.

Everyone listens respectfully, eschewing, perforce, the destructive solution of saying something aside, to his neighbor. None of that! Thus, even the shyest person at the table has a chance and receives encouragement to take it. Little by little, he learns to be bolder. He waits for his opportunity. He stores up his sentences, knowing and trusting that he will be attended to. You know, it's quite difficult to have mustered up the courage to speak, only to become aware that others are whispering or otherwise not paying attention. Nowhere else in our utilitarian world will he be given the chance to run with the big boisterous ones, but without the danger.

That is what a family is—a safe haven to be yourself, only better, and to be loved for who you are, not for what you can contribute. Paradoxically, this quality of the family makes the person a better contributor to the outside world!

4. *Children can be asked to stop talking.* Here is a strategy I would like to print up on a card and hand to ladies in the dress shop and gents in the food line at the game:

You can tell your child to stop talking.

I mean, you can be kind about it, but you can do it. If you have half an hour in the shop and are concentrating on what blouse goes with what skirt, which do you think is better: to let your child babble on, getting louder and louder, "Mommy, look at this toy! Mommy, can I have this truck? Mommy, MOMMY!" Or to say, "I will talk to you in a bit, but now I have to concentrate. Please be quiet." Which would *you* rather overhear at the game: "Dad, get me a hot dog. Dad, I need a hot dog. DAD!" or "Now we are going to watch the game, son, and at the break, we'll see what we can find. Quiet now!"

At the dinner table, discover the wonderful, peaceful, amazing world of occasionally silent children. If your family is anything like ours, most of the time the children will be brimming with the day's news, the latest argument, the entire plotline of the book they are reading, and let's not forget the "what-ifs"—a mode of discussion that turns any situation, no matter how mundane, into a flight of hypothetical fantasy with no exit strategy.

That's all great, and it's what makes time with them fun (as long as there is one conversation and everyone takes a turn listening as well). It's also what convinces your children that you really are interested in them. If you don't listen to the entire catalog of the doings of Calvin and Hobbes when your child is ten, don't expect to hear about his deepest thoughts about his encounter with his mentor when he is sixteen.

But keep in mind that the greatest gift you can give your kids is your love for each other, husband and wife. This love is developed, among other places, at the dinner table, and you and your husband need to be able to talk to each other. You also need to be able to respond to what the children have said and maybe even offer a few ideas, anecdotes, or plot summaries of your own.

What holds you back is that you can't imagine saying to a group of friends, "I am going to ask you all to be quiet now. Mr. Lawler and I need to talk." What you are forgetting is that, unlike your relationship with your friends, you have authority over your children (who are your friends, but also your "subjects," and I mean that in a very royal yet loving way, first and foremost). So what would be fairly shocking to your friends is not only appropriate but also necessary with your children; and I am begging you to employ this strategy, for the love of all that is peaceful.

An excellent rule is that the first ten minutes after grace are a time for *quiet* concentration on the meal on the part of the children. Set a timer if necessary and allow only the lowest whispered request for more butter and so on. Silence from children for the first ten minutes allows mother and father to exchange news and opinions and sets the tone.

One more point here: Do you know the book *Cheaper by the Dozen?* Mr. Gilbreth, undoubtedly one of the livelier and more eccentric heads of household you will ever read about, would keep his many children from hijacking the conversation by bellowing, "Not of general interest!"

In our house, where the conversation can quickly descend into the minutiae of details as various as the distinction between lawn and voile cottons or the relative merits of gun cleaning methods, but most of all, the latest adventures of imaginary Lego people, this phrase comes in handy. It's an escape hatch for the truly desperate. Don't overuse it, but don't overlook it either.

5. *Take care of each other.* It's at the very heart of what the family *is* to cultivate a sense of *the other* in each of the members—the parents learn this right along with the young ones. It's very easy to learn practical love at the table. Passing things, getting up for each other, big children helping little ones—this is how those habits of real virtue get formed!

In our family, I would say that one of the hardest things for me to do is to have a dish of food be finished off. Everyone is so careful to leave some for the others that sometimes I have to get up and just distribute the few spoonfuls that are left to avoid having to put them away! What a beautiful problem to have! It's the fruit of many years of reminding, "Be sure to leave some for your brother—he'll be home soon" and "Let's make sure this dish makes it around the table!"

A priest friend of ours from a large family shared with me that his mother would warn, "FHB!" That meant that when they had guests, "Family hold back" was the rule so that the guest could be sure to have as much as he wanted of something that seemed to be running out. Our children need to learn over the years these little rules of charity and hospitality, for there's nothing worse than a person who is intent on eating as quickly as possible to get his share. Such an attitude bespeaks many other habits that will not serve him well in life.

6. *Be understanding of the younger ones.* It's really hard to sit still if you are young and everyone is talking about whether the value-added tax constitutes an opportunity for reform or merely more confiscation of our

hard-earned cash. Yawn. Let the little ones go play. They can put the milk away on their way out.

7. *Younger ones are low on the totem pole.* It's important not to let everything always swirl around the youngest, most demanding (because least well behaved) child. We focused on him all day with his endless demands. Dinner is time for Mother and Father to catch up with each other and the older kids. Thus, we provide an incentive for good behavior. If all the attention is on the most poorly behaved, the bad behavior will be its own reward. Later, we'll talk about how the older ones fall off their pedestals and the attention goes to the youngest, who have become the age that the eldest were when they were this age. But for now, concentrate on the older ones.

These are my strategies—mostly number 3: one conversation.

Everything will be revealed if we cleave to this rule. Suddenly we will be struck by how rude, unkempt, dirty, and squirmy our children are, because we will be listening to some sort of narrative about a cowboy on a spaceship and really, there won't be much else to think about.

But after a while, really and truly, hang in there, because we will also notice how genuinely funny and smart and thoughtful these children are, and once their faces are wiped and their hair is cut or braided, depending, how very good it is to be with them!

Picky Eaters

Somehow, we have gotten to a funny place. We obsess about every micronutrient, so that we can't have even a drink of water without feeling we should be shoring up some languishing yet mysterious part of our bodies' immanent decrepitude. At the same time, the fact that the only booming businesses, in our area at least, are fast-food restaurants as well as the fact that the grocery store has expanded its frozen-prepared-food section, go to show you that people are just feeding—just shoveling it in. Or, not, if they are kids.

This funny place is making it so that we just don't know what do to about food. We are anxious. And one of the things we are anxious about is that our children seem so picky.

There are two basic kinds of picky eaters, I think.

I am not going to talk about the first kind, other than to tell you to wake up and see if this is what you have going. These children, with their insistence on clinging to the familiar, and their sense that things will come apart if they are forced to eat something different, are desperately trying to control their untenable situation. So if you are divorcing your husband, drinking before lunch, self-medicating, or otherwise destabilizing your child's life, then take the picky eating for what it is: the only way your child has to communicate with you. It's a message in a bottle. Open it up and understand that it's not about getting him to take a bite of broccoli; it's about getting your life in order so that he can trust you again.

A subset of this kind of behavior is the child who has his own, really serious, issues. I know that autistic children often become frantic about food, but that's all I know. I'm no expert in this area. I will tell you that only you, the person who loves him, can ultimately know what is good for your child. Again, treating the symptom—the picky eating—isn't the answer.

It seems to me that the way to distinguish this kind of trouble is to try to see your child objectively. Does your child look unhealthy? Too pale? Lacking bright eyes? Too thin? Unable to run, jump, and shout? This objectivity is hard. It's hard to admit that things aren't right, and I don't really know how to help, except to say that we all do *say* that we would do anything for a child.

Things might be normal in the ways I am describing, but your child might have a physical issue, such as celiac disease or a zinc deficiency. Listen to your instincts if you know that something is not right. The pickiest eater (within the parameters set in this chapter) will appear perfectly healthy even if eating only two things, whereas someone who is sick or has a food intolerance will be sickly even if he eats lots of things, although he may also be picky. In other words, if your child is not thriving, examine the big picture. If he's growing and has energy, don't worry too much about pickiness; just keep at it.

That second kind of picky eating is less dire, so let's talk about that.

It's just a normal child in a normal (that is to say, odd) family who, for various reasons, which we will discuss, won't eat anything other than, well, fill in the blank! And, on top of everything, the doctor is getting on your case!

Here's an e-mail I received—does this sound familiar?

Dear Leila,

My six-year-old will not and has not touched a fruit or vegetable in a long time. Spaghetti sauce and pizza sauce and some occasional apple pieces or blueberry or strawberry kefir or some juice would be the closest he comes. Trust me, I try. I remove dessert and sweets and crackers; nothing shakes him.

He does seem to have a texture aversion. Even reaching into a pumpkin to carve it makes him sick. He tried a carrot and threw up. I'm really stuck. I do try to make sure he eats well otherwise; milk or water to drink; vitamins; he loves fish and yogurt and meat. But anything, even baked beans, that comes close to being a veggie or fruit makes him run the other way.

His well visit is coming up, and I cringe. The doctor always asks about his diet. I do worry about his health, though his weight is good and he appears quite healthy.

What to do?

Josie

Here's what to do.

First, get a grip on your inner alpha. Act, don't react. And don't worry about the doctor. I've known lots of doctors, and I can say for sure that their children aren't always eating from all the food groups, to put it mildly. Children don't, as a rule. Just tell your doctor that you are working on it and that you are glad your child is healthy.

Figure out *when* your child needs food and *what kinds* of food he will eat, and do what needs to be done to *provide it in a timely manner.* We'll work from there.

A baby needs you to prepare the food and sit down to help him eat before the family's meal, because most babies are too distracted to eat much at that point. If you think that, say, scrambled eggs and toast and some cut-up fruit is a good breakfast that he might possibly eat, then serve that, encourage him to eat it, and figure that sitting up with the family at the table will take care of the rest if he rejects it. This is why nursing right through toddlerhood is helpful, because then you can rest easy that all the spinach *you* are eating is doing him good.

Yes, you do have to coax some children to eat. Everyone in our family can tell the Goldilocks story with lots of pizzazz, because it's how we got the youngest eater to eat his porridge. Don't make the mistake of thinking you don't have to do this if your child chooses not to eat.

Besides not getting enough sleep, children suffer most from current parenting advice, that they will eat what they need to. Not exactly true, necessarily. Some are troupers and get the job done, but some are too distracted and have to be confined (as in a high chair with a harness) and coerced (as in that old standby, Airplane, and the always handy Choo-Choo Train), at least enough to clear your conscience that you tried.

Very young children will survive on nursery food; you can leave it at that. (Consult your favorite British children's story to know what nursery food is. It is not eggplant. It is not salad.)

Try to work with your child. If you see that it won't cause a core meltdown, start your "just one bite" program now. This is the rule that states that you don't have to eat it, but you do have to try it, and trying it means trying it this time (last time doesn't count). I do make exceptions for foods that have a track record of causing gagging. Potatoes don't count. Take a bite of your potatoes. "Just one bite" starts at the age you think you can get away with it: sometimes three, sometimes seven. You can call it a "no thank you" bite if that seems to help. I have known at least one child (at the age of four) who, upon eating that bite, almost always declares, "I love it!" and proceeds to down the whole thing.

Later, this program will be a cornerstone of your mealtime regime, but know that *there is a trap*. It's called Battling Your Two-Year-Old. Like land wars in Asia, this type of thing is never won. Perhaps your two-year-old likes a lot of things but exhibits secondary pickiness: the pickiness of rejecting perfectly well liked foods for *the most* liked foods. The remedy? Enlist his older siblings to insist that he take a bite of the less-favored item before being allowed to have the more-favored one.

Don't have older children? There is your mistake! Attend to this as soon as possible.

One reader wondered about her two-year-old going to bed hungry because she wouldn't eat the rest of the chili on her plate (although she did have one bite) but wanted the bread and butter. She thought that her friends who had instituted the "eat this first" rule had good results, but it wasn't working for her.

My response is that if she would eat the bread, well, that's fine. You put the chili in front of her, she tasted it, and she chose what to eat. Sometimes you'll find that if you let a child have his fill of bread and butter, he goes back and eats the chili! In any case, if it was tasted, you've made your point. But even if it wasn't tasted, the bread and butter are necessary to sustain him. You can just overlook noncompliance because, with a two-year-old, it's in your best interests not to engage in a battle of wills.

Next time, you might try giving the child the bowl before the rest of you sit down, if it's something she would normally eat. In any case, you have to assess just how hungry the child is when this happens. Sometimes there is a digestion thing that needs to happen, if you know what I mean, and in the morning, the child wakes up and eats a good breakfast.

Sometimes you can give the child a bowl of oatmeal with milk and a little cinnamon sugar in bed. Why not? She tasted everything at dinner. If she's truly hungry, she won't sleep well. Don't trap yourself into any kind of box you can't get out of. Don't make rules for the sake of making rules. You didn't get up and make the child a new supper, so victory was yours in the only sense it will be in this case.

Do things the way you think is best, not necessarily the way your friends do them, if those ways aren't working for you.

The Tactile Hater must be respected yet helped along. Since I am in the Tactile Hater Hall of Fame (but have largely reformed, so there is hope!), I do sympathize. Since I'm also the alpha, I make rules, but I apply them with mercy. If a child really does gag, I won't make him eat certain foods. But next time, I'll make it differently, and then we will see all over again whether he will gag. (That the next time will be long from now is the mercy part.) I will also have an eye out for whether he is *making* himself gag, which would result in sanctions.

If a child favors cooked veggies and fruits (won't gag on them), then why are you fixated on raw? Just give him cooked. If he likes raw, don't insist on cooked.

Here's the thing. In most places, and at most times, the variety of foods that most people have eaten has been very small. And the children's likes and dislikes have been largely ignored! The variety that most children in most places at most times have had is even smaller. Yet the human race survives! Let this be your consolation.

Notice that, although in winter months here in the north, children might have survived fine on something like Laura's corn pone and salt pork, in the summer, they ate from the garden with lots of choices. In a way, our amazingly *available* panoply of foodstuffs deadens the palate. If you never *lack for* a tomato, you are probably unmoved by a tomato.

I know I said that about variety, but paradoxically, having more than three things on a plate helps children acclimate to oddities. So, for instance, if you served only beans and rice, they might not want it, but if you serve a (smallish) Mexican-style plate with an enchilada, rice, refried beans, and guacamole, all arranged just so, somehow all these completely unacceptable foods (to a non-Mexican child, I guess) become doable. Even if they only eat two things, that's a meal. Try just having more things on the plate, rather than heaping portions of a few things. Make them well. Some children respond to a little plate with dividers.

Here I am going to go against what the experts advise. Let's say that you are tired of your picky eater hating zucchini. Why don't you fry up some zucchini in beer batter? I have seen mighty towers of pickiness fall to the ground when confronted with the crisp goldenness of the deep-fried zucchini. The gates of pickiness will not prevail.

Similarly, if you make sure that your veggies are well bathed in butter and salt, or a nice cheesy or creamy sauce (homemade, of course), you will not get the same fight as before. Remember, despite the craze for bare veggies, many nutrients require a bit of fat to be made useful to the body. Little by little, as you let the veggies emerge from their disguise, they will be appreciated for what they are.

Don't get me wrong. I am too lazy to be in the school that thinks you should *hide* the veggies, but I do think that putting the spinach in ham and cheese and spinach pie is a valid way of getting children used to spinach. When they hear everyone oohing and aahing over a favorite savory pie, you can bet that they will have at least some.

I personally never ate a salad until I was about twelve or so, and then only because it was iceberg lettuce (the hearts! crunchy, not slimy like most lettuce!) smothered in blue-cheese dressing. I too, like Josie's son, had the clear thought that I would probably scour my insides, die, or choke if I ate a salad. I was so veggie-averse. I ate only yams (roasted with butter and salt—still my fave!). Maybe peas. Or, maybe not.

Now I'm fine. There is hope.

So, to be clear, this is the difference between our peculiar American pickiness problem and the cultures of the world that don't have it. For us, the concept of the meal as a ritual is fairly gone; that is what I'm trying, in my own little way, to revive here. It is what those other times and places have going for them and we don't have.

Plan your menus (even the very simple ones). Set the table. Make your husband and yourself the alpha pair, or, if you like to think of it in more human terms, the head and heart of your family.

When you think this way, you don't make a mistake that leads directly to pickiness. I saw it once, dramatized, in the grocery store. Dad was walking down the cereal aisle with what can only be called a baby—a child possibly twenty-two months old. Definitely not two. And Dad was crazily and irresponsibly asking this infant what kind of cereal he wanted!

Truly, this is completely outside my sense of what is possible. My kids will attest that if they want a particular kind of cereal, they must not only have reached the age of reason but must petition for weeks, possibly months, to get it. And not even then. I have a very limited notion of what constitutes cereal correctness, and I would certainly never solicit input from a baby! That way lies madness.

To train up a child the way he should go, you should definitely take note that initiating this kind of conversation in the cereal aisle will lead straight to juvenile delinquency and reform school. We taxpayers will not be grateful.

Have certain foods at certain times and on certain days. Don't leave everything up for grabs. My children really would not willingly eat lentils and cracked wheat (mujadara) most of the time, but on Ash Wednesday or Good Friday, they eat it. That's what we eat. Every Friday we have meatless meals. That's how it is.

My favorite example of something an American child probably wouldn't eat is the classic French bite of a thinly sliced radish on buttered bread. But it's the ritual of it (and the goodness of the elements, of course) that makes it appealing! Being the one to add the little shake of salt makes you own it.

Why was popcorn a treat for the pioneers and ho-hum for us? The ritual of making it, of course, and the challenge. Open a purchased bag of already popped corn, and life's the less for it.

Recovering the meal, and even the snack, as a *ritual* leads directly to another important factor in overcoming childhood pickiness—arriving at the table with a good appetite. The satiated child is perforce the picky child because, not being hungry, he can afford to turn his nose up at things. If you are constantly plying him with goldfish, gummy bears, cookies, and cereal bars, don't be surprised that he doesn't eat at a meal. I can't bear to eat real food after mindless snacking—appetite clean gone!

In our prosperity, we tend to placate our children with food. Rather than dealing with their actual problems (such as being bored in a car seat, or tired of shopping, or not going outside), we just pacify them. I'm not against snacking. As someone with blood-sugar spikes, I know the importance of a well timed snack to get you through. But our constant eating has no thinking behind it.

If you haven't assimilated the fact that you simply must know what is for dinner before your little ones break down in crabby whines, you will be caught up in this other self-defeating strategy: the pre-dinner snack. If your children can grab a bowl of cereal at 5:30, don't be surprised that they complain about the kind of dinner you are giving them at 6:15.

Instead, you should be ready to refuse to feed them when they are begging, even if it makes you the meanest mother in the world, and plunk the meal down (with their assistance, of course) by 5:30, or whatever is a good bit earlier than the time you've devolved to (because, of course, in the back of *your* mind, "they've had a snack").

Take note of the rhythm that develops. If you'd rather eat at 6:00, but every day at 4:30 there is a major shattering of mood and happiness, then serve a "tea" at 3:30 (not really tea—that is, not caffeine). My dear husband suggested this to me! So practical. He understood what I didn't: that they just couldn't make it to dinner. Of course, he was picking up the pieces by the time he got home from work, so he was motivated.

One last thing: You are the adult. You made the rules, you can make exceptions gracefully without giving the impression that you are losing. As long as you keep the discussion courteous (meaning, be courteous and require courtesy from your children), you will not lose your dignity.

But, it's not as if I haven't gotten into a struggle over that bite of cole slaw with a seven-year-old. I have. No harm done either way, honestly.

Dinner Together When the Children Are Older

No sooner do you get everyone more or less behaving, conversing, and enjoying dinner together—such a wonderful, happy, delightful time in family life—when the older children get older and start coming and going. They even have their licenses and can drive themselves, and they slip out with a quick "Bye, Mom!" and you are almost too busy to notice that they've gone, until dinner is almost over—and you do miss them so.

Sometimes they have activities and commitments elsewhere; sometimes they are home, and what do you know! They have their own ideas about things. Maybe some of your kids don't live with you now but come home for a bit during holidays? What about when they dash out again to visit friends?

So "quieting down" refers to the absence of the older ones, even when things are still lively with the others. It also refers to how things feel at this moment for me, now that I have lived through this stage, after the many years when they hadn't happened yet.

Open yourself to a larger family, and chances are, if biology cooperates, you will feel like you live inside a giant pinball machine most days, and when your children grow up, *their* children will come and liven things up again. Quiet turns out not to be that quiet! Yet nothing compares to those years of baseball and shows and places you have to get to: meetings, conferences; your children's friends eat over; your kids head out to eat supper with others. Eventually kids grab the keys and head out; before you know it, they are gone for months at a time at school and then, just ... gone!

For so long, you worked hard at the family dinner, and now you have to ask, "What is my family dinner supposed to be like? I'm not in control!"

Roots and Wings

Did you ever hear the expression "Your children need roots. Your children need wings"? I remember the sweet lady who gave me this response when I asked her about her wonderful children who married, had children of their own, but still lived nearby and loved coming home. "You have to give them roots [here she delicately gestured with both hands to the ground] and wings [fluttering her hands delicately toward the sky]. Roots and wings [quick repeated gestures]!"

What is the soil for those roots? Your marriage; that you and your husband *sit down to dinner together*, on as many days as you can manage, and at least on Sundays. If you have circumstances that keep you busy in the evenings, maybe a midday meal is the way to go. You will figure it out.

Believe me, I understand when circumstances intervene. Some constitute a good excuse, like a husband deployed by the military. Someone who is gone is just gone. You do your best to hold his place for him. For many, though, circumstances mean something more like "I didn't have time to prepare dinner today—we grabbed what we could." I understand when this happens, but is it the norm? "We have meetings every night" or "We watch the news" or, well, you know.

If this is the case, it's time to figure out how you can show your devotion to your marriage, to your husband, by preparing dinner *for him*. Even if he is the one cooking, there is more to the meal together than plunking the food down! That's the root and source of grace and love for your family: your marriage, your relationship with your husband.

Dinner together with your family, at the core, means dinner at which Mama and Papa sit down together to share bread and conversation, not letting anything disturb them, not letting their peace be disrupted, with lots of room for ordinary, human error. Don't get frustrated by imperfection.

Your younger children need to feel that as the marriage bond radiates outward, it encompasses them and takes their real needs into account. When your family is young, it's sometimes good to shower benign neglect on the toddlers, indicating to them their need to fit into the family. But when the last toddlers are finally older, they need you to separate yourself from those who are getting to be (or already are) adults.

If your baby is seven, or nine, or fifteen, then focus on him. Worry about where he is going, whom he is with. Eagerly look forward to talking with him. Let the twenty-two-year-olds fend for themselves for a bit. Avoid seeking affirmation from them by letting them take all your attention.

The "wings" are the willingness on your part to let them go, with a diligent, loving freedom. Don't be afraid, and don't fret over your feelings, which are bound to be a bit fraught. It's normal, judging by me, for you never to want anyone to go anywhere. You just have to know when to voice that and when to refrain, and it takes a long time to figure that out, so be patient with yourself.

Be flexible and don't worry. New drivers, for instance, need that reminder to be home by dinnertime. It says so much to them about responsibility, about what matters, about the limits of liberty. In fact, your simultaneous concern and confidence give them just what they need, these young people who are making their way in the interesting, dangerous, wide world.

Even more than physical activity of little ones, mental activity of older ones can make you wonder if you are doing things right. When the kids are young, you and your husband control the discussions, at least in theory (those long plot recountings and imaginary conflicts with inanimate characters notwithstanding). As everyone matures, suddenly their conversation might make you feel as if you've failed or are seriously going to be reported to the family police!

Spouses who have a long habit of unity—which is refined at the dinner table—and of making their relationship the foundation of family life, *talking to each other*, can face this challenge with equanimity. When you listen and reply calmly and with a sense of humor, when you accept that they will come and go, you don't relinquish anything. Be comforted in knowing that if the way I've done things is any indication, there is lots of room for making mistakes! Keep those home fires burning for the younger children, and let the older children have their wings.

On Dressing Children
in Cold Weather

arents ought to provide the environment in which an ordered life can occur; discipline is how we accustom ourselves, our poor fallen selves, to that order.

The environment includes what we wear, how we dress.

Strangely, this topic is not one people like to discuss, as if information about how to stay warm somehow infringes on people's personal freedom. However, I'm trying to restore some common sense on dealing with external circumstances such as the weather; interestingly, as I hope will become evident, the topic has implications for discipline (in the sense of acquiring self-control). Bear with me.

It's true that in America today most of us don't experience extremes of temperature with our ubiquitous air conditioning and central heating. You may live where it sometimes really does get very cold, but for the most part, you have the luxury of keeping your environment warm enough so that you don't give much thought to survival-mode dressing. Nevertheless, if the power goes out, it becomes unusually cold for your area, or other circumstances intervene, you may need this information. We simply don't know that we'll always have this advantage, either as a society as a whole or within our own personal journeys.

Indeed, one of my aims here is to give the reader the tools for living without luxuries. I want to collect the memories so that we don't have to invent these wheels at inopportune times.

I also hope to show you that when your children learn to do what is expected of them in such matters, it's a means of learning self-control. Every time I hear someone say, "Oh, she insists on wearing that cotton sundress even though it's twenty degrees outside" or "My kids complain that the house is too cold" or "He refuses to put on socks," I think of this topic of dressing children properly, *how* to do it, and *why* it affects children's future life in ways unbeknownst to you now.

It may be that it is warm where you live. I commend your foresight on choosing such a temperate or even hot climate, and you can skip ahead to other chapters, though you may wish to come back and consult what I say here when job relocation or even an extended holiday lands you somewhere with temperatures that simply require a way of dressing that is different from what you are accustomed to.

Changing Seasons

Many children run around not properly dressed, for various reasons.

First, we all know how hard it is to switch the clothes each season—those of us, that is, who are not squandering our salvation by living in the tropics but, rather, are working out our Purgatory here in the dark North. (Plain English: I get it; you live in Southern California. But many of us need two sets of clothes. You have to experience it to understand why your light khakis will not work in our winter just by adding a cotton sweater.) It has to be done. Putting away clothes. Taking clothes out again. Putting the other ones away ...

You can avoid maximizing the upheaval of this Great Seasonal Clothing Switch if you use the laundry process to make the switch. Try doing the girls first and then the boys. That is, take those beloved T-shirts and shorts (at the end of summer, for instance) and put them in the wash. Take your normal time to process them through the cycle. This gives you a breather. Now, instead of putting these superannuated garments into drawers (or causing them to be put therein by one of your helpers), squirrel them into their respective bins. Soon the bins will be full and tucked away.

And if you play your cards right, you'll work it so that the children who are capable of finding their shorts in the spring or their cardigans in fall get it done before you work up the courage to face the challenge, saving you a few steps.

See in volume 3 the chapter "Laundry Problems Start with Clothes." For now, let me say, get rid of anything that isn't helpful. And then put away, quite away (into bins or some other storage), what is not seasonal.

Your four-year-old won't wear that favorite tank top in late November if it's in a box in the attic. Get her excited about winter clothes instead. Tell her next year is another year. Bribe her with candy. Just get rid of temptation.

Use this transition to implement some rules that may be new to your family — if you want people to be dressed sensibly. You see, between fashion dictates issued by hot cubicle dwellers and overheated cars and schools, people have lost a piece of the collective memory that relates to keeping warm. Some of us who can't afford to crank up the heat until our little darlings are comfy in T-shirts and flip-flops in the middle of winter have had to figure things out for ourselves. If you want to live simply and save on heating, as well as be the proud mom of the kid who doesn't get frost-bite when the car breaks down on the side of the highway in an ice storm, listen up.

Dressing Babies

Babies are a special category, so I'll discuss them first.

I don't know if it was Dr. Spock or T. Berry Brazelton, but some silly man came up with the patently false idea that babies' feet don't need to be covered — something about their circulation being undeveloped so their feet will feel cold to you, so why bother doing anything about it? When I passed along this bit of nonsense to my mom, she sensibly pointed out that if their circulation isn't good, maybe you should put socks on their little feet.

The main thing to remember about babies is that when you completely undress them, you let out all their body heat. So, when changing a baby's diaper when the air is cooler, you need to be careful to keep his middle covered. Did you ever wonder if the reason he cries when being changed is that the cold is like a knife on his skin, only made intolerable by frigid wipes? Keep him warm during changes.

An underwear shirt (for babies, a onesie) is for keeping the warmth in. Don't change it all the time unless you have to. Keep the undershirt on and just change the outer layer. Undershirts are for the purpose of not exposing the skin needlessly to the cold air.

When your baby has that mottled look—like tea-dyed eggs—on his arms and legs, his little body is too cool! That's how you can tell your baby is cold, even if you don't feel cold yourself. Even if you are overheated from your nursing hormones or from chasing toddlers, even if that brisk wind feels heavenly to you, you can tell Baby's temperature by how his limbs look. Many a baby portrait has been spoiled for me by seeing that mottled skin! Those little purple veins—I know that the baby isn't warm!

Some silly moms overdress their infants to the point of smothering. I guess that's what those baby doctors were addressing. You have to use your common sense. If your baby is pink and fussy, he's too hot, but don't suddenly expose him to a draft. Just remove a layer, take off the hat, or loosen the wrappings.

If he's blotchy and a little paler than normal, he's too cold. But be aware that wrapping him up at that point won't help. You have to warm him up first, which is why a chilly baby is a fretful baby, seeming to want to nurse more than usual. It's his survival mechanism, trying to get warmth from you. By all means, nurse him. The problem is that when you put him down, he gets chilly again if he is not well dressed for the temperature. You might be fine with holding him constantly, but just trying to stay warm, he may be losing valuable energy needed for other activities!

The effective method is to first change his diaper, put on his onesie, then a soft, warm outfit and socks. Then nurse him with a blanket covering both of you. Don't let the heat warming his belly escape from his back!

When you switch him from one side to the other or put him down in the cradle, don't lift the blanket completely off to reposition it. Just sort of slither him around under it so that the warmth doesn't get lost. At that point, you can put a little cap on an infant.

Always have a blanket nearby. When I see a mom out with a baby and no blanket, I get anxious. A blanket (light cotton in summer, warm wool in winter) often comes in handy: going into air conditioning, protecting from sudden changes in the weather (especially wind), mitigating a wet outfit when you didn't bring a change, preventing loss of body heat during sleep (in the normal sleep cycle, body heat rises and falls). Even in the warmest weather, a baby needs a blanket handy just in case—you know, that soft, light cotton kind—to keep off the breeze, which troubles a newborn in a way that it is not a problem for an older baby.

Dressing Older Children

Now, on to the older children …

The most important principle is layering. I'm not advocating bulky sweaters and sweatshirts for young children. First, as a child whose skin was exquisitely, painfully sensitive to wool and anything oddly textured, I sympathize with children who have tactile issues of that kind. Acrylic sweaters are not particularly warm and get strangely stiff and pilled as soon as they are washed. That sad, tired, pilled look makes the child look unattractive and feel unsettled.

An unsupervised child will put a sweatshirt on over his bare skin to warm up in the morning. Later, when it gets too hot for it, he can't take it off, or he'll be quite naked! So he overheats. Whether girl or boy, the child should wear an undershirt and a shirt (long-sleeved). Girls should wear tights or leggings *and* skirts or jumpers that go down below the knee, or socks and pants with undershirt and shirt or blouse. Boys should wear socks and pants. Pants, skirts, and jumpers should be twill or corduroy or denim or velveteen (for girls). Shirts should be knit or broadcloth or flannel.

Leggings are fine as a base layer, but never allow a daughter of yours to sport the egregious fashion of leggings in place of pants. First, they are drastically immodest. For a prepubescent girl, it's that awful sort of borrowed immodesty, like a child wearing a bikini—there's nothing to flaunt, and that makes it all the more pathetic. Spare the skinny girl and the plump girl their respective premature exposure. Second, leggings alone are not warm enough. If her top is shorter than a tunic coming to the knee, the child needs something proper on her nether regions, and a jumper (sleeveless dress) is what that is.

In extreme cold, children should wear a light sweater, vest, or sweatshirt or fleece. I believe in taking stock of the temperature and then insisting that they put that thin third layer on if it's weather *you* would wear a sweater for—the you, that is, who's going out into the weather, not the you who will sit in a warm car. Later, if they want to, they can take it off. But they have to start with it on. Usually though, the undershirt and warmer shirt with a vest if it's nippy (but not in the single digits) will be fine for children ages two to about ten.

Now, the same principle of not exposing the skin applies to children as well as to babies. Help them understand that the undershirt is the layer beneath which they don't go, until the warm weather comes back. Keep the undershirt on when changing from pajamas to dress clothes, say. That way, you stay warm and getting dressed in the morning isn't such a shock.

It's your job to make sure that your children are dressed appropriate to the situation. It's not good enough to think that you *told* them to dress warmly and then accept it when they don't. A child can't foresee that although he feels warm now, he will be cold on that walk in the wind or in a chilly school room after the sun has stopped streaming in. And, if he's headed out the door, you won't see him later when he is unable to function because he's only wearing one thin layer.

It's even worse for girls who love to wear pretty dresses but don't have the habit of putting on an undershirt first. It's fine when they are running around the warm house or are in the warm car, but later the chilled air goes right up their front! They end up huddled with their skinny arms inside their dresses. And though dressy dresses are often sleeveless, even for the holidays, it's still your responsiblity to find something to go under them, and maybe to provide a pretty cardigan.

Now, a word about the imaginative child who isn't so much getting dressed as entering an alternate reality. I am familiar with army guys who can't part with their camo pants or princess fairies who don't feel comfy without their tulle. My affinity for superheroes knows no bounds! I also understand that child who, for whatever reason, just feels more *himself* wearing that certain outfit. But just as you wouldn't let a child eat cake for dinner or gummy bears for breakfast, so you have to do what's best for a cowboy who is going on a hike and just won't make it in tight boots and no socks, or a ballerina who needs to brave the snow banks. And a child's self-image will only improve when he finds that he stays the same person *even in a different pair of pants.*

Don't tell me, "She just won't wear tights" or "He hates undershirts." That's not good enough, and I'll tell you why. If your child learns now to obey your thoughtful, reasonable guidelines for dressing, even though it seems hard (for both of you), that child will be ready at age fifteen to obey you when you say the dress is too short or the pants are too saggy. When the battle seems too much for you when your combatant is three, think what it will be like when he's seventeen! If you can't talk him into a T-shirt *now*, how will you tell him that his old, ripped jeans are no good for church *then?*

One reason this does seem like warfare is that we have succumbed to the "choices" school of child-rearing. However, there is no reason for a child to shoulder the responsibility of figuring out so much about life before he has any experience. It's hard enough to know you must brush your teeth without throwing meteorological variables into the mix.

Children love to be told, "This is how we do it." Notice that they allow themselves to be buckled into a confining car seat each and every time you take a trip! That's because you are afraid of the police.

But you need the confidence—without the arm of the law backing you up—in other areas too. You need to be the grown-up who simply presents a fact: this is how we dress in cold weather. You have to take the time with your toddler who is learning how to dress to say, "First, clean undies, then a T-shirt, then a shirt ..."

You have to have the guts to send someone back upstairs to get something warmer on. If it doesn't matter if he's wearing his space suit, it doesn't matter—let him wear it. But if he will be unprepared for something important (such as frigid temperatures), your responsibility is to do what is necessary to get him into the right outfit.

And let me tell you a perfectly valid reason to insist: do it because it makes other people comfortable! Other people can't be happy if you are wearing shorts in the middle of winter! Other people won't relax if you have bare arms when the weather is arctic! Your child certainly doesn't have to dress as warmly as the coldest person in the room, but he does have to take others' peace of mind into account—or at least you do, until he's old enough to take over. And that means wearing seasonal clothes.

Once it's below forty degrees or so (this all depends on the sun—in damp, cloudy places, forty can seem colder than twenty where it's sunny), break out the mittens, hats, and scarves. Make sure the jacket zips. Teach your children to stow their gloves in their pockets when they are not in use, or tether mittens with a long cord or clips for that purpose. No one likes seeing children with frozen, red, chapped hands and chattering teeth! If we weren't so reliant on our warm cars, we'd be more careful, and yet, who is to say that the car will always function, or that you won't find yourself, contrary to best-laid plans, somewhere exposed to the elements?

Much of what passes for fashion is actually arrested development. It's young people, especially girls, acting out a role rather than presenting themselves in a reasonably attractive and appropriate manner. I believe that it's the little girls who were allowed to totter around in dress-ups no matter what the occasion who then have no realistic idea of what to wear later and who also haven't had the experience of being *required* to abandon their self-consciousness in favor of practicality. When you are five, you just accept the reality you are presented with (although I admit that sometimes there's a battle first). When you are fourteen, that is hard to do if you don't have practice.

I have noticed that parents think they can put off demanding things of their child until some undetermined time when that child is "more reasonable." But your child will be reasonable later on if you quietly present him, *now*, with opportunities, in the area of food, dress, sleep, and behavior, in which to obey you and meet your standards. Do you worry that your teenager won't respect your authority? That your daughter will be immodest? That your son will be slovenly? Start now, and you won't have trouble later.

In an excellent essay, Rabbi Daniel Lapin expressed what I'm trying to say here. He's discussing the discipline of keeping Kosher (and of course, Orthodox Jews also have strict dress codes), but the reasoning is the same:

> Another case of the Law conferring hidden benefits, Kosher establishes the basis for self-discipline and desirable discrimination between the permitted and the prohibited in the most simple of the body's appetites. From toddlerhood, the religiously raised Jewish youngster knows the difference between kosher candy and the other kind. This strength, learned by even the young child with respect of food, will later stand him in good stead with respect to other, more compelling desires. It is obvious to everyone but secular humanist educational establishment ideologues that, for the most part, high school girls who only eat kosher food do not get pregnant.... Children who are raised kosher learn to "just say no" long before they are subjected to the compelling and irresistible calls of adolescence. By then it is much too late to start teaching "just say no."[23]

I'm not arguing for rigidity, just for a practical baseline. Be flexible enough to allow the fringed cowboy vest with each and every pair of pants and shirt, or the tutu over the (warm) skirt and tights. When you go grocery shopping, you will care very much if your child can't make it through the parking lot because he's too cold, but not at all if he's wearing a fireman's helmet. Then, when it comes time to go to church, you just inform him, "We'll leave the army boots here and get them when we get back."

And by the way, it doesn't hurt for *you* to have the proper tights, underwear, shoes, gloves, and hat either!

More Common Sense on Dressing to Stay Warm

When it comes to dressing, use your common sense. I, for one, am not shocked by children running barefoot outside in fifty-degree weather, when

---

[23] Daniel Lapin, "Judaism Today: Why Jews Still Obey the Law," *Crisis Magazine*, March 1, 1994.

Southern children are in their fleece jackets. I think babies need socks when it's cold, but seven-year-olds running through the house probably don't, until they're ready to go out. (But putting bare feet into sneakers or boots is a bad idea, because you need the layer of clean cotton to absorb sweat and keep foot fungus from growing.)

I don't think men should walk around without shirts on, but I wouldn't blame a guy for shedding a few layers, whereas those used to very hot weather can't believe that we New Englanders don't get out our coats until the frost hits.

For most of the time, everyone dresses for the normal round of getting in and out of the car and in and out of heated buildings. You want to be aware of what one needs for the elements, should one be caught in them. But as the parent, you must also know how to dress when it's legitimately cold. It's up to you to anticipate that your child will be out in the cold and wind for a long time.

No matter what, once it gets below fifty-five degrees or so, an undershirt is a must! Even with only a shirt on over the underwear T-shirt, a child can be comfortable whether things get a little warm or a little chilly. In a big range of moderate weather, no sweater will be needed.

What I'm trying to get at is this: once it's cold, once you have the heat on (and some hardy souls here can't imagine touching the thermostat before Thanksgiving—but then, they also know how to dress!), you have to protect your children against *sudden changes*. Sometimes they are going from overheated schools straight into biting winds. One sweatshirt on bare skin is not going to keep them warm.

Please note well: for true protection against unremitting cold, you must dress in a very specific way. Wool socks in sturdy waterproof boots, a set of long johns under corduroys, an undershirt, flannel shirt, and sweater, a warm parka with hat, mittens, and scarf—with the scarf wrapped *inside* the coat. Not to mention snow pants for staying dry.

Obviously, any child would expire on the spot if put into a warm car dressed this way. In fact, I always told my kids to wait to put on their coats because I knew they would start suffocating in the mudroom if they got completely bundled up too soon.

Once a child is dressed in the way I've described, expect him to start shedding layers as he sleds or skis. But also know that if the wind chill is high and the sun disappears, there is serious risk of hypothermia and frostbite, and the stuff has to go back on.

Chilblains, that quaint ailment we vaguely note in Victorian literature, are real. Many a child in our times has redness and pain and even damage to the tissues of his extremities simply from not being dressed properly, even in the house.

You Have to Tuck It In!

Tuck the T-shirt into the underpants and, if the shirt allows it, the shirt into the pants. Then not only are things warm, but they don't slide around, and as a bonus, the pants stay up. For girls, tuck the T-shirt into the panties, and that way, the tights or leggings won't bother their middles, and their dresses will be comfy. It's not modest or warm *or comfortable* to wear a skirt with one's belly sticking out!

You think your child doesn't mind when his belly is exposed? Maybe some aren't bothered. But the more sensitive to his surroundings a child is, the more careful you need to be about getting his core nicely tucked in smooth cotton. The more fretful your child, the more reluctant to join in games or go outside or put down his book, the more you should pay attention to what I'm saying here.

For the very reason that your child has "sensory issues" you need to know these things. I know because I had these issues, and I remember that dressing the way I'm describing is what freed me to be able to move around, run, and jump, which is what children *should* do.

I didn't like it when things felt loose, even though I probably said I did, and I probably resisted taking the time to dress this way, on the grounds that "I hated it" or "I didn't need to." I probably flailed and collapsed on the floor in a heap—and that's probably why for a long time I wasn't dressed properly. Sensory issues often go along with impatience and a wild horror of being made to do things one doesn't want to do, and parents often cave in the face of such behavior.

Nevertheless, the more a child has these difficulties, the more he needs clothing that fits, that can feel firm on his body, that doesn't leave him too hot or too cold. And really, only someone with experience—a *grown-up*—can figure it all out. How can a child know what things will be like in a few hours or in a different location? You're the mother, you're the father: you know that a child has that constitutional reluctance to invest time and effort now for a future gain—in fact, that is the definition of immaturity!

So you have to pay attention to this, using your common sense! Say, "Put on a T-shirt under your shirt and wear your jacket. You can take it off *later* if you are too hot."

The Lesson of *The Miracle Worker*

work of art can convey truths in a way that no textbook ever can. If that art is based on, as they say, "a true story," it can be even more compelling. The insight we gain is irreplaceable.

Yet, I would say that in our day-to-day lives, *especially when it comes to child-raising*, we increasingly base our principles on textbooks, not on art or experience or even common sense. Textbooks (and studies, and scientific literature based on studies, and posts shared on social media) carry an air of authority, but often we forget to ask about the ontology behind the conclusions presented. In other words, we accept the findings of the experts, but we don't inquire into their worldview. What do they have in mind when they advise us on how to treat our children, difficult or otherwise? What do they know about what it means to be a human being—about human *nature*?

What are their goals? What is the picture they have in mind when they speak of "normal" or "appropriate" or "acceptable" or even just "possible" behavior? What expectations do they have for the parents? What resources do they think the parents have? Do they take into account their limitations?

Yes, my observation is that the experts view parents as very limited, but in a self-defeating way. They think that parents are hopelessly lacking in insight into their own children (which can often be true but not fatally so!). But they utterly prescind from the question of *virtue*—of whether the parents have any, are seeking any, or even know that it matters.

When I was very young, I read *The Miracle Worker*, saw the play, and watched the movie. It's about the blind, deaf, and mute Helen Keller, whom Annie Sullivan, a difficult and strong-willed young woman, rescues from a terrible fate—a life of being treated as less than human. And the story formed my attitudes about child-raising in general.

In reading this book, you must try to forget what you know about the influential (and not entirely admirable) figure that Keller was to become and consider the point of view of the other family members. She was truly spoiled, as a result of the combination of her willful temperament, which was to stand her in good stead when channeled, and her family's combined indulgence and dislike. She had seemingly overwhelming physical limitations. She was dirty (as mentioned in the play). How hopeless it all seemed.

The short play presents in dramatic form much wisdom about the human condition, not least of which is that a person must have suffered in order to be of use to someone else who is suffering. Annie can help Helen because she has struggled with her own shortcomings—physical and moral—and the struggle has made her virtuous and wise, well beyond her years. Helen's family cannot help her because they don't struggle, not even against their helplessness, although they do pity and they do worry.

Literature, as so many before me have observed, offers us vicarious growth. (Thank goodness, as there is no way that any one person can undergo all the experiences necessary for acquiring all the virtues. Yet completely virtuous we must strive to be!) So we ourselves undergo a moral transformation as we are offered, in turn, all the choices available to us, through the various characters in the story. As we are offered these choices, we can feel paralyzed by our shortcomings and our uncertainty; we can merely pity; we can impatiently dismiss; we can contemn. We can do the worst thing of all, which is succumb to acedia, the apathy of not wishing to exert the energy necessary to turn to the good and change accordingly. Parents do often lose hope this way. We fail to act on what we know is good for our child.

The crux of the matter—as it is in the story—is *reality*.

Annie Sullivan must overcome the household's desperation to connect Helen with reality, against huge odds. But pay close attention as you read: The greatest obstacles she faces are not Helen's physical handicaps. No, the obstacles are the other people and the fact that, in their diverse weaknesses, no one has had the wisdom and courage to treat Helen as if *they*, the others, exist. They have not given Helen any of what we, at our house, like to call *reality feedback*. Don't fail to notice that among other things, they think she's too young to benefit from realistic responses from them.

Annie expresses this in terms of *manners* after her first encounter with Helen. Pay close attention to how *manners* connect with the very thing that restores Helen to her own humanity: finding meaning in her connection with the world.

This lesson is one that every mother and father must internalize in order to succeed at raising children, because the whole task can be summed up as introducing the child, hopefully gradually and with firmness and affection, to the reality of the world outside him and the self-control to deal with it. If parents don't embrace this task—including with the "special needs" child—they often find that they have consigned him to facing the task alone, later, with painful abruptness, often entailing what seems like cruelty from others (as when Annie isolates Helen from the family and their destructive pity).

Indeed, a whole category of literature deals with this very situation: having been cheated of the curriculum of self-control in the school of virtue offered by a virtuous family, the child must endure an agonizing rehabilitation at a later point.

What the story teaches us is that each child is unique and incomparable, with a spirit all his own, however buried under whatever we might characterize as handicaps; and the whole adventure requires *our own moral growth*, available to us, provided we don't settle for merely *managing* the child's behavior, the unspoken goal of many experts.

Had it not been for Annie and her virtue of fortitude, the world would have not received the gift of the extraordinary humanity of Helen Keller, with all her flaws and all her energy. And we would not have received the gift of a compelling lesson in overcoming our shortcomings for the sake of our children, because we would have no idea that this is the way to proceed.

I consider this book foundational to restoring the collective memory. It's a book that a parent might spend time reading early on in the family's journey, so that the message becomes integral.

The play is also an excellent choice for your sixth to eighth grader who is a good reader but too young for the heavy-duty classics.

Don't Wear Out Your Child's Name

Are you wearing out your child's name?

I have noticed that some otherwise lovely children from good families do not respond to their own name. I have talked to my husband about it; we agreed that we can hardly imagine it. In fact, he remembers thinking, as a young child in school, that one's name, spoken out loud, had an actual, physical effect on one, as of an electric shock. He assumed this was a universal phenomenon, well known to science.

But everywhere you go, there are children running around whose response to their name isn't an electrical shock; it isn't a "Yes, ma'am?" (oh, how I wish I were born Southern and could have taught my children to say "ma'am" and "sir"!); it's ... nothing.

Why? Because their families have worn their names out. Their mothers have desensitized these children to their own names!

Here's how it goes. Whether knowingly or not, you may have subscribed to the disciplinary method that has its roots in the writings of that well known child abuser, the eighteenth-century philosopher Jean-Jacques Rousseau. Rousseau, at the very time that he was abandoning his offspring, convincingly argued that children are born in a state of nature, possessing a personality that will gently unfold into perfection, if we only would not interfere.

I say convincingly because even those who profess the opposite—that we are born into a condition known as Original Sin and need to learn self-control—in effect raise their children as if they opened the wrong philosophy textbook by mistake.

Unwittingly operating as Rousseauians means that parents don't have a coherent way to deal with the inevitable—that is to say, the naughtiness of children. They take advice from Rousseauians, whose own children are not well behaved (if they have any). Why? Because it seems nicer and demands nothing at the moment of them. It's far easier to explain things, after all, than to put your phone down, get up, and be that mean, authoritative parent who administers the appropriate reality conditioning at the moment. Unfortunately, this brings not "the peaceable fruit of justice" of discipline but the long-term unpleasantness of bratty children who don't even answer when you call their names!

The child does something wrong (or heck, just acts like a child) and there is one response, and one only: to *explain* to him why he should reconsider and, becoming one with the darling flower child he was, deep within, act nicer.

To start that process, they say the child's name. "Timmy, Timmy, Timmy, no Timmy, Timmy, don't hit your sister, would you like to have someone hit you with a Lego, Timmy, Timmy, TIMMY, TIMMY ..."

What would you do under these circumstances, which include precisely *no* consequence for the action, other than interminably hearing your name? Why, you would stop listening!

In fact, everyone just stops listening ...

Here is my solution.

First, admit the loss of effectiveness. Knowing is the first step.

Then, resolve to say your child's name under two circumstances only, for a whole week:

1. In an outright, honest bellow, to prevent him from chasing a ball into the street
2. With great affection, like the name of a long-lost friend

I met a lady with many children (double digits), from adult to toddler. By the reckoning of our age, this lady should have been a basket case, sitting in a corner, putting straws in her hair, mumbling gibberish into a stiff drink. You would have expected her to do nothing other than randomly, peevishly say her kids' names over and over, purely out of habit.

But I noticed that, to the contrary, she was poised and attentive to all, and when her ten-year-old ran through the kitchen at a good clip, she stopped what she was doing (which was attending to her many guests) and, with a smile and eye contact, said, "*James*! I haven't seen you in a while! How are you doing!"

In other words, what I was struck by was the real affection with which this child's name was spoken. I paid attention then, and later when they stayed a few days with us (always the test), these parents said all their children's names this way—with affection.

It made me think about how I feel when someone greets me, saying my name with warmth. I feel wonderful. It makes me examine my conscience about how I say my own loved ones' names, let me tell you.

I have another friend (also with a stunning number of children—just so you don't excuse yourself) who calls them Beautiful or Handsome, depending. That's right—all day long, "Handsome, put this over there." "Beautiful, come here by me." Softens the edges, doesn't it?

Give your request, order, or direction clearly, having considered within yourself if it's really worth it. (Otherwise, skip it.) Move the child's body where it needs to be. Put the naughty miscreant in the corner (facing it—much better than time out). Or administer a spanking. If the child is over the age of about seven or eight (too old to spank), you will have to get creative in your punishments, but make them immediate and painful (not threatening), like doing an extra chore, giving you five push-ups, or going to his room.

Eric Metaxas's biography of Dietrich Bonhoeffer opens with a sketch of his father, Karl, who was calm in his authority, imparting high moral standards and a firm sense of identity to his brood, with love. His mother was energetic, artistic, and idealistic (it didn't hurt to have a bunch of servants, I'll grant you that, but it seems that Paula was also practical). Karl, in a letter, said, " … we endeavor not to spoil them, and to make their young years enjoyable." She taught the children at home until they were eight or so, being "openly distrustful of the German public schools and their Prussian educational methods."

Dietrich was a man of wonderful temperament (even as a child) who ended by heroically sacrificing himself for others in WW II. Yet "he was often mischievous and got up to various pranks," a maid remembers, especially "when the children were supposed to get washed and dressed quickly … to go out. So one such day he was dancing round the room, singing and being a thorough nuisance. Suddenly the door opened, his mother descended upon him, boxed his ears right and left, and was gone. Then the nonsense was over. Without shedding a tear, he now did what he ought."[24]

I think there are so few examples for us of what confident, experienced (Dietrich was among the younger children), devoted mothers do. We listen to "experts" instead of being able to pattern ourselves on what works. Maybe if we can be honest about what is *not* working, we'll be able to find a good way of fixing things.

Saying your child's name until he stops hearing it is not working!

It will take about a week to change things if you work on new habits, such as simply saying your child's name less often and with either more affection or (rarely) warnings of danger, using more effective methods instead to ensure obedience.

[24] Eric Metaxas, *Bonhoeffer: Pastor, Martyr, Prophet, Spy* (Nashville: Thomas Nelson, 2014), 13.

Six- to Eleven-Year-Olds
Need Less Patience from You

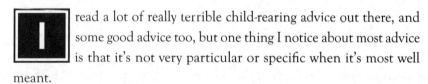read a lot of really terrible child-rearing advice out there, and some good advice too, but one thing I notice about most advice is that it's not very particular or specific when it's most well meant.

"Establish a home of peace and goodness" isn't exactly a road map when you are dealing with siblings who spend every waking moment together sniping, whining, moaning, and groaning. Wrapping these children up in quilts, depicting them in a hazy photographic glow, feeding them whole-some organic food, offering them vast opportunities for creative expression—none of these things compensates for lack of harmony together or provides the means to that end.

Here's what you need: obedient children. Obtaining them starts with teaching them to trust you from the very first moment of life—yes, in the womb—so start being trustworthy now.

Children need to know that there's a world outside themselves and they play a part in it. Don't expect great results in this area until around age six, but there's never a time when gently encouraging awareness is not appropriate. It's hard to draw a line *here* and say this is what you do now and this is what you do then, but even very small children are learning in a radical way that there is a world outside themselves. A two-year-old needs to begin to learn to do what you say. This is so that he will be safe. It's also so that he will *feel* safe and not afraid. It's a mercy to a child to require obedience from him (in keeping with his age), and it is the worst dereliction of duty to neglect to do so.

Less patience, more short, declarative sentences. More yelling, if you really need to yell, with, of course, more hugging and laughing, and then a renewed resolve to cultivate your own pleasant voice. Don't worry. If you are guiding your children in this way I am describing, rather than tensely and artificially trying to keep some sort of impossible peace, the yelling will subside.

WWMD? (What Would Ma Do?)

When Pa Ingalls was away and a bear came to the Little House, Ma told Laura to get inside. And she went, even though she didn't see the bear at first. Would your little girl do what you said in that situation?

Today, with children raised in the false comfortable world of prosperity, where parents think they have the luxury of listening to "experts" (who have no obedient children themselves), we'd read this scenario:

"Laura, get inside!"

"Why?"

"Sweetie, get inside, please. Mommy needs you to get inside. Mommy doesn't want to scare you, but there's a big bear, and she needs you to make a good choice now and do what she says."

"Will you buy me a treat?"

"Yes, sweetie, please, go inside."

"Where's Daddy?"

"Mommy knows you have questions, and that's very smart of you. I'm so proud of you. Please go inside now."

"He's never here! Why isn't he here? You *told* me he'd be here!"

"Sweetie, when you argue with me, you are making a bad choice. What did we say about bad choices? Now, you'll have a time-out if you don't do what I say."

Meanwhile, the bear eats them.

Why? Because Mommy is so *patient* that she allowed every interaction with her child to be an exchange between equals rather than a strong wall that a child can't breach, even for her own sake.

Do you know that today, teachers must build "arguing time" into the school day? Today's children have the habit of questioning every directive, and of course, teachers can't just lay down the law, because then the school would be sued. So instead, they allow more time for arguing!

Pause to shake head.

People often say that I must be very patient to have seven children, which is quite amusing. People think that I never yelled when my children misbehaved; that I never felt as if they were ganging up on me; that I never wanted to pitch them out the window.

But really, patience is learning to accept all of that and yet still demand of yourself that you ask your children to be the obedient, kind, smart people you know they can be. Your children teach you *that* kind of patience!

You don't want them to be good children according to some model of a good child. Your goal is for each child to be the best *he* can be.

The Right and Wrong Kinds of Patience

I am the advocate for not being so patient with your children, which I realize seems odd. Obviously, be patient when they ask "Why?" for the ten thousandth time, or when they need to pick up one more "pretty rock" (i.e., piece of gravel), or when they are crying from a fall.

Be patient with yourself. Forgive yourself for losing your temper and go on to be a strong demander of good behavior. Don't react to every little thing, and don't look for affirmation from the little stinkers.

Here are some mental exercises for you to ascertain whether you have the right level of patience with your little ones (say, four to six, with the two-year-old toddling after the four-year-old because she's modeling such good behavior) and are succeeding in the prompt-obedience project:

1. My child would pick up a designated beach bag and walk toward the car if I said it was time to go, whether I meant that it's dinner time or there's a thunderstorm on the horizon.[25]

2. My child puts toys away at a friend's house and gets ready to leave when I say so.[26]

3. My child would go inside the house if I told him to, whether or not he actually saw the bear.[27]

4. My child would get me the rifle or a Phillips-head screwdriver without whining.

5. My child of three or four buckles himself in the car seat.

6. My child gets me a diaper for the baby.

---

[25] Nothing so astonishes me as seeing a mom laden like a packhorse with the kids' beach toys and a baby on her hip, trying to herd her unruly brood to safety when there's lightning near the water—and they won't obey. I am mad at her: she did it to herself. My children were just as naughty, mischievous, and interested in staying as long as possible at the beach as anyone else's. But I put the work in to convince them that they had better listen to me without arguing and whining. Not that I wouldn't give an answer to a reasonable question or take into consideration something that was pointed out to me.

We talked all the time! But if I said "move," they had to trust me and move. If they didn't obey in easy, normal, non-life-threatening circumstances, they would get a spanking.

That way, in tough and dangerous situations, they were on my wavelength. So they were buckled in the car and eating their snacks for the drive home while all the other rotten kids were out there getting struck by lightning.

[26] You have to say "time to go" when you *really* want to go, not at some vague point before, when *you* still have lots of conversation with your friend to get through. Stop talking, get up, and go. I guarantee you, if you do this five times in a row, your children will always obey you cheerfully.

[27] It's especially hard to get a young child to *go away* from you, but sometimes it's very necessary. If your child really trusts you and has learned to be obedient, he will do it. Getting you a diaper or other things in other rooms is good practice for going away from you.

7. My child will duck under the table if I tell him to (yes, we made our kids do this and all these things, and they're fun to practice).
8. My child will stop talking if I say so.

If you answered no to any of these questions, well, this is what this chapter is about.

Discipline at the Age of Reason

A child from the age of five to thirteen (children differ, and girls and boys differ from each other) is in a time of latency as regards sex, violence, and world affairs. Without getting too Freudian about it, it helps to know that, once having mastered their bodily functions (including being able to resist physically disintegrating into a sad puddle when things go wrong), children enter a phase of mastering the world around them. If you respect that phase and protect your children from anything that will disturb this process, while helping them to grow in awareness of the needs of others, you will have the joy of experiencing truly happy, well adjusted kids.

That seemingly shallow label, manners, can help us understand how to approach this time. So often manners are something people think of as pasted on to basically narcissistic behavior, a way to manipulate others so that you get what you want and they don't get mad at you. But manners truly are the tip of the charity iceberg, and charity is simply treating people with that very love and consideration you would like to receive.

Of course even a one-year-old can learn to say "thank you," and that's a great, indispensable start, but it's a six-year-old who needs to become aware that people are doing things for him all day. It seems to me that if you've trained your children in obedience when they are little, this stage offers you two challenges:

1. Getting them to be good companions because they are more thoughtful about others every day, wash their hands, and don't smear ketchup on their faces

2. Getting them to see that although you encourage them to experiment, just because they have a bright idea about something (Daddy's ax, Mommy's sewing machine, the baby's carriage and that hill, the package of nails and the toilet, etc.), they probably shouldn't act on it without consultation, because you can't make rules about everything.

The difficulty of the second challenge is that these things are hard on you and have a tendency to interrupt naps. But they aren't that bad, and if you provide enough of an outlet for your children's physical energy, these things should be mostly avoidable.

So really, it's about manners, isn't it? Standing up to greet grown-ups entering the room; looking people in the eye; not chattering incessantly; passing food; speaking up when asked a question and answering with clarity such questions as, "Would you like milk or juice?"

"Umm ... I don't care." *Wrong.*

Right: "Milk, please. Thank you very much, Mrs. Jones."

"He says I have to go downstairs." *Wrong.*

Right: "Mr. Jones says I have to go downstairs."

Wearing appropriate clothes for the occasion, whatever it may be; quieting down so that you don't disturb the baby or others in church; eating without complaining: these are steps in figuring out that the world exists outside of oneself.

Ten Rules for Mothering a Thirteen-Year-Old Boy

Dear Carlyn has a simple question:

> I surely would appreciate your input about parenting teenage boys. My son will be turning thirteen this summer, and I need some wise counsel about navigating these strange seas.
>
> Love,
> Carlyn

I admit I did chuckle a little when I read this question, because it brought to mind a time when my two eldest were so little. I was visiting a friend whom I admired for embracing her large family with a can-do attitude. When I met her, she was having twins, her sixth and seventh children; and far from feeling oppressed, wearied, or confused, she took it all in stride. She had so much experience! *Her* eldest child was thirteen, a boy.

Imagine my surprise, then, when one day she casually exclaimed, "Ugh, I just hate [name hidden to protect the innocent]!"

How shocked I was! He seemed a perfectly nice boy, and she really was a good mother. She was laughing, but *how* could one say such a thing about one's very own son! I clutched my precious baby Rosie protectively to my bosom, looked at my little Nick, the cutest two-year-old on the face of the earth, and thought, "Well, *I* would never say such a thing about *my* sweet boy."

You know how that story ends. The day I found myself saying, "Ugh, I just *hate*—" I clapped my hand over my mouth! I realized that, yes, indeed, my darling had just turned thirteen. And sure enough, one year later, my cheerful buoyant son was restored to me.

I'm still amused as I often console a friend whose son is approaching his thirteenth birthday! Of course, it isn't always so drastic, and maybe the age varies a bit, but not much!

However, this question is a hard one. Auntie Leila doesn't know where to start. It's been truly said that building character in an adolescent begins in early childhood, which is why I spend so much time talking about that phase, even though I get lots of e-mails like this one begging for help with older kids.

But I would deplore giving the impression that I think that if everything goes right in the early years, the period of adolescence will be easy, or, conversely, if things have gone not quite right with the little ones, we have no hope with the teens. Neither is true, necessarily.

And, among other issues, when our child's growing-up period hits us, we're still struggling with ourselves. How dare these little cuddly infants get old and needy and critical of our way of life, when we are pretty much adolescents ourselves, barely starting to figure things out, trying to get control of our whims and fantasies, unsure of our commitment to the fight to achieve our own maturity?

Most advice I have read on the topic amounts to this admission: "The entire culture has given up on even the pretense of overcoming its own arrested development, so lose all hope of seeing your children mature before they have permanently damaged themselves somehow. We understand that you yourself have infantile needs you can't resist, so we'll help you come to terms with handing over your responsibilities to those who don't have your child's best interest at heart. Lie back and enjoy."

An honest look at the culture confirms my assessment that parents have no support from the "experts" when it comes to the teen years. So here are my thoughts on dealing with teenage boys, those mysterious creatures who so recently delighted you with their openness, their cuteness, and their unquestioned sweet love. It's not unusual for an eleven-year-old boy to hold Mom's hand while walking down the street. And then, a blink, and suddenly you overhear him on the phone with someone, mumbling and literally grunting! He can no longer speak! He has lost the power of communication! He must also have something wrong with his neck, because he can't look up! He might have narcolepsy, because he's never awake!

Yes, the time of childhood is outward directed; the child is simply learning about reality. The time of adolescence is inward directed; he is finding out who he is *at the same time* he is experiencing a tremendous physical challenge.

Don't worry. Persist for a year, applying to the best of your ability these rules that I have developed just for you. I'm quite sure that after a year from the time the grunting and mumbling is first noticed, you will see improvements. He'll still be growing, but he'll be more interactive; more, how shall we put it ... human.

And what do you know, that whole time you have to be working on yourself too.

Remember my golden principles of parenting:
- Reacting is not a valid parenting technique! You are the adult. You act.
- Don't seek affirmation from your children! You are the adult. You get affirmation from doing what's best for them. Take care that "attitude"—the first reaction you get from your teen, the response that seems not to take into consideration the considerable devotion and tribulation you've put into your efforts to bring him to reason—doesn't bother you.

Don't be surprised when things are not perfect!

And my usual disclaimer: whatever I have learned has been from the SOHK (School of Hard Knocks) and most of it can truly be said to be

DWISNWID (Do what I say, not what I did) or at least LFMM (Learn from my mistakes).

The first three rules, which I'm getting to, seem so lacking in lofty insight. But I'm surprised and shocked and chagrined that I search in vain for them to be mentioned in the experts' advice. So pardon me for being obvious or mundane or not taking it for granted that you already know these fundamental points.

1. *Feed him.* At this stage, everything turns inward for the simple biological reason that these boys are, in the next two years, going to grow a foot or more in every direction. This process requires a lot of food. Snap out of your lentil soup and carrot salad mode and serve up a double cheeseburger with that dainty morsel. I'm not telling you what to eat; I'm just saying that you need a lot more of it, and it needs to include more than some greens. Always offer good hearty bread and butter. What you used to consider a meal—a taco with two tablespoons of meat and some lettuce, plunked on a plate—is really the beginnings of a snack. For it to be a meal for this man-child, it would require rice, beans, guacamole, and slaw, followed by a bowl of oatmeal. Make sure that you plan extra servings in your favorite casserole—go ahead, double it! You'll be surprised how it disappears.

2. *Make sure he sleeps.* Much—much—of what we take for a serious psychological problem requiring outside intervention can be simply (and cheaply) solved by more sleep. I call it Intensive Sleep Therapy (IST), and I'm willing to market it.

It goes without saying that there should be no electronic equipment of any kind in the children's bedrooms. I will allow an alarm clock (an old-fashioned alarm clock, not a phone). But no computer or texting device. Keep the computer very much under your eye in a nice public place, such as the kitchen or den. Bedrooms are for reading and for sleeping.

A thirteen-year-old boy might be mortified to be sent to bed at eight or nine o'clock, but he can retire for quiet reading. If you start to see a lot of zoning out, napping, and lying on the sofa as if stricken by a mosquito-borne disease, make that bedtime earlier!

If the events of the previous night have caused a lack of sleep, then be sure to be even meaner about IST tonight and save yourself a lot of grief. For instance, returning from a sports tournament will require two nights of early bedtimes to recover from.

While you're at it, go to bed yourself, because more food and more sleep are the answer to most of life's problems, as far as I can see. More food, more sleep: the first two steps in any protocol worth following.

3. *Let me just suggest that you cut his hair, making sure to trim the sides and clean up the neck fuzz.* Take it from someone who survived the seventies. No one can relate to an ungroomed, shaggy, unkempt mess. I'm so sorry that this look has returned.

Part of you doesn't want to deal with it, and part of you isn't sure it's worth it. At the very least, if you can't fight this battle, insist that his hair not be in his eyes. Hair that covers the eyes and requires fussing just feeds his desire to take refuge in the world of his making. It takes a lot of energy to hold one's head just so, to keep pushing the bangs not quite out of the way, and energy is just what he doesn't have much of! Hair on the face also provides an environment for acne, another problem he can certainly live without.

It's unseemly enough in a girl to have a hairstyle that requires constant attention and prevents interpersonal communication. In a boy, it's unmanly. It's no coincidence that the shaggy style (if you want to call it a style) continues to gain traction. It corresponds to even more narcissism in our society, if that's possible.

Thinking only about oneself—the central problem of adolescence—goes hand in hand with not presenting a fresh, open face to those who have to speak to him and who would like to be given the chance to love him. (In other words, it's not just you. Everyone is having trouble with this thirteen-year-old boy.)

Why make things hard? Or rather, why not endure the *present* hardship of insisting on grooming, in order to make it easier for others (and face it, you yourself) to react well to him?

Just as you require a jacket in cold weather or breakfast before a hike, you mandate grooming for your son's own good. And you already know that other people, who may not love your children the way you do right off the bat (or ever), respond better when the little darlings are clean and nicely dressed. Same goes for their hair. So just give him that assist, will you?

NB: I've noticed that as a child grows at this time of his life, he by no means grows proportionately. Sometimes one feature—usually the nose—gets weirdly out of whack, giving him a temporarily goofy look that doesn't help you take him seriously. If he's at least tidy, you'll find it easier not to give up on him as hopelessly gawky. I know you can't imagine that I'm telling the truth, but I am.

4. *Treat him as if he's older and younger.* Show him that you know he's on his way to growing up by understanding if he doesn't want to do kids' stuff or be surrounded by little kids all the time. But keep him in the family circle.

Having him share a room with his brothers is never a bad idea, even if it seems so to him; it's better than being off in the basement by himself. A thirteen-year-old gets lonely but doesn't know how to say that (or even admit it to himself) and doesn't know how to reenter human society. You feel a bit intimidated by his sudden retreat from what the younger children are up to, and that's understandable. As I said, it's a learning curve for you too. But try not to exile him too far.

If you can provide him with a baby brother or sister, or at least a puppy if no human companionship is on the horizon, you will be rewarded with the knowledge that at least he's hugging something! Sneak in a few hugs yourself. Don't let him set the hugging agenda, because it will have no items on it.

5. *Insist on real learning*: real books; real discussions, even if they consist of grunts on his part. Don't give up, because this is the most crucial time for young people, in which they are desperately seeking coherence in themselves, you, and the world. Don't let him down by giving in to what amounts to attitude (that uncontrolled reaction—I mean, what do you expect, for him, in his current state of molecular upheaval, to show in his expression what he will really feel only later?).

If anything, renew your determination to provide what is true, beautiful, and good in the education you give your children.

If you have younger children, be sure to include your young man in read-alouds. If you don't have anyone younger to read to, the direct approach might work anyway. "I would love to read this book aloud. We'll do it after lunch." How about listening to books in the car?

Try to choose books that will appeal to him as well as the younger ones—adventures, classics, anything that is substantial. In the resource section of this book, I have good booklists for you; and don't be afraid to choose something that might seem too young for him. Let him enjoy being a child for a while longer.

When you have interesting guests, include him at least for a few minutes. Children should be taught from the earliest age to take coats, help get guests comfy, and offer food. This is so that when they are thirteen, they can converse and perhaps learn something!

6. *Make sure he gets exercise.* He needs to be active. Sometimes he feels so odd in his own body that he doesn't want to move it around too much. It's worth the effort to keep him on a team or to be sure he gets together with friends to play basketball. And anything that includes nature—hiking and camping!—is perfect.

Some experts emphasize exercise because they see it as a release from the tension brought about by sexual development. I think these same people are a bit obsessed with sexuality, from what I can see, making it the *whole* of what's going on in adolescence.

It's a good thing for *overall* health for a young person to be active. Dealing specifically with their sexuality requires that and something more: it requires that we see that sexuality is given to man for the purpose of marriage (or the offering up for a higher purpose of virginity for the Kingdom). In other words, sexuality is a gift that has to do with vocation, commitment, and covenant. You can read about it in the Bible, especially in the books of Genesis and Matthew. For a boy to understand this truth about his body is the work of two things: family life in general (see number 10) and confidential talks with his dad (see number 9).

7. *Work.* It's hard to believe that this child, this kid, this immature grunting person must, in a few short years, decide on or at least develop some notion of what he will do with his life.

I hope that from the first days he could toddle, you've been getting him to haul things and build things and move things and in general help out. Even if you haven't, it's not too late to start. And here's where not being too well off financially really helps. After all, if a company does your yard work, it's pretty hard to motivate your teen to rake. But if everyone has to pitch in, there you go. Building a deck, repairing a shed, shoring up a wall, stacking wood: these are wonderful things for a young man to take on. He may even have ideas on how to do things; it doesn't hurt to ask.

Keep your eye on what really energizes him. Don't be content to put him through the mill of school and extracurriculars, thinking that you can cover all your bases that way. Better for the family to find opportunities for him to take an interest and learn something about it with someone who knows the subject (also known as apprenticing, a venerable and glorious tradition that we would do well to recover).

8. *Demand manners and civility.* If you haven't taught your child to look someone in the eye and shake hands firmly, now is the time to do so (see number 5). Well, his dad can teach him (see number 9). Remind your child that shaking a lady's hand or the hand of an elderly person who might have arthritis requires firm but *gentle* pressure, which is quite different from limp or fishlike or noncommittal. I have encountered young men who've had the idea of a firm handshake so drilled into them that they cannot be firm yet gentle with a lady, no matter how it's presented to him ("Be chivalrous!" "A gentleman never hurts a lady!"). That's the opposite end of the spectrum from failing to teach the manly thing and is just as unmanly in its own way.

Speaking of manners, no matter what you have allowed in the past in some misguided attempt to refrain from repressing your child or harming his self-esteem, when you have teenagers, you simply must require, and yourself live by, the rule that while anger can be expressed, a fundamentally loving and respectful attitude must be maintained. Everyone loses his temper occasionally, and we all shout things we don't mean. Those times call for a quick apology and reconciliation.

But if you let *habitual* unpleasantness of tone and words reign, you are in deep trouble. Parents aren't always right, but they always deserve respect. It's just a *bad habit*—a habit the parents have tacitly accepted—for a child to give snappy answers, use a put-upon tone of voice, and say mean things.

The way to stop a habit is to stop dead in your tracks. Don't nag, don't explain, don't yell. Just stop. Stop the car. Stop the meal. Stop the discussion. Do not take one more step until what's said is said in a way that would be acceptable to a mere acquaintance or a total stranger.

Of course, this means that *your* normal tone has to be friendly, that you have to smile, that you must be pleasant! If you have to yell, then yell. If you're mad, then be mad! But don't fall into the strained if-I-must-speak-to-you-it's-under-duress way of dealing with each other, much less hurling insults and I-hate-yous!

One thing my eldest child and youngest child have taught me is to say "I love you" frequently, especially when saying goodbye. What if that's the last time you ever speak to someone? Look at the child coming in; look at him, in the eyes, when taking leave of him.

9. *Wait 'til Dad gets home.* My dear fellow mother, you must accept that you have done your best or at least had your chance. From here on in, yes, you can gently correct and you can guide, and you can cry (don't lightly discount crying), but more and more you must allow your husband to handle your son.

A common complaint and justification for being the gatekeeper, so to speak, in the adolescent's life is that the wife finds her husband ineffectual, lacking the advanced intuition and superior sensitivity that she possesses. This certainty that only *she* can solve the problems, if confronted, is an indication, a warning sign, to pay attention to a new phase of life—namely, that the marriage has new challenges that it must meet.

Just as your child is developing according to well known stages, so is your relationship with your husband (but the changes are not as well known). Yet all the advice I've ever read assumes this very element, the marriage, to be static. You can't see it, because you're in the midst of it. No one tells you, because so few people survive beyond the early stages with enough energy to explain what happened! Many find that the second decade of their life together is too much, and sadly they split up. Many lose concentration and lose their children in the process, even if they manage to stay together. Not necessarily literally lose (although that can happen), but sort of passively allow the culture to take over and do its thing, because if they try to resist, they find the strain on the marriage too great.

Your marriage comes first. Having his conviction, and acting upon it, is how you help your children.

So this moment—of permitting your own influence over your son to take its natural course into a less dictatorial mode, while your husband's influence increases—is God's way of helping you realize that, though exerting the Herculean effort of organizing your family for the past dozen years has been indispensable, you must now readjust your thinking to allow for others' ways of doing things. This stage is how the mother is rescued from the fate of always telling everyone what to do (unless she happens to get into blogging and authoring and bossing around perfect strangers).

Your husband has had to provide for a home fit for babies, which has required a lot of change on his part. Now comes the new task of getting his family to face the world. You realize your expertise is in managing the household, but not teenage boys.

What's beautiful is that, as your bossing capacity wanes, your powers of loving guidance increase, so do not fear this stage. By the way, this is why I think it's completely misguided to waste time complaining that men don't bear the burden of baby nurturing or housekeeping. The people who want perfect parity just don't understand what life in the second decade of raising children is like; they don't seem to have any insight into the responsibility a man feels when he realizes that his wife has done a fine job of making a home, and now it's his task to help his precious young ones obtain a stable vision of reality out in the world. His wife can help him most by understanding that this test comes just at the time that he is perhaps experiencing real doubts about his success so far.

There has to be *something* your husband can do, and this is it. No, I'm not saying that he has nothing to do with the early years—obviously not (although permit me to note that it's feminists with their endless demands for chore equality who are most critical of men's contributions at home; they never seem to stop complaining about men's shortcomings).

My husband changed a million diapers and rocked seven children to sleep; he hauled laundry baskets up and down basement stairs and did a lot of dishes. But he also respected my innate understanding of what these little children's needs were. He knew his time was coming, when they would be too much for me to handle; when his deep voice was wanted with a new urgency; when those grunts were baffling me.

Amazingly, your son's inability to communicate meshes perfectly with your husband's inability to communicate! This is a partial, but only partial, jest. You see, just as your son is reaching this difficult age, your husband is most likely also reaching a stage when he isn't sure he wants to talk about things so much anymore. That is undoubtedly *not* wonderful, just as you have really hit your stride in that department. While we complain at just this point in the marriage: "He doesn't listen to me!" perhaps what's happening is that a new horizon is opening, one where, with your encouragement, your husband can step in to relate to someone he can understand—no, not you! That difficult new teen.

Start with the conviction that, *with your affirmation*, your husband will find the right way to reach your son. The encouragement you offer him has to be very much behind the scenes and fortified with a lot of real trust in his methods, something you achieve with all the effort of convincing yourself that you may not know everything. And effort it will take! *He* may be the expert on adolescent boys, having been one himself! We have to accept that there is something there, *something male*, that we don't understand.

Then we will find that we have facilitated something we wanted all along, which is strong bonds in the family. We find that our husband and sons have mutual respect and a wonderful friendship—one that, yes, may sometimes seem to leave us out or even cause gentle teasing about our womanly ways.

Well, fine—we mock them all the time!

10. *Cling to Sunday more than ever.* This is the most practical thing I have to say. Right about when your first child gets to be an adolescent, you will be overwhelmed by how complicated life seems to be.

How will you survive? By means of worship and rest. On Sundays, be together. Enjoy each other's company.

The mother must do whatever it takes to make it possible for the day to be a happy one. Remember, no one can figure out what to do about life without a peaceful moment.

As the children get older, they naturally show reluctance to do things they've always had to do. That's to be expected, and parents have to be flexible and understanding, but don't let go of your Sunday! It's the center of your family life. It's nonnegotiable.

In worship, don't demonstrate a loss of confidence by choosing a Liturgy you've been told is relevant to a young person. This approach, though well meaning, is doomed to failure. Either you take for granted a false idea of sophistication in the things of God, inadvertently promoting what you hope to avoid (for do we really want our children to be in the habit of continually moving on from permanent things?); or you expose yourself or the Church to the one thing from which you can't recover: the charge of being lame.

The worst thing for someone who is unsure of himself (e.g., an adolescent) is to appear ridiculous. And trust me, "youth ministry" church will always, eventually, be that. Thus, the safest and best course is to search out the form of worship that is highest, most beautiful, fullest, most traditional (and hence immune from obsolescence, having already proven its endurance), with the greatest spectrum of kinds and ages of people available.

Do you really want your child to outgrow worship? To outgrow the Third Commandment, of keeping holy the Sabbath Day? Yet this is what will happen, eventually, if you go to an age-specific service.

And, of course, having to rub shoulders with toddlers and old people couldn't be a better prescription for overcoming what ails your adolescent—namely, nigh-terminal self-absorption. It worked for the Jews for five thousand years and Christians for two thousand, to worship and raise their children to worship in a universal way. Why would we tamper with such a successful record? Can we be sure we are so smart?

As to the rest of the Sunday, cling to your family meals. Of course you should eat together whenever possible, but Sunday dinner, when Dad is truly resting and the day is devoted to being together, is sacrosanct. The time when the children are becoming teenagers is when your family truly gets its identity, and the supper table is where this identity emerges. I can't begin to catalog all the advantages when you keep hold of the family table, but consider: when you emerge from this difficult stage and realize you all really do love each other, you will be hard put *then* to recover a custom you never had.

If you do one thing for your teen, let it be that you lovingly keep the Lord's Day.

Mothering the
Twelve-Year-Old Girl

Now let's turn to the girl who is approaching adolescence. I called this chapter "Mothering the Twelve-Year-Old Girl" because truly, the year she turns twelve is when you question your skills. But to be honest, the equivalent in girls' development to my chapter above, about the teenage boy, would have to be stated thus:

From the age of about ten and a half to approximately fifty-one, she is going to make you crazy.

Since, presumably, *you* are also between the ages of ten and a half and fifty-one (I know I was at the time I wrote this), you see the problem.

I think we women can relate to the hormonal issues that a girl is facing, and we can understand intellectually that puberty begins remotely. The difficulty lies in being able to separate our difficulties from our daughters' and to accept that they *are* facing them when they seem to us as if they should still be little girls.

I want to remind you, as I did in the chapter on adolescent boys, that all this isn't just about physical changes and the drastic amounts of energy, physical and mental, that they require. It's also about this child, whose task up until now has primarily been to assimilate the sheer facts of the world around her, developing her inner self. She has an adulthood to rise to, and that work starts right now, in the body of this child, in her soul. Suddenly now she must find out who she is.

Again, as with the adolescent boy, I offer a list of strategies to help both of you across this torrent, safely to the other side:

1. *Worship, eat, sleep, learn, and work.* I'm bundling these together because they are covered in the previous chapter pretty well. I emphasize the importance of renewing your commitment to Sundays. Don't let "attitude" (the outward and possibly less than optimal expressions of the child) take away your delight in the Lord's Day.

Just as with boys, and for that matter, babies and toddlers learning to speak and eight-year-olds hiking up hills, and husbands during tax season: more sleep, more and higher-quality food.

Don't fret if your daughter is not thin. If your food is homemade and wholesome and you are careful to have her (and everyone in the family) eat at mealtimes and not constantly graze, it should sort itself out. Most girls are a bit chubby in this period between childhood and womanhood, something that our society doesn't acknowledge, with its weird obsessions. (We have been receiving *Vogue* magazine—as some kind of promotion, I think. I've noticed that 99 percent of this publication consists of photos of emaciated, almost deformedly elongated women, and of the 1 percent devoted to text, about 90 percent of that references eating disorders. Well, yes.) Some girls are a little pudgy. If you adjust for today's processed food, I think you'll find that pudginess is mainly genetic and biologically keyed into hormonal changes. If they are going to be rather tall, they do tend to be oddly shaped for a while, because a lot of material gets compressed into their bodies before their growth spurt. By the time they are done with puberty, they thin out—again, *if* they eat well and are active.

Now is the time for making sure your daughter is reading the "thousand good books" so that she will be ready for the "hundred great books" when she is older. (I cover book choices in volume 2.) Girls at this age tend either to read trendy material, the equivalent of junk food, or to jump right to classics that are too involved for them.

Work is important—Mom is often happy to have a girl around to chit-chat with, but that girl should shoulder real work around the house and a paying job if one is available, but have a care for her safety. A partying dad isn't always the best person to bring your babysitting daughter home at night. Don't let her be alone life-guarding at a lake if your warning bells are going off. Don't let her waitress somewhere where she'll be subjected to disrespect.

2. *Treat her as younger* and *older.* It's a hackneyed truth about adolescents that they want to be treated as children one moment and as adults the next. What the hackneyed-truth-purveyors don't tell you is this: act, don't react, by *anticipating* that she will need a warm hug, just as if she were seven again; and that at another time she needs to be given a responsibility and the trust to make a mess or success of whatever it is that she has undertaken.

When emotional explosions come (see number 6), don't lose your peace and *don't lose your sense of humor.* Kids at this age don't expect you to bring them in on the joke, because for as long as they can remember, the joke has sort of been on them. But they are delighted when you do. The sooner you start sharing your laughter with them, the better. It's a rocky road, otherwise.

3. *Hygiene and exercise.* It's important for a girl to be active, although team sports may not be her thing, sometimes because of the extreme self-consciousness that some girls experience. Still, hiking, swimming, and running with siblings are always good!

But where you simply remind your son to take a shower and put on *clean* clothes afterward, with your daughter, hygiene is a little more involved. Help her keep bathroom and mirror time in balance. If the hairstyle is complicated and the clothes are complicated and the hormones are leaping around, too much energy is diverted to such pursuits and away from being a rational human being. Help her simplify. At this age, my daughters actually welcomed a cute, shorter bob that doesn't need a lot of attention.

Her comfort level will be elevated by not having hair in her face or otherwise demanding a certain immobility of head or features to maintain, just as with boys. And of course, hair around the face encourages acne, and who needs that? How emotionally crippling some styles are!

Mind that she keeps her fingernails short and unlacquered. You can just do more without nail polish, and who knows what dirt lurks beneath that sparkly blue coat? My Egyptian aunties used to say, "She looked like the cat that ate her kittens!"—referring to the dark red nail polish and lipstick then fashionable. You can be sure hearing that comment discouraged any thought I had of wearing those colors! Now girls look as if they ate their kittens and then died of gangrene.

A book can help. Choose one that confines itself to matters of hygiene and hormonal changes, without venturing into sexual matters.

4. *Taking care of others is a womanly art.* Where boys, left to themselves, will talk about cars, sports, or some other topic often involving movable parts or levels, girls will tend to focus on relationships and their feelings or dreams. This can quickly deteriorate to the most unpleasant cliquish behavior imaginable, and I'm sure you have memories of being on the receiving end, if not perpetrating, this kind of thing.

Our girls need to be taught at this age to be kind to others, to choose good friends, and to be good friends. Now is the time to share things you've learned along the way. Your daughter wants to hear that she can change and that someone she thinks she doesn't like could change. Speaking ill of someone, besides just being wrong, thwarts friendship. It's hard to convince your friends that you will defend them if your conversation consists of always tearing others down. And this sort of conversation is truly the hallmark of the insecure. To be less insecure, a girl must *act* less insecure!

Everyone needs to vent or to talk things over with someone. That's what parents are for. Let your daughter know that she can tell you what's bothering her, and do be understanding. Listen closely, just as you would to your best friend. Sometimes you have to agree—yes, that girl was mean, or what she said was. This agreement is what she would look for from her friends, and she momentarily needs it (and *not* sanctimonious commentary, which you might be tempted to bestow upon her confidences).

You can give her that sense of having expressed herself. Encourage her to leave critiques of other girls (and teachers and parents even) out of her conversations with her friends. How strange if we never acknowledged the obvious or needed to discuss events. Let your daughter learn to acknowledge and even explore the ramifications of *bad conduct*, as Jane Austen would put it, while also excusing the person's behavior somehow and, most importantly, learning to put the best interpretation on it when speaking to others (without, however, descending to preachiness with *them*). In this way, she builds trust, and her friendships grow stronger.

Her self-consciousness is best overcome with real efforts to be generous and open to girls who might seem uncomfortable, shy, or, indeed, self-conscious! Learning to see that others have the exact same feelings we do is a big step to graceful womanhood.

How many times have you been in a group of women (or, on its outskirts, to be more exact) and experienced a lack of kindness? That behavior started right here in puberty. For some reason, boys don't seem to suffer the way girls do with this. Let's have *our* girls be the ones to overcome this defect, starting now.

5. *Demand good everyday manners.* Because our misguided culture glorifies bratty children in entertainment, and because we are a bit unsure ourselves about what manners are, our girls will often sass us, say mean things, and generally fail to please. If we took characters in movies as our guides, we would think that the normal response is to accept this behavior—sometimes even to apologize for our *own* responses!

If you take away one idea from this whole discussion, it's that we can give ourselves breathing space to solve a lot of issues if we just keep working on treating each other respectfully and requiring respectful behavior from those we have authority over.

Look at it this way. If there is some deep-seated problem and the family culture is to snap, backbite, mock, and be rude (or to allow all that from some terrorizing members who might be hormonally challenged), then even if you address that problem, you still have the culture. Whereas if you insist on *at least the minimum owed to a stranger* — looking up, saying "please" and "thank you," smiling once in a while, and answering audibly and with respect a question put to you — these habits make it possible to recover your happy home when the dragons are slayed.

6. *This time is also* your *developmental stage; don't be surprised if it isn't comfortable.* You are entering a new phase of your own life when your children start becoming adults. It's comparable to when they stopped being babies and could run around and "do it by myself." You matured then too, as you realized how much more was going to be asked of you! You are now going to learn so much about yourself, about how moody you are, about how self-conscious you are, about the long game, which requires the virtue of longanimity (patient long-suffering), and how hard it is to trust.

The difference between a boy and a girl at this age is this: whereas a boy tends to mumble and disappear, a girl develops an amazing capacity to take any small issue and suddenly explode over it. Things seem so impossible. Life is so horrible. And unlike her brothers, she will make you feel it all as your fault.

It's good to know that if the family does their best to help her with goals that seem realistic or, at least, truly important to her, when the dust settles in about eighteen months, she will be more at peace. That seems like a long time, I know, but there it is. Whether it's finding clothes she likes *and* you approve of, or figuring out how to become whatever it is she is dreaming of, let her know you are on her side even when it seems you are making life difficult.

Encourage her by showing that you are praying to find ways to meet her needs and desires. Especially when the large, busy, and impecunious family comes up against the vast dreamscape of the blossoming pubescent spirit, hope must be preserved! She must know that we are trying our best to help her achieve her aspirations, even if we think that in a few months, she'll be onto something else. Maybe so, but let's not be gloomy and know-it-all about it.

Remember what I told you before: keep your emotional detachment when it looks as if you're in danger of acting twelve yourself. Be very much above your daughter. Understand and sympathize and demand and require, but don't take the fallout personally!

Don't seek affirmation from her, but affirm her with your steady hand.

A *key question*: Are you the arguing type or the folding type?

Whichever you are, you have to work hard to do the opposite. I am the arguing type, for sure. When offered the sliver of an opportunity, I will go to the mat. I had to learn that arguing with a child is unproductive; that my daughter needed to obey and take the issue up with her father if objections persisted. If what I had demanded was unreasonable (usually because I slipped and acted as if she were eight), refraining from arguing helped me to see that it was so and that I had to apologize and amend.

But if what I was asking was reasonable — let's say I told her to put on her coat, or to process the laundry, or to take out her Latin book, or that she couldn't go somewhere with friends — then the correct procedure is to wait for her to obey without starting the air-raid sirens, meaning, of course, arguing.

If you are the folding type, however, you have to learn to stand your ground. Courage comes from knowing that you are doing what is best for someone you love! Once again, this is where your husband is your best ally. If you know you tend to do anything to avoid a confrontation, just refer the whole thing to him. Soon she will learn that she prefers to respect you than to bother him.

If you treat your daughter firmly but fairly, refrain from letting her pull you into wrangles, keep your perspective on your standards and goals, and admit to her that you find all this development painful as well, you will emerge from this as friends — friends who sometimes cry together, but very good friends.

ASK AUNTIE LEILA

Bossiness Cure

Dear Auntie Leila,

Do you have a cure for bossiness? If there were a Mrs. Piggle-Wiggle chapter on bossiness, my four-year-old daughter would be the bossy child! In her (my?) defense, she is the eldest child (I have two others). She comes from a long line of them.

I know I have to tone down my bossiness. On the other hand, I am her mother, and she does need to mind me, which sometimes requires a (very) firm tone. What can I do? She bosses around everyone—her brothers, parents, grandparents, friends, et cetera. Not that we do as she says (especially when delivered in *that tone*), but she is relentless.

Thank you for any insight on the bossiness cure!
Gratefully,
Mrs. Bossy and Being Bossed

Dear Mrs. Bossy,

Gosh, there must be a chapter somewhere in Mrs. Piggle-Wiggle that addresses this! Is there not? Calling all Piggle-Wiggle scholars!

I will do my best; I can relate to your issue, as I am also bossy and have some bossy kids. For instance, one of our children, who is also very kind, so fear not, somehow had the notion that everything that was said or that happened required a response from her. In her defense, she was, like your daughter, still very young.

The moment of truth hits on that day when you're sitting around the dining room table with everyone, and comment from young Johnny gets a response from Miss Bossy, comment from Grandma Bossy gets a response from Miss Bossy, and so on. Every interaction has to go through Miss Bossy!

Sometimes considering the family as a kind of pack helps to bring the picture into focus. A person who has a rather choleric temperament can take on the alpha role (yes! even tots!). And the temperament of others can enable that person—for instance, when the parents tend to be rather phlegmatic or too melancholic to rouse themselves to the necessary pitch of resistance and proper benign dominance. Or this bossiness trend may give rise to conflict, if a parent is also somewhat choleric. Once you identify the temperament or alpha issue, you can take steps. (And we can ask ourselves: Do *I* need to comment on everything that is said? Do I suddenly realize that I am doing just this? People *can* chat among themselves—this can be a revelation. Just let people do their thing! Hmm ... novel idea for some of us.)

You and your husband are the "alpha pair" and that (vital, indispensable, God-given) status is mostly conveyed by gestures and quiet admonishments. Simply putting your hand on a child's head, looking away at a moment when she is getting geared up, raising an eyebrow, emitting a well placed "tsk"—these gestures are worth a thousand nags.

Note well: when correctly ordered, each temperament has its benefits and blessings, so teaching self-control is absolutely critical. That choleric person will manage things very well for you and for the world when she's older, although you will always have to be sure that she isn't taking on more than is appropriate, until she is no longer your problem, having reached the age of majority! Even then, your wise, calm voice will be of immense help to her.

As the alpha pair, you are the arbiters of the interactions in your home; this is a teaching matter. When things are humming along, you let everyone do their thing and all is well. But there are rarely plateaus of calm in a family. So when one person steps out of line and takes an inopportune role (like bossing), you can help her get control over her tendencies.

Try this. Softly: "Be quiet and let others speak." Head her off at the pass. It might take a week to get a little traction on this new habit, and maybe more like years, so see how it goes. It might take repeated gentle reminders and explanations to get the message through. "You can't speak up whenever you feel like it. Listen first to see if you are being helpful." "You don't have to say anything right now." "He's littler than you and it takes him a while to say or do this; you were the same way when you were little. Let's be patient." "He can do it." "Mama said, 'Be quiet.'"

Then of course, let her know when she's been helpful; encourage her when she handles things well, because you know, our faults are our strengths; our strengths are our faults. You can't actually change how you deal with life; you can only somehow, with the help of others and God, make the way you deal *better*.

When she's bossing, quietly go over and remove her from the situation (and work on that raised eyebrow so that you can manage from afar). Explain that she wasn't letting her brother do things his own way. Everyone has to have a chance to figure things out for himself. (This is true for her as well.)

You know, one thing I appreciate about the Arabic culture I half grew up with (when I was with my father) is the paramount importance placed on showing respect to elders. Sure, pertness can be cute, and Americans seem to have a good deal of patience with such behavior, but at some point, you just say, "That's disrespectful. Stop." Say it quietly and keep saying it as the occasion demands, without embarrassing her but without letting her off the hook, either.

This is a work in progress. So sometimes there's naughtiness, and you prudently just wait until later and say, "Sweetie, in this situation, I don't want you to be telling your elders what to do." Correction should rarely be carried out in front of others in this case, because she doesn't mean it—she's *learning*.

Give the words for a better way of saying it: "Grandma, may I take your coat for you?" (In contrast to: "Put your coat over there, Grandma!")

In the next couple of years, you want gradually to give her the idea that she ought to be using her above-average observational and management skills to figure out how she can help people and make them more comfortable.

This effort is really teaching manners. Manners are not some form that we use to get points from people; they are set ways of behaving that are designed to put people at their ease. Manners are the way we show kindness, and kindness is what makes family life pleasant. Our children need to learn to serve in practical and concrete ways and to be kind! It's good to talk about this with them in a gentle way.

Scolding and bossing are rude when the person doesn't have authority (and need to be carefully controlled when the person does!); it's as simple as that. Life becomes intolerable when you are a little kid and everyone is scolding you! We have to make life pleasant for the littles!

Don't worry. Lots of four-year-old girls are this way. Younger brothers have to suffer a lot, but what doesn't kill them makes them stronger.

Keep thinking of ways to express how each person fits into the family structure; ultimately everyone relaxes when the roles are clear. You are on the right track in identifying the problem, and it will sort itself out little by little.

Thanks for writing! God bless,
Leila

Later I got a follow-up (and I do love to hear how things are going!):

I found myself coming back to this e-mail from you today, after a particularly bossiness-filled day in our home. Once again, your advice proved to be a treasure and exactly what I needed (again!).

Truly, thank you. You hit the nail on the head with my daughter, who happens to fit into both examples you gave—alpha dog (or trying to be) *and* feels that all interactions must go through her. But you have given me hope to begin again tomorrow!

Mrs. Bossy

The Back-Talk Cure

You know the back-talk syndrome? The child obstinately says the opposite of what you say to him. Sometimes it is funny. Flush the toilet contents down? He wants to flush them up. But mostly, it's "No come inside!" "No pee on the potty!" "No eat my dinner!" "Yes, grab the cat!" And in response to the reminder or warning, "That's back talk," he'll spurt, "No back talk!"

Ignoring it doesn't work. Saying that it's rude and disrespectful, don't do it, results in more back talk. Punishments don't seem to work either, but you're not sure if you need to double down. Who wants this to be the way everyone interacts?

I recommend, in order but also just according to what works, the following.

Explain calmly that it's naughty to say anything other than "Yes, Mama" or "Yes, Papa" (and honestly, there is nothing wrong with the Southern "Yes, ma'am" or "Yes, sir").

Then say, "You have a bad habit of answering us disrespectfully. You need to stop, as I've told you before. From now on, you will get a punishment if you do it—no warning—because you are old enough to understand, and I'm not going to explain it again."

It's important to understand that the *explaining* and the lectures *enable* the behavior. Instead, you need a quick response to *counter* the behavior.

So the next time you have a directive to issue, say, "I'm going to tell you do something now; if you give me back talk, which means saying no when you should be saying yes [or whatever fits here], you will get a punishment, so don't be surprised! To avoid that terrible outcome, just answer me respectfully by saying 'Yes, Mama.' " Then give the directive.

The child either doesn't quite understand or does understand but needs to test. Either way, if back talk (or whatever other naughty behavior) is the result, immediately, with no further warning, do one of the following:

1. *Put him in his room.* Physically, without a word, march him up there. At that point, tell him you're setting a timer and you will get him when you are ready. Leave. The problem here is that he's interacting, but in an unpleasant way. Removing him from the situation can be a reset. However, completely banishing a child is really hard on him and should be, in my opinion, the last resort. On the other hand, sometimes some silence can elicit the desire to do better and a reset of bad behaviors.

2. *Put him in a corner (facing the corner).* This is my preferred punishment for four-year-olds. You can keep an eye on them, but they are removed from the action. They experience the salutary discomfort of hearing all the fun going on (or just normal family life) but cannot take part. If it's a battle to carry this out, put a stool there and make him stand on the stool. Somehow that's more immobilizing.

3. *Give him a swift spanking.* Be sure it counts. Spank and then move on with your directive. If he talks back again, see number 1 or 2. (You can look up the spanking section here if you want a more elaborate explanation and defense of spanking, see the chapter "How My Husband Convinced Me That Spankings Are Good Discipline.")

4. *Ignore him.* It's useful to substitute a task that results in a benefit for him, such as "Please go wash up for lunch." If he is naughty, well, he's also probably hungry.

As one reader said, "I've learned quite a bit from observing our older son's karate lessons. The master never flinches when the children do naughty things. He corrects them, doles out a punishment (usually push-ups), and moves on with the lesson. It takes him 10 seconds."

Interestingly, hierarchical realities have not been eliminated from sports and the military. We can indeed learn from them and regain the knowledge for family life.

Of course, in the family, we act with kindness and love, but firmness and discipline are still needed. Dad can certainly dole out push-ups. It's fun to learn them together at some other time. Moms can require jumping jacks. (Somehow push-ups are very masculine, and jumping jacks are inherently funny, which can change the atmosphere from exasperated to hilarious, and after all, he just wants to amuse you, this miscreant, when he's not trying to make you insane.)

In short, stop explaining and start exacting a price for bad behavior. I don't believe in elaborate consequences and threats, because who can remember what she has said, and follow through? Stop threatening and depriving. It doesn't work. Discipline should be nothing elaborate. You can decide right at the moment what you want to happen. Do you need a break from this kid? Off to his room he goes. Does he need to know that everyone is having fun without his obnoxious behavior? In the corner, where he can hear but not see. Is he pushing buttons? Ignore. Does he seem a bit frantic? Jumping jacks (and maybe running around the outside the house).

Whining Whiners and
How to Cure Them

 ids misbehave, and as far as I'm concerned, I would rather see or deal with a naughty child than a whining child. Whining is the worst.

However, whining—and, mind you, I'm not an expert, have done no studies, and don't have a degree of any kind, other than from the School of Seven Children—in my humble opinion, is not primarily a behavioral issue.

I think it's kind of crazy that, in our world, real behavioral issues such as "a bear is about to eat my child but he won't obey me because I never demand obedience" are considered management problems. The experts' advice? Calmly explain things to your child. Well, no. That child should trust you when you tell him what to do and, thus, not get eaten by a bear. He trusts that you understand him and normally listen to him in a reasonable manner, and he trusts that when you aren't interested in listening but need a response, he should respond or there will be a consequence. His only question when you ask him to jump is "How high?" This is known as saving his skin, which is a worthy goal.

And furthermore, in our world, lots of stuff, such as pure innocent mischief, is also considered in a management light, so that perfectly normal everyday activity by a child is somehow seen as needing intervention by someone or, possibly, medication.

Thus, the poor kid who needs only to run, jump, yell, and climb is constantly hearing his name and having everything explained until he just wants to run away and join a circus.

Yet a real management problem, such as whining, is looked at as a behavioral problem! I don't get it. What is the point of trying to modify the behavior of someone who is simply signaling to you that he needs you to deal with his issues—which is what whining is: a signal. It's about a kid feeling as if nothing is going to be worthwhile, ever. So why try?

Here is the checklist for interpreting the signal. If your child whines, go down the list, checking the things off. By the end of it, I really think he won't whine anymore. If he does, well, we'll see if there's something missing from the list, or else you will have to seek a higher authority than Auntie Leila!

For the normal child who suddenly starts to whine:

1. *He needs more sleep.* The number-one problem in interpersonal relationships of all kinds is lack of sleep—length and quality. Whatever the age of the child (or might we dare to say husband or wife?), take an honest look at his sleep needs and whether they are being met.

There are books by sleep experts that lay out exactly how much sleep each age group needs, and you could also probably just do an Internet search. But common sense will tell you that a three-year-old who has given up his nap needs to go to bed at a time that incorporates that sleep time that he was getting during the day. If he had been getting a 2½-hour nap and going to bed at 8:30, he now needs to go to bed at 6:30 p.m. at the very latest.

Also, a toddler who gives up a nap won't necessarily never need a nap. Some children transition by taking a nap every third day, but moms tend to assume that from this moment on, things will be different.

Some moms let their kids who don't nap set the pace for the day, not always intentionally. But it's worthwhile to impose a rest time after lunch.

Many children just keep going out of a sort of inability to stop. It's mom's job to manage things so that there is an intentional rhythm to the day that helps the body recharge at key points.

Every stage of development, when you're going through it, takes a lot of energy. Be attentive and realize that if a child is learning to walk or talk or read or deal with bodily changes in puberty, he needs more sleep.

A child who is waking up in the middle of the night and wandering around, crying, needing a drink, needing to be settled, too cold, or too hot is going to feel whiney during the day. You can't cope if your sleep is constantly interrupted. (This is why it's so hard for mom to deal with a sleep-deprived child! She is sleep-deprived too! Perfect storm!) Sometimes foresight—knowing the temperature will drop and adding a layer to the jammies—or a little tough love—insisting that the child go back to sleep quickly—in the short term yields big payoffs in the long term.

In short, this is a problem, and you can't ignore it. Think about sleep in your house and try to tackle it. Most chronic whining problems magically disappear when everyone gets more sleep.

2. He needs more calories. The sorts of things that adults eat are often not suitable for children. You might be fine with your kale salad and your handful of nuts and your quinoa carrot stew, but a growing child needs fats and protein and nursery food—and plenty of it.

I have an issue with the advice given by leading star pediatricians who claim that a child will eat when he's hungry. There's a big difference between saying that a child eats what he needs from what he's offered (which I agree with in a limited way—some children do need coaxing) and saying that a child will be able to get his own food (which is how it looks as if it works out in practice). Since even we adults have a problem figuring out what to eat, spending inordinate amounts of time staring into the fridge and fruit-lessly raiding the pantry, I don't know how a toddler or a nine-year-old or a twelve-year-old is supposed to manage it. Some kids don't tell you they are hungry because they don't realize it. No, Dr. Brazelton (to name one expert who reigned when my children were young), it's not okay to leave the question entirely up to the child.

Like it or not (and you'll like it better if you accept it), you are the food manager. Every morning, noon, and night, children need a meal that has been planned out beforehand (and it doesn't hurt adults either). It's one thing for them to scrounge something once in a while—that happens to everyone. But if every day is a hunting-and-gathering fiasco, hunger is the result. And whining.

When you notice a marked rise in whining, put peanut butter and butter in the oatmeal, cheese in the eggs, extra butter on the toast, chips and fruit next to the sandwich, ham with the rice, cream in the soup, whole-milk ricotta in the lasagna, whole milk in the glass, cookies with the milk, and ice cream for dessert. (You knew I'd say that!)

Make sure the whiner gets a protein-rich snack between meals (but not right before a meal—sit him down and feed him instead—it hardly matters what, just so it's filling).

Give the whiner his meals at least half an hour earlier. It's okay: he can eat alone or with the other whiners. You can read out loud to him so you don't have to listen to his whining. Then put him to bed.

All this advice works for adults too!

ASK AUNTIE LEILA

Six Strategies for Sibling Rivalry

Dear Auntie Leila,

Being an only child, I am sometimes flummoxed by the bickering the children engage in and am not sure whether to ignore it or constantly get involved; if I don't stick my nose into it, will I miss a "teachable moment"? Shouldn't the kids act more loving to each other most of the time? What's with the teasing and, what appears to me, mean-spiritedness? Am I creating an environment that encourages bickering? I don't think so, but what else do I blame?

My husband has one sibling, an older brother, and says they "fought" all the time and our kids are perfectly normal and fine. (But really, is he an expert?) I know you'll say you aren't either—an expert—but I would appreciate any advice.

Thank you,

Jacki

Dear Jacki,

The trouble with parenting advice is the expectation that things will go perfectly when you implement it. After all, when you take your car to the mechanic, you don't want him to tell you something like, "Do these things, pay this money, you'll still experience noise and the occasional breakdown, and in a few years things will look up." Family life is different. We can't fix things in that sense.

But what do we know? You're an only child; I'm an only child; many times, we take advice from people who only have one child! It's crazy!

What I'd love for you to understand, and I hope you can see me *here in the fifth decade*, alternately wringing my hands and waving my arms, is that the first decade is one thing, and the second decade is another and yet builds on the first, and so on.

All too often, the advice you get is for that first stage only. Ninety-nine percent of it is designed to make you *feel* super wonderful and avoid the reality of how very uncomfortable being a mother or father is. One percent of the advice is harsh, with no attention to how everyone grows in virtue little by little, according to human nature—parents too! There's no immediate fix, applicable in the first two weeks of baby's life. But this latter kind is such a small threat that I address it only to strike it down as a straw man, the only real function of which is to frighten us back into wimpiness. Yes, we are paralyzed and dare do nothing more than cajole, bribe, threaten, sigh, and deep down feel as if we were cheated.

After that? Got brats? You're on your own. No experts to be found.

Well, indulge me by working backward on the premise that we don't want to end up with unruly teenagers, an unhappy (or worse) marriage, and a sense of missed chances.

Believe that your marriage, which has already weathered some big changes (having children!), is a friendship that is growing. Your habits toward each other, husband and wife, are those of kindness and delicacy, but you haven't lost your sense of humor. Your children are people you like to be with.

My hope is that you see that if, when they were little, you didn't quite notice anything in particular about their interests or personalities, you will be surprised now to see how much *themselves* they are becoming; and if you knew from the start that they were headed in a certain direction, you will rejoice in seeing that it turned out to be a *good* direction.

I also hope that you do more than simply react to everything your kids do! (My first rule of parenting, remember? Act, don't react!)

In the second decade, you become aware that the babyhood and toddlerhood and childhood of these persons were important for the bonds that developed between you—the trust, the love, the respect—and not for the success or failure of the individual days that you went through to arrive here. (My second rule: Don't seek affirmation from your kids! Why? Because true affirmation takes a long time!)

Making it to the second decade isn't easy because of the traps, which include thinking the "little" stage lasts forever; not *liking* your children (because you fail to teach virtue; they have no self-control!); not being united with your husband because you blame him for your discontent; and in general not building up your home in the first years, when the opportunity was ripe.

So in a way, you have to live through the first years with your eyes on the prize beyond. It's a paradox of time: While you are living in the here and now, appreciating the good things that surround you, you must also look ahead at yourself looking back and seeing these children as *very little*. Look at them from far above. Move your face closer to God's and try to see things as He does, with the long view.

You will have all the grace you need to meet the challenge if you have the right goal in mind. The grace comes from God and is the fruit of marriage. Marriage isn't just a handy way to save on rent. It's the one and only institution that gives a man and a woman a fighting chance at surviving that second decade without wandering away from each other; marriage enables you to offer the world children who will be a blessing to it.

God will give you the grace. I'll give you my six ideas for avoiding sibling rivalry, as long as you understand that nothing is perfect in this world. Jacki, your husband is right: Some sibling rivalry is part of growing up. Especially a girl and a boy are not going to get along well, not the way we moms want them to; and maybe that's a biological safeguard, you know? Because if you love your brother in the way we wish our daughters did, how would they ever have the desire to leave home to marry anyone? It's hard enough as it is.

Six Ideas for Quelling Sibling Rivalry

1. *Cultivate good manners.* Children bicker and fight because they are in the *habit* of doing so (and because yes, they get some sort of attention for it). A habit is a repeated behavior. Right now, today, start creating an atmosphere of good manners and kindness. It's your job to rebuke, correct, and punish, and God has given you the authority to do so; but you also have to be loving.

Strict. And warm. Think and pray about how you can be both.

Don't *tell* your children to have good manners; *enable* them to have good manners, but warmly. Have you ever heard some moms? They are *so rude* in the very act of telling their children to behave. Some mothers interrupt their children at the moment they are greeting Mrs. So-and-so in order to "correct" them and tell them to greet her!

Listen to yourself. Would you talk to your best friend in that strained, artificial, frankly *obnoxious* tone? Not that you do that. Those other annoying moms do that. Still, these are your precious children! Use a reasonably normal tone of voice.

Tell them beforehand how you expect them to behave, and then see if they do it, even if in their own way. There's always next time. Have an occasional role-playing session where you make a game of showing them *exactly* how to make eye contact, shake hands, and be heard to ask and answer politely.

Be polite to your husband and don't treat him like one of the kids. Insist that your children be polite and kind to you and to him. No "free passes" on this one. They shouldn't whine or yell disrespectfully! Do they have the habit of whining just to get your attention? Let them say what they like, but if the tone is not at least respectful, stop them and demanded a redo. I'm more likely to let a child have his way if he's shouting in outrage than if he's whining. I get anger. I don't get whining.

If you are in the car and everyone is whining and bickering, stop the car. Just pull over and tell them you are not going another inch until they can talk nicely. It's funny, because they usually don't care about going anywhere, but somehow, it gets their attention when you won't move.

For one week, make this a priority—clear your mind and work on *this*. Tell them: "We're getting in the car now. If you make one noise that isn't pleasant, I will line you all up and give you each a spank." "We're getting out of the car now. If you can't do it pleasantly, you will stay in for five minutes and try again." Imagine getting in and out of the car with harmony and no bickering! This dream could be yours!

Make your child hand the toy to Sister over again, this time with no grabbing. Make your child walk by Brother again, this time with no shoving or barging. If one is shouting, "She bumped me!" then make her say it again. I bet you corrected the bumper but not the shouter! "How about, 'My dearest, darling sister, please don't bump me!'" If we are all laughing, we can't be bickering, right?

Don't lecture. Get them to do it—kindly but firmly.

2. *Don't be the judge.* Children are opportunistic little mischief-makers and will take whatever advantage they can get. It's all a power play to them. Adult power plays are cases of arrested development, I think.

Now, developmentally, it's unrealistic to get a very young child to see things from others' points of view. That comes later, and much *bad advice* results from doing what is developmentally inappropriate.

Concentrate on letting small children know that there is no reward for their attempts to gain advantages over one another, rather than on trying to get them to *feel* what you consider to be the proper *feeling*. (Please, just give up on that. It's seeking affirmation from them—a no-no!—in a very sneaky way.) How can you know what they are feeling? Do you remember being a child? Do you see how the adults had no idea what you were feeling, unless they had extraordinary insight and could see beyond your *attitude*? Concentrate on the action and overlook the attitude for now.

Teach your children to give full, complete apologies. The best way to do this is by example, but sometimes a little direct teaching is in order. The apology should be commensurate with the offense and should include some indication that the perpetrator understands why he offended (e.g., "I'm sorry I broke your toy," not just "I'm sorry"). Many times a word is sufficient. Sometimes reparation is necessary and can be quite healing. Teach the offended one to say, "I accept your apology" or "I forgive you" or "It's okay."

Don't allow tattling. The tattler should be punished. If there is evidence of wrongdoing but you didn't witness it, punish everyone! Yes, you need to know if something truly dangerous is going on, but you can tell within two seconds if this is the case. One clarifying question: "Are you trying to get him *into* trouble or *out of* trouble?"

Watch carefully so that you are not manipulated into the role of judge, because if you didn't see it, you will be an unjust judge! Even physical evidence can be misleading. I never knew the depths of childish depravity until one of my children, then grown, admitted that she *bit her own arm to produce tooth marks in order to implicate her brother!* Oh, I hear you thinking, "My children would never do that!" But you don't understand. I have the best children anyone has ever had. This particular child would *never*!

Punishments include taking away the ball or the doll or whatever is the bone of contention of the moment; making them all sit on the stairs; putting the game on the high shelf; sending them all outdoors; and depriving them all of dessert if it's just about time for dessert. Something *immediate*.

The result will surprise, astonish, and delight you (in the long run, to be sure), because what will they do? They will unite with each other against you! They will giggle, find something useful to do, enjoy some long-neglected game, or decide to read to each other. In short, when you are the bad guy, they cease to find one among themselves. And that's what you wanted all along.

3. *Observe them carefully, however, and act, rather than react, to their tattling and complaining.* Don't react to the situation as they present it to you, but admit (at least to yourself) that you should have intervened five minutes earlier because you knew someone was getting tired or pushed beyond his limits, only you didn't have the self-control to stop what you were doing to

handle the issue. You talked an extra five minutes on the phone or took advantage of their absence to stay on the computer. If you have self-control, they will (someday). If not, they won't.

Don't leave well enough alone; structure their time, even their free time, if only by limiting it. At their age, even if they become absorbed in something quiet, it won't last too long, and then mischief will ensue. Do guide them so they learn to take turns, although you must balance this with letting them work things out on their own.

Notice that they were getting bored and should have been put to work. *Notice* that one is truly picking on the other. Make him stop by giving him more hard work that he can feel satisfied with. *Notice* that one is intentionally passive because he knows you will come to his aid. Make him take his punches and stand up for himself. Better now than later.

The child who yells the loudest is not necessarily the one most offended against. The child who has the readiest excuse is not always the innocent one. Become a student of human nature, and don't be manipulated by appearances.

Some children are indeed more compliant than others, but don't let this turn into a negative trait. Have you ever met adults like this? The ones who apologize when someone is rude to *them?* Auntie Leila says nip this in the bud.

Not all siblings will be close in the same way because of temperamental differences. Help them gradually understand the differences and even overcome them by being understanding of each others' needs for more or less activity, quiet, solitude, and so on.

4. *Give the elder child more privileges.* It's hard being the eldest, and he or she should get something out of it. First dibs in certain choices: whatever the contested seat in the car might be, the spot next to you while you bake … Yes, they have to carry heavier bags and chase toddlers while you are nursing. Let them have some favors as well.

As the children get older, give the younger ones more responsibility for chores, being willing to do the dreadful job of training them all over again (it's all over again for you, but the first time for them, remember!). Don't simply put more of a burden on the eldest.

5. *Don't expect a younger child to be developmentally the same as an older one, even if they usually play together, and especially if the younger one is a bit on the large side.* Big and tall children often have a hard time, because they are expected to act more mature than they are able.

But don't let him be a pest, either. Be fair and sometimes punish the younger one. He can't always be the victim; it's just not possible. Everyone has to try to be polite and kind, according to their abilities. Even a six-month-old can be taught to stroke a cheek, not scratch!

6. *Most of all, build family honor and unity.* Put it into words. Say, "Smiths don't act that way."

When you are out somewhere, remind them to help each other and defend each other. Talk about "the honor of the Smiths" and how "no one messes with a Smith!" Remind them that "we Smiths stick together" and "we're troupers."

Sometimes it's best to simply say, "We don't do that."

I'm for less talk overall; less coercive speech from Mom. But if you must talk, make your talk be not about how disappointed you are, blah blah blah, but about how their friends will come and go, but sisters and brothers will be one another's best friends and have each other forever. Tell them to be good to each other.

Quote Psalm 132 (133, in other versions): "Behold, how good and how pleasant it is for brethren to dwell together in unity!"

Discuss with your husband the whole general idea of building family unity, according to your own tastes and hopes and dreams. Not for today; don't expect much today! For the second decade.

PART 6

On Living within the Patterns Set by the Year

There is Liturgy with a capital *L*, there is the rhythm of nature, and then there is the liturgy, or rhythm, of family life as we live it uniquely in family celebrations and remembrances; this is the threefold strand that is so decisive for building the culture.

A few years ago, David Clayton and I wrote a book called *The Little Oratory: A Beginner's Guide to Praying in the Home,* and that book was my best attempt to show that having a traditional prayer place in the home is the best way to grow in prayer along with the liturgical year.

Liturgical time is a mystery in its connection with life in Heaven, and it's what connects us to God's purpose for us here on Earth. The amazing thing is that if we make the most of liturgical time, we never again have to worry about missing something in the spiritual life.

Isn't that a relief?

Whether you are aware of it or not, the universe carries on a rhythm—a hidden pattern of time. You can hear it better if, wherever you are, you live the seasons united with the seasons of the Church. As winter comes, for instance, we naturally carry on a certain preparation. What about the *supernatural* preparation? This observation, that there are two preparations, goes beyond analogy. It isn't just that something in our souls is *like* what is happening out in the world; it's that grace builds on nature, takes it into account, and makes a unity of it all.

The pattern of the liturgy can be lived on many levels. Family life, including educating our children, becomes less onerous and more organic when we allow the various rhythms of life—liturgical, seasonal, national, cultural—to guide us, rather than relying on what we happen to have thought of, what experts drum up for our consumption, or what randomly pops up.

Since *The Little Oratory* is already out there with the systematic overview to living the liturgical year, I will confine myself here to touching on just a couple of examples that I hope give you the template for a different way of thinking about time, both in the Liturgy and in nature, to give you the sense of how allowing the year in its aspects to guide you will bring a sense of fittingness into the home and be fruitful for others beyond it.

Advent: The Beginning of Order and Wonder

How paradoxical! The consideration of order immediately brings us to the liturgical year, for, of course, Sunday is the fulfillment of the commandment to worship, the celebration of Easter every week, and of the wonder of God's mysterious act of creation and Jesus Christ's entry into it, for our sakes.

Besides Sunday, the observation of which is the first step toward living the liturgical life more fully, the entry into the sacred order of time begins in Advent. Over the years I have written a lot about Advent. I find it beautiful that what seems accessible only to the philosopher in his ivory tower—that is, the life of wonder at the mysteries of wisdom—is available to the simplest child and the poorest peasant in the observance of Sunday and of the liturgical seasons, which begin in Advent.

To discover the Order God wants to reveal, try not to plunge right into holiday decorating; restraint reveals one mystery of the season: the Lord of all creation choosing poverty on earth. This choice—the lack of accommodations, the stable, the manger, the cold night closing in—we have embellished over time with our creativity, because we love it so. It's our gratitude from being saved from the darkness that makes us love this time of Advent.

Each embellishment of the season takes its meaning from that original beautiful paradox of the eternal choice to be born a king, yet naked on a hillside; until we find ourselves loving stars, sheep, pine cones, and holly as if each one of these things were baby Jesus Himself. We even find ourselves gilding straw, the overflow of this tender wonder is so great.

And all this is fitting, because Jesus showed us that the material world, mere and previously overlooked *things*, take their loveliness from His entry into our world. Who in his right mind would venerate the food trough of an animal? This is the extravagance of love!

Jesus further made it clear that His family was intact wherever they were. They were not a family because of the quality of the inn they could afford, although it's worth noticing that they were able to pay for that inn; it's just that there wasn't room. How delicate of our Lord to make that clear as well, that it was simply His choice to be born somewhere so poor. That fact—the "no room"—He uses to give us the assurance that mere circumstance can never take away the love of those three, the earthly trinity, who in some way clothe in flesh the unknowable cloud of the heavenly Trinity.

Once I lamented to a neighbor that I was afraid that our frequent moves at that time were not giving our small children the security they needed. She said something quite wise, that I think reflects a little of the light of Bethlehem: "Sometimes you have to pack your security up and take it with you!"

It's not in the places or the things that we find security, but in the heart of the home that allows Christ to be born in its midst. Order begins here, in the home, with the keeping of the seasons.

Advent is the beginning of that way of life. It is a season that prepares us for Christmas, the Incarnation. Without any need to invent things, we are moved along with the Church's observances to Lent, Easter, Pentecost, and then Advent again, always ancient, ever new.

Don't Let Go of Advent
for Anything

The world has something to sell, and that's fine, because we certainly need to prepare for Christmas and it takes time to figure out what we need to buy (even if it's supplies for making what we have planned). We could succumb utterly to the world's ways by going full Christmas already, by decorating and listening to the "holiday soundtrack" that certainly does not contain any actual religious content, but I digress.

As adults, we feel that we could do that. It's tempting. Many of us are tired and demoralized; and the reason Christmas endures, even in our utterly secular and pagan times, is that it offers respite and solace on a natural level (for that is the point: God made man; —but don't forget the rest: —that men might become divine).

Advent feels like a denial of all that. And because the Church herself has relinquished some of her ancient wisdom, even she seems to acquiesce in putting this season to us as a sort of blank, a waiting period at a dreary bus stop. Who wouldn't rather just go ahead and, well, not celebrate ("Holly Jolly Christmas" always seems forced to me) but ... anesthetize?

But Advent is not just four weeks of waiting; it's not a pinched denial of pleasure (as paltry as the "pleasures" of the commercial season are). And each week is not just like the others.

If we pay close attention, trying to recover what was lost, blessings will abound. The liturgical year offers us a chance to enter into God's will for our spiritual lives at every moment and to ponder truths and realities that, if approached analytically, would fill encyclopedias of theology and never be complete. How can we reject that offer and still claim to want to know God's will and to learn more about Him?

During Advent, if we care to hear, the messages offered in the liturgy have to do with salvation history, prophecy, darkness, light, Our Lady in her splendor, the angels in their myriads, the impending Incarnation, and the Second Coming. Each week has its own texture and emphasis. Each week also has its own feasts to lighten the gloom. St. Nicholas, the feast of the Immaculate Conception, St. Lucy's Day—each with its message of the Kingdom of God. If we are jingle-belling ourselves into jolliness prematurely, we will miss it all.

But most importantly, if we recover all this along with the season's own music, traditions, and anticipation, our children will benefit from the only "curriculum" that has the power to sustain them as the world tries to steal them away.

The world also effectively deprives us of Christmas, for it folds down its festivities, such as they are, on the twenty-fifth of December. Our children will wake up on the twenty-sixth to its dryness.

We may feel safe from worldly ways (but perhaps that's merely hubris), but our children have no defenses, other than what we give them—and make no mistake, very few ramparts are built with words and admonishments. They are built with our way of life. Past generations gladly denied themselves and held sloth at bay for the privilege of passing along this patrimony intact.

There must be a few who will stay with the old ways, keeping the "for every time there is a season" verities alive. We said we would, we like the idea in theory, but at the first striking of "It's Beginning to Look a Lot Like Christmas" we surrender to the mall mentality, which, may I point out, is itself on its last legs! Talk about selling your birthright for a mess of pottage!

Enjoy Thanksgiving, and shortly thereafter, start some Christmas gift making with your children. Sing the Advent carols: "Sleepers, Wake!" "Lo, How a Rose E'er Blooming," "Alma Redemptoris Mater," "The Angel Gabriel from Heaven Came," "On Jordan's Bank," "Come, Thou Long Expected Jesus," "Comfort, Comfort Now My People," and maybe, beginning only on the seventeenth of December, "O Come, O Come, Emmanuel." (You may notice that my list here follows the Propers of each Sunday.)

The liturgical seasons are rich, with richness beyond imagining. Only by living them will we begin to uncover these treasures! And our children will accompany us; truly, the consolation of their wonder, of the light in their eyes, will give us more heart than any blandishment the world has to offer.

Celebrate All Twelve
Days of Christmas!

have hesitated to write about this because often people think, "Celebrate all twelve days of Christmas! Sounds like too much." And I'm no expert, nor would I set myself up as an example. On the other hand, we really did this, all those years, learning as we went, thanks to my husband's insisting on our living Advent, my first three children being born in December, and living on one income with all that implies. So maybe you'd like to know about it.

I'll give suggestions for shopping (since, like me, you probably didn't make all your gifts, starting last January, nor did you thrift any of it—but next year you will, and so will I, no doubt). The gift-giving questions in my in-box can be more or less summed up by this one from dear Shawna and form the basis for the crazy idea of celebrating *more* instead of *less*:

Christmas is coming, and I'm dreading the stress and expense. Then there's the "hangover" that follows the spending. I have seven children (ages seventeen to seven months) and even with the idea of magi gifts (three: one to read: one desired; one needed),[28] it's expensive. Plus, the children are so fixated on the gifts that they fail to understand the gift of Christ as the real reason for Christmas. Additionally, the well-thought-out and hard-earned gifts are frequently forgotten shortly after Christmas day. We do a traveling nativity, we do sacrifices, we attend Mass. How do we simplify Christmas and make it meaningful and affordable?

Dear Shawna,

The way our society celebrates Christmas really does put a lot of burden on the parents to be magical and fulfill every wish of their child—even if the child doesn't seem all that interested in our contortions at the end of the day because others swooped in with far more enchanting gifts—or he just liked the box the gift came in.

Like a lot of other things (unsupervised play for children, less pressure for outside activities, lower college tuition), if more people had more children, gift-giving wouldn't seem so high stakes. Well, we just have to do what we can, keeping in mind that children are hardwired to find just about everything magical, if only we could just relax a bit.

I've found that living liturgically, as always, contains the key to the answer; it must, however, must be done in the context of our own families, with their likes, dislikes, and unique ways of doing things. In other words, Christmas is a time for us parents to rely a bit more on the grace of our own family life and a bit less on comparisons with other people and, thus, with the utmost naturalness, to begin to teach our children to do the same (and isn't that the point?).

What if we, having lived Advent, also live Christmas, a *season*? I'm going to take it for granted that we are on board with the appropriateness of gift-giving at Christmastime (because gifts and Christmas are delightful *and* magical, and because we simply *must* do something to respond to the sheer generosity of having been given the gift of existence), but we are indeed

---

[28] We've also seen four, which includes one to wear.

overwhelmed. Let's try spreading things out a bit and not burdening that one day with all the "magic."

At my house, on Christmas Day, the children opened their one—count 'em, one—Santa present (and their other presents from guests and in their stockings, because we did not have the good sense to do stockings on the feast of St. Nick back in the day when we should have been foreseeing this craziness; in my defense, I was always getting ready to have a baby around that feast and in no condition to be foreseeing things). In the stockings are maybe new socks, a tangerine at the foot (do collect them after a day or two to avoid yuck), a bunch of special candies, and some fun little toys or special things such as tops, jackknives, and so on. With seven children (in your case and mine), that is already a boatload of presents!

Then, in the following days, gift-giving arranges itself.

Tip: Make a chart or, as I did, use a long strip of paper (such as adding-machine paper because this was before we learned to make everything worthy of a photo for social media) and have all the days with their gift or activity written down with little sketches for nonreaders, and posted for all to see. I wish I had taken a picture of it! It was cute. This builds anticipation and keeps you on track.

Don't be scared. The management key is this: half the things you were going to do anyway, and (almost) half are actually quite peaceful. But you are spreading them out over the days rather than squeezing them all at once into one day or making them something separate, like vacation activities.

If there is a need (for those in cold climes), give the mittens and hats on the feast of St. Nicholas. Give PJs and nightgowns on Christmas Eve.

Let me give you a typical scenario at our house (you must adjust according to your particulars and based on which day of the week Christmas falls on in any given year).

Second Day of Christmas (December 26). Visit extended family, which includes inevitable gift giving; or — and this became a tradition with us — make gingerbread houses. Turns out that this "little project" we always think we are going to do is a full-on day-long (at least) extravaganza of marathon baking, decorating, and general sugarcoating of the kitchen. Since we had birthdays during Advent, with their own baking requirements, the gingerbread got pushed to after Christmas. As the kids got older, our modest efforts became "gingerbread villages," "gingerbread forts," and "gingerbread Fenway parks." (Bonus: the candy is all on deep discount.)

A "gingerbread family" cookie-cutter set is a boon, but beware: it's only the beginning! For instance, once a gingerbread church was built that had a stained-glass window *and* flying buttresses.

Third Day (December 27). Give a whole-family present such as a board game that all can play (it's okay if the littles aren't absolutely included in this; they don't really care or are napping or can be on someone's "team" until they go play with cars) or a special piece to add to a collection you have. A train bridge for your wooden train set is an example of this latter sort of gift, and it results in the pulling of the train set out of the bin and the communal building of a fabulous new track. In other words, you are renewing interest *in old toys* with *one* gift for everyone.

Now is the time to put the bee in your relatives' bonnets about these items. You know the ones I mean: The well-meaning people in your life who shower you with things you don't want and toys that are inappropriate. These toys I'm suggesting are still in my toy closet after all these years because they are awesome. See if you can gently nudge these generous people to give the family one of the pricier of the following things instead of their own dreaded selections: train additions; a wooden castle for all those little building-set knights, ladies, kings, and queens; a dollhouse for action figures or dollhouse families to put in one you have; and Calico Critters, aka Sylvanians.

In the evening, we might have had a simple supper and gone caroling, which usually astonished people because *they* thought Christmas was over.

Fourth Day (December 28). Go to a museum, to a performance of *The Nutcracker*, or ice skating—yes, we were going to do some of this anyway. Sometime around Thanksgiving, scout out the free or discount day.

Fifth Day (December 29). Open the box that a far-off relative sent (which you cleverly did *not* put out on Christmas Day). Do jigsaw puzzles. It's good to have a quiet day at home, and, it's okay, by the way, to have one day be more for the older kids and adults and one day be more for the younger kids. Children learn to enjoy each other's enjoyment. They have things to do on their own. This is all good.

Sixth Day (December 30). Focus on books. For many years, we lived not far from an amazing bookstore called the New England Mobile Book Fair. On a day during Christmas, we would plan an afternoon to browse. With seven kids? Yes, with seven kids; it's that kind of place (I mean, I don't know what the staff thought, but it's sort of a warehouse and I have no shame). I would get lost in the remainders section; the older kids would hunt down Tintin books; the Chief would find his favorite publisher (the books are somewhat maddeningly arranged by publisher) and settle down; the younger kids would sort of run in between us. Baby was on someone's hip. The toddler was parked in the cart with a board book. Everyone could get a book or two.

If you don't have a bookstore near you, one of the days of Christmas is perfect for giving the books you ordered. Unless someone really wished for a certain book on Christmas Day, having a dedicated book day prevents these treasures from getting lost in the dazzle of all the toys. Another idea is to start a read-aloud book on one of the days.

Seventh Day (December 31). This is New Year's Eve. When you have older children who might be lured out on the dangerous roads this night, a party with compatible families can be so much fun. Maybe you have a family tradition on this day, such as eating Chinese food. Go for it as a Day of Christmas *and* New Year's Eve. When my kids were under fourteen, we would often bundle them up for a trip—thrillingly, *on the train!*—into Boston for "First Night," a citywide celebration of winter activities, all free. We'd eat street food and get really cold. That we didn't do the more sophisticated concert or party or midnight-revelry things was never even on the kids' radar. It's dark by four o'clock, and to them, it's late.

At our New Year's Eve party, which we inaugurated in later years, we would feature smashing and eating the gingerbread creations and lots of fun party games, followed by Christmas carol singing (*all* the verses of the really beautiful old ones). Schedule the gingerbread smashing in *somewhere* so that you don't make the mistake either of eating them right away (unseemly) or leaving them too long (gross).

Eighth Day (January 1). This is New Year's Day and the solemnity of Mary, the Mother of God. Go to Mass (it's a holy day of obligation) and have a family movie. In the years we did First Night on New Year's Eve, we had a party with a family or two on this day, very relaxed and enjoyable.

Ninth Day (January 2). Enjoy that box of candy that keeps getting overlooked or another very small treat that can calm down the hectic schedule yet still be festive.

Tenth Day (January 3). Go for a family walk. One of these days is bound to be mild(er)! Bundle up and get out there!

Eleventh Day (January 4). Have a reading day, made special by elevating it to "Books at the Table Day." (Anything can be a Day of Christmas! Just give it a name! Nap Day!) Just make something not very messy for supper. Other thoughts: delve into that one gift (such as the game Axis & Allies) that takes forever to figure out and set up; visit an elderly relative who is a bit far away, stopping for donuts to bring; have breakfast for supper; make a model or do a craft; assemble the bikes that were under the tree.

Twelfth Day (January 5): This is Epiphany. Bake a crown cake. You and your husband can give *your* gifts to each other and to the children, versus the *one* Santa gift you gave on Christmas Day. Often I would buy these on deep clearance at some point during the week, having now ascertained what each child wanted.

As I said, this reflects what we did—including my getting confused about when Epiphany is! It's January 6th. The twelfth day is the vigil of "Little Christmas." And further, the Church (in the Novus Ordo calendar) celebrates Epiphany on the Second Sunday after Christmas. So I very much would choose when we would celebrate based on the day of the week and what the family at large was doing. For instance, if the twelfth day fell on a Sunday—making January 6 a Monday, we'd do our Little Christmas on the twelfth day. If January 6 was on Saturday, we'd do it then. If I was going crazy with everyone's schedule, we'd do it on the Second Sunday after Christmas, somewhat over the protests of the Chief, who nevertheless realized I was hanging by a thread. This is called rolling with the punches.

My list is based on my family having been thrown very much on its own resources. But it might be that you are in a community or a large extended family that supplies many activities of its own. Any special thing on a given day is the gift for that day! Any particular interest your family has could be encouraged in this season! See how it works?

And do you see that it frees up Christmas Day to be calmer? If you are thinking, "Well, no," I offer the following testimonial from Rosie: "I always felt that my one Santa gift was magical; I secretly thought my friends were deprived because they didn't celebrate Little Christmas (Twelfth Day)." "The stockings were the best and most fun," I remember Nick saying, not long ago.

I haven't surveyed all my offspring. I'm a little afraid to, because I always feel that I didn't do a good job and that the magic *wasn't* there. We parents are hard on ourselves. But Rosie encouraged me to tell you all about this, so I have.

New Year's Eve

Every year we have a big New Year's Eve party. It all started when the Chief and I got panicky because our teenage boys wanted to drive to friends' houses down a dangerous "highway" (read: scary fast road with no barriers dividing the traffic).

We do our best to host something that combines a family party with a celebration that lasts into the wee hours, complete with crazy party games and a champagne toast—and singing. We try to make a gathering that satisfies the teenage need to party yet establishes a benchmark for real fun, excluding, I hope, the idea that simply *drinking* constitutes fun. Because we have wonderful friends, they have been on board with the concept of a party that *significantly* interferes with our generation's need to sleep.

Don't get me wrong: the kids have sometimes mightily resisted this party. When they get safely out of the teen years, they are free to do something else, and we concentrate on the next ones coming up. They might, even now, be sort of mocking me as they read this. And not every family can make the investment to make it happen, which has sometimes made it hard for us to keep going.

Believe me, I appreciate the thought of staying home with Chinese food and board games! As long as your gang is happy doing that, go for it!

But my kids are so sociable that it has been worth the effort to keep this tradition going. They humor me, and I hope that someday they will understand what we are trying to do. I mean, the *really* big picture of what we are trying to do.

Some years, when New Year's Day isn't on a Sunday, we can go to the Vigil Mass for the Holy Day (the solemnity of Mary, the Mother of God), and the party is a supper that goes on into the night. Since it's also the seventh day of Christmas (until it becomes the eighth), we ring in the New Year with Christmas carols, singing *all* the verses to as many carols as we can manage.

The party, in the past, has ended as late as 3:00 a.m., with Joseph and his friends playing jazz in their little band for us, and Will, as always, managing the logistics and general hilarity. (The grandparents of friends had to miss the party for the first time in ages when they were well into their nineties! In the past, they had been the party closers, keeping everyone laughing with their antics. And we have tried, somewhat in vain, to convince little ones to lie down on blankets in the living room and just drift off.)

Suki always led our caroling on the piano when she lived at home, and she and I have a similar mission to exclude all "mall" versions of holiday songs, putting the kibosh on "Jingle Bells" in any form. Once you begin to explore the world of carols, you realize how very lovely, wonder filled, and catechetical they are, teaching in their beauty and poetry all the lessons of the miracle of the Incarnation that take theologians volumes to convey.

If New Year's Day is on Sunday, or for some other reason (such as a changing demographic that again includes younger children), we move everything up to more or less *end* at midnight, which is fine with us.

Parties—celebrations—are an important way to form the culture. In a way, the kind of parties you have says a lot about what your culture *is*. You see, culture itself arises from the celebration that accompanies true worship. This isn't an abstract notion. It's as real as can be.

As worship has degraded into entertainment, celebration has seemed increasingly unfulfilling, it seems to me. Josef Pieper speaks of the vapidity of artificial festivals. He connects true festivity with worship:

There can be no festivity when man, imagining himself self-sufficient, refuses to recognize that Goodness of things which goes far beyond any conceivable utility; it is the Goodness of reality taken as a whole which validates all other particular goods and which man himself can never produce.... He truly receives it only when he accepts it as pure gift. The only fitting way to respond to such gift is: by praise of God in ritual worship. In short, it is the withholding of public worship that makes festivity wither at the root.[29]

Each family, to restore the culture, has to find a way to rejoin the two in their organic relationship: true worship and lively celebration! Order and wonder! Ritual and imagination! We can't be satisfied with weak liturgy, and we can't be satisfied with superficial and ultimately barren fun.

And we can't be satisfied with our own warm memories, if we are lucky enough to have them, or dreams of *someday*. We have to try, here and now, with our imperfections, to get going on the project of saving Western civilization. I beg you, don't make the Super Bowl the most satisfying thing you do all year! (Enjoy it if you love football, but put it in its place.)

A party that contributes to flourishing, then, will often be linked to a really big feast day (and every day in the Christmas octave is a big one!). And it will almost always include all the ages. Of course, there is a place for the strictly age-segregated event. I enjoy a couples' dinner or a cocktail party as much as the next person. For young people, there is a time when they benefit from being together on their own (kids enjoying snowball fights, teens making bonfires). They need to form their friendships and have silly fun with no adults around!

In my opinion, New Year's Eve isn't one of those times. It's just too darn dangerous and late, and besides, with the next day a holy day, with the need to get to Mass, it's a great opportunity to make the connection between worship and celebration so that it doesn't lapse into the profane sphere (and if you think about it, without this "vigil" aspect, New Year's Eve doesn't make a lot of sense and can be depressing, in fact).

---

[29] Josef Pieper, *In Tune with the World: A Theory of Festivity* (South Bend, IN: St. Augustine's Press, 1999), page 71.

I hope this makes sense, but to keep it practical I will give you the nitty-gritty on what we do, keeping in mind that the whole shebang is our best effort, but by no means the last word on great parties. Don't get me wrong here and start thinking that this is an unreachable ideal. Far from it. I'm sure *our* guests would tell you all sorts of ways that things could be better, and I'm only here to tell you that *if we can do it, so can you!*

Party Essentials

- A room where kids can hang out at the beginning of the party, maybe with a Foosball table or board games. Keep an eye on where the beer is going.
- Food and drink. It's important to have something you serve every year, I think. In this case, it's ham and a big pot of potato chowder. Somehow, people look forward to things' being the same—with, of course, interesting variations as they appeal to you, as well as contributions from your guests.
- Carol booklets or hymnals with good old-fashioned carols, all verses. If you *must* have "Frosty the Snowman"-type songs, get them over with at the start, and please, for the love of all that is merciful, keep them to a minimum. As far as I am concerned, the stores have destroyed these songs, and they had very little value to start with. This might take some work—collecting beautiful carols in one place and having enough copies for everyone. I recommend using *Take Joy* (well worth even thirty dollars for a used one in good condition), *The Trapp Family Book of Christmas Songs*, and Benjamin Bloomfield's *A Collection of Christmas Carols* as resources for your own family songbook collection.
- Champagne and sparkling cider for the toast
- The singing of "Auld Lang Syne"
- Toasts from guests, if they are up to it
- The singing of the Salve Regina to herald Our Lady's Day (It happens that most of our friends and family know this chant very well. If that's not the case for you, you can learn it!)

- Fun-loving friends who are in it for the long haul! Start when your kids are young and go to bed early. By the time they are teens, they will be up for this kind of thing.

Party Games We Like to Play

You can easily find more information about these party games online. I touch lightly on the basics:

- The Murder Game (although, one year, we had a guest who had actually been the victim of an attempt on her life—yikes!—so we changed it to the Thief Game). Our version is quite scaled down, with little pieces of paper determining the roles—murderer or thief, victim, judges, lawyers. The conversation at the beginning of the evening is punctuated by screams from "murdered" guests. Some of our friends really relish making the most of this dramatic moment! At the end, before the midnight toast, we have a raucous trial to determine the perpetrator.
- The Guess Your Famous Character Game. Everyone loves this one, and you can have fun matching your guests to their alter egos or nemeses. We tape the name to the person's back, not to his forehead, which just seems a little invasive, but then he tends to forget to ask others questions about his identity.
- The Party Quirks Game. One or two of you come up with amazingly funny scenarios beforehand. Some examples from our past: You are watching your sister's kids in a china shop. You are a dentist trying not to notice people's teeth. You are obsessed with the color red. You fall asleep unless you are asked a question. You think the world is ending tonight and are trying not to panic. Announce the quirks to the group while the host is out of the room. (Be warned if you choose to watch the online videos of the "Whose Line Is It Anyway?" skits, from which we borrowed this game: they are hilarious but often quite rude. We are G-rated only.)
- The New Year's Resolutions Game. Write resolutions (stay away from "losing weight"-type ones, and go for "learn to Irish Step

dance"–type ones) on slips of paper. One guest picks from a hat and chooses another guest to give it to. Start off with pickers who understand that the less matched-up the recipient is with the resolution, the funnier the moment will be. If played correctly, this game capitalizes on juxtaposition for humor; if played incorrectly, it just hurts everyone's feelings. Be forewarned.

- Charades. This is one of my favorites. A reader suggested using Christmas carol titles!

We have a lot of fun despite our shortcomings. The parking in our dark yard is always an adventure. Here in New England the weather is often prohibitive. And I'm sure my guests could give you an earful about how I am just a tad aggressive when it comes to making them play games and how I berate them when they try to sing "Jingle Bell Rock." That's okay. I don't claim to be perfect, only trying. I will say this: if no one *makes* them play or sing, they won't do it, but that's what they enjoy in the end. Hard my row is to hoe. I sacrifice myself.

Over the years, we have invited the families of our children's friends. That has meant that not everyone we love has been included, and that can be hard. Every year we think we are not doing it again. But this and similar things *need* to be done, organically and according to your own circumstances. You can do it.

And everyone needs a nap before the party!

Live Your Lent

You know how you really love making things, and will neglect even the most basic responsibilities to fashion, say, knitting needles or dish mats? And you know how you love when your kids make things and have a walk-in closet full of supplies for every known craft from stamping to woodburning? You know how you jump to assure others that homeschooling does not mean "crafts with kids" to you, and they give you that blank look? Like, "You?"

Yes, you are so crafty. But you are not that fond of "activity" crafts, right? You know how you have every intention of getting your kids to do projects in religion, but then things fizzle out and you just take a nap? You know how bad you are at praising God with a paper plate?

But, enough about me.

Well, what if it's okay not to stress out about finding things for your kids to do for liturgical seasons? Well meaning parents, especially the intense homeschooling kind—but really the intense any kind at all—tend to feel that if they are not *actively* teaching their children something, the children aren't learning it. These parents are results-oriented, and they unintentionally violate my second rule of parenting ("Don't seek affirmation from your children"), not getting the connection at all.

They think I mean (I mean if they've ever heard of me and my rules, which is doubtful), "Go ahead and make your kids mad" but that isn't it. That's more Tiger Mother stuff, and we don't really believe in that. What I mean is more like "Don't expect obvious results right away; in fact, get used to plowing ahead with your simple vision and seeing no outcome whatsoever."

Very much in line with this no-affirmation approach (which, by the way, fits in neatly with a lazy reluctance to drag out crafting supplies for which the mess-to-learning ratio is far too high) is my advice about liturgical seasons. Which is this: *try living them.*

Instead of setting out to teach your children about Lent, just try living Lent. I'm only saying this in case you are a little overwhelmed and in the dark about what to do. If you have a really great plan in place, don't let me interfere! But if you tend to see a Liturgical Season as a specifically child-raising burden, perhaps I can help.

In the few hours left to you once you realize that Lent is upon you, gather everyone together (preferably during dinner, and preferably let your husband gather everyone) and have a big discussion about what you will give up as a family for the forty days. This might be TV, movies, or video games during the week; sweets, ice cream (sadly for me), and snacks, although go easy on that last one with growing children who seem on the skinny side. But choose your own sacrifices to make as a family.

In recent years, we have made a special effort to give to a local charity the money we save because, to be honest, you don't save all that much by not eating sweets, and a family in your town whose child is sick with cancer will likely have more use for your $48.65 than the Red Cross will. I think it's good to make something in your community a priority. Put a jar in the center of the table and put the cash in there, along with any spare change that you run across.

When our kids were little, my husband and I agreed to work on not just giving things up during Lent but on doing charitable works for others, works that engendered more virtue at home. For instance, getting things cleaned up cheerfully for when Papa came home. Do you know how much easier it is to do a chore when it's for someone you love whom you're excited to see? Do you know how much children love to see their mother wanting to do something for their father?

That is what Lent is for: to work on virtue, especially the virtue of love.

Also, take a few moments to speak to each child alone about what virtue he could work on. Do you realize that you and your husband are your children's spiritual directors? It's true. You are there with the grace of God gently to guide them with your wisdom, even if you don't feel that wise. So it's a learning experience for you—to be approached with humility. Guide them with little steps to do a little better, with the help of the Lord, working on one thing—answering nicely, prompt obedience, watching out for a younger sibling, doing things without being told (take care to encourage with this last one, especially, as it's easy to take the effort that goes into it for granted).

As you do this, you also learn a lot about how the Father works with us, one little step after another, often using a time set apart to do His work.

Many parishes make it easier to get to Mass during Lent, which almost seems counterintuitive. It's far more important to put your energy into getting everyone to Mass than into extra activities. Mass, Stations of the Cross: these are the things our children will remember. This is what the Church wants us to do. I mean, if you want to.

And then, you know, as you quietly go about your devotions with your family, and your extra sacrifices, if the children take out the colored pencils and start drawing, well, that's wonderful, isn't it?

Entertaining and Family Fun

 ou know, it's up to us to restore happy times to our tired, sad world. Sometimes we just don't know how! I think we've *almost* lost the art of knowing what to *do* with our time together.

Bonfires, hot dogs, marshmallows—it's good clean fun!

This city girl had some trouble with the concept of a weenie roast. I can host a dinner for sixty, but a campfire like this was beyond me. I don't know why I couldn't wrap my mind around it, but you know that's what I am here for—to make you look good!

While boys standing in a patch of poison ivy chucking random flammable items into a giant fire can't be improved upon, from their point of view anyway, it's worth putting in some effort to have a dedicated spot of some sort for this activity.

A bonfire is a wonderful thing. It can be enjoyed by all the generations, and it can be enjoyed by teens alone.

I find that people are divided into two groups when it comes to thinking about how kids socialize. One group, by far the larger, has accepted our society's norm for separating generations right down to segregating ages quite rigidly. Schoolchildren tend to adopt a hostile stance to anyone not in their group (grade); our culture reinforces this tendency to a frightening degree.

The second group today comprises mainly homeschoolers and those forming around small religious schools, who have discovered the virtue of mixing ages and generations, and it tends to lean toward family parties, which is overall the healthiest way to spend social time.

As beneficial as this recovery of family parties is, we need to understand that young people, even those who are used to partying with all ages, want and do need time with each other—precisely *not* with adults and small children. The young people I know can keep a good balance of including friends who aren't only in their grade; nevertheless, they do need some time away from toddlers and middle-aged persons.

As a developmental stage, this one is also fine and important; it shouldn't frighten us. At the same time, these young people also need to be guided to choose activities that are grounded in nature or traditional fun—at least, that don't always require screens or the expenditure of money.

Bonfires fill these needs, but they are wholesome. There's that whiff of danger, but the adults are nearby. They are a wonderful way to mark liturgical times, such as the Vigil of the Nativity of St. John the Baptist (June 24). When you are looking for something for sixteen-year-olds to do, this is one really good thing. And of course, it's good for everyone. Running around the yard, roasting your own hot dogs, telling ghost stories, dancing around the fire, staring at the fire: these make good memories.

An Old-Fashioned Summer

he seasons in nature are part of the rhythm of living with the Church, though today we tend to restrict ourselves to only the liturgical seasons with a capital *L*—if we think of them at all. Let's enrich our life together; let's recapture all the patterns that we can.

I whimsically (yet utterly seriously) suggest, in order of desirability (using my highly objective inner scale that detects these things with utmost accuracy), the following. As you read, consider whether you must leave home to find one of these places or activities, or if perhaps they exist near you, even on your own balcony, in some cases:

The ocean. The ocean has its rhythms. It has wildlife everywhere. There is constant white noise that somehow patterns the mind for peace. The saltwater is healing. The swimming is demanding, the waves are challenging, the sand is inviting, the tidal pools are interesting, the kayaks are fun. The bugs are minimal. I realize that the downside is sharks.

The lake. The lake is quiet. Swimming in a lake can't be beat for refreshing, cool fun, and if there is a floating raft a few dozen yards out, you need do nothing more to provide entertainment. Canoeing, kayaking, rowboating, fishing—what's not to love? The downside is murky water and mosquitos. Hearing the loons across the water late at night can't be beat for magic.

The river. Rivers are beautiful, as are big creeks. There is so much to observe, and you can often swim in them. Canoeing a river brings you right back to the Indian days—you can play Lewis and Clark and Sacajawea, or Tom Sawyer. The downside is currents—and also mosquitos.

The pool. Pools are fun, clean (hopefully), and often have diving boards. Nothing wrong with a pool, unless it's not clean.

The kiddie pool. Don't underestimate it. The smallest kiddie pool in the backyard or even on the deck or the porch will provide hours of entertainment even for big kids and will provide you with the means to cool off your feet. Even a basin of water ... The downsides are obvious, but the benefits shouldn't be overlooked.

The hose. Who doesn't love running through the sprinkler or just getting hosed? Not kids! They love it. The older ones like hosing the younger ones and secretly enjoy this pleasure themselves.

Can you tell I think water is essential? Water makes summer fun!

June Thoughts on the Flourishing of Holiness

Order and Wonder is just my odd way of saying that what we long for is already there, given to us; we simply have to conform to it, this river that pours out of Heaven and is free for all to come and drink. The trees planted by this water flourish (Rev. 22:1–2). If we love and follow God's holy law, and live the liturgical year, we will be able to teach our children what they need to know, without any stress.

Pope Benedict XVI's Wednesday addresses on the saints make great spiritual reading (and are collected in a book called *Holy Men and Women of the Middle Ages and Beyond* as well as being available individually online). At the end of the series, he has a little talk on holiness, with this consoling reflection (my emphases):

> However, the question remains: how can we take the path to holiness, in order to respond to this call? [This could also be the question for us parents: How can my children take this path?] Can I do this on my own initiative? The answer is clear. A holy life is not primarily the result of our efforts, of our actions, because it is God,

the three times Holy (cf. Isa. 6:3) who sanctifies us, it is the Holy Spirit's action that enlivens us from within, *it is the very life of the Risen Christ that is communicated to us and that transforms us.*

It's our Baptism that gives us this life. Pope Benedict XVI goes on to quote some deep teachings about all this and then says:

Perhaps we should say things even more simply. *What is the essential? The essential means never leaving a Sunday without an encounter with the Risen Christ in the Eucharist*; this is not an additional burden but is light for the whole week. *It means never beginning and never ending a day without at least a brief contact with God.* And, on the path of our life *it means following the "signposts" that God has communicated to us in the Ten Commandments, interpreted with Christ, which are merely the explanation of what love is in specific situations....*

We might ask ourselves: can we, with our limitations, with our weaknesses, aim so high? *During the Liturgical Year, the Church invites us to commemorate a host of saints, the ones, that is, who lived charity to the full, who knew how to love and follow Christ in their daily lives. They tell us that it is possible for everyone to take this road.* In every epoch of the Church's history, on every latitude of the world map, the saints belong to all the ages and to every state of life, they are actual faces of every people, language and nation. And they have very different characters.

... And I would like to add that for me not only a few great saints whom I love and whom I know well are "signposts", but precisely also the simple saints, that is, the good people I see in my life who will never be canonized. They are ordinary people, so to speak, without visible heroism but in their everyday goodness I see the truth of faith....

In the Communion of Saints, canonized and not canonized, which the Church lives thanks to Christ in all her members, we enjoy their presence and their company and cultivate the firm hope that we shall be able to imitate their journey and share one day in the same blessed life, eternal life.

Dear friends, how great and beautiful, as well as simple is the Christian vocation seen in this light! We are all called to holiness: it is the very measure of Christian living....

I would like to ask all to open themselves to the action of the Holy Spirit, who transforms our life, to be, we too, as small pieces in the great mosaic of holiness that God continues to create in history, so that the face of Christ may shine out in the fullness of its splendour. *Let us not be afraid to aim high, for God's heights; let us not be afraid that God will ask too much of us, but let ourselves be guided by his Word in every daily action, even when we feel poor, inadequate, sinners. It will be he who transforms us in accordance with his love.*

As we live the liturgical year, many subtle and gentle lessons emerge when we notice the *placement* of the feasts, their relations to each other. In every season there are such delicate invitations to go deeper. Let's look at three June feast days (and I'm just picking three out of the many beautiful feasts in June). These are good examples of the hidden treasure we find when we approach the gift of the liturgical year with a humble receptivity (and of course, I don't pretend to have plumbed all the depths!).

Solemnity of the Sacred Heart of Jesus

This solemnity is about nothing less than what we read in 2 John 7: "For many seducers are gone out into the world, who confess not that Jesus Christ is come in the flesh: this is a seducer and an antichrist" (DR).

To convince a weary world that had gone over to abstraction, forgetting that God came to live with us with *two* natures, one fully divine and one fully human, this devotion to the Sacred Heart came to be. David Clayton has an appendix chapter about it in our book *The Little Oratory*, in which he quotes Fr. John Hardon:

In my forty-two years in the priesthood I have dealt with many souls and have been involved in many problems. I believe the hardest mystery we are called on to believe, when everything is against it, is that God does love us.

Fr. Hardon goes on to say:

> Margaret Mary was chosen by God to provide the Church and through the Church all mankind with a deep and clear understanding of God's love for us and the love we should have for Him. In spite of the trial and tribulation, including the reputation in her community for being out of her mind, she never wavered in her loving trust in God.
>
> Love is mainly proved by suffering. No wonder Margaret Mary could ask in one of her letters, "What can keep us from loving God and becoming saints, since we have a body that can suffer and a heart that can love?" Margaret Mary became the catalyst whose mission was to restore to the Catholic Church what some had lost and to strengthen what was so weakened the mystery of human freedom in responding to the merciful love of God.[30]

June 22: Feast of Sts. John Fisher and Thomas More

Here begins the "June Triduum" (or three feasts of June that I have, in the past few years, become more in love with for the particular times we live in). Would you die to uphold a commandment of God? Would you be a martyr, for instance, for what marriage says about human nature? But this is what St. John Fisher and St. Thomas More did: they went to their deaths because they would not sign a statement ratifying the king's wishes.

There are actually two commandments involved here. There is the one that prohibits adultery. There is also the eighth, which so interestingly does not flatly state (although it does comprehend), "Do not lie." It says, rather, "Thou shalt not bear false witness." To sign a paper, to swear an oath ("for what is an oath but words we say to God," admonishes Thomas More in that great play *A Man for All Seasons*), to say what you know to be

[30] John Hardon, S.J., "Doctrinal Foundation of Devotion to the Sacred Heart," *Faith and Reason* (Summer 1990), posted at EWTN, https://www.ewtn.com/catholicism/library/doctrinal-foundation-of-devotion-to-the-sacred-heart-13692.

false—these are ways that we make ourselves false witnesses when we ought to be honoring the truth.

Do they seem little things? Why not sign the paper and live another day to defend God's rules? But as Fr. James Schall says,

> [Thomas] More was a scholar who saw the intimate connection between mind and reality. He saw that the function of the Successor to Peter is to uphold clearly, wisely, and compassionately, the truths handed down to be explained and affirmed in every age. He saw that he must "witness" to this "abstract truth," even if he must stand alone, and lonely, in an obscure cell to do so. Had his "witness" not been so firm, Henry might well have laid claim to rule, not only the city, but the mind.

In our day, the enemies of the natural and supernatural order *do* wish to rule the mind, to interpose themselves between us and the truth, which is to say between us and God. Devotion to these two saints will give us the courage to imitate their virtue.

June 24: Feast of the Nativity of John the Baptist

This feast rounds out all our themes, helping us to meditate on God's law, which He so graciously gave on Mount Sinai, and the Incarnation, the "becoming flesh," which overcomes our inability to reach the heights God has in store for us. John is the prophet who connects the Old and the New Testaments, and the feast of his birth is called "the summer Christmas." At the furthest possible point in the year from Jesus' birth, we who follow the Church's year receive a beautiful renewal of our love for the piercing event that saves the world. On our own, we wouldn't be thinking of the crèche with Mary and Joseph and the baby Jesus in it, but now it is brought to mind.

John's birth comes just after the summer solstice, as the days begin to grow shorter. Do you see how the heavens declare the truth of the Gospel, that "I must decrease, that he may increase"? The old ways wane as the New Adam arrives (at the winter solstice, the point where the days begin to get longer!).

Of course, St. John, too, was martyred for the faith, specifically for the truth about marriage. When we think about someone's birth, we also think about his death, so even here we have another reminder about God's law and its goodness.

The feast of the Immaculate Heart of Mary also comes around this time (it is a movable feast in the Novus Ordo calendar); the proximity to the Nativity of St. John the Baptist, when it happens that way, can be a little reminder of motherhood, so intimately connected to babies and their births, and the great Mother of all, Our Lady, with her heart that was preserved from sin from all eternity.

We could tediously try to explain a lot of abstractions to our children; we could read a lot of boring books. Or we could celebrate the feasts and *know* ever more deeply what God is showing us!

And this is what I mean by Order and Wonder, by living the liturgical year. If you are wondering how, why, simply begin with the feasts that are coming up.

For the feast of Sts. John Fisher and Thomas More, certainly bake a cake (honey would be a fitting flavor; hold the locusts), but more importantly, try to go to Mass on these feast days; at least tell the stories of each commemoration, that they not be lost. How about watching *A Man for All Seasons* (a favorite around here)?

Praying each day's Vespers will put you on the right path. Afterward, and especially for St. John the Baptist, I recommend a bonfire or a festive party. Traditionally this would be held on June 23, after the Vespers that anticipate the feast.

Let's reclaim the culture for our own, with Order and Wonder!

Practical Civics on the Glorious Fourth

In case you aren't used to an old-fashioned Fourth of July, you need just watermelon, something to grill, and a few games; even simply throwing water balloons fits the bill. Badminton, volleyball, horseshoes—if you want to get fancy. All American.

I remember how I used to think of Independence Day. Fireworks and the above-described party, perhaps. My husband's parents, whom we lived near for many years, had a rather staid commemoration of the day—one that included salmon and peas (a traditional New England Fourth of July menu, and I hadn't heard of it either) eaten in the dining room, and the hanging of a small replica of the Declaration of Independence from the fireplace mantel with Scotch tape.

As we visited, I thought further back to big barbecues at the state parks in the South where my Egyptian father lived with my stepmother. In those days, immigrants were relatively fewer, welcomed by the hospitality of a people firmly confident in their own traditions, enough so that they were interested—really, enthusiastically eager—to know more about their guests' ethnic customs.

On the Fourth, these warm neighbors good-naturedly included us in their un-self-conscious celebration, which, however, did not include any lore or sense of participation in a historical remembrance. Looking back, I think I detect in them a sense of retaining the instinct to rejoice, but only the instinct. The collective memory—the knowledge of the particulars that cause the celebration—wasn't passed along. It could be that they thought the schools were doing that part of the task. I can see how those same people, forty-five years on, might be unsure of how it has come to be that certain precious things are no longer remembered.

At this moment we are at a crisis of liberty. It's not enough to drink lemonade and hold a sparkler. But just getting angry, or worse, despairing, doesn't fix anything. And certainly only talking about what's important might make us think, but it's not actually doing anything about the situation.

Remember, I'm that rootless person who has spent my life trying to build things from scratch, with only a few scraps from the lumberyard—little pieces of memory and information pounded together to form some sort of structure. I saw the little Declaration posted there on my in-laws' mantel; I ate my salmon and peas; I thought of those Southern softball games and hot dogs. Of course there are the many books I've read; that's how I learn a lot of things, as we know. But translating into my here-and-now life can be tricky.

Thanks to friends whose gatherings are more centered on the building of culture rather than only preserving its outward manifestations, one day it all clicked: what we should do to build this part of our culture—the part where we attend to the human side of how we live together in freedom.

We should have the party, and we should not only display but should read the Declaration of Independence with our children! And talk about it! And tell stories about how it came to be!

So, somehow, almost two decades ago, it became dear Suki's job to write out the whole thing on a long roll of paper I happened to have. I don't think any of us had really internalized how long the Declaration is (yet how short for such an important work of human genius, the foundation of our freedom!), and it took her quite a while to transcribe it.

I think that if I had to do it over, I might give each child a section, to spare any one child from such onerous work. But she did it. Just as in the original, there are mistakes. Don't sweat over those. It's just fine. Actually, I think she did a beautiful job and marvel over the straightness of her lines.

Every year after some outdoor fun, we give an older child, usually the oldest boy of the hosting family, the task of reading the whole thing in a nice, loud voice to the assembly. Shouts of "Hear hear!" and huzzahs (or boos at the appropriate moments, such as the recounting of the wrongs inflicted by foreign tyrants) are encouraged. (And you need someone with a steady arm to hold the thing up for the reader!)

Asking the children to sit and listen quietly to the ringing words, even if they don't quite understand them, forms them in piety and respect. Hold the toddler on your lap.

In coming years, they will come to know the events and the Declaration well. It's good to know by heart the preamble, "When in the course of human events it becomes necessary," and then discuss the particulars (imagine if you had to feed and house a troop of soldiers from another country!).

If your children are very young, maybe Father could proclaim the Declaration for a few years until the eldest son is ready. Our guests (including the youngest to hold the pen) love the chance to sign the bottom of our copy, with the sober words ringing in their ears, "for the support of this Declaration, with a firm reliance on the protection of divine Providence, we mutually pledge to each other our Lives, our Fortunes and our sacred Honor." (I usually tell our guests, "If you haven't signed in the past, please do today!" just because the space on our document is limited. But I think children from previous years like to "do a better job" on their signature, and that's fine with me.)

Of course, it's hardly a celebration without music, so as it gets dark, it's wonderful to sing patriotic songs, maybe around a bonfire. You might need to make your own booklet with the lyrics printed out; some candles or flashlights will come in handy.

Stay with it. The important things are the work of years, not the assignments of a day. Civic lessons are one thing, and necessary, of course. But celebration is what fixes the meaning. With love and patience we can recover our patrimony and raise a new generation to love freedom!

78

A Procession for the Feast of St. Martin; or, Building the Culture with Celebration

Did you ever hear of the tradition of a procession in honor of St. Martin?

This great saint's feast is on November 11. (Isn't it interesting that we celebrate Veteran's Day on the feast of this military saint?) This day used to be the sort of unofficial start of Advent, which makes sense when you notice the days getting so much shorter and your thoughts do turn to the coming preparations for the feast of the Nativity.

If we're thinking about building authentic traditions to build our culture—the culture of our family but also our neighborhood, circle of friends and relatives, and ultimately the whole of society—it's things such as the St. Martin procession that stand out as really meaningful.

For one thing, no one will ever be impervious to a great story. You can read about St. Martin in your saints' book or online. When we think about our boys, we want for them this strength and big-heartedness—the man on his horse who stoops to share what he has with a beggar! Note well that he *shares* his cloak. He and the beggar will be facing the cold together, in a fraternity of charity. When we think of our girls, we want them to admire men like this—magnanimous men!

For another, it's lovely to go out in the darkness with lanterns, and that is part of this traditional procession!

Prepare your lanterns, which can be candles in simple jars that you've collected in the previous weeks, cleaned out, and decorated with tissue paper applied with watery glue or Mod Podge. A long string can be a handle, wrapped around the neck of the jar and made into a long loop (you don't want the flame to burn it). Sticks with notches work perfectly for carrying these far enough away from our bodies to be safe.

A beautiful and fitting hymn to sing for your procession is "The Light of the World Is Jesus." It will take a few weeks beforehand to get it memorized. The "Iste Confessor" chant is traditional.

If you have the day off, maybe the festivities can happen on the evening before. The evening of the feast day or the Sunday before are good too.

A feast needs food! It's traditional to serve roast goose. Now, this you might not be able to swing, and for us, if it's on a Friday, we will share some delicious clam chowder and other soups, in solidarity with the poor and in remembrance of the suffering of Our Lord. But it can still be a special meal, with treats. On another night, you could serve a festive meal with goose-shaped cookies or gooseberry fool.

The children love to hear the story of the saint while they are drawing or coloring a picture of him. In my religion class, we made prayer cards. The way to do this is to give each child a half page of card stock (cut the sheets with a paper cutter). Each one gets a small picture of the saint (you can download one from the Internet and print it) to cut out, color, and glue to his card. Then the child writes on his card the name of the saint and his feast day. The card can be bordered with decorations of the child's choosing and embellished with St. Martin's symbols. If the child wants to, he can write down the things that St. Martin is the patron of. You can tell him the story while he works. When he's done, the card can go on the family oratory or in the child's personal oratory near his bed.

PART 7

On Creating a
Family Culture

F amily culture is a blend of what the two parents bring to it (including their memories and resolutions), what the children's personalities contribute, and how those factors mingle with the community and are formed by it in turn.

Young parents often become caught up in the first two aspects, understandably, and don't understand the importance of the last one. We all need a wider community—and we are here on earth to build it after heavenly patterns.

St. Gregory Pockets

S t. Gregory Pockets is the name I gave to the little "pockets" of people in a given geographical area (not online—what we used to call "the neighborhood" in a quainter era), pockets of people who would like to get together naturally, to share the seasons together, to help out when a mom has a new baby or someone is sick, to have kids who can play together, to have picnics where men can talk to other men who care about raising strong families in a countercultural way.

Bold Friendship

I had the idea to name these pockets after this great saint because he is beloved by Protestants and Catholics and Orthodox alike. Gregory was senator and prefect in Rome; then a monk. He had to leave the cloister to become pope, and in his life, we can see how God uses every experience in a man's life to carry out His providential goals. Gregory rescued the disintegrating city of Rome by bringing true worship of Christ to the people, ransoming slaves using the treasures of the Church and restoring the Liturgy with, you guessed it, Gregorian chant. The antiphon for his feast hails him "Father of the city, the joy of the world." He's a fitting patron for those who have to work to build a life together in a community that probably doesn't already exist (but if it does for you, count your blessings and pray for the lonely people who are adrift). All it takes is a couple of families who can then welcome more families, and sooner or later, there will be a group and then a real community—you'll see! This building, to be fruitful, must be rooted in beauty and fraternal love.

I've learned over the years about how to be part of a community that will support you on your way, and in which you will be a trusted supporter of the others. Be advised: I've learned these things the hard way, by making *all* the mistakes in interpersonal relationships, and the easy way, by having the blessing of good friends despite my shortcomings. These are not things that come naturally to me. So there's definitely hope for you! If *I* can do a tiny bit of all this, *you* certainly can do a lot!

Practical Thoughts for Your Pocket

Start a Pocket to find people and get together on a regular basis to enjoy each other's company. Invite other families for a Sunday meal, after church. Find other homeschoolers and have them over to discuss curriculum.

Bring your friends dinner when they need it (do use the easy online trackers to organize); throw a (modest and fun) baby shower when a baby is on the way; watch one another's kids when there's a doctor's appointment. By helping one another in these practical ways, the enjoyment part of your friendships will be deeper and based on a firm foundation of real charity.

You are not looking for your bestest friend ever when you are working to establish your Pocket. Instead, content yourself by looking for other people who need some friends too. Find the people. ("Who is my neighbor?" Not necessarily a person who agrees with every single thing I think or does just what I do or is exactly my age.)

When you get together, enjoy each other's company. Share snacks to enjoy together. Everyone can bring the kinds of things they like best, resulting in a nice spread—some for grown-ups, some for kids, some for everyone. Leave the leftovers with your host unless seriously urged to take them home.

When you have these enjoyable get-togethers, suggest (and eventually encourage others to suggest) something (preferably short) for everyone to have read beforehand. That way, not only do you have a topic to discuss, but you can steer the conversation toward matters that edify. People sometimes limit themselves to niceties or banalities in conversation, especially when they are feeling insecure. A way to have everyone remember the gathering with a positive glow is to have a substantial topic to advert to when chitchat lags. In this way, you will set the tone.

This idea of the St. Gregory Pocket is different from and broader than a book club for the purpose of forming a community, though it includes the feature of having something to discuss. The difference turns on the focus; the group of friends is getting together to enjoy the company, food, and possibly needlework or other crafts if you are in possession of older children to whisk babies away (more on that below). Having something everyone has read is not the purpose of the gathering, but it's really conducive to energizing the group.

I know that the distinction may not seem a real one at first, but somehow it is productive of a longer-lasting community that is able to weather the normal changes that life brings.

The reading I recommend could be gleaned from essays, longer articles, older papal encyclicals, and shorter books by thoughtful writers. Sharing posts from my blog or chapters from this book that muse on family life, a woman's role, and liturgical living creates a connection and reveals kindred spirits who prioritize wanting to live differently and placing importance on honoring the collective memory. A discussion on menu planning can easily expand to include important reflections on family life and devotion to it.

Experience suggests that you might want to stay away from sharing mere punditry or click-bait-style posts that are reactions to reactions. Rants seem to get everyone angry and tend to polarize even people who normally agree. We want contented, not contentious, meetings and to promote deeper thinking about everything in general.

Women who've had the foresight to have older children can encourage the younger ones with handiwork of some sort. Mothers need a chance to chat, nurse a baby, and knit or mend a tear in a pair of pants; the gift of a willing nine-year-old to whisk that baby away cannot be estimated. Simply encouraging this sort of creativity and housewifeliness can be a real benefit of these get-togethers. One crafty lady can teach another a tricky crochet stitch; someone who needs help assembling materials for a children's project will find willing hands. If you need 150 cloth napkins cut out, as I did for Suzanne's wedding, you'll know where to turn! And if you really don't know how to darn a sock, someone can show you, or you can all watch a video about it together and figure it out.

If you are a bit older, consider that far from not being interested, the younger women you see at church or in the library might really appreciate getting your perspective and relaxing in your big yard.

But younger women who are juggling that baby all on their own should regard nursing as a form of "handiwork" and enjoy the chance to converse and snack at the same time. Choose your readings on the basis of how well they can be held in one hand!

In all cases, try mixing up the ages.

For couples, think about at least a quarterly get-together with dinner or a sort of tapas-like, "heavy hors d'oeuvres" event (often the most fun and least labor-intensive—once you're all together, that is). Don't forget dessert! Being able to have a deep conversation about something of potentially life-changing substance—such as the importance of Sundays or the possibility of purity in our teens, to mention two topics discussed by yours truly—will make the time together a treasure.

Don't be daunted by the thought that you are the only one in your entire state (or country, or continent) who reads this book or anything at all, or that you may not be the organizing type. Start the group anyway and invite a few people. Make it clear that they can invite others. Let the organizers do their organizing on your behalf if that is what it takes. One of life's greatest pleasures is introducing people you know to things you love.

Mistakes about Making Friends

We go online to make friends, because we are a lonely society. Over the years, I have found that many of my readers are isolated, both physically and psychically, often because of the choices they have made to prioritize family. Sometimes the demographic pressure is enough; there simply are not many young families visible today.

But there are a few fallacies that can prevent a person who desires friendship from finding it:

- *The fallacy of thinking that everyone else already has friends.* Hopefully we're not in seventh grade and can make the leap to understand that everyone can always benefit from more friends! Why, I have a friend, a ninety-plus-year-old lady, who just a few weeks ago made new friends after Mass by inviting a couple she could barely see with her failing eyes over to her house right then and there for donuts. And they went. And they enjoyed it very much.

- *The fallacy that you can't break into an already established group.* Well, avoid the mean girls, I guess. But otherwise, just plunk yourself right in there. Try to be of service, and you will see that it will be fine. Groups can give off the air of being quite self-contained. It's hard not to do it if you're the group. But sometimes, if you are looking at it from the group's point of view, a person just won't be pulled in. She refuses. As long as you're trying to avoid being that rather difficult person, you should be good. Just barge right in (but delicately, acknowledging that you must learn their culture, so to speak). Assume the best.

- *The fallacy of preconceived ideas.* This is when you think that you can be friends only with a person who thinks just like you or looks just like you, or contrariwise who thinks and looks the way your ideal, imaginary friend thinks and looks. The thought that the married woman with no children isn't longing to be your friend. The thought that the woman with grown children wouldn't like to talk to you. "Who is my neighbor?" Right. I already asked you that one, but it's a good one.

- *The fallacy that everyone who is your friend will be your* best *friend.* But this is not necessary. It's fine to be just friends, not particularly close, but she can depend on you in a pinch. And you can leave your kids with her if you need to go to the doctor, and you will bring each other dinner when you need it. Cultivate this sort of friendship, and the other will be added unto you. Remember, it's the "just friends" who are able to build a whole community.

Hospitality Thoughts

Here are some little ideas for making people feel truly welcome and comfortable in your home; the generous touches of warm hosting I have observed in others, that establish a culture of friendship, peace, and festivity.

Prepare for Your Guests

Your preparations should be as fabulous as you want them to be (and sometimes you're aiming at simple, so by all means, do that), but for your own calm presence and that of your family, you need to *plan*. If you are in the kitchen frantically dealing with things, it's no fun for anyone. For the sake of your guests, it's better for you to forgo those extra (and time-consuming) details you pride yourself on, if it means that you can sit down and enjoy the conversation.

I have found that I am most peaceful when *almost* everything can be made beforehand, but there is one task that I can have a friend help me with. This depends, of course, on the gathering, but often people do feel more comfy if they can help with something. It's a balance, because you don't want to be so harried that they end up with the sense they have to take over for you — or escape the kitchen entirely for self-preservation!

In other words, don't be so stressed out by your vision that you're just not good company. Knowing your own limitations requires humility, a virtue. The reward is learning that guests enjoy being taken care of and truly won't know what they … don't know.

Greet Your Guests Warmly

Greeting your guests warmly sets the tone for everything you want to happen! Think beforehand of things you will say as people come in. No matter what your temperament, rely on a set ritual to get you through. It's no good saying you're an awkward introvert! Get a ritual and use it. Anything else is a lack of charity.

"So good to see you, thank you for coming, wonderful that you made it, please come in, welcome, welcome!" Not as comfortingly ritualistic as "Blessings of the evening," "God bless the evening in you," "May we find you in good health," "God is good," and other exchanges found in more formal cultures, but these efforts of ours will have to do.

The physical entryway might not be the most graceful. At my house, the large front door is ignored, New England style, in favor of the mudroom door, followed by a tight passage hemmed in by a brick wall and an ill-conceived counter, after navigation through yet another door. Just do your best with the inevitable fumbling. Take coats, step back while leading the way past the obstacles (maybe keep an eye on your spouse to see who will take which task), and try not to pay more attention to your obnoxiously ill-behaved dog than to the duty of greeting your guests! (At our house, said animal's behavior has been much mitigated by the advice I picked up from a dog-savvy friend: if your pet sees it as her bounden duty to guard you from and alert you to these intruders in the most aggressively loud and jumpy way possible, *put her on the leash*. It's the entrance that makes her crazy. It's just not hospitable for people to be greeted not with hugs but with shouts of "ROXIE, BE QUIET! BAD DOG! SIT! LIE DOWN! SHUT UP! NO! BAD DOG!" I hadn't realized this, as our previous pets had been better behaved and more responsive to commands. But Roxie is a border collie and just can't help herself when it comes to protecting the fold. So leash it is. I find that after the initial bustle is over, I can just take her off it and she is fine.)

Do Greet Your Guests

If the party is so large that people are coming in without knocking, as one does when the festivities are in full swing, and you're already in deep conversation with some guests, take a moment to say, "Excuse me," and *greet the newcomers.*

Never let someone stand uncomfortably while you finish up your point. Don't assume people will be fine with sidling into the fray. If you see them charging up to the beer cooler without you, fine, carry on with your stinging rebuttal or hilarious punch line; but make it a point to welcome that person within a few moments.

If your interlocutor doesn't pick up on the signal that you need to turn from him, and you find yourself caught in a hostess gridlock, use the tactic of the arresting hand on the interlocutor's arm, accompanied by a "John! Good to see you—Harry is just telling me about the time he was caught in a flash flood in the Andes!" and then turn back to Harry after a few beats. Your physical contact assures him, Chappie A, that you will not abandon him while you greet Chappie B. It also reminds you not to abandon him.

Keep an Eye on Needs

In any large gathering that you are hosting, be prepared to say, "Excuse me," to tend to a guest's needs at any time. In general, all the people in a gathering should make eye contact with anyone on the periphery; don't form a tight little knot that others can't easily enter into.

Even if you're not the host, do look around and smile and at least nod at other guests, if you do not verbally greet them. A party is not the time for that intense tête-à-tête that leaves others out in the cold, as it were. Cultivate the art of the *mingle.*

Serve the Food

When it comes time to serve the food, do it with some sort of ritual flair. Gather people (I have a bell for larger parties. People do make fun of me a little, but it works—perhaps they are envious). Reiterate your gratitude for their presence. Say grace.

Above all, especially at a sit-down affair, do not get your own food before your guests have theirs! Lifting your own fork and muttering, "Help yourself" or "I guess we should dig in" is not the way! Serve them first. Be sure they have everything—the rolls, the butter, the condiments—before you attend to your own plate.

A rule to discuss with your family beforehand is "Family hold back" (FHB). I mentioned this rule in "Seven Strategies for Dinner with the Barbarians." The concept was introduced to me by a monk of our acquaintance who is from a large family. When his mom would suddenly realize that they didn't have as much of one dish as she had thought, she'd whisper, "FHB!" and they all knew that they were relied upon to restrain themselves in favor of the guests. Now the monks do this, too, when they entertain the populace, and so do we. Relatedly, MIK lets your family know that there's "more in the kitchen" and they can help you replenish if necessary.

Make Connections

Have a few questions to ask your guests to draw them out. Don't filibuster or dominate; let them speak. Some people are shy and need a little encouragement.

When dinner is at the table—say, up to twelve people—do your best as hosts to maintain one conversation. Perhaps your guests will engage in little side discussions, but try not to do it yourself, or if you do, make an effort at a break to pull people together again in case *they* would like the opportunity to extricate themselves from being monopolized by a side talker.

Be diligent about letting your guests get to know each other. Don't let them go the whole evening interacting only through you. A well placed tidbit of information—"John, did you know that Tom also used to live in

Bangalore?" "Grace, Mary is an expert at training falcons, and I know you love birds of prey"—can foster a conversation while you tend to something (or someone) else.

Let Your Guests Go

Graciously allow your guests to begin making little winding-up comments ("Well, this has been lovely!"). It's a little dance; know the steps.

Hopefully, you won't be driven to change into your pajamas to give them the hint that it's time to leave, so enchanted will they have been with the evening's conviviality, but things do wind down on their own, usually. Maria von Trapp says that it's better to end things a little before they seem really to be over (actually, she recommends stopping at the peak of the fun), rather than to keep them going for too long.

If you've offered coffee after dinner, followed by a small nightcap (I'm not saying you have to, but as an example), if an hour or so later, you say, "Would anyone like a coffee?" usually people take this as a cue to say, "We really should be going." If you *want* them to stay, you can say, "No, really, I'm having some—what can I get you?" But if the party's really over, it's a good hint.

Give your guests a fond farewell, remark on how enjoyable it has all been, and help them move along out the door. Observe the little ways people have of doing this, and make them your own. Your warm hospitality will stay with those who have enjoyed it.

ASK AUNTIE LEILA

Relocation Priorities and the Desirability Quotient

Dear Auntie Leila,

When one's husband is unexpectedly at the end of a career path and searching for something new (and urgently), what should we try to prioritize as a family, assuming any of these might be factors: making ends meet, geographical location, his vocational fulfillment, school options for the children, moving nearer extended family (kind of spread out, unfortunately), low cost of living, good parish? Just generally, how does a wife support him in this and help recraft our family vision?

Thank you,
Wandering

Dear Wandering,

I think that God has a way of getting us to where we need to be, especially if we just ask Him outright. So don't forget to do that!

Usually, though, He just makes it clear with one criterion: *whether we can afford the thing we are thinking of!* So mundane, no clouds parting, but it's the truth. You can be pretty sure that if you can't afford a certain house (school, dress, trip), you aren't meant to live in that house (or what have you)! (Not that, if you *can* afford it, you are assured that it's His will that you buy. This is a negative test.)

The other sign is the location of the job. This is what you don't know and where the discernment comes in.

You need to be where your husband can find his new path. The family goes where the father goes, and he goes where he can support the family. Sometimes, alas, that is far from the extended family. But, wither thou goest, and all that!

Finding a good solid parish is also very high up there on the priorities list. It's difficult, because pastors get moved, parishes close ... The only thing I see trumping even a job is if you find yourselves somewhere where there is no place to worship in a way that will allow your children to grow up in the Faith. Remember, God has no grandchildren, only children!

Adults can put up with a lot of nonsense, because we have an interior world where we can cling to what we know is right, by means of our memories and imagination. But children must first be formed.

Normally (I mean, barring a miracle), our children's faith is learned and kept because the place where we worship is truly oriented *to* worship — church is not a self-affirmation project, a little club, or an entertainment center. The family really can't do this alone.

Ideally you would find a community supporting true worship that includes *some* like-minded people — others, even one family, who are trying to live differently and who have the fortitude to commit to a life that is a bit different; other moms who are devoted to home; other families who sacrifice and aren't putting material things first; a group of people who are more daring in terms of family size ...

Nothing's perfect, but having friends is very important!

My husband adds: When I talk to kids about courtship (or friendship in general), I point out that you are a somewhat different you in different circumstances and with different people. So you want to choose a spouse (or friends) who make you the you that you really want to be—the good you. There may be something similar about choosing a community: try to imagine yourself living in Town A; then imagine yourself in Town B. In which place do you see your family being what you really want it to be—and what God wants it to be?

So now you get down to the real work of finding a place to live.

And now, the überscientific approach to relocation, a veritable algorithm, cooked up by your resident math geniuses, the Lawlers.

The Desirability Quotient!

When the Chief and I were making this sort of change in our lives, we made an informal spreadsheet or glorified list. We assigned points to a house based on all the criteria, from trivial to vital, that we could think of. We really made a science of it, if science is when you try to quantify the subjective by means of a changing metric, and it passed the time when we were driving all over tarnation looking at properties.

Here's how it worked: Assign points to any and every attribute that strikes you about a house. Like this:

- Proximity to grandparents (say, 5 points)
- Walkability to shops, library, church (say, 5 points)
- Enough bedrooms (say, 3 points because you can always bunk the kids)
- Enough bathrooms (say, 3 points—you get the idea)
- A back staircase (so much fun! Getting whimsical with the list, but drives are long)
- A fireplace in the kitchen (we added this when we realized this was a thing, and now I would give it 100 points)
- A flat yard or portion thereof (our area is so hilly)

- A kitchen (added this seemingly basic feature when we looked at a house with a fridge, stove, and sink, and that was all—no cabinets of any kind)
- A study (the Chief works at home, so this was worth a lot)
- A short commute (if this applies)
- The ability to move right in, no major rehab necessary (a lot of points, didn't come up much to be honest, in our price range)
- House set back away from the road (added this when the house looked great on the listing but turned out to be three feet from the street)
- House actually on the acreage (added this after looking at a few houses with tiny yards and the reputed five acres that came with them were attached by the merest of paths, way back yonder)
- A hallway upstairs (added this after looking at a house where each bedroom was reached by walking through the preceding bedroom)

And so on.

Add the points up. Divide that number by the asking price of the house (drop any zeros) to get your Desirability Quotient (DQ)!

For instance, if a property scores 40, and the asking price is $250,000, drop the last three zeros, divide 40 by 250, and voila! DQ = .16—so, 16 for that house. If another one is the same price but you gave it 50 points, that gives you a DQ of .20—so, 20 for conversational purposes; that one is superior (as long as you are considering houses you can afford, of course).

Like its close relatives, the Ben Franklin and the Decision Matrix, this process tells you which house or location or life you really want in your heart of hearts, because you find yourself secretly manipulating points so that the DQ comes out the way you want it to.

But again, making ends meet is the brick wall! Good thing, or we'd never be sure what God's will is.

A little tip: a wife doesn't make the burden heavier by worrying and fretting and posing hypotheticals that involve failure. Just do what you are doing, trying to analyze the situation and help your husband figure things out.

Serenely assume that God has an amazing plan for you. Trust. (Entrust your family to St. Joseph, the patriarch whose mission is to protect and guard you, just as he did the precious family entrusted to him.) Be patient, and meanwhile, use your cleverness in the many areas that will become clear as you forge ahead (being frugal, getting organized, traveling light).

There is no perfect place to live on earth, but when you're together, figuring things out as a family, that's heaven.

Where Children Can Play

hildren really shouldn't play with their friends in their bedrooms, for the most part. If they are all the same sex, *and the door is open*, being in bedrooms can work for a while when they are young, especially if you have a one-level layout; but in general, I think that, for the sake of the habit of openness and chastity when they are older, it's better to have the general sense that guests are entertained in public spaces of the house.

You would be surprised how quickly children grow up—I mean, how quickly they go from being unaware of much of anything to being open to opportunities, good and bad. It's best to be practical about your hopes for them, early on. If your hopes include their purity, which, in turn, is their best shot at happiness and happy families of their own, then start now to give them the tools for keeping their (perfectly normal and healthy) appetites in check. Self-control is a gift we give them by means of our expectations and clear limits.

At the same time, kids are noisy! The best idea is for them to be outside! Even at night (Ghost in the Graveyard, anyone?)! Even in the rain! But of course, in they come ... and then what? Put thought into where they will be together in your home.

ASK AUNTIE LEILA

Raising Our Kids Together Now That They Are Older

Auntie Leila,

I have five children. My friend Jen has ten. Our families, along with several other dear families in our community, have enjoyed raising our kids together, and our children have played countless hours in one another's backyards while moms have had coffee and solved the world's problems. Most of our close family friends also homeschool, and we are very blessed to have a community of mostly like-minded families.

Over the last year or so, we have seen a marked shift in the way that our children interact with one another, as many have crossed over into early adolescence. Flirtatious behavior, hurt feelings, insecurities, and a concern for feeling accepted have somewhat overshadowed the easy play times that our kids used to enjoy.

I realize that this is normal, as hormones factor in and our children transition to adults. However, I am wondering if you have any

456

practical advice for helping kids negotiate peer relationships, in a family setting, in a more graceful way. Already, we largely go against the norm by homeschooling, and our kids' peer time is usually, almost exclusively, at our homes, with parents. We are here to help, but sometimes I just don't know how.

What is your best advice for moms with a house full of eleven- to fifteen-year-olds—their own and their friends'?

Thanks!

Shawna

Shawna, you are so lucky and blessed to have a wonderful community of friends. This is the way to raise children!

I think that your question touches on the larger one of building the culture: precisely the work of bringing children into adulthood. Every traditional culture has a systematic way to ease young people into their responsibilities, taking into account the developmental realities.

Maybe this is what people mean by "socialization," without realizing that conformity isn't the goal, but raising responsible, self-controlled adults is. One learns self-control just the way one learns any other skill—by being put to little tests that don't have a lot at stake, so that when the big ones come, one is ready.

A good start is having rules and plans and standards for your teens, just as you do for your littles. You have to stay out of the picture more, giving them their freedom and time together, but you must stay just as vigilant.

You are right: it's healthy in young people to show interest in one another. It's the adults' job to channel it all in the right direction. Their environment matters. Is the TV where the bed is? Even if it's just your guest bedroom that you've made into a TV room, that needs to be rethought.

Better ideas: bonfires and other outdoor activities; a rec room that's not off the beaten path or never gone into by adults but is more central and open; contra dances and swing dances; hikes and swim parties; Monopoly tournaments, Foosball tournaments—heck, poker tournaments.

As they get older, finding places other than the homes works well to offer more freedom. A local sandwich shop once in a while for some fries, hiking, bowling ... But they have to be reminded how to act, how to show courtesy to the shop owners—and not to pair off. Girls must be guided to dress modestly; boys must be led to dress respectfully.

Young people don't like being told that it's not a good idea to loll around, pair off, or engage in horseplay with the opposite sex or what have you—but they have to be reminded. Don't let the "attitude" get you down. Have standards and voice them. Let them know that you want them to have a good time together as a group and that singling others out makes the rest feel uncomfortable. Don't be afraid to let them know that you take their feelings seriously enough to want to protect them from being exposed too early to things whose consequences they cannot foresee. Encourage your husbands to set the bar high as well.

Make sure there is some sort of plan for their get-togethers, such as games or projects—and fixing up their own get-together spot is a great project—meeting at the beach and so forth. Guide them. They are like big toddlers whose playdates have to be managed, only with finesse. Even letting them "just hang out" is fine, as long as you know what is going on, unobtrusively.

When they get mad at each other, acknowledge that they might have a point, but keep their eyes on the big picture: we're in this together, these are our friends, let's take a breather, let's overlook faults. Remind them that they can be just as annoying to their friends as their friends might be to them. Remind them that these kinds of hurt feelings often arise because too much time, or too much undirected time, is being spent together. Bored people or pointless activity leads to issues between friends, as does lack of sleep.

Now, one problem gets to be that other parents have their own ideas, and you can get vexed with your friends when it seems as if they aren't paying attention or don't think something is important. But hang in there. It's true that they have their moments of exasperation with us too. I am sure that some of my friends thought my girls weren't properly dressed at the same moment I was throwing up my hands about how their daughters were dressed. I'll bet I thought their sons were being goofuses right when they were fed up with mine.

So do talk about it with other parents. Parents really help other parents by saying no to certain things. When your friend wonders if that movie is appropriate, it helps you remember to check the movie out, and that's a good thing!

Gather your own children at some point in a busy time for a comfy talk, maybe on your bed. Know that teens *do* want to talk, but not with "the littles" around. Going over the day's events helps them remain close to you and gives you a peek into what's going on. When you have overnight guests, scheduling in separate family time helps keep relationships peaceful, as does making sure everyone gets sleep.

Keep your sense of humor, and acknowledge that sometimes things won't be exactly right. The main thing is to prevent the kids from being left entirely to their own devices.

Let your standards be known and don't worry too much.

Standards and Solidarity: Ten Ways to Give Your Child the Gift of Purity

Blessed are the pure of heart: for they shall see God.

— MATTHEW 5:8

You are justifiably worried about your child's being exposed to porn, bullying, and invasion of privacy due to social media. Our most serious thinkers pen essays worrying about the dire effects of these things on our children. They call for marches. They call for Internet blocks. They want someone to do something.

Well, Auntie Leila is here to tell you what to do. It's simple. It's not easy, but it's simple.

No one can fix things but you, the parents—not the school system, not the technology, not the government. I'm all for society's doing certain things, but it's not going to help unless parents make decisions, sometimes tough ones. The reason is that there is too much money to be made as long as parents are clueless.

So, it's just you. But you can do it.

You can give your children a healthy, happy childhood. Will doing these ten things guarantee that your kids grow up to be pure and see God? No, alas, there are no guarantees. But that shouldn't stop you from doing your best. Be realistic, but be confident. Mistakes happen; I've made my share. I'm not a perfect parent, and neither are you, but we can give the question the effort it requires.

1. *Decide on your standards and stick to them.* The most important thing is to have standards, and this will necessarily be somewhat relative. What I mean by that is that each family can figure things out without being exactly like other families. It almost doesn't matter, as long as you're somewhere on the "standards playing field." I am not going to get into how many inches the inseam of a pair of shorts should be, or at what age the child can go to the store by himself. I'm just saying, decide for yourselves how to handle things and then handle them, even if it means making sacrifices—and it will.

The truth is that almost *any* standards will do. This is not about being strict or running away from the world in fear but about staking your claim wherever you can, showing your kids that you care, and when they are older and can really talk back to you—in the second decade—sticking to what you've decided.

In general, it's a good idea to have lots of standards for lots of things, so that, when the day comes for you to say no to an inappropriate mode of dress or an unlimited texting plan, you will have had practice.

2. *Wives, encourage your husbands to protect.* Let your husband say what he needs to say to be protective, even if sometimes it seems like too much. You can talk about it later. If it's too little, encourage him when you're alone. "The girls really appreciate it when you make rules for them; they may not show it, but they know you care, and they have pride in their strong father." This sort of comment will work wonders on his willingness to speak up.

Sometimes you can work with a silent but willing husband when you realize that he accepts your saying something like, "Daddy says you can't do that [dress that way, use your phone that way, talk to a girl that way]." Some husbands are by nature not on top of the details—they are happy to delegate. It's better for the unity of the family for rules to come from him, so this is a good compromise: letting you channel his "wishes." As long as he backs you up ("Um, right, you are absolutely not wearing that!"), this strategy works. Keep your discussions with each other private. Better to err on the side of setting standards than of being permissive. Be grateful to each other for your solidarity in this battle!

3. *Don't allow, and then strictly limit, social media.* There is no way that a child needs a phone, a tablet, or whatever device is current now. An older child might need something, but you are the guardian of his soul and the payer of the service bill. My recommendation is to keep such devices from him until he's old enough to drive.

Remember that even an e-reader has access to the Internet. Gaming devices (including handheld ones) do as well. Try to think of what children ever did without phones, and then make your decisions without reference to your children's whining, their attitude, your need for peace and quiet, and so forth.

4. *Be the gatekeeper for visual images.* It's up to us to know what our children are looking at. Parents decide, but deciding means you have to know beforehand what the content is. Stall for time if you are caught off guard. They can rewatch a favorite movie if you didn't have time to check out the one they want to watch now. It is not unimaginable for you to make your child call you from his friend's house to ask if he can watch a certain movie. If he knows it's a rule, he'll do it, especially if you ground him from that friend's house for a time when you find out that he broke it.

There was a popular show from maybe fifteen years ago (but it's still very popular), in which parental bedroom activity was discussed—not acceptable content for an eight-year-old, no matter how amusing the show is overall for older kids. "So, sorry, older kids. You don't get to have it on, because there is no way I can preview every episode. Concern for others is what we're all about!" Don't go by ratings. Often PG-13 movies are far more rude than the R-rated ones.

Feed the imagination with good things. Offer your children beautiful images—good books—and good movies.

5. *Mind your own viewing and conversation.* If you think your kids don't know when you're being a hypocrite, you're wrong. Practically the only thing that matters to them as they go through adolescence is figuring out whether you are committed to the things you profess. It takes a lot of virtue for an immature person to overcome temptations; if a mature person can't do it, well ...

Appropriateness expands with experience, of course, and your kids can be taught that distinction, but there are lines to be drawn. Sometimes the best lesson you'll teach your children is the example you give when you turn off what you were looking forward to watching because of inappropriate content.

6. *Actively seek out friends who will share the journey with you, even a little.* Your friends don't have to agree with everything you believe (see number 1) to be in solidarity with you in the child-raising journey. Most people these days are suffering from utter collective memory loss. The current generation isn't operating from a position of strength: when they were young, all-night prom parties and middle-school sex-ed demonstrations became the norm. And now they (you?) are parents.

When you share your struggle, you help those around you who would be in solidarity with you but are not quite sure how. When you mention that your children aren't going to see a certain movie, their ears will perk up, and they are the ones who will join you for a different way of life with youth. Even if they join with only some of your plans, a real community of like-minded people can be formed. If nothing else, they will remember your comments about making choices that involve your kids. You want that to happen.

This outspoken attitude can help you reach out to the parents of the children your child interacts with—at least be open to friendship. Don't dismiss people out of hand because they don't *look* like the sort who will be up for the community you have in mind. Share your thoughts honestly (with a cheerful, even humorous, attitude), as the situation allows.

Thanks to your outspoken yet friendly willingness to air your views, you will almost certainly find friends who also won't be doing it (whatever it is that your children think is indispensable), and this serves a purpose: your children will be more likely to forgive your intransigence. At the minimum, they will know you aren't the only crazy parents in the world—a valuable state of affairs.

If everyone is silently deploring the conditions that their kids are exposed to, but no one knows that the others are as well, how can things change? So go outside your comfort zone and express your opinions to your acquaintances. You don't have to be that wild-eyed crazy mom. Just ask them if they've read the headlines, and see what ensues in the way of conversation. Even if they don't seem interested or actively oppose you, don't worry. The important thing is that you tried, and the door might open to getting some people together to discuss the problem, maybe read something informative about it, and make concrete plans for a better way.

My seat-of-the-pants assessment is that if five families made a commitment to these ten points I've outlined here, in a way that leaves room for family freedom of expression (that is, not a cult), you'd see a big difference made in the community. At a minimum, you'd have enough kids for a fun bonfire.

7. *Provide healthy interactions with friends.* It's not enough to refuse to allow your children to go to the pool party on the grounds that the ten-year-olds were uploading videos of themselves dancing in bikinis (true story). The burden is on you to provide a party where the kids innocently play games and enjoy their time together. (It's also on you to be the adult who walks over and says something to the effect that the phone needs to be put away, after verifying that the photos are deleted.)

I'd say that one goal of the first ten years of your family life should be to end up in a living situation where *fun can be had*. In other words, try to plan for hospitality and conviviality. It's hard if you're like me and didn't grow up with anything like that, but just keep trying and keep making mistakes.

Contribute what you can to the community in terms of fun, whole-some entertainment, great music (think of old-timey tunes of some kind that's easy for everyone to join in), and whatever kinds of culture you can dredge up.

8. *Provide peace and quiet.* Most people, children included, don't want to be stimulated all the time. Social media makes the possibility of down time much more difficult. Bullying has always existed, but a child could get away; once he got home, he'd be safe, at least. I remember my father telling me to get off the phone. Part of it was that if anyone wanted to call, the line would be tied up, but part of it was the truth that after a certain amount of time, enough is enough, interaction-wise.

Texting in particular makes it so that a person has no recourse, no refuge, no inner space. Only parents can make the necessary rules to keep the inner life of the child (even older teen) safe.

9. *Trust and show real affection.* Most advice from the world accommodates parental irresponsibility. The peer culture among young people is so strong that even adults don't dare point out to other adults what their duties are. And yet, where does that peer culture come from? Some authority of some kind is establishing and maintaining it. Experts enable peer culture and undermine proper parental authority by urging us to trust children, without offering a plan to build the foundation of trust, which is parental guidance and vigilance, patiently bestowed and prudently lessened.

Be confident. Know that when you don't panic but show firm confidence in your principles, your children will respect you, even if they err. Don't make your children feel as if you are certain they are doing something terrible. Don't create a paranoid atmosphere of distrust, no matter how bad things seem out in the world, and they are bad. Stick with the adage: trust but verify.

Many people equate being strict (or even just having some standards) with lacking affection. What I have learned is that the best way to raise children is to be warm *and* demanding. When you aren't smacking them upside the head (that is a figure of speech), you should be hugging them.

Trust, smacks, hugs.

10. *Pray.* Pray together as a family, and pray on your own. What else do you have a family for, other than to see the children grow up happy and healthy, with blessedly pure eyes with which to behold the Lord? Why else would you go through the trouble, if not to make things better for everyone? What are knees for, anyway?

Trust that God will give you the grace to do what you have to do, even when it seems hopeless—as long as you do your part. No giving up, no giving in, no making your peace with the popular culture.

Especially, live Sunday as a day of rest that bestows the peaceful connection to God's will. Enjoy one another's company! Your family needs this. We all do. Things are bad, but there's hope. God made families to protect their children.

Dating for Teenagers?

I've had conversations with older people about the topic of teenage dating; in their vehement enthusiasm for dating, they are remembering something from a time so long ago — maybe from the forties — when there was plenty of cultural support for virginity before marriage, and the whole context was that the young people were aiming at making a family.

Because of the generation I belong to, which barely emerged from hippie craziness with any sanity at all, I know how very far from that context things went. But somehow, even at this late hour, we continue along with the idea of dating as if somehow our children will manage to reconcile the various meanings this word conveys — in the teeth of our own experience.

To give your children a good chance at being able to respond to God's call when the time comes, you have to get to the heart of things. Start with this thought: dating is not really about being at a particular age. I fear that when we say, "No dating until eighteen [or sixteen or whatever]," we are still operating in that weird mindset that brings you two-piece bathing suits for toddlers and couples' dances for tweens and Disney programs about little prepubescent boys falling in love with taller, curvy girls. In short, though we might reject *those* aberrations, we are still buying into the notion that the mystery of union between the sexes is about feelings only, feelings with no plan, no responsibility, and above all, no risk—feelings period.

Start the necessary paradigm change by discussing with your husband this question: What is the purpose of dating, in the form we would wish it to take? Is it not to discover whether the person is someone you would like to marry? Thus, if a boy or man, of whatever age, is not in a position to get married, should he be dating? If a girl or woman is not in a position—that is, ready emotionally, physically, and spiritually—to get married, should she be dating?

I believe that an eighteen-year-old (or one even younger) is very much capable of falling in love and having deep feelings about another person. We parents forget about the interior life of children, despite having been children ourselves. We think they are impervious, unaware, superficial—when really, they are, if anything, *more* passionate and *more* wholehearted than we are about many things, simply because we are getting worn down and they are young!

Remembering this, we have to be very careful and delicate. An eighteen-year-old certainly *can* be finding his vocation. Our job is to offer prudence and wisdom and freedom. We are showing him that it's not about feelings only—a monumental task in today's environment. What's needed at this stage is work and dedication to become that person who would be the one *for his love, before she appears—or if she is there, before the relationship develops.* It may happen, in the meantime, that he finds out she's not the one, and if so, little harm has been done, since nothing transpired in terms of emotional involvement.

And as to flirtation (innocent little sparks between the sexes), well, it's normal, isn't it? Here we see the true extent of the virtue of modesty, and how it applies to a fellow. A young man should be encouraged to refrain from indulging in too much flirtation or responding to flirtation—not because he's a prude, but because he would like to show respect. The respect is due not only to the girl, but also to the whole concept of the mysterious and beautiful relationship that a man will want to have with his one and only love.

Learning to moderate (for a purpose!) the exuberance and natural attractiveness and attraction is part of maturing. We want our children to love life and be fully human! And all of this comes under the idea of *gaining self-control*. It's not easy, and there's not one thing that solves it all. It's a matter of the person's getting to know himself and God's plan for his life.

If he is not in a position to get married, then is it wise to put himself in the position of having those feelings encouraged and acted upon?

For instance, a girl may be ready at eighteen to start a family in all the ways that I mentioned. In our times (and ever since college became a universal goal and marriage got later and later, or even just dispensed with), we can hardly believe it, but it's true—and many a girl would be rescued from a lot of heartache if she could just get married to a good man already.

In our society, however, it's unlikely that she would be dating a man capable of providing for her, although it's possible even now. (I myself met Mr. Lawler at a young age—he's ten years older than I am.) But an eighteen-year-old fellow—well, there are extremely few in our society who are able to set out providing for a family. There are some rare, very responsible young men who own their own businesses or farms and could do it. Their parents' job would be to make them prove it. Thus, unless he is one of those few, he should not be dating.

What I wish everyone would understand is that keeping your son out of the dating scene is *not* because he isn't capable of being serious about a girl. It's because he is.

If young people were encouraged by their parents to see dating as a means to marriage, not simply as an inevitable expression of their affection, they would accept the idea that it's unwise to begin if the answer to the question "Are you ready to get married?" is no. Look at it this way: It seems unreasonable to say, "You are too young to love a girl, kiss her, and have amazing feelings about your time together." But even a headstrong young man can understand "You are not prepared to support a family."

For a girl, dating before the time for considering marriage at least as a possibility is even more harmful. Girls by nature go straight to imagining their future and become emotionally wrapped up in their dreams. Continually pulling away from one young man after another is too much on the emotions *and* the dreams.

Auntie Leila hastens to add that these young people should be encouraged to make friends, go in groups, see how their friends interact with family members, get to know lots of people, observe and judge their conduct (as dear Jane Austen puts it),[31] and, in general, have fun and think about what makes a good and attractive companion.

In our family, we developed this rule: there is no reason to be alone with a person of the opposite sex if they are not in a position (at least in theory) to pursue marriage with that person—if they don't know the person well enough for that to be a possibility. In other words, you and the other person would have to be good friends already and be mature enough to consider marriage.

This is simple prudence. A fellow can avoid much unpleasantness in the way of unfounded accusations if his father talks seriously to him about not being alone with a girl he barely knows (even if he thinks he knows her). And of course for a girl, the reasons are obvious. Seriously, my friends! Please consider the necessary prudential steps to preventing the conditions that result in pregnancy out of wedlock in the first place.

It isn't so much about "rules" as about helping your kids to take responsibility—but this one rule really helps. Deirdre tells me that she carried this one rule of ours with her to college, and it gave her freedom without her ever thinking much about it. As she put it, "There's really no reason to be alone in private [as opposed to taking a walk or otherwise being in public] with a boy!"[32]

---

[31] I recommend *The Jane Austen Guide to Happily Ever After*, by Elizabeth Kantor. For girls, it is a great discussion starter—*if* they are very familiar with Austen's novels. It's good to be clear on one thing that the book somewhat assumes: that it's a sin against the sixth commandment to engage in premarital sex. But with that as a given, it's an intelligent exploration of how to attain happiness with another person Jane Austen–style. I particularly appreciate the author's explanations of the importance of judgment of character and conduct. Today we are indoctrinated with the idea that it's wrong to do so. The careful corrective offered in the book can help us overcome this dangerous mistake.

[32] I can expound at much more length on this rule. Suffice it to say that there is a big difference in having alone time with someone you know and trust,

Of course, in college, it's even more important, since to college students a dorm room feels like their "home," but it is, in fact, a room with a bed. Keeping the door open whenever she had a male visitor kept her comfortable and prudence satisfied. Shut that door, and these young people are in a danger zone, to be blunt.

Let's protect our children. In the era when dating was carefree, fun, and a great way to get to know someone, it also was shored up with many taboos and standards, and romance wasn't the hyped unrealistic nonsense it is today. I'm afraid we just have to let go of that dating idea, at least for now.

Our children should know that we think it's wonderfully normal for attractions to happen. The nicer and more wholesome the kids, the less surprised we should be! Our job as parents is to keep them on track with their real goals, which are, at this age, to get themselves in a position to be ready to say yes to God's will for their lives. Getting into position requires a lot of hard work and practice with self-control.

When the subject comes up, discuss it in these terms. Merely by commenting on behavior (or *conduct*, as Jane Austen puts it), you'll lead your children, eventually, to mature thinking on the subject. If they become infatuated, it's good to help them see that these are normal and natural feelings, but that it's unjust to pursue them if they can't offer the person what he or she really wants in his or her deepest heart, which is a lifelong commitment.

Playing with those feelings is incredibly unwise. Most kids who date are indeed playing—playacting—and setting themselves up for a sad future of using other people or being used. The purpose of choosing a mate is to have a happy family someday, to which you are bringing a clear conscience and a pure heart.

---

when you are prepared to think about marriage—and even then, you ought not to go in the bedroom! Let's grasp the realism here.

Helping Our Children
Get Married

This book has, I hope, helped you to overcome your own past or the influences arrayed against happy home life; you have found a way to establish a family, against all odds. Now your children are, perhaps, growing old enough that you can see the same dangers you faced looming for them, despite all your devotion and prayers. Auntie Leila, you ask—how can we help them do what they ought to do and not fall prey to the forces that are pulling everyone apart?

For young people today, hookup culture is the undefined norm that replaces finding a lifelong marriage partner with using others for self-gratification in serial relationships with no goal in sight. It can mean meeting up with someone; it can mean having anonymous sex. We need to restore sanity, one family at a time.

Our advice to our older children is fairly simple (keeping in mind, of course, the moral law): just get to know the person in a way that doesn't create unmanageable expectations. Beyond getting a cup of coffee or an ice cream, we suggest inviting the person you think you might be interested in on a walk. Liking walks is normative for a happy life! It has the benefit of costing nothing (unless you get ice cream cones and take them with you). It allows you to talk. It keeps you moving. It's invigorating. You can walk somewhere beautiful or to something interesting. It allows you to talk without worrying excessively about your appearance or how the other person is reacting to you, but it's not a conversational roadblock the way a movie is. If a person looks askance at a walk, that person likely won't be for you.

When trying to make new rules to recover dating, it's important to remember an almost lost truth: women have a deep *desire to be pursued*. Prof. Kerry Cronin of Boston College has created rules for dating, and she makes the argument that this sort of "getting to know you" event is not courtship; it's just coffee. In her model, men and women should be equally free to propose such a date, and whoever does the inviting does the paying. Prof. Cronin hints that as such, the noncommittal coffee date is more like a green light to be pursued, perhaps, in the future.

That is a good point, but like most contemporary handlings of relationships, her plan, as encouraging as it is, fails to address the difference between men and women and indeed, the tricky issue of paying. Why do I call it tricky? In this day and age, who cares? Does it matter? I think it does, because when a girl offers to pay, she implies that she accepts the reigning ideology of equality. Since one purpose of the interaction is ultimately to indicate to the other person what your worldview is, giving this impression is counterproductive: marriage can't be conducted along those lines.

Prof. Cronin points out that our society simply doesn't support a more hierarchical model at the moment, so it's important that if a man is being asked, he doesn't get the wrong idea about expectations going forward. What Cronin doesn't say is that men's failure to understand is in large part because women have collectively, and to their unacknowledged grief, trained them out of any natural instinct to act according to hierarchy rather than equality. Why should the man ask and pay? Because he ought to be the pursuer, and by spending money, would be demonstrating to the woman that he can, and is willing to, support her if they should decide to marry. This is decisive for their future happiness, since marriage isn't a sort of business arrangement, but a sacred way to build a life together *complementarily*.

In *The Dating Project*, Prof. Cronin's movie that shows her methods, the excellent point is brought out that knowing how to ask people questions and have a give-and-take conversation is just good manners in society—not particularly dating related. Perhaps it would help to consider the early phase of getting to know each other more broadly, as a desirable interaction for any two people, not necessarily those who have romantic possibilities.

Mothers with young children are probably the only adults left on the planet who know how to say to each other, "Want to come over for a cup of tea?"—simply because they have the pretext of getting their children together for playing. They are the only ones left who can pull off a new acquaintanceship without awkwardness.

Because we now e-mail and text—but most of all, go on social media to relate to one another in groups—we have lost the art not only of dating but of just getting together with one friend of any description. (Being with *one friend* is a key element to Prof. Cronin's analysis of the lost art of dating.)

In general, let's think about how to model and help our children to be able to say to a friend, "Want to get together for a wee chat?" The lucky mothers who have this privilege might encourage their husbands to stop for a quick beer with a friend after work once in a while. We adults should make time to meet up for an hour of conversation with a friend over a pastry and to make a point of meeting an amenable couple over a drink.

If we have more practice having real conversations, one on one, our children will too, and then when it's a matter of a date, they won't be so disadvantaged.

The role of friendship *in* romance is a neglected one. One person needs *to get to know another*. Romance and physical attraction are important, of course, but nature has a way of keeping her advantage. If we were better at having friends in general and knowing what to do with them even for an hour, we'd be better at the kind of dating that will lead to marriage.

Those who manage our cultural input have duped us into thinking that the goal for men and women is sexual hookup; but the goal is marriage.

Another key element in finding a mate is to resist the fatal urge to discuss "The Relationship" or "What I Want out of a Relationship." Help your children understand that getting together for a simple date has the purpose of allowing the two people to look outward at interesting things, conversationally, so that they get to know each other (which is why taking walks works wonderfully—you can't really look at the person very much when you're walking). You want to know simple facts about the person so that you have context, such as where she is originally from, how many siblings he has, what he studied in school, what she's reading now.

Obviously, it's not good to invest any time with someone who expects to jump into bed! But people can change their shallow ideas simply because it's worth it to them to get to know this new person who has such novel attitudes! Perhaps we need to bring back wearing a crucifix around the neck so that at least the other person has an early distant warning.

Preparation for dating (that is to say, for the process by which one finds a spouse) is primarily *remote*; it starts very early on in life. There is no program capable of bestowing on the young person what he needs to know to find a spouse. We all understand very well that you don't get a lovely ripe tomato from your garden a few days before you want one. We understand the importance of loosening the soil, preparing it with compost, leaving it fallow at the right times, letting even the frost do its work on its structure, carefully planting the seed at the right depth in the spring, and on and on.

The same is true in the family. Prepare the ground as best you can. The fruits are up to God.

The Tranquility of Order
and the Wonder of All Things

The peace of all things lies in the tranquility of order;
and order is the disposition of equal and unequal things
in such a way as to give to each its proper place.

— ST. AUGUSTINE, *CITY OF GOD*, XIX.13

This whole book (including the other two volumes) and the thrust of all I have written in the past decade have been about Order and Wonder and how these two concepts, so paradoxical when juxtaposed, can give our life its proper orientation. In my own way, I have tried to show that there exists a hierarchy in the universe, a hierarchy that is benevolent.

I have observed in myself and in others a dread of routine that causes longing for excitement, but the determination to liven things up is shortly followed by weariness and yearning for less stimulation and more predictability.

What I have called "wonder" is more than excitement, though—perhaps it's C. S. Lewis's *desire*, "an unsatisfied desire which is itself more desirable than any other satisfaction. I call it Joy, which is here a technical term and must be sharply distinguished both from Happiness and Pleasure."[33]

But making wonder or joy the goal of your pursuit is to ensure that you will not find it. Those who insist on living by spontaneity and whose creed is "Live, Laugh, Love"—implying a rejection of predictability or routine—find themselves with a false smile determinedly fixed on their faces; that oxymoron, a sort of routine gaiety or ritualized fun, soon plagues them. "The inherent dialectic of desire itself had in a way already shown me this," said Lewis in *Surprised by Joy*; "for all images and sensations, if idolatrously mistaken for Joy itself, soon honestly confessed themselves inadequate."

The person who wishes to be liberated from this fate turns to routine as a panacea, determined to seek safety from disappointment that follows chasing elusive longing. But how long can he be satisfied with an utterly quotidian life, plodding along and never looking up?

After some time, we may be given the grace to realize the need to stop chasing one or the other of these modes in turn. We need to heal the whiplash that creates an interior soreness and strain we feel right into the muscles of our being, lest we be tempted to give up. Instead, the remedy is to pattern our lives, to embrace the creative tension of living according to an objective order, that we may have peace. For the end or goal of joy—of desire, of wishing to be satisfied, is the peace of possession of the good. Just as the point of thirst is to bring the person to a glorious quenching, so the desire for we-know-not-what is to keep us searching for peaceful hearts.

In the quotation at the beginning of this chapter, St. Augustine speaks of tranquility in the larger sphere of "the city"—of our life together in the community. That tranquility is made up, surely, of the peacefulness of each family's life, for what is the community or state but the joining together of

---

[33] C. S. Lewis, *Surprised by Joy: The Shape of My Early Life* (New York: Houghton Mifflin Harcourt, 1956), 15.

these building blocks or cells, consisting of two people, man and woman, coming together cooperatively to form a unity that organically becomes part of the larger whole. The passage that precedes the one I quoted makes this order clear — peace within the body, body and soul, and man and man. "Domestic peace is the well-ordered concord between those of the family who rule and those who obey. Civil peace is a similar concord among the citizens. The peace of the celestial city is the perfectly ordered and harmonious enjoyment of God, and of one another in God."[34] In God's plan, the small patterns resonate with the larger, not only those of society but of the universe; even the angels are ordered in their hierarchies, as St. Clement teaches.

It's surely worth mentioning that Lewis came to see that "the experience [of joy, or of wonder, as he and we so often long to capture], considered as a state of my own mind, had never had the kind of importance I once gave it. It was valuable only as a pointer to something other and outer." The qualifier "as a state of my own mind" hints at the stunting that occurs when we observe ourselves, trying to capture something, to hold it and really consume it. Instead, the "other and outer" he speaks of is ultimately God, but along the way, along our journey, is the order of tranquility that God Himself offers us.

The pattern, though, must never be allowed to descend to a lifeless routine. In this volume and the ones that follow I have tried to offer the deeper reasons and some of the practical assistance to prevent the fear of doing things well. What I hope you, the reader, have come to see is that order is kept from lifelessness by one thing only, and that is devotion. Woman is devoted to home; man is devoted to woman. By these connections, these energetic, fecund bonds, we can flourish and be part of establishing peace around us that alone can give true wonder and joy.

Only love can animate the liturgy of worship and the smaller patterns that participate in it, found throughout our lives. This love gets its motion from the love that moves the stars, the love of God.

---

[34] St. Augustine, *City of God*, XIX.13.

Appendices

APPENDIX A

A Reading List for Marriage

When you get married, you need to know a few things. You need to know what marriage is, first of all. That's tricky, because, as with most important concepts, one learns by living—in this case, ideally from growing up in a good, happy, fruitful, loving marriage —not any easy experience for many to come by. And then, it would be helpful to have the definition clearly stated, and even the best-intentioned books don't do this.

I was once asked to read the proofs of a book about *Catholic* marriage (the publisher was seeking an endorsement from me), that, to my shock, did not mention that it is a sacrament. Needless to say, I passed on that one. Even a book for non-Catholics needs to point out that marriage is a divinely instituted union between man and woman for a purpose greater than the two of them (see the first two chapters of Genesis) and that what God has so joined, man has the expectation of receiving His assistance to protect.

You need some practical insight on how to become virtuous (hopefully, to *continue* to become virtuous, as virtue is not a project for marriage only). You need to know that people are different in how they express love and in how they feel inside, and that men are different from women, and vice versa. Often we need these books *after* the wedding, not having gotten the memo before. I mean, there is a certain fugue state that those about to be married dwell in, combined of equal parts romance and wedding-planning insanity. Sometimes this state needs to clear up before the practical work and deep thinking can begin.

Some books are about how to manipulate the other person, how to apply lessons learned from management experts, or how to get the most satisfaction from the other person. But marriage is a journey of sacrificial love, so in the end, those books aren't going to help.

You need a book with wisdom, a commodity that is sorely lacking in today's market, including in the marriage-advice category of the publishers' offerings. In particular, seek the wisdom that reflects the reality of marriage as a hierarchical enterprise. Books that treat husband and wife as mere equals who approach life in the same way will not ultimately offer you the assistance you will need.

I am going to give you a short list of wise books that I have found personally helpful and that have stood the test of time. They are good for marriage preparation, but they are also good both for what I like to call "remote" preparation (well before marriage is on the horizon) and for any marriage that could use a little remediation.

To Answer the Question: What Is Marriage?

I had often seen Fulton Sheen's *Three to Get Married* but had never read it. I guess I assumed it was a popularizing kind of book. Now that I've finally read it, I recommend it as excellent and by no means lightweight. *Three to Get Married* is basically the meat of Pius XI's encyclical *Casti Connubii* (On Chaste Marriage) presented in book form, which is to say that it combines theology with natural law and is very deep indeed.

Sheen offers a treatise on what we now call the "theology of the body," or Christian anthropology—so much so that, as I was reading, I began to think that Pope St. John Paul II simply scooped up the important bits of this book and used them to work out his opus by that name. The key ideas to be found in John Paul II's works are already here (because they were already in *Casti Connubii* and, thus, already in the long teachings of the Church, rooted in Scripture). But Sheen, while rigorous, is easier to read.

Even so, if someone finds this book to be more than he expected, it might help to begin with chapter 18, "The Dark Night of the Body," and read to the end, and then go back to the beginning. A wonderful work of mercy for an older couple or two would be to host a reading group with those preparing for their wedding or recently married, to offer them guidance.

Both husband and wife will benefit from reading Pope St. John Paul II's *Mulieris Dignitatem* (On the Dignity and Vocation of Woman), as well as his exhortation *Familiaris Consortio* (The Role of the Christian Family in the Modern World). Marriage is about making a family through the "unity of the two," man and woman. Did you know that the word "matrimony" means "making a mother"?

I have written a guided reading of *Casti Connubii* called *God Has No Grandchildren*. Lives have been changed by reading this encyclical, published in 1930, against the acceptance of birth control by the Anglicans and the increasing acceptance of divorce. Far from being a purely negative teaching, *Casti Connubii* puts forth the vision of the Church for the family in the world, and especially for the vital role the woman plays in it.

On the reasons for not using contraception, read Pope St. Paul VI's *Humanae Vitae* (Of Human Life). When read in the light of *Casti Connubii* (as, of course, it must be, since all Church teaching builds on what has gone before), one finds, contrary to what the world implies, that the Catholic teaching against contraception is not a capricious, arbitrary rule cooked up by bitter old men, but emerges organically from the meaning of marriage itself. Anyone—not only a Catholic—can follow the reasoning and come to the same conclusion. (I hope you appreciate just how many Vatican documents I want you to read!)

Practical Wisdom

Once you know what marriage is, you need some practical wisdom on how to live together. I never really got that much help from any of the books usually recommended, except for these two really stellar ones:

The Temperament God Gave You, by Art and Laraine Bennett: many books make assumptions about how husband and wife will communicate and about what "meeting in the middle" or "meeting each other's needs" might look like. But few take into consideration a basic starting point—namely, each person's temperament. Even a seemingly traditional sort of book such as Father Lawrence Lovasik's *Catholic Family Handbook* assumes a lot about each spouse's temperament, making it not that helpful if there is a significant difference from what he takes for granted.

For instance, what if, far from being henpecked (common enough, I grant you), as Fr. Lovasik posits, the husband is so choleric that he just can't let his wife do anything her own way? What if this situation is exacerbated by her compliant personality? Your usual book about marriage won't treat this possibility at all. But if you are given the tools to figure it out—namely, knowing that a certain kind of reaction goes along with a certain temperament—you can learn to live peaceably while striving to correct faults.

I think that *The Temperament God Gave You* is a good book to read long before you begin to date anyone seriously. Knowing that people are *not* necessarily just like you in their reactions to things helps immeasurably to understand them. The book can help you to know if you are a good match with the person you are interested in, or perhaps why you are finding someone frustrating or opaque. It might also help you understand why you are drawn to a certain personality type. (Is it just easier? But will it be harder in the end?) Not that two particular temperaments can't have a great marriage, but it's good to know.

As I said to my daughter, never in a million years would it have occurred to me that a person might *prefer* to approach a disagreement by retreating for a while to think about it. Before reading this book, I would have assumed that the person was acting with ill will.

My poor husband.

The Five Love Languages, by Gary Chapman, also offers self-understanding, which, in turn, helps the reader to understand what he is looking for from the other person. Where the temperament book is good well before marriage (a high school student could read and discuss it with profit), this one might be good for the marriage preparation phase and definitely for later in the marriage.

People do have different ways of expressing love and affection—giving *and* receiving. Perhaps five languages are not enough to quite cover the myriad ways of expressing love, but the book certainly gives the basic idea. As you read, keep in mind that the point could be made a bit more explicitly that you can't change the "language" a person uses to express love, but you can accept the expression for how it's intended. Sometimes this acceptance is actually the sacrifice God is asking us to make, and sometimes it's the one that goes most against our will.

Most marriage advice and counseling tends to center on verbal communication; this unfairly weighs in favor of the more communicative person in the relationship, which is usually the woman. Men (or the person whose love language is nonverbal, but usually men) are willing to try to do better, but in the end they become frustrated and even despairing, because verbal communication simply isn't how they express their truest feelings.

This book remedies this problem, and believe me, it is a problem. My husband and I read it maybe thirty years into our marriage (at this writing, we've been married for more than forty years). It did two things for us. First, it made it possible for us to simply say what we need in order to feel loved ("Please turn on the light on the porch for me if it gets dark and I'm not home yet"—me; and "Please say encouraging things to me at the end of the day"—him). But it also helped us to accept that the other is "saying" "I love you" in our own way, since that is always going to continue. It's not that the person has to change completely, which is good, because that wouldn't be possible!

We take for granted that we are working on our friendships with our non-spouse friends. Obviously, we don't have to deal with them morning and night and day after day, so in that way, these relationships seem easier and somehow fresher, more doable. Yet we fall into the thinking that the relationship with our spouse is just supposed to be perfect, with no effort from us.

These books have the effect of helping the reader to be more kind. Once we realize that how we react is not how everyone reacts, we can be more flexible. Kindness toward each other—forbearance and understanding—is how we build that community of life and love that is the goal of our existence here on earth.

For a nice vintage read on family life in general, as well as a chapter about very specific issues relating to the marriage act—but put in a respectful and loving way, very much in the context of the personhood of the two (and with no unsavory overtones so often found these days)—I recommend *A Marriage Manual for Catholics*, written by Catholic doctor and married man William Lynch. It's only available used. It's pretty old. But if a couple is having—how shall I say this delicately?—*technical* problems in their married love life, this is the book to go to. Just pay no attention to the author's diet advice, nor to the advice about breastfeeding, which is sadly typical of the time and not helpful.

For better advice on breastfeeding, read Sheila Kippley's *Breastfeeding and Natural Child Spacing*. Marriage is for making a family; having children is the goal of marriage, after all; we need to trust that the whole issue isn't stacked against our peace and well-being—even biologically.

Having a child every year is not the biological *norm* (I'm speaking in general here)—if we shed our modern expectations of how taking care of an infant will go. Kippley explains how, for the vast majority of women, the natural act of nursing a baby will space children. I consider this vital information for every engaged couple, to relieve any anxiety they will be overwhelmed by childbearing if they follow what the Church teaches about contraception.

I want to encourage you to consider one possibility, which is that you might not end up with as many children as you feared—or perhaps even wanted. Children are a gift from God and not to be feared! Sometimes you just need a book about how things will *probably* go, not a book about each and every possibility. Sheila Kippley's book is that book. (I do not necessarily endorse her other work.)

When a friend who is a practicing psychologist asked me for a list of books to recommend to couples, I couldn't help adding to the ones above *The Little Oratory: A Beginner's Guide to Praying in the Home*, written by yours truly and David Clayton, with charming illustrations by Deirdre Folley (yes, our Deirdre). Why? Because when you're getting married, you might not know that you are setting up your own little "community of life and love and prayer"—but you are! You need a *visual* expression of just that, and we help you make it. It's a kind of "little prayer table kit," complete with beautiful icons, easily and inexpensively framed, as well as extensive instructions. With your home altar, you have the organizing principle of prayer in the home, in union with the Church. Praying together brings the Holy Spirit to help us in marriage and in everything.

To help you further with building the domestic Church, I also recommend *Around the Year with the von Trapp Family*, by Maria von Trapp, and *The Year and Our Children*, by Mary Reed Newland.

APPENDIX B

Books to Help Solve
Sleep Problems

Sleep is a human right! If you read my chapters on babies and nursing, you will know that I am a strong advocate for feeding babies when they are hungry and for sleeping with infants in or very near your bed.

Parental lack of sleep with newborns is *completely normal* and will adjust itself after a few weeks if you calmly accept that this time is disruptive, sleep when *you* are able, and don't project the current season way into the future, causing you to panic (imagining you will be pacing the floor with an eight-year-old or nursing your college student at 2:00 a.m.).

Fragile babies depend on their mothers' being totally responsive, and healthy babies thrive on the closeness of their mothers. Sleep-training *infants* using cry-it-out methods (distinct from learning their rhythms, as I explain in the chapters on nursing) is a bad and destructive idea.

There are, however, some older babies who are well nourished and healthy but who do not let their parents sleep—ever! This is a problem of what I call "failure to establish hierarchy in the pack." For the good of the family, everyone needs to sleep, and it's up to you and your husband, the "alpha pair," to fix things. Parents whose children don't have difficulty often underestimate the seriousness and stress of lack of sleep on family life; it sometimes even results in the determination not to have more children! But I get it. No one can survive for years without sleep!

If your seven- to ten-month-old baby is in this category and you have reached the point of desperation, having tried all the methods (including having him sleep with you—but he won't sleep!), here are the books I recommend that you check out of the library:

Healthy Sleep Habits, Healthy Child, by Dr. Marc Weissbluth. Excellent understanding of and sympathy with your situation; good advice about sleep cycles. However, the author's warnings are too dire. Nothing permanently bad will happen if you don't get sleep under control right away. Eventually you will work it out. Take the author's advice on adjusting the child's schedule; leave his predictions.

Solve Your Child's Sleep Problems, by Dr. Richard Ferber. This book will give you the confidence to let your child cry when other methods have failed. You allow your child to cry in his car seat because you are confident that he will survive best that way and you know what is good for him. He cries when the doctor has to put in stitches; you would never refrain from a procedure simply because it was distressing him at the time.

Similarly, bad sleep habits can be overcome (and Ferber insightfully explains what these habits are), but human nature is such that a period of adjustment is necessary for his own good, and a baby only has one way of expressing disapproval, after all! Ferber's method of checking on baby according to a timetable is brilliant; it allows you to take necessary steps while assuring you that all is well.

The proof that this method works is unarguable: baby goes from being aggravatingly clingy, whiny, and demanding to cheerful and contented once it has been implemented, and in most situations it takes twenty minutes to three nights. There is no lasting trauma. My babies even began almost leaping into bed, and they woke up cooing and babbling. I have many e-mails from readers offering testimony to the efficacy of Ferber's method, usually after only a few days' trial—because it's more a matter of parents taking charge than anything else. Everyone is merrier. Sleep is indeed magic.

The St. Gregory Pocket Reading List

Christianity spread throughout the world by means of people living quietly, raising their families, loving their neighbor, and being friends. That's what the St. Gregory Pocket is about. I encourage you to make in-real-life friends for the long term. Don't waste your time with endless Facebook group discussions or forums where you will never meet the people you are talking to. Your children need to grow up thinking "these real people are my people"—people who sacrifice for each other and who also enjoy each other's company with a right goodwill.

The St. Gregory Pocket is not (or is not only) a book club, but we do encourage members to read articles, documents, and books to share with each other in conversation, whether women together, or couples, or men. (You can read about what the Pockets are and how to start one in the chapter "St. Gregory Pockets" in this volume.)

My experience is that when people are reading some of the same things, the opportunity is there for a real exchange of ideas—and it comes in handy, too, when the conversation needs a little direction. Using the *Like Mother, Like Daughter* (LMLD) blog or this book as a touch point will ensure that you will have something in common with the people who join—more even than that you all baby-wear or use cloth diapers (to name two reasons groups of women with young children often congregate).

Shorter readings work well for gatherings of friends. Committing to a novel or polemical book can seem formal and even overwhelming, but very often people find that discussing an article is what they are going to do anyway, and the conversation is greatly facilitated if the reading is not left up to chance.

If you find that your friends are too busy to read a book, certain of my LMLD posts or chapters from this book, short articles, and documents of the Church work perfectly. That said, there are some books that are a joy to have read together and have in common; these days when we find our own education has let us down, we can do something about it on our own, together! You can take a long time if you want—no rush! And if you are homeschooling older children, you can take the opportunity to read some of their material with your friends; this will help when it comes time to discuss their content with your children.

I have put together a reading list, a sort of Summa Domestica hive-mind (or collective memory, if you will) to dip into if you need suggestions for readings that specifically relate to moral and family life and general intellectual stimulation.

These are not in order of importance, obviously! Maybe more in order of what you could suggest as you get started, and then as you go along and have known each other better.

Certain Posts on Like Mother, Like Daughter

The blog has a menu bar that lists the most important posts gathered for easy reference. I know that could be better; even better would be a book, and so voila! I wrote this book (and its two companion volumes). Some mothers' groups have printed out the menu posts and just hashed them over, for instance, to see how they would implement them in their families, for mutual encouragement; some have taken the laundry and cleaning methods and done the same thing.

Essays

The {bits & pieces} feature on the blog always has links to great articles! So you can browse those most profitably—they constitute a vast appendix to this appendix. Some articles I would suggest especially (but I chose them mostly at random from my archive of articles):

"Why Young Readers Need Real Books," by Maura Roan McKeegan (*Crisis Magazine*, February 6, 2018)

"Will Rascals Defend Our Civilization ... and What Books Will They Read?" by William Fahey (*Crisis Magazine*, February 24, 2012)

"Morning Time and How It Can Change Your Homeschool," by Pam Barnhill (published on her site, pambarnhill.com)

"The 3 Characteristics of an Educated Man," by Brett and Kate McKay (published on The Art of Manliness site, artofmanliness. com, October 30, 2011)

Here are a few examples of the sorts of essays that don't take too long to read but would provide a good basis for lively conversation at a couples' get-together:

"On a Small Point of Doctrine," by James Schall, S.J. (*Homiletic and Pastoral Review*, April 15, 2015)

"A Little Mother Prevents Big Brother," by Stella Morabito (*Federalist*, May 5, 2016)

"Manhood Is Not Natural," by Glenn Stanton (*Public Discourse*, December 17, 2017)

Documents of the Church

Why do I recommend church documents? People are always making things up about what Catholicism (and Christianity in general) holds as true. Why not do some studying and find out what is really taught?

Casti Connubii (On Chaste Marriage), by Pope Pius XI. Lives have been changed by reading this long encyclical. I have a reading help for it: my book *God Has No Grandchildren: A Guided Reading to Pius XI's Encyclical* Casti Connubii, *On Chaste Marriage* (2nd edition) is available from Arouca Press on Amazon.

Divini Illius Magistri (On Christian Education), by Pope Pius XI. Read especially for Pius XI's explanation of how the "three necessary societies" of Church, state, and family work together, and why boys and girls should be educated separately in schools.

Humanae Vitae (On Human Life), by Pope St. Paul VI. This is best read after *Casti Connubii*.

Mulieris Dignitatem (The Dignity and Vocation of Women), by Pope St. John Paul II

Books for the Pocket

A truly eclectic collection of books; well, they are united by my conviction that excellent conversation will certainly ensue if any one of them is chosen.

The Restoration of Christian Culture, by John Senior

The Abolition of Man, by C. S. Lewis. This can be a difficult read, short as it is. I recommend reading the novel *That Hideous Strength* along with it. You could always start with *The Screwtape Letters* (and that would make "Ten Ways to Destroy the Imagination of Your Child," by Anthony Esolen, easier to discuss if people aren't familiar with the satirical genre).

Planet Narnia, by Michael Ward, if everyone has read Narnia and Lewis's space trilogy, of course.

Any Jane Austen novel! (*Persuasion* has the virtue of being short.) And then, when you've read and enjoyed them all, *The Jane Austen Guide to Happily Ever After*, by Elizabeth Kantor. (The footnotes of this book are a delight.)

Return to Modesty, by Wendy Shalit. If you want a book to help you and your friends throw off the shackles of feminism and find a different vision of how men and women can interact with social virtue, I highly recommend this book. I have a guided reading of it on the *LMLD* blog.

The Hiding Place, by Corrie ten Boom. An incredibly moving story, *The Hiding Place* contains many bits of parenting wisdom as Corrie recounts her wise father's actions and words. In our quest to raise our children to be saints and if necessary, heroes, the book is a resource, as well as an important historical record.

Peace Like a River, by Leif Enger. Pay attention to the names. This book is full of biblical imagery and beautifully recapitulates salvation history as a classic American tale.

Vipers' Tangle, by François Mauriac. If you happen to have a group that can handle an unreliable narrator in an epistolary novel, this is the one for you.

The Temperament God Gave You, by Art and Laraine Bennett. I've written about how I recommend this book highly in the reading list for marriage, above, but I recommend it here because Deirdre says this was the most enjoyable read for her St. Greg's Pocket. It really got everyone talking about themselves and their families—a great ice breaker!—and it's really extremely helpful to understand everyone better.

A well received book for spiritual reading in a group is *A Mind at Peace*, by Christopher Blum and Joshua Hochschild. This book is about the four cardinal virtues in practical life and combines good scholarship with an approachable format, including study questions that facilitate discussion and meditation.

Discrimination and Disparities, by Thomas Sowell. This brilliant economist (and all-around thinker) explains the intricacies of race in America; required reading in our era of the ascendance of Critical Race Theory.

APPENDIX D

How I Cure a Urinary Tract Infection

I include this information about urinary tract infections because it has proven to be an important resource for many, collecting into one place remedies that really work. Cystitis is similar to mastitis: a malady that is debilitating if it can't be controlled; it's largely preventable and treatable without antibiotics, but we've lost the memory of how to go about curing it. My own experience confirms that knowing how to ward off this infection can make the difference in being able to cope as a woman.

Some women are prone to urinary tract infections, or cystitis. The pain is overwhelming, and then there is an emergency room or urgent care visit, because the symptoms somehow always become acute at night, usually going into a long weekend, when the doctor is far away.

Then, when you finally have antibiotics in your hot little hand, it's quite possible that they make you feel sick as well, and you have to recover from *them*.

I have come across a way to treat a UTI without antibiotics. I will tell you exactly how, and then I will give you the reasons you might be having a recurring problem.

If you already know the details of this sickness, you can skip to the list of treatment elements, toward the end of this chapter. I wanted to put everything in one place for the sake of the collective memory (and really for my own reference as well), so this information is quite detailed.

But first I want to say that if you have pain in your side or back, which is where your kidneys are, high fever and chills, vomiting, or nausea, or both, you do need to go to the doctor. If the UTI goes back into your kidneys you may end up with damage and a long hospital visit, so do pay attention to those symptoms.

Also, of course, I'm not a doctor—or a nurse or anything at all!

But I have had a lot of these infections, and I got sick and tired—and scared!—of taking so many antibiotics. My experience is that a UTI makes me feel wretched and causes a lot of pain; however, I don't get a fever (or just a low-grade one). You might get a higher fever, because everyone is different, but if you have the other symptoms of a kidney infection, you need to see a doctor.

Burning, frequent urination, passing only small amounts of urine despite the urge to urinate, blood in the urine, cloudy urine, a certain smell, pain in the pelvis—these are the symptoms of a UTI. It's debilitating and makes you panic.

The antibiotic will usually take care of the bacteria, true—if it is an infection, that is. These symptoms could also be inflammation and irritation that may or may not develop into a UTI, and so all the more reason to be wary—because of course, we all should be taking fewer antibiotics!

So if given the choice between taking antibiotics and not taking them, with the same outcome, of course we prefer not to take them. (I have also noticed that sometimes a rather weak antibiotic is prescribed, which lends credence to my theory and experience that a UTI can be cured without an antibiotic.)

But even if you *want* meds, it's not so easy, is it? You know the drill; you drive yourself to the office or ER, and the visit takes hours, all while you feel as if the fires of Hades are in your nether parts.

You get the dip test, it comes back positive, they send the culture out for further tests to match with the kind of bacteria you have (more than 90 percent sure it's E. coli however), and meanwhile you go on the antibiotic that may or may not be the right one.

I'm allergic to penicillin so that whole category is out. That means they give me Cipro, which has disturbing side effects. Plus, UTIs end up scarring the tissue in your urethra, so you are only more prone to them as time goes by, increasing your dependency on antibiotics. This is all so unfair.

Now that I am part of a cost-sharing plan instead of having insurance, I have a further incentive beyond not wasting time and suffering agony, sitting around waiting to be treated: I also don't want the people in my sharing plan to pay for those tests and that visit when I already know what is wrong with me. (Not that you aren't paying, indirectly, when you have insurance!)

Maybe if they just prescribed the only antibiotic I can take anyway over the phone, I wouldn't have been so motivated, but those days are gone when the doctor would just help you without the insurance rigamarole. But then, so many courses of antibiotics—it's not good. So I needed another way!

Try this treatment (with the caveats mentioned above!). It has worked for me when I've been *in extremis* with awful pain and bloody urine.

Suki told me that there is a sugar, D-Mannose, that has a molecular structure that bonds with E. coli, the bacteria most responsible for UTIs. A helpful midwife told me about marshmallow root, which provides mucilage and soothes smooth muscle, including in the urinary tract.

You need to address the pain. Ibuprofen (Advil) alone for the pain might be enough; if not, take Phenazopyridine (AZO), which is also available over the counter. It turns your urine bright orange (and don't touch your contact lenses without washing your hands!) but it takes away the pain. And that is the key!

Once you feel that the pain will be taken care of, you can do what needs to be done, which is to force liquids so that you can urinate copiously and wash away the bacteria that have bonded with the D-Mannose.

UTI Natural Treatment Protocol

Take the pain killers according to the dosages (this is not the natural part but thank goodness for ibuprofen and AZO).

D-Mannose. This is a sugar whose molecular shape has been clinically proven to bond with the most common bacteria (E. coli) that cause the infection, resulting in improvement of a UTI infection.[35]

You don't need it in pill or capsule form; it's sweet but otherwise tasteless. Just buy it as a powder and dissolve a teaspoon at a time in a small amount of warm water. It works best if you give it a chance to rest in your bladder before you begin forcing fluids. As soon as you realize you have a UTI, take a dose of D-Mannose, wait for about twenty minutes, then begin hydration. (Subsequent doses can be taken while hydrating, without waiting the twenty minutes, although if it works out that you are less hydrated when you take it, the dose will be more effective, as the bacteria bonds with it and then washes out in the urine. But of course, hydration is essential for treating a UTI, so don't worry about this.)

Take one teaspoon about three times a day. You are aiming for three grams a day, so go by the amount per dosage listed on the container and spread it out over the day. It might have the effect of loosening your bowels; if so, cut back. I have not found this to be a problem, myself.

Hydration. Besides water, try dried hibiscus flower tea. You can drink it cold, warm, or hot, and it's delicious. It is related to marshmallow root and so may have the same effect on the mucus membranes; it's also very healthy with plenty of vitamin C and antioxidants. Buying it in bulk is much cheaper than buying it as tea bags, and it usually comes as relatively large dried flowers, easy to brew (it's called Kerkaday at Middle Eastern markets and Jamaica at Hispanic markets).

An experienced OB/GYN recommends taking a large container of water and a cup into a warm bath. His thinking: you are afraid to pee because it hurts so much; the bath relaxes you, you can drink from your container (a pitcher with two quarts of water), and you can pee in the bath (the urine will be so diluted that it won't matter). A heating pad

---

[35] L. Domenici et al., "D-Mannose: A Promising Support for Acute Urinary Tract Infections in Women: A Pilot Study," *European Review for Medical and Pharmacological Sciences* 20, no. 13 (July 2016): 2920–2925, posted on PubMed, https://pubmed.ncbi.nlm.nih.gov/27424995/.

across the pelvis is also very soothing (not in the bath, of course! But, for instance, in bed . . .).

> IMPORTANT NOTE: Don't force fluids beyond your capacity to take them in. Just focus on drinking enough to allow your bladder to fill and empty quickly. It is possible to overdo this step. You don't want to take in so much that you dilute your electrolytes and feel dizzy or faint, nor do you want to induce vomiting. Take in enough to increase your urination, but not so much that you cause other problems. Common sense, my friends!

Marshmallow root. This comes in capsules unless you grow your own or find it in bulk somewhere to make into tea. You need to take two capsules four times a day. That's a lot of swallowing, I know. Keep at it. The tea is very nice and can count as your hydration. Marshmallow root and hibiscus both add to your interior mucus, which can help if the trouble is arising from tiny kidney stones or irritation in the urethra from something you eat.

The following suggestions are listed in descending order of helpfulness:

- *Vitamin B6.* Helps with urination. You can take a complete vitamin B capsule. According to the Mayo Clinic, the recommended daily amount of vitamin B6 for adults fifty and younger is 1.3 milligrams. After age fifty, the recommended daily amount is 1.5 milligrams for women.
- *Mullein.* I have dried mullein gathered from my yard. This useful plant helps with many infections, but it has many spiky fibers that you will need to strain out through a cloth for the purposes of a UTI, so that you don't irritate your bladder and urethra. Pour 2 cups of water over 3 tablespoons of dried mullein leaves or flowers. Steep for ten minutes before drinking; you can spread your consumption out over the day.
- *Raw honey.* Real raw unfiltered honey has antibiotic properties. Take a teaspoon a couple of times a day; sweeten your hibiscus, marshmallow-root, and/or mullein tea with it.

- *Propolis.* A study[36] shows that propolis (a substance made by bees and available in capsule form, although we collect our own from our hives—if you keep bees it's not difficult at all) can help prevent the adhesion of E. coli in the urinary tract.

I recommend having all these things on hand in your cupboard and traveling with them as well (at least the AZO, D-Mannose, and marshmallow root), because it does take a bit of effort to round them up, made only harder by an unfamiliar location. Make yourself a UTI kit and keep it handy.

Another caution: Don't take too many capsules at once! It can be too hard on your stomach. Spread them out. If you start to feel as if it's too much, just rest. The main thing is to overcome the pain and hydrate (although I've been so anxious to drink liquids that I've vomited from the sheer volume! It's hard not to overcompensate when you are feeling bad).

Of course, talk to your doctor if things don't feel right.

My approach is that this natural protocol is worth a try. It's a lot cheaper than going to the doctor's office or the ER and you can always go later (by which I mean in the morning, when the doctor's office is open) if you need to.

Ongoing Care to Avoid UTIs

You can take D-Mannose on a regular basis, maybe just a teaspoon a day. Mix it into your tea or coffee, or take it with warm water. It works better if it can sit in your bladder, so take it at a time that you are not as well hydrated—say, first thing in the morning with your first cup of tea. Likewise, marshmallow root and hibiscus can keep your urethra calmed if irritants are provoking an infection. Some people take propolis regularly as well. (There is some evidence that taking marshmallow root along with hibiscus

---

[36] Jean-Philippe Lavigne, Xavier Vitrac, Louis Bernard, Franck Bruyère, and Albert Sotto, "Propolis Can Potentialise the Anti-Adhesion Activity of Proanthocyanidins on Uropathogenic Escherichia Coli in the Prevention of Recurrent Urinary Tract Infections," National Institutes of Health, November 29, 2011, https://pubmed.ncbi.nlm.nih.gov/22126300/.

can cause an allergic reaction in some people. It has never bothered me, but be cautious by starting out with one or the other.)

Be better about staying hydrated. Have a set amount that you will drink all day, or certain times that you stop and have some water, iced tea, or kombucha. Don't let yourself feel parched; if you do feel parched, get a big drink *right away.*

The first urine of the day should be a light yellow—you should barely see it. If it's dark, you are not drinking enough.

Urinate before and after intercourse and *make sure you're hydrated.*

Wipe front to back when you go to the bathroom. Don't wear undies that are made out of anything other than cotton in the crotch.

Don't use those menstruation cups that fit inside your vagina if you are prone to UTIs. The pressure of the rim of the cup presses against your urethra and can cause a backup of the bacteria that cause UTIs.

By the way, little girls can get UTIs too. I have a friend whose ten-year-old daughter was not doing well for days, acting listless and tired. She realized that the girl had a very low-grade temperature when she finally thought to take it at different times of the day. She called the doctor and the UTI was finally diagnosed. Just something to have in the back of your mind. Children need to be reminded to drink at regular intervals too!

I also want to say that the one thing you usually hear—*drink cranberry juice*—is not very effective or the best thing to do. It's not effective because the active ingredient that helps you (the D-Mannose present in the juice) is too diluted. It's not the best because it's so acidic that it will inflame your urethra and bladder more, causing more difficulty.

INDEX

thrush, 166–167
toddlers. *See also* two-year-olds
    babying, 261–262
    control issues, 243
    grocery shopping with, 192
    as helpers, 193
    at mealtime, 298–299, 301–302
    napping, 385
    nursing, 168–170
    outings with, 192–193
    physical activity needs of, 265
    spanking, 235
toilet-training, 271–272
tongue-tie issues, 162
traditions
    abandonment of, 11–13, 31
    enjoyment of, 11–13
    New Year's Eve, 410, 412–415
trash treasures, 62, 64
trust, 197
two-year-olds. *See also* toddlers
    crankiness of, 259–262
    help from, 307
    laundry and, 235
    patience and, 351
    picky eaters, 320

unity of family life
    accepting children, 106–114
    dining together, 105–106
    friendship, 114–119
    keeping Sunday, 103–105
    protecting, 102–119
    siblings and, 395
Universalis (app), 94
urinary tract infections (UTIs),
    495–502
    antibiotics and, 495, 496, 497
    care to avoid, 500–501

children and, 501
collective memory and, 495–496
cranberry juice and, 501
natural treatment protocol, 497–500
symptoms of, 496

Vipers' Tangle (Mauriac), 494
virtues. *See also* hope; patience;
    self-control
    Aristotle on, 234, 236
    cardinal virtues, 50, 90, 94,
        197, 238, 494
    fortitude, 197, 239
    justice, 197, 225, 236, 239
    practical insight on, 481–482
    prudence, 50–51, 197, 238–239
    temperance, 197, 239
vitamin B6, 499
Vogue (periodical), 371
vomiting, 158–159n, 213–214, 299
von Trapp, Maria, 487

Ward, Michael, 493
weaning, 169, 199–204. *See also*
    feedings, solid foods
weight gain
    anxiety over pregnancy, 135
    body image and, 176
    clothing and, 179, 180
    older children, 371
Weissbluth, Marc, 489
"What's Wrong with the World"
    (Chesterton), 68
whining
    cure for, 384–387
    siblings and, 391–392

Sophia Institute

Sophia Institute is a nonprofit institution that seeks to nurture the spiritual, moral, and cultural life of souls and to spread the gospel of Christ in conformity with the authentic teachings of the Roman Catholic Church.

Sophia Institute Press fulfills this mission by offering translations, reprints, and new publications that afford readers a rich source of the enduring wisdom of mankind.

Sophia Institute also operates the popular online resource CatholicExchange.com. *Catholic Exchange* provides world news from a Catholic perspective as well as daily devotionals and articles that will help readers to grow in holiness and live a life consistent with the teachings of the Church.

In 2013, Sophia Institute launched Sophia Institute for Teachers to renew and rebuild Catholic culture through service to Catholic education. With the goal of nurturing the spiritual, moral, and cultural life of souls, and an abiding respect for the role and work of teachers, we strive to provide materials and programs that are at once enlightening to the mind and ennobling to the heart; faithful and complete, as well as useful and practical.

Sophia Institute gratefully recognizes the Solidarity Association for preserving and encouraging the growth of our apostolate over the course of many years. Without their generous and timely support, this book would not be in your hands.

www.SophiaInstitute.com
www.CatholicExchange.com
www.SophiaInstituteforTeachers.org

Sophia Institute Press® is a registered trademark of Sophia Institute.
Sophia Institute is a tax-exempt institution as defined by the
Internal Revenue Code, Section 501(c)(3). Tax ID 22-2548708.

THE SUMMA DOMESTICA

THE
SUMMA
DOMESTICA

Order and Wonder in Family Life

❧ VOL. 3 ❧

Housekeeping

LEILA M. LAWLER

Illustrations by Deirdre M. Folley

SOPHIA INSTITUTE PRESS
Manchester, New Hampshire

Sophia Institute Press
Box 5284, Manchester, NH 03108
1-800-888-9344

www.SophiaInstitute.com

Sophia Institute Press® is a registered trademark of Sophia Institute.

paperback ISBN 978-1-64413-398-9

ebook ISBN 978-1-64413-399-6

Library of Congress Control Number: 2021940523

First printing

CONTENTS

THE SUMMA DOMESTICA

Order and Wonder in Homemaking

To an open house in the evening
Home shall men come,
To an older place than Eden
And a taller town than Rome.
To the end of the way of the wandering star,
To the things that cannot be and that are,
To the place where God was homeless
And all men are at home.

G. K. CHESTERTON, "THE HOUSE OF CHRISTMAS"

---

rder means first things first. For the family, first things are the journey on earth toward heaven in the company of those we love; first things are also mundane realities such as making sure the kids are fed on a regular basis and have something to wear, while keeping clutter from swallowing us with nary a trace.

I myself have gone on a journey of discovery about order and wonder in the home, and it has led me to the importance of trying to do one's best with what one has. When our children were very little, on the other side of the wall in the side-by-side duplex house we lived in was a lovely couple who had never had children. They were old enough to be my parents, and they were friendly. Bert would come over on some neighborly pretext, and before I knew it, he would be neatening up all the reading material on my coffee table, which was a lot—magazines, mail, books—everything just thrown on there, as was my habit. He would make tidy stacks of all my stuff, even putting toys in the baskets; only then would he sit down and chat with whoever was around. He loved the children.

I noticed something, even as I interiorly demurred at what I saw as the uselessness of his effort: tidying the piles made my living room look instantly better. I started tidying them myself (rather than waiting for my odd middle-aged gentleman neighbor to do it for me, you ask? Yes, I reply, humbly). It took someone literally meddling in my affairs (as opposed to telling me to do it or ignoring it until I figured it out) for me finally to assimilate that such a detail made a difference.

Much of what I write here is taken up with so many seemingly mundane details of *order*, such as menu planning, laundry organization, cleaning methods, and even frugality tips, that the reader might be forgiven for not seeing the connection with educating children, which is the underlying motivation of these volumes, after all. But let's think: if you sincerely want to educate your children, but if, on any given actual day, you don't know what is for supper by suppertime, how will you have the peace of mind to help your children explore the world with delight? If anyone asks me how to go about homeschooling, I always want to answer, "Are you at peace with your duties? Have you fed your children recently? Washed their faces? Gotten up on time? Read a book of your own, having made time for such a pursuit?"

There are indeed many amazing facts for children to learn. But how can they learn them if you, the person they rely on for an environment in which to learn, are frazzled by the exigencies of survival?

Without a peaceful, orderly home, we have short tempers, crankiness, and most importantly for the strict understanding of education (even when the children attend conventional school) no mental space for oversight of what is being learned and what needs to be learned. Many a parent laments that his child is falling through the cracks and doesn't see that the disorderliness at home is the cause—or at least isn't aware of the necessary (if, granted, insufficient) condition for a flourishing life.

As you read, keep in mind that I wrote almost all of this one bit at a time, to help the woman who feels incompetent gradually to find her way to keeping her own home the way that suits her and gives her a sense of accomplishment, of mastery, and of creativity. I have tried to keep that incremental approach intact while also delivering a complete volume. I hope that you will find real encouragement in these pages, even where topics seem to overlap; my aim is to help you discover in a gradual and peaceful way, the wonder of the hidden life of *home* in the satisfaction of living its order.

PART 1

On Making a Home

Much of my writing has been to encourage people who are not naturally tidy, clean, or prone to decorating to find satisfaction in creating order. If someone who has trouble with being orderly resolves to improve, that person might start with the particulars of cleaning, organization and so on—and might find the task overwhelming. In a development that may strike some as paradoxical, making things beautiful (or, as I like to say, pretty—it seems less stressful) can be the motivation to find that order and the means by which it can be done without feeling suffocated by the sheer amount of work involved and the paralysis of not knowing where to start.

Sometimes the incentive to do necessary work—even drudgery—comes from a creative vision, and then the slog, the long march through the swamps of housewifery, becomes a joy—or at least not so bad as we feared.

Xenophon, ancient philosopher and chronicler of history, wrote of the beauty of order in his book *The Economist*, "After all, my wife, there is nothing in human life so serviceable, naught so beautiful as order." His narrator, Ischomachus, recounts the pleasing arrangement of things on a merchant ship:

> There is no time left, you know,... when God makes a tempest in the great deep, to set about searching for what you want, or to be giving out anything which is not snug and shipshape in its place. God threatens and chastises sluggards. If only He destroy not innocent with guilty, a man may be content; or if He turn and save all hands aboard that render right good service, thanks be to Heaven.[1]

---

[1] Xenophon, *The Economist*, trans. H.G. Dakyns, chap. 8. I am indebted to John Cuddeback for introducing me to this ancient author's domestic musings.

He turns from the ship to the home, where he extols the same order, not only for the sake of being ready for danger, but for something higher:

> let me harp upon the string of beauty—image a fair scene: the boots and shoes and sandals, and so forth, all laid in order row upon row; the cloaks, the mantles, and the rest of the apparel stowed in their own places; the coverlets and bedding; the copper cauldrons; and all the articles for table use! Nay, though it well may raise a smile of ridicule (not on the lips of a grave man perhaps, but of some face-tious witling) to hear me say it, a beauty like the cadence of sweet music dwells even in pots and pans set out in neat array: and so, in general, fair things ever show more fair when orderly bestowed.[2]

I think if we can bring some of this "sweet music" into our lives, some harmony and order, we will find the same sort of pleasure and enjoyment—in the *home*.

[2]   Ibid.

Competence versus Perfectionism

Whoever is diligent will soon be cheerful.

— GEORGE MACDONALD, *THE PRINCESS AND CURDIE*

There is simply no way that you don't have *more* ability than I to make a home, with all that *making a home* entails. I fail every day, at that and at many other things. I started writing about how to do things because I suspected that the perfect images we see online are a bit defeating. When I began, I had the vision that maybe it would help to see someone *just doing her best*, with a little competence.

I've always posted photos on my blog, with the aim of drawing people into the text. Sometimes it has happened that the photos did the opposite: they functioned to make readers think that I was far, far more competent than they. This is partly because the pictures are taken from a certain point of view, so that you don't see what I don't want you to see (though

Heaven knows, I thought the pictures were humble enough). Partly it's due to the fact that the only child I had as I began the blog was the one who wondered why on earth I don't sweep the hearth after putting logs in the fire—and then did it for me.

It wasn't always thus, as you can imagine. It was just like it is at your house if you are a little conflicted, easily distracted by books, and prone to flights of fancy regarding what your true destiny might be. Only, worse, because I'm not actually driven by any obsession to cleanliness—just to a sort of good-enough order.

However, in the interest of slaying vanity disguised as false modesty, I will say that I seemed to have shown that I am able to get readers of the blog to tackle some of their problems. I found that I just took a guess at what those things were—probably based on what I myself was reading on the Internet at the time—and left it to them to take what I said in that spirit of random projection. I was always amazed when someone would comment that I had addressed *just* their issue at the time.

Above all, my hope was that they came away from the posts knowing that the stuff *they* need to deal with is their very *own*. That is, I always tried to keep from making my problems the readers' problems; my aim has always been to facilitate a good look at oneself, whatever the circumstances might be and however little I could imagine them. Sort of an operating principle, if you will, to be applied as necessary to specific cases.

Speaking of what ultimately is about our relationship with God—this tricky ability to figure out what our very own struggle is, and not continually make other people's our own—a while ago I read a blog post, the author of which was embarking on the project of finding out what God's will for her could be.

She thought that finding God's will for her was going to be a vast, immense project. As I remember, she was allotting a year, maybe more, to get the job done. She even left home in order to devote herself to the search, as if God is in a certain place (but that place is never where we are, when we approach the search this way).

Do you sometimes feel as if you have no idea what God's will for you is? That you would need to take time off and go away to focus on that one problem in order to make head or tails of it?

What would you think if I told you that you could find out *right now* what His will is? That it's a "problem" of a day or an hour, not years? His will for you, specifically? (And I'm not going to trick you by saying that God's will for you turns out to be "love everyone," or "work for world peace," or even "lock and load"!)

It's not really a secret, and it's so simple that it seems as if it couldn't possibly be true. It's just this: trying to do all what you must do, *today*, with a loving heart—not everything you could possibly do but what you *must* do.

Knowing what those things might be couldn't be simpler, and it counts as the most meaningful prayer and also the *remedy* for the distraction of *other people's priorities*. In God's presence, think of *your* obligations; most importantly, the people to whom you are obligated.

You have obligations to God, and again, they are quite simple. He doesn't ask for much: worship Him on Sundays, give thanks, ask Him for your needs and desires, keep His commandments.

You have obligations to your husband. He has obligations to you too, and the best way to get him to live up to them is to live up to yours; don't fall into the trap of thinking he has to go first.

You have obligations to your children—it's all you! They owe you nothing until they can learn the Fourth Commandment,[3] and even then it's a work in progress.

You have obligations to a boss, if you have one. The newsletter for the committee if you said you'd do it. A class if you're teaching one.

And you have obligations to yourself: to take a shower, get some rest, eat a proper meal, and stop running around like a crazy person.

You could sit down right now and make a list of these things. If it's just what you *have* to do, *today*, it won't take long, especially if you take into account your limitations: illness, nursing a baby, tiredness, importunate toddlers, someone unpleasant you must deal with . . .

There's a word for all these things, one that isn't often used these days, and it's "duty"—the thing you should be doing today, the *one* thing, for the ones God has given you to serve.

---

[3] Honor your father and your mother.

Duty. An elusive, if not repellent, word. I mean, we feel repelled when we haven't been doing it, our duty. It hides itself behind strange ideas that come from nowhere and everywhere, thoughts such as looking for God's will somewhere other than *here*.

But I've noticed a paradox, perhaps embedded in the Gospel injunction that we must die to live and that the stone that was rejected becomes the cornerstone: that when you joyfully and wholeheartedly do *the things you have to do* as coming directly from the hand of God, then other unforeseen other things open up, and you discover the big picture, the adventure, the outrageously perfect plan God has for you—if adventure is what you wanted. If not, you discover the marvelous rest God has for you!

In other words, you find your heart's desire—so don't be afraid!

Therefore, while you are waiting for the big reveal from on high and thinking, "If only, if only!" (the number-one sentence starter for losing your bearings: If only I lived somewhere else! If only I were married to someone else! If only my children were like those children! If only I could do things easily like that person!), and wondering *what* in Heaven's name God's will for you could be, and whether you should go reform the slums or climb a Peruvian mountain or rescue flood victims—and maybe those are things you should do, for all I know, it's not up to me—just make a little list, a teensy list of things that you should do *today where you are*: get supper ready, make sure everyone has something clean to wear tomorrow, make the bed, give the baby a bath, call the doctor to make an appointment, wash the dishes.

Don't be like Dickens's Mrs. Jellyby in Bleak House, whose eyes "could see nothing nearer than Africa!" "It must be very good of Mrs Jellyby to take such pains about a scheme for the benefit of natives—and yet—Peepy and the housekeeping!" Maybe it was just that she didn't *know how* to take care of anything nearer. Maybe she wasn't *competent*. I happen to think that trying to be competent helps you have a loving heart for God's will!

I think that you love what you do *when you know how to do it!* Whether it's something the world sees as important *or* something it sees as drudgery, what's stopping you from tackling the stuff you have to do is not really knowing how to do it, how to get started, how to make it a habit.

Not only cleaning a bedroom but doing a good job of it, because you just know how. And clean it you must.

Getting a good supper together, on time, frugally; there's a satisfaction in that, not pride in a bad sense. I think it's the same good feeling you would have for anyone who did that, as when you say you are proud of your child for a good job. You are allowed to be proud of yourself in that same way, you know.

Love your neighbor as yourself means sometimes taking pleasure in a job well done just as if someone else did it, and this very pleasure glorifies God when it's offered to Him. I think there's some confusion on this very point.

On the one hand, you could demand a perfectionism in the daily round that would get in the way of more important things. Losing peace over a messy room just isn't worth it. And it is pride to think that our worth is bound up in how other people view us. Perfectionism often has its roots in a sense of inferiority, as if we lose our standing with others if we show a crack or flaw.

But that's not realistic. There are valid things that interfere. I remember times I just had to go shopping because the need for underwear had become acute! That meant the cleaning was put off. Or if someone dropped by, the priority at that moment was serving a hospitable meal, not whisking away toys. (Someone who doesn't have a lot of kids around can hardly imagine these problems, but there's a critical mass of humanity that makes the smallest errand or chore turn into a bog of quicksand.) At those moments, we have to console ourselves with the knowledge that tomorrow is another day to make another list and try again.

On the other hand, there's a scorn for doing things competently, as if there's something almost shameful in knowing how to keep things clean or teaching a child to read—as if real, intelligent, loving moms shouldn't care about home and children and husband! (Unless they can be shown to be dabbling in a high-priced way—"I used my *fabulous* designer squeegee to get this window *fabulously* clean—now, off to the resort with the *hoi poloi!*") But a daily commitment, usually without benefit of any kind of designer anything, is not going to be appreciated by many.

Maybe the confusion is not seeing that the Gospel injunction "be ye perfect" means, I think, that God wants our perfection in love. I think it's consoling to know that He is more patient than we can imagine with imperfections in everything else. There really can't be perfection in material things—they are just too prone to entropy. So don't you see the go-ahead there, written into the natural order of things, just to do a humble, competent job when it comes to the "everything else"?

Do your best to do each thing competently (not perfectly), and add your own little touches for your own and the Lord's enjoyment. Enjoying life's order is something God Himself did, on that seventh day, and this restful attitude can be reflected in the smallest things we do.

Don't get frustrated or negative with yourself if your duties are not carried out perfectly, but don't think it doesn't matter. If taking care of your home, your husband, your children doesn't matter, what does? But what's important is the effort and the sort of "background love" that goes into becoming the sort of person who really wants to do the given job.

And maybe that little list really will be all, as far as God's will goes, and you will be given the knowledge that it is. On the other hand, maybe there will be another thought of something He's trying to tell you, and that thought will be a quiet inspiration from the Holy Spirit. And, don't worry, it will be clear quite soon, either way—no need to run away from home to find out! And know that, with this calm determination to do what you ought, you can be serene in knowing that you are following God's will.

Beauty

he English philosopher Roger Scruton points out that there are two kinds of beauty: (1) the individual, expressive, and revealing gesture, and (2) ordinary harmony and fittingness:

> In everyday life it is the second kind of beauty that is important, and it is exemplified in home building, gardening and the design of squares, houses and streets. It is important because it expresses and amplifies the human desire for settlement, for an environment in which things fit together and people too. It is an instrument of peace.

Summer is winding down here. The bees are working hard, but there won't be a large harvest this year; the weather was too dry. The grass in my backyard has recovered somewhat; in the front, it's still pretty stressed. However, it was never impressive, even on its best days.

I see all the weeds I haven't pulled. I see them clearly. I see my plans, and how I didn't get to many of them. The garden is what it is. I dream in June, and I pick what I can in September: plenty of tomatoes this year, kale always, and raspberries—which are just a treat!

Inside, there are shelves to put up in the laundry room. We could have done that job over Labor Day weekend, but we went to a wedding and took advantage of the proximity to children and grandchildren to make the rounds of their houses. And certainly, that is all good!

I feel the urge coming on to make some quilts, but I'm not quite ready to get started. Hopefully I will be soon; maybe when the cooler weather settles in for real and the tomatoes are safely inside.

Scruton speaks of how ordinary beauty is imperfect, unlike the perfection of the grand gesture. But it reconciles us to our own imperfection while allowing us to remember that there is perfection, giving us a home in the world while reminding us of something beyond.

I believe that these words resonate particularly with the mother and the father of the family, however large or small that family may be. If we serenely pursue this *ordinary* beauty in everyday things and relationships, we build our home. This beauty gives us what Scruton calls settlement, and it gives others settlement as well. It gives them a glimpse of what they can have, themselves, without the anxiety of thinking they must somehow be perfect; paradoxically, it's that very homelikeness, the imperfection, that most reminds them, and us, of the perfection of Heaven.

Take the Reality Test and Straighten Out Your Life

What follows is actually one of my most loved and read posts—not because it's so profoundly written, but just because it's my pep talk about something you don't often hear, which is doing the *least* you can do, not the *most!* The advice in this book is aimed at just this: helping you figure out the details of the two things you simply must get control over in your home—the least you can do—before you can start implementing your life's dreams.

A Practical Resolution

Do you make a bunch of New Year's resolutions every January—resolutions about being a more loving wife and mother, taking care of your husband, keeping your home, and raising your children better? Do you feel a little twinge of doubt (maybe even anxiety) about whether you will keep those resolutions?

I'm going to tell you the secret to doing better. It won't sound like much. But it really works, and I know it does because it's how an overintellectual yet undereducated, impractical, and undisciplined person like me has been able to keep house for all ten of us—not as you see in a magazine; not as you see on some blogs; but enough to be called housekeeping, and on a tight budget too!

And here it is, the incredible secret that no one but me will tell you (unless you call up the friend who told me), and it's really amazing in its simplicity:

> Do better in the minimum that anyone can expect from you, and you will do better in everything else.

This counterintuitive revelation was vouchsafed to me one time when I was really sick. I had given birth to my dear Will, my sixth child. It was a very difficult time that left me recovering from major surgery and double pneumonia. And then I got the flu.

As I lay on the sofa, cradling the phone, lamenting to my friend (whom we call Auntie Sue) about my seriously miserable condition and the mountains of duties beckoning to me—no, hurling themselves at me—and especially the fussy baby who was not quite getting enough milk due to my illness, and my phenomenally, epically, heroically messy, dirty house, she told me this: basically your family needs food and clean laundry from you right now.

Just think about tackling those two things. Just two little tasks that the minimum in housekeeping comprises.

Now, maybe you are not sick and not recovering from a major trauma, and maybe you don't have a passel of kids. And maybe you are sort of a perfectionist and want things really clean and nice, as in a magazine. And maybe you are great at all that and should write a book.

But just maybe you are sort of keeping things going by dint of a boom-and-bust cycle, and no one really knows where you will land today. Maybe you are the way I was, and things are sort of okay but not really the way you want them to be. They will never be perfect—you know that—but they could be better.

Maybe you are like me, and can manage with functioning appliances from the last decade; maybe you don't really care whether things are brand spanking new. But as you look around, the dismalness is starting to get to you.

If the foregoing is the case, I can help you!

Let me ask you: When you are making your resolutions, do you have at the top of your list these two items: feeding and clothing your particular horde? Because if you do, things will go well for you this year. And this is why: no matter what other duties you have, the two biggest challenges you will face will be—ta da!—cooking dinner and doing the laundry.

Conversely, if you have a grip on these two areas—if you have serenity when contemplating the dining table or the washing machine—you will be rational in your approach to all other areas of your life: losing weight, saving money, cleaning up, using your time well, loving your family more, having reading time with your kids, teaching them Latin—you name it! It will all go better if you have order in these two fundamental duties. Or at least our inevitable failures even in this minimum won't upset the peace of our family as much, when we find ourselves knee-deep in horticulture or building violas da gamba or whatever our real passion might be.

I call these duties for a reason. Some mothers look at dinner and clean clothes as chores assigned by a particularly demanding, even cruel parent. This attitude, of course, begs the question of who that parent is! At the same time, in their heart of hearts, these mothers consider the basic duties to be optional.

They whine! They complain! They live with a laundry room that has piles of dirty laundry, and a master bedroom that has baskets of unsorted clean laundry! They get annoyed because their kids are hungry! They hate cooking supper!

They think that someone else will come and fix all this for them (perhaps that invisible yet demanding parent)! They spend money, the household's hard-earned cash, on takeout dinners, or frozen dinners, or drive-through dinners, because they can't figure out what to have for supper; and on new clothes, because the old ones are dirty! And then they say they have to work because they don't like being home and the family is not able to live on one income.

Does this describe you, perhaps a little? Then only you can solve this problem, the problem of your life; and this is the year to do it! I will show you how! Now, I can't show you how to make your home like what you see in a magazine. Can we all remind ourselves that our design mavens may actually have no family and that a crew, perhaps several crews and a staff, make their every whim a reality?

If I can do it, so can you! If a girl (I was nineteen, after all) who got married without really knowing how to sweep can keep house, so can you! If a girl who thought that *Mastering the Art of French Cooking* was a good manual for meal planning can keep three squares on the table within a budget, so can you! If little old me, who would rather read a novel than scrub a toilet (and I don't think I'm alone in this), and who shorted out a whole apartment building ironing a shirt the first year of her marriage, can do it, so can you!

Look at it this way: if you had the profession of managing, say, a hotel, you would be darn sure that, first and foremost, you had a plan, a system, and a clear idea of how you would provide food, clean sheets, and a warm atmosphere for your customers. You would not whine. You would pat yourself on the back for having such a great career! If you did not do this, you would be fired!

Oops—are we in danger of being fired from our jobs as moms? (Hmmm ... while pondering our resolutions, we probably should add one to be grateful to the long-suffering good humor of our families!)

Now, I know you are actually not like those babies I describe above, those terrible whiners. And you probably have a better work ethic than I do. But still, have you achieved clarity in these two important areas of your home-keeping duties? That's where I come in, with the clarity.

You know, your whole life is preparation for one thing or another. Jumping forward to when you find yourself a mama, you replace your sponge so that your kitchen will be clean. Your kitchen needs to be clean so that you can cook in it peacefully (and not get people sick or grossed out).

Your baby needs to be nursed (held, cuddled, fed) so that you start a good relationship with him so that later, when you give him a needed punishment, he knows you love him and learns to obey.

He needs to obey you so that he will stay alive long enough for you to tell him a few important things he needs to know before moving out—such as, that he can escape being whipped around by his moods and by his desires (see volume 1).

You plan meals so that you aren't surprised every day by the necessity of making dinner, so that, by the time your kids are old enough to sit at the table and listen, having learned enough manners not to roll their eyes so that they can participate in an actual conversation, your mind is just clear enough to realize that you need your husband there too so that the kids will listen to him, since you can't remember what it is you wanted to say, though you know it was important. Clearly, I am not the expert on these things, but one thing I do know: these are things you must figure out quickly so that you will be ready for the next challenge.

I see many people thinking that those things (cooking, cleaning, laundry, and the rest of the details of order) are ends in themselves, and they aren't. They are some of the practical things that go into mothering and making a home, but they are all for a purpose. Even making a home is for a purpose: so that we have a place in which to find out what God's will for us is and are able to take a stab at carrying it out.

Since one can wear dirty clothes, but one can't last long without food, I will start our journey to Order and Wonder with meals.

PART 2
Menus and Food

Meals don't just appear; food doesn't just buy itself! Nor can we simply be told, "Plan your meals" and know what to do. You need (well, I needed) exact directions and specific strategies. Feeding a family turns out to be a complex enterprise requiring thought and skill—and time.

Becoming competent in this area will happen and I will help.

How to Make Dinner
Every Day and Like It

I have dished up enough grub to satisfy up to eleven people on a regular basis—five of them hungry teenage boys (those were the days when we hosted a couple of boarders too!). I've fed my own seven children, husband, and mother, day in and day out, shopping for them with a bunch of them in tow. (Joys of homeschooling!) And I've been doing this in a semi-quasi-mostly-orderly way for about a quarter of a century.

I've planned meals while pregnant, nursing, convalescent, on the run, and under the weather. I don't always do a great job. Sometimes my family members have looked at me with a "this is your idea of dinner?" look, but usually it gets done, it's usually tasty, it doesn't break the bank—and those are my credentials.

And if you've read volume 1, you can see now how important it is to eat dinner together, at your own table at home, on a regular basis. But making this happen isn't magic, especially when you've also seen the importance of living on one income.

So we will start out here with the most basic issue of this whole project, and hold at bay all provisos and quid pro quos, as the Genie in *Aladdin* says. We will refine. We will be frugal. We will get fancy. We will discuss the ins and outs of deep freezing. We will discuss the true pitfall: eating out.

But for now, let's grapple with the first step.

This step is simply not covered in any of the guides or books or manuals that I have read. Everyone else starts by saying, "Make a week's menus to create a shopping list." That's like saying, "Make a dress for the ball from a pattern" to someone who doesn't know how to sew! They've skipped the important part.

Or these helpful experts give you their menus, which maybe you (or more likely your family) have no interest in; very importantly, as you will see, their menus certainly have nothing to do with what's on sale at your grocery store and don't take into account the schedules of a busy family.

Make Your Menus: The Secret to Successful Meal Planning

How did I come by this secret knowledge? Well, I'm the kind of person who could be found, long ago, *either* serving up Farce de Porc, Pointes d'Asperges au Beurre, and Soubise, *or* staring blankly at a package of frozen ground beef at 5:15 p.m., wondering what the heck to do with it. Not very practical, either way!

Then a more experienced friend told me that I simply had to know what I was going to have for dinner by 10:00 every morning. Good advice.

And then the long-suffering Phil pointed out to me that "we" were spending six hundred dollars a month on groceries. In 1984. For the five of us, three of whom were babies. I cried that day.

But it must have been an angel who whispered to me that if I planned my menus for the week, I'd do better. And I'm here to tell you that if you do nothing else but this one little step, and shop accordingly, you will cut your grocery bill by at least a third.

I once read that the average single American woman buys chicken breasts, broccoli, lettuce, and yogurt. And that's it. Granted, that was single women, but perhaps some of us haven't quite made the transition. Does frozen pizza count as variety if you have a family? I'm afraid not.

Others give you ideas for individual dishes, but I find that whole meals, all planned out, are what make the difference between failure and success. But don't be overwhelmed, because they will be *your* menus, and you won't have to wrack your brains every week to come up with them.

My secret, the key to success at last, is to have a master list of menus (most of which will be fairly simple, even humble) that you created along with your very own family, and you can consult it whenever you need to. You will be confident, knowing that when you plan out this week's offerings, everyone will be pleased, you will use your pantry and other food stores well, and you will shop efficiently.

Simply ask your family and yourself what they like to eat, and write it down! You don't do this every day, of course. No—once and for all, you all brainstorm together and create a Master Menu List. Then you use that to make your weekly or monthly lists, without troubling your family any further, except occasionally when you see their tastes changing or you become inspired.

If you think you get it, then go! If you would like more detail, excruciating detail *and* step-by-step instructions, keep reading.

Eating Out

But first, let me say a few words about eating out, and why your menus need to include things you would normally order in a restaurant.

Eating out (all the time, I mean, and all of these comments include takeout and delivery as well) is ... well, it's sort of a snare and a delusion. You think that you can afford it, but that's because you don't put it in your grocery budget. If you did, you'd be appalled.

If you charge your meals, you are probably still paying for things you ate years ago! At normal credit card interest rates, if you carry a balance on your credit card, you might be paying many times what the meal originally cost you. Eating out has ruined many a family's finances. At least if you charge a chair, it isn't gone the next day!

Yet there's something so enticing about being enveloped in the warm, cozy, food-swathed environment of the restaurant. Something so appealing about letting the kids choose what they want. Something so comforting about not having to think about cooking. It makes you so happy.

Eating out is a nice treat—I'm not against it. But let's examine it as a way of life.

Think of what you are missing when you eat or order out several times a week. Let's leave aside the money issue. Let's even leave aside the health issue, important as that is. Let's look only at what we are missing when we don't interact on a daily basis at home.

Kids need to be served balanced, nutritious meals that they basically have to eat without complaining. They shouldn't have choices at a particular meal. (You will ask them their favorite menus—and I will explain this below—and that's enough.) The discipline of eating what's set before you turns your mind to other, more important issues.

Sitting together at home, the whole family is discussing matters of consequence or laughing over common experiences. The members are interacting and getting to know each other (including children getting to know their mother and father!), which also means putting up with each other. Soon the family is making decisions together and building a life together. These are priceless times, incredibly formative, and all too fleeting—and a whole lot of them happen at the dinner table.

Someone, and that someone is you, has to make that all happen, and that means staying out of eateries unless the trip is planned, affordable, and all the more enjoyable. I think that because you also have to taxi people around, go to games, check homework, and do the laundry, a little part of you feels that it's not decisive if you eat out a lot. Please reconsider this. All those other things serve this one thing, your time together, bonding as a family.

But it's true that we are tired and haven't planned well. So let's do that now!

You know what? I found out I could make cheesesteaks (one of my favorite eat-out choices)! I found out I could make guacamole, fish tacos, breadsticks, and onion rings (using the deep fryer I got at a yard sale for seventy-five cents)! I found out my kids love my homemade pizza! I even made a creditable stab at the eggplant salad we had at the divine Persian restaurant in the city.

We don't need no stinkin' restaurants to be happy. We will enjoy these things if we do go out, but as long as I plan well, we can also be happy right here at home.

Master Menu Work Plan

his part is fun and almost feels like work avoidance. Everyone will help you, unlike in the next steps, where you will use the information they have given you so that you always know what your family will be eating and when.

Creating Your Family's Master Menu List

You will need a pen and a few sheets of paper. Any piece of paper will work.

Sit down with your family—all of them. I tend to think things will go better if you haven't just eaten something. On the other hand, it would also help if everyone isn't so hungry that they can't concentrate on talking about food without getting upset.

Ask them this simple question: What are your favorite meals? We'll concentrate on the main meal for now. Stick with me, because this is a process that builds on itself.

Do try to get your family to tell you the whole menu, not just a certain dish. A complete menu means a meal with all its components. This could be three or four dishes in the traditional sense (meat, starch, salad, rolls, for instance) or something more one-dish (spinach lasagna—but don't forget the breadsticks if that is their favorite part). Write all their ideas down.

Getting all this information might take more questions, but it's worth it. Perhaps the family will be most helpful if you make it a game.

Here are some prompts to get everyone to tell you just about everything they like to eat. Let them go right through one category before you ask the next prompt.

- What are your favorite meals right now? (Make sure you write them all down! Make them wait while you do: it helps them remember more.)

- What were your favorite meals when you were young? (This applies more to your husband and you than to the eight-year-old, but I bet the eight-year-old has something to contribute!) What unusual or special meals did your family have growing up? What did your pals growing up have that you remember? Taco salad? Oyster stew at Christmas? Grilled fish? Chicken and dumplings? What did you have with that? Applesauce? Fritters? Squash? Corn on the cob?

- What are your favorite ethnic meals? Chinese? Italian? Greek? Portuguese? Your family includes certain ethnic traditions, I'll wager: be sure to include those, whatever they may be, with whatever goes with them. Since I grew up with a lot of Egyptian food, I include my favorite dishes, and they have become my family's favorites also. My husband is quite Irish, and we enjoy a boiled supper with brown bread as well as some old Boston favorites (baked beans, fish pie).

- When you went to a friend's house, what were you served that you enjoyed, that maybe we don't usually have? A casserole? Fried chicken? Soup? What did the mom serve with that? Biscuits?

- What meals in books or movies appeal to you? (Think *Farmer Boy*, Dickens, *Anne of Green Gables*, Dorothy Sayers, *Big Night*, etc.)

- When you go to a restaurant, what do you most like to order? If you could go to any restaurant, what type would it be? If you could order anything without regard to cost, what would it be?

Onion rings? Chicken Caesar salad? Beef Kempinski? Duck à l'Orange? Cheesesteak? Shrimp cocktail? The last few times you went to a restaurant, what did you order that you really liked? Fajitas? A deep-fried onion flower? A cheeseburger?

- What are your favorite "easy" supper meals (that are not spaghetti or pizza)? Sloppy joes? Hot dogs? Breakfast for supper? Fish tacos?
- What are your favorite fancy meals? Roast beef with Yorkshire pudding? Salmon and peas? A turkey dinner? Peking duck?

When you are finished, you should have a fairly long list of menu ideas. Take your list and sit quietly by yourself. If any menu reminds you of another menu, write that one down too (for instance, if a lasagna dinner reminds you of a baked ziti dinner, write that one down). It's very important that you try to put them in menu form. If someone says "spaghetti," try to get him to tell you if he would like salad or green beans, garlic bread or rolls with that. Don't stress out; you can easily add ideas later as they occur to you.

Now as a final step, you could put all this data into the computer and organize it by type, or you can wait for the next step in the plan, which has more tips, to do that.

I got myself a durable and waterproof binder and some of those nifty plastic sleeves to put papers in, and I made a place for all my food info. Don't worry, we'll come back to this. And remember: yes, if I can do it, so can you!

Congratulations! This was the hard part, and it was fun!

Why My Menu Planning Is Different

It took me a while to realize that I needed to write down detailed menus when planning meals for the week, which is why I emphasize this method here. For a long time, I'd just jot down "pork chops" and then stand in the produce aisle, getting all wound up inside my head, probably thanks to dear Julia Child, that culinary paragon who both taught me to cook via her *Mastering the Art of French Cooking* and rendered me a bit of an overthinker in the kitchen.

Sometimes you just need to write down "broccoli" next to your "Chicken casserole" so that you can move on with your life as lived in the grocery store. Sometimes you are in such a broccoli rut that you need to write down "salad with pear, blue cheese, and pecans" or even "chou-fleur blanchi" if you remember what that means, so that your poor family can move on with *their* lives at the dinner table.

For shopping purposes, you also need to be able to see at a glance of your list of menus just how many heads of lettuce you will need (because you have actually scheduled salad for four out of the seven nights) and whether to check the cornmeal supply (because you want cornbread with your chili, days from now). Those items won't turn up if you haven't thought out the whole menu, and efficiency will suffer.

After working on this menu making, we will have learned about ourselves that we can't look at a package of chicken thighs in the grocery store and somehow, at that moment, know what to do with them and what to serve them with—not while quelling two toddlers and figuring out unit prices of boneless versus boned, we can't.

The grocery store is not where we magically become inspired.

Do you realize that everything—*everything*—hinges on knowing what is for dinner?

What is the difference between a reasonably tidy home and living in a pit dug out by spatially challenged warthogs? Between being able to have a good homeschooling day and feeling as if you are in charge of a bunch of illiterate savages who figure out the speed of passing trains with knotted ropes and their fingers? Between starting a creative project of any kind, working on it, and finishing it, and feeling as if all you do is go in and out of the grocery store?

The difference is knowing that dinner is under control.

Why is this? Because, and I realize this might be news to you, so hang on: *dinner happens every day.*

Now, one reason I started writing for others about my menu system is that I often read elsewhere about people's meal ideas, and they always amount to something like, "Make your menus, shop, and cook." It did seem as if *something* was left out.

On the other hand, I was somewhat daunted by the amazing proliferation of really wonderful blogs, magazines, and books with barges of recipes.

Yet recipes are not really the issue, since the chances are slim that you have the ingredients on hand to make something truly different and exciting, and how can you either rely solely on "things you have on hand" or shop effectively for more variety without knowing which recipe or sort of food you will make on which day?

In a nutshell, I'm telling you that it's not enough to say, as articles I have read do say, "Monday we'll have spaghetti; Tuesday we'll have rotisserie chicken from the grocery store; Wednesday we'll eat out; Thursday we'll have pasta; Friday we'll have leftovers; Saturday I get the day off from cooking; and Sunday my mother will rescue me."

We can see that the expert here is hardly cooking at all. Going by this list, she's spending a lot of money on prepared food, planning on eating out because of her inadequate plan, and leaving herself open to an emergency trip to the store or yet another restaurant outing with that deceptive "leftovers" entry.

Another source tells you simply to come up with a bunch of menus without regard to the day of the week. As I contemplate a different schedule every day, brought on by the plethora of children around me, I wonder what her life is like. I also wonder if her plan is too much cooking, since, with my detailed plan, I can *schedule* making chicken, broccoli, and rice one day and using the extra I've planned on in a casserole a few days later. Now that's "leftovers."

Most "weekly" menu plans I have seen factor in a day *or more* of eating out. Maybe those writers are living in New York City, where eating out is a must, as far as I can tell; or maybe they just can't imagine cooking seven days a week, or maybe they haven't checked their credit card statement lately. But a family living on one income doesn't plan to eat out once a week. That is not a hardship, however. Once you learn to plan, you eat very well and come to see normal restaurant fare as not worth the expense.

Think of it this way: Taking three children to a fast-food restaurant is the equivalent of purchasing a couple of nice steaks—the ultimate fast food at home!—grilling them, and serve them sliced with baked potatoes, salad, and garlic bread, with money to spare. And there would be leftover steak for sandwiches the next day.

Or if time is the issue, purchasing a bunch of cold cuts and making subs to go would leave you with plenty of dollars left over for your ice cream fund. Buy cashews, dried apricots, and string cheese, and everyone would be satisfied until they reach home, with money and extra snacks to spare.

Anyway, try using my plan for making the week's menus. The key is not to think up things all the time. Spend some quality time planning and render them already thought up.

Menus versus Mixing and Matching

Why do I insist on spelling out a menu for each day's dinner? Wouldn't it be just as easy to sort of mix and match, putting together a week's worth of ideas and then just deciding at the moment what to make?

Maybe for some people it is, and building in flexibility can only help you, but if you have a busy household, try to follow the liturgical calendar, and also have a tendency to space out over a good book or phone conversation with a distant friend, my way, where you think out all the elements in advance, might be for you.

Remember, you don't have to make the same menus I do. After you have made your very own basic menus, as described earlier, according to your own preferences, you'll find that you make better use of all the inspiration that surrounds us in the form of magazines, online sites, and cookbooks.

Perhaps your whole family is invited out for dinner. Lucky you! You get an extra day in your meal planning! Push everything down the list or skip over one of the night's menus.

Some flexibility comes from *unexpected* leftovers. If you end up with enough food from one night to carry you through another, that's a bonus day in your menu plan (distinct from planned leftovers). Another use for unforeseen leftovers is to pool them for "leftovers day," aka "bits and pieces," "fab buffet," or whatever name you give this meal for maximum family approval. Pull out everything, warm up what needs to be warmed, arrange it tastefully and appealingly, and let people take what they want.

Supplement with a good loaf of homemade bread, butter, and cheese if you need it. Again, just juggle your days and pocket the bonus.

Cheap and Not Cheap

The next step in making that master plan isn't maybe what you are thinking.

The next step is to get these menus sorted out into "cheap" and "not cheap" (or use any words that appeal to you—you might prefer "affordable" and "fancy" or something less abrupt), because when you are managing a household on one income, you need to have good control over your food expenses. You need many thrifty menu ideas, meals that appeal but don't cost much. And they need to be written down in advance, because the enemy of thrift is last-minute deciding, which always defaults to spending more.

The exercises below will explain it to you if you'd like more information, and there are examples.

Simply think about what you would make if you had only a small amount of money to spend, and put those menus in one list. Think about what's more elegant, special, and expensive, and put those in another list. It helps to do it in a computer document so you can shuffle them around.

That's all there is to this step, but it's an important one.

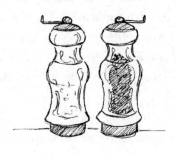

Menu Planning

Now that you have that list of menus or at least a few grudgingly imparted vague ideas garnered from your family, and you've begun to ponder the importance of eating meals at home, at the table, together, do some brainstorming. Get out your recipe clippings and your cooking magazines. Open up your inspiration file or site. Flip through and write down anything that seems as if it would work for a family meal. Make sure whatever you write down is in complete menu form, for the *menu* is the key to good planning.

And as I said, as you go through your list, try to figure out which menus seem to be fairly inexpensive. These will all go into one document (do it on your computer if you want and file it under "recipes" as "cheap menus").

In this section I will give you examples. They tend to the very traditional "American" sort of category because those are the tried-and-true backbone of feeding a family in our country.

Believe me, I can get just as fancy, global, and eclectic as the next person, but in my examples, I have kept it somewhat plain so that you can see that not every meal has to be super inventive. My sense is that the consumerist-driven food industry has exhausted us by making us feel that every meal must be some sort of culinary epiphany, when really, what is important is that the food is of good quality and the company is loving. These are just examples—in your own mind you can easily translate them into what you have come up with and what your own cultural background suggests as "plain family fare."

Thrifty Menus

Here are some examples from my own "Cheap Menus" list—meals designed to make the most, especially, of a small amount of meat or none at all, and still be nutritious and tasty:

Sausages or hot dogs
Baked beans
Cole slaw
Brown bread

Chicken Caesar Salad
Oven fries
Garlic bread

Chicken enchiladas
Orange and romaine salad
Cornbread

Spaghetti and meatballs
Green salad
Bread

Spinach lasagna
Mixed stir-fry vegetables with ginger and soy sauce
Bread

Chicken and broccoli stir-fry
Rice

Quiche
Three-bean salad
Rolls

Cannellini bean, sausage, and kale soup
Grilled cheese sandwiches

Chicken noodle soup
Pumpkin muffins and cheddar cheese

Pizza (homemade, of course — "bought" is not cheap!)
Salad

Chili
Cornbread
Zucchini in cheese sauce
Rice

Bean burritos
Corn
Guacamole

Do you get the idea of how these are thrifty menus? One chicken breast can be plunked down in front of one person, and then it will serve only that person. Or you can put it in a big salad or an enchilada casserole, and it will serve three or four people.

Notice that I have included everything I would serve at that meal. Notice that every meal includes bread, pretty much. In a large family, this is a must. You will avoid a lot of grief if you are not worried that your child is starving by having only a taste of each dish; the bread and butter will see him through. Your teenagers need rolls and butter.

Of course, you can swap things out, but believe me, food planning is simply easier if you start with menus, rather than individual dishes. If you can arrange the menus by type (Italian, Chinese, bean, chicken, and so forth) the process is even easier.

Regular Menus

You can also think in terms of the season. Many of these menus I've mentioned seem suited to the school year and cold weather. When summer comes, you will add to the list with all the great grilled foods, salads, and cold suppers you will suddenly think of (and inspiration for which will be all around you in magazines and on food sites).

And that's another thing about menu making: often I've found that I just can't think of anything to make for supper—have drawn a complete blank on any foods at all—because the season is changing and I just haven't realized it. At the end of summer, I get energized for menu making if I stop thinking about grilled chicken and start thinking about soup—and vice versa.

Make a list of "regular" menus with main dishes such as stew, pot roast, pork roast, chicken bake, roast chicken, and so on—menus with meat as the main course, so not thrifty in themselves—and be sure to add the sides that you enjoy.

Here are some examples of less cheap weekday menus, which I would suggest alternating with the more frugal ones:

Pork chops with apples and onions
Green beans
Roasted squash
Rolls

Honey-ginger chicken
Rice
Broccoli
Rolls

Beef stew with potatoes and carrots
Green salad
Rolls

Grilled steak tips
Garlic mashed potatoes
Grilled Italian vegetables
Focaccia

Pulled-pork sandwiches
Cole slaw
Oven fries

Special-Occasion Menus

Next, make a list of the special-occasion menus that you and your family have come up with; they are more Sunday fare or menus you would make only for holidays or other special occasions. Keeping a record of your festive meals makes menu planning much easier the next time you do it.

Here is an example of a restaurant meal that would be a little pricier than your normal home-cooked fare and takes a lot more preparation for each element. Note, however, that making it at home costs a fraction of what you would pay at the restaurant.

T-bone steak
Mushrooms and onions
Salad with blue cheese dressing
Twice-baked potatoes
Parker House rolls

Here is a Thanksgiving menu (my own Thanksgiving menu has many more dishes, but this is the basic thing we mean when we say "turkey dinner"):

Roasted turkey with gravy
Cranberry sauce
Squash
Mashed potatoes
Brussels sprouts with chestnuts
Potato rolls

Here are two Sunday menus:

Baked ham
Roasted sweet potatoes
Green beans
Applesauce
Biscuits

Roasted chicken
Roasted squash
Kale salad
Rolls

Any menus that you make need to be what you and your family like. I would also encourage you to make them doable. If you like to get fancy (and I often do), you can embellish, of course. But so often with a busy family, we are rushing and tired; keeping expectations (for yourself!) reasonable is the difference between success and failure.

Cookbooks such as *Joy of Cooking* and the *Better Homes and Gardens Cookbook* have menu sections, and you should consult them—they have gotten me out of a rut many a time. However, those books have to appeal to a wide range of tastes and unknown desires, whereas you are free to leave out things that no one in your family likes and put high on the list things they do like! It's your own personal compendium, and no two families' lists will be the same.

These menu lists are the backbone of your weekly menu planning. For a while, you should consult them faithfully, and then, voilà! you will have memorized them!

Writing Your Menus for a Given Week

You want to make menus for *at least* a week. It's more than possible, as you get good at the process, to make them for two weeks or a month. But for now, let's just get the week under our belt, on the theory that it's a doable goal that won't overwhelm you.

With your menu lists in hand, all printed out, make your plan for the week. Yes, you are ready to do it. And it won't be that hard, because you already have a "stockpile" of ideas that you know your family likes.

What do you need to do this? You could use an Excel spreadsheet, a PowerPoint presentation, a PDF file that you download off an organizational website, or any other technologically advanced method you choose. But I usually grab a scrap of paper and jot down:

M:

T:

W:

Th:

F:

S:

S:

M:

I like to make them for one extra day so that I have that leeway if I don't get to the store. I can always roll the plan for that day into the next weekly list.

Then I look at my calendar to see which days I'll be in the car at four in the afternoon rather than able to be cooking at home; which days I know I'll be tired because I have a meeting the night before; and which days I know I will have time to bake or roll up tortillas or something like that.

Then I choose my menus accordingly. In another section, I will go into depth on what I call "Save a Step Cooking" — making extra of various things and then using them at various times. For now, let's just go through the week together.

Here's my thought process, which I hope will give you the idea of how to make a week's worth of menus that will fit your schedule, pantry, and energy level like a glove:

Monday: This is a day I when spend a lot of time in the morning cleaning up from the weekend and making sure I am up to date on my bills and checking account. Mondays are a day of anxiety over the coming week's demands or at least a sense of extreme busyness for most people, so it's good to have something easy and hearty for dinner. I usually have an Italian-American type of dish on this day. Knowing that I will probably be making spaghetti with meatballs (that I have already frozen) or pasta with meat sauce or easy no-boil lasagna makes this day a cinch.

- Spaghetti with meat sauce: I've already frozen my browned and seasoned meat that I did in one big session—more on that later.
- Salad: if my stores of fresh veggies have gone down, I can easily serve carrot sticks instead.
- Garlic bread: I stockpile enough bread to know I can pull a loaf out of the freezer, and if I'm short on time, a nice warm loaf without the garlic is fine too, if a bit disappointing.

Tuesday: On this day I teach a religion class in the late afternoon. I can do my grocery shopping in the morning, but I can't do any cooking in the afternoon. I like to use something left over from Sunday on this day.

- Leftover stew: I make enough for my Sunday meal and for at least one more meal.
- Noodles (the stew goes further if you serve it *over* the noodles; just make sure you have lots of gravy)
- Green beans tossed with olive oil and salt
- Bread: I make all our bread other than bagels and pita—and sometimes I make the pita!— and usually have a bunch in the freezer. If not, I can easily make biscuits.

Wednesday: I like to serve soup on Wednesdays. It's a good way to be simple in our eating habits, and it leaves me time to bake and do other things on this day when I don't *have* to go out until 3:30. When you serve soup, you might want to have some little nibbly things such as a bowl of peanuts, tortilla chips and hummus, and cheese and crackers out on the counter for the older ones who need more calories. Those things can be added to the table after the littles have had some soup and bread.

- Split pea soup (using a hambone from the freezer)
- Cornbread

Thursday: Since our meals have been simple for the first days of the week, I tend to be more elaborate on Thursdays. Kids are ready for a hearty meal, and its leftovers are helpful on the weekend, when more people are around. However, we have a lot going on on Thursdays. I have a busy afternoon that never ends. It's also a good day for a chicken menu, most of which can be popped into the oven and left to roast without much oversight.

- Roasted chicken: Never, ever roast just one chicken! The leftover meat can be frozen and pulled out of the freezer another day; the carcasses can go into the stockpot for broth.
- Squash or roasted yams: leftover from Sunday, or roast along with the chicken in their own pan.
- Salad
- Biscuits, made from my homemade mix (found in the breakfast recipes in the appendices)

Friday: We go meatless on Fridays except during the Octave of Easter and on solemnities. Almost always we have homemade pizza and salad. Occasionally we have a fish dish or a pasta dish, so I'm highlighting that here.

- Salmon cakes with yogurt cumin sauce: I keep canned salmon in the pantry for this simple meal; the sauce is just plain yogurt with cumin and lemon juice.
- Waldorf salad: all the ingredients store very well for when you're low on fresh veggies: apples, walnuts or pecans, celery, raisins or dried cranberries, tossed with a little mayo, vinegar, and salt.
- Rice
- Pita bread

Saturday: Usually we have leftover pizza for lunch, which is pretty hearty (I make an extra one with meat on Friday night for this purpose). So, by Saturday night, we don't need anything too filling or complicated. In addition, I've usually worked hard on chores and don't want to cook! My husband grew up having hot dogs and baked beans on Saturdays. I'm not a huge fan, but it *is* easy! If we have lots of leftovers, we'll have a "bits and pieces" night—meaning a meal in which I bring out all the little leftovers there may be and set them out, along with good bread and an assortment of cheeses, saving those hot dogs for a busy day when I really can't cook.

- Hot dogs with buns
- Baked beans (homemade or from a can)
- Cole slaw (homemade)
- Oven fries

Sunday: It's worth it to do a traditional big Sunday dinner. You will get at least one more meal out of it in the coming busy week; maybe more, if you play your cards right. More importantly (and sometimes we do have something very simple), it's good to have a family day, emphasizing being together and resting. A roast is restful to make—more so than a casserole! Try to make something with bones you can use for soup another day. To make your Sunday even more restful, prep the work on Saturday so that all you have to do is turn on the oven.

- Pork roast: Make extra for barbecued-pork sandwiches later in the week.
- Mashed potatoes: Make extra for shepherd's pie later in the week; use cooking water for bread making.
- Broccoli: Make double for broccoli soup for lunches.
- Rolls: Keep a lot of homemade rolls in the freezer!

Monday: I like to make a "weekly" menu of a little more than a week, in case I get thrown off somewhere. Having an extra meal up your sleeve without any extra preparation really helps.

- Chili: It's easy to make a large amount and freeze what's left over; serve with sour cream and cheese.
- Rice
- Orange slices
- Guacamole
- Tortilla chips

These menus are what the Lawler Family tends to eat when we are not being fancy. You can certainly use them, but you should feel free to make menus that reflect what *your* family likes to eat, for that is the entire point of being successful at menu making!

An Example of Planning Menus around Activities

I'll show you why I like to assign a specific menu to a specific day, going so far as to write down, in my menu plan, what is going on that day—in other words, making the menus part of the activity calendar. Here's how I prepared for a week in the life of one spacey mom, when I still had children at home and many activities. Imagine we're sitting down on Sunday evening, March 15, to make the menus for a Monday shopping trip:

Tuesday, March 17, is St. Patrick's Day, and I will be out in the late afternoon, not coming home until 5:30. I'll be making what I always make on this day: corned beef dinner and Irish soda bread. But I spell it out on my menu, because if I don't possess cabbage, red potatoes, and buttermilk, then this simple dinner will not come off! The detailed menu enables me to make a detailed shopping list *without having to rethink everything.*

Wednesday, March 18, is my son Will's birthday. I have to remember to ask him what he wants for dinner (I guess I'll catch him after his soccer practice), and I have to schedule baking a cake. I also have to get Bridget from choir practice to dance practice and won't be home until 7:15 p.m.

Thursday is the feast of St. Joseph. This glorious saint, wonderful protector of the family, of virgins, of the Church, of the soul—intercessor to God for all our daily needs—deserves a proper commemoration. I want to prepare for that. But it's a day when I have a religion class to teach in the afternoon and Bridget's dance class from 6:00 until 7:30 with a half-hour drive each way. And I have to be at a committee meeting at 7 p.m. in the next town. Great! I'll bilocate! I can do this! Or maybe not. All right, I'll have a lasagna in the oven and good ice cream in the freezer.

On Friday, we will have a Lenten supper with friends. Again, simple: I can make soup and bread, and people will bring things to contribute—but I'd better be ready. I'll be gone all morning with Bridget's orchestra.

And this schedule represents only the ridiculous activities of two children, one of whom can drive himself! I remember when I had five children playing soccer (three on travel teams), three in dance (obviously they overlapped, but still) and on and on. And on top of everything, I'm someone who exhorts others not to overschedule children. Dinner must be served, though.

What do you do about games, meetings, classes, and errands? We simply cannot afford drive-through for those days. No wonder people think they can't afford to give up the wife's income: they are spending it all on activities and fast food.

I know that on Saturday I won't want to be cooking anything complicated. It will be a day for franks and beans (which my husband loves, luckily!).

Sunday we will have another family visit for dinner. I want to make the ham-and-leek pie that came out so well on the feast of St. David (patron of Wales). The ham and the pie crust are in the freezer, but I have to put leeks on the grocery list.

Sure, there can be interchangeability, both in the days and in the dishes. Just because you wrote "salad" doesn't mean you can't do green beans. But if you have the plan written out according to the activities and events you have on the roster, you will experience the satisfaction of order.

Plan for a Week or a Month?

I suggest beginning by planning a week's worth of meals, but once you are used to working this way, going by the month might work better. When I had all my family about me, I planned menus for a month. It was more effective in terms of effort to put in the work all at once, and by not starting from scratch every time but working from your trusty menu list, you soon realize that the meals are on a basic rotation that makes planning ahead easy.

Lunches

Lunch is a touchy subject for me because I detest it. I can hardly even say it. Are you ready for "br-lunch?" "su-lunch?" I am always blurting. I like breakfast and supper. I don't like lunch!

So, as with all the other resisted-yet-unavoidable things we do, we need a plan. Those of us at home eat leftovers that aren't earmarked for future suppers. That third of a pan of lasagna, a bit of meat and a bunch of rice that can be heated up together, a few meatballs that can be sliced up and tossed on leftover pasta. If you don't like making sandwiches, it's *even more* important to make more than you plan on eating at supper so that you have something to eat the next day at lunch.

Important note: these little tidbits are not dreary at all if they were well cooked to begin with, and crucially, *if the first meal had not been previously frozen.* Leftovers of food that was already not fresh will indeed be dreary. This fact is one of the main reasons that I endorse what I call Save a Step Cooking as opposed to freezer cooking, but more on that below.

A big pot of macaroni and cheese will be supper and lunch for a few days.

Soup is a great lunch dish; it's very flexible, as you can always add a little water, broth, or milk to stretch it.

The occasional quesadilla or salad rounds out the menu plan here. And yes, sometimes I make sandwiches, grumble, grumble.

On Saturdays, when I would rather walk barefoot on tiny swords than make lunch (as opposed to my normal weekday aversion), we have leftover pizza from the night before. Making that one extra pizza is so worth it for the next day, when you are knee-deep in chores and errands. And if takeout pizza is your fallback during the week (because you didn't plan menus), it will be enjoyed. It can be rounded out with other leftovers or a peanut-butter sandwich for a still-hungry child.

Again, make your grocery list with *your* favorite lunch menus in mind. You should know how many loaves of bread you need in a week (and if you make bread, how many sacks of flour!), how much ham, how many blocks of cheese, how many cans of tuna, how many packages of pasta—the things you need for each lunch each day.

On Packing Lunches: A Secret to Keeping Your Sanity

When the kids were packing lunches for school, and I had up to six people heading out the door with a brown bag, I realized something important: don't expect to make lunches during breakfast. It's a bad idea.

The counters are already strewn with bagels, butter, eggs, cereal, and milk. Add to that mayo, ham, plastic bags, chips, and all the rest, and you will spend the rest of the morning just putting things away. And you'll be cranky while you do it and after everyone leaves, because the breakfast- and lunch-making scene is so unpleasant and chaotic.

No. Make lunch at lunchtime, the day before. While you are making sandwiches for those at home, make them for the next day as well! While you are heating soup, get lunches ready for the brown-baggers! At the very least, make them at night before bed. Do whatever it takes to avoid the morning chaos.

I like to make them myself or delegate the task to a responsible older child, because it's the most efficient and frugal use of the food for me to oversee and manage the preparations. The children can't be expected to use that last chicken breast to make chicken salad. No kid is going to know to put the extra half a slice of ham on each sandwich to avoid leaving behind a slice and a half, good for nothing. Something will end up shoved to the back of the refrigerator if you are not there to supervise.

But, once the sandwiches (or at least chicken salad) are made and wrapped or discussed with a competent executor, it's up to your children to get a bag and put into it a piece of fruit, some snacks, a cookie, and the sandwich. Keep a good supply of brown bags in a handy spot. You children can even get a napkin. They can do it.

And they have to be sternly warned never to throw good food away! "Give that sandwich to a classmate and then tell me if you are getting too much or don't like something." (Not that they are allowed to be super picky, but if there is a genuine distaste for mustard or meatloaf, they'd better let me know and not just throw it away!)

Frugal Grocery-List Making

Now we somehow have to get from a nice, tidy menu list to having food in the house with which to prepare all those meals. And if you're like me, with a strong preference for reading a book, taking a nap, or really anything other than figuring this stuff out, and, to boot, you have a bunch of kids, no money, and a fair amount of homeschooling thrown in, you might like to know how to approach the grocery list.

Buy Low, Sell (Eat) High

First, when I'm making the menus, I start with those that *must* be made this week because (1) something needs to be eaten or it will spoil, (2) someone needs some particular dish or *he* will expire ("Make meatball subs or I will expire"), or (3) something in my freezer might as well be taken advantage of because nothing like it is on sale this week.

In my mind, this way of doing things is related to the economic principle that one must buy low, sell high. Just as you don't go out and buy stocks when they are at their highest price—necessitating a sale later when the price is low—so you don't use food willy-nilly but try to always make the most of the lowest-priced food you can obtain or have obtained so that you can eat high (eat well!). Since we consume food (and thus can't sell it later for a profit), it's a little different, but this is how I think of it. That roast that's in the freezer, the one you bought on sale three months ago, will serve you well this week when there is no sale roast to be had in the stores.

So much for what's already on hand. To make my weekly menu, I need the flyers for the grocery stores I know I want to go to—the ones I know have reasonable and not inflated prices across the board. I make my remaining menus based on what is on sale. (Remember, as you do this, that your master list is so you don't churn your wheels every week, getting deeper into a rut of not knowing what's for dinner. Pull it out every time you plan your weekly menus and shopping. I often have to remind myself that I have already thought things through, and making menus shouldn't be a new experience every week!)

Aha! I see my handy local market has ham for seventy-nine cents a pound; we are having ham for Sunday dinner next week for sure, and I am confident I have several ways to use it on my master list. If nothing else, buy at least one for the freezer so that you can buy low and sell (eat) high another day. (In the section on organizing food, I will address the issue of where to store all this food.)

You should quickly be able to fill your menu list with foods that you already have on hand that you "bought low" *and* with things you will "buy low" this week. In a few weeks, you should have a good enough stockpile, in pantry and freezer, to be able to do most of your shopping with sale items only, or at least at your targeted low price. And that is how you permanently lower your food budget while eating very well.

If you have no extra money to spare for this project, put the money you save by buying sale items into your next week's budget. Then use that little extra to buy more sale items. That way, you will soon be ahead of your budget.

Now examine every item on every menu. Do you have enough flour to make this week's bread? Do you have enough beans for the soups you've planned? Celery? Noodles? And so on down the list. Your menu plan will be derailed if it turns out that you can't make something because you lack an essential ingredient.

Once you have all the items for your menus, go over your needs for other meals and snacks. You should have some idea of how many eggs, gallons of milk, boxes of crackers, and so forth you go through during the week. If you don't have any idea, that's something for you to observe in the next month and ascertain. All that goes on the list, and off you go!

This trip is your main shopping at the store that has the best overall prices. You can stop at a store for some specials if it is more or less on your way to somewhere else.

Every week, I stop at a store that has good unadvertised markdowns on meat, but I know that bargains on other items await me elsewhere.

If you are lucky, you have a child who enjoys scouring the flyers for good prices, understands unit pricing, and gets the "lowest regular price" idea. His reward is that he will come across something he wants that you might have overlooked, and he can put it on your list. One of my children helped me like this, and it made list making so much easier! (He went on to be an economics journalist!)

Keep in mind that if you are spending hundreds of dollars a month on groceries, you need to think big. Saving a buck here or there isn't as important as saving on *everything* you buy. It's also not as important as getting a real bargain *all* the time on *all* your meat or produce.

Don't wear yourself out and use up a lot of fuel running around, and don't go to a place just because it's closest or is a big-box store. The pasta at my local big-box store is more than 20 percent higher per pound than at my local market, and the tuna too. But the dog food is much cheaper. Don't be tricked by their tricky flyers. Use your common sense and your price notebook! (Do take note of a particular store that has a low price on, for instance, milk, but not much else. Perhaps your husband can make a stop once a week to stock up just on milk.)

Start-Up Costs; or, Don't Use Up Your Pantry Supplies

Your motivating idea should be to buy low (get stuff on sale, marked down, on clearance, at a good price—consistently) and sell high. Again, the sell-high bit doesn't exactly apply, because you aren't selling your food; you are eating it. But to me it just means "eat high"—eat well despite high prices—and "time is money"—consider your time something you have to buy at a high cost, and use it well.

Here's another economics principle for you: keep start-up costs low. Start-up costs are the up-front expenditures made in a business before delivering the product to the customer. You are the business. The customer is your family. The product is the meal. The costs are in dollars and time!

Now to this one, there are two parts. One we have talked about, and it's mainly about time: saving a step every time you cook. But there are other start-up costs that are real costs, in actual dollars.

Adding to Your Stores

Does it make sense to use up your pantry items entirely?

Sometimes I read the advice, supposedly frugal, to use up everything you have on hand before buying more food. And I don't think this is actually frugal in the long run.

Now, to be clear, I realize that it happens that you are at the end of the money and have to be clever. I've been there too, and I think it's worthwhile to know how, in an emergency, to get by for a while on what you have.

The problem, though, with using up all the beans, rice, and onions you have as a regular practice, before buying anything more, is that very soon you will need those things and not necessarily be able to get them at a good price! You will have to start up your process of building the pantry all over again, which costs too much in time as well as money.

So I want to talk about the normal case, which is that you have a certain limited amount to spend every month, and you need to make the most of it.

For long-term frugality, constantly adding to your stores by buying low is the best way to squeeze every penny. It has to do with start-up costs! You have to look at everything you buy as representing a certain amount of time and effort as well as money. You hunted down the best price for flour, sugar, beans, coffee, canned tomatoes, pasta, oil, and so on. You invested in a certain quantity of these things—more than you need for the present moment, to tide you over to the next sale—with the idea of saving money overall.

With the money you save buying these things at a low price, you are able to buy other things at a low price as well, stocking up on meat, vegetables in season, and fancy things like nuts, chocolate, dried fruits, and so on. Very likely there will be a time lag between getting them into your pantry and the next time the price will be right.

Meanwhile, you do your weekly shopping, continuing to roll your extra money (gained from stocking up on low-priced items) over into supplies for future meals. And it's essential that you do this if you are able to, because every week there will be some things that are priced low that you can stock up on. Some weeks are better than others, and it is true that you can spend more or less depending on how good the prices are, if you are willing to use what you have.

Saving Money Takes Time

It's hard to start doing all this. It takes effort. You have to change your thinking. You have to research prices. It's a start-up cost.

It gets easier if you don't have to do it all at once. It's easier if you don't have to get the machinery grinding up from zero each time!

Now, your menu plans, in addition to the goal of providing interesting, nutritious dishes for your family in a timely manner, should also take into consideration this ongoing process of using your own stores of food to the best possible advantage ("selling high").

If there are bags of frozen broccoli (from when you cooked extra when making a side dish) at the bottom of your freezer (I will tell you below how to organize your deep freezer!), *and* whole chickens are on sale this week, then I would plan to make a big pot of broccoli soup. That way, you take advantage of both the stash you have and the bargain you can get.

Your menus shouldn't just be a reflection of what you feel like eating that week but also a judicious use of what you have on hand and what's on sale this week.

More on Lists and Shopping

Time to examine your list. It's essential to organize your list in the order you will shop for things, *not* in the order they occur to you. Arrange your list by aisle and fill in categories as you think of them. If you have a random list going, take a moment to rewrite it by grocery-store aisle; it will save you lots of time at the store. You have a mental picture of the store (enhance it by looking at those signs they have hanging over each aisle). You don't need a specially printed list; you just need to make your list visual.

If something is on sale, buy a few extra at least—if the price is below the lowest *normal* price for the item (see "Price Notebook," below). Your pantry should have depth to it, so that you are not always shopping for staples, but replenishing when sale prices are good. This is the backbone of saving money on groceries, and you won't see the effect for many months. But then your food budget will stabilize at a lower level.

When turkeys are on sale at Thanksgiving, buy a frozen one and put it in your deep freezer (at the bottom). When ground beef is on sale, buy twice as much as you need for that week. When zipper freezer bags are on sale, buy extra so that you have freezer bags to store your ground beef in!

When tomato paste is on sale, buy twice as much as you need—more if your budget allows for it—and store it in your pantry.

Beware of the sneak attack, price-wise, in the staples department. If you save on ground beef but at the same store pay much more for flour, sugar, canned beans, canned tomatoes, bread, milk, and so forth, then you haven't saved, and it would be worth it to shop where the basics are lower, even if the ground beef isn't on sale.

Big-Box Stores

I used to shop at the big-box store when I had more people to buy for. If your household is little, it's not worth the membership fee, unless you have a pet (pet food is a lot cheaper there) or the store sells alcohol (the ones near us don't). When I had enough shopping for both the big-box store and the supermarket, I could discipline myself to buy only the things that are truly cheaper at each. If you do all your shopping in a big-box store, you will spend much more. As an example, the last time I checked, although flour and sugar were cheaper there, pasta, rice, and other staples were considerably more. (This depends on your region, of course.)

Since right nearby is a good, large, cheap grocery store, I make the special trip to that one to get my large quantities, figuring that the membership fee goes a long way in paper products and other things I would have saved on.

Again, if you have a large family and pets, it could be worth it to go there. How to tell? You must know your prices!

Price Notebook

Do you know your grocery stores' prices well? To save money, you must know your prices! You do this by keeping a price notebook (until you eventually memorize the prices). Why? Let's work through it.

Grocery store A has a name that is designed to appeal to people like you and me, making us think we will save money there—something like "Super Thrifty" or "Cheapo's." And indeed, their flyer prominently displays seemingly amazing deals. Pork chops for ninety-nine cents? Chicken legs for thirty-five cents? Cheap. (Well, around here it is.) But I'm telling you, everything else in that store is much more than even at "Elegant Market"!

That means that unless you are willing to go there for the pork chops and go to another store where you know the prices on all the other things you need are 20 percent on average cheaper, you will end up spending more.

For instance, the same store advertising the cheap chicken legs has the mayonnaise you usually buy, and it's fifty cents *more* there than at store B. And the same for 90 percent of what you are going to put in your cart. Store A even advertises that mayo in its flyer *as if* it's a bargain! It's a total mind game—they are counting on your *not knowing* how much you pay for all those other things, the hundred little things you fill your cart with. They put the price of a dozen eggs in that flyer, as if it's a low price. They are assuming you don't know the average price of eggs in your area! Do you?

If you did your weekly shopping at this store, you would spend a lot more than anywhere else, regardless of the bargains. And I bet those pork chops are not cut right. Stay away from this type of place; it's simply not worth your time.

Keep a price notebook. Write down in a small notebook the *unit* price (price per pound, per ounce, per liter, per hundred, or what have you) of the things you buy. What kind of things? Everything, but especially the pricier things. Yes, there are bargains in beans, but you really need to know the *regular* prices of ground beef, flour, sugar, broccoli, bananas, apples, pork roasts, condiments, cans of tuna, bottles of ketchup, and so on. This is especially important for buying from Amazon, because Amazon doesn't list its prices by unit in a way that items can be efficiently compared, frustratingly. It's up to you to figure it out, which can take a lot of work—and your time is worth something!

Keep in mind that things such as eggs are tricky to figure out, because one dozen eggs does not necessarily equal another, even though each carton contains twelve eggs. You might need two small eggs to equal one jumbo, and on top of that, some stores' "large" eggs are another store's "small"! Really, eggs should be sold by the pound, and even that wouldn't work, since the shells of different-size eggs would weigh different amounts, not to get too picky about this. So you have to get smart on how you compare them, and intuition is sometimes needed.

I have noticed a trend in selling vegetables such as red peppers individually priced ("by the each," as they sometimes hilariously say!) rather than by the pound, which is incredibly obnoxious. Feel free to take them over to the scale and weigh them—then mark down the per-pound price in your notebook. Soon you will know what a good price on peppers is.

For most things, go by the amount in that orange square on the sticker on the shelf, not the price for the box, bottle, and so forth.

Start to note approximately how much snacks cost, for instance. White flour, oats, and sugar are in the one-dollar-a-pound region, and butter is in the two-dollars-a-pound region. But boxed prepared snacks can be from four to ten dollars a pound! Sometimes everyone needs to buy a box of granola bars, but it's really important to your budget to know how much you are paying for them *per pound* and to have it in your mind that, for instance, ribeye steak might be in the same price region! (Let's see, which would I prefer, a granola bar or a ribeye steak?)

Non-Food-Item Pricing

There's another area of price awareness that has to do with nongrocery items that you buy sometimes at the grocery store and sometimes elsewhere: toilet paper, laundry detergent, lotion, toothpaste, and so forth. Sometimes the grocery store has sales on these things; you might save yourself money and an extra trip by buying them at the grocery store, but you need to know the prices.

One of the very hardest items to price is toilet paper. In theory, there is a unit price, but unit of what? Squares? But the thickness of the paper affects how many squares one uses. And then there are fat rolls and tiny rolls and super soft rolls. Sometimes you are to be forgiven for not knowing how much you are paying, but do your best.

Spend a few weeks *paying attention* and *writing down*. Keep updating your notebook. Eventually you will know the prices by heart, and this will save you time when you are deciding whether a sale is really a sale or just a come-on. It will help when you are somewhere unusual and see a putative bargain. Things are tricky out there in grocery-store land. Sometimes the larger box of an item isn't cheaper, per unit, than the smaller, counterintuitively. Sometimes a discount store is expensive. Sometimes even a coupon doesn't make the purchase worth it, if you compare with the store brand.

The only way to navigate these waters is to know your prices.

Save a Step Cooking

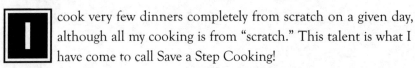

I cook very few dinners completely from scratch on a given day, although all my cooking is from "scratch." This talent is what I have come to call Save a Step Cooking!

Make menus with an eye to the little extra things you can squirrel away for another meal as you go about your normal cooking routine. Getting into this habit of saving steps will streamline your dinner preparations and make the kind of cooking that moms of big families have to do enjoyable—or at least not burdensome.

If you are clever, you can schedule your week so that you put in a big cooking effort on only one or two days—at the most—and usually you will take advantage of some time-saving steps you've done when it's convenient and efficient. You still make everything you want from scratch, but efficiently!

I think of this as "buy low, sell [use] high" as applied to the precious commodity of time. Use your time when it's plentiful—say, on a day when you are home for at least a morning, rather than doing errands all day—to build up a food stash for a day when you have little time (when time is "expensive" for you). Use the hour that you are already making a roast chicken to roast two chickens (or three!). This costs you no more in time for the actual roasting and only a little more for cutting the extra cooked chicken up and adding the bones to the stockpot. Later, when you need cooked chicken or chicken stock for a recipe, it will already be there for you.

To use another economics image: you are applying efficiencies and economies of scale by using your means of production to increase output. So, for instance, if you are already making bread, you increase the dough and make a couple of loaves to freeze. Even an extra pan of rolls in the freezer will take the edge off the work of a future meal. Your setup and cleanup are not significantly more, but you end up with a lot more of the product.

See, when you have put "meatloaf, mashed potatoes, peas, applesauce, rolls" on your menu list, you can make the menu lists of future weeks a lot easier if you make enough to produce two meatloaves plus a tray of meatballs and freeze what you aren't eating that day.

Save a Step versus Bulk Cooking

In contrast, the idea of bulk cooking that is often written about and promoted has you taking many steps all at once—shopping for many meals, cooking many kinds of foods—for later. Realities of life in a large busy family don't get factored in—nursing a baby, illness, extra guests ...

No matter how many articles I read about it, it's never going to happen that I get all my food using coupons or that I cook once a month and freeze all my meals. In forty years of doing this, it hasn't happened. But I'm still frugal, and I'm still fast. (I'm almost never on time, but I am fast.)

I'm committed to fresh, simple, delicious food, and I'm very efficiency-minded, being an engineer's daughter. If I find a coupon, I'll use it, because I like saving money, but coupons are not a system—not a food system. They don't get your dinner made every single day!

Bulk cooking is efficient in one way, but it doesn't address certain issues. One is that if you are like me, you get tired easily. (I bet you are stronger than I am, though!) Food is better made fresh, for the most part. So I just can't imagine my entire meal (as opposed to components of that meal) being defrosted. And I don't think one person with a very large family can do it all in one or two days.

I don't like the boom-and-bust way of doing things, perhaps because I'm too prone to burning out and then getting depressed. I like to be on an even keel, knowing that each day will have its own pace. Everyone experiences days of nonstop activity, but I'd rather not force myself into such days as part of a long-term plan.

If I cooked for a solid day or more (apart from the many hours it takes for a holiday dinner or another special occasion), I would not recover in time for the next bout! And then, what about nursing the baby, reading to the kids, and taking a nap? I couldn't have spent two days not doing *those* things!

Worst of all is the recommendation to prepare for the week ahead with a bulk cooking marathon on Sunday, when Sunday has enough for moms to do, and we, too, have to rest on Sundays!

I think it's a healthy thing for kids to know that Mom will usually be in the kitchen at a certain time getting things ready. They help, of course, and they also have those great free moments that seem like hours, with the smells wafting around them as they play or read. They need an opportunity to find you there, busy but also able to talk.

Those are great memories for them! Do we really want to eliminate that part of life? To do so would have the unfortunate consequence of enabling the frantic, activity-oriented child-rearing we see today, something that I am devoting this book to alleviating.

With Save a Step Cooking, you do *whatever you are already doing*, only you see how you can use the existing setup to give yourself a little edge later. The devoted mother does need to be organized and efficient; that calm presence in the kitchen relies on having set up a good rhythm in household management. In just a couple of short weeks, this system will pay off, and you will have even more free time to create efficiencies in even more areas as they occur to you.

By the way, my friend Sue wrote a ditty for our readers, since Save A Step Cooking is her idea, which I stole (well, I stole the name and most of our conversations). She is the most frugal person I know, and someday she will write a funny book in which she recounts to you the doings of her family of ten children. Meantime, this is what she offers you:

> Make ahead,
> Do the prep,
> Double up.
> Save a Step.

Use Your Menu Planning

Now, concretely, the menu planning stage is the place to do most of this thinking. I find it interesting that mothers of the past did what I'm suggesting as a matter of course, because they were very busy with many activities, many children, and few resources. Mothers like Ma Ingalls of the Little House books would make their roast (if they had one) on Sunday and then use what was left from it in the coming week. Even without freezers, they had a stash of preserved food, stale bread, and what have you that awaited clever use in many dishes. They used up the less stable items first, and then moved on to those that kept. They had common sense!

Here are some ways to get started on this today. You will think of lots of others. My point is this: Don't do all your work all at once. Work and stash as you go, saving your steps along the way.

1. *Plan for roasts at least two Sundays a month.* It's fairly easy to do, and everyone loves a roast with gravy. The frugal way to do this is to make whatever roast or large piece of meat is on sale. Try to get one that is at least a few pounds larger than what you would normally buy, or two chickens if you usually roast one, three if you usually roast two. It will repay you many times in the coming days! You can prevent people from eating too much meat by serving enough side dishes, along with hearty rolls. Make them take those first! (This strategy is behind such foods as Yorkshire puddings, the idea being that working men needed a little filling up with tasty gravy-soaked morsels — eggs and flour, for instance, being easier to come by than standing roasts — before they moved on to the meat. Wisdom.)

You don't have to take care of the leftovers right away. You can cover the pan with foil, put the whole thing in the fridge (if you have enough room; I do think a second fridge is worth the cost in a big, busy household), and deal with it the next day. Meat is easier to cut up when it's cold anyway.

I have been known to set a pot (with a tight-fitting lid, of course) out in the cold garage on the workbench when my fridge is full. However, once you get used to cooking this way, you will find it doesn't take very long to divide leftover meat into slices, chunks, and bones.

Wrap the meat up separately, labeling each package clearly. (Have supplies for this activity at your work station.) Many times I even divide leftover meat into categories based on the size of the chunk and whether it's white or dark meat. Label a package of small bits of ham "ham for soup" and one of lamb "roasted lamb for shepherd's pie."

Either wrap the bone up for freezing, or go ahead and start a stockpot as your family helps you clear up after dinner. Just throw the bones and any handy onion, carrot, and celery in, cover with water, and set to a boil. If you want, you can just do the bones and add vegetables at another stage. You can add leftover gravy if you won't be using it in the next two days. Certainly scrape any pan juices and drippings into the pot. All of that will enrich the broth nicely. There is not really any precision to this! Set the timer for two hours. Many is the time I've boiled down and burnt a pot of broth after leaving the kitchen! That's not thrifty!

Once the broth has cooked (the bones will be soft or, in the case of big meat bones, all the connective tissue will have boiled into the liquid, and any meat in there will be bland to the taste), pour it through a colander into a bowl large enough to allow quick cooling. Put it in the refrigerator until the next day. If you have ever tried vainly to get liquid fat out of a bowl of stock in a rush, you will thank yourself many times over for doing it this way. The next day (or the day after, up to a week—no rush), scrape off the fat (or lift it off in one piece, depending on the type of broth) and throw it away. Note: Some fat is well worth saving in a clean jar in the fridge: snow-white pork fat, duck fat, beef fat. You can roast your potatoes in it, and that will be lovely. Since I always have at least two jars of bacon grease in my fridge, I do not keep chicken fat.

Spoon the congealed broth into containers, leaving headroom (at least an inch, for expansion as the liquid freezes), and label them clearly. I write with a Sharpie right on my plastic containers. New writing goes right over the old. These containers can go in the freezer. Broth in the fridge that doesn't have a seal of fat on top will keep for about two days. With its layer of fat, it will keep for a week. This broth will be the lynchpin of your food stash, saving you many steps in the coming weeks.

Now, any recipes on your handy Master Menu List that call for cooked meat will be a breeze for you. Barbequed-pork sandwiches? Check. Chicken enchiladas? No problem. Ham and bean soup? Yup. Turkey potpie? Got it. Minestrone? The broth is already in the freezer, as are the ham pieces. You won't have everything you need for a given dish, of course, but you will be well on your way, without having knocked yourself out on an all-day cooking spree.

2. *Make more of whatever you are making.* Let's say that you have scheduled roast sweet potatoes in their jackets for a side this week. (Sweet potatoes are my favorite food. I love them so! Nothing could be easier, either. Just choose a bunch of uniform size, put them on a sheet of tinfoil on a baking tray, and roast them at 425 degrees. They make an awful mess as they ooze their sugars, so do use the foil. Then serve, split open, with a little butter and salt. Heaven!) Roast twice as many as you need, and let the extras cool completely. Then remove their skins, slice them into a container, and freeze. Another day you can have sweet potatoes as a side dish, premixed with butter and salt, without the hot oven or the messy tin foil.

Making a potpie? Can you make another one, even if it's smaller? I could never face making potpies on a day I was also making every other meal for the month, but if I'm already making one, it's not that hard to make another.

Making more is particularly important with baking. Making a pie? Make an extra crust or two—it will freeze perfectly if wrapped well, and then your potpie will be that much closer to realization.

Homemade bread freezes beautifully. Make sure the loaf has cooled completely—at least a couple of hours on a cooling rack. Sometimes I leave loaves out all night if I bake them at night—after all, bakeries do that! Then freeze, well wrapped. When it's defrosted, it tastes as if you baked it that day. You can wrap it in paper towel and microwave it in a pinch, and it will be just fine. It's always worth it to freeze at least a loaf or enough rolls for a meal.

If you are making cookies, scrutinize the recipe. It's almost not worth doing if you are not going to make extra. It takes so much time to get the ingredients out and mix them. Go ahead and make a quadruple batch! You can freeze the dough if you can't get to baking all the cookies now.

A lot of things can be frozen that you wouldn't expect, and it's easy enough to search online to find the answer. Ask yourself if you can make more for later, and then do!

3. *Save a Step on basic recipe building blocks.* Don't get caught without bread crumbs. Not only do you used them in many recipes, but any otherwise lame dish can be made so much more appealing with a topping of bread crumbs.

Save all the bread bits and bobs, and put them in the food processor. I used to balk at doing this because I didn't want to have to wash the processor out after such an insignificant use. Then I realized that either the crumbs are so dry and inert in terms of anything else I would put in the processor that a simple wipe would do, or I was going to use the processor soon after for something that would not be affected by my having processed crumbs in there; I could wash it afterward. (If the bread is very hard, use the blender instead. Don't forget that you can use a regular-mouth mason jar: the blade assembly fits and then your crumbs are already in the jar! Leave off the rubber gasket for dry grinding, as with crumbs, it tends to get pulled into the jar to disastrous effect.)

Put the crumbs in a ziplock bag, press out the air, and keep them in the freezer.

Almost every conceivable savory dish calls for chopped onion, minced garlic, and perhaps chopped peppers. Sauté up double, triple, or more, freezing the extra for next time. Go another step: if the recipe calls for doing all this with ground beef, cook a large amount and freeze the extra!

I can't count how many times my skin was saved, dinner-wise, by having this mixture in the freezer, ready to go. You can make spaghetti with meat sauce, chili, sloppy joes, meat enchiladas, burritos—all without firing up the skillet.

Most recipes using boneless chicken breasts are enhanced by pounding the breasts first. If I'm making boneless chicken breasts, it's almost certain that I'm in a rush! So when I buy them, I take them out of the package, pound them all, and repackage them in sets of three with a layer of plastic wrap in between the sets. They store all flat in a ziplock bag and are ready to go right out of the freezer—much better than trying to handle them half frozen and all bunched up.

You can also skip pounding, the object of which is to make the breasts an even thickness, by simply slicing into each breast partway to even up the thickness and opening it up like a book or fanning it out a bit so that heat can be distributed evenly.

Chopping nuts for a recipe? Why chop half a cup? Chop the whole package, and then freeze the extra. (Buy two packages if you think you will need whole nuts for something else.)

Even cutting up carrots and celery can get you a step ahead when you make your broth. Pop the bits you've trimmed (assuming they are not rotten) in a ziplock bag in the freezer. You will be all ready to go on Sunday evening when you get out that stockpot for the bones from your roast. By the way, mushroom stems, parsley stems, and parmesan cheese rinds are great additions to the stockpot. Just pop them in that same handy bag as you acquire them.

Making mashed potatoes? Drain the cooking water into a bowl, and then transfer it to a clean jar. Any bread recipe is enhanced by substituting potato water for some of the liquid. If it's salted, remember to adjust your recipe a bit. It keeps for a week or so in the fridge.

Cooking bacon? We have bacon at least once a week. That's a lot of bacon fat to throw away! Drain the fat into a clean jar and keep covered in the fridge (not in a can on the counter, no matter what your grandpa did). Use it to make your pancakes and as the shortening in savory pie crusts. If you decide one day to do a deep fry, use the bacon fat! It's so tasty.

4. *Store things well so they will help you later.* Make it a priority to do the best you can with what you have. If you buy a lot of broccoli, cook it all right away. Cooked vegetables save their freshness better than raw. You can use the leftovers in soups and casseroles or just reheat it if you didn't overcook them to start with, but a bunch of raw broccoli in the fridge will lose its savor pretty quickly.

Stocks and broths that have been strained into a bowl will keep very well under their seal of fat in the fridge for a week or so. But they won't keep forever! So keep track of what you have.

Put whole grains, nuts, flours, and spices in the freezer, well labeled. Left out, they go rancid and stale quickly.

If you are not inspired now, store the item in question for maximum freshness and decide later. You may come across just the right idea when you least expect it.

Do a little more when you can, not all at once. Now you are getting the idea. If you are cooking something anyway, think ahead and cook some more of that particular thing. Choose your dishes to produce other dishes another day.

Don't be afraid of leftovers. As long as they are handled correctly, leftovers are the goal here! Don't be afraid to build your stash and Save a Step!

Twelve Things to Stash That Will Help You Get Supper on the Table

Some people (who write articles you might see) scoff at the idea that you need to plan a week or more's worth of menus, or even that you can do it at all. They say you just need good recipes and nice fresh food. But these people, whom I sure we would find delightfully spontaneous and witty, should we ever meet them, simply don't have as many small children or teenagers as we do, and they undoubtedly have a sushi cart rolling right by them as they type. I bite my thumb at these people!

You really don't need recipes, which are all around you—you need menus.

How are you going to go shopping, efficiently, if you don't know *just* what to make? And how will you know just what to make if you don't figure out, once and for all, what you and your own particular family actually like to eat?

Yes, someday you will be so experienced that you can pull things together using what's on hand, at least some of the time; and certainly when the garden or farmer's market is burgeoning with fresh produce, supper seems to make itself and inspiration is just floating in the air, ready to be plucked and put to work. That's great, and you'll be happy knowing that you still know how to plan menus for meals if you need to.

Another thing: sometimes the menu doesn't work, no matter how careful you were to plan it with your day's activities in mind. Someone is sick, you forgot to defrost, you ran out of a key ingredient, someone ate the very thing you were counting on—these things happen!

You Need a Thought-Out Stash

So you do need a few things up your sleeve and in your stash—"anytime" resources that can be relied upon to fill the gaps. Once you understand how building a stash works, you can collect these resources as you move through your day in the kitchen and at the store.

One day, I had bread dough rising in the fridge, as I often do, and then I remembered about it and put it on the wood-burning stove, which I had just lit, so that it could come to room temperature and be baked.

Then I went into the other room, because experience has shown that I will definitely remember that I have something going on in the kitchen when I'm elsewhere, and nothing stupid will happen.

When I came back into the kitchen, the fire was roaring and the dough was risen, all right. In fact, the bottom half of it had started to bake (in the inadequately greased pan). What to do?

Well, I might be doomed to repeat some mistakes, but I knew that I could get something out of this mini disaster. Not a nicely baked big loaf of bread, but something. So I gently pulled off the part of the dough that wasn't already baking, formed it into a little focaccia-like lump, put it on a properly greased baking dish, and popped it into the oven, letting it continue its rise as the oven pre-heated. It was fine as a little bit of bread for the family at supper; actually, they loved it, which is so sweet of them and why I don't give up entirely in the face of my distractedness.

The other bit, the part in the pan, I just baked as it was. It was not lovely, and it was impossible to get out of the pan without serious hacking and muttering. The substance itself tasted fine and not even sour, as I thought it might after being prebaked on the wood stove. I could have used it for Breakfast Casserole (see the recipes in the appendices) or bread pudding, but I chose to make it into bread crumbs to stash away for another day.

Later and unrelatedly, one of my daughters remarked on how I am able to "pull out" things from the fridge, such as bread crumbs, to get supper together. Now that she's seeing it from her own perspective as a homemaker, she was wondering how it's done.

I kept reassuring her that it's something that comes with experience and, to be fair, definitely results from having a certain number of people around to cause the build-up of food you can later use in this seemingly magical way. Save a Step cooking (delved into above) is the best, most painless way to keep from having to come up with a meal from scratch every day or go broke trying.

I'm not going to list the usual things you find in magazines about what to have in your pantry. I take it for granted that we all know we shouldn't buy pasta one box at a time, and that jarred tomato sauce has its place. You have your cans of tuna and beans (or maybe some beans you've soaked and popped in the freezer). You understand that you need to have a supply of milk and eggs. You have rice.

But what else would be helpful to have around? I will tell you:

1. *Pie crust.* When you make a pie, make extra crust by doubling the recipe, form it into a disk, and stash it in the freezer well wrapped and labeled. A pie crust makes a small amount of stew (beef or chicken pieces with potato, carrot, and peas or really any braised meat and vegetables) into that wonderful, magical, filling substance known as potpie. One pie crust, rolled out thin, can make a tasty galette (an open tart piled with any little tidbits and free-formed by folding the edges of the crust back over the top) that rounds out a pot of soup or some leftover slices of meat or what have you. Sweet-potato galette with sage, onions, and goat cheese is delicious. Just pile the ingredients on your pie crust in layers and bake.

2. *Pieces of ham.* A reader asked me what kinds of things I would make with the little bits, since I'm always referencing them. *What wouldn't you make?*

Soup is better with bits of ham. Mac and cheese becomes dinner with pieces of ham. Galette (see number 1, above) is heartier with little bits of ham strewn upon it. You can make Hawaiian pizza if you also have a can of pineapple in the pantry. You can toss pasta with ham and green beans and feed eight people with half a cup of meat. So next time you serve ham, carefully divide the leftovers into nice slices, chunks, bone, and little bits you've taken off the bone (although you don't have to be obsessive about it since the meat on the bone is good for the soup). Place each sort in its own ziplock bag, label it, and stash it away.

3. *Pieces of bacon.* You'll have to squirrel these away before the barbarians attack breakfast, but even two slices (I always get thick-cut bacon) will crumble up nicely on a salad with blue-cheese dressing. That galette I mentioned above will be lovely with bacon. You can add crumbled bacon to mayo to make lettuce, cheese, and tomato sandwiches that aren't BLTs but do have a sort of bacon-y aura.

4. *Stock.* When you have a roast (and making a roast on Sunday is the best way to keep work to a minimum on Sunday and still serve a nice dinner and also save plenty of steps for the weeks ahead), put all the bones in a pot with the bits of onion, carrot, and celery that you've collected along the way (see "Save a Step Cooking"; you can keep those in a plastic bag in the freezer as well, along with parsley stems and mushroom bits). Add any pan drippings if you haven't already used them for gravy or sauce.

It's not beyond me to ask the family to put their chicken bones in the pot when they're clearing their plates. Add water, and simmer it for the rest of the evening (it doesn't take days, as some think) with a tablespoon of vinegar, if you remember it. Even if you add nothing, just simmer the bones. Then strain the liquid into a bowl over a colander and set the bowl in your fridge (sometimes in winter I put the pot, with the lid on it, on the workbench in the garage; being able to handle such things is a good reason to have a second fridge but sometimes even that gets full!).

The broth will keep with its layer of undisturbed fat for a week or more. Before using or storing the broth, scrape off the fat (you can keep it if you want—I usually don't if it's chicken, as I have lots of bacon grease handy, but I keep duck and goose fat, for pâtés and roasted potatoes). Pour the stock into mason jars (leaving two inches of headroom), and freeze or use within a day or so of removing the fat. Defrost stock by putting the jar in a container of cold water, completely submerged (you can crack a jar if you only put it in only partway); after about fifteen minutes, you can slowly microwave it or add warmer water to your container.

Stock is essential. With stock you are ready for any gravy or nice sauce, and you can make good, hearty soup. The stock you buy at the store, even in the pricier organic brands, has many additives, often soy or MSG in some hidden form, to give it the umami taste that homemade has with the addition of celery or mushrooms. Homemade stock is not hard to stash (boil it down if you have space issues—you can add water later), and it's so good for you!

5. *Pieces of cooked chicken.* When your supper of roast chicken is over (and remember, you should never roast fewer than two chickens at a time), separate it into big pieces, bones, and little bits. The latter will be your special stockpile for chicken salad sandwiches, chicken Caesar salad, and chicken quesadillas. Making chicken soup with your stashed broth? Add a cup of pieces of cooked chicken at the end, and the meal will stick to your family's ribs.

6. *Cabbage, carrots, celery, and apples* in your fridge drawer. In winter especially, when you can't get to the store for fresh veggies, you can always pull out ingredients for one of my three favorite side dishes: coleslaw (shred cabbage and carrots, toss with mayo, vinegar, a little sugar, salt, and cumin), carrot sticks (obvious), and Waldorf salad (cut up celery and apple, add raisins or dried cranberries, toss with chopped nuts such as pecans, and dress like coleslaw minus the cumin, or with it, for that matter).

7. *Garlic-ginger paste.* This is easy to make by crushing equal amounts of fresh garlic and ginger and adding a teaspoon of salt for every quarter cup of the resulting paste. Keep it in the fridge. Add the paste to coleslaw along with bacon or cashews. The paste also makes stir-fry fast and extra authentic.

8. *Sausage and beef mix.* When Italian sausage and ground beef are on sale, buy extra packages of each. Then fry and drain the meat, divide it up, store it in ziplock bags, and freeze. With this mix you can make spaghetti sauce, chili, tacos, shepherd's pie—all super fast. Always make more than what you need for the dinner you're cooking, because you will use it, trust me.

9. *Cooked veggies.* Cook your green beans, sweet potatoes, squash, peas, whatever—with another meal in mind. They keep well in the fridge (make sure you know how to cook your green vegetables to the proper point and no further). Two days later, pull them out and heat them up. Most veggies (not green beans, it's true, although even those will work in minestrone or stew) freeze fine. A part of me dies a little when I see a recipe for a casserole that instructs you to cook its elements separately. That takes so long! Plan potpie after you have previously cooked the meat and veggies and want a delicious way to serve the leftovers.

10. *Frozen corn.* Suki says that corn makes everything better. It's true. You can add it to potpie, chili, or soup to stretch it out a bit as well as make it tastier. Peas and spinach are also good to have in the freezer for when you don't have another fresh veggie on hand.

11. *Bread dough* in the fridge. Almost any dough will be just fine in the fridge, rising there slowly until you are ready for it. Homemade bread makes the simplest meal seem wonderful and warm. You can always make supper of a tray of dough, spread out, topped with your sausage and beef mix (see number 8) and cheese. Cheeseburger pie! Delish!

12. *Bread crumbs.* The most ordinary casserole is just a million times better with a layer of toasty bread crumbs on top. Use any regular-mouth mason jar with your blender blade[4] to grind them. (You may be able to source a

---

[4] Don't use this blender trick with hot liquids—there's no room for expansion and the glass could break. It would be great to source a couple of plastic mason jars for this purpose. Making a frozen drink works well with this method—it's ready to drink right out of the jar. When grinding dry ingredients, leave the rubber gasket off, as it has a tendency to be pulled in and chopped up.

plastic mason jar, which would be best and safest for this purpose.) Collect all those heels of bread and leftover toast—you can keep them in a bag in the freezer until you are ready to grind them.

With bread crumbs you can quickly make chicken breasts with a thin spread of mustard, topped with buttery crumbs or mac and cheese for dinner. Your meatloaf and meatballs need them. And does your market sell thrifty bags of red peppers? Cut the peppers in half, or in quarters if they are large, and arrange them on an oiled pan. Mix some kind of cheese (goat, feta, or even cream cheese), with some bread crumbs, parsley, and maybe a small amount of finely diced tomato or sundried tomato; drop a tablespoon of the mixture onto each piece of red pepper; top with a little grated parmesan; and roast for twenty minutes at 400 degrees. Serve with a pasta dish. You can't pull that one out of a hat without bread crumbs, but you could serve it at your best dinner party!

Save a Step at Breakfast

Now that you have mastered the dinner-menu idea, let's do breakfast.

Do you wonder why your kids are crabby? Are there meltdowns at your house as you start math? Do you have a child who gets headaches? Do you feel shaky sometimes? There must be breakfast. Cereal alone doesn't cut it. Children will be better off having some protein and fat; some even need to wait a bit before eating.

Do the same thing with your breakfast menus as you did with dinner: find out what everyone really wants to eat, and add your special dash of common sense and practicality. Then make a shopping list based on your preferences.

For breakfast, the process will be simpler than for dinner, because most people eat more or less the same thing every day for breakfast. I find that I just need to have a few basic breakfasts ready to go; the creativity comes in with Sunday's breakfast, which at our house is usually quite hearty.

Breakfast must have protein, and milk alone isn't enough. Personally, I am subject to fits of low blood sugar, and I am aware of how I don't function unless well fortified.

A teacher tells about a high school student who seemed really hungry by midmorning. When the suggestion was made that the child needed to eat breakfast, the student's mom's response was a dreamy "yes, that would be a good idea"—she seemed unaware that it was her task to accomplish this goal!

If your child is involved in a sport along with other after-school activities, has a lot of homework, and goes to bed a bit later than he should, he is not going to be able to get breakfast and make himself a lunch to pack unless you make it possible by shopping and doing some of the prep work.

So there is flexibility but also the need to manage the whole process. At our house, the weekday breakfast selection looks like this (recipes are included in the appendices):

- Toasted bagels and cream cheese. My local supermarket has a store brand of good bagels with unobjectionable ingredients; I stock up on cream cheese, which stores well, when the price is good.
- Eggs, scrambled or fried, with shredded cheese and any leftover breakfast meat crumbled in; toast with plenty of butter.
- Papa's Special (method in appendix A)
- Pancakes on the weekends, with breakfast meat left over from during the week crumbled into the batter. (This is incredibly easy with my pancake mix.)
- Oatmeal Porridge Like Mother, Like Daughter—filling and yummy. I confess that we don't eat this often, because I'm too spacey to get it ready the night before, but when I do, it's appreciated! Also, leftovers are easily microwaved; make a big pot.
- Cereal. Since mostly we like eggs or bagels, there isn't a lot of cereal consumption around here. But it is handy in a rush, if used cautiously and with guidelines:
  1. Mix the cereal. At first, this concept was not appealing to me. But then I saw that if you insist that a child mix a small amount of sugary cereal with granola, the child is happy and you know he's getting more; it's actually tasty. No eating even whole-grain Cheerios by themselves around here. And by sugary, I mean what most people consider health food. The really sugary ones are not for breakfast or even for anything at all.

2. Make your own granola.
3. Include a piece of hearty toast with lots of butter, some yogurt, or a piece of cheese. Teenagers will get away from you on this, but by that age, they know how they'll feel by ten o'clock—it's up to them. But no six-year-old is having a bowl of cereal and calling it breakfast!

A lot of this can be done by the children themselves. I let them more or less choose, although if someone is feeling wan or acting up, I make him some eggs.

Not all breakfasts must feature hot food. Do you know what Egyptian children eat for breakfast? Pita bread, feta cheese, and olives. Sometimes eggs with dates and fava beans mixed in (the Egyptian version of which is like refried beans).

You decide if you will have everyone eat the same thing or if you will let each choose and make his own. Do track how much chaos ensues if everyone is pulling things out, toasting, scrambling, and so forth, and think through the system so that you aren't left with an exploded kitchen when they've all departed.

Here, we each get what we want during the week, I fix some things for some people, if they want. When the kids were little, I got their breakfast for them. On Sunday, I make one big breakfast for all, often featuring something someone has requested. Do what you want! But do it.

All of this decision making works its way to your grocery list. Try to figure out how many packages of bagels you use in a week. Next week, adjust. Store extras in your big freezer.

Buy more than enough eggs. Eggs are cheap. They last. You want to get many dozens at a time, so that you'll have a good supply for more than a week.

Buy good sharp *shredded* cheddar cheese along with the brick form, if you find that it's no more per pound. Add shredded cheese to scrambled eggs to make them heartier. If the cheese is already shredded, you are more likely to use it than if you have to shred it yourself.

Stock up on oats and other grains for porridge. Buy a few cartons of buttermilk. (I don't hold with dry buttermilk. By my calculations it seems much more expensive, and buttermilk isn't going to spoil around here with all the pancakes and biscuits everyone likes!)

Get extra bacon on sale, cook it on Sunday morning, tuck some away before the family gets at it, and hide it way back in the fridge or in the freezer to use during the week. Same with sausage.)

Don't practice false economy by skimping on breakfast. What you spend in bagels you will reap in snacks: the pricey fruit roll-ups can be foregone if the tummy is anchored.

Process Veggies for the Freezer

Gardening helps a lot with the food bill. Having some of your own home-grown produce stashed away couldn't be more satisfying, and you don't need a lot of room to grow at least some of your food! Here are my issues with putting up veggies in the freezer. Maybe you can relate—probably not if you grew up on a farm, but maybe if you have tried a little garden too.

1. The veggies are not all the same size. The ones you buy at the store are, the ones you pick are not, whether we are talking about beans, peas, broccoli, or asparagus, which are what I'm likely to be dealing with in this manner. This bothers me into paralysis.

2. There are often not enough all at once to process, but too many to eat right away. Stalemate.

3. What exactly is blanching, how is it different from plain old cooking, and no matter how well you define it, I will still feel that I'm doing it wrong. More paralysis.

4. I don't have a vacuum sealer thingy. Wandering around ... looking for a book.

5. Even if I go through it all the way you are supposed to, won't they come out mushy and gross, like regular frozen veggies you buy? (I like frozen corn and peas, but broccoli and beans—sort of unpleasant.) Feeling the energy draining out of me.

I think I've conquered my anxieties.

1. Sort them into sizes. Let's say we're talking about green beans: teeny baby ones, medium ones, sort of leathery ones that might be good in a stew, and ones that need to be shelled.

2. Do this over a few days as things ripen out there; nothing bad will happen. Keep them in a cool place covered with a towel or refrigerate.

3. Before freezing the extra harvest, blanch it. Blanching just means boil quickly—we can do this. It brings the food to the temperature at which the enzymes that cause breakdown will be killed without fully cooking it. The books say boil three minutes but with super little beans or tender snow peas, just cook until they brighten slightly—maybe between one and two minutes. Use your common sense, and you will be okay. See a useful resource, *Putting Food By*, by Ruth Hertzberg, Janet Greene, and Beatrice Vaughan, in the latest version (which will have all safety updates). The book is up my alley, being chatty and also strict about stuff that you should be strict about.

4. Use ziplock freezer bags, and simply press the air out, or suck the air out with a straw. It might be undignified and a little dizzying in the heat, but it works fine.

Five Food Thoughts

It seems pretty clear that keeping food simple, making (and even growing) our own if possible, and avoiding highly processed food makes a difference to our health and to our finances. And then we venture into the topics of "organic" and "grass fed" and "locally produced," and it all seems so complicated again.

It's funny how even the question of which potatoes to buy relates to our goals and our vision, isn't it? We have to know what our "things" are if we are going to make "first things first." It's paralyzing to contemplate the many facets of a very elemental issue in our lives: food.

One important point: we can't always be throwing out all our resolutions when a new one comes along! Who needs this revolving door of anxiety, I ask you? The prudent thing is to make do with what we have and with our own limitations, staying calm and trying always to learn more.

I care about food; too much so, actually! Once Suzanne and I were laughing together about how we have to remind ourselves to do something other than cook, clean up, and eat!

Branch out a little with some other activities once in a while!

Instead of having crises over food, whether about its production, purchase, preparation, quantity, quality, or any other issues, may I suggest a few key "first things," ordering principles if you will, that help me to stay on the right track?

1. We are committed to living on one income, with my role being to make the home on the day-to-day basis. Being the homemaker isn't drudgery; it's the most creative thing most people will ever do! It's important because it brings peace to your family.

But yes, that means that I put a lot of effort into making good, wholesome, healthy food for a large family, and yes, our budget was always tight when our children were growing up. I've made up my mind to accept these realities.

2. We have to trust that God sees that we are doing our best. Ultimately, our well-being depends on Him. We can't guarantee good health or good fortune merely by our efforts; far less by trusting in our dollars to bring us security. Our priority has been to have good family life for the nurturing of the whole person entrusted to us. Health, as good a gift as it is, isn't something to worship or to lose peace over.

3. This excellent observation from Joel Salatin expresses what I think (not just about food, either): "Now that the high prices [of food labeled "organic"] have attracted unscrupulous growers who enter the movement for the money, people realize that no system can regulate integrity."

No system can regulate integrity.

As parents, we have to use our common sense. Just because something seems to promise purity doesn't mean that it will deliver. Just because it's labeled "organic" doesn't mean it's better for you or even that much different from the one that isn't labeled that way.

There are serious issues with our food production, but I personally am not in much of a position to change things on a large scale. Sometimes I remember my trip to Egypt when I was a girl. I remember the meat hanging out in the market (on a hot day, of course) with flies all over everything. There are always going to be problems.

At some point, we have to trust that if we do our best, we don't have to worry. (We shouldn't be worrying anyway. It's pointless.)

4. I have to accept where I live. If I were to "buy local" all year, I'd be living on kale and parsnips for a good bit of it.

Maybe some of you live somewhere with a desert climate. Maybe you live in California, and I am not bitter about your CSA box being all avocados, blood oranges, and strawberries (although these things also come at a price in water use). Be realistic and thankful that you *can* get food from elsewhere if you need to.

When you are able, get your food from nearby, but don't make this a stress point. I do appreciate that the smallish supermarket (with good prices, for which I'm grateful) where I usually shop often sources things from our area. The reality is that, in our climate, this means that the local produce begins appearing in July, and by the beginning of October, it's all gone, other than the winter squash, which I have a bunch of already, from my garden!

My meat and veggies might not be labeled organic, but they are very good. And my ice cream is amazing and is made right here in New England, so I'm all set! But it's not my first priority for things to be organic *or* local, because I'm not convinced that it ought to be.

We are amazingly blessed in our country to have good food, basically when we need it. If things are otherwise for you, you will have to get clever (and start a little homestead farm). But do it peacefully.

5. If I return to the system I've devised, knowing what's for dinner (and lunch, and breakfast), and Saving a Step as I work, and knowing that my stash will support me in a pinch, I can provide simple, wholesome food for my family (thanks to my dear husband, who works hard and provides so well). My system doesn't wear me out, and I don't think it will wear you out either. You can still nurse the baby, go to the kids' games, and even read a book—most days.

My system will work for your family because you can tailor it according to all your needs. It will help you take into account your schedule; you'll finally figure out how to have the meal you need for a rushing-around day, a leisurely feast day, an ordinary day—whatever you have going on, you will be ready, because you will key your meal planning to your calendar. Your food will be as much from scratch as you hope it will be, but you won't be in the kitchen all day—unless you want to be!

Even with lots of kids and not much money, you can eat well. You must work at it; don't get me wrong. And you won't be able to buy everything at that upscale organic national chain, but as Salatin explains, you probably shouldn't even want to, even if you could afford it.

Thrifty Eating on the Road

When, for one reason or another, you are on the road and need to eat, consider packing food for nutrition and frugality—and also because it will likely be much better than what you can buy, even supposing the option is available. Here are some suggestions:

- A loaf of sliced bread with jars of peanut butter and jelly, plus plastic knives. *Don't* make the sandwiches ahead: avoid the risk of a smooshed, soggy, unappetizing mess.
- Cheese and crackers, especially with a bit of dried fruit on each one. Cheese and crackers might not excite you if you are getting the bland versions of the key ingredients. Try the sharpest cheddar you can find and the nicest crackers. Brand-name crackers have a lot of salt and sugar in them. Try water crackers, pita chips, or any other European-style ones. Usually they are crisper and let the cheese shine through. A little dab of fig jam on each one is so tasty, and kids love it.
- Sandwiches with cold cuts and cheese. Try buttering the bread the way Germans and Hungarians do, with a little brown mustard on one slice.
- Summer sausage, cheese, crackers, baby carrots, and fruit.

- Hard-boiled eggs with a little container of salt (try a seasoned salt of your own making, adding dried parsley, chives, dry mustard, or cumin) for dipping.
- A hot container of refried beans in a cooler, a bag of tortilla chips, and some shredded cheese for spooning on-the-go nachos. Make this your first course, to avoid having the beans cool down to the point at which they are not safe anymore.

For a baseball-game kind of picnic, take a good, heavy, cast-iron pot and fill it with the bean soup of your choice. When the soup is good and boiling, and has been boiling for at least ten minutes, set it in a cooler padded thoroughly with towels or a cheap camping-style "emergency blanket" in case of spills. Some muffins on the side will round it out.

Plain yogurt is easy to flavor with jam, and Greek yogurt doesn't make much of a mess. I make my own by straining a whole batch of yogurt at once with a potato-sack towel set in a colander over a bowl. (I use the whey in my breads and as a substitute for buttermilk in pancake and such-like recipes.)

- Any kind of pocket bread or pastry type of dish: calzones, pasties, empanadas, and so forth
- A container of hummus, or one of guacamole, or both, and pita or tortilla chips
- Chicken salad, along with a loaf of bread, some large lettuce leaves for wrapping, or tortilla chips
- Nuts

For something more along the lines of supper, cold fried chicken is always delicious! You could put it in a cooler, and bring some heated baked beans in a thermos. If everyone has a thermos or if you have one large enough to share, red beans and rice (perhaps with ham or sausage included) works well.

If it's an evening game that is throwing you off, have your big meal at lunchtime and something more snacky at supper.

How about keeping a "picnic bag": pick up plates, cups, bowls, and silverware from yard sales and such. It cuts down on forgetting important items, because you store them in the bag. The bag with the silverware also contains a can opener and a wooden spoon. Wash the items later and return them to the bag for reuse.

Organizing Food:
Refrigerator and Freezer Talk

 f you follow my "buy low, sell [eat] high" recommendations, and of course you should, you will soon find that you have to organize your rapidly filling freezer space.

When your family is small, if you have the opportunity to choose, prioritize a refrigerator with a larger freezer area, preferably one large enough to have a shelf. Eventually, you may find that a second fridge is helpful (especially because, if you follow that advice, your fridge area will necessarily be smaller, but your children will be drinking a lot of milk, which takes up so much space). Also prioritize a large freezer in that second appliance.

You can get along for quite a while with these two fridge freezers. Think in terms of what the best cost-space ratio is: you will save more money by freezing meat you've gotten on sale than in freezing bread, which is bulky and not as pricey (though it's not cheap either; I feel your pain). Don't waste precious space on items that don't save you much money when you stockpile them.

Eventually, if your family gets large enough, you will *also* need a deep freezer. I prefer a chest style on the grounds that it is more energy efficient.

The food stays fresher for a longer time, because an upright freezer has to go through a defrost cycle, meaning that the temperature fluctuates, with a negative effect on long-term quality.

Organizing the Chest Freezer

The problem is that a chest freezer is quite the challenge to organize! For the longest time, I had been put off by the thought of a large chest of food with everything all tumbled in there, covered in frost, unidentifiable, trackable only by the use of a clipboard—only how are the inventory and actual items correlated if the latter are all thrown in?

Here's my low-tech solution:

In the produce section of the grocery store, you will be able to catch at certain times the stock boy piling up nice sturdy cardboard boxes that have plenty of holes for ventilation; these often have handle grips punched in the sides. Nab a few of these in various sizes; you can always put them in your own recycling if they don't work.

Broadly and mentally divide up your food into categories, such as big roasts, precut meats, breads, produce, and partially cooked stashed food (which I explain in "Save a Step Cooking"). Use a box for each kind of thing (or miscellaneous smaller items that tend to get lost in the deep freezer).

Stagger the boxes as you pile them up, with the big roasts below or between them. You see that not every single thing goes in a box: the boxes are for organizing anything that is not a large ham or a leg of lamb or a big carton of hamburger patties.

I'm very visual, so I found that the extra step of recording the freezer's inventory on a clipboard did nothing to help me keep track of all the undifferentiated frozen things in that big chest. Instead, every week or so, as I'm making my menus and grocery list, I lift out my boxes to see what's in there. (This is made significantly easier if you remember to label everything, so keep a Sharpie handy in the kitchen. And in case you've forgotten to label something, keep a Sharpie by the freezer as well, along with paper towels to dry off the plastic so you can write on it.) The box method is simpler than keeping up a written inventory, but it's definitely compatible with it if you do want to have a written record.

If you have an upright freezer, arrange the boxes on the shelves. You can pull the boxes out like drawers to remove the items you need so that frozen items aren't constantly in danger of sliding out and burying you or breaking your foot.

I keep bread in the section that the freezer manufacturer helpfully divided off with a rack, over the motor, which you may or may not have. If not, fruit box to the rescue!

The wire basket that perhaps came with your freezer holds the little odds and ends that would otherwise fall to the bottom. If you don't have one, it might be worth scavenging one from the recycling center or online; the basket uses space at the top of the freezer that might otherwise be lost. I might use this basket to hold freezer bags containing small amounts of ham for soup, breakfast sausage rolls, a concentrated broth of some sort in a jar, a bag of frozen fruit that I've already opened, or a small container of ice cream that I'm saving for a treat. A lot fits in this way but it's never just a pig pile. The pig pile is the downfall of the deep freezer, and what makes it so scary: things (often small) are there at the bottom; not only have you forgotten them, but you can never really reach them (if you're short like me, anyway). The boxes solve this problem.

A Handy Surface

You'll need a horizontal surface of some sort next to your freezer—any narrow table or shelf will do; mine was a roadside find. There is no way to avoid frequently moving items around in the freezer, and you need a separate holding place for this activity. When you are putting things away after shopping or simply rummaging, you can set things down on the shelf or table instead of on the garage or basement floor, while you reorganize. Long-term success with freezer organization depends on the boxes and on this staging surface.

You do have to *think* each time you put things in. Sometimes, for instance, bread has to be put near the meat so that it freezes solid before you can fit it into the bread section without crushing it. So there might be a brief period of seeming "disorganization" while newly added items freeze properly, but then, when the meat is well frozen, the bread is safely hard, and so forth, you can apply logical storage by category. You are never quite done with food storage, I find!

The Real Secret to Planning Menus and Having Peace in the Home

We will start with a reader's question, and then I will tell you the secret that will set you on your way to success in homemaking.

Dear Auntie Leila,

I can't get past the step of making a huge list of potential meals. My husband and kids aren't much help. My kids, five years old and under, can't tell me what they want to eat because their likes and dislikes seem to change from day to day! My husband says, "Make what you want!" I feel paralyzed when I sit down to think about it. I don't like being in the kitchen anyway, so the thought of all the time I'll be spending making this stuff and then cleaning it all up is depressing, to say the least.

Then the dilemma of what to make? Should I stick with fun and delicious, but decidedly not-healthy things? Grandma's Jello fluff salad? Chicken-cream cheese pockets made with Pillsbury crescent roll dough? Nigella's pasta? Then there's that diet plan I'd theoretically like to follow, to lose the last little bit of baby weight (or, since I'm newly pregnant, to keep from gaining my usual sixty pounds).

Will my kids even eat what I fix? If I make something they like one day, they'll turn up their noses the next day, or one child will love it and the rest won't touch it, which definitely adds some unpleasantness to our mealtimes. Then there's the health angle to consider: Am I struggling with anxiety, depression, and exhaustion because I'm gluten/dairy/soy/sugar/food-intolerant and don't know it? (Or is it just because I'm a constantly nursing or pregnant mom—sometimes both—and life is hard!) I used to eat anything, all the time, and it didn't make me anxious. In fact, it was rather enjoyable. Should I be drinking kefir and making my own bone broth and fermented sauerkraut? Would that magically make me a new person?

And then don't even get me started on the budget side of groceries. Yes, we are very poor, and the less we spend on food, the better, but since sticking to a tight budget seems impossible, we don't even try! My husband says, "Spend what you need to!" and I take him up on it because why stress myself?—even though it still stresses me because I know we're spending too much! Help!

Love,

Frazzled

——————————————

Dear Frazzled, and all of you out there who *know* you should be making menus, however simple (also known as planning what you will eat for at least a week so that you are not spending all day staring at a package of ground beef and wanting to run away to a circus or a convent or anywhere where they will just plunk a plate in front of *you*); dear reader who needs help overcoming this obstacle to the first step of a life of peace and order, *which is making the menus*: the secret of the French and the Finns and all the other cultures with which we are daily browbeaten, who are so superior to us and never feel overwhelmed by the necessity of feeding their families:

> Every person in the house must be polite and respectful and grateful for the food that is served.

If anyone doesn't like it, that's okay. Lots of people don't like lots of things. They can even let you know what their preferences are. But it must all be done kindly and with courtesy.

Talk to your husband about training your children to speak respectfully to you about the food. It will require both of you to make an effort, but you can do it, and honestly, a requirement is that you—husband and wife—speak to each other kindly and respectfully about everything.

All this won't happen on its own. Training must occur, and you must do the training. It will take time and not happen overnight. But one day you will realize that it's a pleasure and not the burdensome task you imagine to plan your menus (relatively speaking) because it's a pleasure to sit down and eat with your family.

How to bring this impossible state of affairs about? Auntie Leila will take you through the steps.

1. *Talk to your children beforehand about what they are and are not allowed to say.* I grew up being told, "We don't say 'hate' about the food." I wasn't even allowed to say "stuff" as in "What is this stuff?" My stepmother thought it was disrespectful. Begin by saying, "We don't say that about the food." Work up to making it clear that if *one word* that is not polite—"Oh, gross." "Yuck!" "I hate this!" "I'm not eating this!" and so forth—comes out of their mouths, they will leave the room. You will know when enough is enough.

I would not threaten loss of dessert. We are trying to cultivate true enjoyment here (see number 4). Simultaneously, give your children the exact script that you want to hear from them. "This looks delicious." "Thank you, Mama." "I like the [mention something they do like here]." "You are a good cook, Mama." "Don't worry about the burned green beans, Mama; it's okay." (This last one often has to be said to me, for some reason.)

An option: Silence.

2. Surround your meals with ritual. Whether, as sometimes happens, you feed the children first or they are sitting with you at supper, and no matter how simple the meal, have the table set beforehand (note I do not say *you* set it beforehand—distribute tasks as necessary and possible). Light a candle.

Teach your children not to eat until Mama has sat down. Daddy has to do this. He must wait for his beloved wife to collect herself. Of course, he has pitched in with the prep (perhaps by distracting hungry children elsewhere) and then sat down to model patient waiting. There is something shocking, in the normal course of things, about a man who begins eating before his wife has collected herself or guests have been served. When Mama sits or otherwise indicates she is ready, he leads grace.

For a ritual to occur, you must be prepared. Rituals are never spontaneous. Great care goes into their maintenance. It's up to you to realize that every single day you will need a drink, glasses, napkins, silverware, serving utensils, salt, pepper—a whole host of things! Instead of getting those items *after* everyone is seated, as if visited by a daily revelation regarding these matters, think it through beforehand. Keep the things close to or on the table, possibly on a tray. Minimize fuss at the table by supplying what

Here is my dear friend Emily's solution to one of the tasks:
a utensil caddy. This honestly never occurred to me, but I think
it's delightful. Later, another one could be added and they can be
kept on a sideboard nearby if the table becomes too crowded.

is necessary with forethought. Try not to be continually surprised by the things you need.

Even the other meals need a bit of ritual, appropriate to their lesser status, but still, this sense of orderly preparation will considerably enhance the experience. If you take care of the details beforehand, you will notice that when you sit down and pray, there is peace. The agitation comes from jumping up, not being ready, and general disorder due to lack of forethought.

3. *Every member of the family should bend over backward to be sure that every other member is well supplied with what he needs and what he prefers.* I have a friend who says that her father would take the sweet part of the watermelon on the grounds that he was the father. Well, this is not my experience of fatherhood, based on how my husband acts. He holds back and makes sure that I have what I like. If left to himself, he takes the least appealing portions. He notices what the quantity of food is and how it will be distributed. I usually have to urge him to take the last bite of something left on a platter or in a bowl.

Actually, I have to watch like a hawk lest all my family members leave at least what amounts to one small serving, no matter what the quantity of food has been, such is their habit of restraint. Sometimes I have been known to insist—with a sense of gratitude for their forbearance, but still, to insist—that ten people surely can manage to relieve us of the burden of putting away a quarter of a cup of chicken potpie or one lone broccoli spear.

But this forebearing attitude comes from habits instilled long ago: to have consideration for others and their needs. Even small children can helpfully pass what is next to them and can notice what other family members especially enjoy.

In volume 1, I told of a priest friend, a monk who hails from a large family, who had mentioned the principle of FHB: "Family Hold Back." This means that when there are guests, the family is already aware that something might run out, and so they hold back to be sure that the guests have enough—a simple guideline for hospitality, but a beautiful one. This kind of courtesy comes with practice! Practice with each other.

Young children can be taught to jump up and get the butter or the marmalade. Rowdy boys can be encouraged to pick up someone's dropped napkin. Older kids who aren't absolutely riveted by the adults' discussion of the latest world crisis can take the baby for a turn.

4. *Enjoy the food, however humble it is.* One issue with grumpy children is that we parents (and mothers in particular) do not feel free to enjoy our meal and to be confident that we did our best, however humble. We are hovering over our children with great anxiety that they (a) eat enough to ward off sudden expiration and (b) affirm and approve of us. We somehow feel that our worth as parents hinges on how they behave at the table, and yet we do not supply them with the proper behavior or even attitude. Thus, grumpiness occurs.

If someone truly does not like something, he can, if asked, answer, "It's not my favorite." That is the extent of the negativity! For instance, if offered more liver and onions (after his one bite which he must eat unless you know it's a real aversion), the child may observe, "No, thank you, I'm full." If pressed, he might say, "It's not my favorite." He can certainly have more of whatever else is offered, especially bread and butter. However, and see number 3, he can't hog the delicacies, because that is rude.

It's possible that a given child is simply too young to be at the supper table. It's fine to feed that child earlier and either let him sit up at the table with some bread and butter or play quietly nearby. Maybe dinner can be scheduled late enough so that he can go to bed early after his own simple meal.

5. *When finished (and for a small child, this might be in ten minutes), each person should thank the cook.* "Thank you, Mama, for this nice meal; may I be excused?" When your husband thanks you, thank *him* for being a good provider. (Remember Ma and Pa Ingalls in the Little House stories? So gracious to each other, while eating corn pone and salt pork or some such starvation meal.)

At least implicitly, we should be thanking God all over again, and there are those who say a little grace after the meal as well. It can be as simple as "Thank you, dear Lord." I remember my own father, who was not Christian, saying this prayer in Arabic after the meal, as is customary in Muslim culture. You can go on sitting there and enjoying the food and conversation with whoever is left. See "Seven Strategies for Dinner with Barbarians" in volume 1 for how children should leave the table and what is expected of them.

Wait, that's one secret?

Yes. Having a culture of kindness and good manners. I'm just telling you how to get that culture.

Once you institute this culture or feed it if you already possess it, you will find that you feel much more free to plan your meals. You won't worry as much about who will or will not like what you decide on. Since with my method you are consulting your family (or observing them if they really aren't forthcoming or are very young) and taking their preferences into account, your fairness *with* them meets with good will *from* them.

Only, you have to teach them that goodwill. I'm giving you a sketch; feel free to do it according to your own family style!

But a warning: do not fall into the trap of thinking that the family style is to have no manners. No way.

Once you plan your meals, you have an amazing amount of time and a lot of confidence quickly to take care of the other tasks that face you, including addressing the issue of getting kids to help. And then your environment, which is the key to educating your children, is orderly and, thus, open to wonder!

Manners (kindness and courtesy) are the secret.

Dear Frazzled, I think you will benefit by reviewing the "Menu Planning" chapter and trying to internalize what I'm saying. You will really get things in order if you try to make some lists. You can probably make all the things you are dreaming of, one at a time. Let's be patient with ourselves, and you know what? We can ask the family to be patient with us too. Kindness and courtesy.

One thing at a time. Worrying about it all at once is a good way not to succeed.

Most of all, let's enjoy one another's company, the good food, and life.

PART 3

On Conquering Laundry

N ow that you are serenely sure of what your family will eat in the foreseeable future (or for three days), you are ready to systematize your laundry. Remember, if these two areas are orderly, your days will open up with possibilities for the many activities you *really* want to do. Spending a week scrutinizing and rationalizing your laundry will pay you back a hundredfold.

Laundry Problems
Start with Clothes

So, here it is: the secret. The one thing you have to grapple with to be able at last to emerge from the mountain of dirty clothes blocking your access to the very machines that can help you, and to navigate the ocean of clean clothes piling up in your room. It's not all you have to do, but it's the indispensable first step: *Have fewer clothes.* And I don't mean this just for the shopaholics among us or the victims of the overgenerous grandmas and aunties. I mean it for the frugal, thrifty, "simple living" ones, who have a lot of kids and not much cash.

In some ways, we have it worse, because we're afraid of letting go of something in case it could come in handy later on, what with the little sprouts outgrowing their togs faster than you can find them at the thrift store.

Our family got by for several years when the kids were little entirely on bags left on my porch by kind neighbors. Yet this posed a problem. Anxious to keep anything with any possible use, I made a lot of work for myself and prevented my children from helping me effectively.

The truth is, children tend to wear only a few outfits on a daily basis. They don't like change; they like predictability. Not only is it no use fighting this trait; it's counterproductive. Their drawers and closets are so full of things they don't wear that they live out of their laundry baskets most of the time. They simply can't put things away because there's a clog in the works—namely, the clothes they aren't wearing.

In addition, they function within a paradox: they want to wear only a few things, but the knowledge that they have many things gives them implicit permission to overuse the laundry system. Clothing doesn't fit in drawers, so it ends up on the floor or, if you are lucky, in a hamper. A garment on the floor is by definition dirty! Everyone knows that instantaneous contamination sets in as soon as the item is cast off! Also, how much easier it is to throw it in the hamper than to put it away! Thus, you are overwhelmed with unnecessary laundry.

Here is what your pre-adolescent children need (or at least use this list as a starting point, because of course, we all have to think): a few, five at the most, bottoms (say, two pairs of jeans and two corduroys in winter); a scant week's worth of tops; two light sweaters (for Sunday and other formal wear, girls need a simple but stylish cardigan, and boys can possibly use a vest); and for church: for boys, a good pair of pants and two good shirts; for girls, two nice dresses or two church-worthy skirts and blouses. Much more than this, and you will find that it all sits in a drawer getting stuff heaped on it. If the child has six drawers and they don't close, you have an issue. (My older kids shared dressers and basically had two drawers each—for all their clothes.)

Now, at the same time, each child also needs more underwear than you might think.

First, socks. Please, for the love of all that is good, try to buy socks in a minimum quantity of six to a pack. And buy two identical packs at a time. Why? Because, this way, if you lose a sock, and then you lose another sock, you still have a pair! But with the cute unique socks you are getting your children now, lose one and you are out a pair of socks. I once met a poor lady who had an entire laundry basket full of single socks. You couldn't hope to find the missing one in that pile even if it happened to be there. Or was it just a basket of single socks? Who could tell? I suppose, in a pinch, you could include figuring it out as a particularly challenging intelligence test for your children in your homeschool curriculum, but maybe there are better ways to spend their time.

Buy the style your children like (but avoid low ankle socks in winter). Never buy tube socks. Don't skimp on quality; get the good kind at your favorite discount store. Get good tights for the girls and one pair of dress socks for each boy.

Try to have at least eight pairs of underpants and at least six undershirts. You will be doing less laundry by the time I'm done with you, so your children will need to have enough underwear to survive the gap, including if you are sick and can't get it done, the power goes out, or some other disaster befalls you.

Go through those drawers with an empty laundry basket, a mending basket, a trash bag, and a donation bag by your side. If something is out of season, throw it in the laundry basket. As you pull each item out, ask yourself (in the case of everyday wear) whether you have seen it on a person in the past two weeks. If the answer is no, give it away or put it aside to try on the next kid. Maybe it's too small, too big, or he just doesn't like it. It's hard to accept that last one, but there it is. Just get it out of your life, at least for now. If it has a hole or tear, it can go in the mending basket; if it makes whoever wears it look pathetic and not a credit to the family name, throw it in the trash bag.

If it's pants or jeans that have holes in the knees, put them in a separate bag. Schedule a day to cut those pants off at the thigh and hem them (pretty easy: just turn under, turn under again, press, and sew). Now you have shorts to store away in the appropriate place for summer. (In the appendix I offer a tutorial for patching jeans if you need them long.)

Fewer outer clothes, more underclothes: that's the beginning of the path of laundry wisdom, according to Auntie Leila.

On the Subject of
Clothing Oversupply

You're sitting at my kitchen table, and you take a sip of iced tea. "I just don't know what to do about my laundry," you say. "Nothing I try seems to work. Sometimes I find folded laundry in the hamper, ready to go through the wash without ever having been worn! I can't get to my washer or even see it over piles of dirty laundry. What am I going to do?"

Laundry problems start with clothes, as I am hoping you are starting to see. You need quality control. Sorting and folding are two tasks I like to do myself most of the time, because they help me with quality control, and I realize I am going against popular opinion here. Some aspects of the laundry can be delegated, and I'll talk about that later, but if you ever want to crawl out from under the crushing weight of your laundry problems, stick with me here.

As I am sorting and folding, going through the clothing in its clean state, I can easily notice whose undies need replacing, and who has been wearing one shirt over and over. I make note of a pair of pants that turns up in the wash without really having been worn (maybe it put in an appearance for an hour or so)—a sure sign of a wardrobe misfit (or possibly a person who doesn't understand the concept of putting a clean article back in its place without having it go through the whole system).

Something not really worn is not worth keeping around. Or it could be a sign of a problem in the storage system. If there's no room in the drawer for a pair of pants, and the rule is "No clothes on the floor," then into the hamper it will go, worn or not. But that gets us right back to where we started: too many clothes.

While you begin to implement the suggestions below, use the laundry process itself as a step in the system to reduce unnecessary items. As you are folding, you can throw away shabby underwear and add replacements to your shopping list; you can remove that blouse you've noticed is just too small for your daughter; you can make note of the kinds of colors your son prefers.

As you put things away, look in the drawers and closets. Yes, usually everyone should put away his own clothes, but once in a while, you have to do it yourself to see what's *really* in there, and I am aware of the horror factor here. First and foremost, are the clothes in season? Why are shorts cluttering the world up if it's winter? Note to self: establish a place (with its own system of shelves and well marked bins) for out-of-season items.

When was the last time you saw the items worn? Encourage everyone to weed out items that don't fit, are the wrong color, or otherwise don't meet personal or family standards. Once a quarter or so, as you get people to do this, grab two big trash bags into which you put those items that can be given away and those that should be thrown away. Then hustle them (the clothes, not the people, regardless of the temptation) out the door.

The number of items each person possesses is a personal decision, but it's clear that some quantities will not to work. Usually people don't need twenty T-shirts, or eight pairs of pants, or ten sweaters. Often when children are wearing hand-me-downs, they accumulate these things, or we accumulate them on their behalf as a hedge against the odds of finding something to wear.

But the hand-me-down system *can* work if you exert quality control. Think of it this way: if you were buying the clothes, you would be more careful about size, color, and suitability. Just because something didn't cost you much or anything at all, it doesn't mean you should keep it. Be just as fussy about bargains as you are about items you pay a lot for. The point isn't how much you paid for it, but how much it's worth to you. A blouse that fits and shows quality workmanship should be cared for no matter how much it cost. Regardless, something suitable will cost a lot to replace, because good clothes are hard to find.

Any clothing you buy will stand you in good stead, both for the person it's purchased for and down the line, if you keep in mind some criteria:

- For children, avoid clothing with pictures or animated characters printed on it. Those things look *instantly* tired and mismatched—how will they look in a year?

- Trends such as unfinished edges, deliberate tears, or pre-distressing are anathema to the thrifty family, not to mention a scam and an insult. One washing (never mind the hundreds we have in mind) will put the article out of commission.

- Fitted clothing is best, but make sure that sleeves and waist are in proportion, with enough length to allow for growth. A sweater with reasonable sleeves but short in the waist is useless for what it's intended for, which is keeping the person warm.

- Some things must be bought new (as opposed to a thrift store) and are worth spending a bit more for (as opposed to getting a cheap version that doesn't last), and here is where you have to think carefully. Underwear falls into this category. Even in our most direly penny-pinching days, I never found a way to avoid buying socks!

The Laundry Process

I f you have a good system going for your laundry, then good for you! I affirm you! And a lot depends on whether you have a dedicated laundry room with plenty of workspace, or whether you have to make do in the basement or the mudroom.

I'm going to tell you about my way. This is a kid-tested, decades-honed, homeschool-proof, flexible system that does not take over your life.

Fair warning: it also does not produce a home free of laundry baskets in various stages of delivery. If you are looking for such a system, one in which a basket of clothes is nowhere to be found, I suggest you take one or more of these steps:

1. Hire a laundress.
2. Give up ever doing anything other than laundry.
3. Go naked.
4. Get rid of almost all of your children.

Otherwise, welcome to my world, where there is always a laundry basket *en route* to somewhere! If you are seeking permission to have clean clothes on a reliable basis *and* laundry baskets wandering around your house, under control but in various stages of the process, consider it given! I don't know any other sane way to go about it.

Everything I tell you is based on a family of at least six. If you have fewer, you may not need so many baskets.

Dig Yourself out of the Piles

In the beginning of this journey to laundry order, you will need to rid your laundry area of the piles of things you have in there. Most likely, you have a lot of stuff that you thought at the time, "That is an unusual load of things. I'll get to it soon." A bedspread you're not sure your machine can handle? Some sweaters you think might shrink? Some very dirty towels?

Whatever it is, get to the bottom of it. Dedicate a day to this project.

Take the bedspread and a couple of other oversized things to the laundromat. Start some loads of towels before you leave—with hot water, detergent, and bleach (1/4 cup per load). Pick out the sweaters for a later "hand washable" or "delicates" cycle or get them to the dry cleaner by putting them in a bag and taking them out to the car (meaning, this is not a mental exercise but a real one!).

On this laundry battle day, pull everything to the middle of the room and plow through all the piles until, one way or another, they are gone. Put all the clean things into a different room to be sorted later. If you don't have extra space, use the dining table and eat in the kitchen until you're done! Motivation!

Now, while the bedspreads are at the laundromat, go to the store and get yourself four plastic hampers. This is what you need: one for lights, one for darks, one quite large one for towels and sheets, and one for "special needs" loads (not large; I'll explain soon). There are also good hampers to be found at those nice discount stores; they look like wicker but are plastic over wire (necessary to avoid mold).

You also need an airy hamper (real wicker is fine) for ironing, and something for the kitchen and mudroom area, where a lot of laundry is generated but might not make it to the laundry area right away.

If you don't have any already, you need four ordinary sturdy plastic laundry baskets, preferably stackable. These should be rectangular with handles on all sides.

Now, find a place not far from the bathroom or bedrooms for the four hampers. They can go in a hallway.

Here is where you have to convince yourself that your children can and will understand what they have to do. And they can and they will!—if you insist. They must, every night upon disrobing, place their dark clothing in one hamper and their light clothing in another.

I am here to tell you that even a two-year-old, if a girl, and definitely a three-year-old, if a boy, can learn this. Usually they interpret it to mean that outer clothes go in the darks and underwear into the lights, and if you firmly explain that a light yellow T-shirt counts as light and black socks count as black, you should make headway. Yes, you will have to remedy the occasionally misfiled object. Sometimes a girl gets it into her head that one of the hampers is for "pretty" things and the other for "not pretty" things; see what you can do.

Insist that your children put *two* socks into the hamper. Spend a week making a point of directing them to put whatever socks they have randomly thrown about into an appropriate hamper. That hamper in the kitchen or mudroom is fine and now you see why, besides kitchen towel management, you need this downstairs (or not bedroom-oriented) landing place for dirty things.

I am death on taking socks off wherever one happens to be. Any perpetrator will be dragged from kingdom come to dispose of them properly. This is why most of my loads come out sock-even. When your children master putting their socks in the hampers, train them to turn the socks right side out first. We're talking brutal efficiency and strict adherence to the norm; there's no mercy in socks.

The reason single socks proliferate is that children take them off in random places. You will thank yourself if you establish early on your clear disapproval of the placing of socks in any receptacle other than the hamper. Children regard a wet sock as a sock they want to forget about. They think nothing of leaving such a thing in the middle of a room. They get hot playing in the den, and off come the socks. If you register disbelief that anyone not inhabiting primordial ooze with the dinosaurs would throw his socks behind a sofa, and immediately require rectification of the error, you will find that these sorts of terrible misadventures rarely trouble you.

Towels and bedding[5] go in that larger hamper.

Laundry Tip

By way of a little drill-sergeanting and cheerleading, let me comment on something I've noticed when people talk about laundry. They seem to think that you must sort, wash, dry, fold, sort again, and put away—all at once! Do you think that? Go back over the info here in this section. If you have more than two children, how about viewing each step as different chores that you cycle through at different times of the day?

Let your children give you a hand with or even completely accomplish the various parts of the process, and let them put away their own clothes. If there are too many to put away, there are too many clothes!

But don't try to do the whole task all at once. Don't consider it a failure that it's never all done; instead, redefine. Otherwise, it all seems like—and is—too darned much!

More on Sorting: Hampers and Towels

Hampers

As I said, and it bears repeating, even the youngest child, if he is able to remove clothing, has the ability to distinguish between at least two kinds of hampers—the lights and the darks! If he can toddle, he can toddle down to the designated spot and place his garments therein. Well, you can tell him what to do until he gets older, but the older children who are doing the laundry will handle it better if they don't have to touch dirty clothing to sort it.

---

5   If several beds are being stripped at once, you won't have room in one hamper for all that bedding. This situation is my only relaxation of my "no dirty clothes on the laundry-room floor" rule, as there is not much else to do with them. But the good news is that you can work through them quickly, and they don't disappear behind the appliances the way small items tend to do.

If you have room, deploy four hampers, two of which are approximately laundry-basket-sized; they hold one or two loads: one for lights and one for darks; a large one for sheets and towels; and yet another for items that require special care of some sort (permanent press, delicate, or hand washable; also for lingerie, bras, and pantyhose).

The reason the laundry room gets out of control is that there is no hamper for occasional sheets and towels, so these items get piled up in front of the washer. But clothing gets priority, so the piles of larger items become fixtures; people literally climb over them to do more urgent loads.

But—and this is important—wet things should not go in hampers! They will become a moldy mess! So you need to think through how you will get dirty things *dry* before they are placed there. Bath towels should be kept on a hook or a rack to dry after use and collected frequently for laundering or placement in the hamper, but there is always that one that has been left in a heap or used to dry the dog; it needs to be hung over a railing until it is tossed directly into the washer or is dry (if dirty) and can be put in the hamper.

Any special clothing, such as sweaters, dress shirts, nice delicate cotton knits, dress pants, silk tops, and lingerie go in the smaller permanent press or "special needs" hamper. I have always taken care of those things myself, since a mistake can spell disaster here, where the other categories are more forgiving. You can point out to the little person that his item needs to go there, as needed.

Think about it. If the laundry is presorted, doesn't it make life easier? Do we really enjoy sorting through *dirty* laundry (left in heaps in front of the appliances or jumbled into one big hamper) on washing day, to get it in the right place? Is it necessary to add this dreaded step to an already Sisyphean, thankless task? Yes, no, and no. And this is my secret: *presorted dirty clothing*. It's worth it.

Towels

Some mothers wake up one day with the realization that half their laundry is doing towels. Some never realize it; I have heard of some who do towels every day, and I am all astonishment.

The solution is to get each child his own color of towel, or a monogrammed one, or something (color-coded tag, for instance) for when they are tossed around (the towels, not the kids). Install hooks (or buy the kind that go over the door, if the children are tall enough to reach). This system saves you money: washing those towels constantly and replacing worn ones is costing you! Show the child how to hang up his towel after he uses it.

If the hook is low enough, even a toddler can do this. But it must be done, because bath towels can remain clean and usable for days *if they dry out between uses.* If it has not been hung up, it's easily identifiable, and the offender should be made to hang it up. A week's worth of training and enforcement will yield a habit.

Dirty towels go in the towel hamper, but they must be dry, or the hamper gets smelly and the towels become difficult to get really clean. (An adult has the responsibility to decide when a child's towel is dirty.)

With this system of towel management and hamper sorting, doing a load of laundry shouldn't present a problem for anyone who can lift a full basket. After all, how much finesse does it take to put a load in the washer, measure some detergent, and get it started?

Well, it takes training, but it can be done. And with the grossness factor of sorting dirty laundry removed, even an eight- or nine-year-old can be taught what to do.

Laundry Solutions

I f you and I were sitting and talking about what highly intelligent folks talk about ("The problem with you women is that you just want to talk about the price of potatoes!" a male friend once scolded. Hey, we can talk about the stimulus package or the One and the Many if you want to, but we are interested in the price of potatoes as well!) and also about laundry, you will say to yourself, "I can do that, and I can do better than that." Yes, it's as I've been telling you: if I can do it, so can you.

So here are some notes on simplifying the laundry. This part is blah-blah-blah ... it just goes on and on. Oh my goodness. I'm so sorry.

Those of you with high-tech nuclear-powered washing machines and dryers are on your own. Read your manual and figure it out. Actually, everyone should read the instructions that come with household appliances. These machines are expensive to replace, and they are not magic!

It's easier to explain to a child how to use an appliance if we really understand it ourselves. Have you completely internalized the fact that if you consistently overload your washer it will fail you long before its time? (I know of one family whose washer failed that one time when their returning college student put *all* her laundry in it at once!) This knowledge will help you explain to your minions how to choose a water level or cycle.

Laundry Detergent

Choose a detergent that doesn't have a scent. Some tend to try to save money by buying off-brand detergent that has an overwhelming scent at the expense of effective cleansing agents. Be sure that you are smelling your clothes, not the detergent.

Really clean laundry has a clean smell of its own. Some people's laundry smells clean from far away, but if you get into it and really smell it (as when they're giving you a hug), you can tell it's not clean deep down. So your scented detergent might be masking this sad truth from you.

To provide deep-down cleanliness, you need a couple of other products and the occasional run-through with warm or hot water, and outdoor line-drying in the sun if the weather allows.

I realize that we are all trying to be frugal and washing in cold water, but permit me to say that refraining from using warm or hot water when you need it is causing you to wash certain things more often than they need to be washed, which is costing you in electricity, water, and wear-and-tear on your machines and your clothing.

What makes things smell, for the most part, is body odor and molds. To handle the former, use warmer water; often presoaking does the trick. As to the latter, towels need bleach and at least warm water. In the summer they need hot water or line drying. One summer, we stayed at a beach house that supplied towels and sheets. I ended up washing all the "clean" linens before we could use them. I had to go buy bleach and proper detergent to do it. They were so musty, yet overpoweringly perfumed with the cheap detergent the owner had on hand that I couldn't bear even to be in the house with them.

Mustiness is that "whiff" of something that's not dirt or sweat, that you get from damp towels, sponges, washcloths, rain gear, old shoes, or anything that has been sitting around in damp. That "whiff" makes me crazy! The only cure is bleach, hot water, a hot dryer, and a good airing in the direct sun.

If you find that laundry in drawers after a few days no longer seems clean and fresh, try doing your wash in warm water for a while and add a little bleach to the whites. The problem may be your "thrifty" homemade laundry soap; commercial detergents have surfactants, which are chemicals that bond with dirt *and* water, making it possible to wash the dirt *away*. Homemade soaps will not be able to do this.

Stains

Here are some of my secrets to add to your usual stain-removing aids:

- *Lestoil* (a cleanser with pine oils, which will remind you of those old-fashioned floor cleaners, plus sodium tallate, a soap) will remove those grease spots on knits and chino pants. (I realize that this is possibly a regional product, which is why I gave you the basic ingredients to check against what you may have where you live.) You know how you always seem to drop a bit of salad on your favorite polo shirt? Or how your husband seems to plunk pizza on his new khakis? How about that ring around the collar of winter jackets? Rub Lestoil into the grease spot, let it sit for a few minutes, and launder in warm water. I've never used a more effective grease spot remover, so I don't buy the others anymore. I pour the Lestoil into a squeeze bottle (for condiments) from the dollar store so I can target stains precisely—better than trying to pour out of the big bottle.
- *Ammonia.* For articles that seem yellowed and for sheets and other vaguely greasy objects, try ammonia according to the directions, and warm or hot water. Your pillowcases won't get really clean with bleach. You need ammonia! (And remember, *never mix the two.* A toxic gas will result that will harm your lungs if it doesn't kill you outright.)
- *Oxygen-type bleaches.* I do like oxygen-type bleaches for some things. You can even use straight hydrogen peroxide. You can make a paste with the powder and warm water and rub it into berry and wine stains. Then wash the item and dry it in the sun if possible.
- *Soaking.* Giving soiled articles a good soak is a time-tested method of removing stains. Unfortunately, many washers today don't

have a soak cycle. If yours doesn't, here's a tip that works with my top-loader (I don't know if it will work with a front loader, but you can puzzle it out): After you treat your stains, fill the washer as usual and let it agitate enough to distribute the water and detergent evenly. Then pause the machine and unplug it. If you just pause it, after a certain (short) time, it will drain, so that won't work. Set a timer so you don't just forget this soaking load; I suspect that one reason manufacturers eliminated the option to soak is that it's not good for the machine to be left a long time this way; it's certainly not good for the clothes to be left with bleach or detergent for days, which sounds unlikely, but people do get distracted. Anyway, when you're ready, simply plug the machine in again and press the start button. Give it a minute to recover its senses. It should just start up where it left off.

- *Bluing.* For whites that have yellowed, try bluing. It works! So old-fashioned!

Drying

In cold weather, I use one-quarter to one-third of a dryer sheet (really all you need) in my regular loads to prevent static (not with towels — fabric softener works by adding a substance that attracts a little moisture; this would defeat the purpose of a towel, which needs to be *dry*). The cheapest, most generic dryer sheets are just fine.

You really need a folding drying rack for lingerie, delicates, spandex, and whatever else shouldn't go in the dryer, but always ends up there just because you don't know what else to do with it, and that will not be good for them; alternatively, your home will be draped with washing.

A line outside is so comforting, and of course there is the bleaching power of the sun. If you can't have a clothesline outside for some reason (or it's winter), perhaps you can put one in your tidy basement or cleaned-out utility closet, where the furnace keeps the air dry. The Irish call this *the airing cupboard,* because they don't have basements, and their climate is so damp. This sounded oxymoronic to me, as a cupboard seems the opposite of airy, but my Irish friend explained it to me, and now I would really love to have one.

Distributing Folded Clothes

Remember those baskets I had you buy? Get the loads out of the dryer (most days it will be two loads) and take them somewhere handy for folding, if you don't have a laundry room with a counter. I use my bed. That way, I have to finish the task—or I won't be able to sleep! If all else fails, bring the baskets to the sofa, make yourself comfortable, put on a show, and get all your laundry folded!

As you fold, place the piles carefully in the baskets by *room*. If, for instance, your four girls share a room, place their clothes together in one basket. I would put the big girls' clothes on the bottom, side by side, and then the littler ones on top of those. They know whose is whose and the older ones can help the younger ones. Ditto the boys. If two girls are in one room and two in another, use two baskets. The point is to get the clean clothes to their destination. When the children have put their laundry away, the baskets get returned to the laundry area near the hampers. Sometimes you have to call a "basket roundup minute" to accomplish this last step.

Some families have the space to have dressers by or in the laundry room, and that is a system that could definitely work, on the principle that things should not travel far from where they are taken care of.

Dish-Towel Talk, an Interlude

Speaking of good and bad and having standards, what is up with dish towels that are coated, impregnated, or otherwise imbued with some substance that prevents them from absorbing moisture? Is it that people generally use paper towels and consider the dish towel an ornament, not called upon for actual use? I use paper towels on occasion. But I need my cloth towels to dry things.

Too much to ask? I think not.

I sometimes find myself with a stash of dish towels that is getting tired. It's a carefully curated stash, purged of anything lacking in absorbency. But I find it's a tired stash. So I go shopping and refrain from the cutesy and the seasonal. I resist. I have criteria.

Waffle-weave dish towels are my favorite. I like potato sacking okay, but I find the fabric thin. The simply flat-woven doesn't measure up. It's damp where I live. I want my hands to feel less moist after a wipe. I want my dishes to be lacking in dampness after contact with a towel.

So I find some towels that seem promising. They are big. They are beefy. Some are waffle weave, albeit only partially; a dubious characteristic that makes me tremble at portents of future distensions. But I spring; I purchase them.

Then, I am boiling—with rage against the unjust treatment of cotton, yes, but also literally, with water on the stove, in an attempt to rid the towels of this bad coating of water resistance and to provide myself with new towels that actually dry.

How to Remove Mildew Stains

Continuing in a dish-towel vein: What if yours is mildewed? It may be that you need to throw that thing away. Other than rust, I don't know of a harder stain. Until recently, that's what I did. Just gave it up for lost.

But I, your friendly laundry consultant, will share this immensely important discovery I have made of removing mildew stains.

The worst has happened. You've somehow left a towel or bib or blouse damp and wadded up. Days later, you find it and—little black spots. Ugh. Nothing will get those spots out, you think. You've tried bleach, OxiClean, vinegar, vinegar and baking soda, magic elven dust, essential oils, and every other laundry remedy, including sunshine, and you know that once you have those spots, that's it—game over.

But a while back I had an aha moment. If I'm going to throw it away, I might as well try the last-ditchest of last-ditch efforts, right? So that's what this is.

A really hard-core solution. Don't be shocked. It works—or it doesn't and you throw the item away, which is what you were going to do anyway.

Where we live, it can be damp, and we do have a problem with mildew. Having used foaming bleach bathroom cleanser to remove mildew from the grout in the shower, I know it works. (It is merely more concentrated bleach, but the foaming aspect makes it adhere, rather than run off.)

So, I thought, why not spray that mildewy towel? The heavy-duty bleach spray will definitely bleach out anything it falls on that is not resistant, so you have to be careful. It's a strong chemical, a solution of last resort, as when you have black in your bathroom and need to get rid of it.

And, if you spray it on the spots on textiles, they will disappear. Most towels are bleach-resistant—they have to be, because people need to bleach them, most cities put a little bleach in their water, and often people take towels to pools, which, of course, have chlorine added to the water. Some articles of clothing are either white or bleach resistant, and you won't know until you try! The fact is, you were going to throw it away, so why not? And for something like a bib, I'd rather have it be bleached out than mildew spotted. A faded bib or towel is no real tragedy.

Wet the item all over, spray the spots, and let it sit for a bit; then rinse it, and wash it with your normal load.

It has worked for me many a time! Just be sure you aren't wearing your favorite jeans or shirt when you do it, and watch what's behind the item when you spray it.

You Can Beat the Laundry

If you struggle with the laundry, suffering from a sense of overall defeat, I hope that I have helped you to think deeply about all the issues raised here and inspired you to make a plan of action. I must speak seriously, based on the overwhelming obstacle laundry presents to mothers attempting to achieve some sort of competence in homemaking: if you have more than three children, and up to seven (after that, you are on your own; Auntie Leila has only seven children), you will be doing an average of two loads of laundry a day, every day. You will fold at least four loads of laundry every other day. A battle indeed! When you have a baby, you will be doing more. If your husband has a dirty job, you will do an extra load of his clothes. And probably at least once a week, you will do many more than two loads, because you will also do the towels, the permanent-press items, and some bedding. That will be your *real* "laundry day": every other day is just "doing laundry" along with everything else.

You need a new paradigm in which you don't think of laundry as a surprisingly immovable obstacle in your way, one that doesn't have much of a solution, but instead as a constant aspect of homemaking, with its own satisfaction, once you accept it and accept that *it does take time*. There will always be laundry to be done, but it will be under control if you follow my plan.

PART 4

The Reasonably Clean House: Its Organization, Upkeep, and Justification

ow can one have anything resembling a clean house when trailed by a pack of expert house wreckers? What is the point? Should we ask the Almighty to "bless this mess" and just forget about it? Is it possible to have a tidy home?

There is a point, and it can be done. Little by little, using my methods, you, dear reader, can have a Reasonably Clean, Fairly Neat, Comfortably Tidy house!

The Reasonably Clean, Fairly Neat, Comfortably Tidy House

I've always written for people more or less like me: people who would rather be reading than cleaning; people with lots of other people around; people who will stop whatever they are doing to hear a good story; people who like children and dogs, at least in theory; people with big ideas who are continually surprised at the intractability of the material world—its propensity toward disorder, for instance.

We would rather make plans for a difficult and complex project than execute it, and we tend to get bogged down in the details. But, I'll say this about us: we do realize that the details matter, and that somehow we must stoop to conquer. We don't scorn cleaning a bathroom even if it doesn't come naturally, because we know we are happier when things are clean. We know they could be *cleaner*. We're good with clean.

In this section, you will find the deepest thoughts I have on the Reasonably Clean, Fairly Neat, Comfortably Tidy House (hereinafter referred to as the "Reasonably Clean House"), and that will take some time. I will give you some secrets on how to maintain a Reasonably Clean House with a passel of kids, because we all know that if we lived alone, we, too, could be just like any paragon of organization featured in magazines—it's just all these *people* who are causing our problems.

For starters, have you ever read the following books? Look for them at the library. They are the ones that helped me the most, and I'll tell you why.

Confessions of an Organized Homemaker, by Deniece Schofield. The author raised five kids and thought things through analytically, in light of the good of the family. When I had no idea how to get started, this book really helped me a lot. Schofield is realistic and practical.

Schofield's book on organizing the kitchen, *Kitchen Organization Tips and Secrets* is just as good. She applies engineering principles to a sector that could well use them. Not every kitchen is the same, but having expressed principles for organizing *your* kitchen is really helpful.

Sidetracked Home Executives, by Pam Young and Peggy Jones: what helped me in this book was the idea of cleaning a room by starting in the same place and working your way around, every time. Thinking about cleaning rooms rather than the whole house works wonders on this easily distracted mind. The authors are genuinely amusing, which is such a blessing when you are contemplating how bad at something you are.

Is There Life after Housework?, by Don Aslett, shows that using the right tools along with time management to reduce housework can be done. Some of Aslett's books descend into product pushing, but his professional outlook can shake us housewives out of our inefficient ways. If it weren't for him, I would have never spent the money on rubber mats for my mudroom, but twenty years later, the same ones are doing the job cutting my housework time. Good investment! An important point for time management: overlap jobs. While you are waiting for water to boil, wipe a counter. Spray your shower, clean the rest of the bathroom, then wipe the shower down—this gives the cleanser time to work on the scum. Use the waiting time in one job to accomplish something in another. Aslett's whole approach has more energy than others I've read about.

Home Comforts, by Cheryl Mendelson: I love the extensive detail in this book as well as the forthright declaration that an orderly home *matters*. As big as *Home Comforts* is, I would have preferred *even more detail* about the author's experiences, and that, dear reader, explains why *my* book is in three volumes! And certainly, for our purposes, the fact that Mendelson had a career and only one child makes her advice nice to shoot for but perhaps not in my "if I can do it" category—not at all! As such, maybe it is a little unrealistic for large-family life. But that's where I come in. And *Home Comforts* does have a huge amount of really good advice for those who love to delve into particulars.

I haven't read every book on this topic, especially lately. When I do read a new one, I am confirmed in my thought that these authors who might seem somewhat out of date are nevertheless the best of the bunch. It's these that I always recommend to anyone who asks.

I'm going to tell you my own way of doing things, and you'll recognize the influence of these writers on my methods. So if, like me, you'd rather read than clean, tackling this book list is the perfect procrastination!

Tidiness Magic

After I wrote this series on the blog, a new book captured everyone's interest: Marie Kondo's *The Life-Changing Magic of Tidying Up*. Kondo captured the truth that tidiness works magic on life—I think the title is really inspired! It's a great read. The core idea, that you can finally declutter by applying Kondo's criteria to your belongings (especially, famously, the one that asks if each one "sparks joy"—and if it doesn't, instructs you to "toss it in the bin"), helps tremendously to cut through the strange hold that *things* have on us. Later in this volume is an anecdote about my experience KonMari'ing some things.

In the meantime, for a detailed analysis for the truly impaired, read on.

How to Start Keeping House

I am convinced, and often assert, that if you have your meals planned and your laundry in process (I say "in process" because laundry is never done), you can handle other parts of your life in a realistic manner.

If you feel you can say "70 percent yes"—in other words, "most of the time, dear Auntie Leila, I have meals and laundry under control" (Auntie Leila would *never* ask you to be more on top of things than she is herself, or she would be going to *your* blog for advice), then you may move on to the next resolution, which is ...

Preparing to Clean

If you are not a good housekeeper, you will have to be patient and do things little by little, just as with menus and laundry. In a bit I will tell you *where* to start. We will talk about how to do more in less time, and even how to make sure you don't do *too much*. Yes, that can be a problem—please tell your loved ones to stop laughing! How rude!

We will talk about how to have the Reasonably Clean House with a nursing baby and a toddler, all while homeschooling. We will talk about how to get your kids to help you and *why* they should. And we will talk about many other things, all of them fascinating and profound.

For now, we aren't going to clean—we are just going to *think* about cleaning. So don't worry.

But I'm going to tell you my biggest secret to getting things done, whether it's organizing a shelf or cleaning the garage. It seems simple. I hope you won't be disappointed. But I can tell you that human nature is such that doing it sort of takes a leap; consequently, one often doesn't, much to the detriment of progress in this area. I have never seen other guides start with this secret. They seem to take it for granted, if they even know about it; sometimes they tell you the opposite, which is a problem. But knowing it makes all the difference.

First, and I apologize for this further delay, I will say this: I really think you should gird your loins for cleaning by going ahead and taking a shower and getting dressed. This is not the secret. This is the pre-secret, explained in detail in volume 1.

Often, I've noticed, persons who stay at home put off the showering and dressing process, perhaps thinking that it doesn't make sense to tackle a dirty house by getting oneself clean first, and sometimes they refrain just because they feel that they can hardly tackle *two* projects—getting dressed *and* cleaning—in a day.

I beg to differ, however. You will work hard, but you really aren't going to get dirty, not for normal cleaning. While it might make sense to clean the bathroom or the garage before taking a shower, for the most part, delaying the shower is counterproductive.

I mean, don't get dressed up. If you think your normal jeans and top will get soiled, you should wear an apron. Not a fancy frilly one—a sturdy work apron made of twill.

If you don't do as I say, what will surely happen is that you will be tired from your exertions and find yourself not all that inclined to shower and dress after all. And then an emergency will arise, and lo! you will find yourself in the doctor's office with a sick baby; tired, not showered, in sweats, and looked upon with scorn by any passing nannies. And that will not help our cause one bit.

Besides, being clean and dressed invigorates you, makes you ready to take on all your tasks, and, to use an annoying word, *empowers* you generally. If you are in your yoga pants, there are all kinds of ways to put off getting up and getting going.

Another thing (also helped by being dressed for action): make up your mind to try to be fast in whatever you do. Right now it's more important to get through a task than to take a lot of time over it.

Some people are in the habit of working so slowly, they really stand no chance against the forces of entropy. They are like those little helpless bunny babies with a great big entropy cat stalking them.

Watch someone lively do her work, and measure your own motions against hers. Could you be faster? Try!

The Secret

All right, here it is—the secret.

When you are cleaning something, particularly for the first time (or for the first time in a long time):

Start by getting everything out and off; *then* sort. Don't try to de-clutter in place.

Put back only what you have determined truly belongs, and not one other thing, even if it means leaving that thing in the middle of the room.

That shelf you are trying to clean? The table you need to locate under the stuff piled on it? Take everything off it. Vacuum it or wipe it down. Then replace only what belongs there, without thinking about how to deal with the rest.

I can't tell you how often I have seen instructions that have you taking things out of a closet, say, one by one, and deciding which bin to sort it into. I'm all for the bin-sorting method of decluttering, don't get me wrong, and we'll get to that. But unless you don't need me anyway, you will likely never be done with the job if you go about it that way.

First, you need the immediate gratification of the gleaming, shining object (shelf or table or whatever it is) carefully arranged with its proper contents. Second, it's all too easy to stop halfway through the task to do something else urgent, and then you might as well not have started! Whereas my way, you will have the newly arranged space and, it's true, the pile of junk to deal with, but that just means there's no turning back.

It's total commitment and instant gratification all rolled up in one step.

So these are the principles or tips, as it were, with which we will start.

- Get dressed.
- Get what you're cleaning cleared off and all the items out.

This Secret in Practice

Here's a little mental exercise that on the blog was a staged tutorial, lavishly illustrated with photos. Here we will just imagine that it's shortly after Christmas, the school year is resuming, and ...

Oh my! Look at that sideboard. There's so much junk on it. Looks as if people just walked by and put stuff on there. They probably thought: Oh! A horizontal surface! Let me pile my junk on here. Not permanently, no, why would you accuse us of that?

They thought, "I'll put these things here, just until I do 'this one thing.'"

This sideboard isn't pretty or even orderly, it's just piled with stuff. Should I address each thing in turn, walking it to its rightful place?

Auntie Leila says: no, because this would be tiring. And halfway through, you'd wonder if that Latin curriculum left on there is really the right one for your seventh grader, and you'd go search for reviews, or the phone would ring, you'd be off finding your husband's important papers he forgot, and the sideboard would still be a mess.

You can't even get the offenders together to deal with it, because they are finally studying or off at soccer practice, or the truth is, it was you.

Instead of all these traps, here is how you clean it. Provide yourself with two damp rags, a trash bag, and a basket of some sort; place them near you. Now, get everything off the sideboard. *Everything.*

Some things belong there, such as a cake plate and candles. Should I just leave those things to save time?

No.

What about the wine bottles? They can stay, right?

No.

I wasn't too sure about this gift of Amaretto; such pretty wrapping—or the little apothecary jars I got at a thrift store for twenty-five cents each. What should I do with those?

Stop thinking about it. Take them off the sideboard.

I wish my sideboard were refinished. Other people have refinished sideboards. Maybe I should spray-paint it. Would black be too much?

This is your sideboard. You literally got it out of the trash, thanks to a friend who alerted you that a rectory was being cleaned out and a pile of furniture was out in the driveway! It's a miracle you have a decent sideboard. It even had some linens inside! Maybe it should be painted, but *not now!* This is it, and it needs to be cleaned. Let's clean it today and worry about refinishing it tomorrow. Truth is, you will be a lot more contented with shabby chic when it's all clean.

You obey Auntie Leila and take *every last thing off.* That's what I'm talking about. Completely cleared off. Where is all the stuff? Turn around. It's all on the dining room table! But that's okay, and you'll soon understand why.

I allow you to put some things away right now if their proper place is in that same room you are cleaning. So the box of candles can go in one drawer of the sideboard. (And why, pray, were they not put there in the first place? Literally *right there.*) The linens that were piled on the Latin book—ditto.

Otherwise, just live dangerously with everything else on the dining room table, and get your rag. (I favor flannel rags torn from old flannel sheets and pjs, laundered of course. The rag should be either slightly damp or soaked with furniture oil. Do not dust with a dry rag. (You might as well just not do it, especially in January! You will be merely flinging the dust in the air, and shortly it will settle right back where it was.)

Now wipe off every surface of the sideboard. Start at the top and wipe every inch, including legs and sides. If we were cleaning the inside, you would have taken everything out and you would wipe all the sides of the drawers.

Now start putting things back. Put things back on the sideboard only if

- they belong there
- you really love them there because they are so pretty
- they have a function there
- they are clean

With these thoughts in mind, you may begin replacing certain things, wiping them as you go with your rag, if they are wipeable.

The handmade linen lace from your mother-in-law that goes on top: at least shake it out, or, if it has been a while, launder, starch, and iron it before putting it back.

The candlesticks: wipe them with a clean damp rag. Wash and dry them, if you haven't done so recently.

Here on top is where you "store" your cake stand, because it's so pretty, with the cake dome on top of it. If a cake appears in the kitchen or elsewhere, requiring the stand and the dome, you are ready to go.

The Polish pottery dishes go here; nowhere else to put them, and they are pretty. Think carefully, though. Don't put them back just because you always have. Make a decision about them. It might be that some serving dishes that are taking up room in a kitchen cabinet need to go, and that would free up room in there, while these might stack well in a drawer.

On the other side of the sideboard, you place two of the nicer bottles of wine, to protect them from being drunk willy-nilly on an ordinary day. These pass the pretty test and can stay. The third bottle goes in the wine rack.

You may put on the sideboard the candy dish with the last of the Christmas candy in it, so that someone other than you will be eating it. And a certain little decorative plate will soon go on a wall in the den, so it's okay here too—only because it's pretty!

There. The sideboard is clean, it's pretty, and it feels as if you meant it to be just like this.

What about the table behind you?

Take the apothecary jars to the kitchen. They need to be washed out, and then we'll think of what to do with them (they held Christmas candy when everyone was here; perhaps now they can hold cotton balls in the bathroom). Some of that other junk is Christmas decorating flotsam, so it needs to be stored away or discarded in the trash bag you have provided yourself with. The basket is handy to collect this miscellany so it can be moved to its proper place.

The books obviously go on the child's homeschooling shelf. At this point, it might be worth it to you to put them back yourself, and not wait for the child to do it; put them in the basket as well so you won't risk distraction in that other location.

And now the table looks like this: a couple of gifts received that need a home and a table that needs to be wiped. We can live with this if we need to take someone to an appointment right now or if bread needs to be put in the oven. This is nothing! And the sideboard is pretty and fresh.

If you only had twenty minutes (maybe while talking on the phone to a friend?), you could do this. If you were deep-cleaning the dining room, you'd *use this exact process* in every part of the room and only at the end address the table itself. Dust the room thoroughly (another tutorial for another day) and vacuum. And then the room would be clean.

And it starts with this little secret, which you will apply to all your cleaning tasks, large and small: *Start by getting everything out and off, then sort. Don't try to declutter in place.*

The Heart of Cleaning

Now that the secret is out of the way, we are going to get to the core of this cleaning business.

A little note: some of you are very good housekeepers, and this is all going to seem pointless to you. I'm not one of you, and I don't think you understand those of us who aren't naturally clean, or who would be fabulous at it, if only we didn't have life to distract us. Please understand that we have our issues that can be handled only a certain way. We love you and wish we could be like you.

For the rest, well, I need to give you a quick pep talk on why you should strive to have a Reasonably Clean House.

1. *No one else is going to do it for you.* If someone else does clean your house for you, then lucky you! But it may happen that you go through lean times—at that point, you'll be back relying on yourself. Many have given up the second income (or chosen not to have it in the first place), and a housekeeper is not in their budget.

Don't waste time being bitter about this responsibility. Why would you? Because you're so highly educated? Because you used to be an executive?

Because your mom should help you? Because you could be earning a big salary if, if, if ...? Because your friends don't have to?

Well, if you are home today and your house is dirty and no one is coming to clean it in an hour, then you, and only you, have to deal with it. All that other mental clutter doesn't matter. It's as simple as that. But you'll feel better about it if you know *how* to do it—if you are *competent*.

2. *Order is liberating.* You can think about other things when your home is orderly. You can pray, read, cook, and entertain. You can leave the house without dreading coming home.

By being orderly, you will have taken concrete steps to overcome anxiety and depression if you suffer from those ills, for while a disorderly house might not *cause* mental disturbance (although, then again, it might!), it's a necessary, even if insufficient, step to curing it.

Anyone who has seen my blog knows that my house isn't like one in a magazine. I'm not talking about some unrealistic ideal—just a reasonable standard.

I encourage you, if you're not quite ready to pick up a dust cloth, to train your eye. If all you can manage right now is surfing the Internet, then put that activity to good use by searching for images of *ordinary* tidy rooms that glow with a kempt, cozy light. This will take some search strategy, using the right key words, such as "vintage," "bohemian," "English country style," and other terms that exclude matchy-matchy styles that imply a lot of decorating professionalism and expense.

To become a good housekeeper, you need to have assimilated a lot of visual data so that you can arrange things in a pleasing and effective way. Cleaning is only one part of keeping house! You need to clear your mind of all those perfect magazine pictures and find your own order.

3. *You will be nicer to your children and your husband if you aren't constantly irritated and even depressed by the dirt and "visual background noise" in your house.* You will be able to have a conversation with him or read to them without wanting to scream or cry or run away. You will also be able to offer hospitality with a peaceful soul. You may find that you love making a home for how it frees you to interact with people.

4. *You will be content with your things and finally conquer that vague "if only my house were perfect" nagging feeling that makes you waste time and spiritual energy (and, possibly, money).* You will see the beauty in even the humblest object if it is clean and in the right spot. You will also be more able to handle real problems of household organization and decoration if you have a clean slate (I said clean, not blank) to work with.

5. *You will not mind a temporary mess if your house is reasonably clean.* When the kids make a fort with the living room cushions, or take up finger painting, or pull out every pot and pan from the cabinets, it won't be a disaster. Well, it will be a disaster, but not a fatal one—because those things can be set to rights quickly when things are basically in order. But when their mess adds to an already dire situation, it's hard to recover.

6. *You will be better prepared to make structural decisions if your home is clean and tidy.* I've seen people make costly decorating, renovating, and building mistakes just because what they were living with wasn't bad but only dirty or disorderly, or both. People think they need a big addition, only to find that they virtually abandon the former parts of their home when it's done. Doesn't that imply that they were not using it well in the first place?

If you clean and organize something and still find that it's not working for you, then (and, I'd argue, only then) can you think about renovations in an effective way.

When you really clean, you sometimes find that a room's walls, floors, and windows are not conducive to becoming clean; sometimes these elements need to be replaced with better ones before you can clean them. That takes time, money, and effort, but it's well worth it if you can afford it. I can't say that enough. Even my cheap soft-pine floor in the kitchen, which shows every dent, is a million light-years better than the old broken linoleum.

Paint makes cleaning possible, so it may be that you need some repainting done. Paint woodwork with semigloss or glossy paint (oil based, if possible). Paint walls with an eggshell (not flat) finish so that it will be scrubbable. If the color is dingy with years of dirt, nothing you can do will make it look good. Once you repaint, you will be amazed at how much easier your job will become.

If you can't clean your windows because the wood has dry-rot and the sash weights don't work and the screens are broken, repair or replace the windows. This effort will pay you back in energy savings, and your cleaning job will be significantly lightened. Install wood trim moldings (or paintable resin ones) where the walls meet the floors and the ceilings. Before you paint, caulk edges wherever they meet, using painter's caulk. It's easy, and it makes a huge difference. The caulking may have to be redone every few years. Dust and bugs come through those cracks, making things dirtier; see what you can do to tighten things up.

In the process of repairing, replacing, and painting, you have to move furniture away from walls (if not out of the room) and take draperies and curtains down. Suddenly you will be deep cleaning, despite your reluctance. And then the room will be clean. Remember: don't put back anything you don't need or love, and make sure the thing itself is clean before you return it to its place.

What I Learned from the Cleaning Lady about Deep Cleaning

With me on all this? Well, then, I'll tell you a story.

Once, long ago, when I was recovering from a difficult childbirth, my sixth, and feeling overwhelmed, my dear husband and mother put their resources together to get me a cleaning lady.[6] We really couldn't afford it, but something needed to be done. Part of me was completely opposed to the idea. I did feel as if I should have been able to handle my own problems; I thought that the money was certainly needed elsewhere; I was ashamed of having someone else dealing with my shabby possessions.

But somehow I had lost the ability to keep my own house clean! All I could think to do was vacuum, and that didn't seem to help. This lady

---

[6] This story is in no way to discourage you from getting cleaning help if you can afford it. At the time, we really couldn't. The point is that you need to know how to do these things whether you delegate them or not. And you will be happier doing them if you know how, anyway.

was someone I knew to be kind and helpful, and she needed the money too, so I agreed.

She told me that before she came, I'd have to "pick up," and I did, and that was quite an effort because I still didn't feel well. Then she arrived and proceeded to take two full days to deep clean every single thing in my house—one day for the upstairs and another for the downstairs.

She worked in one room at a time. She opened windows. She pulled every article of furniture out into the middle of the room and wiped down every molding and window frame. She vacuumed or wiped the furniture itself, including under cushions. She cleaned the floors around the perimeter of the room. She washed curtains and towels.

She removed every item from every horizontal surface, cleaned the surface, cleaned the items, then put them back. She took out every book from every shelf, wiped the shelves, and put the books back neatly, rather than in the jumbled way I had stored them. She pushed everything back and cleaned the floors and vacuumed the carpets. She worked her way backward out of each room.

And then my house was clean.

But you know what? Every week after that (for maybe six months?), when she came, she just dusted the wood furniture and vacuumed (of course I had to declutter before she came, and I was getting stronger during this time). For a good long while, that was enough. She never deep cleaned after that first time.

And soon I realized she wasn't going to, and the fact was that with things decluttered anyway, I could do it myself! I knew how! I saw her!

As I got irritated with the fact that she was only dusting and vacuuming (I could do that! I had already done the hard part of putting our clutter away before she got there!), I made the decision to take on all the cleaning myself (and really, we couldn't afford her anymore).

I had known what to do all along, and at one time I had done it, but somehow I also forgot it, but then she helped me remember.

Now, when I get to feeling that things are overwhelming, I remember that it isn't enough to vacuum the middle of the room. You have to declutter (and we will talk about that), pull everything to the middle of the room, clean the edges from top to bottom, pull everything back, and clean the middle. You have to do that in each room, one room at a time.

Then you will be set in that room for at least a few months. If the cleaning lady won't do anything about it, you don't have to either, until you are ready to fire yourself, that is!

Keeping Cleaning in Perspective

Now, just because I talk about cleaning or doing laundry in such a compelling way doesn't mean that those things are the basis of our self-worth.

Even though I think it makes sense from a lot of points of view to get good at what we do in the home, they are important in the grand scheme of things only as *things that we do*, in the "he that is faithful in that which is least is faithful also in much" kind of way (Luke 16:10, KJV), and insofar as they make it possible for us to love others better and be more patient with ourselves.

So making a nice dinner or finally getting a room organized really is worthy of praise, and we can hardly be blamed for seeking praise when we do them. But I think it is good to try to see ourselves as God sees us: needing to accomplish a lot in our corner of the world but not ever being perfect, not in the grand scheme of things. I don't know about you, but everything I do could certainly be done better. That would depress me if I didn't also see that the point will never be to seek perfection here on earth. I don't mean that we should abandon the effort to be better. Imagine saying, "I just won't do it then!"

No. We keep striving, with peace. Trying to keep things orderly allows us to attend more to matters that are beyond, and above, the merely temporal. It's a paradox, but it's true. If we have a reasonably neat and clean house, we will be more able to attend to higher priorities.

Maintaining Your Deep Clean: Confine and Corral, Part 1

 et's talk about another issue: dirt and kids. Getting your house reasonably clean requires that you *confine and corral your children*.

Don't do anything yet. You are not ready, by any means. We are only thinking about cleaning, not actually cleaning!

But just think about this: pretty much all the dirt in your house comes from two sources: the outside and food. Oh, there are others: wood-burning stove or fireplace, dog, miscellaneous hobbies that involve glitter and glue. But these are the biggies: the outside and food.

And the means of spreading the dirt around your house can be summed up in one word: kids.

I do think that kids can be helpful in cleaning. But without addressing that issue just yet, let me say that even if they aren't actively helpful, you need to focus on keeping them confined when they eat and corralled when they play.

Confine

One of the most important objects in your life is the table. A good, sturdy, easily cleaned kitchen table (if you have room for it). Children need to be taught that they must eat at the table. If you let them run around the house with food, you get what you deserve: a house that smells like old food and has a greasy film over it.

Children are entranced by having their own child-size table and chairs, and if you can fit those in the kitchen, it's a lovely way to help them learn the skill of concentrating on a meal. Of course, having them sit up at the big table, first in a high chair, then perhaps on a booster seat, and eventually on a big chair, works fine.

For some reason, a lot of moms seem to think that they have no right to make their children sit still to eat. They seem to feel that it would be really hard; maybe just impossible. They think it's okay for their kids to graze, eating at all and any times, so it never occurs to them to make them be still to do it. We can blame some of this on the sixties-style parenting advice that has permeated our culture down to this day, for sure, and it has only gotten worse as homemaking has received less respect. Time to do things differently!

Children will do what you ask of them. The proof of this is that when I was a child, no one ever asked a child to sit still in the car, and now no one thinks twice about buckling even the most active toddler tightly in a car seat, every single time.

Yet, somehow, in that same era, a single teacher could enforce perfect silence and order on a class of twenty children for hours at a time (and my husband, who is older and went to Catholic school, had one nun for fifty young children!). Nowadays, twelve children can't be expected to line up without benefit of counsel.

You must teach children to sit at the table, use a napkin, not get food on the outside of their mouths, keep their hands clean, and get up only when they are excused (which they can request, of course). Keep at it; keep it short; don't let them eat unless they are doing what you say, more or less, and stay cheerful. Maybe at first you have to read to them, play a story CD, or bribe them with sailboat sandwiches. It doesn't matter. It must be done!

If they can't manage it, there is a wonderful invention called a high chair, from which no one should ever be released without a good rubdown with a clean, warm washcloth! A one-year-old with greasy, grubby hands can turn your home into a pigsty in about a week. Think about it. The grease doesn't magically disappear. If you are lucky, it gets rubbed off on your jeans, which can go in the washer. But a sofa, a rug, a curtain—it's all fair game, and like the proverbial frog in hot water, you won't even notice until your house is filthy!

Using a clean, warm dishcloth, wash your baby's hands and mouth before he gets down. Then rinse the dishcloth, get it a little soapy, and wipe down his chair and the surroundings. It takes only a minute.

Even a three-year-old can take a plate, scrape off the scraps into the trash, and put the dish in the dishwasher or next to the sink. Then that older child can wash his hands, because of course you have a handy stool for just that purpose and a clean towel that he can reach.

This way, the food residue isn't being spread, inexorably, throughout your home. Indeed, there is simply no way to keep a house clean if its inmates do not follow these simple rules.

Corral

Young children will pull out their toys and strew them all around. The question is, are you letting them have the run of the house, so that nothing is beyond their reach, nothing remains in its place if they choose to pull it out?

Are the little barbarians wreaking havoc in one place as you are cleaning up another?

Even older children have the tendency to seek out a quiet, orderly spot and sort of make a nest there. I am not sure why this is, but I have observed it many times: no sooner have you tidied up a room than there is a child, plunk in the middle of it. You have to make it clear to your children by whatever means—gates, fences with spikes, massed tanks at the border—that there are boundaries they must respect, whether they like it or not.

If a child can show the maturity to be in a kid-free zone without trashing it, then by all means, let him go. I'm all for it. It's a privilege to be earned, and sweet when it is!

But if you know that a mess will result, your sanity demands that the activity take place within the confines of an easily cleaned room designated for the kids. Where toddlers are concerned, the kitchen and the playroom or den are the only areas you should even think about letting them dwell. They are just like puppies in this respect: super cute but completely untrustworthy.

And don't hesitate to take this policy a step further with a nice, spacious playpen in which said small child can spend a half an hour in the morning while you do some necessary things, as well as another half an hour in the evening before supper. It's his little den, and by age six months or so, he can start enjoying it. This blessed time of confinement won't last too long, but it's worth it for those maximum mobility-to-irrationality months. We're talking about an hour a day. Try it!

Something you will notice is that as you train the children to respect their environment and your work, and as you take the time and make the effort to teach them with love and equanimity, everyone enjoys being together more, and after a while, the big payoff isn't just a cleaner house: it's also a more peaceful home. It might take a while, but it will happen.

Maintaining Your Deep Clean:
Confine and Corral, Part 2

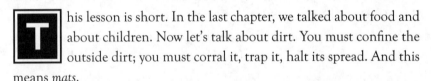

This lesson is short. In the last chapter, we talked about food and about children. Now let's talk about dirt. You must confine the outside dirt; you must corral it, trap it, halt its spread. And this means *mats*.

If you read Don Aslett's books, you should come away with one key learning: there must be industrial-style, that is, *effective dirt-trapping*, mats at the doors. As Aslett points out, what do stores and other institutions do? They can't ask people to take off their shoes. Instead, they place the proper materials at the door to stop dirt from getting all over. (At home, we really ought also to take off our shoes, but that's not my point here.)

We are not talking about those accursed little rag rugs that seem to be made to keep the emergency room in business. We are not even talking about rubber-backed glorified bathmats that might stay in place but are too small and practically leap up into the beater bar of your vacuum.

We are talking about a large (at least 3.5 by 5 foot) rubber, water-absorbent mat that stays put. You can hose it down; you can vacuum it; you can sweep it. There can be one outside the door where the daily traffic is: a good sturdy coconut or coir mat, or a very decorative Waterhog-type mat (they do come in formal designs and this one can be a bit smaller); but place the large one inside the door.

You will come to see this utilitarian object as beautiful once you realize how much work it saves you! Your children and you can take your shoes off upon entering the house. But guests, workmen, dogs—their dirty tracks stop there, on that awesome mat. Trust me. It's worth every penny.

In the winter, if you live where there is snow, you can also lay down an old blanket or quilt on the floor, beyond the mat, for when a bunch of kids are coming in with their snowy boots and togs. The snow will quickly begin to melt, and there will likely not be enough room on even a big mat for everything. It's not nice to step in a puddle wearing socks, so the old blanket is helpful for all the wet things; after taking off outerwear, one can step onto the dry floor.

So, to sum up, we're going to keep the outside dirt from tracking in, and we are going to keep food from getting all over the house. Confine and corral.

Decluttering with Shelves and the Occasional Well Placed Nail

I imagine you already know the theory of decluttering. The practice is hard work. Right now might not be the ideal time if you just had a baby and the baby needs to be nursed all the time. Maybe you are sick? Maybe there are pressing things that have to get done.

If it is the right time, you'll have to schedule it in and be ready for a hard day. But don't exhaust yourself needlessly. Think.

You know very well that you need three things:

1. A trash bag, for trash
2. A box, for giveaways
3. A laundry basket, for internal relocation

Now, pick a spot, and keep it limited. Not more than one room, for sure, but possibly even one dresser, one closet, or one shelf in a closet, depending on how dire the situation is.

People are very different. Some people consider one book on a coffee table clutter. Others are festooned with fake ivy garlands and knick-knacks that wish you welcome; love; luck o' the Irish; Boo; harvest; red, white, and blue; and everything else, as if somehow every thought in your heart must be memorialized on a plaque and displayed. And some people have books and kids.

Fact: I personally am not so uncluttered. But when I clean up the bookcases, I do only the bookcases, nothing else. Otherwise it's too tiring. Only you know who you are, how much energy you have, and how much stuff you want around.

Remember my secret, discussed at length above, which boils down to this: if you have clutter, don't try to clean it up where it is. Get it all out into the middle of the room, even though this feels incredibly messy; wipe down, dust, disinfect, and maybe even paint whatever it is you are organizing. (Do you know how delightful a painted closet is? Paint it white so you can see what's in it.) Now and only now, put back what you really want there, using the criterion of Marie Kondo ("Does it spark joy?") or William Morris ("Have nothing in your house that you do not know to be useful, or believe to be beautiful"), depending on what moves you to do what you must. If it's something decorative, for the love of all that is orderly, just make sure you wipe it before you put it back.

One thing I learned from having that cleaning lady was that if I hadn't decluttered enough for her before her arrival, she simply put everything in a pile in the middle of the room, perhaps having cleaned the spot beforehand. After she left, I had to deal with the stuff, and you know what? It's not that hard when it's all in one spot like that, and you know that the room is clean once you just put it all away or throw it out.

Having applied these rules, look at what is left. Whatever it is, *at this moment* it goes into one of four places:

1. In another spot in the room, the room you are working in
2. In the laundry basket if its true place is in another room. Do not leave the room to put it away, or you will become hopelessly sidetracked! You will start cleaning that other room! You will forget that you are in the midst of a hellish nightmare in this room right here! You will then likely end up in *yet another room*, and only after supper, when everyone is exhausted, will you remember what you were doing, and then it will be too late. Your doom will have been deemed: to live, not in clutter, but in utter chaos.

3. In that box you already provided yourself with, for giving away
4. In the trash bag. Just throw it away if it's not worth anything to anyone. Don't overthink this. Don't let stuff keep you from living your life.

Now, I have another secret for you.

Things that you "store" on the floor, be they children's toys, books, pots, brooms, or really just anything, are always going to seem messy. Keeping things (that aren't furniture) on the floor is inherently cluttery and will make vacuuming and wiping down much more of a chore than they need to be.

This is where the shelves come in. And hooks. And nails.

As you are putting things back, or maybe just a moment before, ask yourself if there is any way to get them off the floor. Or the counter. Or whatever horizontal surface they are parking on. Any way at all?

Do you keep the broom in a corner on the floor, propped up against a wall? This is going to sound odd, and you may not believe me, but if you keep the broom on the floor, besides not being good for it (the business end will deform), *you will never feel like a good housekeeper.* But if you put a big nail in the wall and hang the broom on that, you will feel as if you have it all under control. Don't wait for the perfect broom holder. (I had one, and then I got a new broom with a handle too large for it. The nail I am using now is the upgrade!)

Keep the broom, mop, vacuum, dustpan, and other cleaning items out of sight, not near the front or back door or in a corner of a room. They need to be out of view in the living areas. Could they be hung up along the basement stairs? Just outside the door to the garage? Inside the pantry entry? In a closet? Even if closet space is scarce, once you think about *hanging* these items as opposed to having them propped on the floor, storage space will be forthcoming, I am sure.

Don't wait for the perfect container for the other objects lying around. Look around for baskets, which seem to multiply in the house. Pick up some cheap clear plastic bins at the grocery store and put the kids' toys in them for now. You can always use them for something else later. Put the bins on shelves. Look at thrift stores and yard sales for hutches, bookcases, and old cabinets. You might have something in the garage that could be spray-painted.

Metal brackets are inexpensive at the hardware store. I have spray-painted them a pretty color to good effect. Brackets on the wall with a sturdy pine board going across can transform your space.

Get some nails and hooks—and buy yourself your very own hammer so that you can pound a nail in a wall when you need to. Have a stash of those very secure and removable adhesive hooks if the wall won't take a nail (there is a very secure kind that says it's permanent but can be removed with a blow dryer). Look at your favorite household-goods store's clearance section for those handy racks-of-hooks that can go behind any door or on the wall. Shaker peg racks are so pretty and so useful.

The less you have on the floor, the more you will feel that your house is becoming fairly tidy.

Start in Your Bedroom

f you remember, when we started this discussion, I promised that I'd tell you the best place to start—when you are ready to clean, not just think about cleaning.

Did you guess? Do you care? Do you think it matters?

I do!

Whether you are spring cleaning or just going through your normal routine (I know, I know; well, let's work on it!), you should start in your bedroom, and in the process, express your love for your husband in a hidden yet effective way.

Even if your "normal routine" seems less like a line with a starting point and more like an endless circle, I hope you will come to think of the master bedroom as where you begin. When you're a bit paralyzed by all you have to do, start there. When things are going pretty well and you have the cleaning under control, start there anyway.

I mean, when things are going well, you just keep going around and around, doing a little deep cleaning here and a lot of maintenance there, don't you? And no doubt there are problem spots that are always calling out for attention. And then you might lose your bearings. So, although there is one school of thought that has you start with your kitchen sink, and certainly, much has to happen before the sink gets shiny, which makes this idea clever, I wonder: *If you start in the kitchen, will you ever leave?*

The Sidetracked Home Executives (one of the books I recommend) have you start with your entryway, which I do not dismiss. It's about seeing yourself as others see you; we'll get there.

But after about thirty years of reflection, I am having you start in the room you share with your husband. The reason is simple, but profound. Your home has many areas that express family life, but your bedroom expresses the foundational relationship between you and your spouse; the inner sanctum where the sacrament of your marriage is consecrated and continually renewed with the conjugal gift. If it weren't for the intimacy of your commitment, your family would not be. God has ordained it so. It was that way from the very start. It has always been that way. It always will be that way—the family does not outgrow its need for a foundation.

Express this reality by means of your respect for this physical place, for your body, for the body of your husband. Your first steps should be to make the room—the bed and the places for your clothes—truly orderly. From there, it's not far to make it actually beautiful, according to what you both think is beautiful. It will be a sanctuary.

What good does it do to have, as so many families do, a fancy living room, a gleaming kitchen, a curb with appeal, a huge TV and wet bar, but chaos, piles of laundry, dust, and dreariness in the bedroom? Conversely, some people tend toward narcissism in there, but our aim is loving simplicity, not hedonistic luxury.

So it seems fitting to me that the struggle to bring order to the home begins here, where the home has its origin. It seems to me that whatever you do here to improve your sense of service to your husband and the bond you share will redound to the good of your family, joining the grace of your sincere effort with that of the sacrament, bringing "grace upon grace" to all.

When you make your bed, which you should do every morning, offer up the incense of thanksgiving for your husband and a prayer for his sanctification, which depends so much on you!

In difficult times, when you are tempted to let bitterness creep in, try to think of one thing, one quality, that you are truly grateful for in this person God has given you. Remember that God has foreknown, through all eternity, that you would be married to him. Have faith and trust that, in foreknowing, He also ordained it and desired it. In other words, it's no mistake, if that's what you are thinking.

If you're thinking, "Oh, no! I love my husband; he's so good to me!" then this is a good time to tell God you realize His blessing.

And then, maybe go ahead and change the sheets! Even in the leanest times, it's worth having two sets of sheets so that you can accomplish this task with a minimum of effort (that is, without having to wash the one set on the spot; I personally find remaking beds exhausting enough without that pressure.)

So, on to the cleaning. As I told you, you have to ask, "What belongs in here?" A bed, side tables, lamps, dressers, possibly a chair ... an exercise machine, a quilt rack, an extra dresser because the other ones are quite small, a floor lamp, a small laundry hamper—my bedroom is big, and I want you to know that I have realistic standards. For the sake of full disclosure, I will say that it's my clothes that are usually piled on the chair.

If your bedroom is small, consider keeping the dressers in the closet. Sometimes you can put suits and other hanging clothing in another room.

For years, our bedroom had a bassinet coming and going, and a changing area for the baby. That's part of life, if not of magazine pictures. Can you make these things pretty and keep them clean? Don't let dust accumulate under the changing table because you think it's temporary. Don't let your sheets get dirty because the baby will just spit on them as soon as you change them. In fact, you can have a little stash of extra layers, whether a folded twin sheet or a large towel, for spreading out under the baby.

No matter how little it seems to bother him, don't let your husband feel that he's second fiddle to the parade of little ones marching through your room and your bed, or to anything else.

If your problem is that your bedroom is hidden under laundry, review the chapter on solving that lamentable situation ("The Laundry Process"), and make your first move to clear everything out. Even if the piles have to reside in the hallway for a while, that's fine. The important thing is to get *this* room whipped into serene order.

In an ideal world there would never be a laundry basket in sight. In my world, I fold laundry on my bed. That's a given for me. Decide what level of "less than perfect" *you* can live with, and then stick to it (by which I mean don't go beneath it). For me, a couple of laundry baskets in transit is an acceptable level, not to be degraded to the mountains that could be there if I let them. Beware that this danger is especially real if the laundry room is regrettably placed adjacent to the master bathroom. I do think a laundry room *near* the bedrooms makes sense for efficiency's sake, but it's just too tempting to let it pile up if it's "only in my room."

When the changing of the seasons comes for those of us who have to switch wardrobes a couple of times a year, it's inevitable to find a sea of clothes here in the master bedroom. They have to be somewhere! But get them out as soon as you can!

Even making sure we don't throw all the household clutter in the master bedroom when we're entertaining gives us a haven to repair to after the company has gone.

You may be surprised at how devoting some effort and love to your bedroom can make you aware of and resolve some deep noncleaning-related issues in the home. Once you make it a priority to keep your bedroom *reasonably* clean and tidy, you will notice that you've removed the unspoken tension of disorder and gained your husband's gratitude. You will find, too, that you can more reasonably expect your children to clean their own rooms as they are able. They grow to respect your room—and what it represents—more as they grow older. We think they don't notice such things, but, in fact, their whole consciousness of home and family is made up of such details, which they cherish.

Do you see how that consciousness contributes, however humbly, to their understanding of the preciousness of marriage and the home and the reverence that both you and your husband have for your relationship? Do you see how this lesson, an unspoken and even unintended one, will carry its message to a new generation?

Who knew that you were expressing so much by cleaning a room?

No More Boom and Bust: The Moderate Clean and the Blitz

nce you get the idea behind deep cleaning and decluttering, you'll see that these are activities that can't be indulged in very often. It's exhausting and mighty work.

Some books and guides give you a schedule for deep cleaning your house, but as far as I can see, it's just material for an anxiety attack. Having a schedule for power-washing your siding seems a bit overwhelming to me, I must say, not to mention reminders to refold your linens to avoid permanent creases, as in "take out perfectly folded things in order to refold them." I'm pretty sure the people who do things like that don't need to be told to do things like that, or perhaps have a staff whose life mission it is to do them, in which case, that's fine, they can have the schedule with my blessing.

The truth is that once you know how to pull everything away from the walls and clean underneath, wipe wooden trim from the top down, and dust books and shelves before restoring order, and once you know enough to approach a chest of drawers with a couple of bins for sorting, putting back only those things you really want and need, you will start to know *when* it needs to be done.

Do your deep cleaning and decluttering when ordinary methods fail to please. No schedule necessary other than the one imposed by holidays, season changes, and weird odors.

There is more to life than cleaning. But, paradoxically, in order to get to that "more," you have to have order in your daily life; so cleaning is a must.

Enter the Moderate Clean and the Blitz. These are your ordinary methods, habits that are going to keep that Deep Clean working for you so you can do other things. An alternate name for the Moderate Clean that I'm going to describe is "Sparkle and Shine," but the truth is that I never called it that myself. When I heard it called that recently I thought, there goes a better mother than I, a more cheerful, more upbeat mother—a natural sanguine, sunshiny person. I call it "chores" myself.

Master the Moderate Clean and the Blitz to stay out of the dread cycle known as the "Boom and Bust." Do you know what I mean by "Boom and Bust," that syndrome in which things go downhill fast after the Sisyphean burst? You never really enjoy your clean house, because you're always either exhausted from deep cleaning it or living with it dirty. You boom—get mad at yourself, the house, and all the residents, and go on a cleaning binge—and then you bust, because the binge depresses you and leaves you convinced that you can't maintain that level of energy for long—and you can't.

So we'll talk about how to get on a more even keel. Wouldn't that be nice?

The Moderate Clean

If you're booming and busting all the time—if you are either exhausting yourself getting things clean or not able to enjoy a steady state of a *reasonably* clean house, but instead invest a considerable portion of your decorating budget on little plaques plaintively hoping that God will find it in His heart to "Bless this mess" and affirming that a good mom gives kisses, not chores—you, my friend, need the concept of *the Moderate Clean, or Sparkle and Shine.* Throw the plaques out, and let's get serious.

When I read other people's advice (other than the books I've already mentioned), I find that a couple of things aren't taken into account:

1. The person giving advice often doesn't understand what it's like to live with a lot of children, each of whom you are trying to nurture lovingly according to his own interests, resulting in a house full of gravel ("pretty rocks"), drawings (what is it about a stack of paper that cries out for a crayon line? one line per page?), houses (cardboard boxes, by far the best toy, yet somewhat anti-aesthetic, no?) and enough Legos to shake a stick at.

2. The person doesn't homeschool and consequently has no idea that there simply isn't a stretch of time every day when you are alone, able to concentrate on removing fingerprints, and so forth. On the other hand, sending the kids to school could be a snare and a delusion. I found that I no sooner recovered from the morning and got the baby to nap, than they were home and too much in need to decompress to do anything around the house other than play. Plus, all the *paper*—but I digress.

3. The person doesn't take into account that you will be living for years, nay, possibly decades, with at least one nursing baby, and the subsequent feeling of sheer immobility you feel when faced with dirty floors, clutter, piles of dishes, and so on.

This author wants you to have a *perfectly* clean house, whereas you and I know that we want only a *reasonably* clean house; that is, one that has order but doesn't take all day to get that way, and one that we can whip into shape if we really need to, as opposed to booming and busting.

I have this to say: unless you have quadruplets and some kind of higher education that renders you unfit for housework, and *anyway*, aren't really bothered by clutter and dirt, there are two little secrets that, once you internalize them, will make you grow up and take care of your own home.

Schedule an Hour to Clean Every Day

Some of your time each day has to be devoted to certain things: personal hygiene, dressing kids, eating, checking your e-mail, reading to kids and yourself, and other sundry activities. Let's accept that a certain amount of time each day will be devoted to taking care of the home. It's not the same amount of time each day, and yes, there will be days when you aren't able to do one single thing and other days when you will do nothing but clean.

But if you do some deep cleaning as described above, and then get it into your head that you need to clean for a minimum of one hour a day—just one hour, and that includes dishes!—you will have a reasonably clean house.

Does one hour seem like a lot? Can you picture yourself spending that amount of time on such a wretched activity? How about half an hour in the morning and half an hour after naps?

Can you embrace the hour? Or do you feel somewhat offended that cleaning takes any time at all or maybe that it takes any of *your* time? Be honest.

You'll feel better—more responsible, happier—if you schedule it in. Unlike the deep clean (which I told you would announce its necessity to you in various ways), you really do need to know what you are cleaning and when. Consider it a sacred duty. Consider it an intellectual challenge. You are smart! You can do it!

In my own "education of a girl who couldn't sweep," the stages were gradual but inexorable. First, the Holy Spirit came down with little whisperings and made me realize it was immature to wait for my mom to come clean up for me. For one small detail, she lived 182 miles away. I was in denial, all right! But I was also enabled, since my mom *did* come and help me, quite a lot. But after this revelation, I purchased for myself a real vacuum cleaner and a dust cloth and made an effort.

I still just kind of let cleaning happen, sort of in the way young singles approach mealtimes. If you're hungry, eat. If things are dirty, clean them. No forethought, no plan, just react. Pretty soon, I reached deep into my vast stores of reading memories and asked, "What Would Ma Do?" (WWMD) and pulled out that pioneer idea of "Wash on Monday / Iron on Tuesday" ... and that's as far as I got.

It *was* good start, though. I decided I should clean every Monday, as well as do my laundry, because after all, unlike Ma, I had a washer and dryer. I made a commitment not to go out shopping, not to socialize, and not to read on Mondays, but to tidy, dust, vacuum, mop the kitchen floor, and do the laundry from start to finish!

Granted, I think at the time we only had two babies, so there wasn't a lot of laundry — *nothing* like later. But our duplex had two floors and a basement, three bedrooms (one of which I ignored), and the laundry in that basement, so I was really exhausted by Monday night. What a great feeling, though! To have everything done! To embrace, rather than deny, my duty!

Starting out the week with a clean home helped me overcome the depression I was feeling at living somewhere with no friends to share my journey with, everyone else being either still in college or working on their careers. I had no clue where to find friends, and just imagine life with no blogs! But at least I was on my way to feeling a little more optimistic about myself in my new life.

Then I realized that weekends were miserable with things a mess, which, of course they were when I hadn't cleaned since Monday. So—and this was such a stroke of genius, I must say—I decided to clean on Fridays too! That way, I could enjoy the weekend with my husband and children!

It gradually dawned on me that I could even do a little every day, while still keeping the basic "housework" days of Monday and Friday, and my house would be clean and enjoyable most of the time!

The learning curve can be ever so gradual an incline, but eventually you get there. You get over the idea that "staying home" means "not doing work," and you commit to doing some work!

And now my second secret.

Divide Your Home into Cleaning Zones

All of this will be unfolded as we go—remember, we are still thinking about cleaning—but it's really worthwhile to mentally break up the house into separate areas with a promise to yourself that you will almost always tackle only one zone at a time.

The kitchen is one, not to be discussed now. Bathrooms are another. For me, it's upstairs and downstairs, with the downstairs further divided into "hard use" (the den and mudroom, but kitchen separate for these purposes) and "easy use" (living and dining rooms). If you live in a ranch house, you simply think of the "sleeping zone" and the "living zone" and go from there.

Now, when you approach your hour of work, think in these zones. Most of your cleaning time is going to be devoted to one zone only; maybe even part of a zone. The rest get the Blitz, which I'll save for another section, but I'll bet you can figure out that you don't spend much time blitzing.

So your Moderate Clean will consist of approaching your zone with an eye to getting it into shape in less than an hour. You work fast. You have your cleaning tools ready. You have your helpers (also a topic for another section, but you can start thinking about how even a two-year-old comes in pretty handy as a runner). Start in one room and stick to that room until you are done (which is why you need the runner).

Always start at the door and go around in one direction. I'll let you choose whether to go counterclockwise or the reverse; I'm not picky! But do not crisscross the room, whatever you do. Just go in one direction, once around for decluttering and dusting, and once for vacuuming.

Why? Because there is no point in wasting any more thought on this process than you need to! Instead of figuring the process out anew, just do the same thing every time! It's totally liberating! Try it!

Let's suppose that on the first day, you will be found tackling the upstairs (bedrooms and hallway). Don't forget to start in your own room (where you will make the bed and deal with clothes every day!).

For Moderate Clean, you quickly move everything either to its proper place or the middle of the room. Have a laundry basket at the ready for everything from books to laundry that didn't make it into the hamper. Make the beds. Put away clean clothes. Keep in mind that you can get your kids to do a lot of this, but I won't get into that now, and it's a good thing to know what has to be done and how hard it is before you start delegating.

Dust surfaces by wiping them down with a damp (with water) cloth or an anti-static duster. Every couple of weeks, move everything off surfaces to dust and pull things away from the walls, but for a normal, Moderate Clean, you can feather dust in place. Every other time, make yourself do the baseboards and other molding as well as furniture. You can use the brush attachment on your vacuum for this job.

Put the laundry basket (or other container) of random stuff out in the hall. Make the kids claim their stuff and put it away. If any socks were found under the bed, this is the time for a lecture or sweet reminder about the hamper system, discussed in "The Laundry Process." Personally, I would give penalties for every sock found. For instance, they have to clean a window (which most kids love to do, and it's not as if you'll be getting to it anytime soon).

Vacuum only when all is in place and dusted. If your vacuum spews dust, you need a new one! Remember to go in one direction around the room, then do the middle, then go out the door you came in by. Work your way down the hall and from bedroom to bedroom until you've finished that area.

If this sounds monumental and unreasonable, it's because you have too much stuff—you need to go back to decluttering. *The Moderate Clean works only in a decluttered zone.* Without first decluttering, you will never be able to keep your occasional cleaning to an hour.

It may also be that you are working slowly. All that wiping down and scooping up should be done as quickly as possible most of the time. Challenge yourself to make this your workout.

Now, go do other things, knowing that tomorrow is another day!

Remember when we had a little chuckle because I said that my way keeps you from *doing too much*? It's true, though. There are some ladies who never clean. There are others who can't figure out how to do other things they like because they are so focused on keeping the house clean! The problem is that once you start to love a clean house, it sort of consumes you, and of course there is no end, simply no end, to how much you could clean, when, really, you ought to move on.

It's good to know that you'll get to it, whether you are on one end of the tidy scale or the other. Even if things are messy, you have other things to do. If someone drops by, you have the satisfaction of knowing that you are doing your best, even if it doesn't look that way.

We're not talking about how things look to other people but about how things are done to satisfy God, your family, and you. That's what matters, nothing else! It's a different story when people drop by and things are a mess because you've done *nothing* about it, ever, nor do you intend to. That's when you can be a bit embarrassed. But we're fixing that right now.

The next day, move to your downstairs zone, the "hard living" areas: den or family room, eating area, and mudroom. Here you will want to add to your supplies some strong cleanser and a rag for wiping down walls and doorjambs. The basic process is the same. Start in one place—the same place every time. Start where you enter, go around the room clockwise or counterclockwise, end in the middle, where all the stray things will be piled or placed in a laundry basket.

The next day, you can do the "easy living" areas, which might be very quick indeed if you've made sure to confine and corral, as I told you. In fact, you can probably skip this zone every other time.

Many people with young children don't have two separate living areas. I didn't at first. But you can still keep your children from trashing every room in the house by making sure they don't play in the living room *and* their bedrooms, or by allowing them to do crafts on the coffee table *and* the kitchen table. You will be able to figure it out now that you have the basic principles in mind.

One day of the week, Moderately Clean the kitchen and the bathrooms, and make sure your laundry is caught up.

On a busy day, do only the stairs (which I find get lost in the "zones" idea) or quickly triage the house and do the neediest zone.

On Saturdays, if you don't have a million soccer games to go to, you can make everyone clean everything, especially their own rooms. I don't know whose idea it was to make Saturdays "lazy day," but that won't fly in a big family. Up and at 'em! If you do have games or other activities, take an extra hour on Friday for the Moderate Clean. You can also use Family Movie Night, Friday or Saturday, to incentivize a quick cleanup if activities preclude really getting the house in order for the weekend. I will explain that type of cleanup shortly.

The most important motivation here is to do what you have to do to go into Sunday with a calm and orderly mind and house, so that the family can worship calmly and have a restful day.

Divide things up and work fast. Do things on the days that work for you; for instance, since grocery shopping with children can be truly exhausting, keep that day's housekeeping light. Look at your schedule and figure out what needs to be clean when. If you are hosting the ladies' tea on Thursday, it makes more sense to do a Moderate Clean in the "easy living" area than the bedrooms on Wednesday.

To summarize:

- Commit to an hour of cleaning a day (usually), and you can break this up into half-hour or twenty-minute segments if necessary.
- Divide your house into zones and work on only one zone (or even part of a zone) at a time.

The Blitz

I t's impossible to explain to anyone who hasn't lived through it just how hard it is to keep house with a lot of kids. It *could* be likened to trying to establish order among wild horses, except that I think that wild horses have a limited imagination about what they want to accomplish. I don't know that species well, but it seems to me that they probably just want to run around a lot, and every once in a while, eat.

Whereas kids don't want to do just one thing or two things. Their little minds are firing off in a million directions. They exude dirt and trash. The exponential effect they have on each other means that three kids make nine times as much mess. So really, if you have six kids, they are making thirty-six times more mess than one kid!

This is why I quickly learned that my small-family deep- and moderate-cleaning skills were not enough. Although cleaning on Monday and Friday might work for a family with only one child, it isn't enough for a large family. And, as I told you in my recounting of the time I got a cleaning lady, having a lot of kids made me forget any expertise I had acquired. My brain literally became paralyzed from the necessity of feeding, teaching, and, in fact, defending myself against all my kids, whom, nonetheless, I loved very much; and I really did just forget how to deep-clean a room until another person demonstrated what was required.

Slowly I achieved my new powers of understanding. I grasped the necessity for the Deep Clean; I moved on to the Moderate Clean maintenance theory and practice. Then I identified the self-preservation strategy of the Blitz.

The Blitz is a lightning strike on a room that has been reasonably maintained (in other words, not a room in need of a Deep Clean but simply one that has endured three nanoseconds of kid exposure). The Blitz enables you to live a real life with the sure knowledge that you can whip things into shape in fifteen minutes.

There are two peak times of need for the Blitz.

1. After breakfast and before schooling starts, or you leave the house for the day, or otherwise start your various activities. It's much nicer to know that you have a clean slate and can face the day with a clean conscience.

2. Between 4:00 and 6:00 p.m., or whenever *meltdown* coincides with *Dad's return from work*. I mean, just *before* that point. You will be amazed at how much better you can handle the end of the day if you can rely on your gang to straighten up. (If you don't have a gang yet, train yourself in these techniques because you really want to know that you are up to the job yourself.)

So yes, you will blitz every day. Were you wondering how, if you devoted, let's say, four days a week to the twenty-minute Moderate Clean in one zone (assuming the rest of your hour of cleaning went to everyday chores such as kitchen cleanup and bed making) the rest of your house would stay reasonable? If you are getting the upstairs in order, what happens to the downstairs? What happens is the Blitz.

To implement, you have to have the kids on your side. They have to believe that this is all great fun. They have to understand that we're all in this together and our environment matters. Yet, at the same time, there has to be an undercurrent of real danger. Somewhere in there, they have to believe that if they aren't going to pitch in, bad things will happen to them. Punishment must loom. *So you want an atmosphere of lightheartedness – gaiety even – not uncharged with peril.*

Get a timer or set a deadline. I am bound to say that this worked best in the days when a favorite show came on at a certain time. Those fun episodes of harmless ("mindless," as my father would call them) TV came on at 5:00 p.m., and let me tell you, from 4:45 to 4:59, never was such activity to be seen in my house—and never was half an hour better earned or better timed for maximum predinner efficiency on my part. One little measly half an hour isn't too much to pay for peace and even a kind of cultural literacy, if you look at it in a certain twisted light. I just put them on their honor to mute the commercials, and we were all set.

These days of streaming mean that you must create your own sense of urgency, which is not as easy, I admit. The promise of a chapter of *Little House on the Prairie* works too, but not with that fine sense of finality that TV gave. And you *will* cheat and make them do more than fifteen minutes, which isn't fair. A timer will do, however.

This is bribery, a perfectly useful and acceptable tool in parenting, also known as positive conditioning. Show coming on? Want a snack? Want to play with Legos? Blitz the den. (I use "den" as a handy term for our main living area that has the TV and the toys, but it stands for any room currently in a shambles. By all means, apply to the kitchen, the dining room, the race track, the hall or ninepins alley, or what have you.)

And of course, if you don't participate cheerfully in the Blitz, you can go sit by yourself far away while the rest of us have a great time with *loud music*. Loud, fun, rollicking music.

- Old-time rock 'n' roll: try almost anything from Little Richard
- Fiddling: an upbeat tune from Natalie MacMaster
- Bluegrass: "If Wishes Were Horses" (possibly the best song ever, as heard on the O Sisters CD)
- "Tritsche-Tratshe Polka" with Maurice Andre, trumpet master.
- "Choo Choo Ch'Boogie" by the Manhattan Transfer
- Many Disney songs: the best are from *Beauty and the Beast*, *The Little Mermaid*, and how about "I Wanna Be Like You" from *The Jungle Book*?

In the true Blitz, you limit yourself to one room (or two if you have enough workers for teams, or whatever you can handle in the fifteen minutes). Your aim is not so much to clean as to give the appearance of clean. And what is the appearance of clean? That things are tidy and even pretty. I will tell you how.

- Go around the edges and from the edges to the center, as always.
- Divide and conquer. Depending on your work force, assign picker-uppers for each category: toys, books, papers, crayons, random socks.
- Assign a runner during the Blitz, but only one person should leave the room in question at a time, lest he find some (untidy) game to play elsewhere. It's all too easy to forget about children who are not underfoot.
- Assign a small person to look under furniture for stuff. Finders can put everything on the coffee table or in the middle of the room. Put-awayers can put away.
- Return any throw pillows to their places (assign a susceptible child to "make things beautiful"—there's always one who understands throw-pillow placement), neaten horizontal surfaces, send dishes into the kitchen (although it's strictly forbidden to eat elsewhere, so it's not clear why crockery is in any other room), make sure things aren't thrown into corners and around the periphery.

Now is not the time for dusting, and anyway there shouldn't be much dust because a hard-use room has to be moderately cleaned at least once a week. But if there seems to be some (imagine!), wipe it with your apron or blow it away. This method is by no means a remedy, but we're going for appearances here.

Lastly, sweep or vacuum the room (a task well within the capabilities of an eight-year-old), but only the parts that you can see—for instance, the rug. And put away or train children to put away the vacuum cleaner! Nothing undermines a tidy room like a vacuum left out. You don't *store it out*, do you? It simply has to have a place to be hidden away, even if it means hanging a curtain from a shelf and sticking it behind there. Children should learn to put the vacuum cleaner away without banging it against the woodwork.

Now, the well trained household can accomplish the Blitz without you (note, *not* the Deep Clean, or even the Moderate Clean — they might be able to do it once, but not twice in a row), *if and only if* everyone is trained in making sure corners are cleared.

Otherwise, they will quickly catch on to the Pseudo-Blitz, shoving everything away from the center of the room *into* the corners — a bona fide housekeeping disaster. Everyone needs to learn that the room can't even pretend to be clean, does not even have the appearance of clean, until the edges at least are clutter-free.

What most militates against internalizing this insight about the edges is that we assume that things will be cleanest when horizontal surfaces, including the coffee table, which is undeniably in the center of the room, display only those things that are meant to be there. But since most of us, living in families as we do, almost always have quite a bit of stuff out, the times we can achieve this desirable state are few — so we tend to give up and unconsciously subscribe to the idea that shoving everything toward the periphery is a good compromise.

But if you can't clean up the clutter or the random things you need right now, try making the piles of stuff neat and tidy, without pushing them to less used parts of the room, where, I can assure you, they will simply become part of the landscape. If all else fails, put your clutter into a laundry basket and put *that* in the middle of another room, one that is out of sight. Later, when you are doing a Moderate Clean, you can and will address the piles, which will be right out there in the open. But during the Blitz, you will have to be satisfied with neatening things in place for the most part, because you are trying to use your time well — not use it all *up* on constant cleaning.

When the Blitz is over, all you have to do is inspect! Don't let them turn on the TV or get out their extra-zowie-tiny-pieces-of-death super construction toys without making them do it right!

What Can Children Do?

Pope St. John Paul II tells us this:

> All members of the family, each according to his or her own gift, have the grace and responsibility of building day by day the communion of persons, making the family "a school of deeper humanity": This happens where there is care and love for the little ones, the sick, the aged; where there is mutual service every day; when there is a sharing of goods, of joys and of sorrows.[7]

My mother was fond of telling this joke:

A woman and her son were visiting a new friend. They arrived in a limo. The chauffeur came around, opened the door, and carried the nine-year-old boy to the house. The friend, who was waiting to welcome them, asked the woman, "Oh my, is something wrong with your little boy? Can't he walk?" The woman replied, "Thank God, we're so rich, he doesn't have to."

---

[7] John Paul II, apostolic exhortation *Familiaris Consortio* (November 22, 1981), no. 21.

You see? We are so prosperous (and preposterous) that we consider it a virtue that our children have nothing to do. Little do we realize the damage we are doing with this attitude—nothing less than sending yet another generation out into the world handicapped by incompetence in daily life. The family is the ideal place for a child to learn to help others, to relate to all sorts of people, and to take responsibility for all sorts of things, because it's impossible for one person to do all that has to be done to keep a home running! Yet we are in the absurd position of simultaneously doing it all and resenting our lonely martyrdom.

How about changing all that?

> A fundamental opportunity for building such a communion is constituted by the educational exchange between parents and children, in which each gives and receives. By means of love, respect and obedience toward their parents, children offer their specific and irreplaceable contribution to the construction of an authentically human and Christian family. They will be aided in this if parents exercise their unrenounceable authority as a true and proper "ministry," that is, as a service to the human and Christian well-being of their children and in particular as a service aimed at helping them acquire a truly responsible freedom, and if parents maintain a living awareness of the "gift" they continually receive from their children.[8]

All very well, beautifully put. Let's talk about what can be done and what to do.

A Child's Contribution

Chorewise, what exactly can a child's contribution be? Let's look at some examples, very roughly by age.

Curtain Climber (Ages 1 to 3)

The curtain climber follows you around and make things much, much worse. He pulls things off shelves, then plows right over them. He grinds

---

[8] Ibid.

bagels into chairs. He eats kitty litter. (Keep repeating, "My vocation is gestational in nature" and set your sights for the long distance.)

The main thing is to develop a relationship with your baby such that you are responsive to him and he to you. This age is the time for teaching him to do things in order, rather than worrying about chores.

A two-year-old can sometimes put his underwear in the "lights" hamper and his little jeans in the "darks." Your little ones can get up from the table and clear their places. Washing hands after using the toilet, lining up trucks, tucking dolls in their beds, clicking the cap on the toothpaste, putting pajamas in the drawer, getting the puzzles back on their shelf—these are "remote chore preparation" and plenty to work on for now. And then you give them a bowl of water and a rag and set them to washing the deck furniture. Make sure you call it their work.

I Can Do It by MySELF! (Ages 2 to 4)

Do you know why this stage drives you crazy? Because you have nothing for him to do. He feels as if he's not *contributing*. You think of a two-year-old as an eating, pooping machine that has to be taken from point A to point B. Maybe you carry him around all the time, sort of mindlessly pacifying him. You react rather than act, or you keep him buckled in his car seat. You may not respond at all.

He needs to become his own little self, and yes, that's a bit messy. Put your silverware where he can reach it. Get him his own small broom and dustpan and a place to put them. Give him a damp dust cloth and teach him to wipe down the stairs. Let him fill the dog's water bowl. You have a stool he can stand on to reach the sink, right? What's the worst that can happen? Spilled water! If you can't handle that, you need to get out more. Seriously, just keep a stash of demoted towels handy in a nearby cupboard, and let him dry his spill.

Surprisingly Helpful (Ages 3 to 6)

Start making a list of the things you would like to get to, but don't have time for because you have six children under the age of six, or two children and ill health, or other circumstances that keep you from housekeeping perfection. You'd be surprised how many of them your children can do, if you would just grasp, once and for all, that it's better to have it done by a five-year-old than not done at all.

Dusting, Windexing, appliance wiping, deck sweeping, dishwasher unloading, towel folding, dog feeding, egg collecting: these are all things that can be competently if awkwardly done by those approaching the age of reason. Just give them a tutorial, correct them a few times, and let 'em rip.

A pile of shoes at the door is often all that stands between you and a welcoming entry. A totally wonderful, perfectly suitable chore for a four-year-old is straightening out the shoes! You know, a neat row of shoes by the door is a joy. No basket necessary! (Besides, a basket doesn't really work, because the shoes get jumbled, and who has a basket big enough?) A terrible, thankless job for Mom. A great job for someone closer to the floor.

Our William had this job at our house for quite a while. Once I was taking Rosie (who was maybe twelve) to buy new shoes. He really took a stand! "No! I *wefuse*! Wosie has too many shoes aweady!" Turns out that he was struggling to keep up with her supply, which, of course, included soccer cleats, dress shoes, sneakers, and probably one other pair. Poor Will! We took pity on him and made Rosie take a few pairs up to her room.

Indispensable (Ages 6 to 12)

If you've been patient and clever, you will now have an indispensable work force on your hands. Let's remember that Ralph Moody was herding cows solo at the age of eight. That's why you must read *Little Britches*! Nothing your children could possibly do would match *that* for responsibility, danger, and solitude, I'm guessing; so quit making life so easy for them.

Here's what my nine-year-olds could do: process a load of laundry (not their own personal loads, but every step in the process of the family's laundry), clean the bathroom, wash the dishes, vacuum the den, watch their baby sister or brother, get the trash out of the car, make lunch.

Here's what an eleven-year-old can do: mow the lawn (but please, not fill the gas tank: it's really too dangerous because you need height and long arms, and I'm all for kids doing dangerous things, but we have to draw the line at severe burns or death), mop the kitchen floor, head up a car-cleaning team, get a room sparkling from top to bottom. After this, you will know what your kids can do. They will surprise you with their skills.

And of course, once that child's feet reach the floor, he should always be carrying something for you, getting something for you, and generally not being a leech on society. If there is one thing that makes me weep for our times, it's the sight of some poor woman staggering under a load like a packhorse, while her children whine about how they don't want to be there, don't want to leave, or are hungry. Even a kid in a stroller can hold his own sand toy.

If a task demands a safety lesson, make sure it has been given and absorbed. Make sure your children understand that a machine is not magic. I can still hear my engineer father's voice in my head: "Don't force it!" This is the principle of machines: don't force it.

Inspect the job until it's done to your satisfaction.

And occasionally, do it yourself. Two reasons: (1) usually (not always!) you do a better job, and if you don't put yourself in the rotation, your house will suffer for it; and (2) sometimes your children do need a break, and you build trust and model kindness by showing yourself to be understanding when an unexpected opportunity comes up or they are feeling sick or tired. With a young child, just let it go if he has run off to play and some little thing hasn't been taken care of.

It's good to be merciful; you will know when the right moment is to let up on your demands.

Not Every Child Is the Same, and Perfection Isn't the Goal

Now, let's remember a few things. Some astonishingly small children are dexterous and interactive. Their focus is close up. They delight in order and repetition. Some children have large movements and interests. Their horizon seems so very far away, and it's hard to reel them in. *So don't compare one child with another.* Above all, don't read parenting advice and wonder why your kids don't do everything you read about. There's always next year. I'm convinced that there is a much wider margin than we are told for what constitutes appropriate behavior. I once gave the following advice to a friend with two rambunctious boys: stop listening to your friend with one sweet tea-partying, page-coloring girl! I'm sure she's a nice lady, but *she has no idea what she's talking about!*

Oh, and one more thing—and this is what John Paul is saying in the quote below, essentially—the goal is not for everyone to be behaving perfectly! Expect imperfection!

Meltdowns happen, even Mama meltdowns. Yelling isn't the worst thing. You don't want to be yelling constantly, of course, but sometimes your children need you to yell, *because their bad behavior has to do with your excessive talking and misplaced patience.*

(And honestly, sometimes you and I deserve to be yelled at, let's admit it. What could I do that would make my kid want to yell at me? What about this: She's on her way to do what I told her to do, and I tell her to do something else! *I'm* not even listening to *myself!*) No. The worst thing is a tense, overly bright covering up of the sorry fact that no one is helping anyone else.

Family communion can be sought and preserved only through a great spirit of sacrifice. It requires, in fact, a ready and generous openness of each and all to understanding, to forbearance, to pardon, to reconciliation.

> There is no family that does not know how selfishness, discord, tension and conflict violently attack and at times mortally wound its own communion: Hence there arise the many and varied forms of division in family life. But, at the same time, every family is called by the God of peace to have the joyous and renewing experience of "reconciliation," that is, communion re-established, unity restored. In particular, participation in the sacrament of reconciliation and in the banquet of the one body of Christ offers to the Christian family the grace and the responsibility of overcoming every division and of moving toward the fullness of communion willed by God, responding in this way to the ardent desire of the Lord: "that they may be one" (John 17:21).

ASK AUNTIE LEILA

Is It Too Late for Kids to Become Helpful?

Dear Auntie Leila,

In light of "What Can Children Do?," I see the monster of my own making.

My eldest child, a tea-partying, page-coloring girl can practically run the house without me. She's like a well-oiled machine. Loves to please. Very capable. Loves to be a little mama. So cleaning and matronly duties are considered fun by her.

My second child, difficult from day one, has been carried around by me since birth, not because we are so rich, but because this lazy mama would rather baby him than hear him whine, complain, or pitch fits. I know. I can't believe it's like this either! What have I done?

Here is my dilemma. Where do I start in the retraining of him and his mama? Do I start him at stage one until that is mastered? He does have a very small chore list (make bed, clean up toys, feed dog, clear his dishes from the table) that he completes daily, but never without reminders and rarely without grumbling.

I don't blame him. This falls on my shoulders. The worst part is, I know his wife will not appreciate all this. He's eight years old. Tell me this can change! Help me, dear Auntie. Where do I begin? What do I do when he grumbles? What do I do when he doesn't complete his task?

Yours,

Rebekah

Dear Rebekah,

Well, your consolation is that, especially with boys, training in the home (I mean, specific chores) rarely carries through to adulthood! My sons strangely do not seem to regard an empty beer bottle as a blight (I mean, not that they drank beer as children, but they certainly had to clear their dirty dishes). When they are husbands and fathers, it may be that some of it will come back to them. In any case, they are indeed the problem of their spouses, present or future.

I've come to see that, at least for those of us who aren't so neat and tidy that our children just can't *conceive* of dirt, the thoughts here about chore giving and discipline have two goals: (1) to give the children a merely *general* indication that life could be orderly, perhaps in the form of a distant voice in their heads that resembles yours but, apparently, doesn't come through very clearly; and (2) to get *you* through the days, by getting some work out of them.

We just naturally like our children better if they are working and not lolling about. And that's a valid reason to go to all this effort. (We also like them better if they are clean and well groomed, but that's a rant for another time. Nevertheless, take a good look at your son and ask yourself if you just find him ... grubby. Then do something about it.)

Begin the rehabilitation as if he has been good all along. An eight-year-old can take out the trash, process the laundry, sweep, vacuum, feed *and* walk the dog, and others things that you will find in "What Can Children

Do?" He should carry things for you, particularly grocery bags in from the car, baskets of laundry, and firewood. (People get wood-burning stoves, chickens, and huge gardens not so much because they love these things but so that their children will have strenuous activity to engage in.)

Tell him that he's strong and big and a big, strong boy and that you need him. Praise his big strong muscles and his ability to carry things and bravely handle stuff that makes you tired or cringy. Big. Strong. Brave.

No toys until the chores are done; no shows, games, sitting down, eating, resting, or any other thing that he would like to do until things are done without whining and to your satisfaction. Make a chore list so everyone's clear.

Tell him that in the Bible it says, "If any would not work, neither should he eat" (2 Thess. 3:10, KJV) and you don't intend to raise a deadbeat for a son. Tell him you'd like to be spared visiting him in jail. Tell him that you've been wrong, but now the iron has entered your soul. Be ruthless, yet affirming.

Talk to his father. Hand your son over to his authority. He has the con (that's nautical for "is in command") when he's home, and his spirit hovers over things when he's gone. This is his son. Undoubtedly the naughty genes come straight from him. Let them get dirty and smelly together. Affirm the punishments your husband chooses to hand out, even though, I warn you, they will appear so harsh, due to current levels of enabling.

Meanwhile, read these books to him: Little Britches, Two Years Before the Mast, Captains Courageous, Hatchet, Hornblower: Beat to Quarters, and anything by E. Nesbit. I want you to read them to him so that you benefit as well; as you read, you will understand just how much adults can ask of children, and just how miserable children can be and still benefit from the experience. Reading time should be after chores.

"Auntie Leila, do you think children should be miserable?" Well, here's the thing. Children do spend a certain amount of time being miserable. You might as well have their misery be about something real. For instance, it's far better for a child to feel a little hungry while he finishes putting the clothes in the dryer or moves the woodpile a foot to the left than to grumble because you forgot to buy him the newest version of his favorite video game. The first problem will result at least in his sense of accomplishing something, followed by a meal that he's more likely to appreciate. The second will result in feeding the lazy, disrespectful beast within. Very few things are worse for a child than feeling justified in a grudge against the world, embodied in his parents.

Chore Charts?

Sometimes people ask me if they should make a chore chart. I am all for whatever works for you and makes life easier. There are so many variables: the size of your family, their ages, your ability to focus, the willingness (or lack thereof) of the participants.

At times, we used a chore chart. I put chores on the weekly homeschooling chart. I made lists, posted chores on a board, put chores in a chore jar, wrote the chores on the children's foreheads (not really), and made buddy systems.

I was never very good at following up on rewards, particularly stars. I guess I tend more to punishments, which is silly if rewards work. Just beware: a rewards system easily devolves into endless arguments and comparisons, which indeed make punishments seem simpler. My gut feeling is that if it results in a lot more work for mom, it's not going to succeed as a system.

The Chore Jar

Some years, once we had a preponderance of genuinely useful children, we began each season with a big jar into which I put scraps of paper with jobs written on them. Each job had a level or difficulty number associated with it, based on the time it took, the ickiness factor, and so on. These were not the basic jobs, such as processing laundry or bathroom cleaning, that were assigned by age, but jobs I was pretty sure I wouldn't get to but would definitely be happier if they were to be accomplished by someone else. The kids took turns taking papers out until they were gone. There was a brief exchange or bargaining period, and then the chore lists were written up for future reference. It worked fantastically.

Parents will have to think about the work question in relation to their own circumstances. Ideas are legion, but keep in mind that what looks attractive might be predicated on factors that are not universal. Those with lots of kids have to be more businesslike than those with only one or two. Above all, aim to avoid nagging. Something written down in some form, even graphically illustrated with symbols for the nonreader, really helps.

I'm going to be honest, Rebekah: Your job is harder with only one or two children under that maternal microscope. The two of them are shouldering the whole burden of making you (and the house) shine in the end. But, if this is indeed God's will, then amen, and get them moving.

Schedule your day so that there are certain times when everyone is working. Play fun, upbeat music, and you won't hear any complaining. Make your slacker child miss out on good things if he doesn't comply, but just make sure any punishment is immediate, not remote. Schedule in rests and fun at the park.

Work on the new regime for a week, perhaps easing into it. New habits bring self-control! After a week, set a new goal. Give that a week. In two months, I promise you, things will be better!

You are not failing your child, and you are a good mother! Soon you will like and respect your son again. And he will like and respect you!

A big hug,

Leila

Five Important Strategies for Selling Your Reasonably Clean Home While Homeschooling

I recommend that you read this section even if you aren't planning to sell your house, simply to avoid the trap that has ensnared so many, to their regret; namely, that they applied the energy necessary for organizing their home (and fixing the little things that bothered them) only when they were about to leave it, rather than when they were living in it! I think the ideas here can help a family be more organized even when they aren't selling their house. Maybe reading the following will help you make your house nice enough for a prospective buyer, however imaginary, right now, and hence, more enjoyable for your family.

Selling your home while living in it—especially while homeschooling in it—seems impossible, and if you start to hyperventilate at the very thought of it, I don't blame you. I've been there: homeschooling five children (including two in high school) *and* nursing a baby. It's not peaceful.

The reason people grow old and die in their inadequate and cluttered homes is that they can't face the disruption of moving! But sometimes, face it you must. So here's how.

We will take it as read that you have already searched the Internet thoroughly on the topic of staging your home for buyers. Besides the big things, such as a new roof, that can be negotiated, you know that you need to make a list of little things that need repair or replacement. It's always good to have such a list anyway! It can go in your sticky-note to-do list under a "master household" tab (see the section on note keeping below).

You *know* that you have to declutter, and this Reasonably Clean House section is about helping you do that. You know about renting a storage unit. But chances are that, if you are homeschooling and have lots of kids, you need more stuff than the average advice giver can even imagine. You certainly have more books than the realtors think is appropriate, and that's fine, as long as they are dusted and look neat and tidy (the books, not the realtors). Besides following all my thoughts on how to get a clean (reasonably so) house, there's the issue of these strangers walking in. You can't satisfy their standards, because you don't know them, so the main thing to keep in mind is that whatever you have in your home should be clean and pretty, especially at the front door (this is also known as curb appeal).

I'm going to tell you something that I have learned from looking at thousands of listings. The main reason realtors advise sellers to stage things in the blandest, most "impersonal" way possible—and I say this without judgment in my heart, but it's true—is that most people have trouble making their homes look tasteful. I don't blame them; I blame the mass-marketers who destroyed traditional ways of keeping home and substituted décor that has a built-in dissatisfaction level, to keep people buying.

We can overcome the tension between realtors' desire for us totally to declutter and our need to go on living by striving to fulfill our role as beautifiers of our environment according to principles that you will find scattered throughout this book and in tradition. For a large family with limited resources, it's not possible to render the house personality-free. So please don't worry about it; I believe that the peace and goodness of your home will be attractive to anyone who enters.

To continue with the plan:

You already know that your whole house has to smell good. Now is the time to light that big scented candle you got for Christmas. Put it on your stove, where it won't burn the house down.

You already know that your house has to be warm (if it's cool out) or cool (if otherwise).

Now I am going to tell you how to achieve a sale when your house is not utterly fabulous and high end, your children are numerous, and your school must keep going regardless.

The Blitz

Start at the top and Blitz. (If your house has only one level, start at the furthest point from the door you will ultimately exit.)

Selling your house gets you to deep-clean every zone in your house. Don't try to do it all in one day, but do schedule each zone realistically and get it done. You must be able to declare an area "closed" in the sense of having been deep-cleaned, and then later in the sense of "no one go in there." (It's not a bad idea to have no-go zones for the duration of the selling period if you can swing it.)

Once you have done that, you need to incentivize your children to perfect the Blitz for when prospective buyers come around. Maybe show them the movie *The Hunt for Red October* (if they are older) or take a field trip to the fire station and observe the drill. Once they see that their job needs military precision and a sense of urgency, as for putting out a blaze, they will enter the spirit of the thing and execute.

In the house-selling Blitz, just as with normal living, the goal isn't the Deep Clean or even the Moderate Clean. It's just to make things tidy as quickly as possible so you can get out of the house and have it ready for showing.

You need the Moderate Clean for days you are not showing, or you will end up booming and busting, which is not good when you have so many to take care of; you simply can't do it and maintain your sanity. Sanity comes first, I always say.

The kids need to think this is a fun and exciting process that they do on the run. Besides some sort of model, they probably also need a bribe or a reward waiting for them when they are done. You will end up in the car, so maybe stash some treats there or head out for ice cream.

The Appearance of Clean

Unlike normal cleaning, you are *not*–repeat, *not*–going to clean in your normal fashion according to the areas that need it most or are most used. And you are not going to prioritize actual cleanliness (after you have done that necessary deep cleaning), but instead, *the appearance of cleanliness*.

Thus, pay more attention to wiping surfaces and vacuuming than to getting the area under the sofa cushions crumb free. Windows need to be sparkling more than sheets need to be laundered. (You can do the latter on a non-showing day.) It's more important to get the toys off the lawn than to put your clutter away!

How?

Laundry Baskets

You are not going to put your necessary clutter (as opposed to the unnecessary clutter that you got rid of before this whole process began) away! You would go crazy! You can't do it!

When you get the call, your drill will be to throw any "necessary" clutter that can't *immediately* put in its proper place *into laundry baskets* as you exit the area.

You start to see the importance of starting at the top (or furthest area) of your home and working your way down and out. Besides resolving to do as much eating and playing outside as you can, you must clean yourself out of your house. The children need to go ahead of you, blitzing.

One child (or team) can be in charge of blitzing bathrooms (after you have carefully trained them in the art of making it look clean, which mainly involves wiping everything with the hand towel, putting it in the hamper, and replacing the towel). One team can be in charge of making sure that beds are not only made but that any stray stuffed animals are propped up in front of pillows (which instantly makes the bed look charming). One team wipes down stairs and removes any clutter from them, placing it in a basket.

Put any laundry in hampers or in the dryer. (Identify hiding places for things: bins under beds, the space inside the dryer and inside the washer—but, don't stuff things in the oven or in closets, because people look in there. They won't open the fridge or the deep freezer, though.)

If you are going to stay sane, you can't have everyone running to and fro. No crisscrossing back into no-go zones! No entering areas declared stranger-ready!

I developed this method when I realized that having everyone running around randomly, up and down and around, was giving me panic attacks. My house had three floors and we started at the top (and in the bathrooms, because only so many people fit in one place) and backed our way out.

You are the last to leave a room while your children are tackling the next part—and no one reenters after you have left, as in a fire drill! You are the last to leave a floor.

You give the floor (or zone) you are leaving the critical eye, snatching up personal things as you go, and then attend to the next one.

What do I mean by "necessary clutter"? What you can't face putting away because you know that you just can't. So everyone works their way out of the house, collecting, as they go, toys, books in the process of being read, the ten matchbox cars they were just playing with and can't leave behind, bath towels (and other bathroom detritus), sweaters, shoes, blankets, and the random "personal knickknacks" so deplored by realtors and putting them in the laundry baskets (laundry bags and large trash bags are helpful too). Don't waste time putting every last thing away. Just toss it all in the basket.

Those get put in the back of the undoubtedly large vehicle you use to transport your brood (of course, when you first listed your home, you cleaned out the van too!).

Homeschooling with Backpacks

Consider having your children keep the materials they are using in backpacks or totes that they can grab quickly. Then you can head to the library for the hour or two that it takes to show the house.

If you follow my advice in other chapters, your homeschool will be fairly simple and streamlined, and this won't be too difficult.

Keep in mind two things:

1. If your children were at school, they would have days when schooling didn't go as planned, because of drills and other disruptions. It's not as if every day, every nose is constantly to the grindstone—far from it. So if you use the showing time to run errands or visit a friend, I wouldn't worry about that.

2. Your house has certain basic qualities that make it marketable *if the price is right*. The biggest factor is what other houses recently sold for in your neighborhood. Realtors like to get you whipped up about how important your staging is, but the fact is that most people have decided when they pull up to the door whether they are interested. That your bathrooms and kitchen are functional is more important than whether your furniture doesn't look brand new. That said, if it looks welcoming and tidy, it will appeal to them! So just work on that and don't stress out.

Immediate Homing of Clutter upon Return

This is the key to keeping the system running. When you get home, take everything out of the car and put it, baskets and all, in the middle of the floor in a central place. Spend whatever time it takes to put each and every single item back in its place. Make your children your runners. What you will note immediately is that there are things that you resent having to cart in and out this way, and lo! these things can now easily be donated or discarded because they are right there, probably already in a trash bag!

Thus, the clutter you are dealing with at any point in this house-selling period is what you need right now—not *accumulated* flotsam and jetsam. You start to realize that you can function with much less than you thought. You also notice that this mode is effectively the "post-office system"—collecting things in a central location and then distributing (or discarding) them. As

I say, it's a good method to use even in the times you are not trying to sell your house.

Your children will develop an eye for how things looked when you returned. If you play this period of your life well, you may just end up with higher standards all around!

ASK AUNTIE LEILA

How Do You Prepare for Thanksgiving (or Any Looming Event)?

Dear Auntie Leila,

Could you tell about the things you do to get ready for Thanksgiving?

Love,

Susan

D ear Susan,

You mean the magazines aren't helping you with their advice to set the table the day before? You say you actually use that table at every meal for your impossibly large family? And even if, during those crazy prep days, you could simply hand them food out the dog hatch, telling them that it's normal to eat meals on the porch in November, your

194

nimble toddlers would slip past you and make short work of the china and glassware?

You don't think it would be wise to set the table more than a nanosecond before everyone sits down, even with your linebacker brothers to guard it while you keep the other toddlers from standing on the dishwasher door?

Because you have an infinite supply of toddlers?

I hear you. I don't have any brothers, so it was even worse for me.

Maybe some of these ideas can help. Keeping in mind that this chapter is really for large, busy families with children who aren't old enough to contribute by bringing all the dishes to you, and that I am usually stirring gravy with one hand and forgetting to defrost the pie dough with the other, here are some helpful hints.

General Items to Keep in Mind

Schedule time for your baby. Know that when you have little ones, you are not going to have that one day you can devote to giving the extra turn to your puff pastry, making individual miniature cornucopias as favors, or blanching your almonds.

Remember to sit down and nurse the baby. By the way, this is where I think baby schedules get a bad rap. The schedule is for you—so that you don't push your baby a little past his limit with your busyness but are fully aware that, yes, it has been two hours and he really does need you. Not for a quick sip but for a good, hearty nursing. If you bottle feed your baby, no, you can't just hand him off to others while you run yourself ragged.

The baby is like a big speed bump in the road, but not in a bad way. Slow down; pace yourself. You know for a fact that the baby will need to be held, and, exasperatingly, held more often when your level of frantic activity is up (there is a direct correlation between children desperately needing you and your distractedness—this has been documented by countless women, or would have been if they could have found a pencil).

Even if the baby seems fine as you feverishly work to get the holiday ready (and he's not, because to him it's just a day, not a "special" day, and he wants you), you might get sick if you put him off. At least, if I didn't stay with my babies' rhythms, I would get a breast infection—no fun and no good for anyone.

On the other hand, you have lots of little helpers who can do charmingly naïve approximations of place tags, fashion turkey decorations and garlands, and bring in pine cones. So decorating is taken care of.

Pay your bills and go through your papers before Monday of Thanksgiving week. You will be vexed if you get a late fee because you let yourself lose your concentration.

Do a lot of laundry Monday. Fold it and put it away. Notice today if your family doesn't have enough underwear to get them through Friday. If that's the case, get thee to the store and buy some. You'll still have to do laundry every day (probably including at least processing some on Thanksgiving itself), but give yourself breathing room before the real rush.

No matter how efficient you are, and especially if you're like me and really like to make things from scratch and have them fresh on the day, you will be quite busy on Wednesday and Thursday. You don't want a lot of dirty or wet or jumbled sheets and towels mocking you every time you walk by wherever you stack all your unprocessed laundry.

Clean your room sometime before Tuesday. If you want peace in the few days before Thanksgiving, you need to know that your house is in order. That tense feeling of paralysis comes from the vague sense that you have too much to do, which is, in turn, fed by those little strolls you occasionally take through the house and yard. If you do a big chunk of it—the non-turkey-related chunk—a few days before, you will experience a lightness you never knew you could have.

The fact is that roasting a turkey isn't all that hard. Someone once pointed out, after having fussed over a chipotle turkey with ancho stuffing or whatever, that in the end, Thanksgiving dinner tastes like … Thanksgiving dinner—no matter what you do!

So keep it simple, and rather than thinking that all will be lost if you don't have five-spice squash, just make good plain squash and do your chores ahead of time.

Complicated Thanksgiving recipes are creatures of magazine editors who sit around all year thinking up stuff for you to stress out about—and then get their own Thanksgiving dinners catered.

Actual Thanksgiving, on the other hand, is about the bounty of nature (among other, loftier things). Put butter on it and it will be lovely.

Let your children help. You know those feelings you have: "I wish I had time to sweep the porch!" "I need to vacuum the stairs!" "Ugh, there are cobwebs in this room!" "Under the trash can the cabinet is so dirty!" "The chairs need to be dusted!" "I can't even think about the car!" Well, those are all things kids could take care of. It won't be worse than it already is. Put your children to work and see if you don't get a bit ahead despite yourself.

When the nether regions of your house are moderately clean, your laundry is put away (I know there's more, but you're on top of it), and your bills are paid, you can take a little breath.

The Details

Now on to more details of how a holiday happens without total collapse:

Make lists. Sit down (with the baby, of course) the week before the holiday and start your lists.

These are the lists you need:

Details of the cleaning that has to be done—guest areas and kitchen. Just before a holiday is not the time for turning mattresses or any of that deep-cleaning fancy stuff. Declutter a little, wipe things down, tidy up—including your messes that you can't deal with right now; just make them as tidy as you can—and vacuum.

By Monday of Thanksgiving week, the unseen regions of your house will at least stop giving you that sinking feeling that you will expire soon. Get the bathrooms in shape. When you wake up next week to the reality of cooking for your crowd, you'll have the satisfaction of knowing that a Blitz will have you in good form.

Nonfood items that you have to purchase: dress shoes for the boys, new kitchen towels (please resist the brown and orange ones, or you'll have to start all over again in a week), a gravy boat (just get one—it's about time—it doesn't have to match), and candles (don't forget the Advent candles—because vexingly for us in the United States, Advent usually begins the Sunday after Thanksgiving).

Extremely specific menu plans for every instant from the moment your guests—including returning children—arrive. You need to try to picture in your mind exactly what you want to be serving for breakfast, lunch, appetizers, dinner, and snacks for the whole weekend. Then throw in a menu for the day before anyone arrives—something simple, refrigerator-emptying, and quick, such as soup or pasta with ham and spinach.

Your menu list should have three parts: the menus, organized by meal; the prep work for each meal, the better to delegate, since even the youngest child can peel a carrot or wash broccoli; and a shopping list. Arrange your shopping list by aisle and department.

The Prep

Armed with your lists, you are ready for actual prep.

Make ahead of time whatever you can: make dessert first; well, make your pie crusts sometime before Wednesday and even weeks before, putting them in the freezer if you are that ahead of things. Once that part is done, the pies are easy and can be baked before you put the turkey in (I really do like mine freshly baked on the day, other than the pecan pie, which can be made the day before—and it does freeze well).

What's really great about this particular dinner is that you can make almost all of it in advance. Since you are likely also having to feed your family on a regular basis until then (why? why do they need to be fed so often?), you probably won't be that housewife who calmly mixes herself a martini an hour before the guests arrive. But here are the things that you can do while you are getting through the preceding non-holiday days:

Turkey: If you can roast a turkey along with your pre-Thanksgiving Sunday dinner, do. That allows you to have already carved meat and gravy, sparing you the last-minute frenzy. You can still roast one on the big day, but it will be mainly for show. One turkey—even a big one, which is mostly bones and cavity—isn't really enough for more than eight people anyway, not if you want the best part of this dinner, which is sandwiches made with leftovers!

Cranberry sauce: Since the sauce has to be cold anyway, make it right now. Homemade is absolutely worth the effort, even if you just follow the directions on the package, leaving out the lemon zest, hand-picked hazelnuts, nori cultivated in special Japanese sea gardens, or varietal red wine reduction.

Canned cranberry sauce tastes like sugar (or, more likely, corn syrup) that met a cranberry sometime in the distant past and can't remember its name. And which one of us hasn't been smacking ourselves on the head on Thanksgiving morning, foreseeing all too clearly the inevitability of warm cranberry sauce, having forgotten about it until then?

While you are at it, make double—it's basically jam, so it keeps and will enhance not only fowl but hams and pork as well.

Stuffing: Any time the oven is on, put a tray of cubed bread in there. Stash it in the freezer after it has cooled.

Vegetables: To give you a peek at how you can prep the vegetables ahead of time, I will tell you about the time I was making pizza and I got the cranberry sauce done while I was already cooking, as well as a nice batch of onion confit, with figs, ginger, and coriander. (Remember, my kids are not underfoot now!) I was slicing onions for the pizza anyway, so I saved a step and sliced extra. If all my dishes are pretty plain (but yummy), the confit will be memorably interesting, and that will be enough variety for an already multifarious meal.

When the oven was still hot from the pizza, I put the sweet potatoes in (be sure to line the pan with foil so you won't end up with a pan of burnt sweet-potato guts to deal with). Those can cool for however long it takes—days, even—to peel them and toss them with butter and salt in a serving dish. And then they are done.

Rolls: When you make your dough for the rolls, make enough for several loaves of bread for the all-important sandwiches afterward. For those, you need some really good bread! Freeze it after it's baked and cooled so no one eats it before the right moment.

Look at your list and try to get a couple of things done each day. Most of the vegetables will keep just fine in the fridge or the freezer—or even, in the case of sweet potatoes, squash, beets, and such, on a cool shelf in the pantry for a day or two as long as they are in a shallow enough dish to cool quickly after they are cooked.

On the Tuesday before the big day you can do your final shopping, knowing that your house is reasonably clean, and if all else fails, you will have pie and stuffing with cranberry sauce.

On Thursday morning, make everyone take a long walk. If they stay inside, they will just get the house dirty. I won't say you'll have that martini, and that's probably just as well, but it's the best it will get until they are old enough to invite you to Thanksgiving dinner!

Seeing Your Home
as Others See It

I can't help thinking that conversation about the role of the woman in the home, including the education of children, is futile without first putting our hands on the tools we need to cope with what happens during the day, at home, with children. On the one hand, there are those who write about the high calling of making a home and give no details. On the other, there are plenty of resources for getting organized, but most don't take into account having a busy household while trying to educate the children.

No one knows as well as I do how hard it is to stay on top of things when you have babies and toddlers and kids running around, because I'm just like you, only with less energy. But keeping a reasonably clean house is part—not *all, but part,* the "necessary if insufficient" basis—of the order in Order and Wonder. A lot of our frustration as women with *life at home,* with implementing all our hopes and dreams, comes from simply not knowing where to start when it comes to housekeeping!

I already gave reasons to start in your very own bedroom. The order we do things in is an order. When we seek order according to the pattern we try to discern in the universe, in human nature, and in God, we find that the wonder increases. Starting with the foundation of the common life in the home—marriage—even in something as seemingly trivial as knowing which room to clean can yield amazing benefits in other less mundane areas.

Once you've conquered your own room, you might find it beneficial to implement the advice I read in the helpful (and amusing) book *Sidetracked Home Executives*. (I fully admit that the books I refer to are mostly from the last millennium. I do read some of the new ones, but I still like these. They are funny and real—and thorough.) The authors suggest something that might not occur to you for housekeeping, although it's often recommended for house *selling*, when it's far too late to reap the benefits for making the home: that you stand outside your house and see it as others see it; then walk in and see what they see.

There's a certain kind of person, self-absorbed, abstract, prone to be found reading novels, for whom this idea is revolutionary! Not only did this advice help me to be more orderly; it transformed my sense of hospitality!

Why is it that we are continually entering others' homes, getting an impression of how they live by what we first encounter, and yet never considering that others are doing the same thing with us? Why is it that we may know some people who never let us have a glimpse of their chaos, if they have any, but we don't feel particularly welcomed in their homes? And others are quite open about having lots of life going on, yet we get an overall sense of peace and contentment?

What's the key to the way those others do things?

We are stuck inside, mentally as well as physically. We are never seeing beyond the dirty dishes. *They* somehow, maybe intuitively, know how to make us comfortable from the moment we walk up to their door. They project something that we need to project! Seeing our home as others see it can be as life changing as that view in the three-way mirror in the dress shop! You will learn a lot about yourself if you do this and do it often (both the home and the mirror, I suppose!).

Take pictures if it helps. My house is just my house. I don't pretend to be any kind of design arbiter. If you come here, you will see lots of flaws. Maybe your house is the same.

A thought, borne out by experience: once a person has an impression, good or bad, of your house, it's hard for that person to shake it. Try to have your friends' first impression of your home be one of tidiness, and they will forevermore excuse messiness as *not you*.

Another thought: everyone has dirty dishes, at least sometimes, but not everyone has stray underwear on the front porch. Don't excuse things because they're *your own special mess*; you know you don't do that with others. If things are basically tidy and clean, a few messes don't register. But if there is a generalized disorder that seems layered by time, *fossilized*, almost, the impression given is of bad housekeeping, and it's really off-putting.

Maybe you always come in the garage but your friends don't. Have you seen your entrance recently? What does it say about you? Possibly it says, "We literally never see this part of our home, but, uh, welcome?"

Maybe your guests enter via the kitchen—here in New England that is often the case due to the way old houses get added on to. Here is the thing: inside, from my point of view, I have a clean kitchen island, only a few things "in transit," and it's relatively neat and clean by at least some standards. But when I enter, I'm tempted to put things on the first surface I encounter. It's not near *my indoor* "center," the sink and the table. It's off to the side, and very handy for stuff that's going out the door as well.

From *my* point of view, things are still pretty tidy this way. But clutter is what greets someone walking *in* via the mudroom, especially because of the narrow entry into the kitchen caused by the brick fireplace hearth which starts to the left with very little room to maneuver. That person may even see an open dishwasher door first thing! It's just the way my kitchen is laid out.

It's all in the point of view. I want someone who is dropping by to sense a welcome, to enter a home that is basically neat and tidy, that is reasonably clean. So I keep that counter nearest the entry to the kitchen clear (which in turn means I need a horizontal surface earlier, in the mudroom, that is expressly for the purpose and won't proclaim untidiness because it's not as high as the counter inside). I try to shut the dishwasher door when I'm not working on dishes.

Instead of making excuses using that false notion that "someday, when it looks like a magazine, it will be nice," we can make others' view of our home attractive *as it is now.* If it's the best it can be, it will reveal itself to be either just fine or in need of something particular that we can realistically plan for; either way, it's good: it's reasonably clean, and its order promotes a sense of peace.

The peace we get when we start outside is not just for guests, by the way; it's for family members too. Kids who are coming home, Papa who has been running errands, even *I* like walking in when the entrance is orderly. Making it so offers me a sense of contentment and happiness.

All these thoughts and efforts come to me after years and years of practice and being patient (or, probably, unaware) as the babies come and grow. I will be honest: *reasonably* clean, neat, and tidy is the best *I* can do, so don't feel too bad or too pressured.

On to Cleaning the Kitchen

I've thought a lot about where *exactly* to start with this mighty topic of cleaning the kitchen, and I've decided that before we get into organization, workflow, and actual *cleaning*, we have to have a little talk about a habit the children must learn.

The Reasonably Clean Kitchen
Starts with Rules for the Kids

Although we mothers begin to find meaning in what we do by understanding it as *service*, paradoxically, an important part of that service is teaching the little ones *how to help themselves*; in other words, in *not* serving them—on purpose! Oh, we will still serve them, all right, but, little by little, we will help them learn to do things for themselves and for others.

Some mothers don't teach little ones this important lesson because they don't respect themselves or their God-given authority, and they find that they can't ask someone, even a three-year-old, to do anything. Some don't do it because they truly don't realize it has to be done, and besides, it requires effort. The truth is, we might be tempted to avoid the effort to think about and act on giving the needed training.

Some don't think it can be done; they are unfamiliar with the hidden resources of children or are fooled by the perfect willingness of children to avoid most of the things they don't want to do, even if they thought of them. And, for the most part, how could they? Most children *of course* have no more idea that something needs to be picked up or put away than that there is a man on the moon; any child who does get the inkling can't be blamed for wanting to escape doing something about it. Naturally they have more important things to do!

Many mothers are waiting for someone else or the perfect time to do it. Some are so caught up in serving others—they have such a good heart, in a way—that they feel guilty demanding action.

But sweep all that away, particularly that little voice inside you that keeps whispering, "It's just so much easier to do it myself," as well as the other one that says, "Who cares, I'm too busy [insert description here, e.g., having babies, reading, surfing the Web, talking on the phone, waiting for my mother, and so forth] to exert the energy to do this." It's as if you have two devils, one on each shoulder, and there's no room for the angel who would like to say to you, "Put in the effort for a week, and you will reap the benefits for a lifetime." (Never mind that *other* devil who tries to convince you that you *like* things messy and gross. Please.)

It's not easy, but it is simple. You know how you dread each meal, and when it's done you feel that the cleanup is a sort of particularly sheer mountain you have to climb, only there's also scree that keeps causing you to slip down to the bottom again? You know how your kids spend the whole time running around and then they suddenly are just gone, off to do something fun? And you are left with not only dirty dishes but food everywhere—on the chairs, the floor, the table, the counters. I'm not surprised that you find it hard to keep the kitchen clean.

Sometimes I think that some people really think that their children are no more capable of helping out or acting properly than a bunch of cute little barnyard animals! They regard feeding them with just as much pleasure and derive just as much satisfaction as they would if they were throwing feed into a trough, and they regard the aftermath with the same resignation with which they would clean a stall. I've heard moms say things like "I throw them a bagel."

Auntie Leila doesn't like this way of speaking of your nearest and dearest.

I've heard that some moms *always* use paper plates at lunchtime! This astounds me.

If you are one of these ladies, I'm not judging you, but consider. Not only are you depriving your children of an important opportunity to learn how to take care of things, but it's all so self-confirming and dreary. And are you going to be caught off guard when they don't act properly when the table is set? (Also, how wasteful! I mean, once in a while, okay, but every day?)

It's amazing what children can do. Let's try it. Let's tackle just one thing (well, really two), and while you are tackling these two things, keep this in mind: children really like, and respond well, when you make rules! They aren't good at following logic or understanding reasoning (which is why it makes me crazy when parents go on and on, talk, talk, talk!), but a rule is something they can wrap their little minds around. Later the opportunity will arise for you to explain the rule, and that's fine, because Lord knows you have some good arguments backing you up, not least of which is that you don't want them ending up being handed their tray through a slot in lockup, which is where they are going with those table manners of theirs.

Paradoxically, the more you make them behave with good habits, the more time you have for engaging in delightful conversation with them! The more you rely on reasoning (and its evil twin sister, nagging), the fewer enjoyable moments you will have with them. But I wasn't going to get into child psychology. We're cleaning up the kitchen!

Let's make those rules! Rules lead to good habits.

Before the Meal

First rule: the child must come when you call him and do what he is told to help prepare; for instance, set out the napkins, get the cups, and so forth.

You choose what each child should do, but don't let yourself get into a situation where multiple people are grabbing food and plates and shoving food in their mouths and running around while you are still wondering about how to clean up from the last meal. And above all, *never let anyone open the refrigerator without your permission*, at least until they are old enough to clean it as well; and wait to say grace *together* (which means waiting for *you* to sit down) before starting to eat.

You are going to have to tell them that this is coming up. Don't blindside them. Let them know that things are changing around here. It's a good conversation to have at dinner when Dad is there to drive home what you say.

If the kids are really little, just tell them before you get ready for the meal that when you call, you want them to come in right away. To work this point, obviously you will have to be ready with the food and ready to sit down with them and sit still yourself. Don't call them in if you aren't mentally ready or just because calling them makes you feel that you have accomplished something. You will also have to be able to give your full attention to them, interacting with them cheerfully. And yes, I mean this even if "them" is your three-year-old.

These criteria apply to breakfast and lunch as well as dinner. The reason is that, although you might be tempted to think that you ought to have a break by relaxing standards—and certainly, there are different standards for different occasions, within reason—doing well at dinner requires practice! Where will this practice come from, especially if you want to avoid turning dinner (so often the only mealtime the children have with their father) into nagging time? From the other meals, of course—from breakfast and lunch.

A question I have been asked: What if there are two minutes remaining in the game, and when you call everyone into the meal, they can't tear themselves away? Well, I have learned to ask when the game is ending!

After the Meal

Second, the helpful attitude—not to mention the gracious manners—you are instilling require beginning and end points: the ritual and order of the thing. There is grace before the meal, and, of course, each child has to ask to be excused before getting up. He should also thank you for the delicious meal. Some people say grace after the meal as well in thanksgiving, indicating that those who wish to be excused may be.

Second rule: on asking permission, overtly or tacitly, to leave, that child must clear his place!

Tacitly means that you notice the child is done and ready to leave; you say, "All done? Good. Time to put your dish in the dishwasher." I'm not suggesting that you raise a martinet, after all. Later, when there are more of them and you need to rein things in, you can explicitly require asking permission.

By the way, help children understand that they must come in to say grace, not necessarily to eat, if you find they are becoming picky or difficult. They must have only a bite of everything or eat what they can. But the reason for this, and why I tell you to have them thank you before they leave the table is that you want to cultivate gratitude and respect for God; for you, the parents; and for the food.

It might take three trips for the child to clear his place, and in the case of a toddler, you might have to get up and help or ask an older child to help the toddler while you help the baby; but the number-one cause of motherhood burnout (other than failure to establish bedtimes, but that is another topic) is being left to deal with dirty dishes alone. It's too much work for one person! Oh, maybe you are escaping consequences now, but how will it be when you are sick or after you have your third set of twins or when your thirteen-year-old invites all her friends over for pizza? (Note well: it's amazing how, if your child clears her place, all her friends will follow suit; you discover this beautiful reality when a visiting child clears *his* plate and your child follows *his* example, causing you to smack your head with your open hand for never having made this rule, when this other, more clever, mother, has!)

Now, for this rule to prosper you, you must have an empty dishwasher; or at least, if it has things in it, let them be already dirty, with space for the rest. Naturally (with forethought) someone has to have emptied the dishwasher first thing, before breakfast for starters, and before every meal, obviously. And when my kids were growing up, it wasn't I who emptied the dishwasher before breakfast, and it shouldn't be you either if you aren't a good morning riser! If you have older children, assign one to do it. If you have a couple of younger children, assign a rack per kid and one to the silverware, and arrange things so that the place for the clean dishes is within reach for them. (Get sturdy dishes and glasses and teach them to be gentle.)

It's in the Bible: "If any man will not work, neither let him eat" (2 Thess. 3:10, DR). It's okay to ask people to do a little before they get fed. If you need a solid pattern to follow, read *Farmer Boy*. Of course, then you will probably be asked to fry doughnuts.

If you don't have a dishwasher, then the sink area has to be clean, the clean dishes put away, and the sink should have a tub of hot soapy water in it. We'll talk more about the system in a bit.

So, to recap, your children are going to help get set up for the meal in a limited but effective way. Then they are going to stay put and eat it, if only for a short time. And then they will ask to be excused, thanking you politely. Then they get up and put their very own dishes in the dishwasher or gently in the sink or stack them on the counter (you think about it and decide), and also any forks and cups; they will throw away or put away their napkins; they will push in their chairs.

They can take their time doing these things, and they don't have to do it all together. I find it perfectly acceptable and even desirable for two littles to go off while the bigger ones sit longer.

Your part is to get the meal ready for them, even if only to the extent that you know what you want served, and to be attentive during the habit-forming period, which really should be a full week with your older children. This week, repeated as necessary, will help you all to get into the habit of being attentive and present to each other during meals, which is a very good thing indeed. By the time you are on the third or fourth child, the family culture will be firmly established, and you won't remember even thinking about it.

Moms dread eating with their children because they have allowed themselves to hate everything about it or, rather, haven't put in the necessary work to enjoy it. But I ask you: If their own mother doesn't want to eat with them, who will?

Will there be messes? Of course! If you didn't want messes, you should have stayed single! I'm talking about *reasonably clean* here, messes you can handle, recoverable messes. The goal is that you could have company over without needing therapy before or after. A lowish bar, wouldn't you say?

Really, Auntie Leila, is this doable?

I always loved having my kids around even during mealtimes and even as distracted and disorganized as I am, and, in large part, it's because I naturally gravitate toward making rules. (But you knew that.)

You are not alone; you can ask your wonderful husband to join you in modeling all these things for his dear children, but let me caution you against speaking to him in the commanding tone you use for them. Don't treat him like one of them. Don't ruin the good habits you are teaching *them* by getting into the bad, even fatal, habit of acting as if *he's* a naughty child. More women have ruined their marriages by this one fault than you would suspect.

Flow in the Kitchen

Work goes so much better—the house will be so much more reasonably clean—if you think in terms of *flow*. Hence my admonition at the start of this discussion to begin cleaning in a predetermined direction, one you don't have to think through every time. That goes double for the kitchen.

The book *Cheaper by the Dozen* may be familiar to you. The sequel is called *Time Out for Happiness*. Being a person who could never in a million years have done one worthwhile thing at all in engineering school, I nevertheless have time and motion management in my blood, thanks to my engineering professor father, who was, in fact, a recipient of the Frank and Lillian Gilbreth Industrial Engineering Award. Believe me, it was for a reason!

Naturally, I loved this book. For one thing, it's a sweet love story of two remarkable people. Early on we are introduced to the young Frank Gilbreth, who wins a lot of bets from veteran bricklayers that he, a seemingly greenhorn wet-behind-the-ears office guy, can outperform the best of them at their job. He does this simply by analyzing the wasted motion the men have accepted as unquestioned components of what they do. Where they bend and heave, he moves the stack of bricks and bucket of mortar to arm level. Where they backtrack, he moves smoothly from one motion to the next. Over the course of a thousand movements, these little savings add up. His walls are straighter, neater, and more quickly built than theirs. They accuse him of cheating!

Thinking about a task, especially a tedious one that cannot be avoided, is essential, so let's think about the routine in the kitchen and start figuring out where to cheat!

I gave you a head start with the idea of training each child to put his own dish, cup, and utensil in the dishwasher or in the sink (which, of course, means starting with an empty dishwasher or sink; put this important step in the routine) and to throw his own trash away. Even a two-year-old can do a little. Do not end up being the dirty-everything rounder-upper.

Now let's think about *flow*. And time. And motion.

Unfortunately, very few kitchens are designed from the get-go with the proper flow. If they were, at the very least there would be one center with a sink for food preparation and one with a sink for dish cleanup. Since most of us must work with only one sink (even if it's a double sink), establishing flow makes the difference between a smooth system and, well, no system.

By the way, if I had to choose between a double sink and a dishwasher — and I think this is a choice that many have to make because of the size of the cabinets — I would go for the double sink and make sure it has a gooseneck faucet, making filling and washing pots *so* much easier.

Here's a diagram of what we are going to analyze.

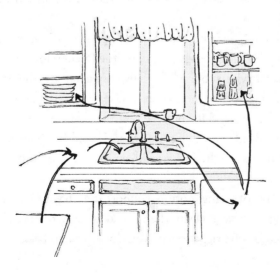

Let's aim for a flow that everyone in your household can understand. It should be simple and should make sense on a basic level of *where things land and where they are headed*. Just as a landscaper takes note of *where the paths already are*, you should see what natural flow already exists.

As with the house in general, it's good to divide the kitchen into zones. There's the food-prep zone, with the subset of a baking zone. If you've never thought about baking in terms of having just about everything you need not more than a step away, you are in for a significant leap in your kitchen's efficiency!

And there's the clean-dishes zone. Even with a dishwasher, you will need a place that is for clean items *only*, and once established, it will be clear to others, including guests, that dirty things don't get placed there. Some hand-washed items will be drying on a rack or cloth. When the dishwasher is unloaded, there are always some plastic containers that are not quite dry. They can't be put away wet and nestled because bacteria will grow in them; these can be placed in the clean-item area to air dry (or, if there is time, shaken out and left on the top rack of the dishwasher until they are completely dry).

Even when you are able to put everything away (an unusual occurrence at my house), removing the drying cloth or hanging up the rack in its spot, keep this area mentally prepared for clean items only by insisting that dirty ones go on the other side of the sink (or in it if it is properly prepared to receive them).

In my kitchen, the zone for food storage—refrigerator and "in-use" pantry cupboard (I have a large pantry off the kitchen for those items not needed immediately)—is to the left of my prep area, as is the bread supply, which is in a drawer below the toaster. I have to keep the pots in the open cupboard on the left, and it's not the best place, since the stove is on the right, but I removed the cabinet doors so I wouldn't have to bend *and* reach behind doors for them. Large, deep drawers would be better than lower cabinets.

As an example of saving motion, suppose that in your kitchen it works to go left to right, dirty to clean; then it makes sense to have clean dishes and pots stored on the right so that you don't have to backtrack through the cleanup area on the left to put things away. For instance, if dirty dishes are being staged on the counter to the left of the sink, then that counter won't be available to place clean dishes on when you are putting away a stack of things, moving them from the dishwasher on the right, because it will likely be soiled with food. (Of course, you can set things up going right to left. The important thing is to have a direction!)

Now let's think about the steps toward establishing the flow.

1. *Think about the flow of clean dishes to the table, dirty dishes from the table to the sink or the dishwasher, and clean dishes back to the cabinets.* Think about how you can establish a routine that makes sense and save steps, even if it's not perfect. You might have to rearrange some things; if you do, wipe out the cabinets before you put things in their new places. Consider putting the dishes in a place that is as accessible to children as possible, both for setting the table and for putting clean dishes away; normally people don't store dishes in lower cabinets, but it might work for you.

My clean dishes should really go in a cabinet closer to the dishwasher, but there isn't a cabinet there. Should I waste my time dreaming about how to renovate the kitchen, or should I work with what I have? Right—work with what I have!

2. *Clean from the periphery in toward the sink.* Don't start at the sink, because it's demoralizing to turn around and realize how much you still have to do. First, clear the table of the meal and the dishes, utensils, cups, and napkins. Then clean it off with a warm, soapy washcloth. Move any cooking items closer to the sink in your "dirty" area, putting warm water into pots and pans for soaking while you wipe down the stove. As food is put away, wipe counters, moving from further away from the sink toward the final task, the washing up.

3. *If you have a dishwasher, fill a basin or large pot or bowl with hot, soapy water;* it will assist you with any handwashing. Clean pots and pans can go back on the stovetop to dry. Now load the dishwasher. If you do dishes by hand: fill one of your sinks (or a basin) with hot, soapy water, place your scraped dishes in it, and as you wash each one, move it to the other sink for rinsing.

While you are thinking this flow question through in your best time-and-motion frame of mind, consider the area above your sink. You probably have a windowsill there, as I do, but whether you do or not, remove everything from the sink area, scrub around the faucet, behind the sink, and the whole windowsill, wall, or shelf. Find a home elsewhere for all the debris that has collected there and put your dish soap into a dispenser, storing the container it comes in under the sink. Then make it pretty, however you would like.

This area above the sink is our own little personal shrine, isn't it? If the bedroom is the altar, so to speak, of our marriage and the dining room table is the altar of our family life, I think the kitchen windowsill is the shrine of a mother's working life. I encourage you to have it reflect that. I think you will find that carefully arranging this one spot will help you organize the rest of the kitchen.

Helping Kids and Yourself to Do the Dishes without Despairing

It had come to Auntie Leila's attention that some moms with lots of kids find that they can't impose on their children the chore of doing dishes due to the terrible burden of it, and right away I could see the issue (from the pictures posted where I was reading about this).

More on Flow

If you want kitchen cleanup to happen without turmoil, you need to establish flow in your kitchen, as discussed above. Think about it in terms of your kitchen's setup, whatever that may be. My kitchen is far from perfect. What matters is that you do not forge a new path every night. Make the path once and for all.

Why? Because if *you* are tempted to run screaming from your life every single night as you face the dishes, so much so that you post a picture of the disaster on social media to gain sympathy from your audience, just imagine how it looks to a twelve-year-old! No wonder that kid hems and haws and has to psyche himself up. These "recurring problems" — such as doing dishes after every meal — have to be subjected to a process, a system, a set of previously thought-out steps.

Important rule that will improve the situation immediately: don't put the baby's high-chair tray on top of the dirty dishes in the sink. This sort of thing is what is making your young kitchen helper die a little every night, and frankly, you are having trouble too. It's what makes the whole job take so long. The piling is not to be faced. Do one of two things:

1. Get the baby out — deploying what we call "the crack cleanup team": one responsible party to wash his face, hands, and arms with a warm washcloth and another to wipe down the chair (and don't forget to obtain a dog for licking up the floor) — and clean the tray at the sink *before* the general cleanup begins, and return the tray to the high chair, with everything spiffy in that area. This makes sense because usually Baby is done before the meal is over.

2. Leave the tray *at the high chair* until the general cleanup is over, washing it last. Just shove the whole thing to the side. Don't forget it.

But do not put it in the flow. It creates an almost insurmountable barrier to cleanup.

Staging Areas

Figure out where you will stage things. Not every time — once and for all. Then distribute and communicate your plan to all concerned. *You* can't handle a sink full of dirty dishes, and neither can a kid.

You need a place where you can put away food left over from the meal (that could be someone else's chore, by the way, and I recommend it be yours, so that you can manage leftovers). At our house, that place is the island, because there's room there for the serving dishes and the containers for packing leftovers away.

Know beforehand where you will stack dinner plates so that they are scraped and ready for the dishwasher or the soapy basin while the food-storage process happens. Even four dinner plates can cover an entire counter; twenty can stack neatly to the side until ready to be cleaned—if they are able to be prepped.

If your dishwasher can handle it and your children are able to manage the plate-scraping process, have them put their scraped-off plate directly into that appliance. It's up to you and how much activity (that is, how many bodies) you want in the area.

A significant game changer (especially during holidays, but really, at every meal): *have a separate basin or shallow pan (such as a lasagna pan) for utensils.* Getting all the forks, knives, spoons, and serving pieces out of the pile of plates works wonders for streamlining the whole process. Children can be encouraged to clear their places in this manner, putting their plates in one place and their utensils in another, *not* just piling everything on the last persons' items, creating a cleaning bottleneck.

Even separating the utensils to one side of the sink while you scrape and stack plates on the other changes the task from tiresome to the work of a moment. If the utensils *can* soak in their own receptacle, they can be picked up by the bunch and put in the dishwasher, as opposed to loading them one or two at a time as you work your way through a precarious pile of dishware.

Of course, sharp knives stay next to the sink until you're ready to wash them, so no one will get cut by a lurking blade under the suds.

The Art of Washing Dishes

Besides all the prep work mentioned above, there is the matter of actually washing dishes, whether in the dishwasher or by hand. Either way, don't just run hot water continuously while squirting dish detergent endlessly.

For washing in the dishwasher, just put the dishes in after they are scraped. If you have stacked them, you can run a little water in between each one so that nothing will be stuck on them; dishwasher detergent works better if there are some particles on the dishes (and repairmen also insist that you don't need much detergent; they say it gums up the works and a dab the size of a nickel is best in the case of liquid; I suggest you try this minimum—for powder too—and work your way up if you need more).

For handwashing, use your hot, soapy water to wash. Yes, you can put a squirt of detergent on your sponge or dishcloth as you go, but don't run water over your cloth as you wash; you will end up rinsing the detergent off it.

Think about camping. Out in the field, you'd heat up one basin of water, get it soapy, wash everything, and then rinse—because you're hauling water from a distance. Use this as your mental template so that you don't waste water and detergent. Remember, the detergent is formulated to bond with solids (dirt and grease) and rinse away. Even if the water seems dirty, it's working for you. You can dump it out and refill it, but don't wash each item individually with the hot water running!

Know how to do dishes and then teach your child how to do them. Don't just burden him with a problem that you yourself can't solve.

Doing Dishes Helps Kids Open Up and Finally Want to Talk

Here's a bit of a mystery about washing dishes, one that addresses that vexing issue of how, though you are dying to go to bed, your older kids, for some reason, can bring themselves to talk to you after only 10:00 p.m.

Suddenly the deep dark concerns come out—so late, so desperately late.

My friend told me that her mother (of eight children) always "helped" whichever kid was doing the dishes. She didn't want to have a dishwasher (the appliance) because she knew that it was during that time that the conversations would happen. She remembers one sister or another saying to her, "I'll do the dishes with Mom tonight." And that was so they could talk.

You don't have to get rid of your dishwasher, but do realize that much of the time, not only do you need to be in the kitchen during cleanup to direct flow, put away food (so that you can put it to best use later, as a good manager), and oversee this not-exactly-easy chore, you will also have a chance to have a little conversation with your child.

Yes, that moment after supper often finds the baby needing to nurse, and you can send in an older child or Dad to take your place in the kitchen. But as you get good at this game we call parenting, you can also use the time when others are clearing up to nurse the baby and then hand him off to another child for play or a bath—just at the opportune time to be there for the kid who needs you by yourself. Or you may sense that Dad is the one who is needed. He will be better equipped to work in the kitchen if there is an established method (and he may be the one to enforce it with children, in any case).

Some nights, it's not deep consultation, but just singing songs, and suddenly you'll have a lot of help as family members naturally join in. Even if your child is working by himself, he can handle it because it's a doable chore, with you giving an assist. It's not the aloneness that is terrible; it's the impossibility of the thing, and you mitigate that by means of simply having thought it through and then being on hand to facilitate. Well, that's the pretext, but the real reason is that this time is good for talking.

That's family life together. The very things that seem like the worst drudgery create the best memories—when there is someone loving who will put thought into how it will go and be there for the quiet moments.

Cleaning Cast-Iron Pans
the Old-Fashioned Way

The information I've seen about cleaning cast-iron pans seems to be written by people who are too young to remember the right way to do it. Not that I am that old, mind you. I blame the sudden onset, back when I was a young bride, of nonstick cookware.

Nonstick brings along with it a set of (plastic and, in my opinion, antiaesthetic) kitchen utensils that are not really good for anything other than using with nonstick. And those kinds of pans *are* very persnickety about how you take care of them. On top of how high-maintenance nonstick is, there's no way it can be good for you as it burns the coating off right under your nose. If you have nonstick, you begin to look at all your cookware as impossibly delicate, easily scratched, quite volatile as to coating, and doomed to ultimate failure.

Cast iron is ... cast iron. You are not going to harm it. It is not going to harm you.

With cast iron, there are two issues: seasoning and cleaning.

Seasoning

You can't season your pan with cooking oil, no matter what the "experts" say; you can only grease it. To season the pan—that is, to give it a hard coating that will last as you cook—you need to use linseed oil (pure linseed oil, not boiled linseed oil, which contains heavy metals to promote drying). Linseed oil is also known as flax oil. This oil polymerizes—it hardens when it is heated (or over time).[9]

To season your pan, clean it with a stainless-steel scouring pad and remove any rust. Dry the pan completely in a low oven. When it's cool, pour a thin layer of the linseed or flax oil into your pan, rub it in well, and then wipe off the excess. I use a paper towel. Place the pan upside down in the oven (so that any excess oil, which there should not be, can run off and not pool), and heat it to the point that it releases free radicals and the process of hardening begins—at least to 500 degrees, for an hour. Then let it cool and repeat the process. The more layers of polymerized oil you can get, the better.

You can achieve this polymerization with animal fat as well, but it is not as sure a method, as its "drying" contents (alpha-linolenic acid) are lower. If this all sounds too technical, I assure you that many a cast-iron pan has gotten a nice patina just from frying up bacon periodically; I use bacon grease for my pans all the time. However, vegetable oils will not harden—they just get sticky and go rancid. Obviously you can use them—and butter—to cook, but don't leave them in the pan.

Foods that are high in acid (vinegar or tomato, for instance) will strip the seasoning of the pan.

---

[9] I am indebted to Sheryl Canter for a clear explanation on the difference, chemistry-wise, between greasing and seasoning a cast-iron pan. See her clarifying, and informative blog post "Chemistry of Cast Iron Seasoning: A Science-Based How-To," *Sheryl's Blog*, January 28, 2010, http://sherylcanter. com/wordpress/2010/01/a-science-based-technique-for-seasoning-cast -iron/.

Cleaning

You don't need tongs to clean (the recommendations I've seen are to hold paper towels with the tongs), although if you are cleaning a very hot pan, they might come in handy.

You don't need salt. You *could* use salt or even sand because you are trying to abrade, but it's not efficient.

A plastic scrubber will do you no good. Nor will the back of your sponge; you'll only ruin it.

You do need one paper towel (you could use a rag but I strongly feel that paper towels have their uses, and this is one of them).

I'm going to give you the quick tutorial on how to clean those pans, because once you learn it, you will love using them.

Using a flexible straight-bottomed stainless-steel spatula (some call it a pancake turner), and occasionally a stainless-steel spoon for corners, scrape off all the cooked-on bits in your pan while running the water as hot as you can stand it. For this, you might need rubber gloves, but the spatula keeps your hands out of the hot water. It is not easy to find the kind of spatula you really need, due to the proliferation of nonstick, as discussed above, and this fact is a sore grievance to me. For some unknown reason, contemporary metal spatulas are all curved on the business end. You can get lucky at thrift stores, so always have an eagle eye out for a stainless-steel spatula with a *straight* edge.

Now use a stainless-steel scrubbing pad (not Brillo-style ones, which have soap embedded — just a plain stainless scrubber) to scour out whatever grease and drippings there might be. You can't hurt the pan; it can't hurt

you! Just scrub as much as is needed to get bits out; use as much hot water as needed to rinse grease off. And stop there.

Remember, hot water only. No soap. Trust me. That is all you need.

You just have to accept that your pan will be *conceptually* greasy; you will come to see that between the hot water and the subsequent wiping with a paper towel, the pan will be really and truly clean.

Now put it on your stove; it needs to be dry. A burner that has been hot (on an electric stove) or a burner set on low (on a gas one) will do the trick. Leave it there until it is completely dry.

It's clean.

Some old-timers would season the pan by tossing it in a bonfire. The pan would be fine, of course, but I think that you'd have to wipe off soot after the pan cooled.

One grandmother spoke of "firing" her pans to clean them, not just season them. If there got to be a real buildup of gunk (and this does sometimes happen on the outside of the pan), you can put it in the fireplace or what have you to burn it off. Some people also have dedicated pans—for instance, one just for cornbread, to be sure that "off" flavors don't transfer.

Of course, cast-iron cookware can be used in the fire itself—a Dutch oven full of soup can just sit on the grate and be none the worse for wear.

Remember, there are three basic things to clean with:

1. *Soap or detergent.* We know about this one.
2. *Oil or grease.* You would never put soap on a piece of wood furniture; you clean it with oil. Baby's bottom? Clean with baby oil. Hands stained from gardening? Yes, you can wash them with soap and water, but then rub coconut oil, Vaseline, or olive oil on them, and see the dirt come off? What's best of all is to rub your hands with Vaseline before you garden, then put on your gardening gloves; afterward it's not so hard to get them clean.
3. *High heat.* You don't soap down your oven or grill; you fire it up to burn away cooking grease and congealed fats and meat juices. Now you know why I keep telling you to use hot water on your pan, and why you can throw it in the bonfire.

One reader asked about storing the pans, and it's true, the outside can be either greasy or rusty, making cupboards dirty in turn. You can wash the outside—*only* the outside—of your pan with detergent to remove grease. Wipe it with a paper towel so that you'll know that it's really clean. You can hang it on a hook on the wall or a pegboard; that way, the outside will not be touching anything. I always keep my pans on the stovetop, in the oven, or on the woodstove that I have in the kitchen. You can also lay your pan on a paper towel or a paper bag in a drawer or on a shelf.

If the flavor of the food you cook in your cast-iron pan is off, you might need to strip your pan and season it anew, but first check to be sure that your cooking oils or fats are not rancid. Store your bacon grease in a clean jar *in the fridge* so that it doesn't go off.

If the pan smokes when you heat it for cooking, do clean the outside of the pan. Don't overheat your pan on the stove, by the way. Cast iron, unlike other pans, heats up very slowly and then stays hot. Try preheating it at a lower temperature so you won't be tempted to turn it up high at the last minute. For instance, when I am cooking a steak, I preheat the pan on medium high. I sprinkle salt in the pan and turn it to medium. I cook the steak for four minutes on one side (for an inch-thick sirloin), turn it over, and cook it for another four minutes. I usually partially cover the pan for the last two or three minutes of cooking. This method gets me a nice medium-rare steak with a good sear and nice, salty pan drippings. Putting the pan on high always ends with the pan juices burning.

It's so simple to clean your cast iron. The trick and secret is to accept that using soap is *not* the only way to get something clean! And in the case of cast iron, it will just not work. Try this method and see what you think.

Horizontal Surface
Management in the Kitchen

The one time I lived (very temporarily) in a development builder-style house with a standard large wrap-around kitchen with lots of counters and cupboards, my counters were always piled high with junk.

These days, I have an oddball kitchen with many doorways, a sliding door, two windows, back stairs, and a fireplace that takes up one wall, and I use the word "wall" loosely. All my walls are abbreviated vertical surfaces for linking openings, but that is another story.

My point is that I have only a little counter space and few cupboards (not compared with some apartments, but for a 5,600-square-foot house and big family). And I am definitely a cluttery person who prefers to have everything in view and takes the short-term view on storage; my thought process is often: "Life is short. Why don't I put this down right here?"

But I aim here to tell you that organization can be had.

I have managed to convince myself that things aren't temporary anymore (and I think I would have been happier overall in the past if I had resisted feeling so temporary about everything and just committed to making where

I was *pretty*). So I've trained myself in a few things that might help you if you share some or all of these characteristics with me. I think I can say that, for the most part, things are *fairly* neat and tidy in these parts, *even taking into consideration* the shortcomings of my personality and surroundings.

I'll never win any awards because I lose concentration at the last minute. My hope has always been, as I've posted pictures on the blog and written about all this, that our readers would look at them and say, "Well, I can do *that!*"

Clear Off and Scrub Your Surface

Start your horizontal surface management with the most important step: clearing every single thing off the counter or table or desk you are working on — every single thing, without exception. Pile all the things on the floor, on another counter, or, preferably, on the kitchen table. Scrub the counter so that, at the end, you could roll out a pie pastry on it with a clear conscience.

One of my girls once complimented me on having counters I could plop bread dough down on! She was about ten and could already sense that it would be inadvisable to do this in many homes she had visited.

Lest you think I am bragging, I certainly wasn't always aware of the possibility of such cleanliness, and the way I came to be a scrubber does make me cringe just a little. I had a friend when I lived in the city, back when I had just two littles. She and her husband had run a lunch place together before her children came, so she was literally a sandwich professional. It was from her that I got the notion that a sandwich had to be accompanied at least by chips and a piece of fruit or a pickle; whereas, before I met her, I just tossed the PB&J on the plate, and that was that. My friend also had a telltale efficiency when preparing lunch for us when we visited her for a play date, a bustling quality that only made sense when she told me how her chef husband had gotten his start.

Anyway, one day, at my house, she was helping me get the children's lunch together as they were playing in the basement — the two of us crowded into my tiny city kitchen. But it did have a butcher-block top on one counter—a butcher block that I never used except to put a sack of groceries on. I simply regarded the thing with utmost suspicion. It wasn't *my* butcher block, and I had no idea how to clean it. I didn't believe it *could* be cleaned. I mean, I suppose I wiped it occasionally, but I would sooner put my food on the floor than directly on that wood. It seemed so insanitary to me—as I'm sure it really was.

Well, whereas I expected her to make the sandwiches on the plates, as I always did, she just turned around and said something like, "Oh, I'll just do these here" and proceeded to suit action to words, working right on the butcher block. I was really horrified, but much more horrified at the thought of stopping her—too embarrassed! Here she *assumed* that my standards of cleanliness were up to hers, and I don't know why! I can tell you that the me of today would not have assumed any such thing about the me of then, given all the evidence to the contrary.

When she was done, she took my no doubt also abominable sponge and really scrubbed after herself. And that's when it dawned on me that *I too could clean the counter, be it butcher block or what have you.*

In fact, the setup of this kitchen was a U—one short wall of butcher block, sink, sink apron, stove, tiny counter; to the right, a window, then on the other wall, the bottom part of a shabby Hoosier cabinet—you know, one of those all-in-one affairs featuring an enameled top at waist height, only the top part was missing. This enameled counter had been painted over, and in my new obsession with bringing my kitchen somewhere in the universe of the standards of my friend, I scrubbed some of the paint off.

That was a discovery! I was able to remove all the paint, and so provided myself with an extra-deep top-notch spot for rolling out pie crusts and bread dough. And thus, in so ignominious a way, I embarked on my quest for clean surfaces!

While you are at the counter-cleaning thing, how about considering how to use the space on top of the fridge? A big tray with tall sides makes the top of my fridge look somewhat tidy. The tray itself is too big to store, yet I do use it to carry meals for families with new babies or with other needs. When it's not in use, it keeps miscellaneous tins and bread baskets corralled.

The cabinet above and behind the fridge is somewhat inaccessible, so I put in there things I use seasonally. I don't even know what's in there. If I haven't seen what I'm looking for in a while, I know it's up there!

Put Everything Back

Now that you've cleared everything off, put things back with these thoughts in mind:

1. Is it in the right zone (see above)?
2. Is this really useful enough or pretty enough to be out in view?
3. Do I need this here, out in view and taking up room on this valuable horizontal surface, or is there a better, more efficient, and more appropriate place for it? How about the cabinet above? Below? How about on a hook that's installed on the bottom of the cabinet above? Or on the wall? What if I could *use* my counter, rather than just store things on it?

This is all very well, and you are getting the idea. But the worst thing about stuff is that more and more of it keeps arriving. What to do about that? Many people put papers, groceries, mail, hardware, and everything else on the counters in the kitchen, because they are entering the house there and it seems vaguely the thing to do. I have a better idea.

Use the Kitchen Table as a Landing Place for Miscellany

The secret to a tidy kitchen with clean countertops and organized horizontal surfaces is to put the incoming items on the kitchen table! Yes! The very thing you feel guilty about doing! Why do I say that? Because by the time you have put the mail in the mail sorter[10] that's by the door, and your bag on its hook next to your coat, and choir binder in its spot—then you must

---

[10] Don't let the mail lie around in random spots. At least by the time you have kids applying to colleges, you simply must have labeled bins for everyone's mail, because I guarantee you that they will not deal with what comes to them, ever. Without something to sort the mail into, you will be forever handling it, and it will overwhelm you.

find a way to get the rest of the miscellany that comes in the kitchen to where it belongs, somewhere else deeper inside the house.

The truth is, you can't do everything at once—and that is how things get put on counters. Once they are on counters, they are out of your consciousness *and* they render the counters unusable. Even one receipt on a counter is an obstacle to efficiency.

Things you or others have brought in—clothes, bathroom supplies, things that belong in bedrooms, anything that doesn't belong in the kitchen, because if it belonged there, it would *already be put away*—put on the kitchen table.

Before the family can eat or do school or homework, all of which take place at that very table, everyone will have to take a minute to put things where they belong. It's all going somewhere else.

If you or your children can eat or do homework right away, sitting down at the table with no issue *because all those things have been shoved on the counters*, the *stuff* will never find its place.

Keep your *counters* clutter free, and make your *table* where you put the clutter. The table doesn't let you get away with it for long. Just don't allow yourself or anyone else to move something from the table to the counter: If you touch it again, it's to put it away, where it belongs.

This kitchen-table thing is so contrary to what you might think that you have to ponder it for a while, but it's how I've kept my kitchen functioning with up to eleven people living here. Always allow a few minutes before meals or studying to put things away. "Come clear off the table!"

Many extremely good housekeepers do not leave their sponge and dishcloth out on the sink at all. But I find that in a busy household, having a little dish on the edge of the sink for those items is a necessary concession. Mine has a drain hole in the bottom; you may be able to find a small, shallow planter that works well. I have the dishcloth hanging over the divider of my double sink.

Putting your dish soap in a pretty pump dispenser is ingenious, I will modestly point out. You can get soap out with one hand, instead of having to hold the ugly plastic bottle with one hand and the sponge in the other. And getting that detergent bottle off your sink is worth a lot in overall aesthetics.

Another Word about Making Things Pretty over the Kitchen Sink

Many women, even after considerable energy devoted to education and career, long to stay home and take care of their family. They feel torn away when they leave home, as if a part of them gets left behind—and that feeling is far stronger for them than the feeling they have when they leave the outside world and feel a little torn about *that*. I think most people understand that you can't have everything, and they make a choice.

But many of these same women do go just a teensy bit insane when they stay home (and I say this because I was sort of this way myself, although I had no outside life I cared anything about at all). And part of that insanity is that it is truly difficult to live somewhere that's probably far from anyone you know or are related to, to have no friends who are willing to do what you are doing, and to spend all your time with small children.

Part of the conflict, though, has to do with not understanding or not being willing to commit yourself *to the little tasks that make up this life*. We talked earlier about seeing things the way others do when they look into your home. The prettiness over the sink is about how, when you finally give in to the reality of your indispensable role, you can allow yourself to be happy; what you see is a little reminder. You are in the heart of your home, looking out.

Just as I suppose a physician or an architect has some little tedious tasks that, when done with finesse and elegance, become pleasurable, so the wife and mother has the ability to turn something that seems like drudgery into a pleasure and even a prayer.

This is not just in the head or the attitude, though, like a kind of mind game. It's very material and palpable. The goodness of little things is visual and appeals to the other senses as well; things have to look nice and smell nice and feel nice and sound nice and taste nice for them to be felt by us to be nice! (Mind that I'm not saying they have to be expensive or nice according to worldly standards, necessarily. Just *fitting*.)

What you see when you stand at the sink could be a confirmation of the respect you have for what you are doing, however humble it may appear to others. So that's why I say to make the area around your sink pretty, according to what you think is pretty! And not just pretty, but maybe even a place where your prayers rise like incense to Heaven even while your hands are in soapy water.

The Things You Clean with Should Be Cleaner Than the Things You Clean!

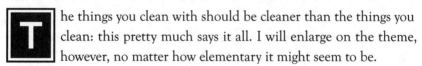

The things you clean with should be cleaner than the things you clean: this pretty much says it all. I will enlarge on the theme, however, no matter how elementary it might seem to be.

It might occur to you, when you are about to wipe that counter that you will then roll a pie crust out on, to wonder if the things you are wiping with (sponges, dishcloths, towels, rags) are clean enough. They sometimes don't look clean. And it makes me remember how things were before I figured this all out at my house, and it further makes me wonder what my lovely friends who were good at housekeeping thought when *they* visited *me*. Honestly, they probably died a thousand deaths. They probably have blogs now, featuring examples of what *not* to do, taken from their visits to me.

I had a couple of dubious dish towels and a sponge. I scrounged for a rag. I can't remember even wondering whether my towels were clean. Once in a while, my mother would delicately buy me a couple of new ones. Some of us are just clueless like that. But we're on a learning curve, and this is it!

It all comes down to this: there is no point in cleaning something with a thing that isn't clean! Think about it! Just because it's *your* dirty sponge, you're used to it, and you are intimately familiar with all the germs that fester there—I mean, they aren't *strange* germs or anything; you know them well—doesn't mean that it isn't gross!

If you use that sponge to wipe something off the floor, even though you know what was on the floor and your sponge is an old friend, you can't use that sponge to wipe a child's face!

Every home magazine and whole shelves of books will tell you how to keep house. I'm not an expert; anyone who really knows me and my house knows I'm not a stellar housekeeper. But I do know this: we need a system so that we can be confident that not only are we cleaning with clean things but other people will be able to step in and take over with confidence as well.

When you are going through hard times and pinching pennies until they beg for mercy, sometimes you don't give yourself permission to buy things you need. Do you buy your feminine products one at a time? Is your toilet paper doled out by the square? Do you run out of soap? Then you know what I'm talking about.

Please get over this. No matter how poor you are, you are going to have to buy those things in some form. Stock up. You can start slowly by using the money you save one month on sale items to buy sale items in bulk the next month, until you have your stash.

Find the lowest price and the quality you like, and go for it. While you're at it, buy a supply of sponges and dishcloths. Not one sponge. Not one dishcloth. Many.

Get the sponges that have a scrubbing side. Everything needs to be scrubbed, honestly, and if it doesn't, turn the thing over and use the sponge side. (For your big pot that you burned potato soup in, you need a stainless-steel or copper pad.) Don't get the kind that are covered with a nylon net. All that happens with those is that the food gets stuck in that netting.

Make sure that the dishcloths are cotton (and *these* can have a mesh side). The microfiber ones will do you no good. They are fine for dusting but don't have the right texture or absorbency for working with dishes and cleaning counters and faces. Under hard use, they pill, which is unaesthetic.

Why dishcloths?

I remember just before we were married, Phil and I were talking about sponges versus dishcloths in kitchen cleanup. (Yes, we were *that* romantic.) He said something like, "I know you'll keep house the way your mother does." It sounded like something he had picked up; you know how you can tell when someone is repeating something they've heard? Let's just say it wasn't the kind of thing he usually said. I thought then I was a sponge person (my mother was a dishcloth person), so I had to laugh, about twenty years later, when I said, "I have to get some dishcloths!" I guess Phil—or whoever told him that—was right!

Dishcloths are useful, I now see, because some things need to be wiped with something that's almost dry, and you can wring out a dishcloth in a way you can't wring out a sponge. As you are wiping something like the counter, you can refold it and have another clean side to work with. With a sponge, after a certain point you are just tracking the mess around unless you stop, walk back to the sink, and wash it out. Too many steps.

Dishcloths have an open texture that helps pick up bits and pieces. And you can throw them in the wash with the towels. Of course, towels should be washed with at least warm water and a bit of bleach. Kitchen towels in particular get quite musty very easily, at least where I live, where it's damp a lot of the time. (This is all discussed in the laundry section.)

I realize that people are passionate sponge or dishcloth partisans. I use both.

Dishcloth people: it's true. How would we clean a floury, sticky counter, egg, or tomato sauce if we had only a sponge, which would simply push those substances around? That said, the dishcloth must look clean as well as be clean. Sponge people: I understand; you want something that holds the soap and feels firm in your hand. Well, the sponge has to be kept clean too! I think we are all familiar with the studies that show that a kitchen sponge is dirtier than the toilet.

That's why I say that you should get a supply, because we all know we hang on to things if we think there's no more left. When your sponge gets a little worn out and not clean enough for kitchen work, let it dry out and then use it in the bathroom to clean the toilet. It's okay to *demote* your cleaning tools! Let them seek their own level, and eventually, *throw them away.*

Always clean the sponge or dishcloth back at the sink before you move on to the next activity. In other words, don't wipe up a bit of sauce and then put the sponge back at the sink. After you use it, rinse it out with hot water and soap, wringing well for next time, and leave it in its dish or, in the case of the cloth, draped over the side. Teach everyone carefully to do the same; the standard operating procedure is that the sponge or dishcloth is ready to go and can be counted on to be clean if it's at its appointed spot.

In an emergency, a sponge or a dishcloth can be left dirty, but then it should be left in the sink to alert the next person (or you yourself, forgetful as you are) of the need to clean it before using it again—because it has to be cleaner than what you are going to clean with it!

And during that sponge's short life span, you can occasionally put it in a bowl and pour boiling water over it or microwave it. Know that very soon, however, even this treatment does not stop the deep-down germs from growing.

Clean the sink itself out well after you finish the dishes. Empty the drain strainers and scrub them. Scrub the sides and bottom of the sink, including the drain opening. Every few days put the strainers in a bowl and pour boiling water over them or throw them in the dishwasher. Clean out the disposal if you have one by running some chopped lemon peel and baking soda through it occasionally.

When we had babies around, we always had a stack of those nice thin baby facecloths for wiping faces and hands. Paper towels are harsh on a baby's face, and it's wasteful to use them for this purpose. At the first sign that Baby was done and about to start clambering out of the high chair, we deployed the "crack cleanup team"—one person removed the tray and the other was ready with a warm clean facecloth to wipe down those greasy fingers and that messy face!

You can also keep a clean facecloth hanging where a child can get it—for instance, on the oven door—and as soon as he has cleared his place, he can wipe his hands and mouth himself. Your whole entire house will stay cleaner if you don't let that little stinker loose to grub things up.

Please understand this: I have no problem with small children getting a bit messy with their food (and babies get very messy!). But commit yourself to cleaning them up when they are done, and you will spare yourself that layer of grime and scent of faintly souring milk that settles on a house where the parents think it's too much trouble to form their own crack cleanup team. When you get down to it, the problem is that they don't have a supply of clean cloths! So the whole house gets dirty. Wouldn't it be a good investment to lay in a supply of washcloths for the baby?

Also, a clean baby is a baby everyone wants to cuddle, whereas a gloppy baby gives babies a bad name!

As for rags, I favor old flannel (sheets, pajamas, shirts) that I've torn into the right sizes for dusting and wiping down. Forget about T-shirts or even the Turkish toweling that Don Aslett recommends; for most applications, I would find that too thick. Flannel is absorbent enough and nicely flexible in your hand. I mainly use rags for dusting, but they certainly come in handy for all sorts of things that you don't want to sacrifice your nice towels to. I have a sizable stack of them, and they are kept *clean*, no matter what they've been used for. If my husband needs one for wiping up hydraulic fluid after testing the plow, I give him a really raggedy rag and then he can throw it away when he's done.

You can wash your rags separately in hot water, although I just throw them in with the towels, also hot water. Don't get into the habit of vaguely designating a rag as "already dirty." You just end up with nasty rags hanging off pipes, draped over otherwise clean sinks, and shoved into corners.

Your life as a housekeeper then becomes trying to assess just how dirty a rag is when you need one, which is too much of a drain on your already overtaxed mind. (And of course, a really greasy toxic rag is a safety hazard, as it could spontaneously combust. In this age of latex paint, people might not talk about not leaving oily, greasy rags around, but maybe they should!)

Keep *all* the rags clean, and that's one less thing to worry about. If it's too dirty to clean, throw it away—this is the beauty of the rag! If it's not that dirty, put it in the hamper (when it's dry)! Knowing you have a stack of clean rags to go to, you'll quickly get into the habit of not letting the dirty ones sit around. You can even iron a few rags and keep them in a special spot for a sort of stop-gap sterile bandage when the need arises.

Now, since your dish towel that's hanging on the hook by the sink is very clean, for wiping *clean* hands, and the dishcloth and sponge are pretty clean, for washing dishes and wiping counters, and the baby cloths, for cleaning baby's faces, are very clean, what do we use to take care of a spill on the floor?

Before I answer that, here's another laundry point: sometimes a towel hanging on the hook *is* clean but doesn't *look* clean, so some people (well, me) are reluctant to use it for their hands (and might grab a paper towel instead, which is wasteful), and some people might use it for something really dirty, like wiping dirty hands on it, or wiping up the floor. When something *looks* dirty, you treat it as if it's dirty. Using a little bleach in the laundry along with hot water, and whatever other methods are necessary, means that your towels will *look* as clean as they *are* and then be used properly.

As I mentioned earlier, before you put anything in the hamper, it should be dry (even though it's dirty!) because it will get moldy in that damp, dark place. Consider attaching a rack to the back of the basement door (if it's handy) or on the wall of the basement stairwell for hanging your kitchen cloths to dry. Don't just throw your used kitchen linens in a heap at the bottom of the stairs or in a corner. Even using a mesh or cotton bag hanging on the back of a door is far preferable.

You can hang clean wet things on your oven door or dishwasher door or what have you, so that they can dry out and be used again, but the dirty wet things should go on a towel rack that you have placed a bit out of the way on your last cabinet side, for just this purpose. I used to have a wooden one, but now I like an old-fashioned metal one just because wood itself can stay damp and get moldy.

Now, back to the spill on the floor. You see that you can grab whatever is drying on the drying rack (preparatory to being put in the hamper) to wipe the floor! The floor isn't that clean, so what you wipe it up with doesn't have to be super clean. A towel that is not clean enough for your hands is fine to mop a spill with. Or get a clean rag for a spill, and once you've used it, hang it on that drying rack so it doesn't get used to wipe a counter.

Things on the drying rack are dirty. Things on a hook or at the sink are clean.

If the towel is hanging on the oven door, we regard it as clean. Sometimes a towel is damp but has been used only to wipe clean plates or something similarly benign; once it has dried on the oven door, it can be rotated back to the hook next to the sink.

I do use paper towels for draining bacon and the occasional wipe-up, especially when the dog barfs (because who wants to use a real towel on that?), but since I know my towels and rags are really clean (are you getting the theme here?) I don't use many paper ones at all.

Sometimes I think that people use a lot of paper towels because they don't understand this gradation, this hierarchy, of cleanliness that I'm discussing here. To them, there's either "spotlessly clean" or "filthy." But just as you should not clean a baby's face with the towel you swiped on the floor, so is it possible to wipe up a spill on the floor with a rag you don't care about much. It's all common sense.

The key here is to make sure the things you clean with are cleaner than the things you clean—by cleaning the things you clean with!

Counting Utensils;
or, Clean as You Go

Apparently, when we were first married, my husband went into work every day and regaled his colleagues with the "utensil count" from the previous night. You see, I had joined the Cooking and Crafts Book-of-the-Month club as a new bride, and new members got four books for a dollar. I got *Joy of Cooking*, *Mastering the Art of French Cooking*, and another Julia Child cookbook. I can't remember if there was a fourth book or if the two volumes of *Mastering* took up two credits.

We had a small kitchen in an apartment in a neighborhood north of Georgetown University (where I had transferred after getting married) in Washington, D.C. I once shorted out the building. Maybe you can picture the little portable washing machine in this kitchen that did double duty as a counter. This washer and my *exasperating* hastiness were the cause. The washer plugged into an outlet above it on the wall, a little to the side. Of course, we didn't have a dryer—we actually had a little laundry line on a screened-in porch, and a little drying rack. But as to shirts, why, I had the idea of hanging them on hangers and letting them dry like that, only I needed something to hang them from.

For whatever reason, at that moment I couldn't think of any better place to hang the shirts than on the plug, which was large and jutted out of the outlet in that way that large plugs do and was *not quite tightly plugged in*. Immediately, as any sane person would have predicted, the wire hangers slipped off the plug and onto the exposed metal.

I think I knew that could happen, but I thought that (a) they would probably slide down the cord onto the floor, so that wouldn't be so bad and I'd be a little more experienced when I thought up the next place to put them, or (b) there would be not much consequence if they went the other way. However, the electricity shorted out the whole building. There was quite the ominous silence after a hail of sparks.

I had to call the super, and he was not excited, and by "not excited" I mean swearing at me, about going down into the basement (which you accessed from outside), where there was about a foot of water standing at all times. I don't blame him.

Anyway, getting back to the kitchen, I was often hungry, as one is, and I think we can see that when confronted with a question, I tend to choose the complicated, or at least, not practical, answer.

And Julia Child's idea of "mastering"—that one, well, mastered recipes in order to learn technique—appealed to me. I have always been analytical, just not practical. Of course, my husband loved to eat too, and he, always nothing if not affirming of whatever interest I have, amiably insisted on doing the dishes, if I wanted to spend my time whipping up French delicacies for him.

After a full day of classes and extracurriculars, I would come home, take a stab at—not housekeeping (I would not use that word; too exact)—but let's say some sort of chaos containment. There was also a good amount of novel reading and studying. Then I would eventually open the cookbook to see what I would make that night. Then I would go grocery shopping. Need I say, dinner was usually quite late. Quite.

At the time and for many years afterward, my husband got about five hours of sleep by preference (I guess. I have no *idea* when he got up!), so he didn't care how late it was, and hey, I was getting up at 9:00 a.m. anyway, having carefully scheduled no early morning classes. He was quite happy and content to start doing dishes at about 11:00 p.m.; he still says that he was just reveling in the good luck of having found someone to cook for him!

And then there was the hilarity of, as he told me *long* afterward, being able to go into work the next day and simply drop the number: fifty-three. They all knew what *that* meant: I had used fifty-three items in making dinner the night before, all piled up in the sink, all lovingly washed by my sweet husband.

Most things are worth going through *for the story*, we have always firmly believed! Even knowing now that all those people were (rightly) judging me doesn't detract from the contentedness we shared. And guess what: I did learn to cook!

Later, when I realized that it was just unreasonable to expect a man to come home from work and clean up after your gourmet productions late at night, I confronted my inefficiency for myself. And that's when I learned *what* "clean as you go" means, because do you not agree that some people are born knowing what that means and others aren't?

The truth is, people like us think it's dumb and inefficient to put things away and wash up as you are working, because there is working, and there is cleaning. It seems like a waste of energy to mix them up, and it is. We're right!

Well, I will explain it, since it all became clear to me when I had one of those days when, even knowing how I can be, I was astonished at the chaos in the kitchen I had caused. I was working on making dessert bars and also meatballs. For some reason (having to do with things not mixing properly or the bowl I chose not being big enough) I ended up using every appliance, not to mention bowls, I own, just about. And the bars were a little weird. But the meatballs were good.

Since I had put myself in charge of cleanup, something had to change!

Clean-as-you-go can be summarized in these ideas, I think:

Make Time

Think about what time you would normally start your supper prepara-tions—not the fantasy you, the actual you. Start twenty minutes before that.

Before you get going, make sure the counters are cleared off in the manner I have already described above in the kitchen-flow section. Make sure the dishwasher is empty. If you don't have a dishwasher, make sure the clean dishes are put away and the sink is at least empty. Go one step further and fill it (or one side of it if you have a double sink) with hot, soapy water.

Make Use of Stopping Points

As you work, think in terms of stopping points or pauses to clean up rather than clean as you go, which may seem too demanding to you, as I know it did to me. When something needs to simmer or bake or sit, use that time to assess the things you have strewn about. Quickly throw away wrappers and other trash (and try to challenge yourself not to leave such things in an interim spot but instead to put them directly into the trash can when possible; it helps to think through where that receptacle is placed for best efficiency). Can the spices be put away all at once at this point, or do you still need them out? Will the food processor be used again? If not, put its bowl in the dishwasher now.

Soak and Wipe

I ask myself: Can I at least soak these bowls, nesting together and conveniently providing myself with a container of hot soapy water for a quick turnaround of utensils? Can I wipe off a counter while I'm stirring occasionally? Great! That puts me ahead.

Make Things in Hygiene or Taste Order

If you have several things to make, plan them out so that you can use certain utensils in "hygiene or taste order," without washing them in between. Examine your work order. If you are going to use the food processor twice in one session, try to wash it only once. For instance, if I'm making cookies and bread, I can certainly make the bread in the bowl that I've already used for cookies, but not vice versa without washing it out first. If I use the sharp knife first on the tomatoes and then on the chicken, no washing in between is necessary, but the reverse order requires careful washing!

And then clean up in between those several recipes as much as possible. It's hard to have the mess of three courses at the end, but not a big deal to clean up after any one.

Tidy before the Meal

Use the twenty minutes you've spotted yourself at the end of the meal prep to whisk everything into the tub of soapy water or the dishwasher; put ingredients away and wipe off the counters. Your dining self will thank your cooking self, and supper's aftermath will seem a lot less overwhelming. Try to sit down to dinner with the food prep cleaned up. It's amazing the difference to your attitude it can make, to have even a few minutes in between the mess and the eating!

Kitchen Drawer Organization

have three thoughts that motivate the organization in my kitchen—two are rather self-evident and the third is easy enough: like things belong together, things that are used together belong near each other, and the Pareto principle.

One of the most helpful thoughts ever to dawn upon the person struggling to make sense of things in general is the Pareto principle, originally conceived to explain income distribution among the population, but applicable to almost anything we are trying to observe—in this case, efficiency in the kitchen. I owe my discovery of Pareto's insight to Deniece Schofield, author of *Confessions of an Organized Homemaker.*

This useful analytical tool asserts that things, whether time or steps or actions or features or people, can be divided into 20 and 80 percent, and the 20 percent will account for the usefulness, output, or efficacy of the 80 percent. Twenty percent of the people in an office account for 80 percent of the work accomplished and 80 percent of the people account for 20 percent of the work; 20 percent of your clothing bears the burden of 80 percent of wear, while 80 percent languishes in the closet.

Note two things: First, the principle doesn't say that this means that the 80 percent is useless or can be eliminated. Second, these numbers are just for purposes of making the point about how things work, typically speaking; the actual numbers might vary.

Even so, it's an incredibly helpful idea to remind oneself of when one is falling into the trap of thinking things distribute themselves equally.

For our purposes here, let's consider the kitchen: 20 percent of the things you use will account for 80 percent of the effective things you do. Identify those things, put them where you can reach them immediately, without moving the 80 percent out of the way first, and you will be much more effective in your work.

Most kitchens are not designed to be very efficient, which is fine if you are young and have nothing better to do than run around in there without a plan. But once you hit the part of your life when you are not only having to come up with multiple meals a day for a crowd but are pregnant or nursing while you do it, you need to save your steps.

Obviously, there are many areas to organize in the kitchen, and you almost certainly have more scope than I, who have only a few drawers to work with. But I thought I'd go through the organization of those few (always keeping thrift and probable tiredness or exhaustion in mind) in hopes of leaving you with a basic structure of how to think about setting things up according to *how you work* and *what goes on in your kitchen*.

In one drawer, keep foils, wraps, and plastic bags together; you want a small open container for rubber bands, twist ties, and a few clothespins and binder clips for closing bags of chips and the like. If you have a designated place in a drawer (a plastic container that has lost its lid is perfect) to pop any rubber band you find, including the ones that come on veggies and other goodies, you may never buy another rubber band. (Please don't store your rubber bands on doorknobs or the faucet. It's not attractive either way, and it's too damp and moldy in the latter case.)

I keep a Sharpie in that drawer for marking zip storage bags and jars lest they be lost forever in the freezer with nary an indication of their contents. A marker also helps with keeping people's sandwiches sorted out.

Consider another drawer near your food preparation area (mine is the one right next to the sink) for extra utensils, separate from your normal eating utensils, for cooking, bread buttering, tasting of sauces, and general activities in the kitchen; for all this you need a separate stash, separate even from the container near the stove with your spatulas, rubber and metal, and wooden spoons and whisks for stirring.

One day early on in my organizing life, I was decluttering the kitchen; all my tableware was in one place—matched set and random ones together—and I thought about tossing the unmatched ones. Then I realized how very useful they are if you simply give them their own category closer to where you cook. Using unmatched ones for meal prep saves your place settings for the table (and thus saves you from having to wash some up quickly as people sit down to eat).

I have two drawers that relate to food prep. One drawer includes those miscellaneous spoons, forks, and knives, along with citrus reamers, thermometers, turkey baster, corkscrew—anything that I might reach for as I'm preparing food—and the drawer has dividers to impose a little order. How did I decide what to put in that drawer? Either by *wishing* that I had such a thing in easy reach or by not knowing where else to put something (e.g., medicine cups and spoons, as one does dole out the random dose standing there by the sink).

In the second drawer, in a separate compartment goes *anything* "knifey," including butter knives, spreaders, can opener, and so forth. When I'm making a peanut-butter sandwich, my spreaders are right there by the cutting board that sits on the counter above that drawer and in front of the toaster.

Sharp knives could be kept in a block on the counter (if you have enough counter space—I do not) or on a magnetic holder on the wall (same thing—I don't have a place for that!). I like keeping mine in a wooden insert (so they stay sharp and safe, not jumbled together, which is terrible in so many ways) in that "knifey" drawer.

Near the table but not too far from the dishwasher, you want your silverware and serving utensils. Those things don't need to be near the food preparation areas, which is freeing.

Every kitchen has a junk drawer. Rather than fight the "catch-all" aspect, organize it, and put it on the periphery of the food prep area. I had a real mental block about accepting this drawer, simply because the random nature of the contents—wire, string, extra felt chair pads, hair elastics, comb—made it impossible for me to know whether to ban it completely or to commit to drawer dividers. But how would I function if I always had to go to a different room for the things in that drawer; on the other hand, how to commit to dividers?

Then I hit on the idea of using plastic containers that had lost their lids (or honestly, it's worth even using cheap ones and sacrificing their lids) to customize this drawer for my own needs with a minimum of expenditure. You can even stack clear shallow containers on top of each other, sliding them as needed. In my drawer, I keep my own stash of tools: my hammer, screwdriver with interchangeable bits, needle-nose pliers, and tape measure; picture hangers and attractive nails (nice brass ones!) for hanging the odd picture.

Cleaning the Bathroom

The bathroom needs to be clean. And it needs to *look* clean and *smell* clean. Here are a few little thoughts having to do with cleaning bathrooms *while* nursing babies, homeschooling, being eight months pregnant and not bendable, and in short, just having lots of kids. It's the reality factor that's missing from the books (less in *Confessions of an Organized Housewife*, as the author raised five children; more in *Home Comforts*, the author of which had one child, and I truly believe you can do anything with one child, including have a clean house all the time!).

Cleanable Substances

First, do everything in your power to get a bathroom made of cleanable substances. When comparing toilets, for example, steer clear of the ones with many nooks and crannies and inaccessible places. Once, when we were remodeling a bathroom, I asked the plumber to move my toilet six inches further away from the side wall, because there was simply no way *to see* to clean in that corner as it was.

Why, oh why, did anyone ever invent the cursed shower door? What's so wrong with a bathtub and shower combo? At least if a shower curtain gets gross, you can throw it out and get a new one. And don't get me started on hot-tub-style tubs. You can't bathe a baby in one for the same reason it's very difficult to clean: too deep. No one can afford to fill one. And no one has time for one. Please just get me an old-fashioned bathtub. Please.

An easy fix, not at all expensive, is to replace a normal shower head with one that has a flexible hose and handheld head (or two heads, one fixed and one on the coiled hose) so that you can take it down to rinse walls and corners efficiently—not to mention soapy kids or one's own feet!

Scrape out old caulking with a putty knife and replace it with silicone caulking, very thinly applied so that it fills the gap but doesn't create a ridge on the tile. Use your finger—you can wipe it off on paper towel later. This task is much easier than it looks if you realize that it all hinges on first getting out every bit of old caulk and then using your finger, firmly pressing that bead where it goes, to finish the new.

Use washable paint (mildew-resistant on the ceiling) and avoid wallpaper. Wallpaper plus steam equals drooping, peeling wallpaper.

Living in old houses, we've always had issues with other people's bad construction choices. I'm dreaming of the day when everything will be tightly sealed, mildew-free, and wipeable! Obviously it's easier to clean a good bathroom than a bad one, so get a good one if you can.

Cleaning What You've Got

Moving on to cleaning what you've got. Personally—and maybe I'm revealing even more of my inadequacy than I intended to—I don't see the need for a bucket unless you are mopping the floor. The bucket idea seems to reach back into the mists of time when the bathroom didn't have running water in it. But lo! it does now. Don Aslett says (in one of his helpful books) to use the water in the sink or tub and then clean those last. I concur.

And there are two levels of bathroom cleaning, just like the other rooms: the Blitz and the Moderate Clean (deep clean about once a month, scrubbing every surface). Here's where having lots of kids works in your favor.

The key to your life with them, obviously, is multitasking. No one multitasks like mother. So, you know how all those kids are always needing a bath? And even when they aren't particularly dirty, it's just a lifesaver to get them in there splashing away?

Well, that time is your chance to get the bathroom into shape with a daily Blitz. You have to be with them because they need supervision so that they don't drown or grab razors and medicine and cleanser and what have you. Yet, most of the time when you *are* in there, they are playing happily and you are doing nothing! So clean the bathroom!

Listen. Don't let them drown on account of me. Use your common sense. You know the difference between a baby who truly has to be watched every second and one who is okay in there because there are so many others in that tub that they are all like sardines, propping each other up, don't you? So you, also on the spot, can scrub down the toilet and sink. If anyone expires, don't blame *moi*.

But this is what I did, and my bathroom was cleaner then than it is now that my kids are grown: I used that playing time (and you really need only five minutes) to get the toilet scrubbed and wiped down. Then, since I've used the sink for my water supply, I clean that, using a different sponge (cut off a corner of the toilet sponge so you'll know which one it is), and rinse and dry it off. Wipe off the mirror. Using the towel you are about to change, give the mirror a final shine, dry the sink, and dry the toilet. Replace the hand towel with a clean one (please do this at least once a day with many kids around).

Maybe you'll try, and your child won't be thrilled that you're not right there to attend to him. No fear! Keep working on it. Some fun things to have in the bath are plastic measuring cups, an old colander, anything that pours, a bulb baster, toy boats, high-quality plastic animals, and fun washcloths that can double as hand puppets. Children also enjoy a "cleaning cloth" and a small spray bottle so that they can help clean along with Mama. Finally, get a bin with holes in the bottom or a small dishrack to put all those toys in; hang it up over the shower rod to drain when bath time is done. (Don't hang things on the shower head, which will stress at the point where it joins the main pipe behind the shower wall; eventually it breaks back there, and that is no fun.)

When the kids are drying off and in various stages of getting dressed, running around naked, screaming, and laughing, wash out the tub, gather up your dirty towels along with the children's various items, and back yourself out of your blitzed bathroom.

It follows as the night the day that your supplies need to be right there under the sink or in a handy cabinet. No running down the hall to a distant closet for Windex. Stock up with the following:

- Two sponges of distinct styling (that have been demoted from kitchen use): one for the toilet, the other for everything else (cut off a corner of the toilet one so you'll know which one it is)
- Comet (it's cheap and is fine on porcelain as long as you don't go nuts scrubbing)
- Scrubbing Bubbles-type spray for the accursed shower
- Foaming mildew spray for the accursed shower
- Toilet brush
- Glass cleaner (store brand is fine)
- Paper towels or rags for the mirror (should your dirty hand towel be just too dirty)
- Squeegee, if you are saddled with an accursed shower door (never mind sprays—you need to wipe that water off with a rubber tool)
- Rubber gloves that don't have holes in them—treat yourself to a new pair
- A basin to contain these supplies neatly under the sink
- A pitcher for rinsing dogs, children, and tubs
- Clean towels and washcloths

Once or twice a week, shake out and wash the rugs, dust the light fixtures, wipe the moldings, vacuum and mop the floor, change the bath towels, and you're good to go.

How do you manage to replace bath towels only once a week? *How, Auntie Leila?*

Color-code the towels. A towel that has dried a clean child will be reusable for many days *if it dries out completely between uses* (this is why you need hooks for each child to hang his towel on). To keep track of which towel belongs to which child, *give each his own color towel*—unless you have it together enough to have your towels monogrammed! Do not rely on the placement of the towels (i.e., hooks or racks). All it takes is for two children to toss their towels on the floor, and you will be sunk.

You know the hygiene protocol that you go through with your children, teaching them to wipe themselves and wash their hands? Let me advise you to revisit that training every year or two, asking them to visualize what will happen to their towels if they do not use warm water and soap to wash their hands.

As you leave, ask yourself if your bathroom *looks and smells* clean. Imagine that you are taking a guest around your house. (This happens often, I find. Sometimes they are looking for their child; sometimes they want a tour.) What would you change right now if a non-family member were there? Do it!

Don't boom and bust in your bathroom; you can keep it reasonably clean by multitasking at bath time.

How to Keep a Closet
Neat and Tidy

I wrote about this topic on the blog after we painted and reorganized a fantastically deep and useful closet in my house that stores all the toys and games of a lifetime (not to mention our record and DVD collection). A reader asked how we would keep it in its newfound organized state.

The problem was never with the stuff itself. When we started pulling it apart to paint, it was remarkably not in a jumble, despite years of neglect on my part. (I mean, don't get me wrong: it was scary. But at the same time, there were few puzzles with missing pieces, because I have learned the hard lesson that such a thing is worse than useless; I kept only the most-loved games; I had early on put toys with many pieces in their own stackable bins, and so on.)

No, the problem was with the closet itself, and I think that if we talk about it a little, you will see how it is that anyone can keep the toy area *reasonably* neat and tidy, with normal fluctuations brought on by life, of course.

Before we painted, I, the household manager, did not ever, *ever* want to go in there. It was too dismal, uncleanable, and neglected. I mean, sometimes I did go in and tidy up, but I hated it. The children occasionally did some organizing or throwing away of superannuated or defunct items.

The proper way to clean something, as I have told you when we went on our Reasonably Clean House journey together, is to pull everything out, clean the space, sort and clean the things, and put back what truly belongs there. This is true for everything. Even things that clean other things—such as dishwashers and washing machines—occasionally have to be pulled out, scoured out, and put back the way you want them! So, how much more a toy closet!

But that assumes that the space *can* be cleaned and that you want to try. Thus, unlike me in this instance, make sure you get the closets repaired and painted before you put anything in them, even if it means having its contents out for a while.

People might be frustrated with where they keep their games and toys and skeptical that my closet will remain fabulous, and I will address their assumptions one by one. Not yours, dear reader, because no doubt you are actually a good housekeeper yourself, but *others'* assumptions.

Wrong assumptions:

1. *The space doesn't matter—it's only for storing things.* No. The space matters. Whether it's a part of the room or an actual closet or under the beds, it needs to be something that you can clean when it's empty. The surfaces have to be free of gaping holes or torn carpet or what have you. They have to be finished in a way that they look clean when they are wiped down. This is something to work on. Having mostly lived in old houses, I know the issues. Just be prepared to consider that it's not your *cleaning* that's at fault; it's the space itself! I learned this when I was in my neighbors' basement and saw how neat and tidy all the little spaces were. Their basement was exactly the same as mine; we shared a duplex. But they had made theirs like a ship's hold. Every inch of space was painted and tidy and held only what it was intended to hold. Ever since then, this has been my (rarely realized) dream.

2. *Shelves don't matter.* They do matter. You can't pile things on the floor and then continue piling. Maybe one thing that I did appreciate a lot about this

closet was the shelves—to the point that I thought the space would work without my immediate attention (see number 1), especially in light of all the other projects in the house that had priority. Shelves make a huge difference in how you can organize stuff. Metal brackets and wooden boards don't cost much in the grand scheme of things. Make sure you find the studs when you are installing the brackets.

3. *If everyone puts things back into the proper place, I will never have to clean.* Well, yes, they need to put things back—we're all in this together, after all!— but no, it's still the manager's responsibility in the end (not that you can't delegate most of that responsibility—but not all).

Are things arranged so that there is a good chance that items would get back in their spots? For instance, the bins on the floor, tucked under the lowest shelf, hold various toys with many—a million—little moving, snapping, or fitting parts. Each bin is large enough to hold its contents, the lids fit, and the bins stack. These are the toys that are most likely to be pulled out, and it's not hard to get the bins back. Things with fiddly (but not a million) pieces are stored higher—in ascending order of likelihood that they (a) would make a terrible mess if spilled and (b) are difficult to put away.

Don't put the thousand-piece puzzles within reach of even a six-year-old. Don't put the dominoes or playing cards within reach of toddlers. Some sort of thought process (or maybe fail-safe button or key arrangement like those on nuclear launching systems) must occur before these many-pieced games get taken down. And maybe a stool- and permission-getting process as well.

So the solution rests partly on how clever you are at arranging in the first place. Low-down things shouldn't be stacked more than two items high. They should be spaced out on the self. If this is a problem, do some trimming of your inventory, because it just won't work to expect young children to cope with piles and stacks of toys. Try rotating toys and storing some in bins under beds. Children certainly don't need all their things all the time.

In considering which items should go on higher shelves, you should consider how annoyed you would be if a box or a container of something were spilled out. I can cope with two containers of plastic army guys being spilled out. But I have an anxiety attack if the bingo game is spilled out without forethought, and that's mainly because if one number is lost, the whole thing is ruined. So the bingo game goes on the top shelf.

The exception to my two-item stack rule is board games that go on the highest shelf and are light enough to move around by a responsible person.

Toy-closet tidiness is also a question of inspection and training. Even a three-year-old will put (simple) things back if you spend some time asking him to, helping him, and making sure he does. It takes a while, but it pays off in the end. Some children will consider putting things back part of the process of playing with it, and *simply cannot understand a child who doesn't do that.* Try to get these children if you can!

But—sometimes you need to rush out of the house, and sometimes the three-year-old has a meltdown, and sometimes ten three-year-olds are over to play, and sometimes everyone was just having a lot of fun and a lot of things got taken out, rules or no rules. So just limit how much they can reach in the worst-case scenario.

Every day there has to be a time (the Blitz) when playthings are sorted through and someone makes sure that, in fact, things got put away properly.

4. *So if they don't put things back where they found them, it's their fault, not mine, if the closet is messy.* Well, no. Not that it would even help to think this!

Occasionally this area needs real attention, and the only person with the big picture is you. You have to notice that a toy placed in front of all the others makes things messy and isn't even enjoyed. You have to get bigger bins or multiple bins for a growing collection of train tracks. You have to throw away broken games and puzzles with missing pieces. So, every once in a while (probably during your once-a-week cleaning of the room—the Moderate Clean, or at least once a month), you need to straighten things up. Rearrange, dust, and tidy. A large child (somewhere over the age of reason) could be given this job with you just coming in to inspect. Certain children really get offended if things aren't kept neat—identify and promote.

5. *Then that should do it—just the Moderate Clean?* Sadly, no. The Deep Clean is still a necessity. I always feel that the thing that needs to be deep cleaned

will let you know it. You just won't be able to take the disorder anymore. And really, only you can do it. Pull every single thing out, vacuum from top to bottom, wash down if necessary, air out, and then put things back.

Be critical. Only what belongs there gets to go there.

The reason things were a jumble in my toy closet was that I couldn't face the closet itself. But now it's a joy even to open the door! So who wouldn't want to make sure that only puzzles are on the puzzle shelf, and only board games on the board game shelf!

By the way, children are perfectly happy being given the job of making sure that only Legos are in the Lego bin and Playmobil in the Playmobil bin. To them, that's as good as playing.

Surfing Your Day, or, You Can Do a Lot in an Hour

Sometimes when life feels a little overwhelming to me, and I don't believe that I can tackle all the jobs that are waiting for me—or, truthfully, I feel as if the jobs would take days or weeks to accomplish, so why bother even starting?—I try to remember that I can do a lot in an hour.

We can waste an hour very easily, so we tend to forget how much can be accomplished in that time. An hour is valuable to the busy householder, but the only way to prove it to yourself is to challenge yourself to see how much you can do with it.

You know that thing we do, most of us—clicking around the Internet? You keep clicking, and there are more and more interesting, fun, distracting, or maddening things to read, listen to, and watch, and soon an hour is gone. I'm not going to tell you not to do that, because that's what the Internet is for, I suppose.

But one day, something occurred to me about this quest for a reasonably clean house. As I was working outside, I kept seeing more and more that I wanted to do; I kept going from weeding one area to raking another. And if I went inside, I kept seeing so many things that needed my attention in there, from sweeping the kitchen to folding laundry.

Most of the tasks were pretty small—just like posts online that promise you "Six Things to Know about Your Car!" that can be read in under a minute. As I moved around the garden, there were "Just Six Weeds Sticking Out of This Low Planting!" Or just as your eye is caught by "The Most Amazing Journalist Interviews the World's Greatest Philosopher," I was tempted by real "clickbait": "Move This Pile of Mulch and Accomplish Two Tasks at Once!" These little jobs didn't take me long but kept me running around: "If I Put This Chair Where It Belongs, I Will Experience Satisfaction with This Room."

To see how quickly things can get done, try timing how long it takes you to tidy up the bathroom or even mop a floor. I think you will be surprised that the time most things take is much less than the time and energy we waste in dreading doing them and allowing ourselves to be distracted by stupid things instead.

You can't flit all day among the little tasks that could use attention, just as you can't surf the Internet all day (you can, but you would hate yourself). But for an hour or so, it's a fine way to get things done.

You can do a lot in an hour. And what do you know: it keeps you off the computer!

The Day I Rolled Up
My Kitchen Towels

One day my husband mentioned that a camera crew would be arriving to interview him for some news show. Usually they go into his study, and that works fine; it's book-lined and oak-desked and generally has the air of respectability, enough for head shots with blurry backgrounds, anyway. But this particular day, he felt that his office was not up to snuff. And believe me when I tell you, that means it was not up to snuff. (I remediated later.)

So naturally, realizing that a news reporter and a man with a technologically advanced apparatus of digital moving photography would likely be in the *living room*, I was suddenly seized with the need to apply what I knew of Marie Kondo's principles (as found in her book *The Life-Changing Magic of Tidying Up*, which at the time I had not read but had read articles about) to our dressers in the bedroom and to the kitchen island, going through all our linens according to her organization guidelines.

Yes. Yes, I did. Two areas of my home that were definitely not going to be featured or broadcast anywhere at all became the intense focus of my laser concentration.

Suddenly, all that really mattered to me, impending interview or not, was this video I had seen somewhere detailing Marie Kondo's recommendations for rolling items of clothing that are stored in drawers, rather than laying them flat and stacking them.

Skipping lightly over what transpired in my dresser drawers, I will reveal that I had, all piled up in the kitchen island, the following:

- nice kitchen towels
- okay kitchen towels but really excellent for covering rising bread, as they are the right size and tightly woven, which prevents their sticking to the dough (I suddenly realized—the camera crew was about an hour away—that I wanted these particular towels not to be in the towel stack, but elsewhere, because they really just aren't that great for drying your hands—certainly not as good as the others—but I'm not the only person grabbing a towel here.)
- not as nice kitchen towels and dishcloths, very clean of course (I also have a supply in the pantry; they get demoted and are for sloppy messes.)
- dishcloths
- real rags (These are not to be confused with sloppy towels or old dishcloths, because if you use those as rags, they will inevitably get cycled back into the good towels or dishcloth piles, and then a guest will suddenly be washing dishes and drying hands with something embarrassing. As I have told you before, I use old flannel PJs, shirts, and sheets torn up into rag-size pieces, which would never be confused with a kitchen towel by even the most distracted guest.)
- cloth napkins, which we use every day, so I have a good supply

Usually all of these are folded and stacked. The stacks, up until this moment, had been separate and approximately sorted. But now I found it necessary to roll them all up, even the rags. Why not? We are going full-crazy-Japanese-tidiness-guru, and the crew is still forty-five minutes away. I also rolled up my secret dough towels, which I put on the other side of the island, away from the carefully rolled good kitchen towels, so that only I will grab them, sparing my family from having to memorize my towel preferences.

After much soul-searching and conscience-questioning, with the camera crew a scant ten minutes away by my fevered calculations, I failed to roll up the cloth napkins. I like them stacked.

Here are my thoughts on Marie Kondo's method: it's one thing to take everything out of its place and roll it up and put away what you want to keep. It's another to do the laundry this way; that is, to take a basket of clothes, sort and roll, and then transfer to drawers.

Rolled things roll. They roll while you are rolling them (I normally do this on the sofa or on my bed), while you are stacking and sorting them in the basket, and while you are putting them away. Thus, the work motions are greatly, *greatly* increased because there is a lot of retrieving and rerolling, or am I just a klutz? Yes, even though I've been told it's not so much a roll as a sort of triangular wrapping, I find that the resulting item and subsequent pile is not stable.

I am having trouble thinking that children will not get frustrated with this method, although I could see eight- to twelve-year-old girls getting obsessed as well. Personally, when I was rolling all those things (which included all the things in the dressers as well), I was getting frustrated. Things kept unrolling.

See what you think, because in the drawers and on the shelves, this is very nice.

I did manage, thanks to some *intense* blitzing, to make the living room quite presentable.

And the interview took place outside, on the deck.

Building the Creative Environment — and the Culture — with Furniture

I am not a decorator, but like you, I certainly am in charge of making my house pretty. I haven't always succeeded, but I have been in charge. This aspect of my life as a mother makes me think of how spiritual things are affected by the material things that might or might not be taken care of.

This entire section has been devoted to keeping what you have clean, neat, and tidy in a reasonable way. Let's also look at other aspects of making your home pretty and inviting. These are practical ideas for implementing the vague wish of gathering with your family and have comfortable, happy family time.

Cleaning is fine, but you also need to acquire (probably buy, but do consult the thrifting section below for ideas) and arrange furniture to make this happen. I avoided the need for furniture when I first set up housekeeping; I see that some people also have this difficulty of committing to furnishings.

This discussion is not a worldly one or focused on things that don't really count; on the contrary, it's essential to building the culture—the culture of your family and thus of your hospitality; by extension, the culture. The whole world might be affected for better or for worse by whether people can have a nice chat in your home!

Lighting

You need lots of lighting, but not one glaring fixture up above. Overhead lights are fine (not that we have many in my old house), but lamps are a necessity. You need one for every area where someone will sit and read or knit and chat companionably. Every corner. The minimum in a living area is three. In ours, we have three table lamps and two wall sconces.

Most children won't settle down to read if there aren't lamps. A lamp provides not only light but also that pool of cozy warmth that you have to have for the *desire* to sit and read in the evening.

And please, consider it money well spent to have incandescent lights in your family-area lamps. Those compact fluorescents are never going to give you the ambiance you are looking for (and they are made with mercury, which is poison). People will always feel cold, dreary, and slightly alienated. It's just not worth the "savings" to use them. Even LEDs, which can approximate the *color* of incandescents, are cold, and the light they emit is actually jagged—emitted in quantum, discrete sharp waves—and is potentially harmful to eyesight. This is true on the level of physics—luminescence is a low-temperature result of the excitation of atoms; incandescence produces warmth as well as light, which is *relatively* inefficient, yet necessary. I like to point out that it would be more efficient to cook everything in the microwave, but I doubt we are going to do it, because efficiency isn't the only criterion.

To anyone arguing about these hard facts, I quote St. Bernard: "It is vain merely to give light, and it is but little to burn; but to burn and give light together is perfection."[11] He is speaking of St. John the Baptist ("he was a burning and a shining light" [John 5:35, KJV]), but I think we can apply what he says here as well.

---

[11] See Pius XII, encyclical on St. Bernard of Clairvaux *Doctor Mellifluus* (May 24, 1953), no. 5.

If you want your home to feel warm in the cozy, welcoming sense, keep the cool forms of light out of the living areas (they work well in closets and out in the garage or in the basement storage area). Obviously, the kind of light we live in has a tremendous effect on our well being.

Furniture

The furniture in your living area needs to be sturdy and welcoming. Children will gravitate to their rooms (and thus not be "gathered" with you of a cozy evening) if the only place for them to relax is their bed.

The furniture also needs to be *close together*. You can't have three people sitting in a line on a sofa, attempting to hold a conversation with someone on a chair across the room. In my family, we enjoy watching games and movies together in comfort, not craned over a computer or squinting at a little set. We don't go out to movies very often. Viewing them together in our home is part of our entertainment. Thus, I am not averse to a large screen and comfortable seating where we do that. Having the seating in a conversation circle rather than all facing the screen gives the right impression about our priorities.

Throw pillows express personality and offer comfort; quilts and afghans are pretty and help keep us warm in cold weather. To keep things simple, I like the big furniture to be neutral so that the other textiles can express design style and be changed without too much expense. But the upholstery can't be too light, obviously, or it will show the dirt, and it can't be too dark, or every dog hair and bit of lint will show up. I know that some say that white slipcovers are great, because you can wash and even bleach them. I can't help but wonder if the ones recommending this option have children who are home all the time! If you are looking to redo well made furniture, the truth is that slipcovers (custom-made) can be pricier than reupholstering!

Once when I was reupholstering my sturdy sofas, I found some dark chocolate velvet that I loved and seriously considered, but I realized that it was just too dangerously dark for our den lifestyle. A fabric that has worked for me (and took a long time to find) is a taupe (medium grayed brown) linen-like fabric that can withstand plenty of "rubs" (the industry standard to express longevity, so you don't get pilling or shininess). Full-grain leather would be a practical choice if the exchequer could take the hit, and I was thrilled to find a beautiful leather armchair secondhand, going for a song. I *almost* couldn't fit it into my car, but I made it happen! It's the sort of chair that just gets better with age, and the newer ones I've seen don't have anything like the classic styling of mine.

Leather might seem to be too cold in winter, but lovely knit afghans and quilted throws solve that issue. (Consider that fabric such as crushed velvet can seem too sticky and even dirty in summer; nothing is perfect.)

If your rooms seem small or you are working with a lot of windows and doorways, or both, focus on the floor: Several big, comfy floor pillows with washable covers can expand your seating. Those could all be stacked in a corner when not in use to keep the pathways clear and then pulled out whenever needed. These days, stores have really elegant floor pillows for animals. Why not stock up on those? They always have washable covers and are made for hard use; I doubt anyone would be able to tell they are not for people. Children seem to prefer the floor to couches anyway, and there is a lot of play potential with floor pillows. Upholstered ottomans can be pushed around when needed, and sturdy wooden stools can be stowed under the piano or a desk, to be pulled out when needed.

Position some chairs or sofas with your wide doorways behind them—liberate yourself from the idea that every piece of furniture needs a wall behind it. If you place a couple of chairs with a table with a lamp between them, so the chairs are slightly turned toward each other, it creates a "conversation area." One of the chairs venturing out in the path just defines the space. Or put a couple of extra chairs on either side of a large doorway. Experiment with putting furniture diagonally in corners or putting a sofa in the middle of the room, facing another sofa or a pair of chairs; this works especially well if they can be perpendicular to a fireplace. Or put the pair of chairs in the middle of the room facing the sofa. Try making these "conversation areas" appear; avoid having all the furniture just shoved up against the walls.

When your home is arranged pleasingly for all the activities that go on in it, and especially for conversation, reading, play, and comfort, it becomes easier to care for. The work that goes into making it clean and tidy has a tangible goal that makes all the difference: your life together as a family.

PART 5
Handling Money

In this section I will give you solid tips on how to stay out of debt and to get out if you are in. I've been in debt, and I've gotten out. But before we get into the details, I have to tell you that being in debt is not the worst thing that can happen to you. So bear with me here. I wrote the following chapter ten years ago. Since then, our financial situation has improved, and I'll be honest, having my kids grow up and move away has helped—turns out that people are right when they say that having a ton of kids is costly! I need not say, however, that it's worth it.

The point is simply this: you live your life, and you do your best. In my opinion, trading a life with the kids God sends you for financial security (not that you can guarantee that, since bad things happen to even the most careful people) is a terrible idea that I could never endorse. In this section, I will try to relieve guilt about being in debt and offer a few practical ways to be more financially secure.

Five Things That Are Worse Than Being in Debt

When I got married, I had never heard of saving money, being frugal (although I did know about finding old furniture and fixing it up), or in any way living within one's means. Or, if I had, I certainly wasn't paying attention. And I married someone who basically couldn't say no to his little spoiled brat of a wife, and anyway, I'm not all that sure he knew anything either.

So it's not surprising that we got into debt. For many years, we struggled. I won't say it's over. Along the way, I learned some lessons the tough way; for instance, being so deep in debt that the issue is no longer about a budget, it's about not having any money at all to buy anything. Sometimes it wasn't too bad, but sometimes it was bad, such as eighteen months of no steady job, starting the day after our sixth baby was born.

So yes, I've regretted every dumb meal out (not the fun ones, though), every shopping spree, every stupid purchase we've ever made. I've wept over some big choices too, even though at the time they might have seemed like good ideas.

I've read a lot of books, articles, and blog posts about getting out of debt, and they have been very helpful. Sometimes, though, they veer into a strange land, theologically. They make it sound something like this: you'll never be happy if you are in debt; you aren't doing God's will if you are in debt; even—and not in so many words, mind you—your salvation can be gauged by whether you are solvent.

But I have to say there are worse things than being in debt. Here are a few (addressed to you, wife and mother):

1. *Worse than being in debt is losing your peace.* Now, some might say that you lose your peace *because* you are in debt, and the good Lord knows I have been there. But today, this very moment, the situation I'm in is God's will for me when I'm doing my best and am sorry for my bad choices, as the mommies at the playground say. Every moment is God's will for each one of us.

Everyone experiences adversity. It's called being human. For some people, that adversity takes the form of being in debt—even if the debt is your fault. The main thing is to keep your peace, to know that God is taking care of each of us, and to remember to trust Him to provide—at least to provide a way out, in His good time.

Do you use being in debt as an excuse not to trust God? That would be worse even than being in debt!

2. *Worse than being in debt is not realizing how much good comes out of a real struggle.* We all know that St. Paul said, "My strength is made perfect in weakness" (2 Cor. 12:9, KJV), but we don't like to think that it will work if the weakness—or, for that matter, whatever the present challenge is—is of our own making. If God sees fit to try us by the adversity of being in debt, we can't wriggle out of meeting the test by thinking that it's our own fault we're in the fight at all. Whatever the fight is, external, internal, our own making, a bolt from heaven—we should see all the good things that come from it. Good things can come from mistakes that we repent of.

What real benefits do we obtain from not having enough money? I bet if we really thought about it, we would see many benefits, including, possibly, learning patience with ourselves for being idiots.

3. *Worse than being in debt is not having a baby because you think you don't have enough money.* See number 1, and trust in God.

There might be reasons for not getting pregnant—I used to think there are more than I now do. But not having money is not one of them. If you are reading this, you have enough money.

There is only a limited amount of time in which you can have a child, no matter what you might think now that you are in the midst of financial difficulty. Thirty years from now, you won't be thinking about the bills you had to pay.

Do you know what the Bible calls riches? Children.

In thirty years, you will be telling yourself that you should have been willing to live in a tent and eat roots and berries to have had more children. Using debt as an excuse to postpone having a baby would be what the world calls prudent and what I would say is a lack of confidence.

I know, this makes me very bossy. But what I want to convey is that you can get money later, but maybe not children.

4. *Worse than being in debt is getting a job to make ends meet.* I'm speaking to the wife here. Let's be real. Let's take all the exceptions as read:

If you can do a few heart surgeries and rescue your family from bankruptcy, do it.

If your husband is bedridden or one semester away from a doctorate in moneymaking, I get it.

If you are so used to working while keeping house (and your mother and maiden aunt live with you, contributing their own retirement funds to your household) that no one really notices when you are not there, go for it.

But the rest of us are needed at home with our heads in our game.

Don't fool yourself into thinking that you can contribute more by leaving for work, or, if you have more than one napping baby, even working at home. The chaos, confusion, stress, childcare, carpools, and taxes are not worth it. No, literally, the actual cost outweighs the benefits.

All that happens is that you are so frustrated with home that the center is lost, sometimes forever. In other words, you start frustrated about money and end up feeling like no one values family life as you once envisioned it because you can't find your way to pulling it together.

It can seem like medium-age children can be fine with this state of chaos, and for a while they will be. But older children need very much to have order at home. By the time the need is felt, it can be too late. The habit of homemaking is gone, and it's often too hard to recover while coping with the demands of older children. Their locus then becomes their peer group, with all that that entails.

Don't make the mistake of putting *getting out of debt* in a higher category than *keeping the home*. Don't make the mistake of having a vague idea that things will run themselves without you; that's rating yourself too low, my friend.

5. *Worse than being in debt is having your husband think he's not a good provider.* Sometimes he's the one saying you should get a job. I'm telling you that, in the end, he will feel like he's not doing a good job protecting his family, which is the very worst thing a man can feel—*much* worse than being in debt—and leading to worse problems than money.

Tell him that you will do your part to be frugal and work with the money you have (and there is so much you can do!), and that you know he will figure out a way. Tell him you know he is working as hard as he can, that you admire him for it, and that you will back him up, no matter what. Tell him you don't mind being in debt for longer if it seems there is no alternative.

It's not the worst thing in the world to be in debt.

ASK AUNTIE LEILA

Ten Reasons Not to Have Separate Finances; or, Marriage Is about Wholehearted Trust

Dear Auntie Leila,

I'm getting married soon, and I will be bringing to the marriage my debt and salary, both of which are moderately large. We're thinking of keeping our finances separate until I at least pay off my debt (at least, my mom says I should do this), but the priest has told us it's not a good idea. But it just makes me so nervous not to have mine separate! I have my own credit cards too. What do you think?

Love your blog and thank you!

Maddie

Dear Maddie,

I know. It seems so old-fashioned or just not an issue whether your finances are separate or not. What's the big deal, right? You've been on your own, and so has he. It seems normal to continue this way.

Well, can I tell you something different? About trust? About the "second decade" of your marriage, that you can't see, but I can; when things change?

People talk about later on in your marriage as "losing the romance" or warn that marriage isn't a bed of roses. Sometimes they blame the children, and for that reason, many couples are afraid to have children! But that isn't quite it.

It's more this: you don't just come to a marriage fully formed and then proceed to experience things in a static way. No. You are in the process of changing, he is in the process of changing, and you also change each other. It's calculus, not addition.

It has to do with things interacting in the dimension of time—the way your car doesn't get the same gas mileage at every moment because you have to factor in the effect of the weight of the gas you're hauling, which obviously lessens as you use it. It's only shorthand to express what's happening as miles per gallon, just as it's shorthand to say, "I'm like this, and he's like that." You're the way you are because he does certain things, and vice versa, and time (together) is a factor.

We hear a lot about how a mother bonds with her child, even on a hormonal level. What we don't hear as much about is how the married couple bond, not only by means of their physical relationship but even more by how they meet each challenge that comes their way. (You might even say that the physical relationship is God's gift for smoothing the path of all those challenges!)

In the first decade, every little and big thing is not only something to talk about and solve but also a way to bond—or fail to bond. If you want to worry about something, know that the scary thing is that it's not apparent how or whether this process has worked until your second decade together. Then, the stresses of dealing with the demands and personalities of your growing children, as well as the difficulties of approaching middle age, will break you if you aren't strong.

So I am warning you now of ten issues you will face, if you are thinking of going into marriage with your finances separate, that maybe your mother hasn't taken into account and your priest doesn't think you'll listen to if he tells you.

1. *Marriage is about unity for the sake of making a family.* Money is the means by which you live. If you are not united in the means, it just stands to reason you won't be united in the ends. Do you really want to risk the whole journey to find out that you are actually on two separate journeys? Marriage is about being "all in"—including debt. When a man and a woman don't act as if they are taking on each other's debt, I wonder if they know what marriage is really all about!

If you are really not ready to marry on account of debt, and obviously it would be better not to have debt, separate finances aren't the answer. Waiting to marry until things are paid off or down is the answer. And usually, very-much-in-love couples will find a way to deal with the debt without waiting too long.

2. *Money represents your plans and goals for your life together.* Money isn't a goal, but you won't reach your goal without money. If your finances are separate, you will find that you end up with different goals. The problem is that this won't be apparent right away; it will be revealed only in the second decade, when stress is high and your bonds haven't formed. By then, it will be very hard to fix. Do you want to take this very real risk?

In addition, having two distinct finances makes the goal of having a family more difficult. Even well-off couples get trapped into thinking that they can't do without the wife's income, simply because of the habits they went into the marriage with. For welcoming children, it's better to be used to thinking in terms of one income stream. Remember, having children is the purpose of marriage! (I heartily recommend using *your* income to pay down any debt or to save until babies come.) Taking care of the home and children is its own contribution, but not one with any kind of dollar sign attached. Seeing that value takes real unity.

What will you do when God blesses you with a child? Start negotiations over who buys what? Please. That's no way to live.

3. *Money represents freedom, but dependence is better in marriage.* We like to think of ourselves as far above having secret thoughts about important things—thoughts we keep from our loved ones. But the truth is that we are only as good as the thoughts we have when the going gets tough. If one line of thinking during a tough time is something like, "Well, I have my own money, I'm free to do what I want," then that is what will define you—not what you think in your best moments.

Just as you don't enter marriage thinking that you can still date others, you shouldn't enter thinking you can always spend your own money. It's the wrong kind of freedom. The secret thought that if things don't work out, you will have your own finances is a stake in the heart of your marriage. Better to face that you can't commit now.

Every choice you make based on the thought that you are really free from your spouse is a choice that will weaken trust. Having one set of finances is not only challenging to the woman's sense of independence; it's also challenging to the man's fear of being depended on. Yet, to have a family, these challenges must be faced; the sooner, the better.

4. *Money represents power, but there is no room for power in a marriage.* Marriage is about serving each other. That is why all the money should be shared. Then all the decisions will be shared (including the decision to leave some decisions up to one of you—that's fine! Who wants to have to go over every little thing? Trust!)

It's not that you set out to use money as a weapon against each other, but when things are tough, every weapon seems handy at the time. Just put this very powerful weapon out of reach from the get-go.

5. *Dealing with money makes you confront your demons: how you handle money, debt, priorities, and children.* This is another way of saying that the process of making your choices, not just the choices themselves, strengthen or weaken your bond.

When you have separate money, you remove some of those processes—the opportunities to decide things together with all the conflict that entails. Hashing things out given your resources is how you become a strong citadel, tested for battle against the enemy. If you don't test your abilities to make tough choices when you are first setting out, with lots at stake and nowhere (i.e., another bank account) to go, you essentially build weaknesses into the walls, only to be discovered later.

Now, for instance, having debt seems overwhelming, but you have no idea how complicated things get later. In about fifteen years, this obstacle will seem like nothing compared with what you face, hopefully together, hopefully with trust. Don't think, "Oh, we'll solve our problems later" if you are also keeping separate accounts. That *is* the problem!

6. *Men's worst fear as time goes on is that their wives will leave them, taking their children.* Ordinary men, men who married with cheerful goodwill, become either violent or utterly defeated, depending on their temperament, when faced with this possibility. For some reason, this psychological fact is a subject for mockery or a reason to belittle a man. I can't understand that. Start now, in this concrete way, to show him that you will never leave him (which is what you are about to vow).

7. *Women's worst fear is that they can't trust their husbands to love them in a mature way.* Sweet ordinary women who married with stars in their eyes fear the betrayal of finding out they are married to a selfish jerk. If a woman's husband is in the habit of living a part of his life separate from hers, with his own credit cards and so on, she will start to feel bitter about his lack of responsibility.

8. *Marriage is about growing together and growing up together; how you handle money is part of the process.* Having unified finances encourages maturity, because you have to communicate. Separate finances encourage immaturity, because you can do things, even irresponsible things, without being accountable. Why enable this pitfall from the outset? What purpose could having one's own money serve other than selfish needs, by definition?

9. *Communication, including communication about the details of handling money, is the lifeblood of marriage.* When finances are separate, communication suffers; even little things can't be discussed because a wall has been set up with the money. Even if you think you can contain money in its own category, you will be surprised to find, too late, that you can't talk about little things

that are seemingly unrelated. Everything ends up being about who spent what, even when it's something like too many beer cans in the recycling or the child's copay at the doctor's office. Instead of loving discussion, it will be all arguing.

10. *Children get the wrong idea about marriage when money is separate.* It isn't just about you. It's about how your children ultimately approach building their own families. If we really want our children to be able to make healthy relationships of their own, unified and generous, we have to be living that way ourselves from the start. Go for it—go the whole distance, together. Go all in. Make it about trust. You won't be sorry.

Maddie hasn't yet begun her life with her husband. Maybe you started on the wrong foot. It isn't too late to change things. Once you realize how much shared finances can enhance your relationship, you can start to have a good conversation about where you would like to go from here. Know that you can start over! Beginning again is better than rushing in the wrong direction.

ASK AUNTIE LEILA

Life Insurance Eases the Risk of Living on One Income

Dear Auntie Leila,

I was and I still am stay-at-home mom. But I always wonder: How people deal with fear? What if something happens to my husband, our only breadwinner? I don't have the qualifications to go right back to work and support myself and my kids.

All the best,

Justyna

Dear Justyna,

Yes, what if something happens?

Very often, it's the husband who has difficulty accepting the burden of being the one income earner; it feels too risky.

Of course, this fear, beaten into us as society pushes for all women to work outside the home, begs the question of what if something happens *to both of you*, and perhaps that highlights the indispensable role of *trust* and the need to accept uncertainty, since we really don't know what the future holds.

We should also think about *how even more precarious* things would be at home if our lifestyle were based on two incomes plus all the outside help needed to sustain two working parents—and one parent dies. Living simply does help when disaster strikes.

Nevertheless, as the old joke goes, "Swim, Johnny, swim!"[12] That is, in addition to reminding you to trust and accept uncertainty, I am also going to fix this worry. It's simple.

We live in a modern age in which, thankfully, you can buy life insurance, the purpose of which is to alleviate this fear as far as possible. God put us in a certain time, in a certain place. In the past, some people did suffer financial doom when the income earner died or was incapacitated. Communities worked to help; my husband's great-great-(great?)-grandfather implemented a forerunner to today's Knights of Columbus insurance provision with a fund to help widows bury their husbands. Such were the works of mercy at the time (and still are very necessary).

Your husband needs life insurance. Some experts recommend that the policy be for seven to ten times the amount of his income. Often, his work covers this need. If not, get it on your own. Make room in your budget for this item.

The couple should also insure the wife who doesn't earn an income but whose contribution is difficult and expensive to replace.

I found it interesting, when I read the arguments for insuring the stay-at-home spouse, that when imagining what a full-time worker would do to manage a home with children in it without his wife, financial planners get serious about the difficulty and stress he would face. This shows you just how vital being the manager of the home really is. It's

---

[12] Have you heard that joke? The little boy's rowboat is sinking out on the lake. His mother, standing on the shore, wrings her hands and calls out, "Pray, Johnny, pray!" His dad, also on the shore, also worried, shouts, "Swim, Johnny, swim!"

impossible to put a dollar value on it, yet when we try, we find out that it would be high.

The enterprise of making a family takes a lot of skill and time! Because we women by nature tend to do our work without boasting and beating our chests, we end up accepting the man's view that what men do is worth more and that what we do is worthless and can be done by anyone.

It all depends on how you look at it. When we speak in terms of the woman's contribution, we think income. But as this discussion of life insurance shows, as soon as we think about the cost of not having the wife there, running things, educating children, saving money, and providing breathing room, suddenly we see the value of this manager. One analyst talks about the husband's having time to be with his kids after his wife dies, versus having to use his free time to figure out food, clothing, cleaning, sick care, and so on. Get your insurance as soon as you can, while you are still young. This advice should be part of every marriage preparation course!

This whole book is essentially about the hidden but indispensable role of homemaker. Perhaps you are convinced, but still worried. Thus I recommend: get life insurance!

Two Practical Money Tips

'm a fan of money-saving tips, but too much advice dispensed at once often overwhelms me. I also find that important advice is mixed in with silly stuff, like "refinance your mortgage" with "use your coffee grounds twice"! Furthermore, I have read that men get advice that's global and involves managing the whole budget, whereas women get advice that's very detailed and targeted at saving a few pennies here and there. I don't know if that's true, and I'm no financial expert. But I'm going to tell you two things that definitely fall in the category of "learn from my mistakes," and hopefully won't overwhelm you.

I like to start with where you are this moment, as you open the month's bills. But before I even start with my two tips, I recommend that you put a prayer card of St. Joseph on your desk where you pay your bills, or in the bill basket, or wherever he can watch over your attempts to be a steward of your affairs. St. Joseph will help you; he is the patron saint of the family and of the household; he is the greatest protector and provider who ever lived.

On to my two things:

First, do everything you can, whatever it takes, to pay on time the bills that charge you a late fee. Are you clipping coupons that will save you a few bucks and then forgetting your cell phone bill? Do you realize that a late charge of thirty-six dollars on a bill of a hundred dollars represents a 36 percent interest rate? Would you take out a loan that charged you 36 percent interest? You'd be mighty foolish to do so, and yet that is what is happening when you forget to pay this bill.

So, if you are like me, and have several cards because of the benefits you get (free shipping from L.L. Bean, points at Amazon, frequent flier miles, etc.), your chances of missing a due date are pretty good, and then all your benefits are wiped out. It would have been better to pay eleven dollars in shipping that sweater than thirty-nine dollars in a late fee! If you don't keep your checking account balance up to date, you risk bounced-check or automatic payment fees, which amount to a very expensive loan from the bank.

Solution: get into the habit of touching base with your bills every Monday morning. Make a list of when your bills are due and place it next to your computer. Enter the dates in your tickler file (online calendar, for instance) so that you get an e-mail reminding yourself to pay on time. Do what it takes to stop getting smacked down by these fees! The obvious answer is to enroll in an auto-pay service, but perhaps sometimes you have to juggle accounts and can't manage that. Above all, do not be late with your payment. If you make a mistake but you're normally prompt, the company will waive the fee, and it's definitely worth the call.

This talk of interest rates brings me to my second tip for saving money: take advantage of a good offer to transfer your credit-card balances to a lower-rate card. Get out your bills and check the interest rate; it's printed on the statement.

Get the best rate you can (you can even call the company and ask them to lower your rate; sometimes that works). Just make sure that it's for the life of the balance, not just a few months. If not, transfer to a lower-rate card. It's worth paying a little up front to get out from under a usurious rate.

Then do not use that card for purchases, ever. That's where the company makes money on interest. Keep only your transferred balance and pay it off as you are able. Use a different card for new purchases (and be sure to pay it off completely every month).

So those are two tips from a sadder but wiser budget balancer. I'm no expert, but even I can tell that you will save more money doing these two things than hunting down a cheaper can of beans.

PART 6

Thriftiness, Frugality, and Prosperity, and Ways of Doing

A secret that I wish more people knew—doing my best here—is that you can live on one income—even a modest one—and prosper. Even more, as every boy marooned on a creek or every girl faced with a tree house to furnish knows, thrift, or the necessity of *making do with what you've got*, is the true creative impulse in life, and even, dare I say it, where the real fun begins.

G. K. Chesterton, in his book *What's Wrong with the World*, wrote:

> Thrift is the really romantic thing; economy is more romantic than extravagance. Heaven knows I for one speak disinterestedly in the matter; for I cannot clearly remember saving a half-penny ever since I was born. But the thing is true; economy, properly understood, is the more poetic. Thrift is poetic because it is creative; waste is unpoetic because it is waste. It is prosaic to throw money away, because it is prosaic to throw anything away; it is negative; it is a confession of indifference, that is, it is a confession of failure. The most prosaic thing about the house is the dustbin, and the one great objection to the new fastidious and aesthetic homestead is simply that in such a moral menage the dustbin must be bigger than the house. If a man could undertake to make use of all things in his dustbin he would be a broader genius than Shakespeare. When science began to use by-products; when science found that colors could be made out of coaltar, she made her greatest and perhaps her only claim on the real respect of the human soul. Now the aim of the good woman is to use the by-products, or, in other words, to rummage in the dustbin.

There are a few reasons I started writing, and one of them is my frustration with the idea that families today simply must have two incomes just to scrape by—as if people in the past didn't have far more insecurity and relative poverty than we do now. And I'm not talking about the normal things that a wife did occasionally in the past to drum up a little petty cash; I'm talking about the notion that she must have a separate career with its own full-time salary and benefits if they are to survive.

The problem is that such an attitude undermines family life and orients it toward acquisition and security rather than toward the more important nonmaterial goods that the family must have to be what it is called to be, day to day, year in and year out. And it takes away the real adventure of life together, to be honest.

Those who have figured these things out—frugal people—might not reveal their ways at first glance. It takes a lot of work and cleverness, and often all the energy is directed at the doing and none at the telling. But as with anything else, deciding what your priorities will be determines how you go about the challenge, and then, soon enough, you see who your companions on the journey are. The goal is to raise the family with what one has (that is, with one income), even if it means going without and making do for years and years—because it's worth it.

This section is practical. Even if you have the means to afford a comfortable life (because, say, your husband has quite a good salary), you might learn something about *spiritual* detachment—about not spending *just because you can*. Of course, sometimes it's better to spend than to drive yourself crazy finding the absolute thriftiest way to go about doing something; sometimes your time needs to be spent somewhere else. But even the richest person must always be checking to be sure that he isn't giving in to comfort but is using his money wisely.

Anyway, here I'll talk about the little things that make living on one smallish income possible. It's about detachment from material things, but also about how to get what you need in unconventional ways. I know that the temptation is to assume that, because other people are sailing off to buy brand-new things at retail prices, there can be no other way. But there is another way!

A lot of our possessions come from yard sales or were even free.

We use a lot of spray paint.

We put off buying new things—just put it off. We wash dishes by hand if we need a new dishwasher and can't afford one (and sometimes discover that family time is quite precious, cleaning up the kitchen together); we go to the laundromat if the washer is broken and a new one isn't possible (and some mothers swear by the efficiency of doing all the laundry at once, and some shopping to boot); we hang clothes in the furnace room if the dryer isn't working (and the electric bill is a lot less at the end of the month as well).

And very often we find what we need secondhand; we just have to be patient. Despite all this sacrifice, we prosper. I don't mean we get rich and have a lot of stuff. I mean we have the prosperity of love and creative satisfaction.

Frugal for Beginners

ou can live on one income and start your journey to frugality. Here are five tips on how to change your habits and discover the romance of thrift.

1. *Stop buying things because it makes you happy simply to spend money.* This is very much like a similar syndrome regarding food. You know, the one where you eat an entire package of Oreos? Why? Because you're hungry? No. It's because for a little while, not while you are actually eating them, but just before you eat them, you think it will make you happy.

In the same way, just walking into a store can make you feel elated, at one with yourself, on the verge of becoming someone completely different. (Ever read anything by Walker Percy? He describes this state with great wit and insight. I highly recommend his book *Lost in the Cosmos* for insight into this phenomenon of seeking ways to feel more *real*.)

Instead, face squarely exactly how you feel during and after you shop (and during and after you eat a bunch of cookies). It's like really smelling your house when you first walk in. It's not what you think it is.

2. *Stop treating shopping as entertainment.* This is a little like tip 1, but different. When you shop for entertainment, you aren't getting your thrill from

spending money, but rather from going out somewhere that seems bright, new, and fun. However, spend money you will.

Instead, find other forms of entertainment! Have you ever spent real time in the library, wandering through the stacks, enjoying the magazines? Gone to a museum (the library has passes, you know), gone for a hike? Instead of shopping, go to the playground, take a picnic on a walk, have a tea for your friends, or take some muffins to a friend at assisted living.

Better yet, stop looking to be entertained and start creating! Each one of those projects that you think you will get to "someday" is simply waiting to happen at the very moment you disappear out the door to wander the shops mindlessly.

3. *Stop reading lowbrow decorating magazines. Stop looking at lowbrow decorating blogs. But also stop getting your ideas from perfectionists who have taste but also know how to ratchet up the anxiety level—and, of course, drum up business and sales.* The problem is that certain magazines and blogs work hand in hand with certain stores to create and then "satisfy" desires. You see a conventionally decorated room in a magazine, and then you go to the store to get it, for a hefty price. Everything in these magazines is new, is slick, and makes what you have look shabby. What you don't realize is that very little of it lasts or is truly aesthetic.

Instead, get your ideas from truly classy magazines, sites, and books. They will feature one of two kinds of homes: (1) ridiculously over-the-top professionally decorated environments (they are creating and meeting their own kinds of desires too, of course) that will hone your taste and help you recognize quality when you see it at the yard sale (2) and truly tasteful examples of people using objects and living in homes that show history, that reflect culture, and that are anchored in real living.

I'm always amazed at how a certain class of rich folks don't care if their leather sofas are cracking or their books are piled up and dusty. Their art is often something they invest their money in, true. But just as often, it reflects just what they like, and we non-rich can do that too!

The more you immerse yourself in this "old money" aesthetic, the happier you will be with your own personal history that's all around you—and you will feel rich!

4. *Stop paying retail for everything.* Having grown up poking around in junk shops, I guess it never occurred to me that some people are uncomfortable with this form of acquisition. I was a bit surprised to find that some regard it as, well, unhygienic, I suppose!

But once hooked, you will never look back. Once you realize that you can find a dresser for ten dollars, a food dehydrator for five dollars, or beekeeping equipment for free, you will kick yourself for paying retail for everything.

So, ask an experienced friend take you to a secondhand store, or challenge another newbie to keep you company. Don't be overwhelmed by a place like the local Goodwill. Start slow. Look only at the handbags or dishes at first. Go back another time to check out the skirts.

5. *Stay home and make home beautiful.* The stores seem, well, arranged. They are clean. They are not grubby. You enjoy being where it's like that.

So, clean everything in your home. You will like it all better when it's really clean.

Make tidy piles of your messes as best you can; arrange what you have as nicely as you can. This step is really key for learning to kick the buying habit. Very often we neglect it, thinking that *because it's mine* it must not be officially great, and what I need is something new, which by definition isn't mine (until that moment I get it home—and then of course, I need to shop again!).

After neatening for a while, get a little critical and simply toss that which you don't feel like neatening any more. Clean again.

Enjoy what you have and be grateful. Stop comparing yourself with others!

You might even come across some things in your very own home that you thought you needed to buy. This has happened to me on more than one occasion!

If you must go shopping—and this might seem odd to some—pray. Ask your guardian angel to help you to be a good steward and to lead you quickly to the things you need so you can get them and get out of the store before you spend what you shouldn't!

Use What You Have,
Buy What You Can Afford

I love beautiful things, and it kind of makes my head spin to open a decorating magazine or check someone's site and see yet another thing or look that I could go for in a second! My house can't be all white (which I love—you know, the fresh and simple Scandinavian style) and *at the same time* bursting with color (which I also love—a bohemian and lively style).

The Internet has provided a resource that most print media never could, just by virtue of the hurdles of real-world publication—namely, ready access to people's visuals of what they do. If you know where to look, you can find affirmation in, of all things, imperfection, which is the most helpful of all. This is not a rationalization of disorder and messiness but the really beautiful inspiration for reconciling the imperfect circumstances of our lives with a harmonious vision of something that we know we can never really attain. Instead of a discontented feeling for what we don't have, this affirmation gives a sense of contentment.

But sometimes, an overload on decorating, a sort of glut of images, does create that unsettled feeling. So how to figure things out?

Here's my answer: *Don't think of what you are doing in your home as decorating.* Think of it as creating an environment for your family that is beautiful (or pretty, if that helps you feel less anxious) in a practical, humble way; that helps you keep order and that makes others comfortable. And try as much as possible to use what you already have.

Take some time before buying something new. Ask yourself, "Do I already have something that I could use for this? Does my mother have it, or do I spy my next-door neighbor putting it out by the curb? [The latter happened to me with what is now, after I painted it, my very pretty bed frame.] Could I clean something up, paint something, or fix something to fit this purpose in a pleasing way? What solutions have others found?" This last question could mean doing a search with your query, which is a good, healthy use of the Internet—and you may be surprised at how clever someone else has been.

For example, I'm not a huge fan of my white Formica countertops or standard wooden cabinets, but they are what I have. After getting some inspiration from magazines (and input from my creative children, who guided me and did the work), I tried to use paint and accents to make them beautiful for us. And do you know what? My kitchen is fine.

I know one thing: if we had gone deep into debt to get something all gleaming, matching, and perfect, and then I had come across something "make-do" but still pleasing in a magazine or on a blog, I would be mad at myself. I would really regret not having tried to solve our problems within our means.

Of course, if what you have is gleaming, then you'll just have to go with that! And if you can afford and need a real makeover, then enjoy!

When you *are* ready to shop and upgrade, ask your guardian angel to help you find the right thing; something that fits your purpose and your budget and is pleasing to the senses, not necessarily something that would be right in a magazine shoot. You will be surprised at what you find!

Always try to buy the best quality that you can, given your budget. A full-grain leather sofa will last a lifetime; a fake-leather sofa will last a few years. But even a cheap sofa is expensive. So it does make sense to buy a good one if you can.

Getting Used to Being Thrifty

Don't think that I consider myself a particularly good example. I am not always the most thrifty person in the room. So you know that anything you read here (and especially any photos that you see on my blog, which are included only because I like a post with photos) is offered in the spirit of "If I can do it, so can you!"

At this moment, the "it" I'm talking about is living on one income. I'm talking about having lots of kids if they come to you, sending them to college, feeding your ice cream habit, and in general living with what the world would consider some sort of crazy risk-taking; but, once you get used to it, it just seems normal and actually gratitude-inducing for how much plenty we encounter all around us!

I have some great friends, and along the way I have been edified and often rescued from some fairly silly pity parties by their resourcefulness and can-do attitude. I think everyone needs a friend, someone who will encourage you and tell you that you can do it.

Take, for instance, when you need a rug. You know that I firmly believe that if you make up your mind that you need something, it will turn up. "Something is bound to turn up." (Mr. Micawber in *David Copperfield*, of course; in a slightly different and not altogether apt context for the present discussion, as he was referring to longed-for relief from his pecuniary entanglements. Well, in a way, that works.) Either you will get the money you need to go out and buy the rug, or, more likely, somehow the right thing will surface at a yard sale or even free from someone who considers it a castoff. You must be patient, and thereby you often have the surprise of discovering a better solution after all, one that wouldn't have occurred if you had been able instantly to gratify your desires.

Don't get me wrong. I am all for the more well-to-do spending their money on top-quality things! If they didn't do that, there would be nothing for those of more modest means to thrift! I shudder when I read stories in the newspaper about the well heeled dabbling in secondhand shopping. Such a bad idea. Thrifty finds don't drop from Mars.

But the rest of us have to be committed to spending very little for the sake of a higher good (in this case, so that you can be free to make your home and educate your children by providing a beautiful environment for them). To make things work, you have to be willing to look everywhere, and you have to tell everyone what you need.

A Thrifting Tale

Want to hear the whole thought-and-action process?

In the back of my mind, I had a rug for the third-floor bedroom in mind, something to go under that iron bed from which Suki had the habit of letting her book drop as she fell asleep! (My room is directly beneath.) I don't know what I wanted, but I thought that a rectangular rug of some sort, big enough, would be nice. I checked all the usual places, but anything remotely to my taste was too expensive, even on clearance. We were planning two weddings! And it was not yard-sale season; the junk shops had yielded nothing.

I also had on my mind where I would put all the other returning (grown) children. I decided that what we needed to increase our capacity was a sleeper sofa in the rec room (on the second floor), and suddenly, a deadline loomed when friends who really needed to be near the bathroom were visiting. In our house, rooms near the bathroom are few. My own room is a good solid sprint as far from the bathroom as you can get.

I found (actually, Rosie, doing a search from California, found for me here in Massachusetts) on Craigslist the ideal used sleeper sofa: never even used as a *sofa*, with the mattress still sealed in plastic. Because we can all imagine the issues with buying furniture this way.

As we were picking it up, ever willing to put my needs out there, I asked the seller (a used furniture dealer stockpiling things in a barn) what else he had. Any rugs? Well, among a rather stunning number of dining sets and crazy stacks of chairs from some sort of institution, he had one, and one only, rug.

At first, I wasn't sure. I hadn't thought of a braided rug at all. What if the colors didn't go? It was certainly big enough and in very good, nay, perfect, condition. He hadn't priced it yet. I waited (the sofa, which I paid his very reasonable asking price for, as it was well worth it, was safely in the Suburban) while he mulled the question (and in my own mind, I decided how much I wanted him to say: $30). He said $50. I offered $40. And that was that! In retrospect, I believe he could have asked $250 and gotten it if he had listed it, but I was on the spot and my guardian angel was on the job.

Home we hauled it, and it waited on our truly herculean efforts to get the sofa in the (I now fully acknowledge) inaccessible rec room. (And a big tip of the hat to our neighbor Ben who rescued us from divorce, destruction, and despair by figuring out how to get around the last bend of our small back hallway!)

So Bridget and I deep-cleaned the rec room, got the sofa bed in place, and then headed for the third floor. I was still not sure!

By dint of inching that large rug under the bed, in a display of hilariously exhausting and inefficient and incompetent making do (I think my husband was on a deadline and unavailable for what was clearly a three-man job), we got it deployed. And, voilà! It's perfect!

All this is to say, don't let things out there in the world, where people claim that a family simply can't live on one income, and that it's a luxury for the wife to stay home,[13] prevent you from identifying and homing in on your goal. If you are motivated by what you know to be good, you can do it.

[13] The wife's vocation is to make the home, even though I don't describe her as being a "stay-at-home mom" just because, in the course of history, wives

Remember that it's not fair to compare the probably now-prosperous home of your parents with your own; they've lived through their shabby times (if they had them). You may have even been there, but you don't remember it. These more well-to-do homes and lifestyles might indeed be the result of two incomes, in which case it takes a dose of humility and realism to recognize that you have other, less visible priorities—and that's just how it is.

Instead of comparing yourself with rich people, compare yourself with genuinely poor people. Doing so never fails to restore the proper perspective! You will soon realize the abundance that is all around; how blessed we are to have loved ones to sacrifice for and how energizing the challenge can be.

and mothers have done a lot of things while making their homes. Making a home means that the family lives on the husband's income, as it's his vocation to be the provider. In our economy, which is based on raising one or two children on two incomes, devoting oneself to creating a beautiful environment for one's family will require hard work and dedication and is well worth the effort. If I can help, even just by cheerleading, I will.

ASK AUNTIE LEILA

Thrifting Advice

Dear Auntie Leila,

Some advice, please. I would love to make our home more beautiful. It sounds, though, that it would take a lot of time to go to thrift shops and so forth. When I do go, I usually don't find anything worth buying. I usually buy things we really need (e.g., furniture) on Craigslist, which can take a lot of time too. With two young kids to rear (who don't want to go shopping!), and not being a crafty person who can make pillows, curtains, and so on, am I consigned to live in a bland, boring house until the kids are older? Please help! Thanks!

Frugal Dreamer

D ear FD,

Yes, things in this world take time or money or both! Usually when you don't have money, things take more time.

My biggest tip to you would be to use your Internet time to poke around at the sites of those who are really good at taking castoffs and making them useful and beautiful. Train your eye! Once you do, you will see things everywhere. I have high standards and take it for granted that any given trip to the thrift shop will yield nothing. Just make a lightning strike and get out. When you find something, it will be worth it. Many couples make a pact that, due to the necessity of thrifting for this lifestyle we've chosen, if we can glorify it with the term "lifestyle," the husband will watch kids and get chores started on Saturday mornings so that the wife can go out unencumbered. It may be that a couple likes doing this together, in which case it can be a family outing or a reason to get a mother's helper in to watch the kids.

Beauty in your home starts simply and can be the result of just keeping your eye out wherever you go. Many things in my house have literally come out of the trash or from the side of the road. Ask your guardian angel to help you make your house lovely, and you will see the opportunities pop up. Also, the two things you named, pillows and curtains, are by far the easiest possible things to make, accessible to the least crafty person, due to the mainly straight lines used in their production. Many books from the library will show you just how to do it, not to mention video tutorials online.

The other possibility is to scour clearances at stores that carry the things you like. Again, it takes longer, but eventually you will find things you like.

Focus on a real need: a rug, a sofa, kitchen chairs, plates, a kid's bed. Get ideas online and then go on a mission. You will be surprised at what turns up!

Another question has to do with how to account for the fluid cash needed for thrifting in a budget. Your budget might be very detailed, which is great for keeping down extra spending. But trouble starts when you see a perfect bed or set of chairs or bedside table for forty dollars somewhere, because you can't anticipate that. If you know you need a new couch, we can save up for it, but how to make sure you have the cash on hand when you see at a yard sale something unexpected but important—or even just something that you know will make your home more beautiful?

The answer is to put in your very detailed budget a category for yard sales and bargain shopping. If yard sales are seasonal where you live, withdraw the money and keep the cash on hand at that time. Thrifting saves money on clothes, shoes, coats, household items, and even birthday and Christmas presents for a large family!

If nothing else, start the fund with twenty dollars. If you don't find anything, roll that dough into the next month's budget of twenty dollars, giving you forty dollars to work with. If it's something you know you simply have to have (every family simply has to have a table and chairs, for instance) and you know the prices and you see something special, then eat beans to buy it (meaning, find the money somehow!). Why? Because unlike something in stock in a store, it won't be there next time.

If you don't have twenty dollars, then clearly God doesn't want you out there thrifting, He wants you to make do with what you have. You can always put a board on sawhorses! You won't be the first struggling couple to do it! There is no way surer to know God's will than to see what it is that we can afford! So we can be peaceful about that.

Getting Good at Thrifting

I come from a long line of ladies who like to wander through dusty barns, find old broken-down things, wipe them off, and put them into service. While my friends' parents were going on shopping trips to Bloomingdale's, I was with my mom, poking around junk shops. I didn't necessarily know it at the time (in fact, I disliked the dirty atmosphere and resented being dragged away from play time, just like any other kid would), but I was getting an education in form, line, and construction. I could spot a beveled mirror at twenty feet. I knew a dovetail joint before I could name it. A gummy finish couldn't hide nice wood grain from me. I was wordlessly trained to spot patina.

Getting this expertise is easier when you are committed to not spending much. Ever. On almost anything. It sharpens your eye. If you can't just buy what you want when you want it, you learn to be patient and snap up what you like when you see it hidden under a table in a Goodwill, or out behind the recycling center's dumpsters.

Here are my general tips:

1. *"Have nothing in your house that you do not know to be useful, or believe to be beautiful,"* advises the British Arts and Crafts Movement designer and

poet William Morris. In other words, make standards for yourself. Start to learn what your own likes and needs are. Arrange things accordingly, as far as you are able.

2. *Train your eye.* Examine every photo that claims to feature "flea-market style" or "shabby chic" or "upcycling"; notice the things that you yourself would have passed up but look fabulous or useful. Notice colors and shapes. Notice when the DIY style has resulted in something worse than the original, for that is part of training your eye. Be critical and take note of what you don't like at all. Then look around you.

3. *Avoid the temptation to think that you can restore everything.* If I can spray-paint it, I probably will. But I've learned that I don't have time for real, professional refinishing, much less heavy-duty upholstering or slipcovering, other than the most basic square-of-fabric-stapled-onto-an-ottoman. The best find is one you can clean off and put in its place right away. Second best is a fix that you can do. Worst is a pile of things in the basement that you'll never get to.

4. *See things separately.* Look at a picture; look at its frame. Those are two different things, and even if one of them is not right, the other might be. The same with sheets. It's the pillowcases that go first, so it makes sense to buy those when you can find newish ones on clearance. The truth is that when the bed is made, the pillowcases are all you really see. Vintage ones look really cheerful and often that old percale wears the best.

5. *If it's unique, get it.* I've never regretted passing up someone's Target cast-off, but there was an antique blue hand-painted bed once ... Sigh. Here is incentive to create a "discretionary fund" even if it means having two soup nights a week! If you squirrel away twenty dollars a month into this fund, you will soon be able to dip into this account when the opportunity presents itself.

Realize that doing so is the opposite of spontaneous or unplanned spending. It's more like "planning for the unexpected," and the truth is that you can't live the frugal life without being ready and poised to seize the chance for an inexpensive way to get the things you need and would love.

6. *Know the trash days in your area.* People put good items out with their trash, hoping someone will pick it up. The law, by the way, is on your side, as trash left out on the curb is fair game. If it's not obviously trash, however, you should ask before taking it. Some people who live near me have a nice white bench out by their curb where they also put their trash. I don't think they want anyone taking it (although I do always look twice).

7. *Know that learning to be thrifty is a process.* You won't learn everything at once, and that's okay. Don't wait for anyone's permission. Just plunge in.

Regions differ, making it hard for me to give a lot of specifics. Find out where people in your area get rid of their castoffs and go there. Are there church rummage sales? Yard sales? Thrift stores? Resale and consignment shops? A "shop" in your recycling center or dump where people take and leave things? A neighborhood list-serve site where people post their curb pickups?

Be patient and vigilant. If you love something and it's cheap, go for it. After a while, you will learn from your mistakes. Just remember to get rid of *your* junk if you don't like it. The great thing about thrifting is that things didn't cost you much, so you can let go of them if they turn out to be a mistakes.

Remind yourself on occasion *why* you're being thrifty. People who are trying to live frugally so that their families can prosper without a lot of income are doing a good thing. This is how Mama can stay home with the children. It's how Papa can go to work without a lot of stress. Go at it with energy, look around, and be picky.

How to Feed Your Kids
Fruit the Frugal Way

I am all astonishment when I see moms handing their young children a whole apple, peach, or other fruit.

And then I am further mystified when I read "tips" on how to rescue half-eaten apples to be made into something in the name of frugality. Even the venerable Amy Dacyczyn, author of *The Tightwad Gazette*, a person who would rather make a diaper cover out of old bread bags than buy real ones, advises her readers to save chewed-on apples to make a dessert with later. Yuck (residual saliva will be doing its number on that fruit)—and also, a waste of sugar, flour, and other expensive ingredients. Have you priced butter lately? And I don't know about you, but my time for making extra desserts is limited; certainly, it doesn't keep up with the demand for fresh fruit in a busy family.

Now, I am going to tell you just what to do, but I realize that it will go against a strong American trait, which is precisely an aversion to cutting up fruit. Perhaps this is because, in America, fruit is plentiful, or perhaps we Americans don't have a love affair with our food the way other people do; but for some reason, I find that most of us laugh at the idea of cutting fruit up into bite-size pieces. However, your typical European or, say, Egyptian (and I get this trait from my Egyptian side) is shocked at the offhand treatment of comestibles because in these cultures, one makes a ritual of even the smallest snack.

It takes less than a minute to cut up an apple and put it on a plate or a cutting board. It's also something an older child could do for a younger one.

You can find a nice, sharp paring knife for a few dollars anywhere. (I'll bet your mother has an extra one you could take!) Cut the fruit in half or in quarters or what have you. Deftly slice out the core or toss the pit. Remove the skin if it's objectionable (sometimes it is), or convince your children that it's tasty and the best part. Arrange the pieces (further sliced if you like) on a plate or in a bowl. Put the bowl anywhere at all, and watch the pieces disappear.

Alternatively, you can make what we call in our family a bird's nest, using a melon baller to remove the core of an apple that has been sliced in half—somehow very appealing to a child, and usually, half an apple is all anyone wants and it's more portable than slices.

I'm afraid that, other than while apple picking, or maybe with the smallest fruits, your average four-year-old is not going to (a) have the appetite for a whole apple or (b) stay interested long enough to finish it. Most children seem to take delight in abandoning a half-eaten apple (it sort of does get unappetizing, you know?), whereas few can resist just one more crisp untouched slice. Any pieces that *are* left over will be mercifully free of taint, and so can be tucked away for next time or gratefully consumed by you.

My way (and the way of most of the world) has the advantage not only of saving on fruit and those expensive ingredients subsequently employed to rectify its waste *and* of being more aesthetic, but it also relieves you of ever again finding a mushy, yet dusty brown substance behind your sofa.

Cutting up the fruit has the side benefit of putting your random sweet thrifted dishes into play.

Living without Air Conditioning

When we moved back to New England after a long exile in other lands (nowhere too far, just not *home*), I walked into my husband's child-hood house on a hot, humid day and gasped with relief. It was at least twenty degrees cooler in there, and I knew that his parents, Grandma and Grandpa Make-Do-Use-Up-Wear-Out, didn't have air conditioning!

One clue to their attitude was that, when we lived in the swamps (literal and figurative) of Washington, D.C., they gave us the one AC unit *they* had been given by a concerned relative for their own bedroom, "because the robins had nested on it and we couldn't disturb them by using it, and we'd rather have the window open." (Obviously this was after the robins left and the heat had started in earnest, so you get the picture of how detached they were from the AC.)

I know that not everyone agrees on this, but I'm with Grandma and Grandpa. I detest air conditioning. I am writing here for those who also have the possibility of doing without it.

My mother-in-law was really the genius at keeping things cool, simply because she had learned from her forebears, and I learned a lot from her, much of which, admittedly, would not work *as well* in a place like D.C., although with the right architecture (such as was found in the South long ago), I think it would go a long way.

Here's what she taught me:

Early in the day, close up the house on the sides that face the rising heat.

Shut the windows. This seems counterintuitive, but if hot air is coming in, the window needs to be shut and the curtain or shade drawn until things cool down.

Lower the blinds, draw the curtains, turn off the lights. Start loving the cool darkness in the heat of the day.

Open doors and windows on the cool sides of the house. A bush on the northwest corner will do amazing things to cool the air coming in a window on that side. You want to catch that coolness in the morning.

Later in the day, that western side is the one that gets closed. The eastern windows can be opened as the sun recedes.

Any north-facing windows can be left open all day except on the hottest days. You can feel the air. If it's cooler than what you've got, let it in! If it's hotter, keep it out.

Open the top of a warmer-side window and the bottom of a cooler side to get a flow going through your house. Try opening them a small amount at first to see if you can set up an air current.

A fan placed near a north-facing window will do wonders. A standing fan is great; Grandma always had one by the window behind the piano, and another in the kitchen (which also faced north).

Best of all is a ceiling fan, and if I had the money for it, I would not get AC, I would put a ceiling fan in every room. Even with AC, you should have ceiling fans. Turn the light off, and get the ceiling fan cranked up (in winter, reverse the direction and set it on low; you will be amazed at how much warmer the room feels). Yet, there is still peace and quiet.

If you are lucky enough to have a screened-in porch, keep it shaded with your landscaping or bamboo blinds during the hot hours. The air that goes through it will cool your whole house on all but the hottest days.

I don't have a screened-in porch but I do have a shady deck, onto which open the slider in my kitchen and a window that lets out to a shady nook at the back of the deck on the shared wall. I can leave the window open even during a storm, because it's protected by the little alcove, and it's always cool.

I was thrilled *finally to* replace the less-than-pleasing light over our kitchen table with the fan. I know it paid for itself the first year in heat savings, and it makes the kitchen pleasant in the hot weather.

At night, once you are used to it, a fan is just as cooling as AC and a lot quieter. On the very hottest nights have the children sponge bathe with cold water or take a quick dip in a cold tub right before bed. An indirectly placed fan (or that wonderful ceiling fan) will have them sleeping better than the frigid, unrefreshed air of the AC.

In short, keep in mind that your body experiences cooling as a "zone" and not a temperature point. What matters most is the sensation of air flowing over your body, and that is why air current and, of course, fans help a lot. If you live where you must have AC, make it a priority to install ceiling fans as well; you can set your cooling higher and be more comfortable.[14]

Pace your activity. The hottest hours are a good time for quiet reading. Keep your lemonade cold and take the hot days a bit slower, rather than trying to obliterate them.

In regions where you simply *must* use AC, you will save on your bill with my methods. Yes, you can open a window while the AC is on if the air coming in is *cooler* than your setting. How many houses have I been in with the sun pouring in the south-facing, uncovered windows *and* the AC cranked up? This is madness.

Try not to bake or turn on the oven during the day; use your mornings or evenings and bake enough for several days. Use the grill to keep the heat of cooking outside. Set up a simple outdoor or garage kitchen using a hose in an old sink and an outlet for your slow cooker and hotplate alongside your grill. But for the most part, use the least-intense method of cooking you can, and go for cold food when possible.

---

[14] Lloyd Alter, "Why Are We So Reliant on Air Conditioning? (It's Not Just Climate Change, It's Bad Design)," Treehugger, updated June 5, 2017, https://www.treehugger.com/why-are-we-so-reliant-on-air-conditioning -its-not-just-climate-4861463.

Shading your house with deciduous trees helps. Sleep with open windows if you can. Use an attic fan to pull the hot air up and out, while the cooler night air comes in your windows. In the morning, shut it off and draw your blinds and curtains. You can tint your southern windows! And an overhang that lets in the slanting winter, but not the high summer, sun will be a lifesaver.

If you have forced-air heat, you can turn on the fan (leaving the heat off, of course!) and open interior doors. This draws cooler air up from the basement, circulating it through the house. Box fans pointed outward in the windows help discharge the hotter air upstairs.

Builders aren't required to design for airflow, so they don't. If you have the chance to build your own house, research on natural cooling and heating would pay off. For one thing, what about when the power fails? Look up evaporative coolers if you live in a place with relatively low humidity.

You feel much cooler in appropriate clothing. Jeans are not good for hot weather. Try light cotton skirts, and don't forget that linen is an amazing fabric that keeps you feeling cool.

Living frugally, we become committed to family life without too many needs. Some grew up that way; some learn later. Thriftiness enriches life, because who isn't better off with a screen door slamming, the outdoors not hermetically sealed off, the chirp of the crickets audible, the sounds of the children playing outside wafting in and out of our consciousness?

A life enclosed indoors all the time isn't a good one, I can't help thinking. I know that in some places there is a stretch when nothing can be done because of the heat. Certainly, here in northern climes, there are times when nothing can be done because of the cold and the ice. That's part of the rhythm of life. But when a breeze comes up, you want to catch it, not be oblivious to it because the stale air circulating around you prevents you from noticing. And, you know, kids are impervious to heat that slays adults, as long as they are given a respite. There is no reason to keep them inside when they could be out playing (rather than carting them to organized sports, season in and season out). Even if it's only a whiffle-ball game well before noon or a pickup basketball game in the evening with a kiddie pool in between, that's where memories are made.

ASK AUNTIE LEILA

Keeping the House Warm in Winter, Frugally

Dear Auntie Leila,

I'm hoping you can offer some wisdom on prepping the home (both house and people) for the winter months.

We are familiar with life in the cold, but it was before kids. I've never experienced a winter while running a household or with children. My boys are eight and one. My parents run a very efficient household but have trouble articulating exactly what it is they do and why.

Adding to my confusion is the fact that our new home is older (1940s). It is heated with steam radiators and has all the original windows. I was able to use some of your "keeping a home cool in the summer" tips and am hoping you may have similar tips for winter.

We have steam radiators, and I hadn't planned to install radiator covers. However, a neighbor mentioned that steam radiators get quite a bit hotter than water ones. Should I be concerned?

When is a good time to transition window screens to storm windows? I'd like to do a thorough cleaning while I'm switching them, but what if the weather turns warm again and I miss the screens? I'm thinking late October.

I've heard that large coats aren't supposed to be worn if a child is in a car seat. Assuming that a little one cannot yet take his coat off unassisted, do I put the coat on, walk out the door, get into the car, take his coat off, buckle him up and repeat in reverse order when getting out? Should I invest in a good-quality fleece coat for quick trips from the house to car and use the coat only when my son is outside?

Finally, I'm trying to slowly acquire the outerwear we will need this year. Any tips on brands or items that are a good investment?

Thank you!

McKenna

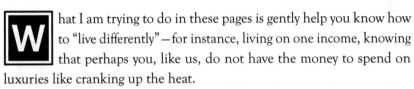hat I am trying to do in these pages is gently help you know how to "live differently"—for instance, living on one income, knowing that perhaps you, like us, do not have the money to spend on luxuries like cranking up the heat.

I'm well aware that readers live in different parts of the country, of course. Some can't imagine temperatures lower than, say, the forties, but I'm not addressing their climate here. I also write with the idea that your children will not be climate controlled at all times but will want to play outside most of the time, regardless of how cold it gets.

Even those who live in the deep South can be hit with a cold snap in the teens or lower. Would you know how to cope? How about if the power goes out (often the case when the weather is extreme)? These are survival skills every mother needs to know. At least you will know which chapter to turn to here!

A lot depends on your circumstances. There's no question, for instance, that schools are overheated, so it really is folly to send a child all bundled up.

Yet, it's also strange to think that even as we collectively feel pretty guilty for using up the world's resources this way, we seem incapable of just turning down the heat in a public building and relying on people to know how to dress.

When this subject comes up, many will respond with a resistance that suggests that they think the heat will always be on, that the car will always be gassed up and working great (and that no crazy person will crash into it, that it will never run over a nail and get a flat tire), that the power will never go out. I get it that even in very cold conditions, the usual thing in our day and age is to go from one warm spot to another. But my point is that we have the luxury to do so.

If we don't, or if circumstances intervene, I myself like to know what to do—how to keep from dissolving into a helpless puddle of anxiety and neediness! So that's what I'm getting at here. I'm assuming that you, dear reader, actually want to know how people cope with, in this case, the cold, when the optimal conditions do not obtain.

With that explanation out of the way, on to the question!

Dear McKenna,

Here is what you need to know! You should install the storm windows in early fall, before absolute necessity sets in, while the weather is nice during the day. That way, it's not a problem for you to get them out, clean them, and make the necessary repairs. It's still warm enough for you to caulk around frames, which will really help keep things warm.

If your house is like my husband's parents' house (built in the 1920s), you also have screens to put away, and you want to be sure you do that in an orderly way (labeling carefully), saving yourself grief in the spring.

The days are still not so short that you would have to rush when you are cleaning windows, and the leaves haven't started blowing around and making things hard to clean.

You will probably find that the storm windows have a mechanism so that you can prop them open. Thus, if the weather is nice during the day, open them up at the bottom and push them out. You don't have to worry much about screens since the bugs are gone. (You can always get a few of those little adjustable half-window screens, but a stray wasp isn't really such a big deal; it will be too drowsy to be a problem.) Even if your windows don't have this feature, you can leave off one or two of your storms on the sunny side of the house and pop them on when things really get cold. You won't need much more than that.

This way, you can set your heat at a reasonable level and enjoy having it on in the chilly nights but still open a few windows during the warm days. It can get cold! Our heat will come on once or twice before the daytime temperatures go down as well, but I have replacement windows, so it didn't take long to close them up. (By the way, the old-fashioned windows work just as well with their storms, so don't worry; just keep them in good repair.)

The radiators probably will need covers. My parents-in-law had them (we have hot water heat, so only a few covers here). Covers give you a little more horizontal space on which to park a couple of kids or a stack of books; there is nothing wrong with them aesthetically (and a nice paint job will spruce them up if they are, in themselves, not presentable).

Figure out a way to make some sort of airlock arrangement where you enter the house, at least for the door you will use most. That is, your house will stay significantly more comfortable if your outside door doesn't open directly into your living area. If you can shut it before you open an interior door to get in, you prevent direct contact with frigid outside air! In my house, the door from the kitchen to the mudroom stays open until the heat goes on, and then I am very strict about keeping it shut! Yes, the mudroom is cold, but at least the whole kitchen isn't cold.

As you move through the year, consider, if you don't have this sort of arrangement, enclosing the porch and installing a door at the entry to the porch, which will then act as the winter "outside door." Or it might be that you need to build such a porch. Such are the joys (and expenses) of figuring out how to keep warm.

Now, you want to notice this year how the heat flow works in your house. Do you have zones for the system? If so, you want to set your upstairs to a lower temperature than the downstairs. The bedrooms really don't need to be as warm as the living areas, and of course, heat rises. When you have good bedding—flannel sheets, down comforters, duvet covers, wool blankets for in between the layers—you find it's preferable to sleep in air that is not too stuffy. When the heat is high, everyone wakes up with stuffed noses and headaches, and the rooms get very dusty.

Babies should wear cotton pajamas with fleece blanket sleepers zipped over them. The cotton is to wick moisture, because they will sweat. I had an eczema sufferer, and that salty sweat really aggravated his rashes. With the cotton, all was well. If it's really cold, put cotton socks on under the footies of the blanket sleeper as well.

Blanket sleepers can have feet or be sacks—the best kind of sacks are sleeveless. That way, Baby can be warm but not overheated, and if it's really cold, you can add a layer underneath the sack.

The children should wear flannel pjs with undershirts underneath. Undershirts are the key to feeling cozy but not overheated.

Here is the purpose of the undershirt, my dear readers: it's so that you have a layer that you do not remove, keeping your body heat close. A child can put his undershirt in the wash before his bath. After his bath, he puts a clean one on, tucked into his underpants. The PJs get put away and the clothes go on, but never is the poor bare skin exposed to that lower temperature in the bedrooms.

That's the old-fashioned way. Maybe today people just pay no attention to that sort of thing (I know I had to figure it out), but it's good to remember it in case, for some reason, it's much colder than you expected—for instance, when the power goes out and you aren't able to check into a hotel for the duration.

Slippers make a huge difference to how we feel about the cold. They should be easy to get on and off, but enclosed and comfortable. Wool socks work well too, but a leather sole helps with slipping. For a full treatment of how to dress warmly in winter, see "On Dressing Children in Cold Weather," in volume 1.

Anyway, back to the house. Even if you only have one zone, you can keep the different areas warm if you have doors to shut. Your challenge will be keeping the warm air downstairs. Yes, you can go on heating the first level continuously all day, or you can keep the heated air downstairs.

You may notice one area where the heat really escapes and there isn't a door. You can install a heavy curtain there. Use a strong rod (conduit pipe works well and is inexpensive) and nice matelessé quilts or heavy velvet curtains (these often turn up at thrift stores). You can even block off a stairway this way, using curtains or quilts and as many rods as you need, attaching them to the ceiling with the appropriate plumber's strap if you need to (just be sure you attach anything like this to a stud).

Just as, in the summer, you kept the strong sun out of your rooms, in the winter, you want to let that sun in. A really well designed house takes advantage of the sun's angles in the different seasons. The overhangs on the eaves of the house can allow the low winter sun in, while shading the rooms in the summer, when the sun is higher in the sky. Even modern glass in the window itself can filter the light, or not, according to its angle.

As evening falls, close your shades or curtains (or preferably both) to keep the heat in. Wooden or insulated blinds, Roman shades, and heavy curtains really help with what are basically holes in your shelter.

That ceiling fan that cools you off in the summer can really help move the warm air down from the top of the room; simply reverse the direction by means of the little switch on the base.

If you have a fireplace, you can see how well it works this winter. Usually fireplaces, unless they are of the Rumford design, actually lose more heat than they provide, which is rather depressing! For more on Rumford fireplaces, read the little book called *The Forgotten Art of Building a Good Fireplace*.

Depending on how it goes this year, you might want to install an efficient woodburning stove in the fireplace, if yours is not one of the good kind. Combined with a ceiling fan and depending on how big and open your house is, you might find that you can use your central heat just to keep your pipes in the basement warm, using the stove as your main source. Just be sure to set the thermostat at the *right* low temperature, lest the woodstove prevent the heat from cycling on, exposing your pipes to freezing and possibly bursting.

In any case, an important part of just *feeling* warm is to have a source for the heat around which you can gather; radiant warmth makes you feel much warmer, as long as it's not whooshing past you on its way higher up, bringing cooler air in its wake; it's the same principle as feeling cooler when air is fanned. Convection heat is moving, so it does not feel as warm; it also tends to get trapped at the ceiling. Radiant heat reduces allergens for the same reason: the air isn't moving as much. (Of course, this advantage is offset by allergens produced by a woodstove.) For this reason, if you have to replace floors, you might want to consider radiant heat under the floor you replace.

Get in the habit of feeling around with your hands as you do things near your walls. It may be that cold air comes in via the outlets, and there is a cheap fix for that at the hardware store: you can insulate them! Window trim might need caulking. When you have to do repairs on siding or walls, you can add insulation. Over the years you can make your house a lot warmer just by paying attention!

Develop the *art* of keeping cozy, and that is as much psychological as anything. Carpets and rugs on the floor feel warmer. Throws and quilts on the sofas help you resist the urge to turn up the thermostat. Candlelight—even one small votive on the table—feels magical when it's dark and forbidding outside. In the warmer weather, you can stow the cozy things away in trunks and benches. I knew some old-fashioned ladies who had different curtains and bedspreads for winter and summer! Maybe such an approach was easier when there was more household help to take care of it all, but it goes to show you how people really did take seriously the change of seasons.

As to the question of children's outerwear: let's please all use some common sense. If it's the middle of winter and in the single digits, don't plan on removing a child's coat to get in the car. Choose coats and jackets that are not overly bulky; get a warm one that allows freedom of movement. Then make sure that the straps of the car seat are secure, especially checking the chest adjustment to be sure it's in place.

At the same time, remember that children tend to get overheated in the car. You can turn the heat down a bit once the car warms up; or if you're on a long trip, take the jacket off—but do have it handy in case of an emergency that exposes him to the elements.

Remember not to let all the child's body heat escape as you are getting out of the car and spending time outside. Conservation of body heat—that is what we are after.

Everyone needs a jacket that goes below the waist to the hips (so that when you sit down, your nether regions have some protection from the cold), a hat, a scarf, and mittens. Put the scarf on *under* the jacket, around the neck; it won't offer warmth if it's worn outside the jacket! If the jacket has to come off, at least the chest is still warm. Choose a jacket with knit wrist cuffs to keep the air from going up the sleeves. For children, the wrist cuffs help mittens stay on securely. A cord for the mittens that goes inside the jacket works to keep them from getting lost, as do little clips.

Little kids don't need bulky sweaters. They usually hate them, won't wear them, and get overheated in them. Instead, choose lighter layers that trap their body heat without confining them: an undershirt, a regular flannel or thick knit shirt, and if anything extra seems necessary, make it a something like a light, soft wool vest or fleece pullover. If the child runs warm, even a thin shirt will work, as long as there is an undershirt long enough to tuck in underneath. You will spare yourself the grouchy, fretful parts of the day if you follow this advice, because the process of getting your body heat back up makes a person cranky.

Girls need real pants, *not leggings alone,* or corduroy jumpers over good sturdy tights or leggings. The ideal outfit for a little girl is tights, undershirt or camisole, long-sleeve cotton shirt, corduroy jumper, cardigan if needed. Warm socks in boots. And most of all, do not let their little middles be exposed to the air. Tuck that T-shirt in!

PART 7

On Getting Organized

Obviously, we need lists, notes, and systems to be organized. Over the years I have been impatient with my discovery that the project of getting organized can itself take time and resources. Just think of the sheer variety of note systems that are offered, both real and virtual—some of them not inexpensive. Mindful of the distraction from true organization that the attempt to organize can represent, and further taking into consideration varying temperaments and concepts of efficiency, in this section I offer some thoughts on a reasonably orderly approach.

Using a Sticky-Note System
for the To-Do List

've finally figured out a list-making system for that helps me get things done, rather than a system that exists for its own sake. I've long abandoned those planners that require their own block of time to manage. As if managing *my life* isn't hard enough—I find I cannot muster the strength to manage the planner as well.

Every morning, this is the conversation between Mr. Lawler and me:

He: "So, Hon, what are you doing today?"

Me: "Oh, getting organized."

Every day, the same conversation! Will I ever be organized? I doubt it, but I know this: lists are our friends. Possibly, with enough excellent lists, we may someday get organized for good; I sometimes think I will have "Getting Organized" inscribed on my tombstone.

My preferred list-material is cut-up scrap paper. I like to grab a pen and a scrap of paper and make a list. For years, that's how I did my to-dos: just jotted them down. Side effect: many lists all over the house, stuck in books, at the bottom of my purse, on the counter by the door, and *not* at the bottom of my purse in the store. Still, I do default to this method, even if I sometimes do take a phone pic of the list after I write it.

There's nothing like a piece of paper that costs you nothing—that you are repurposing and recycling—that you are positively being virtuous by using! This scrap-paper method frees me from decision-making about whether the list in question merits the using up of an official piece of notepaper or page in a notebook. "This note seems so trivial—do I really need to take up my precious notebook with it?" seems to be my thought process.

Besides the frugality of the scrap-paper system, consider its portability. In theory, I can have my little scrap out on a counter or in my pocket and then just trash it—but then this ephemeral quality, which I regard as a feature, is precisely the drawback.

The system of a small notebook and sticky notes, which I will detail for you, has solved this conflict for me to a great extent. It's not as frugal, for sure (and thus I do still write my grocery lists on scrap paper). But it might help someone with my peculiar preferences, simply because, by its flexibility, it facilitates of one of the most important principles of time management: *have a short to-do list.*

Have Only Three Things on Your To-Do List

I read a business-management article arguing that the most effective corporate executive types have only three to five things on their to-do list. As a mother, I know that there are already many, many things that are already on the list before I even get started, such as laundry, making meals, changing diapers, tidying up, and I also have to have planners for homeschooling and menus. So I say *three* things on your to-do list each day.

The big question becomes how to figure out what those three things are?

You need a little chunk of time for finding the answer as you get started, and I recommend sneaking it into whatever you consider your prayer time. This is because what we do with our time is very much a spiritual issue. Although I am no spiritual director, I do consider it *prayer* to sit in God's presence and discuss with Him all those things that make up our day, including *what we should do.*

You might say that the to-do list is where the rubber meets the road in doing His will. Even going to the grocery store is His will for me, if it's what I need to do today. One of the most important questions we can ask each day (and each moment, really) is simply, "Am I doing what You want me to be doing now, Lord?" "Do You really want me to tear out that closet today, Lord, or is there something else on Your mind?" (Also, taking the list to prayer, spiritually and physically, makes it possible to be just a wee bit less distracted, if you are the distractible type, not that I would know about that. Instead of fixating on that important thing I just remembered I have to do, trying to memorize it, I can jot it down and go back to prayer.)

I don't say this is *all* we should pray about or always pray about; or that we should do all the talking in prayer. But I have found it a good practical way to offer God my time; to lay it all out before Him and abandon it to His will.

At first, to set up this system, and every once in a while (on retreat, for instance, or at the start of a new season of some kind), sit with God, pen and paper in hand. Make a list of ten or twenty-five or fifty or however many things you think need to be done. This will be the master list. It should have all the things: getting photos organized, cleaning out closets, calling the insurance company, prioritizing home repairs, figuring out a bill-pay system, planning your school year—all the calls, all the projects, all the commitments.

Now, looking at all those things, which are the top three that you could do today? It's very likely that besides "call the insurance company" and "grocery shop," the third thing may be "make list of household repairs." Maybe the insurance company simply must be called today. Maybe you have to go to the store, or everyone will starve. It's probable that you won't actually start on repairs today, but making a list of them is the first step and a big hurdle. On the list it goes!

There you go. Three things—in addition, of course, to all your other duties, which just get done whether they are written down or not. That is, unless they are out of the ordinary—say, there are four laundry baskets that must be tackled, or you won't be able to do your normal laundry. If you are really just beginning to be efficient in your day as a housekeeper and a mother, then list those "other duties" in the order you see them getting done for today. Cross them off as you go. But as you become more experienced in managing the flow of the household, you can just leave those things off the list, as it can be oppressive to see them there in black and white. Too many items on a to-do list is counterproductive.

Now, what I've discovered is that using sticky notes really helps and represents a significant improvement over the scrap-paper method. The improvement consists in giving a *visual*, which I find important, and also in allowing disposal of that which has been completed, which I find gratifying. I personally don't need an archive of notes that say "call doctor," so I am happy to toss them.

For this method to work well, it seems really important that the notes go onto durable pages. As I was thinking through what I would do, I was picturing a small spiral-bound photo album, the pages of which are smooth, heavy cardstock with a landscape orientation. You don't want too many pages, though, because that's too much pressure to multiply the tasks! We have enough tasks as it is. But I couldn't find what I was looking for.

The sturdiness is hard to find. In theory you could have a "notebook" that consisted of two stout covers—just a folder, really. You would open it up and there would be your to-dos.

I quickly realized that I might have three or however many things to do today, but there are going to be a lot of other things that need to stay near the top of the list. This is the difference between my system and the others. Most other systems have you looking at the whole list. Whatever doesn't get done moves to the next day. You are always "not doing" a lot of things, and it can be discouraging to be reminded of that. With the three-item list you are doing all the things you've realistically chosen for that day.

When they are done, they disappear; the next items move up from the master list onto new sticky notes, according to their priority. Obviously, something will pop up that isn't on the master list; it can easily become one of your few things to do on your main page.

So the prioritized items from the master list, a certain proportion of them (I usually have ten or fifteen), are on the "tomorrow" page of this notebook.

I saw I would need tabs. Fortunately, you can get sticky *tabs*. The main thing is that the ability to change this system around—its flexibility—is very appealing to me. I don't like my organization to be too dedicated. I like to be able to feel that I'm not a slave to it but, rather, that it's serving me. I guess I have commitment anxiety when it comes to organization.

Your master list—that long list of the overwhelming multiplicity of things you have to do (but fear you'll never get to)—can go in the back pages, perhaps under "master list." And you can have other notes under their own tabs. The page you open up to every morning never changes—only the stickies on it change.

On the inside of the cover are prayers and special intentions. When I open my notebook in my prayer time (as described above), I have my intentions right there.

On the right, on the first page, are the to-dos—*just for today*. Some days I need a sort of schedule and almost hourly breakdown, and that's when a large, lined sticky note comes in handy. I can write in the relevant hours very quickly and jot in what I want to do, and when.

But usually it's one task per small note. It works to put three things on one note, of course, but if the jobs are in very different categories, it can help to have the notes separate so that you can visually group them. They can also be grouped in action order.

If I need an archive, there's that master list, and I can cross out the items I've taken care of. But most tasks are not memorable!

On the inside of the back cover, I made a pocket very simply using cardstock (a recycled greeting card you particularly like and can cut down works very well) and glue. I can store a ready supply of various sticky notes there, replenishing when needed.

Other pages in this notebook are for jottings as they occur to me: crafting hopes and dreams, gift ideas, writing notes, and so on. I have other notebooks and an index card file for more extensive thoughts and notes into which these quick notes can be easily transferred; for to-dos, this sticky-note system is the way that works the best for me.

There you have it. I've always wanted a to-do system that's flexible, portable, simple, and visual. I've tried many, many others. This is it for me. I still jot things down on scraps of paper (especially as I say, shopping lists), but now I put most of my thoughts on sticky notes in this little book when they become official to-do items.

Notes on To-Do Notes

If you have a new baby, a houseful of sick children, or are otherwise in a slowdown, know that you must have a to-do list, but your sanity depends on what is on that list. If your to-dos are "wash face, brush teeth," "change diapers," and "defrost chicken broth" then that's a good day's work in my book.

When I first conceived this sticky-note idea, I felt that its drawback is that Post-its are ridiculously pricey (also I'm not a fan of the colors). But knockoffs are fine, and once you get started, keep your eye out for the ones put on clearance in various places. Soon you will have a stash of them. I decided it was worth it to use what turns out to be at most about three a day (usually I put like items together on a note) for me to have a sense of peace about how my day was going. I figure you can buy a lot of marked-down sticky notes for the price of one expensive planner.

Additionally, you can buy a glue stick of the sort of glue that makes sticky notes and make your own sticky notes! This has a strange appeal to someone who cares about paper weight and color.

Grocery Lists

The only effective way to make your grocery list is *in order of the aisles*. You are going to forget things, even things written down. Make it less likely that you will forget by using the layout of the store, rather than the order in which the things occur to you, to organize your list.

Some people suggest having a master list with items you frequently buy, pre-printed and organized by aisle. They suggest that you check or circle the items you need. I have tried this system but quickly abandoned it. Different stores are arranged differently; you quickly memorize the layouts and can jot down items based on the store you are going to. I find that having all the things printed out is distracting and causes me to overlook things. The effort necessary to have a supply of these master lists printed out and to get one before dashing to the store, when you have scrap paper *right there*, makes it not worthwhile to me. I think that having *one* master list could work if you are a consistent item-forgetter; check it before you finalize yours.

Even if you are writing out a list as items occur to you (or have such a thing on a family blackboard, for instance), rewrite it in aisle-order.

The Honey Do List; or, the Psychology of the Individual

What about your to-do list for your husband—that is, those things you would like him to accomplish? I don't know how my husband gets me to do things, but I get him to do things by making a Honey Do list. Somehow, if it's written up there on our kitchen blackboard, he will get it done. If it's not, it becomes one of those things that are just part of the landscape. It's like the bare bulb at the top of the stairs. When you move in, you say, "Wow, how could those people have lived with a bare bulb at the top of their stairs? I mean, every day they saw that thing, didn't they? What was wrong with them?" Then, ten years later, you go to sell the house, and you think, "We could just say 'as is' and then we wouldn't have to deal with stuff like that bare bulb," *if* you even see it anymore, which is unlikely.

Now, the thing about the Honey Do list is that I don't always remember how well it works. But if *I* remember to put something on it, my husband will get to it on chore day. He loves the satisfaction of crossing jobs off his to-do list. Since nagging is not pleasant or even a good strategy, we find that this method is the best way to communicate and still be peaceful.

On Organizing
Household Information

To paraphrase Aristotle, we ought to have right order, which includes putting in the proper amount of time into achieving right order—the time itself must be ordered. In other words, I find that I often fail at my efforts to organize because of two things: I just don't (I am disordered), or I put an *inordinate* amount of time and energy into doing something that doesn't merit it.

Also, know thyself, because if you are the type to go down the rabbit hole of organizing systems, you may never emerge to, you know, get things done.

There is no one master system for complete life organization in list or any other form. It's a collection of various strategies (and they will always fall short due to Original Sin). I will tell you what works for me in the different areas, and perhaps that will help you evaluate the methods you come across and help you find the system that works for you. Just keep in mind the principle that order means that the system itself serves the order, not vice versa.

Menu Planning

In the food and menu chapters, I have offered a really foolproof method of getting the food organized, shopping for it, and keeping notes about it. I like to use a physical binder; among other things, it allows me to archive those scraps of paper that turn out to have valuable information about menu plans that succeeded, shopping lists that need not be replicated every holiday, and notes for recipes I've developed. I include in it the very best recipe for the things our family likes best—the best brownies, the best butter cake, the best lasagna.

My binder has such oddities as cardstock templates for gingerbread houses, along with the best method for icing that holds them together. Having those things all together saves me a hunt through my cookbooks or online. That's just one random example. Basically, the binder is a record of my food brain.

Thoughts and Events

For deep thoughts, I use notebooks, journals, and an online site that captures links of articles I don't want to lose. (I had used Evernote; I now use Pocket—no doubt by the time you read this, something different will have been developed.) I don't save all the links. Just the truly good things I want to return to—bits of info that, back in the day, you would have clipped and put in a filing cabinet.

One very pretty journal holds the birthdays, christening days, and other info on my grandchildren. I use my best handwriting in it. I agonized about how many pages to leave in between each child.

A more battered one is a journal for thoughts, events, and quotes, kept over decades. I have several of these that I have started over the years, and I am not sure what is in them.

Then there is the five-year journal. Let me try to explain the difference: I always thought I would remember the important events of my life (the events themselves, as opposed to how I felt when they happened and my deepest, most intimate thoughts about them), but the years go by, and I don't remember many of them, much less the year they occurred. Things like the names of the couple who befriended us in Rome, or even meeting anyone on that trip, or what my favorite restaurant was, or the sequence of events that time the sale of the house fell through, or what the lawyer's funny secretary said at the meeting. Ever wonder how, in their memoirs, people remember all those names and incidents?

Well, many of them had what amounts to a log. A five-year journal is that for me. It has one page for each day of the year, and that page has five divisions, so that each June 7 in that five-year period has its own section for quick notes on facts of the day.

Any time is a good time to start yours. It could be kept by more than one person in the family, or each member could have something like it when he expresses interest. The point is to log what happened — and that is why, in historical records, you will find "bought six carts of hay" along with "Father died," which seems heartless but — that's the kind of record it is. You write in it, just a little, every day.

Phone Log

Another very good sort of log for family life is the phone log. Now that we have cell phones, causing the central phone for the house to be somewhat superfluous or even nonexistent, this log might not seem that important, but I will tell you how it operated for us and you can figure out if you like the idea and can adapt it.

I had a small notebook and a supply of pens and pencils near the phone in the kitchen. I am the person who used it the most, but others made entries as well. Mainly, it was for information that is important at the moment, information for which you are not ready to make a determination as to whether it will continue to be important in the future.

If it is, you can transfer it elsewhere — to a contact list or an online file. It's for jotting down the number of the plumber your friend is giving you as you chat about her day. It's for recording the names of physical therapists the receptionist at the doctor's office gives you, so you can look them up.

Especially in a big family with many activities, it always seemed like someone was always giving me a little tidbit of information. Where to store it? When the coach tells you which field the practices will now be held on, you can write it down there. The name of a wine you liked, a recommendation for a book, the number for the friend who is picking up your child (but may never again) ... I found it very useful because my short-term memory is not as good as I think it will be, but I didn't want some number that might not turn out to be useful to be entered in a more permanent place. I found I often flipped the pages back a few days or weeks to find that little thing I had quickly noted. What *was* the name of the painter we didn't end up using but maybe should call now? It was in the log, so no problem.

When the doctor is giving you extra information about how to treat a sick child (information that might not be on the prescription bottle), you can write it in the log. Once the child recovers, you won't need those notes again.

The most treasured use for this log turned out to be recording funny things people, children and adults alike, said that we wanted to remember. Our Christmas letter developed into a hilarious collection of these quotes, all thanks to the log, because one wouldn't want to interrupt the conversation to pull out a phone or go hunt down some more permanent journal.

When the log fills up, you have the opportunity to transfer any really important information to more permanent place and then simply throw the log away.

Index Cards

Finally, I learned that, for purposes of writing and giving talks, I need quotes and references on index cards. So now you know how hopelessly old school I have become, reverting from digital efforts (that failed). There is no substitute, I have found, for going through those note cards and being able to handle them, put them in the order I want and need, and then file them back away.

I also learned—too late, alas, but trying to make up for it now—that it's a good idea to write in your books (one of the many good thoughts I learned in *How to Read a Book,* by Mortimer Adler). I used to be very much opposed to marking up a book; it seemed sacrilegious somehow. But I have found that you don't want to be forced to reread all your books in order to remember what you thought at the time. You want to have a conversation with your future, possibly busy-because-she's-preparing-a-talk-or-teaching-a-class-or-simply-making-a-point self. Underline and make notes in the margin in a way that doesn't make the text unreadable.

Online Calendar

The online calendar is a great boon to parents. You can see your recurring and one-time events *and those of your spouse and anyone else you add to it.* If you are both on the go, online is best. Ditto pulling all your calendars together. In the olden days, I had yet another binder for all the sports and activities calendars, and I'd have to transfer them all onto my big kitchen calendar. Now, that activity's calendar can be added to yours. You can color code them, and it's amazing. I used to wonder *why* my husband didn't know that we *always* had soccer on Tuesdays until I finally realized that just because it was engraved on my mind, there was no reason to think he had any awareness at all.

Pinterest

This online visual filing system can help you train your eye and become a better maker of your home. Pinterest can replace binders full of magazine clippings, and if you are working on a design project, whether it's building a house or trying to visualize a more efficient closet, Pinterest can help you zero in on the details that work.

I've used it to find images that help me with a specific problem. If your countertops are brown granite and you want inspiration for trim paint that looks best with them, putting that into a search and pinning the images that you like to a board called "Brown Granite Color Scheme" will help you find your answers. If you need ideas for built-in shelves in a corner, make a board specifically for the images you love that feature shelves in the corner.

Homeschooling

Each child gets his own binder, unless you are doing two in one grade level. The details for this binder can be found in volume 2. The homeschool binder will serve you well through the years.

Efficiency Can Be Taken Too Far

A good planner and to-do list are indispensable, for sure. I do want to say that it might perhaps be misguided to wake up in the morning very, *very* goal-oriented, or at least very aware that everyone *else* is goal-oriented and we are, by comparison, falling behind.

Amid achieving things and decluttering things and making sure we are bursting with explosions of creativity—all of which, of course, I endorse—we might pause each day to think about how much it means to those around us to find us peaceful.

The drive to check off all the boxes can make normal things seem like obstacles. I'm here to report that, for instance, babies are not efficient—but that this inefficiency is what makes babies so wonderful and precious.

In other words, I offer for your consideration that the seeming pointlessness of daily life in making a home may be a result of our not having the vantage point necessary *to see the whole*. And these circumstances of life that seem so, well, not fabulously indicative of our self-realization and, on the contrary, positively derail it, may be God's way of helping, not hindering, us on our path.

At this strange point in history, we have very little direction from our spiritual leaders to help us see that we are here on earth not to perform to some worldly standard and become all we can be, *our best selves, this instant,* but simply to do God's will and be with Him in Heaven.

And yet, each day is *also* full of things we need to do!

Today as I write this, the Office of Readings (from a letter of Pope St. Clement I to the Corinthians) explained the paradox well, and suited my theme:

> It is obvious, therefore, that none of these owed their honour and exaltation to themselves, or to their own labours, or to their deeds of virtue. No; they owed everything to God's will. So likewise with us, who by his will are called in Christ Jesus. We are not justified by our wisdom, intelligence, piety, or by any action of ours, however holy, but by faith, the one means by which God has justified men from the beginning. To him be glory for ever and ever. Amen....
>
> What must we do then, brothers? Give up good works? Stop practising Christian love? God forbid! We must be ready and eager for every opportunity to do good, and put our whole heart into it. Even the Creator and Lord of the universe rejoices in his works. By his supreme power he set the heavens in their place; by his infinite wisdom he gave them their order.

Your peaceful work is a gift to others.

ASK AUNTIE LEILA

Setting Up Housekeeping, Making a Home

Here's a question I received. I hope the answer might help young wives recover this vision of peaceful orderliness and calm wonder I'm speaking of:

Dear Auntie Leila,

How do I organize a new house and new things obtained from our wedding registry? How do I set up housekeeping, and what do I do to keep it all running smoothly? What do you wish you had known when you were young and just setting up house? I'm not married yet, but two weeks from today I will be, and I'm feeling a bit overwhelmed at the prospect of having to make so many decisions about how things will be done! My mother was never the best at keeping house, so I don't have her example to follow.

A New Bride

Dear New Bride,

This book is an attempt to answer just that question! But to put it in capsule form:

Enjoy the honeymoon! Don't worry. You are already far, far ahead of the game just by identifying the *need* to set up housekeeping and indeed be the arbiter of how your house is kept, as opposed to the victim of it.

In fact, since it takes most of us at least a decade or two to figure out that there is anything to be identified, let alone that we are the subject of this identification, you can take some time off while patting yourself on the back. Good job!

As soon as you get home—yes, your new home!—make your bed with the pretty sheets and bedding you received as gifts. If you can possibly wash the sheets first, do, but if not, don't worry; just do it soon. Remember, your bedroom is the sanctuary of your marriage. So this is your first lesson in housekeeping—ordering things correctly. Military wives know to hang your pretty things on the wall right away, not putting it off. This may seem like the reverse of correct order, but they have experience in what makes a new place feel homey.

Put a pretty tablecloth on the table, and make a nice supper, having provided yourself with what you need for supper, even if it means paper plates for now.

As you open your gifts, consider returning the items that don't make your heart go pit-a-pat, even if they are things you registered for. There's no shame in realizing that perhaps, for some of the items, you might have succumbed to a combination of enthusiasm for getting all the stuff, inexperience about what is truly helpful for you in your circumstances, and the store's capitalization on those two states of mind.

I'm not talking about making rash determinations about unusual gifts. Sometimes it takes time to assimilate those unique items. Sometimes they fit a need or desire you don't yet know you have, but the givers are more experienced, and often the gifts are not returnable in any case. But sometimes the return window is small, and it's worth admitting that you need to use it.

Before you completely open every box after unwrapping, be honest about whether the things will fit in your new home (which I will assume is going to be modest, in the approved newlywed mode). Remember, the gift was given for one reason: to make you happy. You might get, instead, something different or scaled down — for instance, only three of the twelve pots and pans in the set. But that is all you will need until such time as you have a baseball-team number of children — at which point you won't need three sizes of sauce pot; you will need one twenty-quart stock pot.

Another way to distinguish what makes your heart go pit-a-pat from what doesn't is this justly famous quote we reflected on earlier from William Morris: "Have nothing in your house that you do not know to be useful or believe to be beautiful."

Ponder the things you have each brought into the house from your previous lives apart as you find places for them. Again, don't do anything rash, but ask yourself if you have done what so many of us do, which is simply move things because they are things and moving is what you are doing. That box of T-shirts from high school? The collection of souvenir mugs from basketball venues? Maybe it's time to say goodbye.

Have lots of conversations about your future together and how you want it to be. Talk about what you really love about homes you have experienced. Get to know each other's hopes and dreams. Don't let people's exhortations and misplaced urgency about enjoying your newlywed state rob you of *this* enjoyment. Yes, you only live once. Yes, there are lots of fun things to do as newlyweds. Yes, you may someday find yourself owning two minivans and incapable of thinking beyond the children's activity schedules. But still, the real fun of this period in your life is hoping and dreaming. Do what *you* want to do to get ready for your future — not what other people deem appropriate, which ends up putting off that future.

In the course of these wonderful talks, use some of the time to set priorities, especially about how you will spend your money. Housekeeping is all about living well, within your means, and using your resources with wisdom to achieve your goals.

I wish I had done that — really thought through what would be important to me five, ten, and twenty years on, and then worked to make those things happen. Some goals I think are worthwhile: a home of your own; the education of your children, should God grant you children; and the environment you want as they are growing up. I wish I had made it a priority to find a modest place to vacation, where the children would make good memories and have a lot of freedom. Think of an enjoyable activity that you, your husband, and your future family can all do together, in terms of recreation, if you don't already have one.

Education here does not mean saving for college, which I think is pointless for most people of modest means. I am talking about having a good home library, musical instruments, opportunities for interacting with interesting people, and access to nature. Now *those* are worth investing in.

Carve out some space for creativity. Use your ingenuity to make it happen where you are. Think about how your creativity can serve your future. If you are imagining a home filled with quilts or knit blankets, or your own paintings, or refinished furniture, see how you can make yourself a little corner to do those things in and a budget for what you will need.

Read. Now is when you have time to read about how to cook, how to clean, how to do those creative things. You can learn more about education, philosophy, and gardening for that someday when you have a little plot to call your own or can access a community garden; you can learn to be frugal! Now is the time to read good novels and to get those thousand good books that John Senior identifies, the solid reading of childhood and youth, under your belt so that you aren't rushing when you suddenly need to get your children's reading in order — and to get a start on the hundred great books, the great and often demanding classics of Western civilization — so that you yourself can join the Great Conversation (that interaction of great minds that transcends time and space), if you haven't already. Now is the time to invest in worthy books and the time to read them.

Use Pinterest, or whatever design and inspiration app that's current, well. Does that sound frivolous? I firmly believe that it's a great tool for the homemaker. Back in the day, we cut pictures we loved out of magazines and kept them in a file. Now there's Pinterest. The Internet is a boon for homemakers, as long as you don't get caught up in fantasizing about perfection. Use it to record how others in your situation *solve problems* and reach their goals. As you seek answers to your questions, keep a record on your inspiration boards of what you find interesting, helpful, and beautiful.

Have a particular problem? For instance, are you wondering what shade to paint the kitchen walls when you have counters of a certain color? Are you gardening with a very specific challenge in your landscape? Do a search for the exact issue, and pin the results that spark your imagination. Go back and edit often. Pay attention, and it will really help you train your eye and learn to find solutions.

Try replacing the category of "decorating"—procuring things to beautify your home—with "putting your pretty things around." For those of us with limited means, the thought that we can't have something perfect makes us think we can't have anything at all. For a long time, I worked that way, assuming that if my dwelling couldn't be architect designed and professionally furnished, well, what was the use? The perils of very high standards!

I would tell myself that "someday" I would have everything "decorated," but "for now" I wouldn't bother, since I couldn't afford what I really wanted. Ah, that "someday"! What a wasting thought! I don't "decorate," although I might occasionally use that word. I just try to make things the way they are, only cleaner, prettier, and happier.

I believe that our homes should serve this goal: to make a proper place for the life of *this* family—one that we, together, think is beautiful and fitting, and one that offers to anyone who visits us a warm, loving welcome.

Remember, you can do a lot in an hour. You can do what *you* want to do and think should be done—especially if you are showered, have a plan for dinner, and have the laundry process under control (this one perhaps won't be as much of an issue for you now, but cast a thought in its direction anyway).

You can also look at your hours and think about how to make them orderly, bringing time into contact with God's inner life. This is liturgical living. Make your Sundays different and set apart, and you will find that everything else falls into place.

Enjoyment and doing what you want to do as a couple are mysterious realities: this week you don't have sanctifying grace to participate in the life of Christ with your true love—next week, after the wedding, you will. It's not up to Auntie Leila to do more than brush you off, set you on your feet, and give you a little push. You will run the race *your way.* And a marvelously unique way it will be!

You are making your home—your contribution to the world, a great adventure! There are means, and you will discover what they are, because you are clever and have an inquiring mind. And those means will lead you to the end: nothing less than God's kingdom.

Hope for When You Regret the Past

We have looked at how to set up housekeeping—and a real home—when starting out married life, but maybe some of you had a pang if, like me, you are already down the road without having done much of the practical or spiritual things I talked about; without realizing what was important until it was too late.

I know some of you do get these pangs, because you have written to me in this vein:

> It makes me tear my hair out to think of how I spent my twenties so foolishly, so disordered toward the faithful family life we are creating now.

Why didn't anyone tell me this before?

I do have a little to say about this regretting of the past, and *what might have been.* Whether it's regretting not realizing the importance of what you do in the home, not having true devotion, or having taken wrong turns, I want you to know what kind of hope God has for you.

Some of you are good with the past and are good with how you've used your time, and, well, God bless you. That's what the Irish say when they *really* mean "You're crazy"—as in "You have seven children? God bless you!" Or sometimes they *really* mean "Are you for real?"—as in "You have no regrets about the past? God bless you."

As for me, apart from the really awful things I've done pretty much on purpose, and all the stupid and ridiculous things I've done out of ignorance, there's just all the falling short and wasted time and serious ways in which I have not been kind or sweet or any of those things that I've recently discovered are important.

One day I discovered the remedy for this feeling—a little lifeline of hope. Not in the "Jesus died to save me from my sins" kind of way, which is, of course, at the back of everything I'm going to tell you—no need to mention it. Not even in the "Heaven will be our reward" kind of way, although sometimes that is all that keeps me going.

It's more a specific prayer that helps me with the actual, specific feeling of having *wasted time and ruined everything.*

Now, feelings are quite separate from objective facts, so even if we've repented and confessed and made reparation, we can still be so frustrated at the feeling (which, after all, is based on fact) that we've *not done what we ought to do,* and now our life is falling short in all these ways. This really is just life, and no one should be surprised that I, at least, wasn't able to wrestle all of it into the shape of my dreams.

Not that there isn't always much to be grateful for, for many are suffering much worse things than I (or you). It's just the defeat of it all ... way back when; some of which may not have been our fault. Sometimes we suffer misfortune, and what could be termed crop failures of the soul: floods and droughts, real and metaphorical; events not necessarily of our own making. And some things very much of our own making.

Sometimes the bitterness is hard to overcome. Especially when we get to that place where we see that things might have worked out, *if we had known then what we know now!*

This hope, this lifeline I'm speaking of first came to me in the form of a little scrap of Scripture: "And I will restore to you the years that the locust hath eaten" (Joel 2:25, KJV). It's a promise from God. He will restore the years.

Now, the chapter in the book of Joel from which this verse is taken is about many things. It's a prophecy about the redemption of Israel. It's apocalyptic and earth shaking and concerns the whole revolution of the universe in the day of the Lord. Its imagery is vivid: the blackness, the fire, the horses, the vats overflowing with wine and oil. The message is not a rosy, fairy-tale one.

And yet there's a tiny bit of comfort there for the *here and now*, for our own interior parched land, and for the desolation of the past. It's not *just* that He will take us from here, leaving behind the mess, and deliver us to a better place (although He will do that if we rend our hearts and not our garments, as He mentions).

He's specifically saying that *He will give back the years.*

Later, as I began doing the Office of Readings, I noticed how often we pray Psalm 90 (89 in some versions). Read it for yourself. Try the Revised Standard Version to get the full effect of what I am trying to say.

The first part of this psalm is about what I've been trying to say here. It's a lament for how short man's time is compared with God's time, and how futile things can seem — even our efforts. The psalmist sees how even our objective successes seem to us, in this light, like the children of men returning to dust; like grass withering. Have we done what we ought to do? This is what worries us, because we can sort of see the answer.

Then He puts the words in our mouths, words *we* should say to *Him*: "Make us glad as many days as thou hast afflicted us,/ and as many years as we have seen evil" (v. 15). Just as we say to our children, "Say, 'Mama, please give me the cherry,' and then I will give it to you," God is saying to us, "Say, 'Teach us to number our days aright.... Give me back the years. Make it up to me.' And then I will."

Now, we aren't babies, so we have to have the right kind of vision to see what He will do. We also have to have gone through those years of the dry times (so it's not a prayer that can be prayed too soon). And it's not that if we have faith, we will prosper — not according to how the world thinks of prosperity, most likely. Certainly, He didn't make His own Son to prosper. On the other hand, there are His words. We must trust and hope.

Pray this prayer of Psalm 90:15 and then have hope, let go, and trust. Remember Joel 2:25, when the memory of the locusts bites. He will restore the years, just as they ought to be, and the work of our hands will grow. And we will be the ones to tell the others of His goodness—we alone, who experienced it in just this way.

Make Something Beautiful

Do you have some handwork that you love to do, or some other creative outlet?

I've been quilting for about twenty-five years. I don't have many quilts to show for all that time, because I was learning when my kids were really little and had to take breaks because I was too pregnant to cut material out on the floor, or had a nursing baby in my arms all the time, or just couldn't get to it.

But you know, it's very fulfilling to be making something—to do something loving and creative even when you feel as if you are too busy. I have found that scheduling the time necessary to set myself up with a project yields major dividends in finding myself prepared later, at unexpected moments, when I can reach for my quilt bag and pull out my handwork. It's the setting up that's difficult. But with some thought, it can be done.

We need to learn to enjoy our days, to take satisfaction in small acts of beauty, however humble.

The recovery of this sense of satisfaction will lead us to be better to the people around us: kinder, more patient, and more affirming. I say "recovery," because I think that before the feminist revolution, the great majority of women, simply and without much fanfare, led quite satisfied lives, in no small part thanks to the little touches they gave their homes, without too much regard to the high fashions of the day.

I know that my grandmother, who raised seven children (without indoor plumbing for a good deal of the time), made lovely objects that were part of daily life at home, and she wasn't alone in doing so. I think this is why I'm drawn to crafts and styles from her day. I am drawn to the idea that women put so much creativity into their homes, with so little to work with. Quilting does have the advantage that the materials are not difficult to come by.

The problem with keeping the household is that many of the things we do each day are ephemeral. Worthwhile, but quickly undone! The same dishes get dirty again, sometimes within minutes. A clean room seems to attract little people with crayons, clay, and grand visions of sofa-cushion-fort architecture. Even a lovely meal doesn't have a long life.

If you have been sort of drowning in the riptides of your life, I encourage you to ask yourself what makes you feel really happy in a homemaking kind of way. Getting the knitting needles in your hands? Making a bag? Doing crewel embroidery?

I have a friend who tells me how energized she feels walking into her sewing studio, and I concur. It's a bracing feeling. And you don't need a whole studio! What if your sewing machine were on a little table in a closet, under a window, or in a corner? Mine is in my pantry on an ugly old office desk that I spray-painted black. I've seen a perfectly tidy, well-appointed little master bedroom with a sweet little sewing machine table against one wall in a corner.

There are many ideas online for creating a craft corner, and I find the visuals extremely helpful. The key is to make it pretty! If your machine is out, you won't dread it. It's only when your crafting items encroach on your main living spaces in that perched way that creativity turns burdensome.

If it's something like working with furniture, pottery, or sculpting, you may also want to take up needlepoint, only because it's hard to throw a pot while watching a baseball game or sitting outside of dance class. You can get a lot done in those hours here and there, just sitting and waiting. I like to talk to other moms—I think most of us are starved for conversation, aren't we? But I don't like to just sit there with my hands idle.

Remember the Middletons in *Sense and Sensibility?* "He hunted and shot, and she humoured her children; and these were their only resources." At least Sir Middleton had the advantage of a warm personality; Lady Middleton was cold. And, as Jane Austen tells us, she has nothing to do.

In contrast to this figure of mindless leisure are the women in *The Quilters: Women and Domestic Art, an Oral History.*[15] These pioneers give an inspiring example of creativity in the midst of astonishing activity: days of backbreaking work in the cotton fields in West Texas that put our soft situations to shame, although they seem not to complain much. And they made the things because they needed them, yet what they made transcended utility.

I enjoyed every moment of reading about these lovely women and their clever melding of their social and work lives into a beautiful and productive unity. Their communities seemed to thrive along with their creativity. I also love how the book reveals the men's interest in the women's handwork and their support for and participation in it (often surreptitiously!). Making beautiful things is a necessity in living the good life.

---

[15] Patricia Cooper and Norma Bradley Allen, *The Quilters: Women and Domestic Art: An Oral History* (Lubbock, TX: Texas Tech University Press, 1999).

Final Thoughts about Keeping Your Home

Wonder (joy and peace) cannot be obtained without Order. The temptation is to set out for perfection; the result of doing that is dissatisfaction. Instead, be willing to ask of yourself the minimum, which, in the case of housekeeping, is food and clean laundry!

When you suddenly feel very busy, I encourage you not to abandon your planning, but to take a little time to plan your menus *around your activities*—easy meals on running-around days, more labor-intensive ones on days you are at home. The truth is, only you can do it, because only you know which days you are running around and which days you are able to spend more time cooking. Only you know you have half a ham in the fridge and sweet potatoes in the pantry. Only you know that on a certain day, everyone needs a bigger meal than usual, but on another day a pot of soup will fit the bill.

But figuring these things out is not difficult if you use my methods. Go back and read how to get this done once and for all, using not *my* ideas of what *my* family likes but your very own family's tastes and preferences and special diets. In fact, your family does the hard work for you! No other method offers you that.

Save a step and tuck a few key things in your freezer as you go, as I outlined in the menu-making section. Personally, I just get very tired if I have to do too many things in one day, or if I have to be on my feet for too long. I can't manage a marathon in the kitchen, but I *can* do a little extra preparation a few days a week to make my life easier most of the time.

If you go from on-the-fly shopping to planning menus, even without shopping your store's specials or employing the really intensive saver's store-hopping method, I foresee that you will cut your grocery bill by at least one-third. That doesn't even count the money saved from eliminating emergency takeout and restaurant indulgences. But even more than the money saved is the peace of mind that comes with knowing that your children are not subsisting on spaghetti and pizza alone.

Once you have made the effort to get to the bottom of your laundry room (literally, to be able to see the floor), staying on top of the washing, folding, and putting away according to my plan (which has you spread out the process rather than impose the impossible task, in a large family, of doing it all at once), you will experience the freedom offered by minimal competence.

Keep your home reasonably clean as I have outlined. Your bedroom is the place to begin (not the kitchen). Every day, leave it with the bed made and things picked up. When you start your cleaning routine, start there. This can be life-changing because your bedroom represents the bedrock of your marriage.

If you do these two things, know what's for dinner, and know that you will get through your house at least once a week—oh, and the laundry: can't forget that, as if the piles won't be their own reminder—yes, if you do these *three* things, you will begin to experience a deep satisfaction in your home life. Your worries, frustrations, and discontents will abate. You will not yell as much. (Did you know that you yell because you think someone else should be dealing with the situation? You think your kids should deal with the disorganization of your life.) You will have at least this much peace, the peace of knowing that things are not irredeemably messy and that there's something to eat and clean underwear to put on.

The Reasonably Clean House is not about perfection, but about competence, about trying to have a minimum of order so that we can experience Order and Wonder — order in the home, order in our days; wonder in our time together as family and friends and with God.

You can't have one without the other, but don't let obtaining them disrupt your spirit. Approach everything with peace, with a sense of confidence that, having understood the mess, the dirt, the hunger of the little ones, or the piles of laundry, solutions will be forthcoming under the gaze of God. Resolve to do the minimum, the least you can do, with a good heart.

Pope Pius XI spoke of the woman's "truly regal throne to which she has been raised within the walls of the home by means of the Gospel." She ascends this throne only by desiring it and by being willing to serve and love and, yes, grapple with all she finds along the path to it. My hope is that these volumes offer encouragement in the journey and, above all, the perspective that our true home is not here on earth: it's with the saints and angels in Heaven, with God.

Appendices

APPENDIX A

Breakfast Recipes

Buttermilk Baking Mix

Make your own mix, and store in the refrigerator. Halve the recipe at first to see how you like it. It's versatile, and the pancakes it makes are very light and good!

Ingredients

10 cups unbleached flour

1 cup whole wheat flour (or just add another cup of white flour, making 11 cups)

1 cup oat flour (process regular oatmeal in the food processor or the blender until finely ground; one cup of oatmeal will give you one cup of oat flour) or 1/2 cup oat bran

1/2 cup wheat bran

1/4 cup wheat germ

1/2 cup flax meal

1 1/2 tablespoons salt

1 tablespoon sugar

2 tablespoons baking soda

6 tablespoons baking powder (I have used as little as 4 tablespoons
when I have found myself short of baking powder)
3 sticks (12 ounces) butter or 2 sticks butter and 1/2 cup coconut oil
Feel free to substitute various flours and meals, using all flax meal
if you are out of bran, and so forth.

Directions

You can process your baking soda and baking powder with your oatmeal
to remove any lumps and facilitate distribution in the mix.

Measure all the ingredients except the butter into a large bowl. Stir
to mix.

In the food processor or a large bowl, cut together several cups of the
flour mixture and a stick of butter until it resembles coarse cornmeal. Set
aside and repeat with each butter stick. Then mix the batches together
before you divide for storage or use.

Store in the refrigerator in tightly a covered container or in a ziplock
bag with the air pressed out. A large, slim, rectangular container is the
most space efficient for the refrigerator. I use a plastic container meant for
bulk cereals. It holds about two quarts and is large enough for all this mix.

To use, spoon, don't pack, the mixture into a cup. Unless you've used
all coconut oil, be sure to refrigerate the leftover mixture so the butter will
not become rancid.

Biscuits

Serves 4 to 6 as an accompaniment to a bowl of soup

Ingredients

2 cups Buttermilk Baking Mix
2/3 cup milk

Directions

No need to measure precisely. Measure the cold mix (cold so that the butter will stay in lumps) into a bowl, add about 2/3 cup of buttermilk (or a

combination with some milk if you like), little by little, until you get the proper consistency, which is somewhat dry—not like a batter but closer to a pie crust; dry enough to be able to knead. Turn the mix out on your clean counter and gently knead it about six times or until it just holds together. Roll the dough out roughly, cut it in half, put one half on top of the other, and roll it out again to the thickness of an inch. Cut your biscuits with a round cutter or simply cut rectangles (this method eliminates the problem of scraps). Put biscuits in a greased pan and bake for about 8 minutes at 425 degrees or until puffed and golden brown.

Note that the gentle kneading and stacking gave you nicely layered biscuits!

Pancakes

Serves 4 to 6

Ingredients

2 cups Buttermilk Baking Mix
1/2 cup flour (whole wheat or all-purpose)
2 eggs
2 cups buttermilk

Directions

Combine the mix and the flour in a large mixing bowl. Make a well in the center. Add the eggs and lightly beat them in the well.

Add the buttermilk and lightly incorporate it into the mix. Avoid beating the mix, which will make your pancakes tough. Instead, keep the part that's mixed very wet as you pull in all the dry ingredients gradually. Stop before you think you are done.

Your mixture should be lumpy and light and battery. As you make your pancakes, you will give the batter a gentle stir each time you dip in your spoon, so allow for that.

Ladle by scant half cups onto a sizzling griddle. Allow small bubbles to form on the surface, flip, and cook until done.

Scones

This mix makes a fluffier kind of scone.

Ingredients

3 1/2 cups Buttermilk Baking Mix
2/3 cup sugar
1 cup nuts or dried fruit
2 eggs
1/2 cup light cream
1/2 cup buttermilk

Directions

Combine the mix, the sugar, and the nuts or dried fruit.

Combine the eggs, the cream, and the buttermilk, and add the mixture to the dry ingredients.

Turn the dough onto a clean, floured counter and gently knead it by folding one side over onto the other using a bench scraper or a spatula, give it a few pats, and repeating until it holds together somewhat.

Divide the dough into four pieces and form each one into a round. Gently roll each round until it is about one and a half inches thick. Using your bench scraper, move each round onto a baking sheet; all four should fit fine. Cut each round into six or eight wedges, pulling the wedges apart slightly.

Brush with more cream and sprinkle with sugar (raw sugar gives a good crunch). Bake at 425 degrees until golden brown, about 15 minutes (less for a convection oven or for smaller scones).

Waffles

These waffles are light, crispy, and tender.
Serves 4 to 6

Ingredients

2 cups Buttermilk Baking Mix
1 cup flour
1/4 cup cornstarch
1/4 cup sugar
2 eggs
3 cups buttermilk
1/2 cup milk

Directions

Preheat the waffle iron.

Combine the dry ingredients (the mix through the sugar) in a large mixing bowl. Make a well in the center. Add the eggs and lightly beat them in the well.

Add the buttermilk and the milk and lightly incorporate them into the mix. Avoid beating the mix, which will make your waffles tough. Instead, keep the part that's mixed very wet as you pull in all the dry ingredients gradually. Stop before you think you are done.

Your mixture should be lumpy and light and battery.

As you make your waffles, you will give the batter a gentle stir each time you dip in your spoon, so allow for that.

Lightly grease the waffle iron, if necessary (the more you grease, the less crispy the waffles, counterintuitively). Pour in the amount of batter your waffle iron's manufacturer recommends and bake.

Place cooked waffles on a rack if you are not serving immediately. You can hold them in a warm oven if necessary; the rack will help them remain crisp.

Night-Before Breakfast Casserole

*There are many recipes like this out there. I prefer mine
somewhat on the substantial side, so I like this one.*

Ingredients

1 1/2 pounds bread (I use homemade; raisin bread is lovely), cut
    into cubes

cooked bacon or sausage

12 eggs

2 1/2 cups whole milk (add more milk for a lighter texture; I like
    mine substantial)

1 teaspoon vanilla

1/2 cup sugar (if you want it a bit more like French toast)

1 teaspoon salt

2 teaspoons cinnamon

1 cup shredded cheddar cheese (optional)

Directions

The night before you intend to serve this casserole, butter a large lasagna
pan. Fill the pan with the bread cubes to within an inch of the top.

Add up to a pound of crumbled cooked bacon or sausage. This is a
good way to use leftover breakfast meat (in the unlikely event you have
any). Even a sprinkling of bacon bits is appreciated. A good hearty portion
of sausage is heaven.

Whisk together the eggs, milk, vanilla, sugar, salt, cinnamon, and cheese,
and pour this mixture over the bread, distributing the cheese evenly.

Cover with foil and keep in the fridge overnight.

In the morning, bake the casserole at 350 degrees for 40 minutes (30
minutes for a convection oven), or until the casserole is puffed and browned.

Serve with maple syrup.

Leftovers can be kept in the refrigerator and microwaved for a quick
breakfast the following day.

Granola

These amounts are approximate.

Ingredients

8 cups oats
1 small package of flaked coconut (sweetened or not), about 2 cups
2 to 4 cups chopped nuts
1 1/2 cups brown sugar (This seems like a lot, but this recipe makes
　　many servings. You can start with a smaller amount at first if you
　　like. You can also substitute honey, molasses, or maple syrup.)
1 cup water
3/4 cup oil (try coconut oil for a delicious flavor!)
1 tablespoon cinnamon
1 teaspoon salt (don't omit: salt is important to wake up the taste buds)
1 teaspoon almond extract (if using almonds)
2 cups of any combination of the following: dried cranberries,
　　chopped dates, raisins, chopped apricots, to be added after
　　the granola has baked

Directions

Preheat the oven to 325 degrees.

Combine the oats, the coconut, and the nuts in a large mixing bowl.

Combine the rest of the ingredients *except* the dried fruit in a saucepan, bring the mixture to a boil, and simmer for 5 minutes, or until the sugar is dissolved and the syrup is slightly thickened.

Pour the syrup over the ingredients in the bowl, and mix well until all the oats are coated.

Pour the mixture into shallow pan (a lasagna pan works well), and bake for 30 to 35 minutes, stirring every 10 minutes, until the mixture is evenly browned.

Remove from the oven. Stir in the extra ingredients at this point.

Cool completely without stirring, for clumpiness, and store in airtight containers (and the granola can be frozen).

Oatmeal Porridge Like Mother, Like Daughter

*This method is similar to the way I cook all grains (except pasta) – namely,
with a bit of fat at the beginning to coat each grain and produce a delectable
separateness and lack of stickiness or objectionable gumminess in the texture.
Try the same method with rice, couscous, barley, and bulgur. Stock up on grains
and keep them in jars or in ziplock bags in the freezer so that they do not get
stale or rancid. If you are using steel-cut oats, soak them the night before.*

Ingredients

1 cup oats (if steel-cut, soak in 2 cups water)
1/2 cup Cream of Wheat (quick-cooking farina)
1/4 cup Wheatena (Do you have this where you live? It's basically
    toasted finely cracked wheat. If you don't, add more farina or
    cornmeal.)
1 tablespoon butter
1/4 teaspoon salt
1/2 cup sugar, brown sugar, honey, or maple syrup

Directions

Bring 4 cups of water to a boil (use half if using soaked oats). Add the
butter and salt.

Stir in the oats, the Cream of Wheat, and the Wheatena.

Cook for about 20 minutes, stirring. If the consistency is too thick, add
water; if too thin, add more Cream of Wheat. I like to make the consistency
quite thick so that cold milk can be added at serving. This cools the porridge
down and adds protein. If you like to cook your porridge in milk but get
annoyed by how it tends to boil over, try stirring instant dry milk (up to
one cup for this amount) at the end of the cooking.

Add the sugar, brown sugar, honey, or syrup. I like to sweeten the
porridge in the pot to a moderate degree of sweetness so that only a little
needs to be added at the table. I have found that if I serve it completely
unsweetened, children tend to add too much.

Serve with maple syrup and milk. Add a tablespoon of peanut butter or chopped pecans for heartiness. The nuts will make this breakfast last until lunch. You can also stir in a well beaten egg for the protein challenged; the heat will make it into a custard.

Papa's Special

I have found out that many families have something
they call Papa's Special, or sometimes Daddy's Special!

Ingredients

English muffin
butter
honey (Use real local raw honey; grocery store honey can contain
    corn syrup! Of course, if you have a child under one, don't use
    honey at all.)
peanut butter (Use real peanut butter made from ground peanuts;
    major brands have a lot of additives and sugar in them.)

Directions

Toast the English muffin. Butter both sides (technically, this makes it a Mama's Special, because Papa doesn't butter the peanut-butter side). Spread honey on one side and peanut butter on the other. Sandwich the sides together.

APPENDIX B

Plain Cooking: Surviving Morning Sickness and More

Q uick disclaimer: I rarely had more than little waves of nausea while pregnant. Before you hate me, I want to tell you that my observation, backed up by multiple studies (or, maybe not), is that those with easy pregnancies often have difficult deliveries, and vice versa. Does that make you feel better? I'll wait while you run to the bathroom. Poor you.

But I have some strategies for you to cope with morning sickness, and some tips. With my admittedly scant experience and surveys of truly morning-sick friends, this post will help. The main issue is how to feel a little better—but also, how to feed everyone when you feel lousy. The answer is to fall back on Plain Cooking, and that is something you learn to do so you can pull it out without thinking too hard about it.

As I see it, we have these levels of morning sickness—call it the Defense Readiness Condition (Defcon), but for pregnancy (or other state that may benefit from preparedness and emergency procedures regarding food supply).

Defcon 5: You are still on Pinterest and can manage to layer dips, garnish salads with edible flowers harvested from your garden, and handle recipes embedded in other recipes. You can stomach the sight of raw chicken for a short time. You are not too tired to have a garden. Good for you! We'll be over for supper.

Defcon 4: You walk rather fast past the chicken case at the grocery store. A dish of squid you mistakenly ate in week 9 has put you off squid forever. Never again will you eat squid. You can barely type the word. Your family wonders why chicken has disappeared from the menu, although some of them aren't sad about this (they are the four-year-old). Ways to make ground beef are not finding any appeal, but you're sticking with it. As long as the six-year-old keeps you supplied with little fizzy hard candies from the corner market, you are going to make it, although your teeth will be the worse for wear. By week 20 you are feeling okay, as long as you have one nap a day. (This may or may not have been me—at my worst. I said I was sorry.) You're doing fine, really, and the troops are fed.

Defcon 3: Dragging from sofa to bed, bed to sofa, barfing along the way. Wishing you had the energy to strangle the next person to tell you to drink ginger ale. Subsisting on saltines. Here is where perhaps we can be of help.

First, let's look at how to feed your family in this case, and, of course, I think your friends and family should be supplying you with generous meals, but for one reason or another, that might not be the case. So let's figure out a strategy.

I think rules are in order, don't you? Thinking and understanding is so hard when you are suffering from morning sickness. Rules have the virtue of standing there, ready to be followed, when thinking isn't an option. So here are three warm-up rules and then on to Plain Cooking.

Rule 1: Get the medical part of it squared away.[16] Have your blood tested for iron. The iron in your prenatal vitamin is probably not enough. Take your Floridix (or Blood Builder—easily swallowed, reasonably sized pills—if you don't think you can handle swallowing the liquid).[17] Iron can worsen

---

[16] Nausea that starts in late pregnancy can be a warning sign of preeclampsia. Check with your doctor or midwife.

[17] Needless to say, check with your doctor or midwife before taking any supplements.

nausea, but so can anemia. Try to take it later in the day when you've eaten something (nondairy).

If you can eat red meat or liver, do. Try liver pâté; either make a simple one with onions and prunes, or buy it. Liverwurst isn't bad, spread on crisp crackers; you may find you crave it when you're anemic. Liver + prunes = iron and may be helpful with consequent digestive issues. There are combinations of vitamins that can help you. Ask your doctor or midwife. But above all, don't get anemic on top of everything else.

There are safe medications for morning sickness. Many ladies swear by the vitamin B6 plus Unisom[18] combination (if you know you get sick, start as soon as you can; you can split the pills to spread the anti-nausea effect over the day, if that's more affordable for you; and there is a prescription version that is slow release) or Zofran, or both. You need to bring it up with the doctor—I've heard too many stories of ladies needing IV fluids more than once, yet the doctor *still* doesn't bring up medical relief. Getting dehydrated is far worse for Baby than taking the (safe!) medication!

Rule 2: Rest. You are making a baby. That's pretty important and amazing. If this is not your first child, you are making a sibling for your other child(ren)—the best gift you will ever give them, besides your marriage. You don't have to do anything else for them in the way of activities, entertainment, and so forth; and your kids will not only survive but will thrive, because they will do for you the things you are not able to take care of. You will see. When you can't, they will.

Sometimes I think this is obvious, to rest, but then I see ladies running around and realize that unless you have my voice in your head, you might not know that you can just lie down. (But if you literally can't move, you might be anemic. See number 1.)

Remember, you might not look all that pregnant, and thus you might think that people are judging you (or you might be judging yourself) for

---

[18] But as with any medication, even if prescribed by a doctor, keep an eye on how you react. Some find that the Unisom can lead to personality changes. The B6 by itself might do the trick.

feeling bad, but all the hard work of making fingers and toes is taking place right now! No wonder you can't cope!

If your other child is only eighteen months old, then it's tricky to have to check out of your daily energetic routine, but you'd be surprised how little an eighteen-month-old needs. If you are skeptical, remember this anecdote a friend once told me when I was lamenting a bout of incapacitating sickness: "Once I was so sick and no one was there to help me. I basically lay on the sofa and held out a banana. The [little] kids ran around in circles in the living room, stopping as they passed for a bite." I don't know how much lower the bar can be, so just think of that and congratulate yourself for holding it together.

Get a fence and let the kids run around outside. When people ask what you need, tell them you need a fence.

Auntie Leila hereby gives you permission to lie on the sofa for as long as you are able.

Rule 3: When you *can* do something, try to do it fast. It's better to do something really quickly and then go back to the sofa than to move slowly for a long period of time. Train yourself to visualize the fastest way to do a particular task, and then do it that way. A sweet reader with severe morning sickness to whom I wrote this thought commented:

> Thank you so much for that advice. It was actually more helpful than you may realize because I can be a sort of "slow to get moving" type of girl. The reminder to work quickly when able is most applicable.

Rule 4: Familiarize yourself with Plain Cooking. When you are able, just cook the food. Do not Pinterest it, do not "Julia Child" it.

Everything is fine with butter and salt.

Cooked meat lasts a couple of days in the fridge and cooked vegetables last for longer than that (but fresh ones don't, so better to cook them).

Boil or bake potatoes. Heck, microwave them. I laughed when I saw a *New York Times* article about "the right way to bake a potato." There is literally nothing easier than baking a potato. Turn oven on. Put potatoes in (you don't even need a pan!). Bake. Place on plate. Cut open. Add butter and salt.

Yes, there are entire cookbooks for how make chicken breasts interesting. But you can also get a pan, melt butter in it, throw the breasts in, and cook them. Salt and eat.

Roast a whole chicken. Just salt it and put it in a medium oven. Roast it for 15 minutes per pound. Take it out. Hack pieces off it. Put it in the fridge. Take it out. Hack more pieces off it. Repeat until nothing is left. If you can muster the energy, throw the carcass in a pot, cover it with water, and make stock.

Put chuck roasts and pork shoulders in the slow cooker (respectively) with some tomato paste and dried onion and salt. You don't need to add water to the pork. You can add a cup or two of water, wine, or broth to the beef. Cook until the meat is tender, six hours or so. If it's not tender, cook it some more. If you can't open a can of tomato paste, don't worry. It will be fine.

Get pork chops. Melt butter in a pan. Brown the chops on one side. Turn them over. Salt. Cover and cook on low heat for 8 minutes (depending on the thickness, more or less). Eat.

Sometimes you need to know that you can open a jar of sauce. Boil pasta. Brown ground beef and add salt. Open jar of tomato sauce (store brand is fine). Pour over the beef. Heat the mixture, and pour it over the pasta. Serve with parmesan cheese or even grated cheddar.

Brown ground beef. Add dried minced onion and salt. Serve over potatoes. Put a dollop of sour cream on top if you want to be fancy. Or put it in a tortilla. Anyone who can open the fridge can get some things to add to that.

Truly, a child can do any of these things. You have only to tell him about washing his hands and the counters with soap. If your child is too young, even your hard-working husband can take ten minutes and do them. If necessary, you can give directions from the sofa.

Just think "meat, starch, vegetable, bread." If all else fails, bread and cheese.

To get slightly more complicated in case the fog clears or someone is there to help:

- BBQ sandwiches with the cooked meat: leftover braised (as above, in the slow cooker) meat, BBQ sauce, rolls
- Ground beef, BBQ sauce, potatoes
- Cooked pork (pulled apart), BBQ sauce, rice

Get the bottled BBQ sauce that is made with sugar, not high-fructose corn syrup. Always have some of that handy, along with bulky rolls in the freezer.

Make a pot of rice and put your cooked meat and vegetables on top, and tell a child to get the soy sauce.

Get a ham (have your husband pick it up for you—one with a bone, pre-sliced or not, but not sweetened), bake it at 325 degrees in a pan with sides. In the same oven, put sweet potatoes on a baking tray lined with foil. (Do not omit the foil, because we don't want you scrubbing pans.)

After two hours, take the ham out, turn the oven up to 425 degrees, and continue to cook the sweet potatoes until they ooze sugar, about another half hour. Boil some green beans.

Open the sweet potatoes and serve them with butter and salt. Once you taste roasted sweet potatoes, you will love them. I literally made it through childhood without eating one green item, thanks to sweet potatoes.

Have a kid take the peels off any leftover sweet potatoes and put the flesh in a container in the fridge. This can be quickly reheated in a bowl or by frying it up in a pan with eggs.

Another day, have ham sandwiches—just bread, butter, and ham, fruit or pickles, and chips on the side.

Another day, soup made with the ham bone—pea soup couldn't be easier. Throw the peas with the bone into the slow cooker, add dried minced onion, and two quarts of water. If you feel fancy or have a child who can help, cut up a carrot and one stalk of celery to add to the pot. Add salt at the end.

Another day, cook some pasta, and add the ham and green beans to the cooked pasta with butter and cheese.

In your pantry you need dried minced onions and dried garlic powder. You can add some of those to whatever you're cooking plainly.

If the defcon level can be downgraded:

Put that chicken carcass that's been picked clean in a pot. Throw in dried onion flakes. Add water, and boil. Strain. Cook noodles in it, maybe a chopped carrot (cook the carrot pieces before the noodles). Shake some dried parsley in.) There you go. Lots of bread and butter.

Caesar salad: send someone out for a big package of Romaine lettuce, parmesan cheese, anchovies (really—you might find you crave anchovies), and Italian bread. They could break Auntie Leila's rule this once and buy Caesar salad dressing, although it's just oil, vinegar, mustard, salt, and garlic (we'll leave the egg yolk out of it for now). Put the leftover chicken next to this salad, and you're good to go.

The main thing is to use your limited cooking time well. If you can do it, cook as big a roast or as many chicken parts as you can manage so that you can put some in the freezer. Have plenty of ziplock freezer bags on hand to make this as easy as possible.

Make a big pot of pasta, and toss it with olive oil. You can have many meals that are pasta, cheese, pieces of meat, and vegetables. All of that has been in your fridge; just microwave it. The same can be done with potatoes or rice.

Don't worry, you will get through this. Someday you will cook with recipes again. For now, just aim to have some cooked food on the table.

Tips for Quelling the Nausea

I realize that so far I've suggested liver and anchovies, but if you are still with me, this advice could help:

Eat whatever you can eat. If that means pastries or ice cream or cheeseburgers or salted nuts, that's what you should eat. You need calories. Don't try to choke something down if you have an aversion to it. We women have been conditioned to cling to the notion of salad as our one healthy option, but salad might not be for you right now. (I suspect that we shouldn't fight an aversion to salad, as raw greens can harbor bacteria that can be quite dangerous when you're vulnerable.)

Try eating before lifting your head up off the pillow. Ask your husband to bring your snack right to you, handing it to you so you can eat while prone.

A cooler by your bed or even a dorm-sized refrigerator in your room might be just the ticket during this time.

Try to eat something with protein if you can. Yes, salty crackers can help, but you need quickly to follow up with (or go straight to) cheese, yogurt, pieces of cooked meat, or nuts. You might be able to eat a sharp, salty cheese like feta.

Eat and drink at frequent intervals. Your aim is to keep your blood sugar level even. Drinking a lot of water is vital. Think of it this way: the reason you feel terrible is that hormones are coursing through your body so that Baby will grow. (You may also get headaches for the same reason.) You need a good fluids balance to have the hormones at the proper levels. If ever you were going to aim to increase your water consumption, now is that time.

Sometimes water doesn't seem to fit the bill. I always drank quantities of homemade iced tea, even knowing that experts frown on caffeine for pregnant women; however, I frown on pregnant women getting dehydrated. Some ladies like the bubbles of seltzer with a little juice in it. It's more important to drink a good amount than to fret over what it is that you are drinking. I would only say, avoid diet sodas because artificial sweeteners are really poison (my husband wrote a book about them!)—and aspartame is the worst of them all, affecting the kidneys and crossing the brain blood barrier. If real ginger ale is too pricey or strong for you, try cutting it with seltzer.

If you can, try to avoid sugars (although I stand by eating what you are able to eat when things are dire). Fats are good. You're aiming at a balance so that your insulin is steady. *Eat at the times of day when you feel less sick.* Set a timer if necessary, because you might be tempted to use your less-sick hours to power through, when what you need to do is eat something during that phase.

Try not to smell the things. This makes the crockpot a bit trickier, I realize, although the advantage is that you can put it out in the garage or on the deck while the food is cooking.

On the other hand, Deirdre suggests sniffing a cut lemon; it has helped her. I found that sniffing a tea bag helped me. Mint works wonders for some. You can keep it in herb, lozenge, or tea form.

Sometimes you can eat something if someone just puts it in front of you. Don't say you can't eat it until you really know for sure. Thinking about it might be worse than eating it. The time I was sickest, I couldn't stand to hear the words "ham," "broccoli," or "cheese sauce," but when handed a plate of just that, I could eat it. Whatever is the thing you can most see yourself eating, just serve that as simply as possible or ask to have it served to you.

Magnesium and vitamin D really help with feeling better, and magnesium is best absorbed through the skin. A foot bath or actual bath with Epsom salts is soothing and delivers the magnesium—far better than in pill form. You can get a big bag of Epsom salts at the drugstore.

Taking cod liver oil can help with the vitamin D. Yes, this is a two-edged sword for sure, and there are capsules. The issue is burping. Deirdre suggests taking it before bed so you are asleep when you burp!

Sometimes nausea is actually from acid reflux, so try to get that under control. Relieve constipation (the sweet potatoes really help with that, as do flax and dates, which you should be eating anyway for your labor). Try Tums or Zantac. Nausea can also be due to low acid, so taking an apple cider vinegar drink or lemonade can help—if you are craving lemonade and it helps, then go with that.

There's still Defcon 2—walking around with a little suitcase containing IV fluids. This is so hard. Please rest and be cared for. I don't know what to say, other than maybe look at the tips above and see if you can manage them or pass them to your husband.

And Defcon 1—hospitalization: Auntie Leila is so sorry and has even less to tell you, other than to direct your husband to this chapter, which will also help anyone who isn't able to be very handy around the kitchen, even if not pregnant. (Hence, the "more" in the title of this chapter. It's just good to remember, for lots of dire circumstances, that you—or someone else—can keep it simple.)

A possibly consoling thought, when anxiety about the rest of your family is making things worse: A friend who does get morning sickness told me recently about a real upside to her most recent pregnancy, and this relates to meal planning directly. She decided she just had to keep it simple and not cater to her other children's pickiness (they were all under six at the time)—because she just could not. She got what she could on the table and that was that, and it was usually the same thing many days in a row.

And you know what? Her children became very hearty eaters!

If none of this helps, let it go, just let it slide. What helps one mom might not help you, and vice versa.

Please join or form a St. Gregory Pocket as soon as you can (I say more about this in volume 1). We all need a community to help us through these times. We can't do it on our own. When you've been through it, you know what to do—which is more than I can say for most people. Be there to help others, and they will help you.

In any case, everyone has his fight to fight, and I want you to know that we all have those times when things fall apart. Do your best, and know that God sees you and loves you. Sometimes I think that we have these times in our lives so that we learn humility and that we aren't meant to be "perfect." How else will we ever empathize with anyone?

Work fast when you can; do the minimum; stock up on good videos and books for the kids. Remember that offering up your suffering is the way God asks us to be united with Him. It isn't wasted—you will never know until you get to Heaven how your lonely, silent suffering helps others. But it does.

APPENDIX C

Bland-Diet Tray Meals

A big part of being a Mom is knowing how to take care of a sick person with love and skill. I think that training in nursing should be required of all women, just as home economics used to be. We need both. Now we don't have anything, and so we have a book like this one.

Early on in my mothering path, of course one of my little ones got sick. I checked with the pediatrician, and he said, "It's the flu. Plenty of liquids and keep him on a bland diet. Call me tomorrow."

So I called him the next day, and he asked, "What did he eat?"

"Spaghetti with tomato sauce and cheese," says I. That honestly seemed bland to me!

"WHAT!" Yes, he was shouting. "What have you done to me!" Yes, that's what he said! What have you done to *me*?

Okay, then, what *is* a bland diet? I asked, and I got an answer, which I put together in the following section. I printed it out and keep it taped to the inside back cover of my personal menu and recipe binder. If you have someone who needs to stick with this sort of regimen, it's useful to have the information written out where you can refer to it as long as you need to.

When Mr. Lawler and I were first married, we didn't have a dining room table. We ate our meals off trays. I still have those trays, almost thirty years later! They have certainly saved the day for feeding sick people: you can't help feeling better when your meal comes on a tray.

The Bland Diet

Bland diet: What to eat when you (or someone you love) have an upset stomach, vomiting, diarrhea, the flu, or the doctor says, "Put him on a bland diet."

Sometimes someone is sick, and he knows what he does and does not want to eat. My experience as "field nurse" to my crew is that there are certain stomach bugs that must be treated very carefully or getting over them will take so long that the risk of dehydration becomes real. When the stomach just can't take anything at all, here are some things you can do.

If *nothing* is tolerated, try giving *nothing* for a few hours, up to six. The stomach needs to rest completely. Keep a sharp eye out for the signs of dehydration, in which case you need to go to the hospital for IV fluids. You can ask the doctor if you are not sure.

If it's possible to give something, try the suggestions on the following page (we placed this list so that it's easy to make a copy of it to keep inside your cabinet door or in your food binder).

Bland Diet

During the Crisis, for Hydration

Give liquids by the spoonful, slowly (every five minutes or so), cutting back if it's not tolerated. Don't give plain water, as it doesn't sit as well as something a little sweet; don't give food, other than a plain saltine if it can be tolerated.

- Black tea with sugar and no milk
- Peppermint tea
- Ginger ale (be aware that big-name brands don't actually have ginger in them, but do have high-fructose corn syrup. Consider stocking up on real cane-sugar soda with real ginger during the flu season.)
- Diluted juice
- Popsicles

During the Recovery

- No fats
- No dairy
- No raw vegetables or fruits
- No beans, seeds, dried fruits, or other high-fiber foods
- No spices
- Soft-boiled egg
- Poached egg
- Very ripe banana
- Applesauce
- Toast—no butter, but honey or jelly is okay
- Saltines, not Ritz (too oily)
- Beef broth (be aware of the non-nutritional nature of canned beef broth, as well as the MSG, and maybe keep some homemade stock in the freezer)
- Plain chicken breast
- Chicken noodle soup
- Chicken rice soup (use white rice)
- Rice (salt, and a tiny amount of butter can be tolerated after a bit)
- Mashed potatoes (without milk—mash with potato water and salt)
- Popsicles
- Apple juice mixed with water
- Black "real" tea—sugar, no milk
- Peppermint tea
- Ginger ale
- Tonic (not for pregnant ladies as contains quinine—but good for malaria, I suppose)

Introduce dairy slowly in the form of plain yogurt sweetened with a little jam or honey. (Ice cream is usually well tolerated, at least by our family!)

APPENDIX D

How to Patch Jeans

I have been a mother for decades and decades. I have three of the male sex and four of the female. Can you imagine how many jeans we have had? Can you further imagine how many holes in the knees we have had? Many.

It's hard to describe to someone who hasn't been through the exigencies of providing that many children with clothing on a tight budget just how defeating, and yet how very common an occurrence, it is when a child puts a hole in his jeans. The jeans themselves might have cost you very little (other than the "human toll" of hours spent in a thrift store with babies in tow, careful labeling of boxes in the attic, and reassuring of wary youths that the style and cut of the garment are correct). But replacing a particular pair of jeans at a particular time is heartbreakingly dear.

(A digression regarding jeans that are sold "distressed" and full of holes. How insulting they are to those of us who need clothing that will look presentable for as long as possible and to the original jeans wearers: thrifty people who have holes in their clothes because they are actually doing hard work that would kill a fancy designer outright. I can't stand the thought of handing over good money for such a thing. How the designers must be scorning us all the way to the bank! How stupid they must think we are!)

In all those years with all those hole-producing children, I never really figured out how to patch jeans. I've done them by hand, I've used iron-on patches (most unsatisfactory), and I've just let the children run around being all "holy."

Honestly, my "solution"—and it's not a bad one—was that, for many years, I rarely bought the boys a pair of shorts. In the spring, I just took whatever pants they had, cut the bottoms of the legs off, and hemmed them! Either the pants had holes in the knees or were going to be too worn out (thus un-pass-down-able) the following year anyway.

But finally, in the twilight of my mothering career, I have figured out how to put a stinkin' patch on a pair of jeans.

Patch Fabric

You could use any pretty or handsome, sturdy fabric for a patch. Cut two pieces the same size, allowing extra for ironing under the edges for a neat look. Putting a patch right across the width of the leg (rather than making one to cover just the hole or the worn part) will alleviate centering issues. Just scoot the folded-under edge of the patch right up to the unopened seam. You should probably do both knees, even if the hole is in just one.

You can also keep some old denim around (either cut up a pair of jeans that are truly dead, or pick up a random pair in the same color denim at the thrift store clearance; you might as well get an extra-large pair and cut it into pieces as large as you can for your repair stash). Rather than making a bulky patch by turning under the edge, just use a more solid stitching to finish off the raw edge. It will take a bit longer, but it will be worth it for comfort.

The Trick for a Durable Patch

The trick is to patching jeans is to break down and open up the seam that isn't double-stitched—the seam on the outside of the leg. Using your seam ripper and scissors, open up the seam a good eight inches or more beside the knee. It will have another seam under it, the one that finishes the raw edge inside, so yes, it's a little tedious. Sometimes, once you have made an opening, you can just rip it. But don't rip the fabric!

Now you will be able to sew on your patch. Using that now open seam, you will be able to sew not only the verticals of the patch, but also the horizontals! This is what was keeping me from sturdily patching the jeans on the machine, the fact that there is no way to maneuver the foot to sew parallel to the hem.

Use a setting on your machine that will give you a durable double-stitch, or, if your machine is super basic, do a close zigzag. It won't take but a moment to sew up the seam you opened, simply by turning the pants inside out and pulling them flat. Just stitch on the line left by the original stitches.

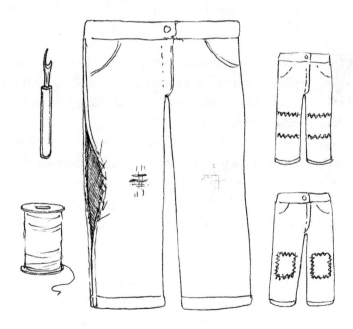

Visible Mending, a Satisfying Way to Make Do

I'd probably need another volume to do justice to the idea of mending, patching, and generally making do with household objects, but I thought maybe a little example would convey a great deal, as well as being amusing.

So many times I was ready to throw away an Icelandic wool blanket; they were all the fashion in the seventies when my mother very kindly gave me this one as a Christmas gift when I was a teenager. Some years later, when it was in use on my own child's bed, our dog ripped a hole in it.

I wavered: I shouldn't keep something that has a big hole in it, but I didn't want to ditch it either, because it was of such good quality. But there was a *big hole* in it.

Finally I figured out what to do. I cut a patch from another blanket that *was* pitch-worthy (it was fairly moth-eaten) to make this patch, thinking that the path to keeping the Icelandic one was to embrace the hole.

I patched both sides with a blanket stitch, using yarn. For the inner sewing, I cut what had been a jagged tear into a neat circle.

I'm glad, because if I had ever seen someone else's story of this kind of patch, I would have been mad at myself for throwing a good blanket away.

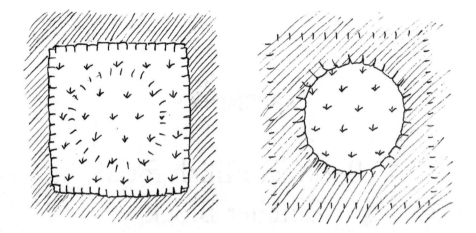

APPENDIX F

Beeswax Finish for a Butcher Block

Here is how to finish a butcher block that you plan to use *as* a butcher block, as well as a cutting board or a tabletop. I use it on my coffee table. You will need beeswax[19] and a food-grade oil. I prefer mineral oil because vegetable oils become rancid after time and some more stable oils are not food grade (but would work fine if your board is not coming into contact with food, of course).

Melt the oil and the beeswax together in a jar, in a ratio of about four parts oil to one part wax. (This sounds precise but is actually guesswork. Do the mysteriously knowledgeable people whose directions one follows mean parts by weight? Volume? I used volume.) To melt them, heat water in a small slow cooker or pot, and place the jar in the water. Stir the oil and beeswax with a wooden skewer or spoon (which will then be nicely

---

[19] We now have our own beeswax because we keep bees, but it's easy enough to order. It's an amazing substance and well worth owning. You won't need much; you can even use stray beeswax candles that may not look as fresh as when you got them. Simply melt, strain, and use according to my directions.

waxed) until the beeswax melts and the whole mixture becomes as one. (I tell you these details in case you are like me and would really like to know.)

As the hot mixture cools, it will become a thick paste that can be stored indefinitely. To apply it to your wood, warm up the jar in the same way, in simmering water. Meanwhile, prepare the wood surface by wiping some of the plain mineral oil on it; using a clean rag, rub it in, letting it soak in for a few minutes, and then rub off the excess. Using the same rag, rub on your warm beeswax paste. After applying the paste, let it cool and then buff it with another clean cloth. These processes (rubbing on oil, then oil and wax paste) may be repeated as needed, and you can store the original rag right in the jar of paste so as not to waste any of it.

INDEX

ILLUSTRATOR'S NOTE

The illustrations for this work were drawn from life, from imagination, and, in the case of a few images, from photos or other reference images. They were rendered first in pencil on drawing paper and then redrawn with either Staedtler or Micron pen.

Some of the domestic scenes were captured in the home of our friend Therese Cross, to whom I express my gratitude for welcoming me for an afternoon of perching myself around her charming home with my drawing pad for this purpose.

My husband, artist John H. Folley, patiently provided consultation and image scanning and editing, as well as nigh-solo parenting of four little ones during my all-intensive week of work on this project.

My thanks to my mother, the author, for entrusting another work to me for visualization, enabling me to pursue my humble vision, and for continuing to tolerate my art supplies strewn around the house. Faithful readers of hers will recognize vignettes of her home in many of these drawings.

My gratitude extends also to Sophia Institute Press and Carolyn McKinney for their accommodating and respectful partnership.

I dedicate these illustrations in loving memory of my grandmother, Elizabeth Day Edwards, who taught me how to draw.

—Deirdre M. Folley

ABOUT THE AUTHOR

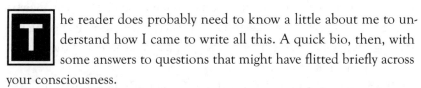he reader does probably need to know a little about me to understand how I came to write all this. A quick bio, then, with some answers to questions that might have flitted briefly across your consciousness.

My name is pronounced "Lye-la"; "Lay-la" is also fine, as it's the Arabic way. Without intending it, my Egyptian father and (mostly) Welsh-background American mother chose the one name that the two cultures have in common. It's also my Egyptian grandmother's name.

I'm the only child of parents who divorced when I was three; wife of Phil, who is American (Irish, and a little German), mother of seven children, grandmother of sixteen with, God willing, more to come.

I'm a convert to Catholicism from vague secular humanism, with a brief, completely uninformed and unconvincing stop as Muslim, sometime in middle school when I was desperately seeking a spiritual home and thought I could find it in the cultural milieu of my father (who was himself agnostic, an appreciator of the good things in life, and a solver of problems, good engineer that he was).

My childhood took place during the upheavals of the sixties and their aftermath; feminists were calling the shots by the time I was in high school. My father had come to this country to do graduate work in the field of engineering. He held academic life in the highest regard. Many are not aware that upper-class women in Egypt had by that time entered professional life, having benefited from Western-style secondary education. My father definitely had the highest expectations for my career.

My father had come to the United States by way of Hungary, where he worked as an engineer in the railways on behalf of Egypt. His experience in Hungary convinced him that communism was terrible and that no one should ever be subject to that system, which he simply described as a police state.

My mother, though rebellious in her personal life when I was young (she later became a devout Catholic), through her reading had become staunchly antitotalitarian. The books and magazines at home (with her) ranged from texts elucidating the most extreme versions of psychoanalysis to the best, most energetic defenses of Western civilization (exposing the ideological flaws of the former category). I also had access to the classics of child and adult literature.

My voracious reading habit led me to the Catholic Church. In high school I met my future husband, who is ten years older than I. He was a journalist working in the same office as my mother, and he had a decisive influence on my life. (I tell a lot of this story in an episode of *The Journey Home* with Marcus Grodi.) And though I had a long road to travel to learn what virtue is and how to get it, I knew in my heart that I wanted to make a home with Phil—that I didn't want a career.

I was nineteen when we married. Being a young wife from a confused background during the early feminist years, in a city where the women my age were definitely *not* getting married and having children, I was isolated and incompetent at what I set out to do. I simply had no skills and no share in the collective memory that had sustained those who had gone before me.

I call how I got from there to here "the journey of a girl who didn't know how to sweep the floor," and I wrote a good deal of what I learned on that journey first on my blog, *Like Mother, Like Daughter*, and then here in this book. My hope and prayer is that it will benefit you in some way, dear reader.

Sophia Institute

Sophia Institute is a nonprofit institution that seeks to nurture the spiritual, moral, and cultural life of souls and to spread the gospel of Christ in conformity with the authentic teachings of the Roman Catholic Church.

Sophia Institute Press fulfills this mission by offering translations, reprints, and new publications that afford readers a rich source of the enduring wisdom of mankind.

Sophia Institute also operates the popular online resource Catholic-Exchange.com. *Catholic Exchange* provides world news from a Catholic perspective as well as daily devotionals and articles that will help readers to grow in holiness and live a life consistent with the teachings of the Church.

In 2013, Sophia Institute launched Sophia Institute for Teachers to renew and rebuild Catholic culture through service to Catholic education. With the goal of nurturing the spiritual, moral, and cultural life of souls, and an abiding respect for the role and work of teachers, we strive to provide materials and programs that are at once enlightening to the mind and ennobling to the heart; faithful and complete, as well as useful and practical.

Sophia Institute gratefully recognizes the Solidarity Association for preserving and encouraging the growth of our apostolate over the course of many years. Without their generous and timely support, this book would not be in your hands.

www.SophiaInstitute.com
www.CatholicExchange.com
www.SophiaInstituteforTeachers.org

Sophia Institute Press® is a registered trademark of Sophia Institute.
Sophia Institute is a tax-exempt institution as defined by the
Internal Revenue Code, Section 501(c)(3). Tax ID 22-2548708.

THE SUMMA DOMESTICA

THE
SUMMA
DOMESTICA

Order and Wonder in Family Life

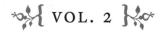 VOL. 2

Education

LEILA M. LAWLER

Illustrations by Deirdre M. Folley

SOPHIA INSTITUTE PRESS
Manchester, New Hampshire

Sophia Institute Press
Box 5284, Manchester, NH 03108
1-800-888-9344

www.SophiaInstitute.com

Sophia Institute Press® is a registered trademark of Sophia Institute.

paperback ISBN 978-1-64413-395-8

ebook ISBN 978-1-64413-396-5

Library of Congress Control Number: 2021940523

First printing

CONTENTS

THE SUMMA DOMESTICA

PART 1

On Family Culture
and "a Thinking Love"

If we look at it a certain way, all the details of the life of man on earth are concerned with the one challenge of preparing children to take their place in the world and in our heavenly home. I suppose first of all we ourselves have to remain alive. But once that pressing issue has been addressed, everything else centers on passing along all that we know to our children; on the necessary task of creating a society so ordered that each generation isn't faced with the same elemental urgencies of mere survival but can build on what exists with what it has learned—for the benefit of the next generation. When a society ceases to be primarily oriented to looking forward in this way, it's a sign that it has lost hope—that its narcissism has resulted in a dwindling supply of children to keep its attention.

"How Do I Educate My Children?"

And what is demanded of her is—a thinking love.... God has given to the child all the faculties of our nature, but the grand point remains undecided—how shall this heart, this head, these hands be employed? to whose service shall they be dedicated? A question the answer to which involves a futurity of happiness or misery to a life so dear to thee. Maternal love is the first agent in education.

We are waking up to our duties and in proportion as mothers become more highly educated and efficient, they will doubt-less feel the more strongly that the education of their children during the first six years of life is an undertaking hardly to be entrusted to any hands but their own. And they will take it up as their profession—that is, with the diligence, regularity, and punctuality which men bestow on their professional labours.

— CHARLOTTE MASON, "SOME PRELIMINARY CONSIDERATIONS," *HOME EDUCATION*

I started writing on my blog in order to try to convey what I call the remote preparation needed to undertake the task. For me, far more important than "What curriculum do I choose?" is "How can I be living the kind of life that offers an environment in which a child can develop according to his nature?"—and my answers to the second question will always be detailed instructions on matters that seem to have nothing to do with the first question.

I told the story in volume 1 about how I stumbled on the vision of Order and Wonder to answer a rather casual question about curriculum, for who can enumerate the answers in a polite conversation with another mom at dance class? There are so many plies that must be wrapped together to form the strong strand of education for a child. Yet this was my situation, time and again—making the attempt on the fly.

The chance to write out my thoughts was my motivation to begin the blog, which then became the basis for this very volume you hold in your hands (along with the other two).

There is no shortage of advice on specifics of curriculum. I am not attempting to join those ranks. I am here offering an outline of organizing principles for deciding how to proceed.

On the one hand, I'm very certain that no one curriculum will fit every child. (Why, even in conventional school, there are options for the children according to their interests and abilities, yet school often feels confining enough to turn parents' thoughts to educating their children at home.)

The "curriculum" I use has always been something I've made for each child. I've resigned myself to the hard, almost insanity-inducing work of doing this—and the unavoidable conclusion that I will fail. When I look at all the resources available—and right now you could be reading any of thousands of homeschooling books, sites, and blogs—I am overwhelmed. I think, "What could anyone learn from me on this topic?"

On the other hand, I do have something to add, after all. Perhaps it's this perspective: that the question of curriculum is too narrow! I'm very certain that education, whether in school or out, can hardly be limited to this idea of curriculum. Do we even know how children learn? There is no magic (or scientific!) formula to transform the (supposedly) raw material of the young child into the fully formed educated mind we all think we can imagine.

Readers (and random interlocutors I met at my daughter's dance class) just want to know how to teach math to a fifth grader; I just want them to take a shower and sweep off the front porch and make menus so that their fifth graders will be well enough rested and fed to be able to concentrate on their math. The connection isn't obvious to everyone—but it is to me! The reader must simply realize that "family culture" will not be separated from this inquiry. So we will return to it often. Volume 3 gives you all the practical help you need.

My words are aimed at homeschoolers, but I always have in mind those who send their children to school; no matter what, the child forms his earliest and most enduring habits of the mind in the home. In our time, homeschooling is almost a necessity, and where it isn't yet, I think it will be soon.

In the ideal (or even moderately reasonable) society, homeschooling would not normally be the best option in the sense of "the most fitting to human nature." The aspects of homeschooling that I think most help a child are the ones that are also compatible with a restrained and appropriate educational system, one that respects its place as a complement to the rights and duties of parents, not a usurper of them.

Freedom to play, benignly neglected by adults, scope for self-motivation, room for daily rest and family interaction: all these characteristics had been features of the neighborhood school up until the second half of the twentieth century, when changes in family structure began to impinge on the balance between the different institutions in the culture.

We simply don't have the possibility of this kind of school today. That is why I homeschooled and why I encourage people to homeschool. Let's acknowledge the undeniable stresses of the undertaking. God sees and knows our efforts and all the difficulties, however. We should entrust the outcomes to Him.

As we go through the topic of education together, you will notice that my thoughts don't develop in a systematic way, simply because by the time I was ready to write systematically about the subject, people had already begun asking me questions about it. In true Auntie Leila fashion, I just went ahead and answered. Sometimes the answers are very specific, but I've chosen to leave them this way here.

Where I've recommended a specific site or program, I just have to hope that it still exists as you read. In any case, you will have the criteria with which to choose among the offerings that are available.

I've chosen to keep the incremental approach so that you don't despair by having too much information piled on you at once; and the truth that I will often repeat is that no one really knows how children learn. My methods here reflect that reality, or aim to, anyway!

A Little about Family Culture . . .

My one little twinge about my blog *Like Mother, Like Daughter* that has given rise to this book, is that, on account of its origins, the title is so female-centric. The idea was that when my daughters moved away, we'd be able to share our crafting and thrifting and so on with each other and anyone else who wanted to join in. In the end, it became a blog that many men read—and I like to think that we have a lot to offer them as well. I love the title even so: it made me proud when Rosie chose it.

Our family blog (which was started by Deirdre) is called *Happy Despite Them*, which is our family motto. Perhaps that name would have been better to continue with, if only so that men, especially my sons, wouldn't feel that I was excluding them from the project, which I certainly don't mean to do. I love men, and I love my man, and I love my boys, and I love my sons-in-law. And my grandsons. I love them all.

Maybe you would like to know that the motto Happy Despite Them came about in this wise:

When the older kids were little and we had time for such excursions, renting a house in the city and not having weekend chores to speak of, Phil and I went to the Scottish games that are held in Virginia in July, which, when you think about it, makes no sense. They wait until it's good and hot and humid, dress everyone in wool, specifically men in kilts, and set them to running about heaving heavy objects—which is what Scottish games are. They don't run races, they don't jump hurdles, they don't swim; they throw stone-like things, sheep-like things, and pole-like things. Presumably this is all traceable to ancient days spent among the rocks and the heather. With the sheep.

We found the whole thing endlessly amusing, from the massing of the pipes to the dog trials. We didn't even know about Scottish fiddling then, or that a Scottish fiddler was in our future (Bridget). As we left, we passed the rows of awnings under which the vendors sold their clan paraphernalia and displayed their individual tartans and, importantly for our imaginations, their family mottos. We're not Scottish, unless distantly and unbeknownst to us, but I would love to be able to claim a tartan.

But a motto! As we walked by, somewhat needing to hurry to get babies out of the hot sun after a long day, we delighted in our quick readings: "Blow Hunter Blow the Horn." "More Smooth from an Obstacle." "Fortune Is Allied to Bravery." "Beware! I Am Present." "Grip Fast."

Some are obscure: "Over Fork Over." "We Have Been." Some imply an approach to life that is not without a certain characteristically Celtic point of view, and *that* we could relate to, in defiant victim mode: "With God's Help, I Shall Conquer Envy"; "Learn to Suffer"; "Keep Silence"; "Deservedly"; "Late but in Earnest"; "I Hope for Better Things"; "Increasing Both in Sunshine and in Shade."

But there was one that struck us particularly as *almost* the right mix of hope and bitterness: "Despite Them." I kept laughing about it and marveling over the naive bravado and unconquerable determination against enemies unspecified (to us untutored passersby, at least). Who are the "them" that we carry on despite? And, hilariously, is that how you would define yourself and your progeny, once and for all?

In the car, as the children dozed, Phil and I talked about the reality for us of this motto. We felt that we also were two warriors on the craggy, inhospitable hills. We felt the rocks beneath the lovely heather all too keenly, and that is just the romantic way we would put it. We were maybe fatally willing to define ourselves, once and for all, by what we were up against. Might as well know who you are! The "despite them" was all too apt! We were well aware that we were exactly those people, the "us," going up against the "them"—who often don't make things easy for others.

We agreed that we needed a motto for our own little family. We might not belong to a clan, but we had the sense that we were founding one; we hoped we were!

Our enemies weren't visible armies arrayed against us, but rather anything that took away from our joy in what we knew was right, good, and true. We wanted to be happy about our cause, not bitter. We knew that we should ask our better selves to be not against, but *for* things, and we knew that our battle was, and is, with the negative, the not good.

Since we are both just as bitter by nature as any Scot plotting by the dwindling fire on the damp highlands, or at as least prone to seeing the dark side of things, we agreed that we had better temper things for our own sakes, and that our very own family motto should be "*Happy* Despite Them."

The "happy," which in any other family would be unpardonable, cloying sweetness, was thus a necessity for us. To be honest, *we* would certainly judge that "happy" in there as saccharine and hopelessly jejune, were the tables turned. But we also knew we needed that "happy."

We have kept to it all these years, even when we have lost sight, for a while, as everyone must, of what we were really after with it. Sometimes, in the midst of a bad, sad argument, when we knew that we were succumbing to the "them" of the motto, the dark forces that want us simply to be

unhappy, we would whisper to each other, "Happy Despite Them." And the motto fulfills its purpose at that moment.

Later, as our family grew, to raise morale we also instituted a battle cry: "Take No Prisoners!" which just means don't compromise your principles. (Did you know that the word "slogan" is from the Gaelic, meaning "battle cry"?) And then, when one of the kids (I forget which one) was apprehensively approaching exam time, Phil recalled the boot-camp routine (no, he never was in boot camp any more than he tramped on the heathery hills!) in which the sergeant asks, "What's the spirit of the bayonet?" and the recruits all yell, "Kill!" To this he responds, "I can't hear you!" and it is repeated until all the recruits are in a frenzy of aggression. This, Phil argued, was the right approach to, say, a math test.

So was born the "spirit of the test."

What's the spirit of the test? "Kill!"

It really rallies flagging students—although Suki found a certain irony in exhorting Will, as he headed off to take the emergency medical technician exam—you know, the one where you demonstrate that you can rescue victims with CPR and other life-saving techniques—to "Kill!"

Conviction was lacking. "Kill?"

So far, we do not seem to have a war dance.

What does all this have to do with education?

Well, only this. Your family isn't a system for inserting information in your children. A family has a culture, one way or another. The best culture is the one for which the parents lay the groundwork in those early days of marriage, when they have the leisure to dream about the future. The family's culture will be partly made up of what each one brings to the marriage from his or her background; it will be partly made up of what they consciously choose to do together and how they use their time.

If you think of culture as the rich nutrient source for what you wish to grow in it, you will see how decisive for the future these little episodes are; where the two, husband and wife, give their hopes and dreams shape.

In a mysterious way that I think takes many parents by surprise, children also mold the character of the family. Perhaps most parents think of their children as offshoots of themselves, understandably; but the truth is that children have their own thoughts and creative sparks. Before you know it, family life takes on a flavor no one had dreamed of before that child arrived, and all of this new life together forms family unity.

No one knows exactly how a child comes to know things. In our technocratic age, family culture is forgotten. But I maintain that it is the *greatest* factor and one well worth developing, but in a way that doesn't cause tension or stress; let it develop organically. I can only describe its formation as a calm, peaceful process borne of the love each member has for the others. Let me put it this way: at a minimum, don't think that experts can give you family culture, and don't let comparisons stifle your own development.

Choosing a family motto is my one silly example of such a moment in one family's life. There are of course, many other such events—some identifiable or memorable but most, undoubtedly, so much a part of the fabric of days that they go by practically unnoticed. It's the delight in life together that builds them into what will become each family's unique character.

So, do you want to choose a motto for your family (presuming you aren't already a Campbell—"Forget Not"—or a MacGregor—"Royal Is My Race")? You don't have to. But if you want to and need some inspiration, you can easily find lists online or in little books. Your motto may help you in times of trouble. Perhaps you will at least be amused!

To Be Happy at Home

*To be happy at home is the ultimate result of all
ambition, the end to which every enterprise and labour
tends, and of which every desire prompts the prosecution.*

**— DR. SAMUEL JOHNSON, *THE
RAMBLER*, NOVEMBER 10, 1750**

Whether you are setting up your home school or simply beginning a new school year, it is easy to feel a sense of urgency and even panic. Even if it's just September that is creeping up on you, there is that impending pressure to sign up for and do all the things or at least to feel a vague sense of moderate self-loathing if we have little to show for what we have grandiosely designated our home "school." (After all, can this enterprise we embark upon, with so little actual credentialing or official benediction behind it, no more than a quixotic ramble in unknown territory, destined to bring nothing but mockery on our heads, be called a school?)

I think of the days of yore when I was given the grace, in my folly and ignorance, to accept being alone (I mean, with my many children, but without a "support network" or "online community"—such a thing did not exist—or "outside affirmation"). I had friends, but that is a bit different from what I'm talking about here.

I was afraid of being isolated with my children. However, I discovered something that I will share with you here, something I think others experience as well.

In his book *Searching for and Maintaining Peace*, Fr. Jacques Philippe says this:

> The more our soul is peaceful and tranquil, the more God is reflected in it, the more His image expresses itself in us, the more His grace acts through us.[1]

When a mother turns toward her home, this turning requires a certain detachment from the opinions of the world and a kind of blind confidence. But if she can do it, she discovers something she may not have been looking for: she discovers peace, and as a welcome bonus, she discovers *that she can think*!

I know that my observation goes against all received wisdom about toddlers not being stimulating, about women needing to leave drudgery behind to do what really fires them up, and about the company of adults being necessary for intellectual stimulation, but the paradox is real.

Thinking happens.

A mother who turns toward her home can think about peace itself, because she is free of the pull of frantic activity. There's activity all right, but it's what she sets for herself, knowing that she can choose not to rush in accomplishing her tasks. Peace doesn't mean "no activity" or "passivity"; it does mean doing only what you are meant to do! This state is very freeing.

A mother can think about how to educate her children, and what education is, and even, astoundingly, she can read a book or two about the

---

[1] Father Jacques Philippe, *Searching for and Maintaining Peace: A Small Treatise on Peace of Heart*, trans. George and Jannic Driscoll (Boston: St. Paul Books and Media, 2002), 5.

subject. And she can even sometimes do it—educate, I mean. She can think about beauty, including ordinary beauty (such as she might bring about in her home and garden), that Roger Scruton, in one of his lectures, tells us "expresses and amplifies the human desire for settlement, for an environment in which things fit together, and people too."

When she considers how chaotic and intractable the world is, and how fickle with its honors, she can, if she gives herself a chance, make her own home a haven for others.

In discussing how to know beauty and judge it, or how to detect its absence, people I have spoken to seem to sense that beauty must go right through all our experience; it must not be confined to art (in the sense of, say, paintings), but must be present in daily life (in the sense of what we might call designing and decorating our homes, for lack of a better expression; and also in our churches and our music).

But how to know what this beauty is?

And indeed, this is the question. The way of beauty is the way that defies a systematic, almost confrontational approach that we are used to when it comes to explaining how the universe is made and the question of what God's nature is.

The trouble is that we live in an age in which we consider truth and morality to be matters that call for a program—a list that we must implement right away to get people to understand. That view has a name that I first discovered reading the essays of Michael Oakeshott. It's called rationalism—a distortion of reason, in which we deny our human nature with its bodily aspect (complete with senses!), preferring to approach things abstractly—and even mechanistically. We analyze but have lost the ability to *see* and to bring what we see into the real world.

Even when we have found the truth and live a life in relation (even though a flawed relation) to goodness, we can find that we are starving for beauty. Our children, whose imaginations need to be formed so that they can have faith (literally, "see that which they do not see"—which requires imagination)—need an education in beauty.

When a woman detaches from what consumes the world, far from losing or burying her creative skills, she can use them, with a serene heart, for those she loves in ever-widening circles, circles that ultimately include whomever she is called to reach. (Know that this woman may never be aware of whom she has reached, just as she has been touched by those she is certain had no knowledge of their influence on her.) It's true that this takes time; the results won't be immediately forthcoming and it does take confidence.

This first part of this book is meant to give you the confidence to accept your role in educating your child. The practical bit, on the schooling of children at home, starts in the second part, beginning with "On Teaching Your Child to Read."

"To Reign Is to Serve"

Devotion to home in this womanly fashion I'm speaking of is the best service, that is, reign, with *leisure to think* thrown in for good measure. In his essay "What's Wrong with the World," G. K. Chesterton says that "to the moderately poor the home is the only place of liberty." He gives us, you and I, leave to consider ourselves "moderately poor." He goes on to demonstrate that the effort to pursue wealth is exhausting, because the home, not acquisition of things, is the end or goal of "every enterprise" and "the only place of liberty."

It was at the wedding of one of our children, in conversation with a friend who was sharing the good news that he was planning to homeschool his children, that I had a moment of perspective of the sort that these grace-filled milestone events sometimes offer.

I suddenly saw that, homeschooling or not, it's worth the effort to commit, to devote yourself to the mission of building your family and beyond into the community and the culture—to do what it takes.

Life brings suffering and disappointment; there are moments when we can't imagine how these fairly intractable people we live with, with their headlong refusal to mold themselves into an approved happy family vision, and especially with all one's own faults and failings (and not to mention the world beating down on one), will come together in some sort of cohesive unity.

And then one day, by the grace of God, they do. And you do. And you are you, the collective you that you were trying to be, only at the same moment—like a wave on the sand that retreats before it quite reaches the tide line—they have their eye on another shore.

It is for this unknown land that we are offering our substance.

PART 2

On a Vision for Education

When my children materialized, I wasn't ready to consider home-schooling (although my husband was). It was all so sudden. Yet it was plain to me that I wasn't going to be able to find a school that lived up to my ideal. Of one thing I was sure: whatever our children learned, it would be more of a matter of developing their personalities and gifts, and what our family style turned out to be, than of any set method or curriculum. You too can have a vision for education in your home.

I Search for My Vision

I had been thinking about education for a long time. My mother was very interested in the "free school" movement; *Summerhill* by A. S. Neill was lying about, and I read it as an impressionable teen. Neill considered the doctrine of Original Sin to be a means for those in authority to control their subjects; he had a Rousseauian belief in the innate goodness of children that views all intervention as deformation. His school, the eponymous Summerhill, specialized in allowing the students to do what they wanted, not imposing any curriculum or requirements, academic or disciplinary (and seems to have provided an outlet for Neill's special brand of narcissism—and laziness).

Perhaps few remember Neill or Summerhill. I don't have the scholarly inclination to ascertain if he was a progenitor of the foundations of our educational system or merely one of its forgotten practitioners. As always, there is a grain of truth (as there is in every theory, no matter how fruity); the educator will succeed if he allows the child to discover what is truly meaningful to him, uniquely. Sadly, our educational establishment kept the elements of Neill's rebellion against what he considered "bourgeois mores" and jettisoned those that contained real insight into learning. Today, schools are a dreary affair that allow for neither inquiry into fundamental principles nor freedom to explore. We retain Neill's amorality but not his creativity.

When I was about seventeen, I was getting to know better the man who was to become my husband. I came across, on his coffee table, an issue of *National Review* with the reprint of the speech by Dorothy Sayers called "The Lost Tools of Learning." (I plunked myself down and read it right then and there. I don't remember if I even said hello. So you can see why he was attracted to me.) Sayers's almost nonchalant familiarity and fellowship with the distant past and classical ideas about education immediately resonated with me. (I can't imagine Sayers giving any time at all to Neill's theories.) Sayers's thesis as a historical matter might be flawed, but as an introduction to something transcending the pedagogical methods of either "free learning" or "pour information into young people's heads," it was liberating.

I began studying medieval poetry and the medieval point of view in general. My fascination was with the thought that everything is connected in an ordered way—from the pulsing of the blood in our veins to the movement of the stars.

All my (short, at that point) life I had thought in analogies, and here, in the Middle Ages, I found a whole time period that made interrelatedness its emblem, sword, and passion. Everything is an image of something else: mind encounters object (both real and imaginary) with delight and hopefulness, confident that beyond it, something even more meaningful can be found.

Sayers seemed to be talking to me—not only with a thrill about ideas from the Middle Ages, but also about my frustration with my own schooling, which seemed so slow and lacking in an interior order. She takes a seemingly modern discovery, the inner life of the child, and, with finesse and wit, illuminates it with what the medieval thinkers had already understood, stripping away false ideas about how to pass on the sheer abundance of information. Her approach is "back to basics"—where the basics are not simply facts but universal ideas and their framework; our patrimony, in essence. She doesn't argue just for great books but for an approach to learning that uses the child's own development to equip him with the ability to learn for himself.

Upon reading her lively and spirited description of the medieval method of suiting the curriculum to the development of the child's mind (and again, she may have simplified and even invented), I knew that I had to remember it until I was ready to make choices for my own children.

The process of developing a vision and sticking with it (not getting side-tracked by others' priorities if they are not resonant with the family's goals) requires remembering that each family is unique. Yes, there are common factors and shared wisdom in education. It would be foolish to scrape up every aspect of the task from scratch. But one's vision offers the organizing principle, the means of discerning what will prosper the undertaking.

Although it's wonderful that so many resources are available to parents today (in particular, the Internet itself, without which I can hardly imagine how I did anything back when I started), they can be distracting and even fatal, rather than helpful, if parents lose confidence that the education of their own children is central to their marriage—and grace will not be lacking.

If you are always looking over your shoulder at what others are doing, you'll never get anywhere, and the most detrimental effect comes from the influence of the overachieving parent who puts a premium on the appearance of activity and results. The wise parent, on the other hand, knows that a show of effort on the part of Mom hardly ever reaps progress on the part of little Jane. On the contrary, you might say there is an inverse relationship: little Jane often knows, at some elemental level, not only that need she not respond when the parental whirlwind is in full force but that the whirlwind will whirl all the more the less she does, causing a net loss in educational value.

Parents who provide an environment of order and wonder, of attention to the hierarchy of things as well as of the child's capacity for awe—and then step back—get the best out of their children, although keep in mind, no one really knows what the deep, internal, mysterious process is that produces a person in love with the pursuit of knowledge, wisdom, and understanding. It's the whole "you can lead a horse to water" question. This is not to detract from the benefit of a strong teacher, a well-thought-out course, or a logical curriculum, but it's well to remember that you just never know when a child will catch fire, or even when something is smoldering within him, invisible to the naked eye—or when he will be impervious to the most imaginative instruction.

I don't like the continual comparison that goes on between homeschoolers (I fell prey to it too and have found myself often in a state of panic over someone else's choices, even now that I'm finished) for these reasons; but that's not to say that good examples can't be found. Usually they are parents who find the balance of providing opportunities and allowing freedom.

One of the first books I read was *Homeschooling for Excellence*—an interesting account of a family who sent their boys to Harvard after keeping them busy homesteading in California. (You can probably get it at the library.) If you read between the lines (armed with your knowledge of how you would report on your homeschooling if you were also homesteading), you realize that the authors, the Colfaxes, did very little in the way of formal schooling or providing a curriculum. I think they, in classic retrospective form, vastly overstate the formality of what they did, as informal as it seems to the reader. It was probably in reality much less than how it seems in their presentation. This is something to think about, because they sent their son to Harvard when homeschooling was a relative unknown.

But they themselves were educated; they provided meaningful work for their children; they clearly passed on to their children their passion for excellence in general; and in addition, they took advantage of the rarity of their experience to capture the attention of the Harvard admissions committee.

Excellence is not a quality you can package. But there are different kinds of excellence, and each family can find its unique path to this sought-after state. As for academic excellence, it pays to listen to those who possess it. By this, I mean, be sure that you take advice from people who are educated, not just in the business of selling education. Don't take advice from people who haven't run the race. I warn against books and sites written by homeschoolers whose children haven't yet gone to high school, much less college or on to a career; yet they abound.

In the following chapter I will offer some thoughts on educators whose ideas and experience I found seminal.

Educational Moonshine;
or, a Reading List

I'm extremely good at reading about doing a thing rather than doing it. I have figured out, however, how to turn my corn of laziness into the white lightning, however raw, of educational conversation. So it is with a truly refined humility that I humbly submit and have been submitting and will continue to submit my distillations—my moonshine, if you will—on the topic of education. These thoughts apply to any child, no matter where his education takes place—at home or at school. Even a child at school needs a home where he can think, converse, and rest.

My thoughts are about how a child learns; and everyone has an approach. Your approach or the approach of the school together with your approach, will determine the success of the endeavor. How we define success is part of the approach as well.

A partial reading list (to add to the items mentioned above) is as follows:

John Holt, *How Children Learn*

John Henry Newman, *The Idea of a University* (he has a section about elementary education too!)

John Senior, *The Restoration of Christian Culture*

James Schall, *Another Sort of Learning*

Charlotte Mason, the Original Homeschooling series

William Kilpatrick, *Why Johnny Can't Tell Right from Wrong: And What We Can Do about It*

David Hicks, *Norms and Nobility: A Treatise on Education*

Of course, there are many more, including the stories of those who educated themselves, such as Ben Franklin and Booker T. Washington.

Now, sometimes people can't get through even some of this reading before they have to make decisions on their children's education. And sometimes it all seems a little abstract when brought to bear on the issue of how to get this particular batch of children educated. Believe me, I know the difference between, say, Mason's ideal of sweet walks in the English countryside conversing about the Battle of Hastings, and the reality of . . . of . . . well, you know. All these people.

Try the article "Against School," by John Taylor Gatto; it's not long. Gatto was a longtime public-school teacher, talking about secondary-school education in our time. His thoughts provide excellent perspective for comparing efforts at home to what we imagine school to be. In this essay (focusing on secondary school), he exposes the immense educational system that insists that each child should be educated in a certain way, to a arrive at a certain point, one that coincides with society's perceived need for docile workers in management positions.

Gatto's book *Underground History of American Education* helps the reader see the big picture of education. The best chapter is the one in which he recounts his childhood in Western Pennsylvania. It's an important slice of American life, evocative of a time and place that should not be forgotten. (Anthony Esolen has written about similar experiences growing up in the same general area.) As you read, ask yourself how much texture your own children have in their lives. How much freedom? Can they roam? Are there busy adults doing useful things with whom they can interact? What can we do to replicate this almost charmed (yet to be sure, somewhat gritty and not particularly prosperous) way of life?

I often have a conversation with someone in which she will tell me that she is so frustrated with a particular child of hers. And she will tell me that although she and her husband have sent this child to the very best school with the nicest teachers and the most clever books (or, contrariwise, they have put together the most well crafted curriculum that a home school has ever known), this child is just *not getting it*.

She will ask me:

"What should I do if he just drags in math?"

"What about writing! I just can't get her to write!"

"He stares at the wall!"

"She won't sit still!"

Of course, we all want our children not only to be educated, but to be well rounded, fulfilled, expressive, and creative. And we want them to excel. And we want all that *now*. But you have to understand something: School as we know it was made by people who specialize in putting things into boxes and selling them. And this is what Gatto is trying to say. Oh, here and there you find an amazing teacher. Gatto was one himself and won awards for his excellence.

And many children do fairly well—fairly, especially if we don't count the opportunity cost—with what they have to deal with. I would say that 80 percent of the children are going to be not completely, fatally harmed in what we think of as a normal American public school (although since writing this almost ten years ago, I think the odds have gotten significantly lower that harm will not be done).

But we all muddle along, which accounts for the fact that school, which is intent on producing a product (a child who can fit into society, conceived as a productive machine), isn't simply scrapped and why most curricula you buy will be more or less fine for most of your kids. And this is why you yourself probably did okay in school, although I bet if we really talked about it, you would agree that you wasted a lot of time, or maybe didn't get to study what you wanted to, or maybe see now that you learned a lot from people who had nothing to do with your school.

So that 80 percent use a lot of energy to get through a system that doesn't really suit them, but once they are done with it, they can go on either to do what they really want to do, and I think only a few succeed, or they acquiesce to fulfilling the goal stated by Ellwood P. Cubberley, dean of Stanford's School of Education, as Gatto tells us: "He had written the following in the 1922 edition of his [text]book *Public School Administration*: 'Our schools are ... factories in which the raw products (children) are to be shaped and fashioned.... And it is the business of the school to build its pupils according to the specifications laid down.'"

Of the remaining 20 percent of the children, let's say 10 percent (and I haven't done a study, but I'm just saying) will be frustrated to the point that their behavior will appear self-destructive because they *get it already* and their time is being wasted; and 10 percent will be truly ground into the dust because they learn in a completely different way from the other 90 percent, and anyway, they don't want to learn what you want them to learn because they have something else they simply must do. (In situations where the children don't have the advantage of an intact family and parents keenly interested in their academic performance, these margins are, of course, much larger.)

And why shouldn't or wouldn't your child be one of these less compliant ones?

The reason I tell parents to read Gatto isn't that I'm railing against public schools. They are so self-evidently a propaganda machine as well as an incredibly inefficient way to spend money that I can't believe we are still trying to fix this system. It doesn't matter. Pretty soon people are just going to do the darn cost-benefit analysis and realize they are on the wrong end of things.

I'm trying to get you to see, or encourage and support you if you do already see, that people grow up needing a rich experience of life on many levels without being hampered by an aggressive system aimed at conformity, and I think Gatto expresses that very well.

Children need the freedom that learning according to the Trivium brings (as Dorothy Sayers explains in her essay "The Lost Tools of Learning"). This freedom allows them to discover their own paths.

In essence, I like reading Gatto because he reminds me to be humble before the true process of real learning, a process that we quite underestimate; and having underestimated it, we then expend vast amounts of money, energy, and other resources trying otherwise to repackage it so that we can feel in control. If we had the guts, we could save ourselves a lot of trouble.

I often recommend that parents read the articles on the Arthur Robinson curriculum site (RobinsonCurriculum.com). Academically he is as strong as they come (in science), and his children have excelled in academe. Robinson has a compelling story. It helps us see our mistake when we don't notice immediate results or when we assume that all knowledge will enter our children's minds by a path that goes through ours—which, when you think about it, is foolish and arrogant. Robinson knew what he wanted to do, and he did it, despite the obstacle of his wife's having passed away when the youngest of their six children was only a baby.

If you are struggling with thoughts of how your children seem to lag or how long it takes them to do the simplest tasks, read his articles. It's a bit of tough love for the spoiled homeschooler, and I find it really helps to put things into perspective. He emphasizes using a simple curriculum and fostering the child's sense of responsibility for his own education (which the parent has chosen).

Disclaimer: I don't endorse Robinson's sect or political responses. And I wouldn't buy his curriculum, because I think children need real books, and he focuses on having everything printed out from online resources. Part of the task of forming a family is to collect the books and other objects (such as musical instruments) they need, just as you feed or clothe them. Those caveats aside, Robinson offers good motivation in staying the course and common sense about how children need to be independent.

On Education and Choosing a Model

The following reflection was prompted by Robert Louis Wilken's article "Culture and the Light of Faith."[2]

You've heard that adage about pygmies standing on the shoulders of giants. Without the past, we cannot build in any meaningful way, culturally and intellectually. Refusing the lift—straining to see without benefit of the height of those who have gone before—is a self-defeating, yet all too common, effort in education.

There are those who want to liberate reason from faith (a pet project of pygmies dating from the Enlightenment, that vexing period of intellectual history) yet don't acknowledge their debt to the very faith they scorn. The debt is owed to the genius of early Christian scholars and artists who, themselves trained in classical artistic forms, grammar, law, rhetoric, and philosophy, ensured the patrimony *of life lived in the realm of reason.* But

---

2   Robert Louis Wilken, "Culture and the Light of Faith," *First Things* (February 2011), https://www.firstthings.com/article/2011/02/culture-and-the-light-of-faith.

even more, they explored how to transform the inheritance they received into tools for expressing *in written words* a new civilization in which reason and faith join to glorify God through culture.

When the parent who wishes to educate his children stumbles across a treasure, say, of the writings of Isidore, the early medieval Spanish author of the *Etymologies*—a vast cultural undertaking resembling something like a one-man encyclopedia of classical learning—he can't help but get excited about how much there is to know, followed by the question of how to pass it all on to the children.

Wilken likens Isidore's "enterprise" of the *Etymologies* to E. D. Hirsch's cultural literacy project. If you, prospective homeschooler in search of a curriculum, ever hyperventilated over a book of that all-too-prolific gentleman, such as the overwhelming *What Your Second Grader Needs to Know,* you will appreciate that I'm not going to give you the grand tour of his work at the moment. What Hirsch did was to warn people that reading a newspaper or a textbook—and understanding it—requires a lot of cultural knowledge.

The problem is, how do you go about getting that knowledge? Or giving it to your children? Some people think you get out the list (which is what Hirsch's books essentially are, lists) and go down it, checking things off.

For adults preparing curricula for schools, or for medieval monks compiling ancient texts, that may seem to be the way to go. But for a child, it's backward. Look at it this way: the newspaper or textbook was written by those who had received *a certain education* (not necessarily formally, mind). Their cultural literacy was high enough to produce a writing that, in turn, requires a reader who brings familiarity with the background material to the task. Therefore, it makes more sense to ensure that readers have an equivalent (or, at this point, another watered-down generation later, greater) education of the same sort, and not, on the contrary, to attempt to remedy the situation afterward by means of lists.

The best curriculum offers children a *start* on the road to broad familiarity with the history, poetry, literature, mythology, and art of the past, such that they can remain conversant with the present and perhaps be the ones to make the cultural artifacts of the future.

What today's pygmies want to give our children is a two-dimensional type of knowledge. They don't want to confront the slow process that went into building our culture and the great responsibility that lies on us to transmit it. They are nothing if not impatient, and they don't like to admit that the child will only drink from the fonts of knowledge of his own volition. He must be drawn to, not crammed with, knowledge.

On the other hand you have Hirsch (and many others, including many "classical"- or "core"-type educators) who, certainly full of appreciation for the vast storehouse of learning that is our patrimony, want to make sure that every child is force-fed as much of it as the frantic parent can manage. This isn't really possible; it is certainly not enjoyable.

Instead, let's simply teach our children the way the writers of those culturally literate people were taught. That is, let's prepare the whole home environment. Let's provide actual, living books: classics and the sturdy time-tested fare of previous childhoods. Rather than pulling ourselves up by our bootstraps or otherwise attempting the impossible to remedy the new situation, let's just go back.

Language is necessary for reason, yet revelation can't flourish without language either. In fact, the Christian revelation is the Word, the Son of God made flesh. And not only did Christians embrace all that reason had bestowed on civilization before the time of Christ in the ancient philosophers; they studied, structured, and preserved it for our time, including for those who no longer see the worth in such a project or who don't even know how to ask where they got their high vantage point — you know, that vantage point the pygmies stand on: the shoulders of giants.

Wilken ends his essay with a marvelous meditation on two of Raphael's paintings: his *School of Athens* (a copy of which hangs in a main building at the University of Virginia where Wilken teaches) and his *Disputa* (Adoration of the Sacrament). His point in offering the juxtaposition is that the horizontal exaltation of reason in the former painting is completed by the horizontal *and* vertical composition of the latter, reason *with* faith, intersecting at the sacrament of the Body and Blood of the Word made Flesh.

The two paintings, Wilken discovers, were hung by the artist in one room in a building in Rome. The deep meaning of *that* juxtaposition is that the light of faith completes reason, putting us in mind of the ancients' dictum that grace builds on nature and does not replace it. Grace cannot normally gain a foothold in our beings without nature, for this is how we are made.

"Raphael's *Disputa* lifts our minds toward things that cannot be seen while putting before us those who, in the words of the Book of Wisdom, obtained 'friendship with God' and were 'commended for the gifts that come from instruction,'" Wilken says in his essay.

Instruction takes place, in other words, by means of the countless little building blocks from the past that make up a full and textured life of learning in the context of transcendent realities toward which we must remain humbly receptive. Reason. Faith. Light from above. These are the elements of education, and the wise parent makes them all his goal.

ASK AUNTIE LEILA

How Do I Homeschool?

Dear Auntie Leila,

I am a mom of six, ages ten months to thirteen years. I have five boys and one girl.

The online school offered by my district is not working for my daughter. It takes her eight hours a day to complete all the assignments. But I am too afraid to do it on my own and try to create what is right for my children. My son resists almost all formal-feeling teaching, so the idea of trying to persuade him to do assignments each day is daunting; I rely on his online teacher to tell him to do it so that he won't rebel.

I'm not totally convinced that homeschooling is the only right way. I can see the good in both settings. I want to homeschool my children. I just feel so overwhelmed and confused on the hows. I've read lots of books and articles, but it all seems more confusing now that the kids are getting older. How do you do it?

Angel

D ear Angel,

In one way, I started writing, wrestling the blog from its intended purpose (of posting crafts and such), for this very reason: to put into words and pictures what I usually end up incoherently babbling to a young mom who asks me, "How do you do it?" "It" meaning, of course, homeschooling.

Because homeschooling—in fact, the formation of our children, pure and simple: in the womb, at home, in school, under the shade tree—is a part of our family life. A man and a woman are meant to marry, have children, and bring them up. That last bit is ... family life! All of it.

So I always look somewhat helplessly at the poor woman sitting in my kitchen. And I stammer some vague things and some extremely detailed things. Usually after the first hour or so, she says, meaningfully (not quite rolling her eyes), "You should write a book!"

I can't help but pause here to note that despite all our post-feminist training, the love parents have for their children really does find the mother worrying about their immediate education while trying to make sure there are clean socks; and their father trying to provide for their education while looking for his socks. He knows he has to get out to work to "fund the bliss." She has seen already that the journey from her arms to her lap to her side is a short one. He would like to be helpful in the matter of socks, but the world presses on him. So the "stereotypical clichés" keep asserting themselves as real life, whatever the ideologies might tell us to the contrary.

Oh, this friend of mine is all enthusiasm: she has hopes and dreams for leading her little ones into the joys of higher learning. But the daily grind that is teaching the three Rs while trying to find socks—that's what gets her down.

But let's assume that you are this friend, and you are reasonably (reasonably, not perfectly!) on top of getting up in the morning, making meals, and doing the laundry—all the things covered in volume 3, including cleaning the house, for no matter how lofty your educational goals, the house must get clean. Let's say that you understand that education means more than schooling, and you are at one with your husband when it comes to Sundays and feast days—that you are slowly trying to live your Faith, day in and day out, with your whole family. Let's say that your children obey you most of the time, as discussed in volume 1, because if not, homeschooling is the least of your worries.

The next thing to realize is that education begins with "bringing up a child to like and dislike what he ought," as dear Aristotle tells us. For a full explanation of this concept (and what happens when it is abandoned), read *The Abolition of Man*, by C. S. Lewis. You will get a crash course on all sorts of things, including moderns versus ancients, epistemology, and first principles. It will be fun; well, not exactly fun, but it's a short book, and it makes you think. Another short read is Dorothy Sayers's "The Lost Tools of Learning." Armed with these two background works, you will be ready to tackle all the other reading I have in store for you!

Now, let's see—you have a vision, right? Let's quote from Plato (this from *The Republic* via Lewis's *Abolition of Man*) about the properly brought-up child:

> Who would see most clearly whatever was amiss in ill-made works of man or ill-grown works of nature, and with a just distaste would blame and hate the ugly even from his earliest years and would give delighted praise to beauty, receiving it into his soul and being nourished by it, so that he becomes a man of gentle heart.
>
> All this before he is of an age to reason; so that when Reason at length comes to him, then, bred as he has been, he will hold out his hands in welcome and recognize her because of the affinity he bears to her.

Right.

And you have the children, who, by no means seem destined to be "men of gentle heart." On the contrary, they are undoubtedly at this minute dismantling something delicate or useful in your very house or are perhaps expressing their inner rage with marker on white walls. They are uncivilized little beasts, and, like Angel, you are fairly sure that sitting in front of a computer for eight hours fails the test of education as expressed by the ancients. And, like her, naturally, you want to find something active for them to do, preferably breaking rocks in a chain gang or hiking a distant canyon.

And to complicate matters, there is no end to the methods, curricula, and options available to homeschoolers. Even my strong convictions can be shaken by a random glimpse into someone else's seemingly magical approach. "Get math geniuses using only these ten musical instruments!" "Learn writing skills with our comprehensive eighteen-volume self-taught manual!"

But, resist. Stick to your vision; do not be sidetracked. You can give yourself a "humility pep talk" by reminding yourself that you are only one person and there are only a few hours in the day for actual "curriculum" as currently understood. You also don't have much money. So you will be keeping things simple out of necessity.

So, how to bring these things—vision and children—into the right relationship, as pertains to actual schooling?

Make sure that whatever you do with your children has this quality: it is related to all the things that intelligent and wise people have ever done to become educated. In simple terms, this means that your plan of study, your curriculum, must be firmly connected to good, old, time-tested, well worn books.

It has been said by John Senior, a seminal thinker in the revival of classical education, that before one can read the Hundred Great Books (those works of civilization that represent the crown of man's thought and art), one must read the "thousand good books." These books are the shared heritage without which all learning and thinking will wither for lack of nourishment from a well prepared seedbed. This is the key! Education is about much more than books, but if the books in your curriculum are not of this quality, the whole enterprise is not going to be worth the energy it takes.

Don't waste your time and money on things that are not time-tested! It's not that there aren't fine things out there. It's that there isn't enough time to get to them *and* read all the wonderful literature that makes us who we are as a culture (speaking of our entire Western civilization).

And don't start fretting about an exact list. People disagree on the margins, but in the main, the books that belong on your shelves are not difficult to find, if you are clever and know how to look for them. (There are suggestions in the appendix.) Here I will encourage reading the works of Charlotte Mason, which can be found both unabridged and in summary on the Ambleside Online website. (Don't attempt to read Mason's unabridged work online. You need her books in your hands, for she is very wordy, and you will need to be able to look up every once in a while.)

Mason's message is that being connected with the past, through what she calls "living books," as well as physically moving the child outside to observe, enjoy, and study nature, is the heart of education. In addition, she incorporates many other activities that in most curricula are considered extras. Music, walks, art, crafts, singing folk songs and hymns — she integrates these into her teachings, and rightly so. The purpose of education, ultimately, is expression. Truth does not remain in the mind, having arrived there by means of reading and thinking. Truth comes forth out of the person, and what we call culture is the synthesis of what people learn, through both study and experience.

Once I discovered the Ambleside Online site, I returned to it often. There are several reasons.

1. As I say, they have a condensed version of Mason's writings, which is wonderful. The woman was a genius, but somewhat prolix! If it's September, you need the gist of what she's getting at, pronto. Save the long version for when you can get comfortable.

2. Ambleside has a book list for each stage, roughly by grade. They include many important books, and although I consider myself a complete bookworm, I have found many gems there, including works preserved online that I never could have found on my own. These book lists alone are priceless, but it's all there for free.

3. The site has lesson plans. I've never used them undiluted, but they have helped me figure out how to do my own plans, based on the books I've chosen. (You probably can't use *all* the books they have in their plans. It's a tremendous amount of material.) The lesson plans will help you realize, if you are as impractical as I am, that the plan is a simple matter, after

all: take the book, divide it into the weeks you have available, and voila! Your plan.

4. Ambleside has guides for nature study, Shakespeare, crafts, poetry, singing ... It's a treasure trove.

I do have one reservation about the Mason approach to history, as organized on this site. The books tend to be Anglo- and Reformation-centric (Mason was an Anglican), which leads to what has been called "the Whig interpretation of history" as explicated in a book by that name by Herbert Butterfield. It's the idea that we are all progressing toward a perfected state from a benighted one. But this doesn't detract from the value of the site as a whole.

Don't be overwhelmed by the vast resources on Ambleside. It's more of a revelation of how things could be done, rather than a set injunction to do them a certain way.

I suggest that you begin with what appeals to you and your children from these lists. It's at least worth a look just for good books from the library or for purchase.

For an excellent synthesis of the Charlotte Mason curriculum, have a look at the Charlotte Mason Education Center (www.thecmec.org).

Overcoming Certain Obstacles

I am not against school. I think school is a wonderful idea. I believe in neighborhood-controlled schools and schools run by consecrated religious; these institutions presuppose neighborhoods and churches with intact families (rich or poor, preferably both living in the same general areas, together) who care more about their children than about what people in other neighborhoods are doing or what the government can do for them.

This is an idea of the past (and maybe for the future if we live our *now* well), when children from all sorts of neighborhoods and parishes got educated, usually on very little money relative to expenditures today. Therefore, you might call me a conflicted advocate of homeschooling, or at least not a "true believer" in the sense of thinking homeschooling is ideal, for I do not think that. The best explanation of how school works with home and church and state is found in the encyclical *On Christian Education* by Pius XI (which can be found online). To its wisdom one can add our American model, long forgotten, of neighborhood schools managed and paid for by residents of the community. I do see the flaws of those public schools; yet they really were locally governed (by parents), as opposed to how they are run today—funded by parents but governed by state and federal mandates.

In a country that approached 100 percent literacy, it's hard to argue that the model was fatal. Nevertheless, today, as a matter of sheer preservation, many of us have to homeschool, enjoyably and fruitfully, even if not perfectly. The reality is that nothing is perfect.

Children must be allowed to develop according to their nature, and parents must be free to teach their own children the Faith. In our time, homeschooling is increasingly becoming the only way to do this, as difficult as it sometimes is.

What about the Future?

With the pressures on families today to do so much that used to be supported by the culture at large, a necessary relief from making overwhelming commitments is to take one year at a time—to do what seems right and fitting for the coming year.

Of course you want to find your place in the community; get your "sea legs" under you as you figure out how to navigate your family. In the early years, many parents crave support and affirmation from more experienced people; this is only natural. And while some children are quite comfortable staying home, especially an outgoing, pert child can benefit from rubbing shoulders with others.

If school kept to its proper sphere, adhered to a proper understanding of authority, and didn't intrude into the child's inner life or that of the family, it would be such a support. School as it was when I was very young was a net help to families. It's now universally too invasive.

Your circumstances might be different; then that small parish or family-run school might work for you. But you have to verify its benefit to your family.

Sometimes even a good school is not what your children need; and your first priority is *their* education. You have a radiating circle of people you are beholden to; you can't let valid concern for others impede your responsibility to those nearest and dearest. These duties, costs, and benefits are discerned by husband and wife in prayer and conversation together.

You have the freedom to act for the good of your whole family. The stress is often less if you decide year by year, and not for their whole lives. You can reserve the right to change your mind—at any time!

When Grandparents Don't Support Homeschooling

The education of children is intimately bound up with marriage—specifically, the adventure that is becoming the responsible unit of culture, and the holy guidance that comes along with that adventure. In other words, as important as the larger community is, as necessary as the input of those who love us is, and as incumbent upon us to listen carefully and understand the advice we are receiving is, in the end, only we, the parents, can make the commitment to do what needs to be done. Only we have the grace to do it. Only we are answerable.

How often I wish I could tell parents who are stressing out about their toddlers' education to *read* about education *now*. Find out more now, while they are young. Being able to respond to others' concerns depends on having ready arguments and knowledge.

The best education a toddler can have is to play, to be read and sung to, to be cuddled by parents, to learn to obey, and to start to help with their "work." So simple! It gets very complicated later. *Now* is the time for you to be understanding what the child needs in every stage of development. Later you will be too busy to do the necessary study without difficulty.

This is why I recommend John Taylor Gatto's *Underground History of American Education*.[3] In some ways its most valuable parts are his descriptions of his childhood.

It's easy for older people (such as well meaning grandparents) to lapse into a dreamy state of idealism about school, even while occasionally getting a reality check about social agendas, poor pedagogy, and general atmosphere of somewhat miserable conformity. Along with my universal rule of 80-20 (the Pareto Rule, twisted to my own probably unrelated purposes and

---

[3]   I found it in the library, but you can read the book online on John Gatto's website: http://www.johntaylorgatto.com/.

further refined here as 10-80-10) you find that 80 percent of the children more or less get through, with damage along some sort of scale from not much to sort of a lot but not debilitating. Ten percent do extremely well. Whether they would have done so well otherwise, given a truly excellent environment, or whether the *sort* of success they have is good for them, no one cares to investigate. And then probably 10 percent do quite poorly, and to be fair, we have to ask if this number of children would have done poorly no matter what.

Grandparents like to suppose that *their* grandchildren are exceptional and should be given every opportunity. If they are educators (as the most opposed to homeschooling often tend to be), your road is an uphill one. My mother-in-law was opposed to our homeschooling, although she had a pretty iron-clad rule of not interfering. It meant that she just remained completely detached—other than, ironically and fortunately, giving me boxes and boxes of those precious old school books I often reference in my advice (more on this below) that saved my day on many occasions.

Grandparents often start to mobilize the pressure to pursue academics when the children are not yet out of their toddlerhood; yet tradition and studies show that boys are not ready for school until they are seven, and girls only a little shortly before that.

The push for early schooling reflects the expert class providing compensation for working mothers. Preschool for children enables the mother (whose own education prepared her to take her place in the workforce) to work outside the home; working requires preschool. You can see how this system is self-perpetuating.

For children so young to cope with a school schedule, including meeting the expectations of people who don't really understand them, a significant internal mechanism has to develop. Just dealing with the smells, the noise, the other children, the coming, and the going takes its toll. When he goes home, the child often can't maintain self-control (after all, he's little), so the parents' interactions with him are not at all satisfying. These years are so stressful for all but the most extroverted children, and thus, for their parents, that going through them is, I'm convinced, one reason people avoid having a larger family.

Anyway, each family has to decide for itself what to do about these important decisions. Sometimes, if helpful relatives are too invasive, the topic has to be avoided.

Remember—it's your call. You and your husband have *grace* from *God* to decide what to do. People can give advice, but it's wrong to force you to do otherwise than your conscience tells you. If their financial control over you causes their opinion to carry more weight than it should, you must do what you can to remedy the situation so that you can have the autonomy your position as parents requires.

On Misfits

I happened on a book review about Rabbi Jacob Neusner,[4] who is called "the most published man in human history," "arguably one of the most influential voices in American Jewish intellectual life in the past half-century." It was the umpteenth reminder for me that the most interesting and productive people in the world were misfits as children. "Neusner's reputation as a difficult person began quite young. Hughes [the author of the biography under review] notes that a comment on his third-grade report card read as follows: 'He prefers not to do as the others are doing, which causes many difficulties.'"

How would you feel as the mother or father of a third grader whose teacher said about him, "He prefers not to do as the others are doing, which causes many difficulties"? Perhaps you've already been told exactly such a thing, and it makes you feel like a failure.

But then, how would you feel as the mother or father of the adult (that grown child!) who received the Medal of Pope Benedict XVI? Or leaving aside Neusner, what if you turned out to be the parent of a person who lovingly and intelligently raised a family of her own, or who could run a

---

[4] Shaul Magid, "Is It Time to Take the Most-Published Man in Human History Seriously?" *Tablet*, August 23, 2016, https://www.tabletmag.com/jewish-arts-and-culture/books/211209/take-jacob-neusner-seriously.

company, or who could engineer something needed, or who could teach others something of great importance?

That is, there is no "one thing you need to know" about the education of the child. There's no denying that, even if you delegate part or most of the formal education to others, it takes energy and trustfulness to raise a child. Not *just* energy; not *just* trustfulness. Both.

The *young child* needs to learn certain things, but somehow, the world itself is set up for him to learn those things, if we mostly stand out of the way, stepping forward only to offer a few key things at opportune times.

The *older child* needs, among many other things, to read a mountain of books; this necessitates a corresponding amount of reading on our part—even of books we've read and studied in the past. Being the mother or father of an older child learning at home is an exercise in changing the whole way we interact with the world, because now we must wrestle with Plutarch and Dickens and Faraday … and very likely a baby or two as well! That is, the mother of such a child finds that it's real work to homeschool.

But we aren't programming a machine; we're guiding a soul, a unique person who *will* learn if we just give him room. Not only learn, but head off in directions we hardly imagined—that's when we find out that we can render even shortcomings on our part into freedom for this child who, it must be said, is not precisely a child *of ours*.

So this is just encouragement on the subject of any anxiety you might be feeling as you raise your children (or any false sense of security you might have when you put your confidence in a *system* or *process* of education).

In one sense, there's no mystery: children have always grown up and learned things, if given half a chance. Of course, that half of a chance consists very much in being left alone to think, and in reading, and in having smart people to talk to and who love them.

In another sense, the mystery is real, and so no one can "fix" it with one easy solution or a complex method. Parents really are in the closest contact with the one thing no one knows much about, despite having been one: a developing human person.

The Neusner review reminded me that the goal of education can't be "to do what the others are doing" or even "to perform well at this level." It really has to be that we offer the child the environment and the necessary support (that is, love) to grow. That means that sometimes even our failures can be useful—which is surely good news!

St. Paul's First Letter to the Corinthians indicates the confidence we have to have in something outside of ourselves when we are faced with such a long-term task as the education of our children. We do our best in God's sight without worrying about how it appears to man. St. Paul says:

> Let a man so account of us as of the ministers of Christ, and the dispensers of the mysteries of God. Here now it is required among the dispensers, that a man be found faithful. But to me it is a very small thing to be judged by you, or by man's day; but neither do I judge my own self. For I am not conscious to myself of any thing, yet am I not hereby justified; but he that judgeth me, is the Lord. Therefore judge not before the time; until the Lord come, who both will bring to light the hidden things of darkness, and will make manifest the counsels of the hearts; and then shall every man have praise from God. (1 Cor. 4:1-5, DR)

PART 3

On the Education of Children and How It Occurs

Now that you have a little reading to orient yourself with on the question of education, we will have an interlude before we tackle the main topic of how to educate the children. You can, of course, skip right ahead to how to teach reading—that part is as practical as anyone could ask for.

Sundry Practical Matters

I find that there are some larger questions to clear up first—questions of family life and culture that aren't easily categorized. How do I attend to all my other responsibilities while teaching my children? What does a day at home with school-aged children look like? Do I need to be crafty? What do I do with my toddler? These are the sorts of anxieties I seek to quell in this section.

When Life Interferes with Schooling

In a subsequent chapter I will explain how to make a curriculum plan, but here I want to say that you must arrange the schedule to take into account interferences; plan for them. Leave wiggle room. Schedule in "catch-up weeks" and recognize those weeks when you ought to put in schoolwork for four days, not five, or mornings only. Actually, almost all school weeks should have only four days, because you need a day that is mostly devoted to household mitigation or visiting or some other un-school-related activity. Homeschooling is vastly more efficient than school, so never have the slightest qualm about compressing the children's work this way.

When you see that anything scheduled hasn't been completed in its appointed week, you are secure in knowing you've built in a way to get it done the following week.

A common complaint is that school just seems never to get done. Find an effective bribe to motivate the school-age children to tackle things very early each day (being allowed to take down a board game that involves a lot of pieces; time to bake or build something they have been looking forward to; a chapter of a gripping book read to them; you get the idea).

Toddlers get into the habit of ruling the roost, although they actually don't like it. Sometimes you have to go through the "Hebrews moment"—Hebrews 12:11: No discipline seems pleasant at the time, but in the end yields the "peaceable fruit of justice." A week of early bedtimes and more alert discipline will be a week of unpleasantness, but it will pay off. The toddler needs the idea that he must start being part of the pack that is the family. Combining discipline with a purposeful schedule of activity (getting outside no matter what, lots of running around in the basement if outdoors is not possible, wrestling with the brothers) will get you through a bad patch with a disruptive toddler.

Always have an idea of the "minimum" that must be achieved—the math and the reading, some music practice perhaps—and be ready to ditch the rest. You can always read out loud during nap time, so don't worry—this is indeed homeschooling in a big family.

Where to Do Schooling

We've had old houses with separate rooms (as opposed to "open concept"), all of which we used for family living. Most builders' houses in developments feature small "living rooms" that can be made into school rooms with bookcases, an easy chair for you, and a work table, and still be somewhat accessible to the kitchen, but also separate. Since we never had that, I'll tell you what we did.

My children did their schoolwork at the kitchen table and on the sofa. They would also disperse to the dining room table or the front porch or the closet under the stairs. Since I found that I was in the kitchen anyway, or needed to sit in the den anyway to nurse a baby or fold laundry, that worked perfectly.

When the children were smaller, we lived in a house with a tiny room off the kitchen that had a window and built-in shelves: the pantry. I did put food in there, but I made room so I could store the kids' books on shelves, within their reach—one shelf per child.

We also made use of little rolling carts that tucked under the counter that was built in there. At first I thought this setup was a sign of failure. Did we not need a dedicated school room? Should each child not have a desk and bookcases and all sorts of places for special materials? But later I realized that it's good to keep things simple and to use the same books over and over—my old, good books that had stood the test of time before we ever got them.

Now I live in an even bigger, even older house that has some good closets. One that pertains to homeschooling is in the den; it can store all the various craft items and the homeschool books that are not in the rotation at the moment. But over the years, I pared down that supply of books, realizing that I did not need the latest curriculum; I needed just the tried-and-true.

What the Daily Schedule Might Look Like

Often an inquiry comes my way: "What does your homeschool schedule look like during the day? How do you manage prayer time?"

A headline might occur to me: "There Is No Way to Answer That Question without Writing a Book"—and right here and now I am writing the book to answer it, but at the time I was writing a blog post, and the five thoughts that follow were sent to our homeschooling group by my very wise friend Therese Cross.

To answer the question about prayer time, she first pointed to my book *The Little Oratory: A Beginner's Guide to Praying in the Home.* And this is also the most complete answer I can give. As the publisher remarked when it came out, "How could it be that there wasn't already a book like this?" It's the book I myself wish I had had thirty-five years ago. It's the book that represents a corporate work—of David Clayton, Deirdre, me, and all of you readers over the years.

The second part of her answer: Don't get too busy outside the home. Keep your mornings without interruptions and afternoons open for fun, family, and friend time.

Third: Don't force things. No two children are the same. They eventually learn to read. My friend says, "I had one reading at five and another reading at nine." These differences need to be accepted because they are real; fighting against them achieves nothing.

Leave some experiences for the kids to discover. They need not play every instrument or every sport activity or visit every museum.

Fourth: Sit down, take a deep breath, and ask Mother Mary to take over for five minutes, and just enjoy seeing what she does with them. You need to do this at least twice a day, if not more. It is a great way to realize that you are not doing this task alone.

Fifth: All teachers in the classroom have bad days. You will too, but none of those teachers will spend as much time individually a day with any one child as you will.

Preschoolers and Their Needs

A question that looms for homeschoolers is what to do with the younger children who are not busy yet with schoolwork. The almost-school-age child finds lessons boring or vexing, but he moves frustratingly slowly in the activities that do captivate him, when you are focused on getting things done.

It can help to remember that the child under the age of reason doesn't have the ability to see time in units. Rushing is meaningless to him. When a little girl "washes dishes," she isn't accomplishing a task—there is no end in sight because the activity is about enjoying the process. Unbeknownst to you, she is thinking and wondering; a lot is going on in her mind. To the child, the forty-five minutes washing the dishes is play time, and yet it is also her work. If you are giving her that time, you help her get dressed quickly, for instance.

Sometimes it is necessary to say, "I'll let you take your time later—right now, we need to get going!" Then, be as good as your word. Young children desperately need their meandering, seemingly pointless time—every day—sometimes for the sake of their digestion alone.

A benefit of keeping the young child at home is precisely to avoid unnecessary rushing. Conformity is hard on the very young (not that it's easy or desirable for anyone, yet it seems to be the one indispensable norm of our society). Home life is more peaceful when we keep these truths in mind.

Is Being Crafty with Preschoolers a Prerequisite for Homeschooling?

Release yourself from dreaming up activities for your three-year-old; instead, make him a place to be—largely unsupervised; a kitchen corner—a play kitchen and baby-doll care area—with scope for activities of a little girl's own devising, a place for a little boys' army guys, a small table and stools for coloring and working with playdough, a truck pit (not just a sandbox), a little workbench, a mud kitchen across the yard where it won't bother you, a nature table inside the door where they can arrange the treasures they find outside and ponder them when the mood strikes.

There are many resources online with good ideas for this type of thing, and it's what kept our lives peaceful. Search for "Montessori at home" sites. What you do in your home doesn't have to be as fabulous as some make it look: it just needs to be what you think of as attractive and what the kids think of as interesting. If you have older children, they will help you set things up, and you may find that in doing so, they become absorbed, reclaiming their innocent time of un-self-consciousness. When one of my daughters and her friends were almost teenagers, they could still sometimes be found playing in four-year-old Bridget's kitchen corner.

Just a little effort to give an otherwise demanding toddler his own space will give you breathing room all year, whereas coming up with crafts will drive you crazy. At least, coming up with crafts (as opposed to doing crafts that we all enjoy) drives me crazy!

Homeschooling with Little Ones Around

Teaching your children stretches you to the limits of what you previously thought chaos could look like. I often get the question of what to do with the littles, and I will tell you that whatever you do, things won't seem very calm.

Here are three fairly old-fashioned ideas for keeping your littles occupied in a delightfully developmental way while you snatch a few moments to direct an older child in his quest for an education.

Playdough is as much a staple in a home with small children as diapers and milk. What would I have done without playdough? Make up a batch without bothering with the dye at first. Later, when your children get more sophisticated, you can pull the dye out of your bag of tricks. Always keep the bar low and manage expectations! Never come out with all your guns blazing. Bath paint or egg tempera paint, depending on how lasting you want your paint to be.

You can find "recipes" for playdough and paint online very easily. But two notes:

1. Keep the little ones confined to one part of the house. Run amok they will; just don't let them run amok all over.
2. I wouldn't do both these things at the same time.

The bean game. Dried beans are cheap. Get a big basin. Pour in one kind of bean at first. Little red lentils are pretty and flow through a funnel pleasingly. Pinto beans are a good size for scooping. Eventually you can mix some together, and time will be spent sorting them if that's the kind of child you have. A note: Don't use kidney beans. They are really poisonous! Even one kidney bean, swallowed not chewed, can make a child sick with vomiting to the point of death. I didn't believe it until I looked it up, but it's true.

Should Preschoolers Have Outside Activities and Lessons?

A four-year-old needs much less activity than most people of a certain (competitive, elite-college-bound) socioeconomic class think. Keep in mind that while many a child that age does enjoy going places and doing things, what he may not enjoy and what may really stress him out is having to do certain things all the time, meaning sticking to a schedule that includes a lot of car time and structure. Many behavioral issues that children exhibit are directly related to this stress.

A boy of four needs time to run around with his buddies. He needs outdoor time and physical activity. It would be ideal to know some families with children the same ages who are up for playground time three times or so a week, or getting together in someone's big yard for games.

If your child has a certain talent, then go with that. Some four-year-olds can play the violin. Others are completely agnostic. Unless there is a clear indication here, it's best to wait until ages six or seven for any kind of formal lessons.

Try thinking back to the day when there were lots of large families and moms stayed home. When my husband was a child in the fifties, in a fairly upwardly mobile suburb, not many children even went to kindergarten. They stayed home and rode their trikes and bikes on the sidewalk and generally just ran around. That is healthiest, as far as I can see—but it requires other families to pull it off.

How can we approximate this scenario? That's our challenge. Take it little by little and try to keep your children unscheduled but playing with other kids as long as you can. Work hard to make friends with other families who see things the way you do.

Homeschooling with Many Children

Paradoxically, when you concentrate on home and all the projects that everyone has, and the playing that everyone has to do, the anxieties become fewer. A normal homeschool day in a busy family involves strategizing: perhaps while baby is napping, the older children can focus on quiet activities such as math and reading. Certainly the goal is for children to work on their own as much as possible.

Usually busy families schedule homeschool time for right after breakfast chores and whatever morning ritual helps to ease everyone into the day—and encourage children to go through their work quickly. Bribery is an option, for necessary but possibly irksome worksheets, for instance; I always kept these to a minimum, but some drilling has to take place—go ahead and incentivize it.

Help your children overcome the tendency to complain. If this habit has become a factor, begin a new day with an alert that all infractions will be met with swiftly, let them know what the consequences will be, and then pounce with separations, imposed silences, and chores, without any accompanying lectures. It's a habit to complain! Only instant feedback—combined with gentle reminders of what we are grateful for—will break the habit.

Get your children into the habit of working as fast as they can with accuracy, and as much as possible without you. Timers are great—twenty minutes is plenty of time to spend on a worksheet. If the work is not done, put it away. If it's done well, offer a treat of some kind until the habit of working efficiently is formed.

Then go on to other things—all the fun and truly educational things, such as gardening, music, camping, reading out loud, playing (versus practicing) music, and whatever everyone enjoys.

ASK AUNTIE LEILA

Should My Kids Play Sports, and When?

Dear Auntie Leila,

How should I prioritize activities for my children? And how will I afford activities, living on one income? I have five boys who spend their days vibrating in frustration at the limited types of exertion available to them. During the summer, it's not too hard, as there is garden work, grass to mow and rake, and so forth. But as we approach winter, I'd like to find something for them to do other than run around outside.

I don't want to run from activity to activity. I would like to pick one thing for them to try, to help burn off all that energy through the long winter days—something a bit more disciplined and with more purpose than just free play.

I also sense in the boys the stretch toward manhood, to begin leaving Mama's apron strings, but don't know where or what to release them to. Being homeschooled and staying home with Mama and the babies from day to day seems to be too limited a scope for them at this point, and I'd like to expand their horizons before they begin to chafe and resent the limitations of our life (of budget, of transportation, and so forth). Also, I think finding some way to provide instruction from an outside person would be beneficial for them.

Sincerely,

Laura

Dear Laura,

Well, of course, you're never too old to run around outside! Having said that, Auntie Leila does have some thoughts about sports specifically, with the usual reminders that she is not an expert, every family is different, and circumstances are different. Think also of what kind of community you live in (sports-mad or less so) and what level of energy your family really has. My disclaimer here for other readers is that if your family is sports-mad, you will know more about it than I! And you will be on top of getting your very young children to be sporty as well. I'm sure you are on it, unlike Auntie Leila.

The suburban practice of signing the four-year-old up for sports is something done because you yourself desperately need to get out (or are the above-mentioned sporty kind). Your leaves are raked, your supper is in the crockpot, and if you don't meet some other parents, your brain might explode on your tile floor.

You kind of want to get going on this parenthood gig, and secretly you are interested to see if your child is (a) developmentally extraordinary, able to catch a spiral from fifty feet and destined for the NFL or this generation's Tiger Woods, or both; or (b) not. There seems no other way to do this than to head out for some activity. Being on a team or going for lessons gets you out of the house, so there's that. That's fine. Everyone does what they have to do.

I myself didn't do this with our kids because sports aren't something I grew up with; I'm a soccer mom convert. My husband did grow up with sandlot baseball and high school tennis, and was fairly athletic, but back then sports were not organized to the extent they are now.

As they got older, our kids played soccer, more soccer, indoor soccer, some baseball, and a smattering of other things. Our girls also did Irish step dancing. We lived in a very sports-oriented place, so although I'd say we did a lot (considering the sheer number of people to be carted around), we didn't do anywhere near as much as most.

The truth is, other than your own enjoyment, there is no point in signing up a small child for sports unless you enjoy watching the antics of little monkeys who have no idea what they are aiming at. It is of questionable advantage to the little tots, although it does make for good mental images when you need cheering up:

- The forwards on the teams of six-year-old girls are suddenly fixing each others' braids midfield, mid-game—completely oblivious to the screaming parents on the sidelines.
- The boys can't figure out how to line up to shake hands—they just can't wrap their little minds around the process of coming at each other so that right hands meet, and their coaches—aka parents—are herding cats trying to get them there. Finally everyone just … leaves.
- A wee goalie has woven her hands through the netting up to her armpits, and consequently can't extricate in time to defend.

Usually practices for six-year-olds end pretty early, and by mid-fall it's too dark to practice anyway. But as to serious travel or club teams with hours of practice more than once a week, I'd say that you definitely have to examine the effect on dinner together and bedtimes.

I once met a woman whose eight-year-old daughter was doing Irish step dancing, private step-dancing lessons so she could make the next level, and club soccer (with games in another state, even granting our states are not so far apart). This mom was wondering why the child wasn't reading well, and why she was doing her homework after 10:00 p.m.

Don't be that woman. (But you wouldn't.) Make priorities and have goals—and discuss them with your husband.

If your goal, and it's a worthy one, is to get your older (over-six) boys to play sports of some kind, because you think they could use the exercise and because playing organized sports does have benefits, then budget it in. If it's to get the girls a skill they've been clamoring for, then go for it.

When you homeschool, you are saving a lot of money. Going to "free" public school isn't free! There are sports fees and a lot of other expenses no one tells you about. Recognize that there is a certain "cost of doing business," as my husband calls it.

Get savvy with used equipment from resale shops, neighborhood on-line groups, and online secondhand shopping sites, and always voice your needs; most people have stuff in their garage that they'd be happy to give you. When a child is old enough to have a job (mowing lawns, shoveling snow, taking care of a neighbor's dogs), he can chip in for things he really wants to continue doing. If you truly can't afford it, then it's not necessary to the well-being of your family.

Getting the kids into sports outside of home is worth it if it meets these criteria:

1. *The child really longs to play.* This is what got us going—our eldest really wanted to play soccer and begged to join a team. To us, it wasn't important. To him, it was. Boys especially love and benefit from team sports. Even when the coaches are just volunteer dads, it is important for boys to relate to other men. Women will probably just never understand what it means to a boy to be in the team environment, even if that boy isn't particularly athletic. Once our first child played, the others followed along for the most part, with varying degrees of interest in various activities.

A child learns a lot when he sticks to something for the time period agreed upon: soccer season, music-lesson semester. He may find things difficult at first, and realizing that he has made a commitment is part of what he learns by participating.

Some children are really gifted at a sport (or an activity such as karate), and you should encourage that, just as you encourage all their talents to the best of your ability, taking everything into account. Some are peculiarly unfit, and while it is fine to expose them occasionally and is probably a good idea at least for a while at some point, don't think they are missing out if all they do is play catch in the backyard. Some are just average, and for those, playing a team sport or doing an outside activity will be a fine experience, kept in its proper perspective.

For most of us, our children are not going to the Olympics, so we should be sure to cultivate other interests!

By the way, Major League Baseball players agree that playing catch and pickle are better preparation for real baseball than T-ball and young Little League play.

2. *It won't interfere with most supper times.* Sometimes there are seasons (especially baseball, which just takes longer to play) where supper gets short shrift. If your family culture is strong, the benefit can outweigh the risk—but only for a time. Don't make it the default way of doing things. Supper together at least four times a week is the goal as your family enters the stage where most of the kids are old enough to sit up and converse. Let that goal slip for more than six weeks or so, and you are in trouble. There is nothing wrong with letting coach know that your child will miss a practice or two. Letting go of supper more or less permanently, as many parents mistakenly do in this phase of family life, is not an option.

Also, consider helping out with the team. Often the coach is a father who is getting out of work as early as he can in order to make the practice. If you can be there a bit earlier, check the kids off the roster, start them on their runs, and set up the drills, he can probably set the time up earlier (and thus end earlier). And you will have helped that father get home to his family as well. Never underestimate the power of an offer to help to put an important idea in someone's head—"Oh, yes, maybe I too should be having supper with my kids!" This is how we help each other.

3. *Sports will have its place in family culture, but not drive out other important activities.* Besides dinner together, those would be reading, sleeping, just being together, and getting work done. Of course, there are times (like tournaments) where yard work takes the backseat, but they are the exception.

4. *Each child also has a balanced schedule, with music lessons and other cultural activities given their due.* A lot depends on what is offered and what the child is interested in, but try to provide different sorts of instruction, not limiting yourself necessarily to conventional resources, but taking advantage

of the talented teen who can teach beginning piano or the enterprising homeschooler who will start a dancing class for the little ones.

5. *The activities enable you to connect with others in your community.* Over the years, I've found it a real blessing to get to know other families I wouldn't have any other way, and they got to know us (whether that blessed them or not!). When you stand out there on the sidelines for hours at a time, you can't help talking to people. This is a good thing, especially for homeschoolers who are otherwise at risk of being too isolated and public-school-goers whose prejudices melt when their kids are on teams with your kids. It's not worth sacrificing family life for (see above), but if it can be put in good balance with your other goals, then do it.

This brings me to another point. If your community is sports-minded to the extent that family life will clearly be impossible—Sunday morning hockey games, practices exclusively at supper time or so early in the morning that they decisively interfere with sleep, competition way out of proportion to the healthy development of the children, the vast majority of whom will never have a chance at even high school varsity-level play—then consider starting "family-friendly" sports and activities through your homeschooling group or St. Gregory Pocket (I discuss St. Gregory Pockets in volume 1). You need only about ten families to get something going at a reasonable time, and before you know it, you will have many more.

Forming your own league might take a few years to figure out, but you start with those seven-year-olds and gradually collect enough interested families to do one practice a week and games on Saturday mornings. That way, sports has a place, but not a usurping one.

Schoolyard or neighborhood games (kickball, tag football, pickup basketball, sandlot baseball) have a value that sports organized by parents and leagues will never attain. It's so sad to see this way of doing things disappear. With adults doing the organizing, neither schoolchildren nor homeschoolers are benefitting; allowing children to get up their own games is in danger of being forgotten entirely. Maybe homeschooling parents can recover, along with other freedoms for their children in this highly structured age of ours, the benefits of letting children organize their own games.

PART 4

Homeschool Planning and the Cycle of the Year

For those of us who can't help making up our own curricula, putting in the work in writing it all down, up front, is gold. Looking back, I can see that I always questioned whether what I was doing would be worth taking note of. I viewed it all as experimental, and so for a long time, I didn't. Don't make the same mistake. Write down what you are doing if only to prevent yourself from repeating the inadequate choice later. I'm telling you these things to save you from my fate. Let's not reinvent those particular wheels!

On Keeping Records as a Means to Clarifying Your Goals

I'm not one for keeping records, sadly. But I'd like to outline how I came to record and organize, and thus plan, my homeschool curricula. I always made my own curriculum for each child, as opposed to the obvious sanity-saving measure of just buying a packaged one. No, thank you, not for me; I am not attached to my sanity!

I went through years of homeschooling without ever really recording much at all. Between using mostly old or free materials and my lack of commitment when it comes to choosing a system, the method I finally developed could be termed low-tech—or bare bones—or simply grossly inadequate.

I record my secrets here, in the hope that they might help clarify certain problems that might not be confined to me. Perhaps my approach can help.

In my state, we don't have to do a lot of record keeping in the home school, which tends to enable a lazy person like me. My children did the work, but I didn't make note of it very well (and, of course, their progress was excellent, which further disincentivized me). But even for me—a person who homeschooled almost solely for the purpose of avoiding record keeping and anything that threatens to require paperwork—having a paper trail is a good thing.

Speaking psychologically and temperamentally, if you have a tendency to meander around, open dozens of tabs on the computer in the course of searching for curriculum ideas, and generally suffer from too many ideas, not too few—it might help to have things written down on paper. It's good to be able to prove to yourself and to anyone who has the power to inquire that you are actually doing something in what feels like a jumbled-up, blurry succession of days and weeks and months when the pregnancies, nights-long nursing sessions, toddler wranglings, chauffeurings, and everyday family-life scenarios erase your memory. Did we read? Did we do grammar? Fractions? French? Did anyone ever write a paper? Good questions.

This observation will be frighteningly obvious to some, but if you keep a good record of what you did with child number 1 in fifth grade, you will have most of the work already done for you when it comes to child number 2, not to mention child number 7, who is coming along when you are distinctly lacking in energy.

The Binder

The binder is basically the complete record of your home school. Since, by the time I figured this system out, I was down to my last three kids, I used one binder for all three, but you could have one binder for each child that will become your record for the grade or level.

This binder is the outline and to-do list for the year: one binder per year. It starts out rather slim, with sections. As the year goes on, the assignment sheet, one per child per week, gets filed after the fact, so your binder will grow in its contents. Note that a three-hole punch is essential to this system; you might as well buy one.

In the binder, you collect your written goals, book lists, any random materials that you foresee printing out and using (or come upon in the course of the year) such as black-line maps, extra math practice, spelling lists—anything that you want handy. Insert pocket separators for storing kids' productions that will need filing elsewhere, eventually. You can record grades, if you give them (and in high school, you might have to, depending on what colleges are in the offing; I know, it's silly, but there it is).

All the forms I used I found on Donna Young's site (DonnaYoung.org) or made in a word-processing program from her inspiration.

I have no doubt that there are more options available to provide these categories, but keep in mind that what is accomplished is quite simple. The binder offers flexibility; you can change or add categories or ways of keeping notes easily. For me, ease and flexibility are the two top qualities in recording anything.

In the binder, on the inside cover, put a copy of your public school district's calendar. Trust me. Many events in town go by this calendar, and it's good to know when school vacations are so you don't choose that week to go to the science museum or other vacationing-kid magnet. As you make your quarterly plans (below), this calendar will help you to figure out when the weeks in the quarter are. It will help you to build in breaks—important if you live in a neighborhood with public school children who will turn up at your door with sleds (and I hope they will!).

I start my planning with a sort of book list of some kind—which becomes the curriculum. It's by no means every book the child will read in the year! Nor is it everything he will do. But it's the skeleton. (In my state, this book list fulfills the required statement of curriculum. With a cover letter stating who's being homeschooled along with their birth dates, the superintendent of schools in my district will be satisfied that requirements are met.)

From the book list, I move from the universal to the particular. After countless hours of intensive preparation and research, complete with grandiose fantasies of the ultimate, classical, Charlotte Mason–driven, and utterly charming year ahead, I would decide on what to do and what to read.

Goals

At first, when I was making my binder and saw Donna Young's simple form for "goals," I thought I could skip it. But then I realized that I needed to be humble and write down my goals for each subject, as knowing where you are going helps you get there.

So for instance, in the junior year of high school, we might have a course called Logic and Rhetoric. As we are planning this course, we need goals, and for that the form is deployed. The first goal (reason for the course) is "to think clearly." This is plunked down in the left-hand column of the form under "Goals." Across from it, in the right-hand column, under "Resources/Comments" we would write (as a resource) "Euclid's Elements," "How to Read a Book (Adler)," and "Aristotle's Rhetoric (Memoria Press)." In the second box under "Goals," we might write (not exactly in parallel fashion) "Essays," and in the right-hand column under "Resources," we could write the several essays we have chosen to study (the Ambleside Online site has excellent recommendations).

LOGIC AND RHETORIC

Goals	Resources/Comments
To think clearly	Euclid's *Elements* *How to Read a Book* (Adler) Aristotle's *Rhetoric* (Memoria Press)
Essays	

You can consider this page your outline or sketch of the course, leaving the exact assignments for another form, called "Assignments," to be filed in the binder after it.

Sometime in February you are going to be wondering why you are requiring and have assigned a certain random essay in your home school, mainly because your equally demoralized young person will be asking why. More importantly, when it comes time to teach the next tenth or eleventh grader, you do not want to have to go through all the effort of finding this undoubtedly inspiring essay again, if you even remember it! But there it will be, safe in your binder—not buried in the assignments but easily accessible.

Another reason to state your goals explicitly: you might want your sixth grader "to write a good sentence." Usually by the middle of the year, home-schooling parents are in the grips of two opposing wishes: to give up on schooling entirely and to teach that sixth grader to write like Hemingway (it's always Hemingway, never George Eliot or Cicero—sad, but that's a different book).

How helpful all around to open your binder to the goals page and read: "To write a good sentence." It comes in handy when all your friends are discussing the latest magic curriculum that gets your sixth grader to write like Hemingway. You realize that your child can write a good sentence, which not everyone can—and you can give yourself a pat on the back.

The Course of Study

Having chosen the books, I would write out a course of study. This is a simple chart with categories across the top: "Subject," "Books," "Times a week," and "Notes."

Subject	Books	Times a week	Notes
Foreign language	Latin I, Spanish 5	5	post vocab lists

In the "Subject" column, write each subject you want to cover. I strongly recommend putting art, music, and religion in there along with English, math, and science. That way, you can see all the areas of study at once and have the immediate sense that you are engaging in a full course of study.

The Quarterly Planning Page

Because I was always putting together a curriculum (no matter how hard I tried to use a packaged one), I needed a quarterly planning page. I used

Donna Young's "quarter planner" so that I had an overview of the weeks. This form makes use of little boxes necessitated by the "overview" format, so you need abbreviations—thus, you must make a key to those abbreviations in your booklist or at the bottom of the quarterly plan. You know, for another year or, for that matter, another week when you have no idea what GWW (*George Washington's World*) could possibly mean.

Now, perhaps you are seeing that if you want to teach a certain book, such as George Washington's World, you don't need someone's packaged curriculum to do so (and thus, I am vindicated, if not completely sane). You need the ability to divide up the book among the weeks you plan to cover it! Looking at it and considering your fifth grader's ability to read and pay attention, you might decide that it will take you five weeks to read and study. (Perhaps the book you are interested in conveniently has five chapters, for instance.) By far, the most difficult thing for me to wrap my mind around in my whole homeschooling career was this: You then plan it for five weeks.

There are other books you want to read and study. Just line them up, divide them up, and record what you want to do in your quarterly planner. The good news is that math books are always keyed to a basic 180-day schedule, so they neatly fill the year (keeping in mind that the first few weeks are review and the last few weeks are filler in the unlikely event that you have torn through the book before the end).

The Weekly Plan

Once you have your quarters mapped out (and there will be three quarters, not four—not in our homeschool, where summer is off!), you can pretty easily come up with a weekly lesson plan. You are just consulting your quarter planner and fleshing out the week's assignments, with other activities scheduled in.

Don't forget music and art, along with their practices and lessons. Since physical education is an important part of school, put in their sports and dance lessons as well.

Eventually I figured out that if I printed out the week's outline of assignments and activities and posted it on the fridge, the child could see what was expected (rather than coming to me every hour or so to ask what to do, or worse, just disappear), juggle his assignments, check them off, and learn to manage his own time. And we'd still be on track to achieve our goals.

When a week's work is done, file it in the binder on top of the quarterly form. At the end of the year, you should have three quarter pages, in reverse order, separated by their respective weekly plans, also in reverse order. That is, when you open the binder toward the end of the school year, the May weekly plans should be on top.

As time went by, I started doing these weekly plans out on the computer and printing them out. Today you can get a lesson planner that is synced with your browser's calendar.

I'm sure all of this can be put online. But do print a paper version so that you have it and so that your children won't have to look at screens to get their assignments.

The binder helps you go from the general to the particular. You start with a list of courses and move through goals to a weekly plan. It helps you keep a record. It keeps you from being at the mercy of your sudden fancy ideas about the one true way to achieve enlightenment, or, on the other hand, from coming up with the same good idea over and over—you can see at a glance that you already thought it through, if you did. And it's flexible, because you can open it up and insert a page when you need to!

Making your own curriculum isn't easy. But a homeschool planning binder really helps.

But How Does the Child Learn to Do It on His Own?

Build up gradually to the child's taking responsibility for his own work. For a second grader, it's not difficult to know what the day's work will be. Wholistic approaches to learning are lovely, but there is room for the math and phonics workbooks, from which a page a day is attempted.

I love the older MCP Plaid math series for its clarity of scope and sequence and also for the ease of saying to the second grader: do a page of your math workbook. Ditto their phonics book—a page in the workbook. (Elsewhere, in my "teaching the child to read" series, I specify which edition of workbook to get. You should know that I do not recommend the newer versions, which, of course, makes things complicated.) The child knows where the math manipulatives are kept. He has his little shelf of books to read—chosen perhaps from the Ambleside booklist. He also knows where books are kept in the house; he can always go get one of those—a nice picture book to read to his sibling, his favorite chapter book ... Yes, Mom will be there directing these young children in the few actual assignments they have.

It seems better in general to have "math time" and "phonics time" rather than a task that seems to go on forever. Keep it all short and sweet. The ponderers in particular are better off with fewer tasks when they are so young. Better to arrange things so that this sort of child is begging you for more responsible sorts of assignments than for you to be in the position of dragging him along.

Reverse psychology works so well with children—it was invented for them! When you put something interesting just out of reach and wonder aloud, "When you are older, maybe you can take a look at this." When there is an attractive notebook and pencil but no touching that just yet ... When you are interested in something and talk about it with your friends but don't actually talk about it with the child directly ...

In fact, this is how I started homeschooling. I was reading extensively on the subject and conversing endlessly with my friends but not with the children. One day, they told the librarian (they did run to the library by themselves; they were maybe eight and six), "We are homeschooling this year!" Well, just to keep face ...

Most of what you do for school with your young children will be reading to them, encouraging them to make their own books and to draw, starting to learn musical instruments, singing some hymns or folk songs, memorizing little poems, and other "life with kids" activities that aren't amenable to a weekly chart with things to be checked off, other than by you. Mostly they just play!

By fourth or fifth grade, you will see a big difference in self-motivation with the weekly chart. When the child reads well, he can handle his assignments on his own; if you speak about the prospect with enthusiasm, he will be eager to do it.

On Losing Hope (or the Will to Live), Commonly Known as "Burning Out"

I was talking to my friend Auntie Sue the other day, and she was wondering what it is about younger moms that makes them want to listen to us. As she said, it's not that we are so great at what we do.

"No," says I. "It's just this: we've lived through a bunch of stuff."

Simply having survived intact means so much in this life of ours.

Dr. Johnson in his Dictionary defines the virtue of longanimity as forbearance and being patient with offenses; he quotes James Howell:

> That innocent and holy matron had rather go clad in the snowy white robes of meekness and longanimity, than in the purple mantle of blood.

Why, this is our virtue! Surely in February we need it, lest we, well, obtain for ourselves a purple mantle of blood. It's human nature to be more than halfway through a project (such as the homeschool year) and be assailed with dryness, doubts, and, yes, let's admit it, despair or even bloodshed. You know what I'm talking about, or you soon will.

What can I offer you as you wrestle with the growing certainty that you should have put the kids in school long ago?

I offer you this: the sure knowledge that it's the same in school. Any teacher will tell you that everyone feels the same way: tired of walking on sand tracked in from the snowy driveway, sick—and sick of being sick—quite sure you're getting nowhere with school subjects, and, worst of all, cabin fever!

Remember why you are trying to educate them in the first place? I did it, however poorly, because I believe that children need order and wonder. The family needs confidence to be this little "society" where the child learns what can reasonably be expected of him; parents provide the framework, the order. Then the mysteries of life, intellectual, spiritual, and artistic, will unfold themselves to our children according to their abilities and openness. And that's the wonder.

Don't expect affirmation from them along the way. Just have confidence in your goals—order and wonder—and the means you use to get there.

Longanimity

Just as by magnanimity a man has a mind to tend to great things, so by longanimity a man has a mind to tend to something a long way off. Wherefore as magnanimity regards hope, which tends to good, rather than daring, fear, or sorrow, which have evil as their object, so also does longanimity. Hence longanimity has more in common with magnanimity than with patience.[5]

February, or anytime you've gotten into a rut and can't talk yourself out, is a good time to clean out bookcases and craft shelves, on the principle that upheaval captures attention.

No one is more disposed to read a book than when he is organizing those books, and nothing is more appealing than a bunch of craft materials

---

[5]   St. Thomas Aquinas, *Summa Theologica*, II-II, q. 136, art. 5.

being straightened up in the cabinet! I don't pretend to understand it, but ask a child to take everything off his school shelf in order to rearrange it, and you will soon find him engrossed in things you despaired of ever getting him to glance at.

Now (February, or the burnout time, whenever it occurs) is the time to go back to your original thoughts about the current year (and it helps greatly to have written them out in some form, which I address in the chapter "Homeschool Planning"). Did you hope that this year your child would learn to enjoy reading a chapter book? Then why are you fretting about goals such as writing a story—goals that you never even set yourself, but maybe overheard some other moms discussing?

Do you know this syndrome? Rather than being reinvigorated by the recent homeschooling group meeting, you found yourself thrown into a panic by someone's mention of her Extra-Zowie Laminated Ancient Greece Unit Study or their Curriculum Packet of Supersonic Intergalactic Genius Makers. Even supposedly classical study methods can have this effect on us. Suddenly it doesn't seem so great that we are reading some poems at bedtime for enjoyment, because we don't seem to have the bells and whistles we keep hearing about.

But if we go by the intelligent people in history, we should rather come to the conclusion that the best thing we could do for our children is to make them spend all day hunting and chopping wood (like Abraham Lincoln), or maybe subject them to outright abuse (like Benjamin Franklin), or maybe just settle for "a difficult struggle to get ahead in life" (like Marie Curie).

We just don't know. So take the "burnout season" as an opportunity to stop and recover your own goals—and enjoyment. Learn some folk tunes. Insist that your children do their math first (or let them do it last for a while, if that helps). Remember that you meant to read out loud every day from a book that's a little bit above them. Go to the library and take out a stack of the oldest-looking books there. Make a lap book. Bundle everyone up and see if the willows have started sprouting. Get out a book on drawing in perspective.

As for me, I'll try to tidy things up, get outdoors more, and get ready for Lent. Before you know it, spring will be here. Longanimity ...

What about Summer?

Summer can stretch out interminably, and I remember the panic, contemplating being home with little children under those circumstances. Maybe the money or the schedule won't allow for a long vacation. School schedules make summer vacation away *seem* to be a necessity, but life on one income (the very circumstance that enables you to homeschool) can make expensive vacations impossible. I used to feel a bit sorry for myself until I realized how enjoyable summers with the kids can be.

I suggest planning an old-fashioned summer with some low-key expectations in which the children can look forward every day to simple pleasures: a few chores (because there can be pleasure in knowing you are all in it together), many books, and lots of play.

Many homeschoolers keep their curriculum going all year long. I never wanted to do that, so no school for us in the summer. But it's funny how when you simply must write your own book, suddenly you get a crash course in spelling. Or when you play certain board games, your math expertise goes way up and you master your addition and subtraction facts.

It's also funny how, when there's a spelling workbook stashed in among the Dover coloring books on the shelf, it has to be done while the children play "school."

Ideally, either way, you will have at least a bit of a chance to take a little vacation (and obviously, if you live somewhere where the better vacation time is not during summer, your circumstances will be different).

Even a day trip here or there works. We would all want six weeks by some shore, but even a garden hose or a kiddie pool provides an unexpected amount of satisfying water fun—and *doing something watery* is how I define summer fun!

This brings me to the question of activities.

Precondition for a Good Summer: Ban All Screens

Hide the remote, close the computers, ditch the tablets—*even in the car*. Instead, listen to good music, including sing-along songs that you will all then know forever. Or just talk things over. Try it; it's nice.

The silences of summer, punctuated by crickets and cicadas, are some of its pleasures. Even if you normally use the AC, try turning it off and opening windows when you are able to.

Reading a book (or, for a child who can't read, looking at the illustrations), coloring on the porch, playing cards on the deck under a tree, playing in the sandbox: your children will do and enjoy these things only if there is no screen or video games to tempt them. Don't use screens to bribe. Just ditch them and be free! (It's fine with Auntie Leila to have movie night, but you understand my point here.)

If your children are older, have a little meeting and let them know how things will go, *especially about the screens and video games* if they have gotten into bad habits. Let them talk to you, but be quietly firm about your goals and hopes for this time. Every once in a while, our children need the experience of *having to give up*. Once they *give up*, magical things happen to their time!

Just playing. Let them play. Their play will be fueled by their imaginations and the books they read (see below). Give them the necessary "tools" of play: a sandbox, an outdoor mud kitchen made of old crates or shelves, age-appropriate board games, balls (including whiffle balls and bats), a basin of water, a bucket of plastic army guys, dolls and carriages.

When I hear homeschoolers say they will continue schoolwork through the summer, the child in me dies a little. Do what you want, of course. But if it's math facts you are worried about, may I recommend having them play games instead? And I don't mean on the tablet. Send them out to the porch after chores to play the card game called "Math War." (Do an Internet search if you don't know it; basically, it's regular War with turning up two cards and then doing math operations to see who wins, with variations including ones that add strategy by using trumps.)

Don't forget Parcheesi for those who just need to do some addition (a super-boring game that takes forever and can be over in an instant if someone jostles the board—what's not to love?). There's Yahtzee. Little girls love playing with jacks—and visualizing the groups that make up 10 is half the battle in subtraction. I bet you can think of ones from your childhood! All way better than worksheets, I promise you.

Activities

Swimming lessons are highly worthwhile. Pack sandwiches, fruit, and chips; juggle naps to give the gift of knowing how to swim. Plus, swimming wears them out. Plan on plenty of high-calorie snacks, big lunches, big suppers, and early bed.

Camps that last for only a week or two. I don't mean send-away camps; I mean little neighborhood camps that give the kids a fun skill. Our older kids and their friends were the ones to offer such camps as teenagers, after attending ones given by kids who were older than they: drama camp, fiddle camp, boating camp, Gilbert and Sullivan camp, tennis camp, baseball camp, basketball camp, art camp: you name it, they can go to it and then give it. If you don't have a group (how about a St. Gregory Pocket? your homeschooling group?), join your neighborhood online network and look for postings at the local library.

Camp gives a nice structure to a short part of the summer, which allows your children to have a good balance between having somewhere to be and enjoying endless days of "doing nothing" (only they will do plenty, as you will see!).

Jump-start your community's economy and interdependence by actively seeking teenagers who will provide this sort of camp for your littles. At first, these teenagers might need a little guidance, but soon you will be able to step out of the way. They will earn some money, and you will have some stellar activities for your children.

Chores, work around the house, and service. Most families could benefit from at least a small vegetable and herb garden, and weeding isn't such a dismal chore if everyone participates in preparing and planting. Towels have to be washed and hung out. There is still the matter of keeping the house, and once a week you have to give it at least a full morning's attention. (Remember: if you aren't *in* your house, it stays cleaner! Go to the zoo! Go to a museum! Go to the playground! Anything not to have to clean!)

Boys must have a lot of good, solid, hard physical work. Read them stories in which little boys do lots of work! Give them big holes to dig way in the back of the yard (if you have one). They can *literally* swab the decks, and everyone will be better off.

If you own your home, projects abound. Children can be workers. They can be in charge of picking up nails, of bringing you supplies, of washing up outside afterward. They can pull the baby in the wagon while you do your work. Soon they will be old enough to take over.

Meals are simpler in the summer but still have to be prepared and eaten, and cleaning up needs to be done afterward. The start of summer is the perfect time to give out new chores and work out new skills around the house.

Neighbors still get sick, have babies, and need their lawns mowed. Send the children out to help with these things. They are your little ambassadors, and if *they* do a charitable work, it will certainly get *you* a check mark! I'm counting on this myself.

I recommend challenging the children to do their big chores early in the day, while it's still cool. If you are heading out to swim lessons or day camp, share with them the satisfaction, the downright pleasure, of coming home to an orderly house after a day spent away. "Oh, coming home to our nice clean house is such a treat!" I found that they did notice.

Reading. Plan a day each week to get to the library (if yours has good books; if not, perhaps try swapping with friends who have good collections or getting to a used-book sale near you, having a treat of going to a good bookstore or ordering online, or "shopping the house" for a rotating crate or shelf of books). For a long time, we were lucky enough to live within walking distance of the local branch. My kids would take a wagon full of books (and sometimes they'd pop Bridget, the toddler, in there) to and fro. They could also ride their bikes. There's nothing like a pile of tempting books, fiction and nonfiction, from the library to keep everyone enchanted for a while on a long hot summer afternoon.

If you guide them wisely, you will find that these books provide all the "educational activities" necessary, when taken with conversations with you and others, with long periods of quiet in which they can think things over, and with the gift of that "unstructured play" we are always hearing about but never know how to implement.

This is it! Summer! That magical time when, if you have a question, you are blissfully free to read about the answers in a book or ask someone who knows. Summer! When you have the whole day and week and month to try building, making, doing.

A great book for summer: *The Boy Scouts Handbook*. Be sure to get an older edition, and be prepared for your children to build traps, light fires—safely, one hopes—and make their own fishhooks. At least they will be leaving you alone!

Dover Publications (which publishes the reprint of the *Boy Scouts Handbook*) supplies so many hours of good activity for the children with their coloring books of birds, fairy tales, and butterflies, and you name it: paper dolls, toy theaters, magic tricks, stickers, and all sorts of things. Their Thrift Editions offer classics at a reasonable price too.

If the children have done chores in the morning and had swim lessons before lunch, they will be ready for some quiet time with their books, after which you can read a chapter of an especially fun one. Reading aloud is also such a treat after the baby is in bed but the sky is still bright.

Praying. Any change of season is a good time to restart prayer time. Summer is the perfect time to use the nature table to transition into a Little Oratory (I explain how in an appendix in *The Little Oratory*, my book on prayer in the home). When you are all together at breakfast, you can say a little morning offering together. Your gratitude at the more relaxed pace can overflow into building the habit of praying grace over meals. The long summer evening is the perfect time to start the Rosary. Even one decade is lovely. Perhaps with everyone getting up a bit earlier with the sun and not having such pressing schedules, you can make it to morning Mass.

Back to summer evenings. If you can have your supper relatively early, the family can enjoy the hours of daylight afterward, especially if Dad can get home to toss a ball in the driveway, have his turn with a chapter book, take a walk with the family (maybe with some ice cream cones, which is such an affordable treat when you buy the cones and scoop yourself), or visit with neighbors on the porch. Those evenings also lend themselves to having friends over for bonfires, s'mores, games of ghost in the graveyard or horseshoes or what have you, and sing-alongs. Older children like to put on little plays for family and friends. The library often has good collections of fun short plays for children (or find them used).

Rainy-day activities. Take advantage of rainy days to pull everyone in and focus on quieter activities. The rain has its own pleasures: tidying

the playroom, doing a little baking, sewing, or building, reading books, tackling an indoor painting job …

Keep a Rhythm Going

So you see, even in summer, it helps to keep a schedule of sorts where you divide the day into periods of activity and periods of relative inactivity. A rhythm.

If you remember that rhythm is your friend, you will avoid that sense that the day stretches out with no relief in sight. It's just that you have to be both rather firm in keeping the schedule and open to summertime freedom—in that good tension that keeps you from going too far from one extreme to the other and shows you just how to hold the reins. Within that good, helpful structure, just let your children have a good old-fashioned summer.

Finally, before you tuck them in, wash your children's faces and feet— do not let your children go to bed with dirty, dusty feet (but do let them run around barefoot!). You want their sheets free of downright grubbiness, and you want the children to have the enjoyment of lying in their beds with tingling toes. Try it yourself—it's delightful.

Don't make the mistake of thinking that unless you purposely include so-called educational activities in there, they won't learn. They will be learning very well.

Let's take a break from trying to make everything educational. Children learn by having lots of great books to read, music to listen to, and materials to make things out of—not to mention freedom to think up in the higher branches of a handy tree. With less stress in the area of official schooling, you'll find that you yourself will feel renewed. You could get to a project of your own (maybe during the baby's nap?). *You* could read a book! When the children see you doing any of this, and most importantly, enjoying yourself, they will figure out what *they* want to do.

Family Travel

Summer travel offers opportunities for family growth and for education in a way that you might not be used to considering. Workbooks have their (very limited) place, but the "visible outcome" aspect of such activities can sap your confidence in less quantifiable ways to spend time.

Children of all abilities benefit from being with their parents. Children who seem a little slower to talk benefit from having to sit tight and listen to their parents talk to each other. Pointing out the scenery as you are contentedly heading down the highway to your summer destination builds their vocabularies as well as their memories.

When you're stuck in the car for long hours, you can sing nursery rhymes and recite poetry (and learn it too). We had some of our best read-aloud sessions in the car, with the cry of "One more chapter please" able to be met with a "Why not?"

If your drive is long enough to justify videos (and you have the technology), decide when you will play them, since Gresham's law applies to leisure activities as well as money: bad drives out good.

Singing together in the car is great fun, more easily achieved when the children are young, but possible, maybe with good recordings to lead the way, when they are older, if you are only now discovering this pleasure. If you don't already have the right repertoire, look for patriotic songs and silly songs (the old-fashioned kind), and traditional American songs such as "Oh! Susanna" and "When Johnny Comes Marching Home Again."

In the appendix you will find a section offering some of our audiobook favorites for all ages. The key for the littles is to read the books beforehand, at home, enough times so that they know the story pretty well. Then, in the car, they can follow along. Audiobooks are better than video because they require active participation from the child. At some point, you can say, "Now you just look at the book, Daddy and I want to talk. We'll listen to the CD later."

Pack a hamper full of snacks: pretzel sticks, tortilla chips and hummus, nuts, carrot sticks, cheese cubes, and cut-up fruit and grapes. Small, manageable sandwiches, cheese and crackers, and cookies will keep you from too much fast food.

Make strategic stops where you can really let a toddler run. Many of the old areas of the country have towns with a courthouse square with a green space to run around in. Big cities that have expanded usually have a few courthouse squares or town greens located along a well-traveled axis, often with picnic tables. Alternatively, a college campus has great green spaces as well—we would let our toddlers run and push their own strollers around! Great for a quick game of catch, too.

Good activities for the car: threading Cheerios on pipe cleaners, enjoying glow sticks in the dark. Magna Doodles are the right size for laps and don't have any pieces to lose. Kids draw on them for a good long while, and

pass them back and forth with Mom drawing funny faces, trains, trucks, trucks on trains—lots of laughter and playful erasing. Water Wow! coloring and painting pads are truly no mess and can be used over and over again.

Don't be afraid of some crying times or some fussy times. It doesn't mean you are a bad mom—it's normal! Children get over their fussiness. What they remember are the good times on the car rides.

Summers with a Newborn

Little babies enjoy just lying on a blanket under a tree looking at the leaves. Do the same things as usual, such as reading books and letting the children run about, but in a different location.

Have "watering time" and give the older children watering cans to water things around the yard. Another day each week, give them a bucket and sponges and let them wash the car or the fence. Another day, it's the kiddie pool or the sprinkler. And then have a snack on the blanket, and that's another half an hour of outdoor time for everyone.

And all the while that the children think you are providing outstandingly fun outdoor time for them, you are resting on the blanket, drinking from your water bottle, and eating your almonds and M&Ms. If Baby tolerates a carrier, walk in circles at a shady park playground while the older children play. You can also get a reliable baby monitor with a long range to take outside if the baby miraculously happens to be willing to nap somewhere other than in your arms. Then you can go outside with the other children.

Sometimes you feel refreshed resting in a breezy spot and can't understand why your baby seems fussy. Bring a basket (something with sides) if you are putting the baby down at the beach, for instance; just laying the baby on the blanket won't work, because newborns are equipped with instincts to protect them from the cooling air. They are too young to maintain their own body temperature, even when it seems hot to us. Always take at least a little cotton receiving-type blanket to keep the breeze off Baby's skin.

Make sure you have lots of whatever you like to drink; don't get dehydrated when you are out and about. Set yourself up where the baby can sleep and nurse. Summer babies are easier to manage in many ways. Keep a basket stocked with all the things that might be needed outside (clean burp clothes, diaper, wipes, sunglasses, book for you, and so on) so that you can get out the door quickly and not run inside for things you forgot.

Babies are portable! Sure, for the first couple of weeks, you stay close to home. But then you're off. That baby just goes wherever you go, with a bit of advanced planning.

A nice, roomy, old-fashioned pram can offer a portable little place to put the baby when you are not nursing (inside the house too, if you have the need to put him down but keep him near).

Older Children Who Are Too Young for Formal Jobs

A niche exists for older children (fourteen to sixteen) who don't want to play but are too young for formal jobs: babysitting, housecleaning, farm work, lawn mowing, pet sitting (for families on vacation), and bagging groceries; offering piano lessons, organizing camps, and watching an elderly neighbor; pressure washing, putting in gardens, and painting fences.

At home, these energetic youngsters can help by putting in raised beds, building their dream firepit, scraping off old paint, and putting up retaining walls.

In their leisure time, they should be encouraged to learn new skills: woodburning, target shooting, sewing, knitting, and woodworking.

Now is not the time to give up on them, because this time at home, while sometimes wearisome, can be the impetus for discovering a real talent or skill and even a vocation.

Fiddle Camp

think that some cities sponsor camps during the summer, and certainly swanky country clubs with expensive memberships have them. But the best kind of all arise naturally from communities that have lots of young people. What we call camps become an excellent means of older children being able to offer the fruits of their talents to younger children. In a homeschooling community they are an unexpected but organic way to achieve continuity and a real blossoming of the efforts put in by the parents when the children were younger. In other words, the light becomes visible in the long tunnel; educating children won't always represent such a vast expenditure of effort and energy on the part of the parents. Eventually, the children grow old enough to become a resource for others.

In our homeschooling group (a handy way to refer to the many families that have grown up near each other rather organically in our area, not all of whom homeschool, actually) we have drama camps, Gilbert & Sullivan camps (music plus drama!), and fiddle camp. My kids have gone to these camps and have taken their turns running them. Our Will even ran a baseball camp, because he really wanted the homeschoolers to know about baseball! It was his personal mission.

To give an example in the fiddle camp, Bridget's students gathered for five afternoons for one week, and her friend Rose helped her teach them fiddle and also a couple of Scottish country dances. The children studied fiddle with Bridget for a few years, and then she went to college, so they caught up during the summer as much as they could.

Offering a camp really gives the children an opportunity to work intensely on their skills and encourage one another to reach ever new heights in fiddle expertise. You don't need professional experts for this sort of thing: you just need mildly competent older children or young adults.

During the week, of course, there have to be breaks, and that offers lots of opportunity for good summer fun. I cleverly bought squirt guns and a kiddie pool half-price at the store, and you know, a kiddie pool is just a surprising amount of fun for a small amount of water!

I used to stress out about having such an event at my house. Even though I have a big kid-friendly house and yard, I thought it wasn't good enough—that you need a real pool, or a lake, or an ocean, or some sort of actual body of water (this is my fixation—can't really explain it).

Not to mention having a yard free of weeds, picture-perfect gardens, some sort of fancy swing set at least ... I had a *serious* case of "not-good-enough-itis," in short. This comes of reading too many magazines or, if you are like this but younger, visiting too many fancy sites online.

I have since relaxed.

To recount the experience of one year with Bridget's fiddle camp: The particular very imaginative children involved in this camp instantly organized games of tag and epic relay races. They all played together—all the ages. And they also learned quite a number of tunes and steps.

At the end of the week, the kids practiced all afternoon and then the families (with all the siblings too) arrive late enough for the dads to join the fun after their workday is over. The finale is a potluck supper with tables out on the grass, and a show on the deck!

Another fun and funny part of the camp is a Scottish or any contra-style line dance that includes everyone—grown-ups too—on the lawn. An important part of the festivities, getting everyone involved!

The children take off their shoes upon arrival at the camp, so they are all barefoot while performing. "Discalced fiddlers," one dad named them.

One funny note was that our normally timid border collie mix, Roxie, couldn't really leave the stage, front and center. I have a photo of her as the campers are playing their tunes in which she is clearly radiating the message, "I'm a fiddler too."

I just want to say: if you stick with your friends, raising your children together, encouraging them to share their talents with you and sharing in your turn—and not worrying about how perfect your life may or may not be—you will see that a culture will grow up right around you. That is my only reason for telling you any of this: to encourage you to start now if you haven't and to keep on if you have.

PART 5

On Teaching Your Child to Read

In the past, there is no question that, with very few resources, children learned to read. Often they were taught by a very young woman with only a little education herself, certainly not the recipient of today's decades of training, costing hundreds of thousands of dollars. Even in cities, this old-fashioned schoolteacher taught multiple levels, with nothing but a small shelf of books and plain old paper and pencil or even just slates and chalk.

Your Child Will Learn to Read

On the list of academic issues that make parents writhe with anxiety, the thought that their children are not learning the basics of reading and writing comes right up at the top. You need to know that no child is exactly like another, and the truth is that no one really knows how a person learns. We tend to think academic success is a matter of prosperity; yet, even children who don't have shoes can learn to read. Literacy in America was 90 percent at the time of the Revolution.

The response to this statement might be that I'm glossing over unacknowledged inequalities—to which I respond that we should not rationalize today's failure. Women could read. Slaves were taught to read by their elders and by tutors. Maybe sometimes they were taught to read so they could keep records for their masters, but they could read, and then they read what they could find, regardless. We have been a nation of readers. Since the goal of early Americans was to make reading of Scripture universal, the definition of literacy was held to a fairly high standard.

The circumstances in which they learned give the lie to the impression these days that only a phalanx of experts and a vast superstructure of bureaucracy can get the job done.

Parents with children in the very best schools worry about reading skills, even though the ordinary mother long ago, with nothing but a grade school education herself, taught her children, often with no access to paper or pencil. No, today's parents are worrying as if they are about to send their child to the moon using nothing but a slide rule (and, actually, that has been done—not by moms with little children, but it has been done).

In a way, they're right. I don't want to sound alarmist, but because education has become a big industry, there is way too much incentive to make things complicated and then sell the schools something to fix what parents already paid a lot of money for (in the form of tuition and taxes). Homeschooling parents get caught up in the anxiety as well.

But I need to ask: Is it possible that we make this too complicated?

In the eighteenth century, ordinary people read so well that *The Federalist Papers*, which are listed in book catalogs today as having a target audience of students in graduate school, were originally published in the *New York Times* as position papers for the ratification of the Constitution. They were written for the citizens of the colony, most of whom were farmers. Don't think that's an exaggeration; even the most far-flung rural area took its news very seriously.

Well, if they were able do it, and achieve such a high level of literacy, one that our school system has no intention of reaching, so can we.

Language and Silence

Some children learn to read no matter what. But reading is about language, and the language our children are exposed to must be of a high order if we want them to want to read.

Most of the language young children (as well as the rest of us) are exposed to is geared toward either making us buy something or making us forget that we are rational human beings (entertainment and advertisements, and noisy background music, respectively). I don't know how we got to the point where language and sound in general have become assault weapons. Thus, it's a little harder to make our children's world one that works for encouraging reading if we don't separate ourselves from the larger culture. The good news is that the world that works for reading also happens to be one that is delightful and conducive to a peaceful existence.

At home, at least, our goal as parents should be to create an environment that has both order and wonder. Even the smallest child should begin to sense that there is a rhythm to most days, with times built in that provide silence and *good* sounds, including those of nature.

Silence. A wonderful, amazing state of being. Every day there should be some silence in your children's lives.

Some good sounds are obvious; the sound of your voice (speaking in complete sentences, singing, and reading to the child); the sounds of babies; the child himself babbling with a book in his hands.

Maybe some are not so obvious: nursery rhymes and old children's songs—these two elements, once so very common in every household, are perhaps the biggest contributors to literacy before the fact, yet the most overlooked today (after a good *old* translation of the Bible, heard during worship). When a child wraps his little tongue around rhymes that mean something to him, he's learning that individual words have the power to delight when paired with other specific words! When he sings a silly song that incorporates alliteration, rhyme, and repetition, he's getting great practice simply in knowing how words work.

I became aware of this somewhat hidden learning experience when we had a French friend visiting. She had trouble getting comfortable with the words "Go tell So-and-so that such and such"—as I'm sure I would, in French. "Go tell Deirdre that supper is ready," I'd say, and she couldn't quite get used to it. But you could get her to *sing* them ("Go tell Aunt Rhody, Go tell Aunt Rhody!")—especially if she had been used to singing as a child. I still remember the dialogues I learned by heart in middle school, when I was studying French and German at the same time.

Words are not just scattershot that you hope hit your target. They should have a purpose and be a pleasure to give and receive. And that takes all the practice of the years leading up to learning to read—years that are hard to get back once they go by.

Children who are learning to read need to run around outside. Parents today—certainly schools—are unrealistic about the vital necessity for a child to, as my husband says, "get his ya-yas out." Part of every day—scheduled into that *order* I keep talking about, the rhythm of life—should be spent simply running around and yelling! Outside, of course.

We smart, strong, intense, discipline-oriented parenting types forget what it's like to be a child. Children today are smothered by the intensive grip of their unoccupied mothers, and yes, I do consider, when compared with families of the past, that we are unoccupied. (Perhaps working mothers are paradoxically the most unoccupied of all when they are with their children, and it's not good for them. "Quality time" is a completely new concept, invented to compensate somehow for time spent entirely apart from one's children.)

Most parents are querulously or limply confining in their approach. These limp confiners don't require anything of their children in the way of focused activity, preferring to regulate them externally with sports and entertainment, but they also never really let them run wild, even for a minute. Their children are still constrained, albeit not to any effect.

Children, even small ones, long ago spent a lot more time just running around. Thus, when asked to sit still for twenty minutes to learn something, they didn't regard such a request as the *sheer injustice* their counterparts today do.

Oh, make no mistake about it. When your child squirms, giggles, slumps, drops his pencil repeatedly, cries, or otherwise misbehaves at school (home or "real"), he's registering (in the only way he knows how, so give him credit) resistance at the *sheer injustice* of your requirements for his day. And I, for one, don't blame him one bit.

When I started writing about these subjects, I was determined to dole out one small homeschooling insight at a time. I knew that readers might think they want the chipper assurance of one long post with all the homeschooling answers. I have found that it doesn't quite work that way.

This business of the education of children is *the* business of your life (if you have children). It can't be solved in a day or with a one-size-fits-all and someone-else-thought-through-it-so-I-don't-have-to program.

Certain components *will* be that way, thankfully. But the whole enterprise is one that each family must work hard at to figure out. My writing is an attempt to help with what really is going to take time and thought and prayer. Simply being together and living family life is a good education in itself; happy family life should bring you great confidence.

Materials for Early Reading

bviously, children learn to read in different ways. Anyone who has more than one child knows how all the preconceived ideas can be surprised into oblivion by that subsequent child. One child will seem hardly to have been introduced to the basics, and he's off with *Tom Sawyer*. Another can't get the hang of reading until he's almost an adolescent.

Let's apply my favorite analytical tool, the 80-20 rule; or my take on it, which is the 10-80-10 rule. I have no idea if those numbers really represent how things break down, but I'll bet they are close. It goes like this: 80 percent of children will more or less do what they need to do to get on in life, including reading.

You would think you could only derive consolation from that fact, but here's what happens: those little 80 percenters create a serious problem for the 10 percent whose quick, effortless mastery leaves them stuck with others' low expectations. And they create a serious problem for the 10 percent who are physically or developmentally out of sync and will take longer to reach a given level than the others. Probably each 10 percent should be further broken down into the 1 percent on either end who make the pigeonholers really crazy.[6]

Being a parent means figuring things out. Use this rough-and-ready true-life guideline to relax just a little! Knowing that institutions can't help but operate on the basis of averages, we, in the intimacy of our homes and the secure knowledge of the grace of our vocation, can make a judgment right out here in the field about this little one who may be having a little trouble, or that one who zooms ahead, leaving us in his dust. And we can adjust accordingly.

This willingness to adjust is the hardest thing to achieve for those of us who are school-minded. We continue to apply a system designed for averages even when we are teaching only one child. Let's shift our paradigm to realize that it's the teacher of a large classroom who's hampered by not being able to tailor the approach to the individual—hence the system or program, which helps him catch as many as he can. The parent guiding her very own child, whom she knows so well, is far freer to spend more time or none at all, depending.

Having said all that, there are three basic things you have to know about how your child will learn to read. And you—only you, especially for that 10 percent on either end of the spectrum—need to find the balance for the learning process.

---

[6] Eyesight can be an issue. If things don't progress normally, which simply means that you aren't comfortable with how things are going, do consider that a purely physical issue might be at stake. A visit to a good optometrist is in order. In my experience, an ophthalmologist hands off the vision correction exam to an assistant, because his focus, pardon the pun, is on *diseases* of the eye.

An optometrist is trained to uncover vision problems, and there are some children who simply can't see the text well enough to make reading anything other than a chore to be avoided.

If the optometrist doesn't find any problem, then seek out a developmental ophthalmologist. A reader of my blog had a child with an issue called convergence insufficiency. He could see, but reading required so much effort that he got tired quickly. With vision therapy, he went from not wanting to read at all to reading the whole *Lord of the Rings* trilogy in a few months.

Choose your materials based on these three things (as well as the other important thing in the next section).

Knowing the Letters and Their Sounds

Letters and their sounds are two different things, mind. Many a child has to sort out that fact, on his own, because we adults forget. Yes, he needs to learn the alphabet. That's easy. Sing the alphabet song, get alphabet books, use Montessori-style sandpaper letters for the child struggling with fine motor skills, and so forth.

What is a little trickier is to associate the name of the letter with its sound. Some letters have more than one sound; some children get it right off the bat. Some need a little more work. Do the consonants first, making a separate list for vowels and doing them later.

In a classroom (because, again, you have to aim at that 80 percent), the best way to teach all this (phonics) would be a system with a wall chart of sounds and cards that colorfully connect the letter with its sound. I would invest in this if I had several children close in age and wanted to get things going quickly.

My eldest, Nick, was taught in school using this method; the publisher was Scott Foresman. I had found out about the program by reading Marva Collins, the teacher who founded her own private school to rescue poor children from failure; it just happened that his school used the curriculum. (Today the materials seem to have been updated to the point that the saturated graphics overwhelm the process.)

Rosie, who was home with me and the babies at the time, was desperate to learn to read, and pretty much forced me to re-create for her, on a long strip of adding-machine paper, the wall chart as I remembered it from classroom visits; the letters with their sounds. She immediately learned to read using this ad hoc "kitchen phonics" program.

Later I settled on MCP Plaid workbooks. I think workbooks have their place right here, in the learning-to-read process (and maybe in early math). There is not a lot of information online about this series (and I'm talking about this *older* series, not the newer editions). I can tell you that they are the ones I myself used in school (or something similar) and have used with my children. They are orderly and clear. They follow a thought-out sequence. They are inexpensive. The child who works through them at the rate of three or four pages a week will learn to read and in later years learn all the basics of usage, spelling rules, and irregularities. (Unless you are teaching a class, you don't need a teacher's manual, I think. Just encourage your child to figure out what to do, explaining things calmly if he needs guidance. After he learns to read, he should be able to do it all on his own.)

They are nicely produced and don't overwhelm the child with visual stimulation—a much more important consideration than most educators realize, because a child who is trying to assimilate *visual* information, i.e., the written word, should not be distracted with *extraneous* visual information in the form of busy graphics.

Somehow people have gotten the idea that things that require concentration, such as schoolwork, should be organized and presented as if they are video games or even with illustrations of the very physical activity that must be suppressed in order to do academic learning—and then those same people fret that children have attention difficulties.[7]

Blending

The leap from knowing the sounds to blending them is, I think, the true stumbling block for the 90 percent who don't instantly get it. For whatever reason, blending C and A and T into CUHaaaaaTTTT—CAT! just doesn't come easily.

Sometimes spending a week with words on flash cards and "cat on mat"-style readers does the trick; once the concept is grasped, reading is but a step away.

For children who have a bit more trouble with blending, a widely recommended book, *Teach Your Child to Read in 100 Easy Lessons*, can be helpful. Using special orthography and symbols, the book helps the child grasp this crucial step in learning to read. I have never used this book

---

[7] See Bruno Bettelheim, *On Learning to Read*.

all the way through. Some children get out of it the ability to blend (but others don't), and if it helps them in that department, it has exhausted its usefulness. As it goes on, the "stories" become inane; that's simply not necessary and can be counterproductive. The whole point of learning to read, after all, is to discover meaning. In addition, it's hard enough to learn letters without someone requiring versions that don't match anything the child will see thereafter.

So, make use of the book for its helpful quality, the blending aspect of reading, and leave it if it's not helpful in the overall challenge of getting from decoding to fluent understanding.

Memorizing Certain Words

To become an expert reader *later*, a child *now* needs to learn the decoding process of language. Phonics simply has to be taught. Now, it's true that reading is something the child is inspired to learn because books contain meaning, and if, in the name of phonics, he's required to read an inordinate amount of pointless nonsense, then he won't want to do it.

But if he wants eventually to be able to go beyond recognizing short words to the point where he can tell the difference between such words as "essential" and "eventual," or "intercessory" and "accessory," or "polynomial" and "portentous"—to the point of real and sophisticated literacy—he absolutely must have embedded in his wee mind the ability to decode quickly. And that means learning phonics—the systematic patterns of the written word.

Yet, the whole-word people have a point, which is that, very early on in the easiest reader, one will encounter words that don't follow any rules. Having drummed home the idea that there is a code and the code always works, we immediately foist on the little earnest trusting creatures "the," "that," "thing," and, most defeating of all, because so frequent, "said."

However, going from that realization to the thought that all words can be recognized without the intermediate step of decoding is a mistake *for the long run*. It's a tricky process, and I don't think we should jettison the tried-and-true method of a reasonable, not burdensome, amount of phonics to start.

So we have to be up front and tell our children that life will be easier for them if they understand that *some* words just have to be recognized, not decoded. That the rules work for the most part, but English is an old, venerable, and many-splendored thing, and like any other amazing work of culture, it has its little quirks.

Yea, Three Things Must You Know, Four I Will Tell You

You need to stock up on stories that are easy to read, but not stupid. Easy readers have to be printed a certain way, with large type and big spacing between lines. They have to be fun. They have to be well written.

If you have a good public library (by "good," I mean one that hasn't been purged of its old books), there might be a section in the children's room with "easy readers." Look for the most well thumbed! This stage doesn't last long, and you need only a few. We always loved *Go, Dog, Go!*, *The King's Wish*, by Benjamin Elkin, *The Best Nest*—my children still quote, "East or West, our nest is best!"—and *Little Bear*, for when they get a bit more skillful.

The idea is to avoid cartoonish books with busy graphics, which describes nearly every book published in the last forty years or so, and this is why I'm making such a point about all this. Choose books that are calm and amusing, and if they contain a dash of pulling one over on the adults in the child's life, that's probably all to the good, as the goal here is to induct him into the mysterious pleasure of being *in the know.*

So that is my first criterion for how you choose learning-to-read materials: *a healthy but not exclusive diet of phonics along with fun books that your children can read on his own.*

Don't ever, during this process, stop reading your normal read-aloud selections—nursery rhymes, fairy tales, stories. These old rhymes and tales teach children about the physical world. They also help children to become sensitive to the spiritual world, and the spiritual is higher than the physical. We get to know deep truths about our civilization, based as it is on faith, by learning to read and being exposed to fairy tales, nursery rhymes, and fables.

Steady Reading Progress
without Parental Panic

Some mornings, you, the newly convinced educator of your offspring, wake up determined to let your children lead the way to what interests them, and other mornings you act like Tiger Mom on a bender. Some days, you so see the wisdom of letting the child unfold like a delicate flower, and the rest of the time you are reacting to snippets of overheard conversations at the homeschooling meeting (or PTA), in which the other moms are comparing notes on the turbo-charged tutorials they've enrolled their three-year-olds in to get them prepped for the writing portion of the SAT.

Take a deep breath and know that children will learn to read. If you have one who shows interest early, you should think deeply and clearly about how to facilitate the process of teaching him (often her, though). You should know *what* you think about teaching reading—and by that I mean, in the most humble way possible, be patient and read what I am saying here. I'm not an expert but I have studied the subject and have been through it, and my friends have been through it, and maybe this collective experience can help you.

Also know that it's normal for a child to take longer than appears strictly necessary, when going by school standards (which, remember, are based on an *average*, which means *not any one particular child*). He (usually he) doesn't get the hang of reading until age eight or nine, sometimes even later.

If the child who isn't ready to read is at school, your challenge is to protect him from being labeled and made to feel dumb. It's your job to advocate for him, though, and armed with the understanding of the difference between the individual and the aggregate, which is all the difference in the world, you can do it with peace.

You should know what you think about this so that the other Tiger Moms don't get you down, or you don't get yourself down on a day when you're feeling like a failure—and so that school officials don't railroad you into bad decisions.

A book that stands the test of time in terms of readability and common sense is *Better Late Than Early: A New Approach to Your Child's Education*, by Raymond and Dorothy Moore. If you are getting anxious about a child of yours who seems resistant to reading, take a little break and read this book. You can probably request it at the library. While you're at it, get the Moores' excellent book *Home School Burnout: What It Is, What Causes It, and How to Overcome It*. The Moores have a commonsense approach to child development. Instead of looking at one aspect of learning, such as literacy, they look at the whole child and how he fits into the family. Is he able to make his bed? Is he helping out with chores as far as he is able? Does he have a sense of family life and his part in it? Does he run around outside freely with his siblings? Will he actually end up being all that academic? It's easy to feel that the homeschool isn't working when we forget all these important aspects of life together and how they relate to learning.

A Note about Dyslexia

I remain convinced that in the majority of cases, it is the kind of reading curriculum used that determines how the child will progress and whether he will develop difficulties with reading (I understand that there is a small number of children with genuine neurological issues). Thus, it is ever more important that the learning environment be controlled by you, that the method be controlled, and that you are ready to stop bad habits as they appear.

Remember, boys usually don't start to read proficiently until they are around eight years old. Before that, a lot of what they are doing could be diagnosed as dyslexia and perhaps would develop into it if they were pushed or made to feel that they are falling short.

Here's where the Moores' book *Better Late Than Early* is very helpful. These authors understand big families, they understand what parents should be aiming for with their children, and they have good insight into boys and their needs.

A frantic, overly scheduled, noisy, distracting environment will certainly not help matters when there seems to be a predisposition to dyslexia. A person has only so much energy to do things. We ask a lot of children in some ways, these days, when it comes to drains on their attention and concentration. A note of warning: it may seem an impossible battle for you to fight, but if learning to read is competing with video games, learning to read will lose. Life can be lived without digital distraction! I encourage you to unplug your children from screens.

Reading Must Be
Connected to the Past

o help your child read, you need a combination of workbooks and simple primers. By not overcomplicating matters, your child will most likely not have trouble learning the mechanics of reading. But if that's all you have, your children will not really read, but remain stuck in the decoding stage. Thus, I emphasize that you must make sure that the books you offer them are connected to the past.

This is true for everyone, of course. We should all avoid the sort of reading that sticks to one layer of time, as if *now* is the only thing you need to know. Even light reading is far more satisfying when it makes connections, references history, and evokes other things you've read — great things.

P. G. Wodehouse, author of early twentieth-century comedy, delights his reader in part because he never lets you forget your Dickens and the preux chevalier, that figure of medieval knighthood, is regularly referenced. You need to know a lot, to have a rather deep background for reference, if you want to be in on his jokes.

Knowledge itself is hierarchical, textured, and spangled—so reading should reflect that reality. It's a big mistake to get lateral in education, as in life. Don't lie down to meet your fate.

If your goal is to teach reading, don't think that you can get there in a straight line. If your goal is to teach morals, the worst thing you can do is to set out a precept as if on a platter. Aesop came as close to doing this as is comfortable, and even he knew that the parable and aphorism are more meaningful than the lecture! Even he *told a story.*

We want our children to know this: you feel small because you—and we—*are* small—*very* small in relation to the greatness of what men have thought and dreamed of in the whole history of the world. Ultimately, we want them to experience the otherness of the greatness of God. The only way they *can* know it is by slow degrees, by the unfolding of experience that shows them that this is so.

In other words, you cannot shortcut or flatten out this process.

I trust you are convinced of this. I trust that you, like me, shy away from ad-copy texts disguised as literature, blunt preaching, and shallow cheery didacticism. Even in the earliest days of learning to read, the child must be enchanted by *meaning.*

The problem becomes this: How does a family that has to take care of the babies, cook the meals, and sometimes run outside, not to mention earn a living, figure out how to get materials connected to the past into the curriculum?

I think I've told you about how, when I started homeschooling, I found that I was already in possession of some books that offered just what I needed. Thanks to Mr. Lawler's mother, a lady who really did not throw much away, but sometimes took it in her head to give me a few things, I was the owner of some truly vintage readers. Amazingly and providentially, they contain a good portion of what I needed for elementary-school literature, when added to that library of secondhand books I had already begun building.

I'll tell you what I like about them as we go along, and maybe that will help you understand what to look for in an old reader you happen upon in a secondhand shop. It would be worth the energy to seek them out. The standards these books offer might help you create your own methods while using what is available to you.

One old reader I found in a box my mother-in-law gave me, *The Progressive Road to Reading*, is hardly imaginable to us as a *third-grade reader*. I strongly suspect that there are many college students today who would be unsure of what to make of it.

The Progressive Road shows that in the early days of the child's educational journey, we mustn't stop reading to our young reader; it's a book was not meant to be tackled by the child alone! He will read a few paragraphs, and we will read a few; the essential thing is that we are reading something worthwhile. The illustrations are all mature and uncondescending. I find them very pleasing, and my children did too. About the only concession to the young mind is the larger type and bigger leading (pronounced "ledding"), the spacing between lines — important for developing eyes to be able to track the text properly.

When you use a book like this along with your workbook (the ones I recommend above), you leave the phonics a bit to the side and simply enjoy the myths, the Bible stories, and the little parables. You might use it for two years, taking bits for copying and dictation, but mostly just for reading and discussing. Of course, you have a lot of other books you read aloud. The virtue of this one (and the point of a reader) is that it helps you keep track of subject matter you want to be sure your child is introduced to.

My other resources were Bobbs-Merrill readers from the 1930s. It's hard for me to express how much I love them. First, there are the illustrations. Maybe it's the limitations of the two-color printing, but the effect is enlivening to the imagination.

Second, there is the help at the beginning of the book. The directions give you leeway, in tacit acknowledgment of the fact that some offerings in a reader will appeal to some students, and others, not as much — that, in short, the student is a person like any other.

My third love is this: each level includes myth, Scripture, poetry, history, and some kind of essay that simply gives information, but in a mature way that assumes an interested reader.

In these readers we find all the kinds of writing wrapped up in one helpful package. Even if today the "informative" essays seem rather dated, to say the least, I see no problem with that. The "latest" news from the cutting edge will always seem quaint after the passage of time. Reading things that seemed very "modern" to their authors and audience helps us be objective about whether we've achieved the final perspective we imagine.

My fourth love is that the study sections at the end of most, but not all, of the readings are perfect, not least because of that "but not all": What reader today would let the poor burdened student get away with *simply reading something*? Is not our whole educational system designed to screw him down in the press until all the study is squeezed out of him, down to the last drop?

We relentlessly pursue every thought to its bitter end, stuffing each one into the student as if we are stuffing an olive or a sausage. We only release him for purposes of mindless electronic entertainment. That he might read something in school without immediately being forced to regurgitate it doesn't occur to us, because we think of *that* kind of thing as a lost opportunity.

In these readers, the voice is elevated yet kind. It leaves room for the present, breathing teacher. The assignments are not onerous, and many can be done orally, if that suits. The vocabulary is demanding. Those who don't take to reading right away are encouraged to draw. Draw! Imagine asking a fifth grader to draw a picture of what the scene suggests to him! Brilliant!

The student can keep a notebook for the varied assignments. Since his dignity is respected along the way, this task will offer satisfaction rather than oppression and the notebook will be an object of pride — more like a commonplace book than a disposable receptacle of tedium.

The poetry in these readers is excellent for memorization.

The retellings of the *Iliad* and the *Odyssey* and other sundry classics (cycled through every year at higher levels of sophistication, so that the child, when meeting the originals for the first time, becomes familiar enough with the stories to be able to follow) are written with delicacy and attention to good writing. You know, retellings have to be artful, because you aren't just forcing the bare bones of the story into a sack. You have a standard to rise to.

The other selections are taken from the best authors.

You *can* find these readers, secondhand. Something is preserved in them that was lost along the way to where we are now: a deliberate, thoughtful leading of the child to the very best of the past, yes; *and* a respect for his willingness to explore it.

By the way, I think that a reader isn't necessary until the child has been reading for about a year, or until he is ready to sit and do "real" work—dictation, copying, and such things.

Based on my familiarity with how publishers kept up with each other, I am sure that there are others with similar offerings, although I haven't come across any as good as these. Other readers I've examined show more willingness to bore the child and make him work to no particular purpose; I have to deplore that.

I offer this odd and possibly frustrating reflection as food for thought, that's all. I trust that somehow, knowing what has been available will help the educator with criteria for choosing or developing something new.

ASK AUNTIE LEILA

Are Fairy Tales
Always Appropriate?

Dear Auntie Leila,

I was thinking of introducing fairy tales to my children (a four-year-old, a two-year-old, and a newborn).

I ordered a collection of the Grimm Brothers fairy tales and a collection of Andrew Lang's tales. I'm unsure about introducing some of the more violent or scary tales to the kids at this point. I've been reading the Andrew Lang book myself and am enjoying it and making a note of the tales I'd like to read to the littles. But last night I read "The White Cat," and though it's a great story, the whole chopping off the cat's head thing gives me pause. Am I being too squeamish?

A few weeks ago, I read my son the story of St. George and the dragon, and he spent the entire weekend hunting and killing dragons. That's fine, especially since he was "protecting" his sister, and he had great fun, but some fairy tales (especially those from Grimm) seem to border on the bizarre. I'm not sure whether I should just let this go, and get my adult brain out of it and let the kids enjoy the stories. (I know I'm enjoying them.)

What are your thoughts or advice?

Candice

Dear Candice,

Without needing advanced degrees to know a child's need to be held on someone's lap (someone loving, like Mama or Papa or Grandma or Grandpa or an older sibling learning to read and so proud to spend time with Baby), to reorganize his little babbles into understandable sounds, to share his delight with others, to learn to put names to the endless phenomena presented to his unformed mind—and to learn the sounds that those funny things make (horses say "neigh," cows say "moo"—incredible!), to learn to read—without government-funded research, without surveys, without focus groups, with no input from PR firms—with hardly any time to spare from making, cooking, cleaning, sowing, reaping, hunting, gathering, defending—our great-grandparents knew exactly what stories and books children need before they are ready to sit at a desk and study for a degree and go into their community and vote and take care of their neighbors and raise families of their own.

Today there seem to be two extremes—the cluelessness of thinking that a child's world is devoid of anxiety, hurt, or worry, with the consequent utter vapidity of reading material; and the backlash that heaps a lot of sophisticated material on his head, not understanding that the child's view of the world unfolds slowly.

Everything children encounter should reach them a little further toward what they will someday know and toward what everyone has always known. To *their* future and the *culture's* past. Yes, even the little word games they play as babies, with laughing grown-ups helping them to, one day, read Shakespeare: Hey nonny nonny!

So what sorts of stories and reading correspond to the stages of growth? There are some good lists in the appendix. Here I confine myself to showing you the *kind* of book to look for—to giving you criteria.

Babies

Don't forget to sing. Beyond that, babies like animals and their sounds, vehicles, and objects that they see all the time, such as balls and rocking horses. Of course they love *Goodnight Moon*, but it's good to understand why they do. It's the repetition and identification of familiar objects, and you can create your own rituals around this fascination.

Goodnight Moon is a type of book that exists more to provide parents with a clue of how to interact with their baby than to be actual literature for the baby. It's informative, for instance, to have a book that illustrates how to play patty-cake—informative for you! It's more fun for Baby to play that game with you than to read a book about it.

No, for babies, books will be objects to chew on, foremost; interacting with the pictures is the second place. What's wonderful about books for babies is that they reinforce the idea that things have sounds that go with them! Names! Words!

In fact, for the first few years, it's much more delightful to a child and peaceful for you simply to discuss each picture, cozily, with no rush, than to try to read most books. Only the most sing-songy, repetitive, well composed books get read! If it's not a pleasure to read, don't read it. If it is enjoyable for *you*, read it to Baby.

After the First Year

Now you want to begin nursery rhymes, folktales, and simple stories of going and doing and observing. In this way you are patterning their little minds and tongues and mouths. Think about this little rhyme:

> Cobbler, cobbler, mend my shoe,
> Give it a stitch, and that will do.
> Here's a nail, and there's a prod,
> And now my shoe is well shod.

Amazingly, in four lines you convey rhyme, meter (sort of! the irregularity at the end sort of cries out for an action from you, doesn't it? like shaking baby's legs or giving him a tickle?), a name for a person who fixes shoes, and the past participle of the irregular verb "to shoe"!

By the way, it's a cruel twist of fate (albeit an easily explained one) that the most common verbs are the irregular ones. Have you ever thought about how difficult it is to ask a small child who barely knows how to speak to tell you that he "went" rather than "goed"? Yet learn it he must. And he will, with very little difficulty, provided you worry less about offering him a wide variety of foods and instead concentrate on a wide variety of diction.

Mother Goose also gets you through the day. If I hadn't had "One, Two, Buckle My Shoe" and the drastically un-politically correct yet somehow delightful "Ten Little Indians," I don't know how we would have gone up and down stairs every day without meltdowns all around. There's something about a sing-songy rhyme that makes putting on shoes, brushing hair, changing a diaper, or eating oatmeal *better* or at least *doable*.

"Folktales" is maybe a better name for fairy tales that are less about magic and more about relating to the complex world this child has to figure out before too long. For the first few years, a child does best with stories such as "The Three Bears" and "The Three Little Pigs." In fact, those are children's favorite stories.

Dear Goldilocks—she simply had to learn her place. There's big, medium, and little. Children are little. They are happier when they accept that for now, and it helps them if there is a delightful "wee, tiny, itsy-bitsy baby-bear chair" that should be taken care of, not broken. They take refuge in Mama's "soft" world, and it consoles them for things seeming either too big or too small. But in the end, it won't quite do! Papa does frighten them a little. So telling that story with a great gruff voice for Papa Bear adds to the thrill and makes it more manageable.

As to the pigs, well, can you see them as stages of development rather than as individuals? That makes their eventual demise more understandable, doesn't it?

Once you see it this way, every time you read the tale, you will understand the appeal for the child of looking forward to being free from anxiety about that troublesome wolf. We always tell our children they have to wait to become more mature; well, that is what this story demonstrates.

The third pig doesn't mourn his "brothers"—and we don't actually care about them much either, except in an overly social-conscious way, because we feel we should and have abandoned our childlike ways of seeing things—because the subconscious recognizes them as symbols of his past selves, the incompetent ones whose demise is welcome so that his new, better self can emerge with mastery. (I have an expanded treatment of this fairy tale in volume 1, in which I explain that it's really about potty training!)

Let this be a lesson in meddling with time-tested stories. We take for granted the skills we have used for years, such as knowing when to use the bathroom; we have simply forgotten how difficult it was to attain them. But we're robbing our children of valuable tools in the fight when we abandon the collective memory in favor of some bland doctrine of niceness that is utterly irrelevant to the situation.

(Even the whimsical stories that riff on "The Three Little Pigs" might be amusing to adults, and believe me, I am not immune to the desire to be kept interested while reading stories to children, but they simply aren't satisfying to that three-year-old struggling with his uncontrolled baby self. Save them for the five-year-olds who know the original well!)

When we consider fairy tales and folktales, we have to be able to suspend our practicality and acknowledge that the child's view of things is so different from our flat, literal one. Or we are so emotional that we insist on relating to the many characters in a given story, feeling empathy for each one.

Silly grown-up. There's only one person in the child's world—him!

But then, the conflict! Because there's you and Daddy too! Horrible siblings! Beloved siblings! It's better for the child to be brought gently into dealing with the conflicts in his life, even as we tease him into reality, which, our tales assure him, isn't so bad after all.

Somehow, these stories achieve that balance. Let's let them do their work without getting fixated on the elements that seem too intense for us. If it were so, and "The Three Little Pigs" were really too sad or violent, it wouldn't be the universally satisfying story it is. (That said, if your child seems bothered by the demise of two of the little porkers, modify it for him.) My poor husband had to read that book more times than he can count! He hates those pigs.

"Jack and the Beanstalk"—how hopeless the world seems, and yet, there are big opportunities that call for quick reactions in the big world. And speaking of subliminal messages, it's not for nothing that this story appeals so much to little boys. Let me ask you, parents of these mischievous young ones: Is there something, something in their lives that grows so quickly and seems to lead to such adventures, both exciting and dangerous? Something, some part of their anatomy perhaps, the sudden overpowering presence of which causes Mama to wring her hands and Daddy to be mysteriously absent? But even this can be controlled—once it's acknowledged as mighty indeed and ultimately best set aside for later, more sublime purposes.

"The Little Red Hen," "The Gingerbread Man," "The Three Billy Goats Gruff," "Brer Rabbit," "Puss-in-Boots"—so many stories of this little helpless person gaining some cunning and strength and dealing with almost insurmountable problems!

Today's "story," by contrast, is likely to try to address a problem *directly*, and that is a bad idea.

First, there is no way to know exactly what it is that troubles any given child. When you are explicit, you do more harm than good, even to the point of introducing issues where there are none.

Besides being imprudent, this practice confirms us in our error of proceeding as if the human heart and mind are not mysterious. We will fall into many mistakes later on when they are more costly if we think we know everything about someone just because he is our child.

Second, adults are often in denial about what the problem is. You might think your child doesn't worry about divorce, but you don't realize he feels threatened to his very being by a small argument you have with your husband. You shouldn't get divorced, but arguing is hard to avoid!

You try your best to explain things, but what about those things you don't know? Read them stories that show that you understand that the adult world is anxiety-provoking but, ultimately, manageable. Where you fail, the stories succeed. You need their help, but in a hidden way.

Let's trust the wisdom of the subliminal message and the indirect approach. It's truly time-tested. Let's be humble when we worry that we are exposing our children to dangers all the time; that even if we're careful, they still perceive the world as mortally dangerous. Rather than choose to ignore this central problem of childhood, let's recover the culture and allow it to do its work, which is a process of natural (literary) selection that happens over many generations, separating the helpful from the less so.

Four-Year-Olds and Up

A four-year-old loves to hear about just life: *Milly-Molly-Mandy*, *The Animal Fair*, *Oh, What a Busy Day!*, *Harry the Dirty Dog*.

As children approach the age of reason (around seven years old — also the time they start losing teeth and learning to read!), you can start introducing the more involved fairy tales.

Now, keep in mind, my dear reader asking this question: the collections of Grimms' and Andrew Lang's fairy tales aren't exactly intended for young children. They are more like anthropological studies, recording for posterity the tales that sometimes were for older people — even adults with children listening in.

Many of the stories in these larger collections are worthy and wonderful, and when the kids are young adults, they may read them for themselves; in fact, I think they should, because a lot of those stories address mature issues. For youngsters, it's up to the parent to pick and choose which ones are read-aloud-worthy. Some are indeed weird—speaking as a reader with *almost* no filter when it comes to classic fairy tales! (One individual collector isn't the last word on the provenance of a tale, either. Sometimes you come across another version somewhere else and realize what was lacking or has been improved upon.)

Here's a good idea, if your public library cooperates by not having trashed its fairy tales: head over there and peruse the shelves. Often you will find them in the 398s, not with the other picture books. (For a long time, I wondered why our library didn't have *any* fairy tales! Then I found out they were on separate shelves in a different room. That was eye-opening, for how will people find what they don't know exists?)

Why not choose some that you think look rewarding? Pay attention to whether they are a pleasure to read aloud; note if the illustrations are child-friendly rather than slick or showy. When you've found favorites, you can start collecting them yourself.

Here are just a few tales our family has loved, so that we know what we are talking about:

The Three Little Pigs, by Paul Galdone

The Three Billy Goats Gruff, by Paul Galdone

The Elves and the Shoemaker, by Paul Galdone

Uncle Remus

Little Red Riding Hood, by Trina Schart Hyman

The Twelve Dancing Princesses, by Errol Le Cain

Hansel and Gretel, by Lisbeth Zwerger

Each Peach Pear Plum, by Janet and Allan Ahlberg, is a rare contemporary book that is pure delight, combining repetition, whimsicality, and reference to all the favorite old tales. After you read it, you can spend time finding the hidden pictures. This is a favorite baby-shower gift in board-book form.

Magic in Children's Literature

"The best kind of book," said Barnaby, "is a magic book."

"Naturally," said John.

There was a silence, as they all thought about this and how true it was.

"The best kind of magic book," said Barnaby, leaning back against the edge of the long, low library table, and surveying the crowded bookshelves, only seeming somehow to look beyond them and beyond everything else, too, the way he so often did, "is when it's about ordinary people like us, and then something happens and it's magic."

To a child, there is hardly a more interesting opening to a story than this one, from Edward Eager's *Seven-Day Magic* (please note: the characters are in a library—no doubt like the one in my childhood and I hope in yours and your children's—one with oversize Naugahyde chairs and quiet stacks). And to the alert reader, the subsequent few paragraphs are replete with allusions to other, equally great stories, sort of a gift within a gift, as the children discuss books they have loved (and we here will reserve the right to revisit especially E. Nesbit, for whom Eager is the gateway storyteller).

Then, this story deliciously continues, they saw "a red book, smallish but plump, comfortable and shabby ..."

When magic is used properly (by the storyteller, not to say by the practitioner, who should abjure it completely), it's about navigating the rules of the universe and solving some issues of your own on the way. This book, with a light touch and a most satisfying voice (don't you love a good author's voice?), will be loved by children of all ages.

If I weren't running out the door right now, I'd sit down and read it again myself.

Two Things to Know about Reading Imaginative Literature

n *How to Read a Book*, Mortimer Adler and Charles Van Doren say this: "*Don't try to resist the effect that a work of imaginative literature has on you*" (italics theirs).

Two things. First, note the "you." The authors are addressing you (and me), but we need to look at the child and say the same thing, but probably not out loud. Consider how can we help our children be open to the effect that a work of imaginative literature has on them. It all goes back to the environment you're making right there at home; what I've called Order and Wonder.

Little steps lead to the bigger ones. However humble your home, you are instilling wonder by means of beauty, the rhythm of life, and, occasionally, silence.

That brings us to the second point.

Whatever curriculum you choose, be sure that at the heart of it is enjoyment of the work of literature (or really, any wonderful thing). The work may be difficult, because what we perceive as difficulty in approaching a beloved work represents the effort of raising ourselves up from our level of understanding—the effort of stretching our minds. But if the beauty of the work isn't enjoyed, there is no point in the exercise.

There are some who agree on one level with this assertion but then demand that we "raise reading comprehension" and "ensure the child grasps the material." The enjoyment and the grasping and the comprehension are not separate. Yes, there are ways to go about increasing understanding, but it's essential to realize that those ways are not primarily mechanistic in nature, although they may be susceptible to analysis.

In the end, what a person ought to learn is to allow the work to have its way with him. Above all, art is a relationship, not a dissection!

Of course, to open oneself to something at this radical level, one must have trust—in the work itself. And trust must be based on reality.

It's not good to open oneself to bad things or even mediocre ones—not at a young, unformed age, anyway. Wonder implies goodness, as does order, for that matter. The question of goodness in literature is one not to be settled here, but as soon as it's broached, it becomes clear that from the earliest days of reading, we need standards.

The best standard is always going to be the one that is formed by tradition, because it's the one with dimension in time. That democracy of the dead extolled by G. K. Chesterton will give us the triangulation we need for judging new things. It's not at all that a new thing can't be good! It's just that one's standard is a tool, the metal of which must be refined by the fire of the past.

On Teaching a Language

Sometimes it's hard to figure out how to give your child something that you yourself do not have, and it might be that learning a language is in that category. If you never studied Latin, French, or Spanish, you might find it daunting to add it to your curriculum.

Remember, though, that educating your children doesn't mean teaching them everything yourself. With younger children, you can learn along with them; older children can study on their own and benefit from a class or a tutor.

The two main advantages that learning a language at a young age offers are that one can then communicate in that language (this one is rather self-evident) and that the brain is patterned at a time when the patterning is good. There is no use lamenting the lack of "critical-thinking skills" in the curriculum when we fail to provide the essential intellectual basis for that thinking.

Grammar is one of the important ways we learn patterns (after all, language is fundamental to human nature); it is akin to algebra in opening the mind to see things syntactically and according to their relationships. If a child is studying grammar, algebra, and Euclid, his mind will become flexible and strong. The patterns these subjects offer are ones of reason, of going from step to step in a supported way, of not making ungrounded assumptions—a skill the lack of which renders the person incapable of higher-level rational thought. Intuition must be backed up by clarity; without formation in analysis, the person is left to bumble about in what Dorothy Sayers calls "the Wood where Things have no Names."

The problem is that English is not an inflected language, so our grammar is hodgepodge: the rules we have must be mastered without the road map of a language where the parts must agree in gender, number, tense, and other qualities.

The preeminent language for this purpose (for the English speaker—a case could be made for Greek, and I wouldn't oppose learning both!) is Latin. The study of Latin provides the key to the grammar and structure of many other languages, and the reverse is not true, as modern languages lack its precision. Besides, learning Latin makes learning the vocabulary of those other languages much easier. And besides *that*, the reader will be lost, in all but the most contemporary works, which don't use them, without the ability to decipher phrases and tags in Latin. For a delightful and informative explanation of the uses and joys of Latin and how to teach it, read Dorothy Sayers's speech on the subject, "The Greatest Single Defect of My Own Latin Education," found on the Memoria Press site.[8] (Of all her observations, this one is perhaps my favorite: "There is also the matter of derivation, as distinct from vocabulary. I cannot help feeling that it is wholesome, for example, to know that 'civility' has some connection with the civitas; that 'justice' is more closely akin to righteousness than to equality; and that there was once some dim and forgotten connection between reality and thought.")

If one is studying Latin, one might as well also study French and Spanish, and really, any language at all (of course, not all languages are derived from Latin, but far be it from me to restrict you to those). Children will have no difficulty learning more than one language at once, by the way; I well remember in seventh grade going from my French to German classes with nary a hiccup. I only wish I had known to study Latin.

---

[8] https://www.memoriapress.com/articles/greatest-single-defect-my-own
-latin-education/

For Latin, I recommend the excellent offerings of Memoria Press for all ages.

For younger children learning French, use Language Together's *French for Kids*, set 1 (ten first reader books with online audio and one hundred vocabulary words). For older children, the excellent, if by now vintage, program (but there are no replacements of its caliber) called French in Action teaches by the "natural method" of immersion. You can find the videos on the Annenberg Learner site[9] and the books online (*French in Action: A Beginning Course in Language and Culture: The Capretz Method*)—both textbooks and workbooks.

---

[9] https://www.learner.org/series/french-in-action/.

PART 6
Teaching Writing

Writing is the synthesis of communicating with words, a putting forth, and it takes time. To write one must have something to say. In this section I hope you will gain confidence in the patient preparation required to help a young person master this skill.

Speaking Well and Reading Widely

he goal of writing is quite simply this: having something to say and saying it so others can read it with pleasure or at least without annoyance. Two notes on this subject:

First, everyone (this means you) should try to express things well. A lot of what I've been trying to say about education in general is that you should not regard it as a stuffing process, as a procedure by which you systematically stuff your child with knowledge.

I've been trying to help you see your home, at least (we'll leave the question of the school and society aside), as a place where everyone, man and child alike, is simply living in and contributing to a culture of learning and expression. Through order and wonder, the home, at least, becomes *more* than a place where we rouse ourselves from a stupor every once in a while to cram some stuff into children's heads. It's where we are free to create and inhabit an environment that facilitates exploring exactly what interests us all. This way, and especially when we find like-minded people to share our adventure, we build the culture, which, in turn, helps everyone to know more about the world, ourselves, and God.

A side effect of viewing education as a stuffing process is acting as if what comes out of your mouth is equivalent to what happens when you take a knife to a pouffy chair: the filling just sort of blurts out. Let's not do this when we speak. When you tell a story, try to tell it well. Try putting the punch line in rather early on and filling in the details afterward (this may seem counterintuitive, but study the rhythms of good conversationalists and storytellers, and see that this is, in fact, what they do).

Remember that "brevity is the soul of wit." When you make a request, use nouns. Be specific. Rid yourself of the habit of using fillers in your speech. Be energetic and use interesting words.

Don't trail off your sentences, allowing gestures to replace the verbs—this is super challenging for the pregnant or nursing mother or any woman who has ever been pregnant or nursing.

The key is to think through what you are going to say before you say it, rather than starting from a foggy place and hoping for the best.

When you up your speaking game, your children imitate you. That's not exactly going to do the trick, though. You sometimes need to stop them and demand that they say what they are trying to say more efficiently.

This demand has its limits, it goes without mentioning—you will have to endure many years of long-winded synopses of cartoon plots and so forth, and with good grace. But still, you can sometimes ask them to rephrase something better. It also works to restate (kindly) what they said with better diction.

When they do turn a phrase or entertain you with their jokes, be appreciative. You can tell they are trying, so smile.

And sometimes it's a good idea to ask your children to stop talking. If children never stop talking, they can't learn.

Any article about students' shortcomings in vocabulary testing will predictably and rather sadly end by calling for "doing vocabulary" in school. A certain amount of looking up words is, indeed, necessary. But if these students simply read good books—even if they did very little other than read good books!—they would definitely know that "puzzling" means "confusing" and that "permeate" means "spread throughout." How can you write well if you have no vocabulary—that is to say, no words at your disposal?

But this is what we are doing to our children when we offer them an ever-dwindling word pool from which to draw, by restricting their reading. It's their *reading*, not their study of vocabulary apart from reading, that will give them the power to write.

Second, I will once again emphasize that children must read and must be read to.

And it's just not true that "as long as they are reading, it doesn't matter what the content is," as so many apostles of mediocrity have tried to tell us. It really does matter, and you'd better purge your home of stupid, clunky, ugly, ham-fistedly moralistic, commercialistic books and replace them with lovely, poetic, and adventurous ones.

You really don't need a list; you just need to look at the publication dates. (There are a few exceptions to this sweeping statement. Some new books are good. But you must know what a good book is in order to recognize one, so stick mainly to the old ones. Your standards will be so much higher! And of course, not all old books are good. You must use good judgment.)

If you want to be able to use interesting words naturally (see my first point, above), you will have to be familiar with them from your own reading. Ditto ways of putting those words together. So reading is the quite massive base of the pyramid you are building, the very top of which you hope will be an ability to write in a way that is expressive. Building this pyramid will take time! Be patient, be strong, be confident.

The Mechanics of Writing

What do we mean by writing?

Do we mean the mechanics of using a pen and pencil on paper in an efficient manner? Or do we mean pouring out one's creativity and ability to synthesize and analyze in three pages?

Start with the former.

Many older children—ones who have reached the developmental stage I like to call "having something to say"—are handicapped by one thing that is easy to identify—an inability to write physically and efficiently—and one thing that is more subtle—an unfamiliarity with models of good writing. (Know the basics of child development so that you can be realistic about what to expect. I look at it this way: if my child exceeds the developmental level exhibited by most children his age, then I consider that a bonus and take the day off. If he's pretty much there, I coast. If he's below, I try to figure out if the lag is due to my lack of diligence. Often it's just that he's tearing ahead in some other area, so I try not to worry, but I do keep in mind ways to unlock anything latent.)

Schools used to be amazingly confident about what to expect from children. There was a collective memory that was passed along, and according to my recollection of my school years, teachers did not get bent out of shape if some children fell behind. They expected it, and they knew something else was going on. They knew that some children aren't very good at school, but in the end, they will find their niche if encouraged.

What they expected of us in first, second, and third grade was to practice the skill and mechanics of writing: first printing, then cursive. We worked at it for at least a half hour a day, and I, for one, enjoyed it!

Nowadays, people expect way more of children at inappropriate levels (for instance, comparing the themes of three books in an essay—in seventh grade, and that is an example from real life!), and then they create a lot of anxiety in parents when a child fails to rise to those levels. So everyone is in a panic, but no one is learning anything. The children who can carry out the tasks asked of them, I suspect, simply have a natural ability to do so, and sometimes, I further suspect, the school is cleverly identifying those children by means of their unreasonable demands, so that they can push them on and claim the rewards of achievement. Both of these traps—not teaching children the mechanics of writing and not giving them good models—can developmentally, appropriately be addressed by simple, time-tested techniques.

First, decide which kind of handwriting you want your child to learn. You can choose an italics cursive style or a more traditional Palmer method.

If a child is truly having trouble with writing mechanics, you can help him by introducing the typewriter and some clever typing software on the computer. Typing has helped many a child learn that he can put his thoughts on paper. Later, as his hands develop their fine-motor skills, he can go back to holding a pencil and working on printing and cursive.

In any case, my goal here is to encourage you to fuel your child's future writing ability with today's writing practice. Use a good, attractive, learnable method. Once the purely mechanical aspect is addressed, supply your child with good things to copy and model. Poems and prayers (including antiphons from the liturgy and passages of Scripture) are the best material for this. Anything devotional can be further embellished and then made part of the family's seasonal prayer time. For instance, during Advent, the child can copy the O Antiphons and decorate them, and these can be used in the lighting of the Advent wreath as appropriate.

In this simple way, you can significantly improve your child's ability to achieve skill in writing, when the time is right.

Teaching Writing: No Magic, Just More Work for You

Writing isn't an obscure and almost magical process, out of the reach of the ordinary person.

You want to believe me. On the one hand, you know I'm right, that it's just common sense that, after all, Laura Ingalls Wilder learned to write, and she went to school on the prairie, had only one dress and two pinafores, and pretty much read only the Bible.

On the other hand, you are suffering from the undeniable temptation to use a big-ticket, complicated, Ph.D.-produced package deal that will allow you to hand over the whole enterprise so you can go back to whatever important thing you were doing before you made the dubious decision to let children into your life.

Then you notice a great big whopper of a usage mistake right there in the come-on of the magical curriculum! The very people who want to teach your precious darlings (and take your money) are dangling their participles! How can they expect you to trust them!

You can't escape: you yourself must know how to write! Yes, you must.

Many teachers, homeschooling and public and private, commit many usage and grammar sins on a regular basis. (I myself found that this chapter needed a lot of editing, in an ironic but probably not unforeseen twist.)

You will know you are a sinner if you find yourself saying and writing "between John and I" or "laying down with the baby." There are a lot of other sins. There is a whole world of grammar sins out there.

Challenge yourself to write well, in just the way that you will be challenging your children to write well—namely, by studying and by making the daily writing that you must do, and that you want to do, of solid quality. Write correctly and aim to say what you mean to say.

I highly recommend that you invest in a few books for yourself and keep them nearby, dipping into them occasionally. These are reference works, by no means the kind of books that you have to read from cover to cover, although if you are anything like me (and I've been accused of reading the dictionary—you too?), you might not be able to stop yourself.

Get yourself an old *Chicago Manual of Style*. Have it handy so that you can answer all your lie-lay, comma-semicolon, hyphen-space, eldest-oldest questions without resorting to questionable Google answers. This is *the* standard. What it says in the *Chicago Manual of Style* goes. When you get a job writing at the *New York Times*, you can use its manual, but for a number of reasons, you shouldn't be happy about it.

The usage books I want to recommend to you are out of print. I will tell you what they are in case you happen to see one at a used-book sale:

Effective English Prose, by Robert Cluett: You may be able to find one for money, big money, in a dark, dusty corner of the Internet. Mine, purchased for me by my prose-master husband because it's what he swears by, is in tatters. The style is no-nonsense and direct. Gold.

English in School and Out, by Roy Davis and William Cunningham: Not available for love or money, as far as I can tell. I got mine from Mr. Lawler's mother's attic. She got it from the school she attended. In the (nineteen) twenties. Much more old-fashioned and comprehensive than *Effective English Prose* (it's aimed at high schoolers, whereas *Effective English Prose* is for college students), it nevertheless has the same virtue—namely, extensive examples from real literature. Occasional references to your "wireless machine" and "locomotive travel" shouldn't detract from the overall value.

Anyway, you know me: I like old-fashioned things.

I suspect that you can find many suitable and similar manuals if you look in the right time period. It used to be, I think, that every publisher had a manual of usage, edited by an idiosyncratic, often downright curmudgeonly Eminence, chock-full of useful advice on proper grammar as well as *development of style*, which is to say, your own voice.

Start haunting book sales and try to find one. In the meantime, go to your library and hope that they have some good, enjoyable, handy usage books right there in the 428s. (Instantly become more educated by perusing any guide to the Dewey Decimal System. Then go and look at the books on the shelves. I guarantee you'll be invigorated—at least, I hope your library still has good books to invigorate you.)

Begin using your newly found usage. Write letters. Make even your e-mails more "you" yet still correct. Maybe even your grocery lists could be more creative! If you have a child old enough to read even a little, start writing notes to him. Start a family journal—a notebook of some kind (you know, actual paper)—and make an example of yourself by jotting things down: funny occurrences, cute things that your kids say, little quotes and poems, prayers. In fact, you can start by copying into a notebook all the adorably funny things that your kids have said that you've posted on Facebook. Who knows where all that precious material goes!

You do a certain amount of writing each and every day. At least make your writing correct, with the goal of attaining your own (grammatically correct) voice.

Writing without All the Torture, Every Day, in School or Out

Now that you are getting the idea that the ability to write is the fruit of a long acquaintance with good books combined with a certain nitty-gritty know-how of your own, you will be more confident about stepping away from the Torture Method of Writing where your young children are concerned.

I guess you could torture your kids with endless book reports, overly cheerful prompts, and grinding drills. And you can torture yourself with complex, expensive writing systems.

Or you can not worry about it until well into high school, using an old-fashioned method of reading and basic mechanics.

You'll end up in the same place.

Only with less torture.

I cannot emphasize enough:

- Read only good books, preferably old ones. It doesn't matter what genre—fiction, nonfiction, poetry, drama—read and enjoy them all.
- Give your child the basic mechanics of writing.
- Know how our language works, and use it well, as well as you can.

Okay, Auntie Leila, but what do we do every day in school?

Use your old-fashioned primers (such as the Bobbs-Merrill ones I wrote about in the reading section). They contain good narration, drawing, and writing opportunities, lightly applied. Children will learn a lot of vocabulary in context, which is the key to remembering it.

Do lots of copy work. Have your child to copy out anything he's working on: Bible verses, a few lines of poetry to memorize, a quotation that strikes him from a book he's reading. A simple grocery list (eggs, milk, butter) for the very, very young (then take him shopping with his list and send him to get the things for you).

Learn spelling more easily. Instead of spelling flash cards, plan in the fall to use MCP Plaid workbooks that teach phonics rules (choose the older editions that are mercifully free of recent bureaucratic criteria). Then simply give a list of words that don't follow the rules, and have the child study *those*, with occasional tests. You can easily find such lists in an online search as well. Many usage books, such as the venerable *Warriner's English Grammar and Composition* (Harcourt Brace Jovanovich), have such lists in the back of the book. There are remarkably few words that need memorization this way. I think I learned most of them by sixth grade.

Teach your child to tell about *a story* (more on this below). A young child can *tell you a story*, but can he tell you *about it*? "And then Cinderella's godmother made her a dress. And then she gave her a coach made out of a pumpkin. And then Cinderella went to the ball." That is telling the story (not very well).

Keep a family notebook that anyone can write in. Set the tone by jotting down funny things everyone says. In our family, what works is a phone log, a medium-size notebook ostensibly used to jot information someone gives you over the phone: instructions from the nurse on prescription dosages; the mechanic's troubleshooting ideas for your washer; a quote from a vendor that you want to compare later with another's. Even in this day of mobile phones, the household might find this sort of log useful, getting the information out of your phone and into the collective sphere, so to speak.

This notebook is so informal that it just works. Everyone feels comfortable picking it up and jotting something down in it. For our family, it has become a place to record the hilarious things everyone just tosses off in regular conversation. In yours, it might be other things as well. The main idea is that it's not sacrosanct, the way a fancy journal might be, although you should do what works for you.

Help your children find their voice with letter writing: short notes to Dad, to one another, and to friends,[10] longer formal letters, thank-yous, letters to authors of books they love.[11] Provide them with the form—you will find letter forms in any grammar or usage book—and encourage proper address (that is, proper to the occasion, whether formal or informal).

Do lots of dictation. Hearing sentences read with the proper inflection and then translating them onto paper takes a lot of skill. It's hard to know how to do dictation if you weren't raised being given dictation. Try to give the phrase, rather than going word by word, and don't worry if you have to repeat a lot.

As your child gets more proficient, try to repeat a passage less as you dictate. Sometimes you may allow a viewing of the passage before beginning the dictation. At first you must specify punctuation as you go, but soon you will be able to train your child to translate the inflection of your voice into commas and periods.

Telling *about* a story is saying (or writing), "Cinderella finds true love when her fairy godmother makes it possible for her to go to the ball that her stepmother is determined to prevent her from attending."

This tip sounds mild; in fact, it is the key to academic success. In order to write well—to write critically and with ample support for his points, whether about fiction or nonfiction—the student must ultimately master the ability to summarize a text. Start slowly and gently with your fourth- to

---

[10] Discipline note: when your children are truly pushing you over the edge with their long, reasoned arguments as to why they should be allowed to do such-and-such, ask them to put it in a letter to you. Require the proper form, sending any sub-par missive back to them for revision. They could make their own stamps, mailbox, and so forth. Hopefully, by the time they are done, they will have forgotten what it's all about.

[11] Homework: read "You Children Write Illiterate Letters" in *Selected Letters of James Thurber* (posted on Waldina, November 2, 2012, https://waldina. com/2012/11/02/you-children-write-illiterate-letters/). Ponder it (while chuckling). Note that he asked the child to write back to him—several times!

sixth-grader, but aim to arrive at this achievement. A productive exercise can be to read summaries found on the back covers of familiar stories; challenge the child to produce his own.

It's a tragedy of today's educational system that teachers and parents put so much emphasis on a certain kind of highly specialized writing (the expository essay geared for standardized tests) that they are killing their children's ability to write on all levels, creative and practical.

Stop tormenting your child; stop letting the school torment him. Your child (and anyone else, for that matter) must have something to say before he can say it. Your task is to get him to realize that he has something he feels inwardly compelled to say, and then reaches for the ability to say it on his own, using the tools you have provided.

Playing and Writing

O ne more thing before we leave the topic of teaching young children (before high school) how to write: let your children play.

Especially encourage one particular kind of play, which is acting out what they read in books. Help them play *Voyage of the Dawn Treader* by making the bottom bunk into a ship. Help them play *Swallows and Amazons* by giving them camping things to take to "the island." Help them search for treasure like any respectable Bastable, by giving them bread-and-butter sandwiches for the adventure.

Hopefully you already see your children do this. If not, the help I have in mind is ever so subtly to suggest "playing the book" after you've read it together ("Would you like to make a box and a treasure map?"), and give them the time and whatever sheets and capes they need. Then step right out of the way. Sooner or later, they will put on plays like the Melendy children or write their own Pickwick Papers like the March girls.

If you can find some benign newspaper to introduce your children to journalism, you may find that they want to produce their own. We were offered *Jojo's Journal*, written by our son Joseph. He began when he was ten. He got thirteen-year-old Rosie to help him figure out how to use what was then a very rudimentary Word word-processing program. He developed his narrative voice with the use of Mr. X (clearly it wouldn't do to quote himself, the editor, in a story!); his wit was sharp, and he produced everything from news stories (a broken arm! a new baby!) to reviews (of siblings' plays and recently watched movies) to ads ("able-bodied workers to submit articles" and "world-class drooler looking for clean shirts to muss, call the milk lady"). Turns out that journalism is Joseph's profession these days, not unexpectedly! I had nothing to do with this production other than providing the paper. I was pregnant and then nursing a baby and only too glad that the kids were busy with something that didn't seem actively destructive.

After about a year, when I had resumed my consciousness, I tried to morph it into some sort of school thing. Maybe the newspaper idea had played out, but nevertheless, that's when all interest in it died. Learn from my mistake.

You provide the lessons in orthography, typing, word processing, copying, and dictation. You expose them to all the worthwhile forms of reading you can. Offer plenty of paper, pencils, pens, notebooks, play time, and printer time. Patiently wait until they have something to say. Encourage saying it. *Enjoy!* And that is the secret to laying the groundwork in young children for the skill of writing.

Learning to Write
Ben Franklin–Style

A book I would recommend for your young high schooler (which can be read during your American Founders study) is *The Autobiography of Benjamin Franklin*. There are so many angles to this work: the sheer history of it all; the pleasure of a genius opening up his mind and letting us rattle around in it for a while; the compelling question of what Franklin is letting us see, exactly, as we do that; and the realization that an education is often the result of a mind hitting an immovable object, greater than itself.

This brings us to the Franklin method of learning writing, which is simply taken from his autobiography and implemented in the classroom or home school; thus, it's worthwhile to read what he himself says about it. You will certainly find the method distilled for you in many a writing program, but you must realize something about that, which I'll get to after I describe the method.

Briefly, Franklin realized that in order to write, he must imitate authors he admired. He set about using various techniques to accomplish this. The simplest way was to take a passage or essay, write out the main points in what we would call "bullet" form, hide the original from himself (cover it up or put it away), and attempt to recreate the original using the points as an outline.

The elegance of this method is that it quickly conveys so many steps without the tedious breakdown and subsequent slog that so many writing textbooks impose upon us all, teacher and student: apprehending that a paragraph, for instance, is meant to incorporate and expound upon an idea and requires some sort of statement; the indispensability of an outline, however constructed; the arrival at the necessity for words—actual words in the form of a vocabulary suited to the task. One quite naturally arrives at an impasse—"I know what I want to say, but not how to say it"—and then, back to the mines to dig out some nuggets in the form of nouns and verbs that will do you some good.

Franklin varied his approach. He used expository writing, but also poetry to sharpen his skills on the stone of good writings. I say "stone" because good writing is concrete, existing, particular. It's not an abstract ideal floating above, separate from its writer.

That brings me to my warning. It's not enough to go straight to this method. It's almost impossible for me to emphasize enough, and I believe most textbooks and programs do not emphasize enough, that *first*, the writing you're copying must be of the highest quality. This is why it's so important to keep the gate of your child's reading.

A person—a child, let's say—has nothing much to say, and certainly won't say even that little bit *well*, unless he has learned and studied and read for a good long while. It's futile to try to get a young child to write (in the sense of producing something synthesized and creative) until you have gone along the path of absorbing what is excellent and patiently trying to imitate it.

The Franklin method is often referred to as the copy method, and that hints at what I'm saying here. Copying is indeed the best way to learn—if the matter for copying is time-tested and true and beautiful. For the young child, copying a Robert Louis Stevenson poem, the moral of a fable by Aesop, or Psalm 23 will be time well spent. In the case of the fable, for instance, he can draw a picture and caption it with the moral, carefully written out in his best handwriting. Be sure to choose a version that is beautifully translated into lofty and elegant language. For the psalm, your child could learn the hymn "The King of Love My Shepherd Is" and then copy it out, stanza by stanza.

For the older child, when your writing program calls for copy work based on an article of your choice, find a classic essay.[12] If you want to read one out loud that will amuse the family and bring a nice sense of irony to the occasion, try Flannery O'Connor's "Living with a Peacock."[13]

But then, it's not enough merely to copy.

The brilliance of Franklin's method is that he doesn't stop at copying; he studies, internalizes, and then synthesizes. The young child starts with copying (and again, simply learning the mechanics of writing is a greatly underrated task); he progresses to expressing ideas on his own, and arrives finally at offering, in writing, ideas *of* his own.

By the way, this method works well with fiction as well as nonfiction. Choose a particularly good sample (from Beatrix Potter to Jane Austen to Henry James, depending on the level of the student), short or long, and have the student copy it. Just copying fiction patterns the student's own work, and contrary to what you might think, creativity does not suffer—any more than the creativity of an art student suffers when he tries meticulously to copy an old master's work hanging in the museum. This is a time-honored way to learn.

"I sometimes had the pleasure of fancying that, in certain particulars of small import, I had been lucky enough to improve the method or the language," said Ben Franklin in his autobiography.

---

[12] You can find numerous essays at Project Gutenberg (http://www.gutenberg. org/). Using the advanced search, type "essay" in the title field.

[13] In *Holiday* (September 1961), https://holidaymag.wordpress.com/2012/03 /30/living-with-a-peacock-by-flannery-oconnor-september-1961/.

Lapbooks

If it were up to me, homeschooling would be about everyone curling up with a book. I guess you could say that's my energy level. In particular, I am not into "crafts" or the "crafty" approach, although, of course, I myself do lots of crafts. I'm here to offer solace for those who are not enthusiastic for the crafts-heavy homeschooling approach.

In case you are like this too, I wanted to share lapbooks, which I myself enjoy in that they do not annoy me by being hard to store or unpleasant to look at, and which I think produce something that is organic to the child's learning.

You know poster projects? Do you hate them? Would you ever revisit them later? I really hate them. Not only are they annoying, but when they are done—and this is where the true white-hot hatred comes in—where do you store them?

Lapbooks are far superior. They are an easy way to do a unit study. (Not that I like unit studies either. You will find that I'm a very impatient homeschooling mom who thinks you should read a book.) With a lapbook, you can pull together several aspects of study into one place, but in a meaningful way that is very enjoyable.

When I first wrote about this subject and pulled out Bridget's creations, she began poring over the lapbooks she had made four years before. I wish I had found out about them long ago. I know that my older children would have loved the process, but I was not imaginative enough to think of it on my own. (My thing is to give someone else's idea a few tweaks, I suppose.)

Above all, being 8½ by 11 in size, these projects are easy to store. Not only do they fit handily in a file box, *they* store the other work, the myriad bits of paper produced along the way. They aren't so much a project in themselves as a way to collect other projects together. They do require somewhere between a tiny bit and a lot of attention in and of themselves, but in a rewarding way.

If you do an Internet search for "lapbooks" or "lap books" or "shutter books," you will find a lot of pictures and information. I would like to share my own little twist that I think makes it a bit less stressful and a bit more colorful.

Instead of using plain file folders, as most recommend, try using colorful pocket folders. Open the folder, gently pry away the glue holding the pocket to the center fold, and then fold the outer edges inward to the middle, to make a folder with two flaps that open outward from the center. A large piece of construction paper will fit into the (now open) pocket all the way across (folding up when the "doors" fold inward); a regular piece of paper will fit in the middle, in between the new folds.

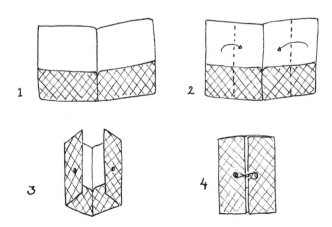

When the "doors" close, they can be fastened in different ways that are fun to brainstorm. Try using buttons hot-glued on and a string going around them; pipe cleaners going through holes made with a hole punch work too.

Aim to do one lapbook per quarter for young children who tire easily and lose interest. A nice one to start with in the Fall is Thanksgiving, which comes sooner than you think.

Now, with lapbooks, you sort of work backward. You don't start decorating your folder right off the bat (unless you want to). No, you start by doing your usual schoolwork, with a theme. First, read some interesting (preferably old) book about the subject — in this case, Thanksgiving. Maybe the child writes a little report on it or draws a picture. That gets tucked into the folder. Don't try to organize yet; just keep the random work stored in it.

Next, maybe the child looks up where England and Holland are on the world map. A map can be colored and tucked into the folder (search for blackline maps and you will have a plethora to choose from). Another day, the proclamation of Thanksgiving could be read out loud, then copied. Again, tucked into the folder.

I'm sure your mind is sparked with all sorts of ideas for studying Thanksgiving. The main categories would be geography, history, penmanship, and reading, of course. You could turn from one subject to the other, keeping your orderly day, but still be working on one overall theme. Each of the assignments can be thought out on a somewhat small scale and tucked away. When enough material has been collected, these items can then be organized by pasting or tucking inside the folder in the order you now prefer.

For geography and reading, we were doing the much-loved Twins books by Lucy Fitch Perkins. Have you heard of them? They are wonderful. Each book features a different boy and girl who are twins and have adventures in their respective country and culture and time period. They have different themes and offer information about countries and cultures in different ways, so they are lively.

I acquired most of my Twins books from my mother-in-law, who apparently kept every schoolbook she ever had, and since she went to school in Boston in the twenties and thirties, they are all treasures for the homeschooler. Later, I found a couple at thrift stores, but for the most part, these books were just on our shelves, to be enjoyed by any child with an interest. And they all really loved them—and loved hearing their father extol his favorite, *The American Twins of the Revolution.*

Now, if you decide to read, say, *The Scotch Twins,* you could find out about St. Andrew and make his cross. The child could tell *about* the story (very different from *telling the story,* and very important to learn—one might say the key to learning to write). He could write his own little book that he makes himself (many tutorials online, of course). That little book gets tucked into the pocket of the lapbook, or the back of its last page can be glued to the folder so that it stands out, ready to be read. The child can decorate the front with some coloring and a couple of plaid-covered buttons.

To continue the Twins and geography theme, when reading *The Japanese Twins,* the child could do some origami one day and haiku another and could learn about St. Francis Xavier, who converted the Japanese to Christianity.

Years later, you will still enjoy looking over what was accomplished. In fact, Bridget at age eleven had so much fun revisiting these projects that she was inspired to make new ones. It's not so hard to see how any age level could enjoy making these with as much or as little sophistication as appropriate.

A very young child might not be ready for the decorating part, and that's okay.

But as he's learning to read, he can draw pictures to go with the text, make his own book to paste inside, and put individual words (to rhyme, to spell, or to learn the meaning of) into little envelopes that are pasted on the pockets.

Copying the beginning of the Twenty-Third Psalm helps with learning it by heart. In fact, a lapbook takes the seeming pointlessness out of copying and penmanship, since now you will have a way to display what has been copied.

When the lapbook is complete, for the love of all that will make you pat yourself on the back later on, write the child's name and the date on the back. Then put it in any normal file-type container—it will fit with notebooks and binders. Hooray!

PART 7
Mathematics

As you are reading here in my guide to homeschooling, wondering where the curriculum is, remember: I try to give you criteria to choose what to teach in the form of an overview of the goals, rather than minutiae, which I think are readily available elsewhere (especially for teaching math).

So here I will identify the three stages of math development and how to facilitate the child's mastery of them.

Math in the Younger Grades: Numbers and Operations

The young child needs to *know numbers.*

This knowledge begins intuitively and can be conveyed (and elicited) by conversations and shared observations. "You give me those two, and I will give you these three." "You have ten; why don't you give half to your brother?" "This flower has four petals; this one has five." "Let's fold this tissue paper so it has twelve points." "How many in that box?"

Threeness and eightness and elevenness must be encountered and internalized. It seems to be built into human nature to "get" the numbers between one and five (interestingly, not zero). After that, things become a bit hazy, and it's this haziness that leads to problems later when operations—addition, subtraction, multiplication, and division—are required.

We adults take this grasp of number for granted, but it does take time for it to develop. Intuition needs a boost from outside, especially, as I say, as the child goes beyond the number five. Seeing larger numbers in groups made up of one, two, three, four, and five helps. Your child needs to relate to numbers on a visceral level before he can tackle operations.

There are a lot of ways to skin this cat. One way is drills. Another is games. To this day, I divide a pot of tomato seedlings or count the up-to-seven eggs I get from my hens the way I divided jacks as a fifth grader, when I was crouching out on the school porch with my best friends (our public school had wide wooden porches where we could play on a rainy or hot day—isn't that charming?). Did you play jacks? It's a perfect game for internalizing number groups that add to ten, while developing fine motor skills and hand-eye coordination. The ability quickly to judge and see, rather than count, small numbers accurately and confidently is called subitizing; it's essential to developing number sense.

A child needs to learn numbers, *and later, their operations*, the way he rides a bike—without thinking about it. If you are having trouble with your seventh grader, it's because he doesn't ride the math bike: he wobbles and is afraid of falling. There is no remedy but to stop everything and get those facts down.

Operations

If your third grader plays Parcheesi for hours (a deadly boring game, you come to find out as an adult; it's really just good for facility with numbers up to twelve, so get another child to play with him if at all possible), then don't insist on spending time drilling the same facts. A simple online search will yield a surfeit of math games, including with dice.

I overcame one child's subtraction resistance by assigning an older child to play blackjack with him for a week in lieu of his usual math lesson (but not hers, poor thing). Problem solved. Truly! He went from answering the question of what twelve minus eight equals with "zero"—so vexing! why must they torture us this way?—to complete facility with addition and subtraction. Assigning a card game seemed preferable to tossing him out a handy window.

There is no reason to shed any tears over this process; *but* the process must be undergone. If your child is "hating" math and you are dragging him kicking and screaming every day, stop everything and just give him games to play that require him to add and subtract, and later to multiply and divide.

Please trust me. It's all about knowing the facts. Who cares how you get there? If calculating batting averages teaches your son averaging, why spend a lot of money on a curriculum for that purpose?

That said, there is a place for drills. I recommend starting out by offering them as a challenge, not as a penance. Sometimes the child finds pleasure in that fresh paper and a timer; sometimes a little reward for finishing quickly goes a long way.

The sort of math books that were in use before the so-called New Math was instituted in the 1950s to 1970s are systematically and pleasingly arranged: a lesson with some examples worked out, followed by drills and problems arranged in ascending difficulty. The type I'm talking about were often still in use into the eighties in some school districts that were slow to adopt the new fashion and can still be found used. I recommend these older texts if you can find them for this stage. By the way, the New Math is the forerunner of what is now called Common Core. Both approaches involve a "discovery" method that simply isn't effective without a certain amount of either drilling or intuitive understanding, and of course, the latter can't be assumed—something proponents won't acknowledge. Both the New Math and the Common Core try to do something that can't be done. They try to replace a universal method of teaching with the particular tips and tricks that arise in the teaching process. A similar attempt is made in teaching catechism: the method discards necessary rote learning only to find that it has discarded the foundation of the edifice it is trying to build.

Once the rote learning and drilling is undertaken, then discovery will occur as a result of the interaction between student and teacher; it can never be prescribed as a general matter. For instance, a hundred chart is a splendiferous thing when you sense your child would benefit from it. Have a stack of them printed out and offer some colored pencils with sharp points. At first, you can sit with the child and point out patterns; soon he will find many more. Finding patterns is how one thinks mathematically.

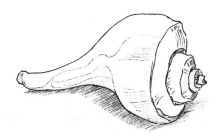

Math in the Upper Grades

he older child, having mastered facts and operations (culminating with short division, also known as fractions, enabling him to work easily with converting units, especially in chemistry), must study algebra.

Algebra

This brings up the eternal Saxon Math question. Saxon Math, a standard curriculum for homeschooling, was developed for a specific purpose: to help children not lose skills ahead of taking the SAT. By rotating through the skills as they build incrementally, this proficiency is achieved, but not necessarily in the most elegant way. Saxon is not good for the earlier, pre-sixth-grade stage, which demands repetition, not rotation. Once you can subtract, you can subtract. I really advise you to use an older "lesson and drill" type text as the foundation of your curriculum. Without a dedicated math teacher for algebra, Saxon will work. It's not the greatest, but it will do, especially if you take it lightly, not slogging through every drill and problem, and not using every book in the series, as some of them are meant as review for students who don't perform at the highest level. You can supplement lessons from another source, such as Kahn Academy, a free online curriculum.

Algebra is the logic of mathematics, akin to the skill of expressing thoughts in language. (If you do the two subjects together, language grammar, including sentence diagramming, and algebra, your child's mind will be well patterned to think about things systematically instead of only intuitively.)

The older, more traditional textbooks are better, though. When I was a girl, we did the odds and often skipped the A and B sections of the problem set entirely (maybe a few at the end, to be sure), going straight to the C, if we were able to do the examples and warm-ups perfectly. The answers were in the back of the book, and we just plowed ahead if we could. The tests were the proof that we had learned the lesson. Many teachers collected *only* tests but went over the lessons with us in class the day after they were done. This method meant less work for the teacher and more accountability for the student—winning all around, and quite doable in the home school.

Geometry

The final piece of math education in secondary school is geometry. If possible, the child should be introduced to Euclid. Yes, working through his propositions would be ideal. However, a traditional geometry textbook—one that has the student memorize propositions and produce proofs—will do. Something along these lines is essential, and the Saxon method of throwing occasional geometry problems in the mix cannot substitute for a concentrated year spent delving into axioms, propositions, theorems, and proofs.

Our intelligentsia are in a dither because children "lack skills in critical thinking," as they are fond of expressing it, but their remedy is self-defeating. First, they provide a chaotic elementary-school experience by design (if chaos can be designed—but to be honest, educational experts are the ones to do it). Then they expect to remedy the not-unforeseen result with a crash course sometime late in high school.

The current fashion is to devise strategies for higher-order thinking, which is an oxymoron. It's simply applying rote learning in the quest to inspire the sort of reflection that employs synthesis, when the only way to achieve that level is to have learned things by rote, to have been given logical tools, and to have internalized them. Rote learning has its place; ironically, that place is rejected by these same experts, who actively seek to eliminate the previous two stages I have described above, which involve drilling and memorization, two modes that are anathema to our critical-thinking gurus.

How can students work through a difficult problem (whether mathematical, social, literary, or other) critically? They must have a foundation from which they may profitably venture into the wilds of uncertainty. The most important foundational stone is to know *when one has or has not proven something*. And to obtain this, the student needs Euclid.

Is Calculus Necessary for the High School Student?

Calculus is a language for science. It's not a sort of bigger abstract mental hurdle for someone who has gotten through the other subjects, to be done apart from its object, which is science (especially high school physics). I encourage you to read Arthur Robinson, a homeschooling scientist who worked on a Nobel Prize–winning project, to understand why a high school student studies calculus.

The main point, though, is that your main goal in terms of offering what Dorothy Sayers terms "the lost tools of learning" as a homeschooler is to guide your child through math facts to algebra and geometry. (Sayers is primarily concerned that the child learn Latin, but as she explains, Latin patterns the mind with its highly inflected grammar, so you can see the pertinence to this discussion of mathematics.) The student can pursue more mathematics later if he needs it in order to learn the science that interests him.

It's Doable, So Don't Worry

Somewhere in his many inspiring writings about learning, the award-winning public-school teacher and homeschooling advocate John Taylor Gatto says that the student can learn any particular skill he needs in six weeks. If you were paying attention in school, you will remember that the first six weeks of every year were spent in review, and the last six weeks were spent making sure everyone was up to speed. I do not remember ever getting to the end of *any* textbook!

If your child suddenly realizes he needs to go to engineering school, he can easily discover the requirements and prerequisites and remedy any gaps—and he'll have the motivation to do it, unlike when he's moping around in your kitchen, not getting why you force him to do math. So don't worry.

Really. I have one child who told me in eighth grade that he didn't want to do any more math (having completed his second algebra year). I agreed. Subsequently, he learned calculus in a high school physics class and went on to work on a delicate and sophisticated biotech project. Another son vowed never to take another math class after high school; naturally he studied calculus in college. It's not *all* up to you! Just give them the tools to learn and they will do the rest.

PART 8
History

History is the most amorphous of all the academic subjects, and perhaps the one that offers the best argument against dividing studies into subjects in the first place. However, since the home educator finds it necessary to choose a curriculum (or perish in the attempt to make his own), I have tried to offer a bit of guidance in the proceeding.

History in the *Very* Young Child's Curriculum

Disclaimer: I developed these thoughts very late, after a long struggle with my own failed education in history. I did not learn history in any systematic way in all my elite education, partly because at a crucial time for me, it was replaced by a progressive idea of social studies.

Therefore, I can't say that my older children, at least, benefited from these musings, because, not knowing much about history as a discipline, it took me a good long time to think out my approach. Add to that a real confusion among even the clearest thinkers about what history is and a difficulty in detecting the heresies of approaches without reading far into them. Still, there is room for "what I would do knowing what I know now" in the advice business!

The style now in classical curricula is to adhere to a "cyclical" method of teaching history. This is how it goes: Start a young child—in kindergarten, say—with something like the "cradle of civilization" (another name for what we used to call the span of time from prehistory to ancient history). Dividing the eras up roughly into four, continue in each subsequent year with subsequent eras. In third or fourth grade, start again, spiraling up and increasing detail for your older child, but efficiently bringing your new kindergartener along for the ride. Continue in this way until you are done, incorporating each child somewhere in the cycle.

I endorse the cyclical method of teaching history. If you are a relaxed, history-oriented homeschooling parent who finds what I'm going to say discouraging, simply know that I'm trying to liberate the anxious, frustrated, compliant homeschooling parent with a few observations.

The cyclical method has its appeal for the overwhelmed homeschooling mother, no doubt about it, because you need to streamline your program where possible. However, I am convinced that history is the hardest subject to teach in any grade, because a curriculum is always going to feel too constraining to the person who sees the varied pageant of man's story through the ages. The material is vast and indeed boundless. It's easy to get lost in details. In particular, imposing the start of the cycle on the *very young* (a kindergartner or first grader) is counterproductive.

Note the verb "imposing." If your preschoolers are building Lego ziggurats or writing their names in hieroglyphics, then your work is done—go get an ice cream cone and put your feet up! But if you are stressing out because they want to run and jump and can't really remember the names of the months, let alone the Code of Hammurabi, then I would like to say, "Don't worry."

In general, the cyclical approach doesn't take into consideration the young child's lack of experience. By using this method, you are attempting to jump-start his understanding of events using those literally furthest from his time and place (unless you happen to live in Mesopotamia, in which case, your job will be easier than ours, once you have fulfilled the other conditions).

It's my strong belief, and I am happily backed up by Aristotle (yes, and he is happy to back me up, that helpful old Greek fellow), that we should begin with what the child *knows*. What he knows is his family and his town—the latter only a little bit.

It's much better to help the child begin an inquiry into events that have taken place as near to him as possible than to wrestle with his undeveloped consciousness of vast expanses of years and of ways of living, so substantially different from anything he has ever encountered as to resemble fiction. *Boring* fiction.

He can be made to assimilate facts about ancient cultures, flooding rivers, early forms of communication, and primitive tools, but they won't be differentiated in his mind from things that are actually unreal. That is, you might want to tell me about a preschooler of yours who truly loved hieroglyphics or spouted off about hanging gardens, but I maintain that to him, such things are no different from Legos or army guys. His imagination is working in a certain way, appropriate to his age, that doesn't include a strong distinction between real and unreal. If it comes up in conversation, he might be enjoying the ideas, but as a method, something is lacking. You aren't getting the product you signed up for, which is the mastery of the pertinent information about the first stage of history, by a child at or before the age of reason.

Most importantly, until about the third go-round of your cycle, he won't grasp the significance of these vitally important observations for the study of history: that man has everywhere and always made laws, laws that we recognize ourselves even at this late date; that ancient cultures formed in a certain particular place; that the origins of civilization uniquely prepared the world for its turning point, the birth of Christ.

I am not sure the purveyors of these curricula *themselves* understand that these are the reasons we are so concerned to grasp the ethos of ancient

times. We are somewhat distracted by our fascination with "the diversity other cultures" and forget that there are other considerations besides this ultimately shallow one.

As a child, I simply wasn't interested in ancient Egypt or Sumer and couldn't be made to be. Later, I discovered the more universal framework from reading Warren Carroll, in his comprehensive *History of Christendom*. His wife, Anne Carroll, developed a version for high school called *Christ the King, Lord of History: A Catholic World History from Ancient to Modern Times*. I wouldn't recommend it as a text, because it's better to have original sources and what Charlotte Mason called living books, but I do recommend it as background and useful outline for you, the teacher. You can generate a satisfying timeline using it as your guide.

If the maker of the curriculum doesn't understand these larger points and the true locus of history—and I find that most of them do not—I question whether you or your child will discover them when you use their products. So, although this observation may stray from my point that the very young child's imagination may not be ready for a study of such distant times, I think that knowing the overall importance of the time period in question will help us when we are deciding *when* to introduce it.

Excitedly poring over books about the Nile, or whatever your lively child is doing to drink in ancient culture, isn't a waste of time, but the expensive curriculum is. Beginning the formal study at the age of nine or older will have a greater effect on his grasp of the arc and of the importance of events.

Also, there is a certain opportunity cost. If what your very young child really needs for his education is large-motor-skill development, fine-motor skill development, and better awareness of his immediate surroundings, then I maintain that introducing the Nile delta is going to impede his progress. A small child will sit still for a limited time. Don't sabotage your efforts by adhering to an unrealistic curriculum. Of course, if your child is interested in a book about ancient Rome, then let him be interested, and take that interest wherever it leads you.

Instead of all this anxiety about introducing the full scope of history so early, I encourage you to tell the young child stories about the place you live and the people who lived there. Help him to see the timeline of his own life and that of your family, which can be as simple as getting to know the calendar and taking walks to see older sights in your area. Have him delve into the tales of "olden days" that his grandparents can tell him. Have him make maps of your block.

Start from what he knows and go outward from there. Start with some simple aspect of state history in first grade and the American colonial period to the Founding in second. If you live near Civil War sites, start there. If you live near pioneer trails, start there. A timeline that is flexible (binder-style or clips on a string hung in your schoolroom) will help you impose the order you so crave. A kindergartener can make a simple timeline of his own life, but it's not necessary. By third grade, you can introduce the larger themes of eras and great movements, always tied as much as possible to stories about people who made them.

All of which to say, don't get discouraged if your *very young child* isn't ready to study Mesopotamia.

In Which I Divulge Tips for Studying History

One of the best aspects of homeschooling is that you can use your intimate knowledge of your children, combined with the flexibility of home life, to make your curriculum work for you. Instead of having history class and literature class and then making a lame stab at "outside reading," you can combine them into one nifty package: a book that they will love to read and learn from because it's just that good.

The Killer Angels by Michael Shaara is such a book. Well written, gripping, based on primary sources yet brought alive by the novelist's imagination, it's a good story about a great moment in history, the Battle of Gettysburg. A book like this can help you figure out how to go about homeschooling the older child—with the two tips (plus a bonus tip) I am going to give you. Maybe thinking about it can help unbend the part of your mind that curls up into a tight ball when you look at the deep resources of Ambleside Online, for instance, with its extensive booklists; or in general think about homeschooling the older child.

If I had known these things from the start, I would have been better off, and so would my kids.

- If you have some method of keeping a history timeline (and even multiple timelines, for certainly American history alone will require several), history will be easy to teach and learn. I like the forms found on Donna Young's site.[14] You can make your own, of course. Choose whichever one appeals to you and works with the amount of detail you are looking to put into your timeline, print them out, punch holes in them with a three-hole punch, and put them into a three-ring binder. (You can pop into your binder other materials, such as papers, drawings, short bios, "letters" from historical figures, and whatever your child has produced relating to the time you are studying. You can see how important a three-hold punch will be to your home school!)

- Keep a commonplace book, or florilegium, as a record of your thoughts on what you read. This sort of journal records particulars about a book—the title, author, chapters, characters, symbols—and any quotes that strike you, any thoughts on developments in the plot, and any questions you might have. It encourages you to become a more careful reader. Don't just assign it; keep one yourself. This notebook will become a treasure of your corporate journey and an archive that you will gratefully return to when you read the same books with younger children. (The commonplace book can also be broadened to include any tidbits, thoughts, quotes, and so on of any kind. For the purposes of getting the most out of reading a book in the curriculum, narrowing it as I have described works best, and not only for history books, of course!)

These two things—the timeline and the commonplace book—work for every age of reader. A third grader can keep a lovely "overview" timeline and a simple journal that records the book information (title and so on). A senior in high school can keep a detailed timeline and a commonplace book that will serve him well in college.

---

[14] http://donnayoung.org/history/timeline.htm.

Extra bonus tip: the amazing Internet will offer you many ideas for study and essay questions. Simply search for something along the lines of "Study questions, Killer Angels, Shaara." Do not spurn these study questions. They are your friend. You can use them yourself to spark discussion or as essay questions, the background preparation for which can be carried out in the commonplace book (finding quotes, musing on possibilities, making connections). You can also search for something like "Civil War timeline" to help with your own timeline.

In any case, *The Killer Angels* is a great read, perfect for late summer. Even if you aren't specifically studying the Civil War, don't miss out on this book. If you plan a trip to Gettysburg (in reality or in virtuality), it's a must-read before you go, to be revisited during and after.

Studying the Bible in a Nondevotional Way

Now, I believe that studying the Bible will always be devotional. The Bible is the Word of God, and, as such, it conveys truth upon any reading of it. The distinction I am trying to make here is probably ultimately not a completely possible one for that reason.

Suddenly I've realized, however, in the course of conversations with people I consider to be truly educated, that they received or are giving their children a more analytical education in the Bible than I had considered possible—mainly because, in my ignorance, I had long thought of Bible reading as *purely* devotional.

I've discovered that until fairly recently, the Bible was known universally *as a subject in school*. Many children arrived at school knowing the stories, but at that point, schools provided a more detached examination of the subject matter and context of the books of the Bible, so that its literature and history were studied in a systematic way. Given that our patrimony of literature and other arts as well as our history were bound up with the story of salvation history, this approach made sense. How can you know what people are talking about if you can't recognize their references?

Then, for reasons masquerading as church-state separation (speaking here of public schools) or lack of relevance (a self-fulfilling situation—the less one studies something, the less important it seems, since it becomes unknown), the "neutral," cultural study aspect was dropped. Now the academic subject we think of as "Bible study" has become very much a matter of "listening to God speak to us" (a worthy approach, to be sure) or more seldom, as a literary inquiry, rather than of simply knowing what this book, the Bible, is—and understanding it in a studious way for the sake of being able to place it in history and in culture.

Those who are fortunate enough to have a deep familiarity with Scripture can hardly conceive of the handicap of those who have it not. Their remedy is often to offer a "crash course" or to provide explanations. But nothing can replace fluency, and fluency must be grounded in these different approaches and attacks on the subject matter, beginning early in life and continuing throughout the course of education.

It's a mistake to rely on background work to remedy lapses, which, after all, are only what economists call "known unknowns," rather than to aim for real familiarity. For instance, when Dostoyevsky mentions the wedding feast at Cana in *The Brothers Karamazov*, does the reader immediately have a full mental image of the episode *in its context*, or is he simply a victim of the "unknown unknowns"—a state from which it is almost impossible to recover?

I've realized that facts I know now and have acquired in a rather random way after a long bewilderment or utter ignorance are already known by a young child who has been read his Bible stories. With this knowledge of the stories of the Old and New Testaments and the timeline of salvation history ultimately comes a certain overview of or perspective on history, and a certain preparedness when the time comes to investigate the claims of truth. Even more simply, with familiarity with Scripture comes the ability to understand cultural references in a visceral way.

All of which is to say that if I were making my curriculum now, I'd be sure to do a timeline of salvation history (there are packaged curricula for this as well), beginning with a simple overview and expanding as the years go on. I'd be sure that we were all familiar with the books of the Bible, what kinds they are (historical, poetic, prophetic) and how they relate to one another. By the time a child graduates from high school, he should know, for instance, what the Septuagint is and what the major theme of each epistle in the New Testament is. He should also know that those scholars who assert that the author of the Gospel of Matthew is not Matthew are not on as solid ground as they claim.

It's interesting that the trend today among the faithful is to emphasize the *religious* meaning of Scripture—to invest a lot of energy in trying to help children understand certain truths. But I wonder if that project can ever succeed in the way that these educators envision. Certainly, the more the child has assimilated *the facts of the material*, the more the ground will be fertile for understanding the deeper meaning when the time comes.

PART 9
Science

What is common experience? Some people say it's generalizations, some say it's stereotypes (when it has to do with people)—but these words are pejorative. Yet there are certain realities we all know without prior analysis. We can hardly grasp how we know; we can't explain it; still, we all live our lives based more on common experience than on anything else.

Science is observation followed by testing (intuitive or analytical); these processes take place in a larger framework of knowing, reflected in the beauty and order of creation. Understanding the study of science in this context of the order of knowledge recovers science and the order of reality. The family can help the child understand the hierarchy of being and the importance of common experience.

Fostering a Love of Science

I have two things to say about approaches detrimental to fostering a love of science in children: (1) a premature exposure to *explanation* and (2) a premature exposure to *proselytism*. As to my first point, Arthur Robinson, a top-notch homeschooling scientist (I don't necessarily subscribe to all his views, but I do think he should be listened to on teaching science), explains in an article on his curriculum site that it's counterproductive to try to stuff a child full of facts about things he can't observe and doesn't have the mathematical tools to handle.

Even if he sees a cell in a microscope, if he hasn't grasped the distinction between *living* and *nonliving* things through observation and contemplation, and hasn't seen and thought about bodies living and growing as a whole, he simply won't absorb the information, and providing it will be futile. Oh, it's fine, nothing bad will happen—until you start making him memorize the Golgi apparatus and recite the steps of photosynthesis. He may get good at parroting, but it won't mean anything. This is why it's so wrongheaded to start biology by studying the cell (which just about every American school—high, middle, and elementary—does)! A child can study the cell when he has made some observations about living things.

The second mistake is committed by ideologues on both sides of the philosophical-scientific divide. On the one hand, you have evolutionists and materialists who want to prevent the unformed mind from assuming nonmaterial explanations for how things happen. On the other, you have anti-evolutionists (creationists and intelligent-design theorists) and philosophy-minded physicists who want to inoculate the student early on against the theories that mistake the origins of the material world and what constitutes different orders of truth.

I love a good controversy, but all of it should be kept far away from the young person's encounter with science, which should be about the here and now, seeing how things work, investigating what is observed. Once there is a good grounding in what turns out to be a huge endeavor—namely, to see accurately and to describe what you see—then, later, you can seek out causes and enter into disputes.

So, instead of banging your head on the wall of your science curriculum, why not set up a nature table, give the kids beautiful nature journals[15] and a set of high-quality pencils, get some interesting books, and consider buying a stereomicroscope. I will discuss each of these ideas in turn, below.

[15] Bienfang Notesketch books are of good quality.

Observation: The Beginning of Science

Science is about observation. There is not much anyone can sell you in order to furnish your children with this prerequisite for a life of scientific inquiry. To learn observation, one must have the habit of … observing! The tools are simple and few.

You need some contact with nature. Science is the study of nature in the sense of the physical world. The outside is free, even for city dwellers. But you have to get out there! And very often you have to bring it inside.

A nature table doesn't cost much. An old wooden table, a metal tray table, or a small shelf works perfectly. It should be just inside the door (or even out on the porch) where you usually enter. Be strict about not allowing any other items on it—practice horizontal-surface management—and refresh it often.

The Nature Journal

The habit of observation is greatly nurtured and disciplined by keeping records, an activity that must be interpreted in the widest way possible. A nature journal is the very best way to keep records until you are doing a scientific study, by which time the specific *form* of the record keeping will present itself—you won't have to worry about it.

The kind of notebook I favor has both a blank portion and a lined portion and is made of substantial paper. Most people, young and old, fall into one category or the other: word users or picture users. To learn the habit of observation, you also want to cultivate the habit of using all available means of communication—words and pictures—and even pasting things, such as leaves and flowers, in the journal.

Start each journal entry with the date and some notes about the temperature, cloud formations, weather in general, and any changes since the last entry. Usually things flow from there.

You can paste seed pods in the journal, make spore prints from fungi, trace leaf patterns, and press flowers. Be casual, relaxed, and open simply to filling the notebook in the early years with raw information rather than any sophisticated synthesis. One inspiring work to consult is *The Country*

Diary of an Edwardian Lady, by Edith Holden. These days, however, a simple search online will yield more inspiration than one family can handle. The main point is to have a combination of visual and verbal records and to work toward noticing details, differences, and similarities. You need books, not textbooks, about the things that you are likely to observe. I recommend looking at all the years (or academic levels) on the Ambleside Online site to get recommendations for books about birds, insects, stars, and other topics. Reading biographies of scientists spurs your young ones to imitation. Older children (say, seventh and eighth graders on up) will learn a lot from reading, with you, two books in particular: *The Chemical History of a Candle*—a course of lectures delivered by Michael Faraday (the first three chapters, mainly)—and *On Motion of Heart and Blood in Animals*, by William Harvey. Following the lead of Arthur Robinson, a really accomplished scientist, I will suggest that these books give the child the freedom of knowing how these very early scientists approached the interpretation of their observations and how they fit into known facts.

When a textbook simply provides the facts about blood circulation in the body, the student is unaware of the adventure of its discovery by the first physician to figure it all out. He may even believe that all scientists simply read textbooks for their information.

But if the student begins with the discovery, then later, the textbook explanation will be more easily assimilated—as will its context, which is more important for his development. The person who first encounters the notion of blood circulation as discovered in history will always remain impressed with how Dr. Harvey was able to make inferences and deductions from his observations—and all without a microscope! Learning this way retains the sense that science can be done by anyone willing to be open to solving mysteries. Yes, there is a lot to learn, because people have been at it for a long time now. But it's not a passive undertaking, and that's what we are trying to teach.

The Stereomicroscope

A helpful tool that is a little pricey, but not as pricey as one sports fee at the public school, is a stereomicroscope. A few years ago, I stumbled upon an article in the *New York Times* by a scientist at Cornell, Thomas Eisner.

Eisner writes:

Say you have a child in tow, you're in the toy store and you're thinking, there has to be something here that provokes wonder, feeds the intellect, awakens the scientist within. And there it is, a pint-size version of the classic microscope, a toy for sure, but sturdy and affordable. "You can see things enlarged upward of 100 times," the clerk says, as if we needed to be persuaded.

Thousands of such microscopes have doubtless been sold over the years. But where are they, and who is using them? Who among professional scientists can claim that it was through the toy microscope that they were introduced to the joys of exploration, that they discovered that science was it, and that it was for them?

Truth is that the toy version of what scientists call the compound microscope receives very little use beyond the day of its ceremonial unwrapping. The instructions with the packaging promise much, but the instrument does not really suit.

He goes on to emphasize this point I'm making about observation:

> How can we make the small loom large in a child's life? After all, progress in science has been, to a great extent, built on the ever-increasing ability to probe the imperceptible. The problem with the toy version of the compound microscope, quite aside from its technical limitations, is that it does not lend itself for scrutinizing reality at that modest level of magnification where you can see in exquisite detail, but without losing sight, as it were, of what you really have.
>
> You will not find it in the toy store, or in many schools, but consider the dissecting microscope. Known to scientists as the stereomicroscope, it is easy to operate, optically outstanding and designed to provide the ideal level of enlargement.

Eisner really is making the case for seeing things at the level that retains the connection between ordinary vision and delving into the secrets of things:

> True, the stereomicroscope is more expensive than conventional toy microscopes because it consists essentially of two parallel microscope tubes, one for each eye. Hence the stereo image and higher cost.
>
> But good models are already available for less than $300. [In fact, you can buy one now for closer to $100.] Increased demand could well bring down the price to that of another great exploratory tool, binoculars. Think of it as a telescope for inner space, a tool for the exploration of the barely visible. Buy it for the children, but be sure to retain rights of access. The instrument may well bring you to the realization that the explorer in you is still very much alive.

I sent this article around to some friends who are interested in education. Mark Langley, academic dean of the Lyceum in Cleveland, Ohio, responded this way:

I read the article and immediately proceeded up to our newly equipped lab here at The Lyceum (i.e., equipped with a lab straight from 1957—donated from the Josephinum College/Seminary). I found that we have at least three beautiful stereomicroscopes, and so I turned one on and started looking at the pencil that I happened to be carrying—then a paper clip—then a small rusty screw.

The article is completely right. These microscopes do in fact unlock the "inner scientist," and anybody can use one. The magnification is just perfect—impressive while keeping things recognizable.

Five Things I Worry I Did Not Teach My Children or You Will Not Teach Yours

I don't spend a *lot* of time worrying about this, because I'm too distracted to spend a lot of time on anything, but occasionally I do fear that I forgot to pass something important along to my children—especially, but not exclusively, the homeschooled ones.

It comes on you as you get older, I think, and lose that wide-open optimism that you can do it all, or at least the sense that there's a checklist somewhere. When I mentioned it to Rosie, she said that Ann, her mother-in-law (and my homeschooling buddy long before she rose to that august position) had recently sent out a message to her children, apologizing for not covering cloud formations adequately.

Exactly.

Here is the list of things I can remember that randomly rise up to bite me with remorse over not having done a good enough job teaching them. Maybe I will remember more things. Maybe not. (NB: They seem to fall into two categories: geography and fire safety. And they seem to be useful really only for doing crossword puzzles — other than the fire-safety stuff, of course, which we hope will never become useful.)

1. *Cloud formations.* I remember having to memorize cloud formations in school. I know nimbus (which I call "nimbulus" in my mind and just looked up, and no, it's nimbus) and cumulus and cumulonimbus. And stratus. So important!

2. *Stop, drop, and roll.* A while back, I read a terrible local history of a woman in the olden days whose skirts caught fire from the open hearth. She ran, with her baby in arms, around the house, burning it down around them. So sad! She didn't remember to stop, drop, and roll, but boy, every time I come across such an anecdote, a handy child gets a lecture about it.

Going to school doesn't seem to confer this knowledge reliably, so it's not as if that's the solution. And Rosie says that in third grade, when she was actually in school, the fire-safety lesson gave her nightmares. That's not the goal, obviously!

My dear friend Nancy, when I told her that I had also given her daughter Katie (who happened to have the misfortune of visiting Bridget when that lecture feeling came on me) this lecture, recounted a story.

Once, after a long and tiring day, she had been resting in the lovely bath her husband had drawn for her, complete with candles on the edge of the tub. Her hair caught fire from a candle, and rather than handily dousing it in the adequate quantity of water provided, simply by slipping down into it, she jumped out and ran out into the bedroom, screaming. Fortunately her fate was not that of the olden-days lady!

Moral: don't count on school to get you off the hook.

3. *Also in the fire-safety category: Don't attempt to put out a grease or oil fire with water.* A commercial during a game reminded Bridget that I had taught her this. I think she brought it up to ward off a lecture, but I was counting stitches in my knitting and missed my cue!

The ad people didn't seem to know this rule. Tsk. Bridget's on it, and maybe now I can let go of this one? Maybe not.

4. *Tundra.* Deep in what Dorothy Sayers calls the "poll-parrot" stage of my education, I also learned the land forms. For some reason, tundra and taiga

really stuck with me. I worry that my children don't know what permafrost is. I really worry.

5. *Oxbow lakes.* Did you know that lakes form for different reasons? And that a river can just jump out of its normal bed and take an entirely new course, leaving a lake behind? Someone had tweeted a photo of an oxbow lake possibly in the throes of formation, and that led me to send Bridget an e-mail with the *Wikipedia* article on the phenomenon and an apology for not doing a good job on certain things.

This was her gentle response:

"Thanks, Mama! I think we already have been over this."

I am sharing all this with you for two reasons: first, so that you are adequately warned that things get worse, sanity-wise; and second, so that if they already have, and you are stuck on the endless treadmill of five things you need your children to know, you will be comforted that you are not alone. Or else, I'm the only one!

PART 10
Music and Art

Music is integral to communication, and as uniquely human as speech! It cannot be sidelined as an optional subject or something precious about our nature will be lost. Let's recover a home-like way of sharing music, especially singing. Performance has its pleasures, but making music together without stress needs to be reclaimed.

Ten Reasons to Sing
with Your Children

Do you sing with your children? I hope you do!

I hope music is part of your day, every day. It's such an important part of raising children. It's an important part of life! Sometimes we bemoan our lack of musical training or the scarcity of instruments, but we can always sing!

Here are a few reasons to overcome your shyness, lack of operatic training, inability to read music, and general stuck-in-first-gear-with-math-in-the-homeschool-itis:

1. Music is joyful.
2. Music transmits culture through the generations by keeping songs (with their stories) alive in memory.
3. Singing makes children happy and disposes them to learn other things.
4. Singing helps verbal children exercise other parts of their brains.
5. Singing helps nonverbal children become more verbal and patterns their speech. Note how a typical song such as "Go Tell Aunt Rhody" contains repetition that isn't tedious.

6. Singing at the top of your voice in the car gets you through some rough patches with the car-averse baby (such as one notorious screamer in our family whose name starts with a "B" and ends with an "idget").

7. Singing cements memories in a way that just speaking cannot, and teaching your children lots of songs from the silly to the sublime will pay off one day at the campfire, the Christmas-carol sing-along, or the Gilbert and Sullivan fest. Your children will thank you.

8. The antidote to bad music (and there is bad *music*, not just bad *lyrics*—I trust you immediately agree, alleviating the need for me to explain it here) is good music!

9. Music builds bridges to others.

10. Music is the universal language.

Start with nursery songs, lullabies of course, and anything you feel like singing to your baby! Musical numbers, patriotic songs, bluegrass, hymns, chant, counting songs … What's your ethnic background? Sing those songs! Play an instrument? Play it, and sing along (presuming your instrument is not the flute)!

Learning Music
with Our Children,
Beginning with Hymns

We need to include music in our home environment.

I know the feeling that everyone should be singing in harmony around a campfire, but also the feeling of having no idea where to start.

Sometimes we can sense a season approaching when the routine is open to change, and it will work to devote some evenings to a project, such as learning some new songs. If you get your simple supper ready early, you may find that the earlier late-fall evenings or the early spring ones are just right to turn your attention to it.

I will try to give you just a few good resources to get you started. I've consulted with my musician children on this, and we are starting you off with hymns. I mean we are beginning the discussion with hymns—of course you should sing all sorts of songs all the time!

If you want to hear the great old hymns as they would be played in a big stone church with a good organ, we recommend the CDs *Abide with*

Me: 50 Favourite Hymns and *Be Still My Soul: The Ultimate Hymns Collection.*
Now, you need to know that not all hymns are best sung so grandly. Many
of our favorites are beautiful French hymns, or the great melodic Welsh
ones that ought to have a more lyrical line than you hear in this type of
setting (organ, big congregation). They were composed for and sung, often
unaccompanied or lightly accompanied, by little gatherings of people who
could really sing. But for us, deprived as we are, the way to begin might
be to listen to the CD, get a hymnal so you can learn the words, and start
hunting on YouTube for some versions that aren't "lush," concert-ish, or
operatic—just ordinary good singing.

If you feel as if you can't sing, remember: Baby doesn't know the difference, and God is pleased. Start with the simple things. In our book *The
Little Oratory*, David Clayton has an appendix on learning to sing when
you think you are tone deaf. It involves practicing in the shower.

Spirituals really will teach you to sing. Queue some up and just let 'er
rip. Some who think they can't sing don't realize that singing is highly
dependent on *listening*. Listen while you sing; cultivate attention to how
your voice blends with the sound you are imitating on the recording or
from the other singers, and you will get it.

Two hymnals we love are the *Vatican II Hymnal* (yes, it's good, and
it looks as if you can download scores for free as well) and *The Lutheran
Hymnal* (Concordia Publishing House, 1941). Older Anglican hymnals are
always treasure troves.

Hymnals always have indices in the back that direct you to the music
by liturgical season (and are often laid out that way—far preferable to a
straight alphabetical arrangement). They also list the hymns by Scripture,
tune, and title. So, for specifically Advent or Christmas music, you will
find a rich treasury. Again, if you look up a hymn online, you will *hear* the
hymn and have a better idea of how it's sung.

You can also look up individual hymns online to find all the lyrics and at
least be able to hear an MP3 of the music. The CanticaNOVA Publications
website (canticanova.com) has a treasury of hymns and chants organized
by liturgical season and refined by the Propers of each week. Propers are
the prayers of the Mass that change according to the day (Introit, Offertory,

Gospel Acclamation, and so on). Tracking the Propers means that you can follow the trajectory of, say, Advent, in sacred music and not get stuck singing the same hymn every week or shuffling them about randomly; it's marvelous and spiritually nourishing to discover that the poetry and Scripture of the traditional hymns follow the development of the season very closely.

For a way to incorporate hymns naturally and easily into your home-school curriculum, visit the Ambleside Online site, which offers a cycle of hymns to learn. It also gives you suggestions for finding hymns and for seasonal selections.

Remember that chant ("O Come, O Come, Emmanuel," "Ye Sons and Daughters," and so forth) should be sung with no accompaniment and has its own special style—very simple, very meditative. It's ideal for children: they pick it up easily and sing it well, once they get that it's relaxed.

Our family, at Mr. Lawler's request, learned to sing the Salve Regina long ago. The children learned it right away (they had learned the English version of the prayer one Lent). The Marian antiphons, as they are called, follow the liturgical seasons. The other three are Alma Redemptoris Mater, Ave Regina Caelorum, and Regina Caeli.

A good recording of monks singing chant will reveal that the "phrases" or arcs of the sound follow the words. When there is a comma in the text, you can hear the voices relaxing; they soften and slow down just a little. Where the music hits a double line in the score, there is a complete pause that is arrived at very calmly. That is the essence of chant, and it's very conducive to prayer.

Sacred Music with Children

The book of songs and pictures called *The Story of the Redemption for Children*, by Fr. F. Adair and Sr. M. Joanne is one to hunt down or look up and print out for your own use, before it is lost.[16] It's really a treasure, a vestige of the liturgical renewal that called upon the talents and imagination of some of our highest intellectual lights. Sadly, that movement's real contributions were drowned by the imposition of a pseudo-populist renewal after the Second Vatican Council. Our children and grandchildren lost a lot.

This book demonstrates a traditional and beautiful way of teaching the Faith to children, using a timeline from Creation to Redemption. You can approach salvation history differently according to the age of the child; teaching these songs is one lovely and gentle way to get started.

The inspiration here is to use ancient chants to tell the story. It seems to me that you would also want to learn the Latin chants as you learn the ones in the book; it is important that we preserve the *semantic*, the special form, of sacred music.

---

[16] *The Story of the Redemption for Children* can be found in PDF form at the Musica Sacra site (musicasacra.com). You can print it out.

To understand what I'm saying, read the instructions found in the text of the book on *how* to sing chant, which differs from more familiar metrical music in that it is more relaxed and is never forced into an even rhythm. Children can listen to monks singing these tunes (with the liturgical texts); recordings are easily found online (or, one hopes, in real life!). In other words, the originals should be the model, and then the little poems in this book can be part of the child's religious education.

Keep in mind a delicate balance: On the one hand, if you introduce sacred things with cartoons and silly ditties, you create a tainted association. Children learn by absorbing the *feel* of the thing. They have an instinctive hierarchy of solemnity. For instance, a child might encounter something that perhaps isn't even holy but has the attributes of something solemn and mysterious, and he will be attracted to it, maybe even in spite of the content. This, I believe, is why today we have young people who are more moved by athletic ceremonies than by religious ones (I mean really moved, even if they dutifully prioritize religion).

On the other hand, if you use sacred modes for anything other than what they were made for, you might ruin their power. A good example of this might be the Rodgers and Hammerstein "Alleluia" from *The Sound of Music.* I could imagine a good choir singing this piece at Mass, except that it is pretty indelibly associated with a Hollywood musical!

If something is going to be used for worship, *it must be set apart.* We don't make altar cloths with the same fabric as tablecloths; we don't grab a handy candlestick from the altar to put in the front hall. It is the same with music. This semantic (imbued meaning) is what makes chant unique and universal as a sacred mode.

I would definitely be sure to sing the original chants, preferably in their context in the liturgy, while we were learning the songs in this book. The text of a chant is much easier to learn if you already know the tune (and vice versa), so I'm coming down on the side of this book.

Go In and Out the Window!

I f you didn't grow up with the kind of songs mentioned here, the best thing to do is to buy a couple of CDs or download some albums and listen to them. You'll learn them, and soon you and your family will be singing away.

With folk and traditional music, you'll give your children the gift of musical discernment, for traditional music differs from the sort of music we tend to listen to in an important way. What we think of as popular music today is a product of an industry, not a homey culture. We have almost lost our authentic folk treasury by replacing it with an individualistic and musically limited genre that we call pop or rock. Having children and wanting to educate them well offers parents the opportunity to remedy this grave problem.

My generation and those a bit older listened to Burl Ives; I remember especially his album *Burl Ives Sings Little White Duck and Other Children's Favorites*. Another old-timey album is Pete Seeger's *Children's Concert at Town Hall*. You wouldn't want to imitate his politics, but the sound of his voice singing "Oh Shenandoah" defines an American moment. At least it defines it for me! You can see some of Elizabeth Mitchell's videos on YouTube; she has recorded lots of traditional children's songs in an accessible way.

Children a bit older love *Peter and the Wolf*, and I particularly recommend the recording narrated by Arthur Godfrey; it's not at all condescending, a fault I've found in other recordings. You can find it online. Children will learn to recognize the instruments in the orchestra through this delightful musical story. I also recommend a really fun recording of *Carnival of the Animals* with Noel Coward reciting the verses that Ogden Nash wrote to fit Saint-Saëns's music; and back when music came on vinyl records, this offering was on the other side of the Peter and the Wolf recording.

If you can accompany simple songs on the piano, guitar, fiddle (like Pa), or banjo, you need *The Great Family Songbook: A Treasury of Favorite Show Tunes, Sing Alongs, Popular Songs, Jazz & Blues, Children's Melodies, International Ballads, Folk . . . Jingles, and More for Piano and Guitar*, by Dan Fox.

Other wonderful resources for authentic folk music: Peter, Paul, and Mary albums, especially the ones specifically for children; a Canadian album by Kim Thiessen *To Such as These* — songs and lullabies for children of the world; and Shawn Colvin singing *Holiday Songs and Lullabies*, which is an American folkways recording (a Smithsonian project for preserving folk heritage, found at https://folkways.si.edu/).

On Teaching Art

A few thoughts about forming your children's artistic tastes and abilities: the goal should be to see and enjoy beautiful works of art and ultimately to learn to produce something pleasing, and it's a completely reachable goal. Just as with music, basic proficiency is within the capability of anyone willing to study.

In the home, for our own enjoyment and to form the child's imagination, we aim for beautiful originals if we have a source, as well as reproductions of excellent art. As with literature and music, stick with what is old and traditional (traditional folk art is far better than the ubiquitous and over-worked prints of masters; seek out less hackneyed examples, if possible). I encourage trips to museums and churches to view original works of art; there is simply no substitute for seeing the real thing.

Have good art materials on hand and encourage their use. Make the joy of creation a normal part of life in the home—creation with no supervision or object, although having you sit and draw with them will always be welcome. Children should be encouraged to play and explore with their art materials. Having them close at hand and in good order will facilitate your children's creativity.

My artist son-in-law John Folley recommends that you supply younger children with a set of colored pencils, crayons, and washable markers, along with tasteful coloring books (we love the Dover coloring book series for their generally good proportions, calm subject matter, and elegant lines), empty notebooks, butcher paper, and individual sheets of paper (I recommend investing in a paper cutter and cutting scrap paper in half; children are often inspired by smaller pieces of paper that they can make into books or cards).

Older children like twistable crayons, fine-line Crayola markers, and Prismacolor pencils. Teach them to use their drawing pencils carefully, not dropping them or sharpening them too roughly, which can damage the core of the pencil, resulting in a tool that crumbles into fragments the next time it's sharpened.

Encourage going outside to observe and enjoy nature with a sketchbook for free sketching. This can dovetail nicely with scientific nature journaling described earlier—two "classes" combined.

Just as children need to learn music composed by others, so they should be encouraged to copy good works of art. As they do, they will naturally seek better ways of accomplishing their object. They will appreciate instruction when they see that it enables them to get closer to putting what is in their mind's eye on paper.

Older children can easily learn the basic principles of linear and atmospheric perspective. In the higher grades, they can pursue other aspects of art: form, line, and color.

I urge you to minimize their exposure to modern art, which rejects form and twists the idea of creativity to mean expression without discipline. It's tempting to go in that direction because one of the rationalizations of modern art is that it claims to imitate what a child does when left to himself, free of so-called strictures, and because a lot of instructors offer this sort of activity. But of course, an untutored child simply hasn't encountered strictures; he isn't rejecting them! The whole idea is something we impose for no reason. In fact, children love boundaries and limits; as soon as they discover them, they respond with more creativity, not less, because the "strictures" or limits of art are precisely what allow expression.

If, after learning proper techniques, the mature artist chooses to use them or break them for his own purposes, so be it, and let posterity decide. But to withhold the accumulated knowledge of the centuries from the child on the spurious grounds that the child can then be more childlike seems to me to be a way of letting the teacher off the hook of having something substantive to offer his pupil.

The parent can't always offer everything the child needs, but we are fortunate to live in a time when information is at our fingertips. Seek out tutors and programs that endeavor to offer your children time-tested principles of artistic instruction, and you will find that they will become proficient.

PART 11

On the Moral
Life of Children

The child has an inner life, and this life is deeply concerned with understanding what is good and what is bad: that is, it is a moral life. Parents above all must know that this life, which is quite hidden, exists apart from them as a direct relationship of the child with God. At the same time, the development of this inner life is entrusted to the parents to nurture with love and respect. This paradox requires thought and prayer.

The Child's Inner Life

O nce, I was sitting with Bridget in the pediatrician's office, and on the TV in the waiting room was on a desperately energy-sapping children's show. I think this show tries to channel Mr. Rogers (which I will be honest and provocative and say I never liked all that much as a child), but this new one transformed his calming messages to a slick version that disturbed me. Do you know which show I'm talking about? I don't know its name. It doesn't matter.

In any case, the topic or theme was sadness. Somehow shoe-horned into the veritable minky quilt of sound that pervades this show—at least, the room was filled with a wall of background noise at all times—was a ditty about sadness. And there was a lesson about sadness. And there were sad, computer-generated, unpleasant-looking cartoon animal characters who were being made to confront their sadness. The message, boiled down, was this: Sometimes you feel sad, and when you do, you should wait. The sadness will pass away.

Is this false hope all we have to offer our children?

We need to develop, nurture, and protect the inner lives of our children. Their inner lives are inseparable from their moral lives; emotions are part of the human experience, and they should be formed for the good.

We need to give our children the gift of knowing when and why things make them sad, and what they can do about it. And we need to give them hope that life is more than a matter of waiting things out until we feel better—that is, according to the message I was watching, until other people do something to make us feel better or until time passes. The view represented on this show (which, make no mistake, is a *world view*) has pervaded even our spiritual life as Christians.

As another example, a series of posters on the walls at our church's religious-education center (as it is called—it is the basement) reference prayer. Among them, a cartoonish child is praying, "Dear God, please take my sadness away." What is this message, exactly? It is nothing more than adults (who, the child is aware, made and posted it) passing along the message of futility, of hopelessness. With these responses, adults are, in effect, absolving themselves of responsibility. Parents and other authorities (including, in this case, the Church) project not to know and not to want to inquire into the causes of sadness in their children. Could that be because they themselves are sad, having lost their moral compass or even the memory of having had one? Or even that they have lost the knowledge of the existence of such a compass?

Much of what I write about is devoted to the upbringing and education of children. My particular observation is that raising children requires a lot of common sense and devotion to order; hence my passion for restoring what we've called "the collective memory" about such things. This mission is ever more important as we observe everyone making things up as they go along, with no frame of reference.

Personally, I had to discover it all for myself. Perhaps some of my readers think I'm more like Ma, somehow knowing how to store squash in the attic and birth babies on the prairie. Not at all. I read a library full of books, struggled alone, and then figured things out, in some cases way later than I would have liked (but that's part of the journey too). My self-appointed role here is to do my part to preserve you from the same fate.

And that is why I write about everything from canning your own pickles to cleaning your bedroom to nursing your babies to homeschooling your college-bound kids. There is much more that can be said than I've said here, of course. I do have a lot about *disciplining* children (mostly in volume 1), which is undoubtedly the topic that most consumes parents' interest: how to get children to behave, to get along, to be happy.

Discipline is important: to understand human nature as it develops and to use your God-given grace as a parent to work toward habits that give the gift of self-control and, ultimately, virtue. Why do I call self-control a gift? Because everything flows from being able to know ourselves and to be able to harness the will. Those who lack self-control desire things, but their desires are not necessarily good and their ability to attain their goals is hampered. Parents by nature want to give their children gifts, but often they trade indulgence for the real legacy they can offer.

Each child is a person who is engaged in a process of growth that can seem like a struggle or battle; it certainly is not effortless, like the development of a flower or a bird. I tend to call it a battle (and anyone who remembers his own childhood honestly will not disagree, I think).

The battle is essentially moral in nature. To understand it, we have to understand that we, as citizens of the modern world, tend to think of things in terms of helpful or useful versus unhelpful or harmful—but these are utilitarian words that don't relate to anything good in itself. They are self-defining. Much of the advice out there, as I have often remarked, tends to comprise techniques of manipulation, because usefulness is its criterion. Even our religion often descends into what has been called moralistic therapeutic deism—a sort of feel-good, nice religion that makes no demands of objective right and wrong, good and evil. These objective realities evaporate before feelings.

We do still experience sadness, of course, even as devotees of that religion. But we retreat into pretending that the sadness has no cause, no remedy, and no purpose.

The child, though, from the time he starts to have awareness of the world around him, is grappling with the things the adults have managed to repress. What is it that they sense? It's the existence of good and evil.

As parents, although we have many, many things to teach our children, developing their moral character defines our mission. Today's "making things up as we go along" mentality stems precisely from the rejection of morality—its centrality to what it means to be a human being—and even its reality.

What ails people most in our society is the systematic destruction of the interior compass, of the conscience. The good draws us to itself; it's in our nature to be drawn. But if our collective project is to destroy nature—to call bad, things that are good, and vice versa—then all that is left is confusion at best, destruction at worst.

It wasn't always this way. People knew the basics of everyday life; they also knew what their purpose in life was, and how to devote themselves to it. They knew that something existed outside of themselves. The message that that *something* is a loving God wasn't silenced, so there was some hope that those who had ears to hear would hear. But more importantly, the organ of receptivity (the ears to hear, so to speak) wasn't fatally damaged. No one was attacking the very nature of the child.

How can we fight this attack? As parents, we need to commit to nurturing the moral life of our children.

Remember, God has no grandchildren. That means that every person has free will and is born under the curse of the sin of Adam. Our aim is to raise *children* of God, not to try to rig the system (that is, to try to circumvent or ignore the nature of things) to try to raise our children to, willy-nilly, become *grandchildren* of God—as if, simply by virtue of having gone through that system and by being our children, they will have a developed moral life of their own. It doesn't work that way.

Let's go back to sadness.

When he's really small, a child is sad because he fell down, because he is hungry, because you left him too long, or because there is some other problem that you need to fix if you are able to. A baby's sadness is not soul-threatening in the normal course of things, although a baby whose needs are never met will simply get used to being sad and it will become a part of his character and harm his soul, in that he will lose his trust—ultimately, his trust in God.

If we are doing our best, we shouldn't worry too much, but just be the parents. The truth is that is possible that a baby might have all his needs met in the normal course of things and still have a childhood filled with a sense of frustration. A lot of that is just human (fallen) nature mixed with individual temperament.

But as a child approaches the stage of life when he begins to think more about what's outside of his bodily needs and interacts with people, he begins to experience sadness that is quite different in quality.

I'll divide that experience into three categories, each of them ultimately decisive in his moral development. (I've put these things in terms of the child's experience, but of course they apply to adults as well.)

External Causes of Sadness

This sort of sadness comes from outside, because something bad has happened or has been said. Daddy and Mommy had a fight; a heaviness pervades the air. The child received a correction that hurts. He falls down just as he was about to reach a goal of some sort. Circumstances such as rain or lack of sleep can make the world seem bleak. He saw something terrible.

An example of the last sort: When I was eleven, I was in Egypt with my father. There were beggars everywhere; an American just can't imagine how it is in a really poor country. In the train station, I saw one poor man whose eye was hanging out of its socket. That this was not perceived as an emergency broke my heart and profoundly shocked me. I know now that I didn't articulate or even betray any sign of my distress. I had to assimilate all at once that, for my father (if he saw) and for that world in general, this man's life had to go on without a response from anyone, other than maybe—maybe—to put coins in his cup. There was so much suffering all around in that place that one couldn't react, or functioning would not be an option.

I was so sad for so long over that. Powerless, helpless. I still feel like crying. I hate myself for not doing something, but what could I have done? I was a child. It was too much of a sudden revelation of what the world could be.

Aside from such a stark experience, even a cross word can plunge a child into that sort of heartbreak, for a child has no ability to calibrate his feelings. Even a word not said with intentional crossness, but simply crossing his intentions in a way that catches him up can cause sadness. "Don't do that now; you have other tasks" — but at that moment, he was particularly proud of what he was doing. His grief is real, but the circumstance is not what he thinks it is.

We can teach the child to overcome the suffering of these sorrows in two ways. First, we can help him understand that present suffering is sometimes necessary for future happiness. Being corrected teaches him right action and is for his own good; he must learn to accept it calmly. Mother and Father reconcile after a fight; forgiveness is beautiful (and arguments are part of life; however, the lesson for the parents is to try to keep conflict out of the child's hearing, but if that fails, make sure the reconciliation is also known).

When a child sees suffering, the parents might not know about it (as with my blind man). We have to remember periodically to ask the child if anything is on his mind. If he can tell us, we help him to know that suffering exists and that it's the mark of a good person to "suffer with" — to have compassion — and we do our best to alleviate it if we are able and to pray for the sufferers.

Second, we can teach the child to join his suffering with that of Jesus on the Cross. Great graces result from learning to offer suffering, from making it a means of union with God. This suffering still hurts, but even a child can learn that the point isn't mere endurance. We aren't telling him simply to wait it out. We aren't teaching him to suspend his soul's experience when we help him find meaning in this sadness.

We can say, "I'm sorry you are hurting over this. Do remember to offer it to God. Remember how Christ suffered on the Cross for us! Let's give Him our suffering as well."

Moral Sadness

The second kind of sadness is when the child has done something wrong. Of course, this presupposes that he knows right from wrong, although it's quite interesting how even a small child can tell the difference. In subsequent sections, I will talk about teaching the moral law. But we should ponder that everyone has within himself the means of knowing right from wrong, which is the conscience. And the conscience can cause actual pain! This may be the sadness your child feels.

In that case, there is only one way out: repentance, sorrow, amendment. Without this, the sadness will only overwhelm the person—begins to define him, even—or he thrusts it so far down that only a hard exterior or callous indifference can contain it.

If we don't know these things, we won't be able to pass them on to our children, but instead we will dishonorably shift the resulting burden of purposelessness—and sadness!—onto the child. How cold, for a parent or a teacher (or a TV show producer) to be aware enough to observe the child's vulnerability but then to proceed to offer a little person, for whom every hour seems like an eternity, the smug advice to wait it out.

An Attack from the Enemy

The third cause of sadness can be what the spiritual masters call spiritual desolation. Sometimes when we're trying to do our best, and even if things outwardly seem fine, we can experience sadness or a tremendous void. It's good to know, again, that conscience and a sense of reality together can see us through.

In this case, waiting is required, but not with passivity or numbness. Instead, we can experience the joy of knowing, apart from any feelings we may have, that we haven't fallen and that, in God's good time, we will again see the light. I'll just note here that it's usually not advisable to discuss these things in these terms with children. Adults are responsible for observing children and helping them without burdening them with ideas beyond their years. Simply fostering a devotion to the guardian angels of both child and parent will go a long way to alleviating this kind of suffering.

The remedy for moral sadness is to grow in virtue. As we pay closer attention to the liturgy and to Scripture, we begin to realize how important learning God's law is. For the child, this means encountering the Ten Commandments as he reaches the age of reason.

The psalmist reminds us:

> The law of the LORD is perfect, converting the soul:
> the testimony of the LORD is sure,
> making wise the simple. (Ps. 19:7, KJV)

You might ask: Doesn't Christianity mean that we don't need God's law anymore, because we are under the dispensation of grace?

Well, if that were the case, why would Jesus have said, "If ye love me, keep my commandments" (John 14:15, KJV)? Let's not forget that He insisted that He came to fulfill the law, not to abolish it. He is Goodness itself. He will make us good.

We have to teach our children the commandments so that they may obtain the sweetness of the moral life.

On Teaching the
Faith to Children

As we teach our children the Faith, let's distinguish the way we learn about most things from the way we learn about God. Generally, we start with what we know and move outward toward the universal and then inward toward particulars. That's why it's faulty pedagogy, for instance, to plunge into the study of the cell before you have observed animals and plants and man and have had a chance to contrast living things and their development with nonliving things, such as stones and water and the sun.

With the faith, knowledge is acquired differently. As we read the Gospels and see how Jesus called people to Him, as we read the Acts of the Apostles and see how the Faith grew in the early Church, and as we see how the Church spread throughout the world in short order, we see that when people are brought before Jesus and His truth, they respond and follow.

Jesus reveals His identity and mission by starting with the things we know, true—a mustard seed, a woman who loses a coin, a lost sheep—but in order to listen to Him, we do not have to be told more about those things than we already know. And in the Gospels, Jesus immediately moves to repentance, forgiveness, trust, sin, salvation—often without any explanation or definitions. Even when He does explain, He doesn't get bogged down in what exactly constitutes rocky or shallow soil or what the composition of a pearl is.

Our observations of nature and common human experience are universally shared. Current methods of classroom catechesis fail to keep this truth as their guiding principle. They begin with what they *assume* is the child's experience of family life or relationships and try to build on them toward the spiritual realm. But how can they know what a child's experience is? How does one know that what the child has lived through is good and pure? If his family is broken, does invoking it condition the way the child perceives God? What about his trust in the teacher?

Today's catechetical programs uniformly begin with the child's presumed context, even though there is no way to predict exactly what that is. And if the child's circumstances cause him to suffer, they offer no solace as they run off with assumptions that suit their purpose.

As an example of this faulty approach, read a chapter about saints in any conventional religious textbook; you will find that it begins with a discussion of worldly heroes (or, desperately, sports stars): Martin Luther King Jr., Michael Jordan (they are always behind the times), Nelson Mandela. The child's sense of wonder is immediately drained into the worldly and mundane—a high price to pay, since it is perfectly possible for a child to grasp immediately what a saint is, much more easily than if he is first distracted in this way.

Contemporary textbooks rely heavily on blandly *narrating* Scripture or summarizing it, rather than reading from the Bible directly. They fail to keep the child protected in the pure light of God's Word. (Note that offering Scripture summaries in lesson form constitutes "value added" in economic terms. No publishing concern makes money from a teacher or a parent opening a Bible and reading to the child.) They suffer from the urge to explain Scripture to the child, rather than simply introducing the child to Scripture and letting God unfold the meaning in the child's heart. (Again, what exactly would their role be in this approach; that is, what would you buy?) Think of teaching your young child the Faith (as opposed to learning about the Bible or history, which I address elsewhere) differently. God has a plan that involves not rushing, not worrying about testing (until you come to prayers and precepts that must be memorized), not subjecting him to your anxieties about learning a certain amount of material in a certain time. While you are comfortably sitting with your child, reading Scripture together (or, for the very young child, well loved Bible stories), take your time. Enjoy silences while you both ponder. Speak about things in a gentle but solemn way that allows your child to chime in with what occurs to him, if he is so moved.

We've done a lot of harm in religious education by interposing ourselves between the Word and the child by using a methodology better suited for the assimilation of any utilitarian subject. A more peaceful and expansive way of delving into God's Word trusts that the child has an inner life and knows that he requires delicate respect from the adults around him. And it trusts that God wants the child to encounter Him.

Parents can overcome their reliance on experts and recover a simple, straightforward, and calm way of learning about God. I was struck how, in his *Memoirs*, Louis Bouyer recalls with simplicity how his mother taught him the Our Father—delicately, in an intimate and trusting way, with very little chatter. Certainly without workbooks to test his knowledge. His mother was Protestant; the Catholic child hears the Our Father at least six times a day, in the Rosary—he can't help but learn it!

The home is not a classroom. The family that has its own place of prayer, lovingly arranged, that prays together (including attending Church together) and follows the liturgical year has only to follow a simple plan of reading Scripture (for instance, the parables of Jesus, the Sermon on the Mount, the Passion narrative, beloved Old Testament stories), to fulfill its duties of teaching the Faith.

Maria Montessori's book *The Mass Explained to Children* (in its older, non-updated, version) is also helpful in demonstrating this calm way of teaching. Most Catholics don't attend the form of the liturgy that was celebrated when Montessori wrote this book (although it may pique their interest). But any parent can learn from her method of explaining important and holy things to children. Just following her example, noticing that she takes her time and delves into the details, becomes a spiritual education in itself for us, rushed and stressed as we are. And this is what we need to know.

Teaching the Ten Commandments

Children are allowed to grow up in ignorance and moral idleness; hence their piety is too often nothing but mere sentiment—a sort of misty and vague dreaminess—which is death to the spirit of prayer.[17]

— ABBESS BRUYÈRE

hrough the liturgical year and ordinary day-to-day interactions, full of affection, our children gradually become familiar with Scripture, prayer, and worship.

The literature we read to our children, the stories they hear us tell, and soon, the books they read on their own all pay homage to the real moral

---

[17] Cécile Bruyère, *The Spiritual Life and Prayer: According to Holy Scripture and Monastic Tradition*, trans. Benedictines of Stanbrook (Eugene, OR: Wipf and Stock, 2002), 93.

truths that our children begin to apprehend (if those stories are chosen wisely): that the good is worth seeking, that actions matter, that inside of us all is a compass that keeps us on the path, if we don't break it. Not that any of the books our children read for enjoyment say so in so many words, but they take it for granted, and they are beautiful. Beauty itself reveals the good.

The baby and the very young child, in the normal course of things, learn that some things are naughty[18] and that obedience brings a delightful freedom and sense of belonging. For children under six or seven, your approval is what matters.

And then comes the time when reason dawns. (Both religion and psychology note that the child seems to turn a corner somewhere around age seven. It's more a stage stretching from maybe ages six to eight, because it really does depend on the child and doesn't happen overnight, either.) The child becomes aware of a world out there and his relationship to it—including the world of good and evil.

A certain amount of actual instruction has to occur. The question of "how to teach religion" or "how to pass on the faith to our children" is more about living than about telling, but telling there must be—just a little, to rescue their spiritual life from "nothing but mere sentiment" as the quote above has it, and to give them something concrete to work with when they start thinking about such things. (This is the brilliance of memorizing catechism questions: long before they can understand the material, it is planted in their minds, where it will grow.)

We need to pay attention to the formal *moral* education of our children! Have you not noticed the crying need? The masses of people who seem to have no knowledge of right and wrong, good and evil? That we keep coming back to the realization that no amount of money or therapy can help them, because they need the *habit* of good?

---

[18] Long ago, when I was just starting to have children and to think about how I would talk to them, I read the advice that one should call behavior "naughty," not the child "bad"—and I couldn't agree more. "Don't be naughty" is a much better correction than "You are a bad boy." It's self-evident, isn't it?

Where did things break down?

I suggest to you that they broke down with the reluctance of parents simply to teach them, and the clergy to teach the parents.

If only, we think—*if only* there were an established *list* of rules or even commandments that covered all human behavior, that we could teach children early on, avoiding the obvious pitfalls of merely responding to difficulties as they crop up!

If only these rules went along with the child as he grows up, there for him to consult in times of difficulty—even when we are not there to correct! They should be permanent, universal—written on stone, as it were.

What a relief that would be!

Well, good news: there is such a list, and I think you know that it is the Ten Commandments. Jesus Himself spoke of them, saying "If ye love me, keep my commandments" (John 14:15, KJV).

I suggest the following plan of action, and everything that I say here is a gradual process to be done in the years between the dawning of the age of reason and the time, around puberty, when a more analytical approach can be taken.

Reading Material

Get yourself a copy of the *Catechism of the Catholic Church*. If you haven't already, start reading it from the beginning. But also start reading the section concerning the commandments. You are really your child's spiritual director, and a director has to know the moral law pretty well. You can't teach what you don't know yourself, and you certainly can't teach virtue without yourself striving for it.

This requires ongoing study, and you might as well go to the source. You can read the latest explanation of the *Catechism*, or you can just read the thing itself. The *Catechism of the Council of Trent* is another resource. Have a copy of each handy. It's the work of a lifetime to go through these treasuries of the Faith—and a challenge and a joy!

The *St. Joseph Baltimore Catechism* for children has been used for generations. Yes, it has old-fashioned pictures. Some like them; some don't. I think the fact that they are in black and white makes them more universal than their style suggests; but if you'd rather, there is a version with no pictures.

Take this book as a curriculum guide for you. It provides you, in addition to the basics of faith, with the *timeline*: Creation, Fall, law, Redemption, founding of the Church, Second Coming. You will refer to this timeline over and over, and soon you will notice that we are living in it, by means of the liturgical year.

The book provides you with Scriptural references. Take each lesson slowly; each one could be a week or quite a bit more! By the time you read it yourself, either read it to the children or say it in your own words, work with them to memorize the catechism points, delve into the Scriptures in a slow, loving, listening way, ask them the questions (again, quite likely in your own words, not as "busy desk work"), and think it all over, yes, a week or two might go by. Dad can hear the memorized work on Sunday morning and discuss it as well.

Thus, one of the books might take two years to complete! That's perfect.

Very importantly, the *St. Joseph Baltimore Catechism* takes you and your child through each commandment, slowly and with a lot of insight. By slowly, I mean that you will return to this year after year! (There are other editions for older children that go more into depth.)

The Greatest Commandment

Specifically about learning the commandments: First, read Jesus' answer to the expert in the law:

> Jesus said unto him: Thou shalt love the Lord thy God with all thy heart, and with all thy soul, and with all thy mind. This is the first and great commandment.
>
> And the second is like unto it, Thou shalt love thy neighbour as thyself. On these two commandments hang all the law and the prophets. (Matt. 22:37–40, KJV)

This is called "the Greatest Commandment," and, of course, it's a summation of the law in Deuteronomy and in Leviticus.

You can print the Greatest Commandment to form two sides of a hinged diptych, as they do on wooden tablets in the Atrium (your de-coupage skills would be very handy for this use!). The sides go together to demonstrate the two parts of the law. (You can also put them in a pocket folder for your diptych.) I do think it's worth making a beautiful one of your own, either printed in a readable but beautiful font or copied in your own hand. That way, the child has a model to aim for, and you will both be meditating on it, just as God tells us to do: "Let not the book of this law depart from thy mouth: but thou shalt meditate on it day and night, that thou mayst observe and do all things that are written in it: then shalt thou direct thy way, and understand it" (Josh. 1:8, DR).

Keep having your child write this out—it makes perfect handwriting practice. He can certainly memorize it very quickly.

Now let's also look at Luke 10:25–37, the Parable of the Good Sa-maritan. We don't often pay attention to the beginning, where Jesus asks the expert in the law, "What is written in the law? *How do you read it?*"

The man answers: "'Love the Lord your God with all your heart and with all your soul and with all your strength and with all your mind' and 'Love your neighbor as yourself.'" Jesus approves of this answer—and do you see how important it is that the man is able to say it to him? We can use this as a model for teaching our children; only then does Jesus go on to explain to him *who* his neighbor is. The man must know the big picture, so to speak, of the commandments, before he can delve into the particulars of loving his neighbor. What he repeats is the "summary of the law." And what is it summarizing? The Ten Commandments, of course. (We must be convinced that the Ten Commandments are not superseded by the New Covenant.) So then you will start studying those. It's easy enough to find or make worksheets that help children put them in order, learn their finer points, and memorize them.

The Ten Commandments

A good work (and it could be weeks or months before you get to this, and you will return to it) is to have the child copy the Ten Commandments on "stone tablets" (two pieces of paper with a stone tablet design, obtainable online). But—important: do not do it as you see it done all over the Internet and in many workbooks, and put five commandments on one side and five on the other! Put the first three on one side, and the other seven on the other.

The reason for this is that the first three relate to the first part of the Greatest Commandment, loving and honoring and worshipping God. The seven relate to the second part, loving one's neighbor. Note that the fourth commandment ("honor your father and your mother") provides the bridge between the two, for through the family the child learns of God's love here on earth as he develops and also learns to love his neighbor. See how God affirms the centrality of the family in this fundamental education of the human person?

As I said, there are many ways to memorize the Ten Commandments: flash cards, crossword puzzles, handwriting practice ... I would take some care to keep whatever medium you choose serious and appropriate (that is, stay away from cartoons unless you want your child to associate God's law with, well, cartoons).

The Commandments Are Givens

As you are doing this, you might keep a couple of things in mind (besides *not rushing*, which I hope you are convinced not to do).

First, don't take the attitude that you are trying to *persuade* your child of the truth of these commandments. They are givens; literally given to Moses by God. They have to do with the reality of God and of how He made us; they also reflect the Fall and our inclination to sin.

Therefore, don't seek affirmation, and you will teach this truth. Be calm, not anxious. The most important thing the child learns in his religious education is that the universe isn't here to affirm him; on the contrary, he must conform to its implacable ways. Blessedly, Our Lord came and died so that he might do that!

Second, be aware that the study of the Ten Commandments is the way we form the conscience of the child and give him the resolve to obey it.

Romano Guardini says (speaking of the commandment to keep holy the Sabbath Day, in his helpful little book *Meditations before Mass*):

> In the conviction of a thing's finality and inalterability lies a peculiar strength. As soon as I am convinced that I should perform some act, I can do it.... Anything but steadfast by nature, man is always ready to let things slide; this definite law in his life is something like the bones in his body, giving him firmness and character.

Here is an example of how we will certainly teach our children without words, when we calmly and matter-of-factly go to Mass every Sunday without fail. How "definite" a life we give them, "like bones in their body"—what an object lesson in "the convictions of a thing's finality."

Ultimately, we hope to confirm in ourselves and transmit to our children that the Law is fulfilled in Jesus Christ. He Himself is the Law. The New Covenant is to persuade the Jews, God's Chosen Ones, to receive in themselves the Incarnation of Goodness (for what is the Law but the guide of doing what is good?). Apart from Him we can do nothing.

In *Jesus of Nazareth*, Pope Benedict meditates on the Sermon on the Mount. He rejects the notion held by many that the Beatitudes *replace* the Decalogue: "This approach totally misconstrues the words of Jesus," citing Mark 10:19 and Luke 16:17. With careful steps that I can't reproduce here, he shows that by His words, Jesus intends us to know that He "understands himself as the Torah—the word of God *in person*." (emphasis added) The Beatitudes are His expression of this new covenant and of His identity as Messiah.

Study God's Law we must (the whole Liturgy tells us this without ceasing); in the end, we can't be good without having the life of Christ within us, and it is for that purpose that He abides with us.

Confession

Knowing the Ten Commandments is obviously the way to prepare for Confession (for everyone, not just for children). Confession is how we grow in the moral life, children and adults alike. How else are we to do it? We need grace; we need Jesus.

So often we are flailing about, trying desperately to think of what we will say. Probably this is the greatest obstacle to Confession—we just can't think! Are we really so bad? But as soon as we delve into the commandments, we realize right away where our fault lies.

I've taught the Ten Commandments to children for years now. I'm always struck by children's *intense* interest in them (especially the ones about lying and stealing). I think it's a mistake to think that children don't commit sins—to trivialize the importance of their failings, either objectively or as it appears to them. Stay away from any resource that downplays their ability to commit sin or their culpability! Their consciences are often stricken. This is the observation that I began this section with; remember that what appears outwardly to be vague discomfiture or sadness in the child, as in everyone, is often a niggling conscience. Once you realize what the trouble is, you can sense their great relief to know exactly how they can repent, be forgiven, and make amends. Of course, they probably will not say any of this, but their riveted attention gives you a hint of it.

I've heard good priests complain that confessions (of adults) tend to include things like "I didn't love myself enough" and "I failed to love God as I should." But really, I fault the priests (different ones, probably)—as well as the seeping of self-absorption into the devotion business—because all the teaching we get today (and all we give our children) is just that vague and useless.

Remedy: the Good Old Ten Commandments.

The *Baltimore Catechism* seems to understand the mind of the child very well. I use it as a guide, reading the points and paraphrasing as I see fit.[19]

---

[19] The only real on-the-fly editing I've done of the *Baltimore Catechism* is to leave off the emphasis it places on immodesty, under the Sixth Commandment, because my classes have been of boys only. Yes, girls should dress modestly; I always add that for boys, modesty means dressing appropriately to the occasion, and respectfully of others; not assuming that going about in your undershirt is appropriate, for instance. I tread lightly on the issue of how girls dress, stressing to the boys that looking in a girl's eyes, no matter how she happens to be dressed, is the proper response. With my own children, I only discovered this book by the time I got pretty far down the line. I think we had enough conversations about modesty and didn't need

Here, I am focusing on teaching and learning the moral law, but you can easily see how to expand this method of using the *Baltimore Catechism* in various parts of the religious curriculum. One really delves into Creation, the goodness of the universe, the maleness and femaleness of man; the Fall, and what its parts are; each stage of covenant giving along the way; the long, remote preparation for Redemption; the life of Christ; the establishment of the Church. This outline can be used for every stage with its own appropriate level of detail and analysis.

For now, I want to get across how simple and direct it is to teach the Ten Commandments. Our world is hungry for people who know and love God's law, who know right from wrong and good from evil, and who desire to grow in virtue.

---

to spend too much time on it. The main thing with this commandment, when addressing a child, is to say that *one doesn't treat someone who isn't a spouse as if he or she is, and vice versa.* I tell them that it's something to think about for later, when they are thinking of whom they will marry.

Nurturing the Moral Life

Our moral life is intrinsic to our nature: we were made to be good, to respond to goodness, to love the good. But because of the Fall, we have trouble being good. If you pay close attention to the readings at Mass, however, you will see how often the Church brings our attention back to *loving God's law*.

I happened upon the familiar reading from the Divine Office on the feast of St. Anthony of Egypt, taken from the sixth chapter of Deuteronomy:

> Hear, O Israel, the Lord our God is one Lord. Thou shalt love the Lord thy God with thy whole heart, and with thy whole soul, and with thy whole strength.
>
> And these words which I command thee this day, shall be in thy heart: And thou shalt tell them to thy children, and thou shalt meditate upon them sitting in thy house, and walking on thy journey, sleeping and rising. And thou shalt bind them as a sign on thy hand, and they shall be and shall move between thy eyes. And thou shalt write them in the entry, and on the doors of thy house.

And when the Lord thy God shall have brought thee into the land, for which he swore to thy fathers Abraham, Isaac, and Jacob: and shall have given thee great and goodly cities, which thou didst not build, houses full of riches, which thou didst not set up, cisterns which thou didst not dig, vineyards and oliveyards, which thou didst not plant, and thou shalt have eaten and be full: take heed diligently lest thou forget the Lord, who brought thee out of the land of Egypt, out of the house of bondage. Thou shalt fear the Lord thy God, and shalt serve him only, and thou shalt swear by his name.

You shall not go after the strange gods of all the nations, that are round about you: because the Lord thy God is a jealous God in the midst of thee: lest at any time the wrath of the Lord thy God be kindled against thee, and take thee away from the face of the earth.

Thou shalt not tempt the Lord thy God, as thou temptedst him in the place of temptation. Keep the precepts of the Lord thy God, and the testimonies and ceremonies which he hath commanded thee. And do that which is pleasing and good in the sight of the Lord, that it may be well with thee: and going in thou mayst possess the goodly land, concerning which the Lord swore to thy fathers, that he would destroy all thy enemies before thee, as he hath spoken.

And when thy son shall ask thee tomorrow, saying: What mean these testimonies, and ceremonies and judgments, which the Lord our God hath commanded us? thou shalt say to him: We were bond-men of Pharao in Egypt, and the Lord brought us out of Egypt with a strong hand. And he wrought signs and wonders great and very grievous in Egypt against Pharao, and all his house, in our sight, and he brought us out from thence, that he might bring us in and give us the land, concerning which he swore to our fathers. And the Lord commanded that we should do all these ordinances, and should fear the Lord our God, that it might be well with us all the days of our life, as it is at this day. And he will be merciful to us, if we keep and do all his precepts before the Lord our God, as he hath commanded us. (vv. 4–25)

"These words which I command thee this day, shall be in thy heart: And thou shalt tell them to thy children."

In his excellent biography *John Senior and the Restoration of Realism*, Dom Francis Bethel recounts that Senior is surprised by his failure as a professor when he, so to speak, brings his students to the waters of Thomas Aquinas and expects them to drink.

The modern student, the student who lacks the basic human formation I've been trying to describe, simply cannot assimilate the rich intellectual nourishment that he's being offered. Senior sees that his students' inability not only to understand the text but even to be sparked by the light of knowledge has to do with a lack of imagination and connection with reality:

> "The *Summa Theologiae* [the text by Thomas Aquinas he wants them
> to read] contains clear refutations of reasonable heresies [by this he
> means simple errors] but scarcely touches anyone who disbelieves in
> the very difference between truth and error." Senior found that his
> students simply did not recognize "the absolute difference between
> 'is' and 'is not.'"

Senior calls this condition an "unreasonable" heresy—there is no reasoning with a person in this condition, as they have not the *faculty* of reasoning.

As I mentioned when stressing the importance of disciplining children in volume 1, the basic habit of "liking and disliking what he ought" must be nurtured in a child when he is very young, as the ancients tell us, or else he arrives at this pitiable state of not being able to move on to abstract reasoning. The child becomes impervious to moral thought and, hence, to moral action. He is at the mercy of his appetites—or, more seriously, of the will of those who are more powerful than he.

This fundamental observation explains why I pretty much despair when someone remarks that the trouble with the state of marriage in our society can be explained by the state of "marriage prep," as if a class during the weeks before the wedding can rectify a lifetime of moral neglect. Proper formation takes the form of organic life, directed by loving parents and teachers, not a program.

Senior came to change his approach to teaching, realizing that the student's preparation takes place outside the classroom *and long before he arrives there*, if his mind is to be open to truth. Dom Bethel recounts that Senior used a metaphor of "the erosion of the 1930s when farmers had to sow common plants in order to nourish the barren land and render it capable of growing food crops." Dom Bethel sums up Senior's recognition of the failure of the "Great Books" movement by commenting that Senior had realized: "Learning is gradual, and first things must come first."[20]

The child, briefly stated, has to be connected to reality at an early age, or the chances that he will be able to function as a free adult (freedom being precisely the ability to control oneself morally) will be low; far less will he be able to tackle intellectually rich fare later in life.

But even if a person doesn't go on to study philosophy, his life will be destroyed by the "unreasonable" heresy: the failure to know that good and truth, above all, *exist*. He will be incapable of living well with others, of being a part of society and treating God, himself, and others with justice. He will, in short, be a slave.

When your children are very young, you might not think you are giving them a moral education by nurturing their imaginations with good stories; their senses with contact with the natural world as it is outside, in the fresh air, under the stars; and with your loving (and sometimes exasperated) insistence that they not be naughty but try to be good. It all seems so messy, and so slow, and so visibly unproductive.

The thing is, everything living must develop according to its nature. There really aren't shortcuts. If you've ever raised tomatoes from seeds, you have experienced this. Every year I try, with my lack of indoor south-facing exposure, but the fact is that a weak seedling ends up as a weak plant that doesn't produce much, despite all the compost I heap on it later on.

Children, too, must develop according to their nature. The great lie of our time denies the vital importance of the *seedbed*. Our experts give everyone the idea that it doesn't matter how the child spends his toddler

---

[20] Father Francis Bethel, O.S.B., *John Senior and the Restoration of Realism* (Merrimack, NH: St. Thomas More College Press, 2017), 151.

years, or what kind of education he gets in elementary school, or who takes care of him. The remedy is simple (but, of course, not easy): marriage as a commitment to each other, husband and wife, and to the life you are building together; and to sacrifice for home life.

You are nurturing the moral life when you say to your three-year-old, "Go wash your hands," and he comes back in a minute and says, "I did," but you see that he didn't, so you say, "Don't be naughty. When I tell you to wash your hands, you must do it"; when you say, "Don't hit your brother, that's naughty! Go help him climb that thing," you are establishing reality for your child, in the only way he can apprehend it, through you. Don't forget that God is Father. He gives us earthly fathers so that we can come to know Him.

Senior wrote in *The Restoration of Christian Culture*: "There is no amount of reading, remedial or advanced, no amount of study of any kind, that can substitute for the fact that we are a rooted species, rooted through our sense in the air, water, earth and fire of elemental experience. 'Nihil in intellectu nisi prius in sensu' (Nothing is in the mind that is not first in the senses)." Where do our roots begin but in our fundamental relationships in the family?

Later, around the age of reason, when the child has the *habit* of obeying and trusting in you and has a growing awareness that the world is a big place, you can start the gentle process of acquainting him with God's law, helping him lift his eyes up from his mother and father to the universe that awaits him. You are bestowing on him a sense of self and of others and preparing for a healthy separation from you at the right time.

Here are a few more resources for you:

As your child moves out of Bible stories and into reading actual Scripture, F.J. Knecht's *Child's Bible History* will help him to grasp the overall sweep of salvation history. This book is not a Bible and not a catechism, but it's very helpful for understanding both. Use the questions after each section as prompts for discussion; a simple narration of the text will be fine and will fix it in the child's memory.

The Penny Catechism is a supplement to the *Baltimore Catechism*. It's really helpful for adults too. Honestly, this little book is worth a million motivational volumes about becoming a dynamic Christian. What we need is for our consciences to become informed, and the Holy Spirit will do the rest.

At the back of *The Penny Catechism* you will find helpful prayers and a short "Christian's Rule of Life." What is a rule of life? It's simply the few habits that you want to have to stay on track. Contrary to what you may think, it's not at all burdensome or anxiety-producing to have a "rule"; far less is it complicated; it's simple and freeing, especially when you realize that you just choose one thing at a time to concentrate on, perhaps mentioning it to your spiritual director (usually the priest you go to for Confession).

For a child, I hope you can find the charming book *A Child's Rule of Life*. Robert Hugh Benson gently and poetically shows the child what "a day in the life" looks like.

On Teaching the Faith
to the Older Child

efore we get to teaching the Faith to the older child, let us see
what we have so far.

- My preliminary musings on a sort of sadness and loss
  of meaning that comes from trying to live life without
  reference to the moral nature of the thing.
- Things grow according to their nature: God gives very
  young children a mother, a father, and family life to
  teach them that things *are*; a child at the age of reason
  starts the simple task of memorizing the Ten Commandments, with a necessary but small amount of
  instruction.
- A bit more about teaching the Ten Commandments,
  with some resources that can take you right up to the
  point where the child is intellectually able to delve
  deeper and more analytically into the truths of the
  Faith and, most importantly, has the beginnings of
  the habits of virtue that must undergird such a study.

Now we come to the older child — that child who can buckle down and study. His mind has taken a turn for real inquiry. In other subjects, he has begun to investigate causes. He is capable of examining a footnote (and I regard a seventh or eighth grader as gearing up for this sort of thing).

For teaching the moral law *and explaining the role of the Church in this task*, the *Catechism* is the clearest, most efficient, and most inspiring way to convey the whole body of teaching. The perceived problem is that it's a *big book*. It has a lot of pages, and that makes it daunting. We think our children can't handle it. But they certainly can, and no one said that you have to read it all at once! Let me tell you how it operates.

There are four main parts, in addition to a prologue, which you will want to read, because it beautifully synthesizes the truths of revelation, history, and natural law. You could make each part a year of your older child's religion curriculum. With the addition of a systematic (not devotional per se) Scripture study, a return, as in every year, to the timeline of salvation history, and of course, your family's living of the liturgical year in unity with the liturgy of the Church, you would be sending your child out into the world with a solid foundation as to the facts and practice of Christianity.

It took me decades to figure this out, with many mistakes along the way; and I'm trying to say that "I alone have survived to tell you" — save yourself a lot of grief and go with this method (you can also use an older catechism, of course, such as the *Catechism of the Council of Trent*).

You can look at the table of contents of the *Catechism of the Catholic Church* to see how it's arranged: one of the parts is "Life in Christ." This section is on the Ten Commandments and their fulfillment in the New Testament, the Beatitudes.

Here's a little sample from the section on the Fourth Commandment, "Honor your father and your mother":

> The fecundity of conjugal love cannot be reduced solely to the procreation of children, but must extend to their moral education and their spiritual formation. "The *role of parents in education* is of such importance that it is almost impossible to provide an adequate

substitute" (*GE* 3). The right and the duty of parents to educate their children are primordial and inalienable (cf. *FC* 36). (CCC 2221)[21]

Looking up some of these words will add value to the overall lesson. How will your child function, intellectually, without knowing what "fecundity," "conjugal," "primordial," and "inalienable" mean? Further, ponder the statement in quotes for affirmation for all the effort this endeavor is costing you.

Each article of the *Catechism* builds on the preceding sections, and everything is shored up by Scripture and sound theology (and philosophy). The parts were given to the very best and most orthodox minds to compose—this is no "committee production," watered down to the lowest denominator.

Every aspect of the question at hand is examined, but there is also a section at the end of each article that summarizes the main points. One

---

[21] This paragraph cites *Familiaris Consortio* and *Gravissimum Educationis*, two of the many Church documents that address the duty to educate.

The first footnote in *Gravissimum Educationis* illuminates the solid foundation of teaching on which the statements are based. I'm just going to plop it here so you can see for yourself how deep it goes into references on previous teachings:

Among many documents illustrating the importance of education confer above all apostolic letter of Benedict XV, *Communes Litteras*, April 10, 1919: A.A.S. 11 (1919) p. 172. Pius XI's apostolic encyclical, *Divini Illius Magistri*, Dec. 31, 1929: A.A.S. 22 (1930) pp. 49-86. Pius XII's allocution to the youths of Italian Catholic Action, April 20, 1946: Discourses and Radio Messages, vol. 8, pp. 53-57. Allocution to fathers of French families, Sept. 18, 1951: Discourses and Radio Messages, vol. 13, pp. 241-245. John XXIII's 30th-anniversary message on the publication of the encyclical letter, *Divini Illius Magistri*, Dec. 30, 1959: A.A.S. 52 (1960), pp. 57–59. Paul VI's allocution to members of Federated Institutes Dependent on Ecclesiastic Authority, Dec. 30, 1963: Encyclicals and Discourses of His Holiness Paul VI, Rome, 1964, pp. 601-603. Above all are to be consulted the Acts and Documents of the Second Vatican Council appearing in the first series of the ante-preparatory phase, vol. 3. pp. 363-364; 370-371; 373-374.

If you consulted each of those documents, you would further find references to the early Fathers and to Scripture.

could certainly go through once using those "In Brief" sections and then go through again, taking the time to expand on them. But you will be drawn in by the excellence and sheer inspiration of the main body of material.

You *could* get a textbook that digests all of this for you. But I'm not going to lie—it's going to make study more tedious. (Sometimes I wonder if we think that serious things *ought to be* tedious! But that's not true!) It's better to approach this compact paragraph as it stands, showing your student how to expand it for himself. Let *him* write you a statement about what it means.

Don't be tempted to add a "slogging factor" to work that requires effort but is basically approachable *if we take our time*. It requires much more energy to read a textbook about Shakespeare than to read Shakespeare!

This is the brilliance of the *Catechism*. It is intentionally compact and succinct. Certainly you, the teacher, can read outside sources to help you explain things to your child, but I would be very wary of eliminating or attempting to override the particular format of the *Catechism*.

The in-depth study of the Ten Commandments is irreplaceable, though of course it takes place over the whole of our lives. When the child reaches the age of reason, the time has come to begin; in his adolescence, as his intellect grows with tremendous flexibility (and potential for good or ill), deep reverberations occur when he continues.

Romano Guardini says in his short book *The Spirit of the Liturgy*:

> We have seen that thought alone can keep spiritual life sound and healthy. In the same way, prayer is beneficial only when it rests on the bedrock of truth. This is not meant in the purely negative sense that it must be free from error; in addition to this, it must spring from the fullness of truth. It is only truth—or dogma, to give it its other name—which can make prayer efficacious, and impregnate it with that austere, protective strength without which it degenerates into weakness.... Dogmatic thought brings release from the thralldom of individual caprice, and from the uncertainty and sluggishness which follow in the wake of emotion. It makes prayer intelligible, and causes it to rank as a potent factor in life.

If, however, religious thought is to do justice to its mission, it must introduce into prayer truth in all its fullness.[22]

The very ability to pray, the gift we want to give to our children, rests on the truth. The Church exists for worship, which requires that she guard doctrine; each person must also guard it, which is why Scripture exhorts us to follow God's commandments and write His precepts on our hearts.

A Good Conscience Is the Basis of the Life of Prayer

In his helpful little volume *Difficulties in Mental Prayer*, Dom Eugene Boylan gets to the root of what might be giving us trouble in our relationship with God in the chapter called "Goodness of Life":

> Prayer will not develop unless the soul is advancing towards the fourfold purity of conscience, of heart, of mind, and of action.... [Sin] is a direct denial of love to God....
>
> Nothing so darkens our gaze on God, nothing so weakens our desire for God, nothing so lessens our striving for God, as a single inordinate attachment. That is the great source of many difficulties in prayer.

The inquiry into the proper orderings of attachment is exactly what moral education is, and *that* begins with the Commandments.

If we want our children to know and love God's law so that they can have a relationship with Him, we have to teach them how to be at peace. Yes, the natural law is written on man's heart (CCC 1955), but this knowledge must be nurtured. Today there's a lot of discussion about conscience and one's actions; what is not so much valued anymore is the role of teaching in forming conscience. The *Catechism* has this to say:

> In the formation of conscience the Word of God is the light for our path, we must assimilate it in faith and prayer and put it into

---

[22] Romano Guardini, *The Spirit of the Liturgy*, trans. Ada Lane (New York: Sheed and Ward, 1935), chap. 1, posted on EWTN, https://www.ewtn.com/catholicism/library/spirit-of-the-liturgy-11203.

practice. We must also examine our conscience before the Lord's Cross. We are assisted by the gifts of the Holy Spirit, aided by the witness or advice of others and guided by the authoritative teaching of the Church. (1785)

That last clause is why we begin with the *Catechism* itself, once the child has grown beyond the years when parents guide him with their dos and don'ts.

That's the "study" part of things (and immediately, we find that study becomes prayer), but of course, such a study forms a part of a more comprehensive education, taken in the larger sense, which has to include other, nonanalytical ways of expressing the same thing; we will discuss these other ways below.

Developing Virtue

The family is made by God to provide a loving mother and father who can deal sensitively with the little moral crises of the very young child. In fact, the child knows God primarily through the parents (in the normal course of things) at this point, for the reason that God entrusts to the parents the privilege of making the child aware of the world beyond the home. Here you get a glimpse of something profound: the three commandments that relate to honoring God give way to the six relating to man's neighbor by means of the *hinge* commandment, the fourth, in which the positive "honor your father and your mother" links the two vital precepts, love the Lord your God and love your neighbor as yourself.

It's sometimes hard to trust in this truth. Our age, having done its utmost to destroy the family's unique role, replaces it with a condescending pedagogy, serving up capsules of dry lessons, explaining its pat observations with unrelieved tedium.

"Sometimes adults can be confusing and mess things up," our apostles of therapeutic helpfulness directly inform the child. But he may not want to hear or be ready for this disturbing bit of information. After all, as Bruno

Bettelheim so admirably explained in *The Meaning and Importance of Fairy Tales*, what child can admit to himself that his parents are weak? What recourse would he have; to whom then would he turn for the stability he needs?

Good point, we say. And then we go on to put our hopes in some variant of this misbegotten form of education, the "character building" program for ethical living. It's like an addiction: even if we know that we are not succeeding in teaching children well, we keep wasting time on failed methods. Or we settle for pacification, entertainment, and quiet (for us, if not for the children)—and neglect.

I hope I've convinced you so far of the importance of teaching the Ten Commandments and their fulfillment in the Eight Beatitudes. Yet I admit that it is possible that even these revelations from God could devolve into the same dry moral dust that chokes (in Michael Oakeshott's vivid phrase), rather than reviving with the life-giving water they are meant to be. The human condition makes it likely, in fact.

That is why I return to the importance of the imagination, the formation of which is the most fundamental step in the moral education of the child and can take place only by gradual degrees in the bosom of the family, with the delicate support of other institutions, if possible. As important as traditional fairy tales are for healthy emotional development, they are even more so for moral development, especially for the virtue of fortitude that is so necessary to accomplish the good. Fairy tales are the gateway to morality. The good ones are all about the truth of what is unseen and the necessity of self-control to happiness.

Perhaps a glimpse of "The Six Swans," a fairy tale I dearly love (but I could have chosen a dozen others), can illuminate another, more time-tested way. This story (as told in Andrew Lang's *Yellow Fairy Book*) opens with a few deft, artful strokes that capture the human condition, with a little commentary from me in brackets:

A king was once hunting in a great wood [and the wood is life itself], and he hunted the game so eagerly that none of his courtiers could follow him. [The king is subject to his passions, which are represented by hunting. The listener immediately hears that he doesn't exercise self-control; consequently, his courtiers, who serve him, but who also merit protection from him, are left behind.]

When evening came on, he stood still and looked round him, and he saw that he had quite lost himself. [This is the perfect way of expressing the situation, is it not? No one did it to him—he lost *himself*. He's king, after all; but the implicit message is that with great power comes the need for great self-control.] He sought a way out, but could find none. Then he saw an old woman with a shaking head coming towards him; but she was a witch.

In exchange for her help in finding a way out of the wood, he must marry the beautiful daughter of the witch. Despite her beauty, the king "could not look at her without a secret feeling of horror." What an interesting warning note that is! Nevertheless, he marries her because he feels compelled to.

He has six boys and one girl by his first wife, whose fate we are not told. Bettelheim points out that the stepmother is the fairy tale's device for avoiding the devastating effects on the vulnerable child of exposing the shortcomings of the mother; once we understand this meaning, we see that any explanation is unnecessary—the mothers are one and the same, and the child grasps the identity without being told.

There is something going on in this story with the needs, desires, and relationships of this king that is not made clear, and this, too, is true to life. Only when they grow up do children realize how complex their parents' inner lives often are or were—parents want to teach the child to be good but have struggles of their own. This is just something about life that we have to accept, and something that the fairy tale acknowledges.

Because of this father's unbridled selfishness, his whole family is plunged into captivity and abandonment.

The boys, who have been turned into swans by the witch, can be freed only by the self-sacrifice of the girl, who represents the soul. The brothers represent the facets of the personality that must be integrated in order to reach maturity, both psychological and moral.

With great difficulty, the girl sews shirts from stinging nettles that will release her brothers from their enchantment; but to succeed, she may not speak, not even to her husband, not even to save her own life from terrible accusations that lead her to execution. You might say that there is a seemingly arbitrary commandment that she must follow, just as the moral code seems arbitrary to the child at first.

Her toil and suffering—and great courage—represent the inner workings of the soul, which must take place without articulation for the most part, even when life seems in danger. As parents, do we know how the interior life develops, and do we respect it and trust in its unseen power?

In the end, the girl is saved from death at the last moment when, determined to the end to accomplish her task, she throws the shirts over her brothers' heads. Only the final sleeve remains uncompleted, leaving the youngest brother to be content with a swan's wing rather than a man's arm. Here, with a masterful and unexpected detail, the story helps us accept that we can never quite conquer our passions in this life; nevertheless, we can be assured that all will be well and we will escape the burning pyre, just as the sister does. When she finally speaks, she gives voice to this promise:

> "Dearest husband ... now I can tell you openly that I am innocent ..." The King and the Queen with their six brothers lived many years in happiness and peace.

If we are honest with ourselves as parents, we realize that we will eventually *and probably continually* commit the fault of the king. Honesty about our shortcomings ought to bring a lot of gratitude for the help that fairy tales offer—that is, that the collective memory preserves for us in our weakness.

I believe that stories like "The Six Swans" help us to understand the mystery of *being good* and that we can't reduce the journey to a more manageable process.

The child listens to the story, reads it over and over, and absorbs not only its meaning on some level, but also the meaning embedded in the parent's approval and telling of it. "If my mother takes time to read me this story," he thinks, "it must have meaning for me."

We need precepts. We need—acutely—the Ten Commandments. We need the Proclamation of the Kingdom, the Beatitudes. And we need beauty with its hidden ways of radiating the splendor of truth. A beautiful story can accomplish what years of explanation cannot.

We need both beauty and precept, and in the family the two strands can be woven into a meaningful sort of formation.

In his *Spirit of the Liturgy*, Roman Guardini writes:

> When life lacks the austere guidance of the sense of purpose it degenerates into pseudo-aestheticism. But when it is forced into the rigid framework that is the purely purposeful conception of the world, it droops and perishes. The two conceptions are inter-dependent. Purpose is the goal of all effort, labor and organization, meaning is the essence of existence, of flourishing, ripening life. *Purpose and meaning, effort and growth, activity and production, organization and creation—these are the two poles of existence.*[23]

I've only looked briefly at one story here. There are so many, including other kinds of good literature that I discuss elsewhere in this book and on my blog. Taken together, they illuminate with the power of imagination the reality that the world has its appearances but that there exists another plane, a *kingdom*, you might say, in which the last will be first, a determined girl can save her brothers, the good will be rewarded in unexpected ways, and the innocent will have grace on their side.

---

[23] Guardini, *The Spirit of the Liturgy*, chap. 5, emphasis added.

How to Talk to Children about Scary News

I grew up with graphic footage from Vietnam on the nightly news, Black Panthers and the riots in New Haven being discussed at the hairdressers', and a vague sense that the Winchester gun factory, which was right down the street, would explode and kill me. On the inside of my world, my family was torn apart by divorce; on the outside, what seemed like total chaos, with no one in control. To me, a child, there seemed no difference: the one was an emblem for the other.

So I'll give my opinion on what to say to children, and what not to say, about scary news. A scary event can be a good examination of conscience, because before we can have a clue about how to protect our children from being hurt, emotionally and physically, by strangers, we have to be honest about whether we are hurting them ourselves.

Children need love and stability from their parents. I'm not talking about superficial stability. You don't need to own a big house before you can think about bringing a child into the world. And as a wise neighbor reassured me when we were moving for the third time in a year, "Sometimes you have to pack up your security and take it with you."

But before you get angry about what the media are doing to our children, be honest about what you might be doing to them yourself. Resolve to make it your priority to make the emotional and physical life of your children as safe as you are able—not by hovering over their every move, but by providing a stable home, a real refuge.

No one is perfect, and children are willing, touchingly willing, to forgive. It's not right to twist that constant (albeit ultimately diminishing) renewal of trust into some sort of justification for failing to protect them, on the grounds that "children are resilient" or that their concerns aren't your first responsibility, because they are. "The kids are all right" is something adults say when they are abdicating responsibility.

One emotional danger our children are constantly subjected to is graphic images, although this isn't a new thing; parents have always had to be aware of it. Just think of days when there were public executions! In the sixties, it's true, the bombardment via TV in the home became hard to escape.

Turning off the TV, switching off the radio, refraining from endless vocal processing of possibly false factoids: these are the ways adults exercise self-control and prevent themselves from falling into idle curiosity and worse.

Having your own habits under control, you can turn to the problem of filtering the information your children receive.

It is a problem, because no matter how careful you are, they will hear snatches of discussion, all the more distorted because partial; they will see images and they will absorb the fear they sense in those they trust.

Even if we try, children will see and hear things we will wish they hadn't, if we are aware at all, and that is probably just how it has to be. I'm not sure that there isn't an immunizing effect, similar to the constant, low-grade exposure to germs, that allows a child ultimately to be able to deal with the big, wide world. I can't quite imagine how it would be if someone were successful in completely isolating a child from anything disturbing until he reached maturity. That might have its own negative consequences.

There's a tension: we must try to shelter young children from hearing and seeing disturbing news and yet accept that some of it inevitably will trickle down to them. And that is an opportunity. It helps us learn how to tease out what they are thinking with a certain finesse, because point-blank questions can be counterproductive, instilling the very fears we are trying to assuage.

We learn to listen. We learn to ask gentle questions such as "Did you see something that troubled you?" "Were you afraid of something today?" "Is there something you want to ask me today?" We learn to interpret unhappiness or lack of peace. And we resolve to tell the truth, according to the circumstances.

The truth is that we can't protect our children from every danger, nor can we do more than try. We must accept a certain level of failure. God willing, the level will be low. But it may end up being more than that. Beware of the danger of promising a child that we will always protect him and keep him safe. We can promise to try.

This is where theology becomes quite practical. Our beliefs must correspond with reality. Things aren't a matter of mind control: wishing life to be soft and flowery and full of basically good people won't make it so. Neither should we give way to helplessness, clutching our babies in despair. Let's not inflict adult uncertainties on them; instead, let's confront our uncertainties alone until we have figured them out.

We ought to know, and live as if we know, that God allows man freedom, including the freedom to do evil; even if the worst happens, He is in control and has a plan for our flourishing—a plan that is nevertheless not free of suffering. For each of us, He wills only the good. The good may not be what was in our plan, but our consolation is that He didn't spare even His own Son.

Telling a child just that, simply and according to his ability to understand, seems to me to be not only the best, truest way to handle scary news but also the best means to restore to him some sense of trust. Little by little, he must learn that it's good to trust in you, his parents, but ultimately, he can trust completely only in God. Many children have lost their parents. Many parents have failed to protect their children. But what we wish for them is to know that we do our best and trust in a loving God.

It would be folly to try to tell your child that you won't let anything bad happen to him. That is simply not true. Yet beware the opposite pitfall, which is to convey the idea that you have no resources and are as frightened as he, which would be tantamount to putting the burden on him. Let your hugs have in them the strong energy of your arms, not their weakness.

Recognize that for your young child, what he most wants to know is "Can you protect me?" He doesn't have a context for the danger, which is likely all muddled in his mind; be aware that no amount of explaining can fix that, which is frustrating. In truth, you must say, and perhaps not in many words, "I am here to do my utmost to protect you" and then to admit that you yourself take refuge in God's protection.

We commend those in need to God's care. Kneeling with a child to pray for those in need gives him a ready example. It is also singularly effective. God listens to the prayers of children! This is how we want the child to help people who seem beyond his reach. You must convey your conviction that this world is not the end of all. There is life after death. The Good God will draw all unto Himself.

That there are bad people is also the truth. Jesus said, "Love your enemies and pray for those who persecute you" (see Matt. 5:44). The enemy of my brother, the victim, is someone I must love and pray for. Loving someone means wanting the best for that person. It isn't excusing him, although Jesus Himself said, from the Cross, "They know not what they do" (Luke 23:34). Let Him be our guide; otherwise, in whom would we hope?

This kind of faith, the faith in the ultimate triumph of good over evil, even through suffering, is what we want our children to learn. Very little of it will they learn from lectures. Most of it they will learn by watching us and in quiet, loving conversations of a few words spoken in answer to questions asked, perhaps silently.

Solidarity, Sex Education, and Happiness

How do I answer my children's questions about what they hear on the news?" "How do I parent in a post-*Obergefell*, same-sex 'marriage' world?" "My childhood was far from innocent. How do I raise my children?"

I propose a few thoughts on human nature to answer these questions, and to suggest some reading that puts parents in touch with the mind of the Church (the great authority on human nature) on the subject of sex education.

We've been conditioned to turn to "experts" for every problem, and we don't realize that the concept of "sex education" as a separate, indispensable subject is as shockingly unexamined as it is new.

The Church teaches that God gives parents the grace to educate their children. The more essential to the core of the human person the subject matter, the more the parents are in charge, and the less the duty to educate can be delegated. No teacher, no doctor, not even a bishop, can insist that you turn your child over to them for instruction. We can't compromise with the world on this matter. As Pius XI stated in his encyclical to the German people *Mit Brennender Sorge,* "None can free you [parents] from the responsibility God has placed on you over your children. None ... can answer for you to the eternal Judge, when he will ask: 'Where are those I confided to you?' May every one of you be able to answer: 'Of them whom thou hast given me, I have not lost any one' (John xvii. 9)."

Sex education is not a matter of finding the right program offered by experts. Instead, the core mission of the family is teaching its own children about life and love.

How a Child Learns Important Things

The enemies of the family have a powerful weapon. They try to get us to believe that "now, in this day and age, when things are so enlightened" (or sometimes, on the other hand, *so decadent*), there is a new way to raise children.

But human nature is given by God and will always stay the same. Children are born into a family, and it's up to that family to help them develop *according to their nature.*

We have to be careful not to project our adult worries and complexes onto our children. "Man and woman He created them," as we read in Genesis. Everyone has a body that was created with a "nuptial" meaning, and ultimately we are all meant to be happy with God in the wedding feast of Heaven. This inner meaning is why children lose hope when we deny them the joy of knowing that God has in store for them *only happiness.*

Giving our children a belief *in happiness* is the greatest gift we can give. It's the gift of faith, of knowing that even with suffering, if we "keep his commandments" we will love God, serve him, and be among the blessed with Him in Heaven.

Certainly, it has been a long time now that society as a whole has tried to foist on parents the remaking of their children. One just can't go on responding to events as they come up, or only *reacting* to stimuli. We ought to be grateful that these schemes are all out in the open now—no hiding behind convention.

Regardless of what is happening in the world, children develop the same way they always have. Human nature is a given. The nature of the child hasn't changed, and we will only do damage if we act as if it has—the evidence of that damage is all around us.

Children have certain needs, including emotional and psychological ones, that undergird proper spiritual development. Grace—the unmerited favor of God—builds on nature; it doesn't replace it. Parents have the duty to try to provide a peaceful, safe home where children, simply by being part of the family, "the domestic church and the school of virtue," as Pope John Paul II called it, can learn about marriage and the meaning of the body.

There is no other way.

Families Provide the Full Curriculum of Sex Education

The family is mother, father, children, and other family members all doing their best to live family life with all it entails, including one another's failures and shortcomings. Parents fight off worldliness—without letting on that it *is* a fight. (For a full explanation of the importance of the family, read St. John Paul II's apostolic exhortation on the family *Familiaris Consortio*, which gave rise to *The Truth and Meaning of Human Sexuality: Guidelines for Education within the Family*, upon which my thoughts here are based.)

In his prophetic book *The Abolition of Man*, C.S. Lewis reminds us of Aristotle's observation: "When the age for reflective thought comes, the pupil who has been thus trained in 'ordinate affections' or 'just sentiments' will easily find the first principles in Ethics; but to the corrupt man they will never be visible at all and he can make no progress in that science." That is, the child has to be taught the right responses to things from a very early age, to "like and dislike what he ought," to know the "right ordering of things."

Educating a child on sexuality is thus a long process that starts early on, very remotely from the goal, you might say. And family life, with its love and affection, its ties of kinship, friendship, and citizenship, is perfectly suited to this process of teaching right responses to things, ugly and beautiful.

Think of the child's first experiences of his own body: being lovingly fed, disciplined, and hugged; roughhousing with Dad; running barefoot outside; carrying bags for Mom ... (If we don't teach our young one self-control in the little things, how will we expect it in the great?)

Think of his experiences as he's taken to church. The music, the art, the awe of worship; of seeing one's parents given wholly over to something apart from themselves ... (If there is ugliness in worship, what hope do we have to inoculate him against ugliness in relationships?)

Think of the home's little prayer corner with its beautiful and heart-breaking crucifix, its serene image of God's own Mother, its strong icon of Jesus' foster-father ... (If the faith isn't in the home, how will the child find it elsewhere?)

Most of all, think of the child with the example of mother and father, loving each other with affection and forbearance, complementing each other ... (What other model is there?)

Protecting Latency

A crucial time period in the child's development is the latency phase, during which important aspects of character, intellect, and emotions grow, undisturbed by premature exposure to sexual ideas and feelings.

Very young children do have a natural curiosity about sex—usually just about their bodies. Wise parents know to give short, accurate answers that emphasize love and marriage, which is the reason our bodies have been created the way they are, and with accurate but not overly particular names for body parts. In this way, parents protect the child's innocence while conveying important lessons of privacy and intimacy—lessons that by their nature, school programs make impossible.

Learn to ask questions to find out what they really want to know. "Why do you ask?" is a good one. "Did someone say something about that, or did you see something that made you wonder about it?" is another. The answers sometimes alert the attentive parent to a situation that needs intervention.

A question about something above their developmental level (and dangerous to their equilibrium) can be answered with a kindly, "You know, when you're older we can talk about it again." Remember in *The Hiding Place*, when Corrie ten Boom's father demonstrates with a heavy suitcase that a child must sometimes wait to be able to carry a burden. He is wisely responding to a question about sex; he is asking Corrie to trust him and to trust God. His lesson carries through to a decisive time in her adulthood when she must totally abandon herself to God's will as Nazis threaten her existence.

The child ought to be left untroubled by excessively detailed factual information and images for which he can have no context. Parents should protect this truly carefree time in a child's life, which is as much a normal part of development as teething or toddlerhood. Let's remember that living things have their own pace and their own way of unfolding, a way that cannot be circumvented without causing damage.

The truth is, there is actually not much to talk about. A good Catholic doctor once said that the actual "talking" takes about fifteen minutes per child. What you *don't* talk about says volumes about what you really mean.

We mustn't be impatient or panic. Some things take time—and not much talking.

Families Need Support from Friends and Church

Parents desperately need solidarity with others as they raise their children, especially in the area of purity. Parents don't need to be managed in groups, but rather encouraged in friendship, and cultivated and strengthened by the Church.

Our priests' most important role is to provide families with the sacraments; in addition, they have a real part to play in fostering connections and community so that their people aren't left to wander. Priests must be willing to sacrifice with the work of restoring and renewing the school, if there is one, and supporting the home school.

We need cheerful priests who are good role models. Fathers of families and priests should be friends; most pastors spend far too much time with women in parish life today, although a little time is good.

A priest should be ready for persecution when he shows solidarity and helps parents to do what is right in this area. It may happen that doing right even entails opposing his own diocese's requirements. It will certainly mean opposing worldly advice and norms.

Solidarity means making real friendships between families, friendships that will endure. If there are two, and soon, say, four or five families having conversations about the importance of setting standards in these matters for their own families, living out their convictions, and, of course, enjoying each other's company, the community will survive and grow.

You see, in puberty, the child emerges from the latency phase and begins to require a bit more information—not only about the "facts of life" but also about himself personally and how he will be able to mature and fit into this life he knows so little about. He will begin to wonder what his vocation in life will be, even at age thirteen or fourteen, although he might not show visible signs of such (or any!) inner development. He will need friends outside of the family. He's not a "teen" in the sense of belonging to a category set apart: he's a young person developing into an adult.

Each person must respond to the Lord's word: "Blessed are the pure in heart, for they shall see God" (Matt 5:8, RSVCE).

And here is where the trouble starts as far as the world goes, even with the family providing the norms of purity, and where solidarity will bear fruit, because the world doesn't value purity. Having cultivated friendships with good families along the way, parents will be in a position to provide children with healthy peers and with other adults for encouragement.

The four or five families will grow to include many others; no need to worry about unduly or artificially sheltering the children. This sense of community doesn't require uniformity. What matters is that there *are* standards and that the community has, over the years, sacrificed for them.

This sacrifice can and will mean standing up to spurious experts, educating children at home, resisting premature exposure to the Internet, and otherwise protecting the children from the barrage of extreme, destructive information. Parents have the right to resist intrusion into their sphere.

Sometimes the danger comes from within the Church. If a bishop insists on a program that exposes the child (such as Talking about Touching or a human-sexuality course such as the one promoted by the Pontifical Academy for Life), then parents must keep their children away and warn others.

The best reality check for the bishop would be to have to meet with a large delegation of angry fathers, but just a few would be a start.

The World around Us

The *Obergefell* decision ratifying so-called same-sex marriage was handed down in 2015. In the Church, seemingly settled questions about divorce are debated. The challenge of raising children in purity has intensified. How do we talk about these things when opposing them calls into question our goodwill?

The context of sexuality is the fundamental nature of man and woman and the original plan of union in marriage (Gen. 2:24; Mark 10:8). Trusting this context, it's not so hard to explain divorce honestly: "Either there was a marriage or there wasn't. You can't just *undo* a marriage that really was, although people do talk as if you can. Jesus taught very clearly about that."

And gay "marriage": "You know that God gave man and woman to each other to marry, to become one flesh. This is God's covenant with us." Such a conversation begins the child's grounding in the Theology of the Body, which is simply Christian anthropology, based on Scripture and the teaching of the Church.

Have the courage to be true to God's word, to be open and honest. We are not worried about offending anyone, because we are *defending* our children's purity—and their happiness.

We often say that children learn by example. Another way to put it might be that they learn most things *incidentally* rather than directly. If a father lets his children call his sister's lesbian partner "Aunt Becky," any talks he has with them about what he really believes will be pointless.

Do we treat cohabiting couples as if they are married? They are not. The man does a grave injustice to the woman, robbing her of her years to bear children and stealing her intimacy. If he were harming her in some other way, would we accept it? It is a sin to use the conjugal act against its nature; sex outside of marriage is wrong, because those are God's terms of the gift.

Is a person presented to us as a girl, when we know he's a boy, or vice versa? We need to tell the truth. There really isn't anything more fundamental on a natural plain than the reality of *boy* and *girl*. We can't lie or be made to deny reality out of a wish to be nice. Where we can be cordial, affectionate, and loving, we are. But good people don't lie, or they break the eighth commandment.

Never treat two people—whether of the same sex or of both sexes—as married who are not married. When I explain the Sixth Commandment (thou shalt not commit adultery) to children, I say, "It means not acting as if someone is husband or wife who is not husband or wife." (And as a religious-education instructor, that is all I say to other people's children; more than that would be inappropriate.)

Where there is a family member who identifies as "gay" and we're being asked to accept that in order to keep ties, we can't, even if it means a break in the relationship. What did we think Christ meant when He said He would pit father against son, mother-in-law against daughter-in-law, and so forth (Luke 12:53)?

The child suffers internal disturbance when he sees or experiences immoral behavior; let's acknowledge this by relating it to the moral life, affirming what is good and asking whether he really understands what God means by marriage. The vital importance of knowing the answer becomes clear when we contemplate what St. Paul says, that it has to do with the mystery of Christ's love for His Church (Eph. 5:32). So the child's relationship with God Himself hangs on our courage in this matter.

Pray for fortitude in truth telling and in child raising. A lot is at stake, and it will cost us. But our happiness depends upon it! And God's grace abounds.[24]

---

[24] This chapter was originally published as "A Family-Friendly Guide to Sex Education," *Crisis Magazine*, October 13, 2016, https://www.crisismagazine.com/2016/sex-education-family-friendly.

Beatitude

nly the chaste man and the chaste woman are capable of true love.
This sentence was written by Karol Wojtyla, the man who would become John Paul II, beloved pope and saint, in his book *Love and Responsibility*, the precursor to his great work on Christian anthropology, *Man and Woman He Created Them.* I came across the quote somewhere, and it took me by surprise. I think things have changed in the years since this pope passed away. I think that a sentence like this now elicits an interior pause in someone who has been exposed to the rising powers of political correctness. Do you feel it? A little moment—hardly a moment—before you assent? To that "only"?

Maybe it's just me. But I feel it.

He doesn't say, "Only the chaste man and the chaste woman can love each other," although that's implicit. (He definitely does not say, "There are many ways of loving that can co-exist with a lack of chastity.") He says "are capable of *true love.*" Full stop. Love of . . . anything and everything. Of God too.

Of course, right away, you know it's a way of saying something Jesus Christ said: "Blessed are the pure in heart: for they shall see God" (Matt. 5:8, KJV). For seeing—contemplation—is how we possess God in this imperfect world of ours. Josef Pieper, in *Happiness and Contemplation*, quotes St. Augustine: "Our whole reward is seeing." And the epigraph of that book, a quote from Konrad Weiss, is this: "Contemplation [*seeing*] does not rest until it has found the object which dazzles it."

That seeing, which is the ultimate acceptance of the gift of God, can be acquired only by means of a pure heart—of chastity, in short.

On Goodness and
Living the Moral Life

Goodness—how we ourselves can become good—this is worth pondering. Virtue is beautiful! We can be discouraged because we lose our peace when we—inevitably—fail and fall and stumble. If, instead, we start at that acknowledged place of littleness, we will have peace, because we won't be surprised! Just like that child who tumbles right over, we will laugh.

But virtue is what we are here for. This life on earth has to be one of making Christ's virtue our own. Our lives together are about growing in goodness.

> Keep innocence, and behold justice: for there are remnants
> for the peaceable man.
> But the unjust shall be destroyed together: the remnants of
> the wicked shall perish.
> But the salvation of the just is from the Lord, and he is their
> protector in the time of trouble.

> And the Lord will help them and deliver them: and he will
> rescue them from the wicked, and save them, because
> they have hoped in him. (Psalm 36 [37]:37–40, DR, re-
> peated often in the Office of Readings)

Pursue this your own way, which you find when you nestle closer to God's way and the Church's wisdom. Don't be afraid! It's the way of peace.

Live your prayer life and efforts to educate your children along with the Church. If you do, you will have Christ's life and His goodness within.

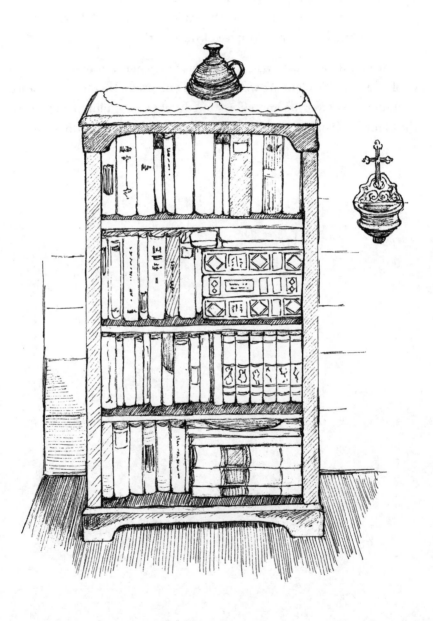

PART 12
Books in the Home

What is more central to education than books? Books are a joy. Today more than ever, the family needs a home library and a solid commitment to reading as a way of life. Reading out loud is a joy as well. In this section, I offer lots of thoughts about books and a small selection of what I have written in the Like Mother, Like Daughter Library Project to offer criteria for selecting a range of reading for children.

On Books and the
Environment of the Home

I simply can't figure out how you would live life (not to mention homeschool) without a collection of real, actual, physical books. Living life, which, of course, includes educating children, takes place in the environment of the home, the unique place where the family—with its uncountable interesting thoughts, works, ways of doing, and creations—forms itself. Not every family can do everything, and lots of things hold no appeal to some. There are a few activities and interests that each one has, and the particular coinciding of these is what make up its uniqueness, developed over time.

All of this is the family's way of relating to the outside world and its ideas, which, in turn, are brought into its life by different means; but among them, surely the books and music in its collection are paramount. Since there is no way to express the vastness of what is and can be in this life, it's good to have a representation of the best according to our unique family view. (The role of the public library, before it became the strip-mall media center, was to preserve the larger archive.)

The environment of the home is part serendipity (books, works of art, music, and even furniture and other decorations that others give us or pass down to us), and part intentionality (things we buy and find). It's only after many years that most families look up from what they are doing and say, "Oh, this is how our home is and feels." It's a certain air that the house takes on, or sense of what our own home feels like. The exact quality of this air will probably always elude us, making itself known only on those rare occasions when we come home from a long journey. Interestingly, others can detect it very well and have a keen sense of what makes our home itself, as we are able to do with theirs! Life is so paradoxical.

The books we read and enjoy (and I really mean *enjoy*) particularly make up the intellectual expression of who we are. For our children to absorb this identity, they need to *see* these books. If the books are hidden from sight, if they exist only on the e-reader, then they are not shared except by assignment, which is by far the very last resort in sharing options, and the least likely to result in enjoyment.

Some commentators who do see the value in actual books put a lot of stress on "reading success" and a vague "intellectual achievement" that they, writing for the general public, undoubtedly know will play into parents' anxieties about the outcomes for their children (and thus to their own success in marketing their theses). But there's more to the "real books on the shelves" argument and how it relates to the heart of education than simply making sure that our kids can get ahead, just as there is more to feeding them than a nutrition-delivery system. A whole culture is at stake in our choices.

Those who want to reduce a book to the bare words on the page, trying to convince us that the delivery system doesn't matter, lobbying for the efficiency of the virtual mode, take for granted that which they effectively eliminate — that a taste for books already exists in the person. But this taste is separate from the act of reading. Just as an aroma tantalizes the appetite, the appearance of the book entices the reader.

The beauty of the book — the visual appeal of the object — is its radiance. Sitting on the shelf, it attracts, even before one knows what the contents might be. By "beauty" I don't necessarily mean any overt aesthetic. The very humbleness of the paperback, the very starkness of the black cover with its simple lettering, the very proximity of the volume to its more familiar neighbor, even its well worn shabbiness, attesting, as it does, to the countless readers who have already enjoyed it: these are the attributes of a book that often draw us to its contents.

Certainly, for the child who hasn't yet learned that the words in a book can be (to a certain extent, but not completely) extracted from its container, so to speak, the book as an object can't be dispensed with. Reading *Tom Sawyer* in your dad's boyhood edition is not the same experience as reading it on CD-ROM in the nineties was (even if it was printed out on printer paper); nor is reading it on the Kindle going to seem the same.

Many a child has picked up *Huckleberry Finn* simply because it was there, next to *Tom Sawyer*, on the shelf. Many a child has picked up a book because the cover beckoned to him—and he had nothing else to do.

By the way, a reminder: it's an undeniable fact that a virtual book may turn out not to be your property. It may be more ephemeral than you meant it to be, disappearing without a trace. Your "library"—if virtual—may become undetectable by those who might later take an interest in your mind and interests, and you may not be able to pass them along at all.

Just Say No to "Books That Build Character"

Recently my eye was briefly caught by one of those "fifty books that build character" lists. I checked out some of them, with their bright, rather attention-deficit-disorder-augmenting covers and pseudo-cheerful titles, and was confirmed in my hunch that these books are a waste of money and, more importantly, a waste of our precious time.

Dear reader, it won't work. There are no shortcuts. You don't get character that way. There is no program.

In fact, programs tend to backfire. You get less of the outcome you're seeking when you tackle things head on. You can actually get more of the outcome you are trying to avoid, and the whole enterprise creates a loss of memory. Because children's books these days tend to be written with a didactic message in mind, rather than to delight, people have forgotten what a children's book should be. Their first impulse, even in reading an old book, is to find the message, tearing off what they consider the hull (the artistic element) to try to discover the kernel (the character-building element). They are like paralyzed people looking at the ambulatory, wondering where the walking mechanism is hidden.

The imagination of these authors seems somehow one-dimensional, or missing altogether. They don't seem to understand the workings of imagination at all, or its relationship to art and the quest for goodness.

They are little moralists who see that sin is the worst possible act (true). They conclude, therefore, that the role of adults is to ensure that little human beings under their care are to be molded into sin-avoidance machines (untrue). They look at art as a way to accomplish this.

Don't try to find the mechanism! (Remember "The Emperor and the Nightingale"? The beauty of the songbird cannot be made into a machine.)

Good literature for children tells a story with delight, contributing to the formation of the imaginative faculties that it assumes already exist; it helps to establish the moral universe it may depict as being under siege. It should offer the choices the children face as choices that build character but not overtly *in order to* build character. The choices exist because a story needs to be told.

Any magic (the rules guiding the universe of the story) should work slowly and deeply. In the best stories, the world offered to the child is simple and mythological, yet imaginatively complete.

Should the Parent or the Child Choose Which Books to Read?

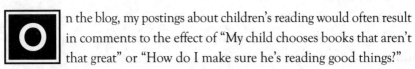

n the blog, my postings about children's reading would often result in comments to the effect of "My child chooses books that aren't that great" or "How do I make sure he's reading good things?"

I know that there is a prevailing wind of child-rearing out there. This wind would not imagine for one moment that you would give your darling any *food* that is bad for him, to the point that the poor kid can't have a cookie. But the wind is perfectly fine with exposing him to any and all ideas. This suits the wind, because it would like to have sole proprietorship of your child's mind. The "wind" is the way of the world. Not content with the normal way of things, which is for the world to have its go at your child once he leaves the sanctuary of the home, the world has made provisions for molding the imagination of the child from infancy, so that he becomes susceptible to its designs.

Somehow, somewhere, we lost the idea that the spirit is even more precious than the body (see Matthew 10:28: "And fear not them which kill the body, but are not able to kill the soul: but rather fear him which is able to destroy both soul and body in hell" [KJV]) and needs even more careful formation.

So what do you do when you are at the public library (or otherwise making a choice)? Who chooses?

Just as your child will survive the occasional bit of junky candy, he will survive reading *Transformers Blast Mars* or whatever unsuitable book he insists on bringing home from the library. If such a book were within my standards, somewhere on a scale—obviously not every book is stellar, but there's a difference between a stupid book and one that is merely harmless—I would provisionally approve it, though often by the time we were ready to leave, another, better one had supplanted it. And then there are the positively bad books, and those must be avoided at all costs.

Children learn to trust you, because when they bring home, say, four books that are marvelous and two that are really sort of mindless, they notice the difference. You can reinforce this experience if, after reading a mindless book, you say something that guides them—"Oh, I thought this would be better," or "I can't read this one out loud again; it's really boring." You'll see: they will agree. Even if they don't agree, that's fine. You make lots of decisions for their own good, and this is one of them. (If they happen to stumble on a gem that you weren't aware of, well, rejoice!)

If they can't let go of a bad book (and this happens when a child is three or so—he just clings to one wretched book sometimes), there's a reason: the book fulfills *some need*. Give that some thought. What is it about this book that makes you cringe but that your child is obsessed with? And then find a better version of the same theme while completely removing the offending item. Like shorts in winter or snowsuits in summer, it just becomes *unavailable*. (This goes for deadening books that well meaning people give as gifts. Just quietly get them out.)

Even a teenager should consult with you about what he reads (and you will find that teenagers want to). You would not drop a fourteen-year-old boy off in the center of town for a few hours without inquiring into his plans (although I'm all for dropping him off if you know his plans). Well, a book is a universe, so don't just drop your children off there.

When you have at your fingertips good things to read (there are booklists in the resource section of this book), your children will naturally fall in with this way of doing things; it will seem normal to them because it is normal.

If they insist on certain books—those, for instance, that are popular at the moment (my middle kids were teens when Harry Potter came out)—you will be able to discuss and figure out what to do. They will have a standard by which to judge something that may be subpar, because you will have given them that standard; don't be anxious.

If you insist that they should just stay away from some things (Twilight books come to mind), they will respect your wishes, because they have been trained in a delightful obedience along the way—a habit of obedience, based on trust.

My daughter Rosie said, "I remember you saying, 'No, let's not get that one. We can get it at the library.' In other words, it's a fine book, and one we'll read once or maybe twice, but not one worth the investment of our money and shelf space. At the library, you'd say of the ones that were fluffy (not the actual bad ones—I'm remembering especially some silly picture books I pulled off the shelves), 'You can read that here, but we're not bringing it home.' This really helped establish a clear hierarchy of books in my mind."

The Difference between
Standards and Censorship

any parents worry, when they think about preventing their child from reading or looking at a certain book, about censorship and imposing their will on the child.

Censorship is when the government asserts its power over citizens, restricting the free exchange of ideas. It's a wrong perpetrated on free adults who have a claim to the world of ideas, directly, without reference to the desires of the state. Anyone who has been given the trust of administering the law, but uses force to monitor people's thoughts and interactions, abuses that trust and is rightly resisted.

And note well that while some authorities simply ban what has been written, in a sort of tacit acknowledgment of the limits of their power, others insult the universe by trying to force the people to refrain from writing, speaking, or even thinking in the first place. That is political correctness, the very worst kind of censorship there is.

Providing your children with good reading material while cleverly distracting them from the bad is different. It's forming them carefully according to your principles, which are based on the true, the good, and the beautiful. Not only is this your God-given privilege; by this process you will ensure that they become alert citizens who won't be vulnerable to censorship—among other things.

If you were to refrain from imposing, and I use that word lovingly, your standards, your children would not therefore grow up free. On the contrary, they would be very much slaves; not to put too fine a point on it, they would be so stupid that they would believe anything they were told and buy anything offered to them.

Clearly the challenge becomes staying one step ahead of them so that you yourself have the discernment necessary to give them the best. Will you goof? Of course. The good will force out the bad, and in a sort of anti-Gresham's law of truth, goodness, and beauty, all will be well.

How a Home Library
Overcomes
Reading Reluctance

Some children read quickly and are hungry for more. But even the books they read for entertainment need to be of a certain standard. Sadly, editors are almost a lost breed. I don't say that every book from the past is good. A lot of what was published was silly and ignorant; some of it was bad. But a certain process (a process that included teachers and librarians who recognized their responsibility to set a high moral tone) enabled the good to rise to the top and the bad to fall away. Now that process has been interfered with by marketing metrics. When books are dumped on schools because they are cheap to produce or have a proven track record of sales, parents must be vigilant.

Your home library is a treasure, but it needs to be refined. Get rid everything that plays into some sort of marketing scheme (such as Disney books aimed to push the merchandise). Good home librarians are always sifting, repairing, adding, and discarding.

Practical Strategies That Help a Child to Love Reading

Boys *in general* often tend not to have time for reading, but that doesn't mean they won't when there's nothing else to do. Work into your daily schedule forty minutes of "quiet time" when babies are napping and Mom needs to rest during which there is nothing else to compete with their attention.

For some reason, teachers have long favored assigning book reports, possibly due to an unacknowledged torture complex. The effect on a child of a looming report deadline can eliminate the will to live, never mind to read. Auntie Leila can barely think of it. Maybe just have sympathy for the victim and let him know that the best way to accomplish the task is simply to enjoy the book, the better to be able to recount it later. Talking over each chapter as it's read can help greatly with this goal.

Keeping a commonplace book, on the other hand, really helps—not as a burden, but as a great record for the future. Everyone will be excited to get a new notebook in which to record the books read and a few thoughts about what made the book great or disappointing. If they can think of it as a "lifetime log" it might have a lot of appeal. Rosie's husband did this (when he was a kid—he wishes now he had kept it up!), and now he enjoys looking over his entries, as does his son.

I make a distinction between one's own list and those supposedly motivational "reading club" lists that libraries have. Good books sometimes take a while to read—it's really not about quantity, is it? Nor is it a competition. Deep pleasures like reading must be carefully cultivated without reference to outside rewards. (I am put in mind of a reading challenge in our old town's school one year long ago. The "prize" for the kid who read the most was, counterproductively, a video-game console.)

1. *Read aloud.* Because newer children's books tend to have an intentionally limited vocabulary and are not morally demanding (at best), the risk is that the child will not ever choose for himself the more challenging ones. The remedy is to *read aloud* very exciting, somewhat demanding books; certainly be willing to read the same book more than once if it finds favor.

2. *Entice or trick your children.* A time-tested strategy is to read one or two chapters out loud to the targeted kid, *just* until the action starts. Then say, "Oh, I have to go close up the chickens [or start the lasagna or mow the lawn]." Usually said kid will pick the book up to find out the rest—provided he doesn't have video games or shows to tempt him away, and if only to avoid having to deal with the chickens or mow the lawn himself.

3. *Leave good books in the bathroom,* in reach. Just a few, or one choice one.

4. *When your children go to bed, let them read if they like.* Send eight- to eleven-year-olds to bed a little early so they can read their good-quality chapter books. Tell them to turn off the light when they are ready for sleep, or perhaps you could ring a discreet little bell or something to signal the end of reading time.

Clamp a lamp on the frame of each child's bed. Please make an effort to get an incandescent bulb for the lamp. I know it's not easy, but the light needs to be appealing and soft. Other types of bulbs interfere with brain function and have a jagged (LED) or dismal (CFL) light that hurts the eyes.

The light for a bedside lamp does not need to be bright. You can even use the chandelier bulbs you find in the grocery store (the ones that fit a standard, not extra-small, socket). A headlamp works too; just make sure it is not too bright.

5. *Sometimes you have to detoxify the mind.* Even a week of being in the "deprivation tank" with only good books makes a difference to your children's mentality. Rotate the books in a crate or basket. Every week choose ten or so that you think will appeal to the different ages. Put the books in a prominent place, and introduce them by saying, "We're going to have a quiet hour; please choose something to read." Let them wander off with a book from the crate, and don't worry about age level—it will all sort itself out.

Detoxifying often means that the middle-schooler who has been reading Judy Blume (how can it be that schools are still pushing Judy Blume?) can't go straight to *Johnny Tremain* or *Swallows and Amazons*. He may need a stop at the "lower reading level" of Beverly Cleary or Tintin (the movie is cute too) or *My Father's Dragon* or The Hardy Boys (get one of the originals).

Good books are good, no matter what the age level. When C. S. Lewis took in children escaping the bombing of London during the war and began reading aloud to them, he discovered that Beatrix Potter is a genius!

6. *Find them good friends who love to read.* Pray about it, because sometimes it is difficult, I know. The problem with school, I have to say, is that the peer group (which is indeed so necessary to the older child) is debased. Children are vulnerable to the influence exuded by a group of children left without mentors, without teachers who are committed to creating a community of virtue and learning. Don't underestimate the power of the peer group to drain all the joy out of reading. But the flip side of that coin is that good friends encourage the lagging to reach for new heights! Perhaps you can gather enough like-minded friends to have a community-wide detoxifying summer.

7. *Communicate the qualities of good books.* There has to be some sort of conceptual difference in your children's minds between the poor-quality stuff "out there" and the excellent books you choose for them. You can start talking this up. With older children especially, you can begin a sort of benign "indoctrination" period, during which you have conversations about books, read lists together, read articles and essays about the importance of good books, maybe watch costume dramas of classics. (There are excellent dramatizations of Dickens's books, such as *Our Mutual Friend*, and I highly recommend the BBC version of Elizabeth Gaskell's classic *North and South*.)

When, eventually, you read chapter 10 of *Little Women* together and realize how much more fun life is when you can read a reference to Pickwick and know what it's about, why, then you will be in business. Who knows, your children may even start a literary club and magazine of their own!

Everyone will enjoy reading E. Nesbit after watching the movie of *The Railway Children*! Win over the elder children and you won't have trouble afterward; younger children tend to live up to what the elder ones hold as a standard.

Why not start reading Penrod aloud, or *Anne of Green Gables*, or *Kidnapped*? Definitely read *Betsy-Tacy*, *Heidi*, *Pippi Longstocking*, and the Narnia books to the six-year-old. Pop some corn, get your cookies and milk, build a bonfire, or otherwise entice the older kids to listen as well.

8. *Don't overlook nonfiction.* Boys will resonate to accounts of Ernest Shackleton, Jackie Robinson, George Washington, and Thomas Edison. Look for Landmark books and the Childhood of Famous Americans series. Boys also connect with books of information, so if you can find some old sets of descriptive encyclopedias they will at least be drawn to the illustrations and the diagrams. Most boys find the following topics interesting: codes and ciphers, technology (airplanes, computers), paleontology, and astronomy—of course, the list is limitless.

9. *Make sure you and your husband make time for your own reading*—when the kids are awake. A good time is after supper, when the dishes are cleaned up and the Rosary has been said. This quiet time yields fruit later, when they are older and need the habit of concentrating to study, and the quiet environment in which to do it.

Reading Aloud

To me, the test of a good book for any age is whether you can read it aloud the required one million times without throwing it across the room. The test of a bad one is that reading it aloud even once makes your head hurt. There are those books that make you really cringe when your child brings them to you, and then there are the ones you enjoy as much as they do.

There are several criteria:

1. *The words need to trip pleasingly off the tongue.* It shouldn't be a chore to get them out of your mouth, and it's really a gift in an author to achieve "speakability." C. S. Lewis came to appreciate what he called the poetic genius of Beatrix Potter when children came to stay at his house during the war. Little books that seemed nothing more than nice pictures and a cute story proved themselves to be masterworks of the well placed word.

Reading them aloud—more than once—is the proving ground. Rhyming, rhythm, and tongue-trippingness are essential qualities especially of literature for very young children.

As much as I love E. Nesbit, her version of "Jack and the Beanstalk" fails in this regard. It's a pain to read aloud, not least because her giant doesn't bother to say "Fi, fie, fo, fum," and what is the point of this story, the thrill of terror for the child, without that murderous chant, I ask you?

2. *The illustrations must be well done.* The child is drawn in by the pictures. The reader is going to spend a lot of time looking at the pictures. Much of what happens when you sit down to "read" a book with a toddler is discussion of the pictures. So the pictures must be good.

3. *The story must be delightful,* which means that it simply must contain something for the adult to contemplate. A dreary moral is worse than useless, but extreme boredom of the reader is part of the bungle.

Best of all is at least a wink and a nod to the adult reader, along with total captivation for the child—which is what makes the classics classic: A. A. Milne's *Winnie-the-Pooh*, Kenneth Grahame's *The Golden Age*, Arthur Ransome's *Swallows and Amazons*. The author gets bonus points for subtle or overt references to other books in the text.

4. *Ideally, you should be able to discover new things in it,* even on multiple readings, because where toddlers are concerned, yes, you will be reading that book again. Here is where text and illustration can create something together that is more than the sum of their parts.

I will give you two examples of relatively new books that I consider worthy of inclusion in the ranks of children's read-alouds that please everyone:

Allan and Janet Ahlberg's *Each Peach Pear Plum* is a winner. We love this book.

The illustrations are beyond adorable, hitting that sweet spot between instantly captivating and rewarding of intense scrutiny. The rhymes are timeless; your whole family can memorize the entire book and recite it on car rides. I think I can still manage it, and not only has it been years since I've read it, but I'm notoriously bad at remembering poetry. It has a forward motion and rhythm that are truly inspired. It's funny and cute and simple and just complicated enough. It will keep the one-year-old interested, even if he has yet to master Mother Goose, and the ten-year-old will appreciate the allusive qualities, discovering the pleasure of seeing the various characters come together in a new way.

It comes in a board-book version. Do get either that one or the hardcover version, because this book is a keeper.

Another book that achieves high marks and deserves a place on the shelf next to the classics is *Flossie and the Fox* by Patricia McKissack, illustrated by Rachel Isadora. I enjoyed reading it to my children and now I'm reaching for it with my grandchildren. The illustrations are evocative and sparkle with the delight of the story, which is considerable.

On one level, it's a simple tale of a girl who outwits a fox in the venerable tradition of Brer Rabbit and other country tales in the black tradition. On another, it's a whimsical exercise in epistemology, for how can you prove a fox is a fox? "A fox just be a fox," as Grandmother says. The cautionary takeaway for the sandy-whiskered rationalists among us is that spending too much time on such matters can be dangerous!

Along with the tried-and-true literature that you'll find in the booklists I recommend (in the Appendix), these two children's books can help you discern the quality of newer offerings, I hope.

Reading Aloud Well: A Tutorial

o encourage that reluctant reader — but also simply to have the beautiful culture of reading aloud — I offer a little tutorial; I will tell you all I know.

Perhaps you already read aloud in your home and your children love the custom. Please do not think that I am here to meddle with perfection or contented imperfection. My tutorial will have a lot of detail because some inquiring minds want to know, but this cataract of particulars should not discourage you. I heartily endorse simply *reading aloud* in any way you feel comfortable doing it; if it's working for you, then we are all happy!

There are some parents who, even if wishing to instill a love of reading in their children, have some trouble reading out loud. This trouble could be just awkwardness or a lack of confidence in how to do it. Even professionals have trouble getting it right. Have you ever started an audiobook only to find that you just can't continue to listen to it? I offer these suggestions for you.

My first moment of awakened listening to a book read aloud — having left behind the childhood comforts and made my way almost through high school to read on my own, silently, like all the mature folks — came in my senior-year AP Lit class. Mrs. Stecchini was the teacher. Far enough into middle age to have solidified her methods, and utterly passionate about each and every book we read, from Chaucer to James, Mrs. Stecchini used her considerable powers of narration to draw us in. For even in this elective class, there were some who weren't enthusiastic—and even those who were enthusiastic needed, she knew, to be shown how to read.

It was in this class that I shed my "devour it quickly" approach to books. I think those of my fellow students who suffered from real reluctance also learned something. Mrs. S. simply carried all along by sheer force of will. At least half of each (double period) class was taken up, simply, with her reading aloud, in a *highly* idiosyncratic manner, whatever work we were studying. Whole chapters of the densest poetry and prose were bestowed on our initially unbelieving ears. She was going to *read* to us? *Like that?*

I had never, ever, heard anyone read the way she did. It took me weeks just to get used to her manner, as she elaborately peered through her impossibly thick lenses at the pages, totally absorbed in the work. But eventually, what I considered her slow pace, elaborate enunciation, and overexaggerated emphasis on parts of sentences I would have just skimmed past, became the norm for me, and the artistry of the author we were examining was able to bloom fully in my intellect. (This was most true of Henry James—not my favorite writer, mind, but one whose polished prose is lost on most high school students who don't have a Mrs. S. to guide them.)

Her class made me realize that I needed *voices* in my head as I read, that a good writer chooses every word carefully—therefore, every word must be given its due, which means not *more* than its due, but also not less; that savoring good writing is its own reward; in short, that the reader is *part of* the art of writing: the writer *depends on* his reader to meet him halfway.

I've been reading aloud to children now for thirty-eight years with Mrs. S.'s methods ingrained in my bones.

So—keeping in mind that your child just loves you and wants to be with you, enjoying what you enjoy; we will overthink things here Auntie Leila style, but stay calm and keep reading to your child!—reading out loud to children, some thoughts:

1. *Choose (and make) a good place.* So many living areas aren't conducive to comfortable conversation or listening. It pains Auntie Leila! David Clayton and I go over this to some extent in our book, *The Little Oratory,* just because family life in general is related to family life in prayer. (Some reviewers called what we said "holy decorating" or decorating for a purpose other than to put things in a room randomly or to make an impression.)

Consider pulling the furniture, at least some of it, away from the walls and into proximity with each other, so that some could sit on chairs nearby and still hear and even be able to see the larger pictures.

Maybe you have a ceiling light fixture, maybe not; but regardless, you need at least three lamps in any given room. Please—I will not tire of begging you—get incandescent light bulbs, if only for these living areas where a warm glow, not a harsh glare, is necessary for flourishing. You can always have an extra soup night to pay for them.

Of course, you might read in the hammock or by the campfire or in the tent or under the stars or in your big bed or by the fire, and that's all good too.

2. *Timing.* It's never going to work to try to read aloud when everyone is bursting with climbing, swimming, jumping, or running energy. Rest time is excellent (although dangerous for the overtired parent; in my later years with Bridget I would sometimes just say, "Mama's going to put her head back right here for ten minutes"); after supper and the Rosary; before bedtime when Baby is finally asleep. Everything has its time and place ... but a really wonderful book will tempt you to "read *one more* chapter!"—which is such a joy, isn't it?

3. *Try to look ahead.* Excellent reading aloud happens when you, the reader, know the book and know what's coming. Even if you can't read it first, you can read ahead in the text as you go, even a little, to make a big difference in how you sound.

Read ahead by phrase; scan the page as you go. Your brain retains the words, and you can speak them *while* your eyes move ahead; this skill is the very heart of successful reading out loud, and I cannot emphasize it enough. Once you get good at it, you can help your children much better to figure it out for themselves, and then *they* become excellent readers out loud.

Reading ahead helps you see the words in *phrases* and plan ahead how you will use your voice to convey whatever emotion, tension, relaxation, drama, or other mode fits best. When you scan ahead, you can usually catch the occasional "he said in a low whisper" direction that's unhelpfully thrown in *after* the actual dialogue, which you might otherwise read loudly or what have you. You can sort out who is saying what in untagged exchanges. You can foresee where a dramatic pause would work best. And so on.

4. *Read poetry and drama aloud.* A reader commented, "One of my husband's pet peeves is that people don't read poetry or plays aloud. 'It's like music; it's meant to be heard.' This was a new idea to me, and when I'd hear his voice coming from an otherwise empty room, I'd ask him if he was talking to himself. He'd give me an exasperated look and tell me he was reading a poem (or Shakespeare). After thirty years of marriage, I think I get it."

This is true. We would never think of *reading* musical notes on a score without playing or singing them. True, we might need to scan them beforehand for some reason, but we accept that they are meant to produce an auditory effect! Reading words isn't quite the same, but thinking about poetry and drama this way can make a difference to how we appreciate them.

In keeping with the musical analogy, *phrasing* enables you to present a thought in a unified way. Because most of us rarely read aloud, and because journalism, not fiction, rules our day, contemporary sentences often just plop the subject at the start of the sentences.

Older fiction is more subtle, uses more dependent clauses, runs on with more freedom; hence, the ability to see where the phrase is going in relation to the whole of the sentence and even the paragraph has a salutary effect on how we read.

How, though? How would we know how to work with phrases rather than just popping out each word as it comes along? This brings me to . . .

5. *Punctuation.* Punctuation is your friend! Mainly, don't fall into the mistake of plowing through the periods and commas. Put the appropriate pauses in at those points—even in an exaggerated way (or so it will feel

at first, until you begin to channel Mrs. Stecchini) — and you will see the difference it makes.

6. *Vary the speed of your words.* One of my pet peeves with even professional narrators is equating *slowness* and *even pace* with effective reading aloud. Yes, fast is not great, but even Mrs. Stecchini wasn't *always* slow; it's just that when she did want to go slow, she really took her time! Some words are getting you to where you need to be; you can't leave them out, but they point to something beyond. Some are tricky to process, or have more importance in the sentence than others, or have an unusual meaning that takes a moment to understand; these are the ones you linger on. The best books are written with a certain amount of irony and a sort of detachment from the narrator and characters; you'll have to vary your pace to catch all that.

Avoid the sing-songy way of reading aloud. Meaning comes through varying the tone. And remember: *silences and pauses are reading too!*

7. *Try voices.* This can seem daunting and silly, but here's the secret: begin with your own natural voice, making it the voice for the narrator. Another criticism I have of audiobooks I've listened to is when the default voice — the voice you are going to listen to the most — is strained and either too loud or too soft, and often overly self-conscious and dramatic. Relax your voice and use its best placement.

How to find this default voice — that is, your own voice? Think of the sound that comes out of your mouth as a soft ping-pong ball. The ball should be just behind your teeth, in the middle of your mouth, *not* in your throat or in your nose or caught in your palate or propped upon your tongue! Relax your throat while you are talking normally to people and make some space there in your mouth for that ball! Soon you'll feel how it should be.

Give the protagonist a slightly higher — *slightly* — or slightly lower pitch than your natural voice, depending on the protagonist's sex. If the main character is a girl, pitch your voice slightly higher; if a boy, slightly lower (if you are a man, make a boy's voice higher than yours but not as high as the voice you will give to the main girl in the story). Otherwise, keep the *manner* of speaking (the accent for instance) the same as yours, for this character.

8. *Listen to good readers and imitate them.* Usually we're caught up in listening to the story, but for this purpose, try to analyze what you like about a well done narration. I recommend finding someone British reading Robert Louis Stevenson or Dickens. The characters in these books are so vivid that you get the full scope of what a good narrator can do. I have audiobook suggestions in the appendix!

The Like Mother, Like Daughter
Library Project

When I was a little girl, I went to the New Haven Public Library, pictured below. I entered on the side on the left, on Temple Street, because the children's books are in the lower level—the basement, I guess you'd call it, but since the library was built above grade

to emphasize the loftiness of the life of the mind, even this level is spacious and airy. I was so little when we started going there that I couldn't help pretending that the double doors were an elevator, and I had to "push buttons" and "wait for the elevator to come"—and of course, that meant that my mom had to wait for me to do those things, which she did, very patiently—even letting other people go in ahead of us so that I could enact this ritual.

I think my first memory of the New Haven Public Library, a mighty and formative edifice, as I'll explain, is of the librarian reading a Curious George book to us children at story hour. I can remember the place very well, which says something, because I have a very shaky memory of most environments; I usually didn't take in the details of my surroundings when I was a child or even a young adult. But I remember the library.

I remember being desperate to learn cursive so that I could sign my name on my first library card. And my last name had ten letters in it, so it took frustratingly long for me to master writing it.

Once I did get my card, I checked out in stacks that I could barely carry. The rule was that you could check out only eight books at a time, but the librarian made an exception for me, whom she knew as a bookworm. She let me take out twelve. Every week, as she stamped the cards, she joked that she'd soon run out of books to lend me.

If you knew how strict people were about rules, especially rules for kids, in the sixties, you would be impressed. For instance, you absolutely could not speak above a whisper, or your mother or teacher would have to take you out of the library then and there, and no greater humiliation was conceivable to me.

I am heartily in favor of all those rules because I think that, like the building itself, they instilled awe for what the library contained, which was wonder, learning, and delight. Fear is the beginning of wisdom.

Yes, even the architecture of the building inspired anyone who was open to it, who had a soul. That lower level was warm and friendly (even with the imposing rules), with fairy tales readily accessible and stacks of chapter books, any one of which was a doorway to the imagination. If you came up by the impressive white granite steps leading to the main entrance, you passed through the dark oak portal to the lofty main floor—a two-story space with comfy Naugahyde armchairs, massive oak tables, study carrels, and huge windows; a place to aspire to enter, if you ever dared!

But—*would* you dare to read books *with no illustrations?*

When the predicted day came and I did run out of books, I ventured up above. I was so self-conscious, so sure that the grown-ups there would, en masse, utterly reject me as the bold intruder that I was, that I could hardly breathe. But then I looked at the books and was transported.

Before this moment, my mother would sometimes leave me browsing in the children's books while she went to look for hers, which is why I had never been to the main floor. But she would sometimes take me all the way up to the third floor to look at art books with her, probably assuring the librarians up there in that aerie, reached only by means of the double marble staircase with wrought-iron rails, that I would be quiet.

By then, I'd have a book of my own to read, my mother would have promised me that we wouldn't be long, and she'd have extracted from me a promise not to touch anything. No fear—it was just too overwhelmingly grown-up there. You couldn't even use one of the two marble staircases because the steps were too worn. (They had roped that side off, and one of my few temptations in rule-breaking was to run up those stairs!) That's how fragile and special everything up there was. And how fitting that the loveliest books about the most delicate of subjects were kept there!

You see, everything about the place was Dantesque, depicting the life of the mind and the ages of man in the form of a building. Even its situation, facing the town green with its open-armed stairs, taking its place with the churches and government buildings, was carefully considered to impress with its importance. It all conspired—the granite, the oak, the marble (and I haven't even told you about the murals and the stained glass)—to convince you that here was to be found the key to life: knowledge.

And it was all free to the patrons, because it was all provided by the city fathers and the good taxpayers, who knew it was in the interest of the city to have citizens who, starting as children (historians think the New Haven Free Public Library possibly had the first children's room), could read books, find information, see the newspapers, and get answers to questions.

Why, a person could educate himself there, for free! And many did. These local projects are a study in how communities can serve the family and all the residents. A small-town library would have been far less grand but would have had just as many of the important books. Books aren't that expensive.

Today libraries are different, I think. They are media centers, you don't have to hush there, and you do have to monitor carefully what your children choose. In fact, they've pulled out and sold off most of the good old books (or not bought them to start with, when they opened the new branches in the strip malls). I'm afraid that quietly, the library has become a monument to political correctness and reflects only the shallowness of popular culture. Today, in our outwardly lovely, small New England public library, the children's section has virtually no biographies of historical figures that I could find. It's all basketball stars and pop singers.

Thus we started on our site, the Like Mother, Like Daughter (LMLD) Library Project, an occasional feature in which we discuss books we consider indispensable for the home. Taking into consideration the limits of budget and space, every choice has to be from the A-list. Our recommendations are books that should be in the public library, a carefully curated collective memory, but they are not, not anymore.

In my posts on the blog, I try to discuss one or two books at a time to try to give you a flavor for *why* I think them worthy, trusting that you will find others, rather than inundate you with a barrage of titles. The truth is that there are many good books and usually, when you name a few, it leads you naturally to the others. In the following chapters I give you a sampling of those posts.

I hope that I can encourage you to replicate the library, or a small part of it, in the sanctuary of your home, until that time when our cities and towns restore sanity and furnish the community (wide-eyed little boys and girls too!) once again with the wealth of good and great books.

Nursery Rhymes

Beware the urge to reduce learning to its seeming bare bones, thinking that this will suffice. As adults who always crave what is new (but who get anxious about the sheer volume of Things Children Must Learn), we forget that to children, *everything* is new! What is old to us is new to them! The advantage of the old things is precisely that they have stood the test of time. We're very foolish to think we should — or can — move on.

Nursery rhymes offer repetition in the context of whimsy and delight. They hone in on the experiences that are familiar and universal (a cross mother, a careless boy, a bad habit such as getting up too late, the sun, the moon), making sense of nonsense but also *enjoying* nonsense.

The sheer fun of language gives rise to wonder at the fanciful world we would like to understand but so seldom can — at least not when we're two but often also not when we're eighty-two. Thus, a great-grandmother can enjoy reading a nursery rhyme to a toddler, which is not something you can say of many so-called educational materials we normally find these days, which are as dreary as they are condescending. (And don't get me started on political correctness.)

And Mother Goose rhymes aren't uniform. Some are long; some are short. A grateful fact when bedtime is late—as well as when you find you do have time to linger with your arm around your little one.

For language practice, you can't beat these rhymes and songs. That little one who can hardly do more than babble learns to wrap his tongue around tricky syllables. Interestingly, our forebears expected the youngest among us to encounter words such as "dainty," "pride" and "folly," "tuffet," "melancholy," "smithereens," "gander," "tutor," and so on. Later, when the same child meets the same words in Shakespeare and the Bible, he won't be defeated, will he?

How impossible, when you think about it, would it be to *begin* the process of familiarity with those words round about high school or college? And yet this is exactly what our educational system today is set up to do, by virtue of having eliminated old books with their rich vocabulary, imagery, and syntax, among other virtues.

The child learning nursery rhymes also learns to count—and to be patient. Many a time I coaxed a recalcitrant toddler of my very own up a vexing flight of stairs by chanting, "One, two, buckle my SHOE!" The older child listens in and suddenly gets certain things he never noticed before (as, for that matter, does the adult reading!).

This is culture and how you get it. Read the old things!

Some collections we like:

Mother Goose, illustrated by Blanche Fisher Wright

Richard Scarry's *Best Mother Goose Ever* (Giant Little Golden Book).

Richard Scarry always satisfies.

Mother Goose, illustrated by Gyo Fujikama

A Child's Treasury of Nursery Rhymes, by Kady MacDonald Denton.

This has the added interest of including rhymes from other traditions.

Some people are put off by the longer (and sometimes stranger) rhymes. Whatever edition you choose, spend your first encounter with it just looking at the pictures with your child. Perhaps the one he gets excited by coincides with one of the shorter rhymes. Read that. In these collections, the longer rhymes are mixed in with very short ones, so you can skip about, finding the ones that your (even very young) child can sit still for. Little by little, work your way up to the longer selections.

If you say certain rhymes as you are going about your day, such as "One, Two, Buckle My Shoe" as you put on his shoes, "Polly Put the Kettle On" as you put the kettle on, "Jack Sprat" when you are cutting up his meat, and so forth, you find that already knowing the rhyme helps the squirmy toddler to sit and look at the pictures.

You can say, "Want to hear about Tom Thumb?" and he will nod yes ... or else no.

Read This, Not That; or,
One Children's Book Is
Not as Good as Another

For a while, an "eat this, not that" series of books became very popular. The idea is to help you make good choices in food and drink to avoid hidden calories that will tank your health. Well, Rosie had the thought that we could do something similar with books for the Library Project: read this, not that.

I'll start with one book I do not recommend: *The Penderwicks*, by Jeanne Birdsall. *The Penderwicks* is enjoyable and well written, in that it doesn't talk down to the child and would keep a reading-aloud parent amused.

The cover is attractive. It's no wonder the book is so popular; the cover takes me to those wonderful books of my childhood that kept me entertained and made me feel I was entering a new, yet familiar, world made just for me. The charming silhouette of children and animals frolicking on the cover can't help but draw the reader in. (And it has an award!)

This genre, children on holiday in the country, is a tried-and-true one. Right away *The Penderwicks* promises to be a favorite, and I wanted to love it.

However, there are many other books with the same theme that are better and don't contain a certain moral ambiguity. So here I will tell you what I don't like and then give you suggestions for what to read instead.

At the heart of *The Penderwicks* is an episode in which the girls' youngest sibling is left unattended by her sisters and is nearly attacked by a bull, only to be rescued at the last moment. The children make a pact not to tell their father about the danger.

This pact begs to be put to the test. For the rest of this book, one is hoping that the conflict will be resolved. And here is the crux of my objection: in a better book, it *would* come to light and the children would make a clean breast of their subterfuge, which clearly ought to have weighed on their consciences. In fact, an opportunity arises later in the book for them to say something to their father; but rather than do so, they lie to cover up the event and their culpability. Astonishingly, this lie is not resolved. The girls also tell another small but unmistakable lie to the unpleasant neighbor and landlady about their dresses, which actually belong to this lady, unbeknownst to her (so there is a bad taste of theft as well).

In some books in this genre, children fail to reveal an episode to their parents; the sense conveyed to the reader is the valid one, that adults sometimes will not understand (usually, the author delicately implies, because they have lost their sense of wonder). This book fails to convey that life lesson; instead, it really does sidestep a moment of conscience.

An author has a responsibility to moral reality. For a children's author, this is a sacred duty. The child is being formed to a great extent by the stories he reads, watches, and hears. It's really important that these stories be completely wholesome.

The child develops morally by learning to heed his conscience. Depicting children failing to listen to their consciences without resolving the issue is disturbing; arousing an awareness of conscience in the reader without satisfying it is a kind of malpractice.

Lying in particular is intrinsically wrong. You can't just excuse a lie because of the circumstances. The moral code has always stressed the importance of telling the truth—even in small matters—and children have to be taught that without trust, people can't relate to each other at all.

That this book treats lies, great and small, as easily glossed over and rather neutral is not acceptable.

There are a couple of other themes that I object to. I don't see the point of exposing eight- to twelve-year-olds (the recommended age group for the book) to any of it. There is a silly one-way crush of the eldest Penderwick girl on the caretaker's son. In a book from a different era, their friendship (for they are friends) would have been handled with appropriate delicacy; in this story, it's really unsatisfactory. The crush kills the friendship, which is exactly the contemporary real-life difficulty that the author should have been able to show an alternative to. Somehow, in older books, children are given a way to handle awkward, premature feelings. It's almost as if the author doesn't know what those ways might be or thinks that in a modern story, a boy-girl crush has to be a feature, even if it leaves the book on a rather low emotional plane.

The neighbor herself, Mrs. Tifton, is problematic as a character in a children's story. I can't remember a children's book in which a difficult adult character is left to be either rather misunderstood or with her failings unresolved. In this case, Birdsall makes a point of introducing the subject of Mrs. Tifton's divorce and her husband's abandonment of their son—rather a heavy issue, no matter how common it might be these days. To put such an unexplored, raw theme in a book for young children is inadvisable.

Mrs. Tifton ends by marrying her obnoxious boyfriend for no good reason; this is just sad, even for her. I remember this outcome really bothering Bridget, who felt that the lady and her son (the "boy" of the subtitle) deserved a happy ending, or at least not a dreadful one. For sure, today's mores are reflected in this plot development: to most people, a remarriage involving two unchanged characters does not register as significant as a moral—or literary—issue.

Of course, to a child reader, who is trying to understand the world and the choices adults make, it's *very* significant and potentially harmful to his sense of whether Providence has in store *for everyone* a happy (or at least a deserved) ending.

Mrs. Tifton is neither that bad character who comes to a bad and deserved ending nor a complicated character who finds understanding. She is just a selfish, weak person whom the author manipulates the children into not liking—but also not understanding. This whole plot element ends up having a "young-adult lit" vibe that is particularly objectionable to me. It has the air of grooming the reader for further, more "realistic" sorts of stories.

It's simply a fact that today, most in this age group *are* reading young-adult fiction or desperately wanting to. We need to protect them and give them really innocent, good literature—the "1000 good books" that John Senior speaks of. They need challenges but not confusion.

Other books offer the fun of a summer-vacation adventure with good morals and solicitude (or justice) for all the characters. And the children don't just get into difficulties; they exercise that most important of childhood qualities, *pluck*, to get out of them.

So instead, *read this, not that:*

Magic by the Lake, by Edward Eager. Children on holiday navigate tricky magic and must use their wits to stay ahead of it. Their stepfather (their mother is a widow, which you discover in the equally excellent previous books) is doing his best to provide; they end up helping him, which is really sweet.

Swallows and Amazons, by Arthur Ransome. Children on holiday have wonderful adventures in a boat and on an island. The adults who, from our own adult point of view, might not have things entirely under control, nevertheless maintain high standards for personal responsibility—standards that the children must live up to in the course of their escapades.

Gone-Away Lake, by Elizabeth Enright. A girl and her boy cousin find an abandoned summer village and make friends with two elderly and odd siblings whom they must learn to understand (and it's well worth it). They also, like the Penderwick children, try to keep a secret from the adults in charge, but the secret is not a guilty one, and it comes to light for reasons not in their power—but also the revelation is understood to be a relief to them.

The Woodbegoods, by E. Nesbit (a sequel to *The Treasure Seekers*). The children in this story try to be good but only cause disaster;

since this is the plight of children everywhere and in all times, the story is most fulfilling, amusing, and clever.

The Railway Children, by E. Nesbit. The mother of the children in this book shelters them from the real reason for their exile, which they take to be a summer holiday (a strangely austere one, to be sure) but which is necessitated by their father's imprisonment. Yet they are the means of bringing about his vindication. Honor is a particularly important subtext in this story. (The movie is delightful—a really fun family film.)

The Cottage at Bantry Bay, by Hilda van Stockum. The children in this story are poor, and the family is loving; they have many adventures, ending with the discovery of a treasure that enables them to procure medical care for their brother.

All of these make great read-alouds. The age level is eight to twelve, but all ages will enjoy them.

Books for the Voracious Reader

I am concerned that a lot of reading lists for children feature books from a twenty-year period—that is to say, from our own time. And they are *about* "now"—about kids "like you"—only, what does that mean? What if a child reading these stories acts more like the child in the stories, who are supposed to be just like him? Maybe that's not such a good thing. Modeling behavior that reflects your own behavior will tend to spiral downward, behavior-wise. We don't want that.

And then, there is another problem: not only do we want our children to read good books; we want them to know how to find good books on their own. Call it a "lost tool of learning"—the skill of being able to find things to read on one's own.

Behold, one purpose of the public library: to allow the reader to follow his nose. Sadly, unless your library is old and too poor to have purged its stacks, you probably can't trust it enough to let your child loose in it.

(Teaching children to be active about finding what they are interested in is another reason I highly recommend the Bobbs-Merrill readers, old as they are, that I mentioned earlier, on teaching your child to read. Many of the selections have, in the "assignment" section, suggestions for looking things up in the library. You will find that they are very helpful for teaching your child to learn to look things up in the library and go on a hunt of his own—again, if your library is trustworthy. Otherwise, they provide a good secondhand-book buying guide for you.)

Thus the importance of having more books, actual, physical books, in your home than you are necessarily reading at the moment, even if it goes against your minimalist tendencies, and even if you do have good reading on the Kindle. It has to do with exposure and externalizing the list—putting it out there where it can be seen, handled, explored, and even abandoned for the moment.

The other day, I took down a couple of boxes I had stowed in the attic. And I came across some books I love, including a series called Best in Children's Books, published by Doubleday. They are out of print, but you can get them pretty cheap. You can probably find them at book sales. You could get them one by one, and it would be like having a hardcover literary magazine for your children, delivered! (You can find a complete list of these books on the Internet.)

Each book has a fantastic assortment of poetry, tales, history, and geography. The illustrations are charming. There's something for each age level, which I endorse, because not only does it challenge the slower or younger reader to do more, but it allows the faster or older reader to linger on material that might still offer something for his development. And then there's always the possibility that your older child will read something to the younger ones. If your child finds a story he likes, why, you can help him find more by the same author.

Now I'm going to suggest some good books that do need a little caution, even though they are books that have been read for generations. Some books are just not worth the trouble they cause—this is how this series-within-a-series got started in the first place: I was impatient with a book that *looked* good but whose content didn't make its flaws possible to overlook.

But there are books on the "1000 good books" list—both the official one from John Senior (see the appendix) and the unofficial one we are compiling here, leaning on his strong arm—that are good reads but not without potential pitfalls—just like life.

This grappling with themes, however, only grows as children get older. Just think of the moral issues in Shakespeare! Think of *Les Misérables*! Think of *Quo Vadis*! I think we can agree that having "themes" doesn't automatically mean that a book "glorifies" them; yet, in some books, certain episodes can be problematic for immature readers.

Your standards may be different from mine—certainly our tastes are different and our children are different in terms of what will cause them trouble. Each parent has to take all these things into account; it's especially up to the parent to be able to discern what's best for his own children.

I am not of the camp that thinks a child must be given a whitewashed version of life in art, because what will surely happen is that we'll have to make up some sort of faux literature for them, which is counterproductive to education (in the broad sense). Children need to read real books—that is, books written honestly for their audience, not out of pedagogy, even if the result is imperfect. Most books are not perfect! The list of *those* is very short. What differentiates an imperfect yet readable book from a book to be simply avoided is not a matter that is susceptible to a scientific formula. And that makes it difficult for us to recommend books to each other with certainty.

The best books make a world for us to inhabit. Even lesser books do this well. For example, I've stated my issues with Harry Potter in various places on my site, but the fact is, it's a world of delight that no pedantry can destroy, and it's precisely the magic that makes it so, because the magic is the rules of that world. But the *magic* in Harry Potter is what many parents object to. My answer is that the imagination formed on Narnia and *The Hobbit* will not likely be led astray, and Harry Potter forms too foundational a text for our current society to be left aside.

I'll tell you the ways the books I recommend below might be flawed, but in the end, I do think that the world they offer is worth the caution that you, the parent, need to exercise when choosing your library. I will do my best to give you the information I have.

So, with those caveats in mind, here are some authors for your older, more voracious readers, both boys and girls, although perhaps the boys will enjoy the first ones more:

The Horatio Hornblower series, by C. S. Forester. A tale of high adventure, featuring a boy who has to overcome or find his way through his unhardened youth and essential sensitivity to survive in a man's world. The TV shows were very good as well, but of course, read the books first.

This series satisfies the adventure-craving reader; so much so that although there are a few places where Horatio's conduct is less than moral, and one place in particular where it is downright immoral, most readers I've spoken to don't even remember them. But of course, we have to be alert; I need to tell you to skip *Flying Colours* (number 3 in the series, although the events take place further along the internal timeline), in which there occurs an episode where Horatio commits adultery. The scene is a bit lurid for the standards that we want for our children. (If you want to ascertain for yourself, it occurs at the end of chapter 9 and the beginning of chapter 10.) The series can be read without this book.

Until you read them for yourself, also skip *Ship of the Line* and *Lord Hornblower*. Just know that this series, besides skillfully depicting that world that most of us would know nothing about without the author's imagination guiding us, helps the growing boy address the issue of *fear*. Horatio's adventures center on his fears and his courage in overcoming them. For that reason, I think these books are worth the read and will be loved by your sons. And again, Horatio's weakness around women—and the failure of Forester to resolve it—does seem to go right over their heads, according to my now-adult experts (my sons-in-law).

The Three Musketeers and its sequels, by Alexandre Dumas. Robert Louis Stevenson loved this book, and why not? Adventure, romance, friendship, swashbuckling swordplay! The only thing to prevent a young person from adoring this book is the first page. Just tell him to keep at it. Again, this is a world of its own; the Musketeers are not stellar people. They gamble, they fight. It would be fine to read an abridged version.

The Scarlet Pimpernel, by Baroness Orczy. This romantic and adventurous tale of hidden identity set during the French Revolution is dramatic and thoroughly enjoyable.

The Count of Monte Cristo, by Alexandre Dumas. Nothing, *nothing* can compare with the beginning of this book, with its tale of unjust imprisonment and impossible escape. Have you ever seen the movie *The Shawshank Re-demption*? I would say that the first part of *The Count of Monte Cristo* is even more heart-rending and exciting than that. Even though the second part of the book doesn't quite live up to the first, it's a story well worth reading. Kind of the ultimate beach book, going on and on. Does this book glorify some bad behavior? Well, not *glorify*. Bad behavior occurs—most notably, the count is motivated entirely by revenge, which is hardly a Christian virtue. He's not a person to emulate in this regard. At the end of the book, however, he definitely has a crisis of conscience. He movingly questions the cost he has incurred in pursuing his goal of retribution. I'm not sure that this denouement absolutely redeems the vast quantity of revenge he has indulged in, but it must suffice.

Don't get abridgments, by the way, except as noted. The whole point is to keep your voracious readers reading!

Mrs. Piggle-Wiggle and Social Engineering

No one expects me to like a new, updated version of mostly anything, but I'm trying to be balanced. There's a new Mrs. Piggle-Wiggle (with more planned). In the new version, the drawings are appealing, which is saying something, because Hilary Knight's whimsical imagination made so many books come alive, and Mrs. Piggle-Wiggle was no exception.

The new Mrs. Piggle-Wiggle tries to have the same lightheartedness as the old, but right from the beginning, it's heavy going, with the first problem for her to solve not even appearing until chapter 3, and she shows little of the original's confidence in diving right in with very little explanation, allowing us to figure things out as we go.

Why don't people just try their own hand at invention? It's quite a legitimate and venerable method to use the old favorites as a starting point. In fact, you'd be hard-pressed to come up with something *completely* new. One wonders (hopefully not too cynically) about the marketing angle: Is the publisher just cashing in on a beloved brand, without benefit of its cleverness?

How is the old Mrs. Piggle-Wiggle not perfect? What needs updating? The reviews say that they were "too fifties"—which means that everyone has parents who are married to each other and Dad goes to work while Mom stays home. This norm, critics say, is no longer our norm. Behind the new Mrs. Piggle-Wiggle is the specter of gender ideology; one character in the stories has two moms, drearily enough. Turns out that the book isn't the work of a misguided author too timid to create her own beloved figure; it's the work of a committee, following a progressive and corrupting script.

Using the smokescreen of rewriting stories to reflect life "as it is," publishers opportunistically deprive children of ever discovering life as it is meant to and could be. As a child with divorced parents, I was grateful for stories that depicted stability; more, I was hungry for them.

The roles are too divided by sex (I abjure the term "gender" in this context), say the critics of the old versions. However enlightened we consider ourselves, the truth is that though parents are oh, so liberated now, and tasks fall on everyone equally because we have decreed it to be so, men still have to think about work and women still fret over household matters (and, often, they fret about work as well). It's just all more stressful now because no one dares admit it.

The intractability of these roles is borne out by all studies everywhere, greatly to the chagrin of feminists who prescribe more of the same failing effort to remake them. Nothing is more common, even today in our enlightened time, than a father who is distracted by his job, or a mom who's focused on the minutiae of the kids' behavior. We just don't have a sense of humor about it nowadays. All the more reason why we need the treasure that is the old Mrs. Piggle-Wiggle!

Casting characters according to type is a time-honored practice that yields much comedy. It would be sad to think that we have to do away with the healing powers of laughter, but I fear that many a smile has been sacrificed at the altar of realism.

It's hard to believe, dear reader, given the sorry, didactic, and even openly propagandizing state of children's literature today, that these older books are not how-tos! They are hilarious *stories*! I still chuckle when I remember "*I thought you said,* 'She fell in the toaster and was burnt up dead!'" from probably the best chapter in the entire oeuvre, "The Thought-You-Saiders Cure"—and when I remember all the times my kids and I rolled with laughter over these books.

They are rollicking good fun, with a healthy airing of human nature. There aren't ponderous morality plays for children, although there is wisdom for parents contained therein, which is why they keep *us* interested as we read aloud. We see in ourselves that astonished mother who can't believe her darling is so bratty! As for children, they can't be blamed for their fantasies: if only our *real* parents would let us dig holes wherever we wanted in the yard! (To be fair, the new version retains this attractive feature of Mrs. Piggle-Wiggle's home.)

Other funny children's chapter books to read aloud:

The Children of Noisy Village, by Astrid Lindgren

B Is for Betsy and *Betsy and Billy*, by Carolyn Haywood. And who thought any of the "updated" covers were in any way attractive? I ask you! Try to find an old copy with its "outdated" drawings, so unironic and charming.

The Henry and Ribsy series, by Beverly Cleary

Amelia Bedelia, by Peggy Parish, for very young chapter-book readers who are trying to figure out why you say such enigmatic things like "dress" the chicken.

Penrod, by Booth Tarkington. This book is for older children, nine and up.

Dangerous Journey

 give you one of the very best read-aloud books you will ever encounter: *Dangerous Journey*, by László Hámori, recommended for ages ten to thirteen but good for all ages really.

This book will satisfy just about everyone's hunger for adventure, and it has the virtue of also having an unusual setting: Communist occupation in Hungary after World War II.

Every chapter is a cliffhanger. The prose is brisk. The story is of mere children left to their own devices, all alone in a hostile environment.

(And so, lots of potential here to discuss all those things you've been meaning to bring up, such as, do you know how to tell which direction you are traveling? And could you discern a helpful stranger from a dangerous one, or know when to run? Could you keep warm? I don't know if you can work oxbow lakes into the conversation, but, for your own peace of mind, try!)

The main character is a boy who finds himself on the road and rail to find his father (so, technically, he's not an orphan—and orphan stories are the most beloved by children—but he might as well be for the duration of the story; extra points, really, actually to have a father!). But there's another boy and a girl too; and there is bread and sausage, which is all I really ask of an adventure.

My fifth-grade teacher read this book aloud to our class after our lunch break. When she finished (and there are twenty-one chapters, so it must have taken at least a couple of weeks), twenty-five rapt children begged her to start it again. We hadn't moved an inch the entire time she read. And she did read it again; but as I recall, she extracted some amazing feat from us first.

I apologize that this book is out of print and you might have to wait a long time to enjoy it. You may find it in a secondhand bookshop. Keep your eye out for it at library sales. Snatch up every copy you find, because I promise you, you will love this book. I found it again in adulthood courtesy of my friend Theresa (of *A Mother's List of Books*), who generously sent me a copy based on my description of "there is a boy, and a train, and it's in Hungary." Which shows you my retention rate of a book read aloud to me twice.

If you are having trouble finding it, you can console yourselves in the meantime with Hilda van Stockum's *The Winged Watchman*, set in Holland, and Lois Lowry's *Number the Stars*, set in Denmark. There are, of course, many more books in this genre. But for a read-aloud, *Dangerous Journey* is at the tippity-top of my list.

The Wind in the Willows

As A.A. Milne so truly put it:

> One does not argue about *The Wind in the Willows*. The young man gives it to the girl with whom he is in love, and, if she does not like it, asks her to return his letters. The older man tries it on his nephew, and alters his will accordingly. The book is a test of character. We can't criticize it, because it is criticizing us. But I must give you one word of warning. When you sit down to it, don't be so ridiculous as to suppose that you are sitting in judgment on my taste, or on the art of Kenneth Grahame. You are merely sitting in judgment on yourself. You may be worthy: I don't know, But it is you who are on trial.[25]

In my work I have tried to catalogue books that fall under this rubric: *They judge you; it is you who are on trial!* Oh, there is room for personal preference, of course. But "the democracy of the dead" (Chesterton) has spoken.

---

[25] A.A. Milne, introduction to Kenneth Grahame, *The Wind in the Willows* (Bristol, UK: Pook Press, 2016), ix–x.

There are some books that are a test of character, and you can excuse your taste, but do not fail to put them on the A-list.

Milne's son Christopher remembered:

A book that we all greatly loved and admired and read aloud or alone, over and over and over: *The Wind in the Willows*. This book is, in a way, two separate books put into one. There are, on the one hand, those chapters concerned with the adventures of Toad; and on the other hand there are those chapters that explore human emotions—the emotions of fear, nostalgia, awe, wanderlust. My mother was drawn to the second group, of which "The Piper at the Gates of Dawn" was her favourite, read to me again and again with always, toward the end, the catch in the voice and the long pause to find her handkerchief and blow her nose. My father, on his side, was so captivated by the first group that he turned these chapters into the children's play, Toad of Toad Hall. In this play one emotion only is allowed to creep in: nostalgia.

Thus, you yourself, a rational grown-up, are expected to sit down and read the whole thing (but slowly and with the trusting mind of the child). Then, taking the temperature of your offspring, you may choose to introduce them to it in its entirety as well (are they bookish and docile—or, will their strong imaginations be enough to quell their restlessness?), or, wisely, to capture them with the adventurous bits (even showing them the movie *Toad of Toad Hall* or enticing them to take parts in Milne's play).

In the end, your goal is to read the whole thing aloud (don't worry—later childhood is a fine time for this; be patient), enjoying the rollicking aspects but also luxuriating in the "numinous" parts (as Lewis called especially the chapter "The Piper at the Gates of Dawn").

This book is about life and friendship. In the chapter called "Dolce Domum," which we might initially pass over as a bit boring, we find a true crisis of friendship and understanding. Rat experiences a moment of conscience deeper than many found in adult novels. He is stricken when he realizes he hasn't really listened to his friend, and he quickly, decisively makes amends.

Our culture gives lip service to diversity, but Grahame shows us how Badgers and Moles can get along. We need to recover a sense of place, and this is what *The Wind in the Willows* offers us: place sanctified by the love of friends.

Toad suffers from arrested development, and not only do his friends rescue (and sometimes enable) him, but in the end, his friendship and kindness redeem him.

Most of all, *The Wind in the Willows* is a delight to read.

I admit I'm torn. In one way, it's so famous; I can't believe I'm adding anything by writing about it; it's not possible that you haven't heard of it already! On the other, I feel strongly that a book like this becomes invisible, completely forgotten, precisely on account of its popularity. For goodness' sake, the cast of Monty Python did a movie of it! On Amazon, you are offered a "premium reading experience" in one version (that makes me tired just reading the description), and in another, a teacher's guide with fill-in-the-blank-style lessons.

Please, just read it. Enjoy it! Talk about it if you like—or don't!

The real difficulty is to choose among the many wonderfully illustrated versions, because every illustrator has taken his turn at this book. Of course, the original Ernest Shepherd pictures are the best, in my opinion, because he was a master of the paradox of *detailed suggestion*. The child's imagination is best encouraged with a deft hand, and so often, illustrators indulge their own vision at the expense of their audience.

But there are so many good editions to choose from. Annie Gauger's illustrations are lush, but I object to the annotation aspect in a children's book. You can try to find the Arthur Rackham version (with Milne's introduction) secondhand. You need this book in hardback and probably in more than one edition.

Just be sure you don't get an abridged one—a smoothed-out, blandified, faux *Wind in the Willows*.

Worldly Themes, Dangerous Topics

Those of us who have been true readers all our life fully realize the enormous extension of our being which we owe to authors.

— C. S. LEWIS, *AN EXPERIMENT IN CRITICISM*

 reader asked about a book beloved by our family and friends; a book that is formative for young men. This worried person offered some selections from *Quo Vadis*, by Henry Sienkiewicz:

Senators, trembling in their souls, went to the Palatine to magnify the song of the Periodonices, and go wild with him amid orgies of naked bodies, wine, and flowers.

I judge, lord, that ten thousand naked maidens make less impression than one.

There would be a new orgy, and moreover a fouler and a viler one.

So let's discuss the idea of introducing children to potentially damaging themes. Probably a lot of us are still reeling over our own contact with worldly culture and downright bad stuff as young people, including maybe being exposed to more prurient material than was good for us. And now we are the guardians of the gate. We are the parents.

We have work, a lot of laundry to do; everything is sticky and hot; Auntie Leila says make your menu plans; and on top of it, we are going to have to read thousands of pages of fiction and fact every year to make sure our darlings are getting educated without polluting their minds? How can this be? How will we do it? Too much! Isn't it easier just to hide it all from them?

Since I hadn't read this particular book, but I know that friends and family have with great delight, I decided to ask my son-in-law John, intelligent reader, former boy, teacher of boys in high school, Christian gentleman of noble thoughts, just what he would say in defense of the book under suspicion. Here is how he responded:

> First of all, I will agree that *Quo Vadis* has adult themes. I probably wouldn't recommend it for kids younger than a freshman in high school (though if it were read with the family, even those younger children might benefit). However, I think that it is really important *how* these adult themes are presented.
>
> *Quo Vadis* does a wonderful job of presenting the lusts, excesses, and pagan qualities of Rome and contrasting them brilliantly with the humility, chastity, service, and real human love (raised to a level of grace) that Christianity makes possible. The author characterizes the depravity truthfully as dehumanizing and deeply unsatisfying.
>
> These images are not meant to titillate. It's forgivable for a mother to be quite worried, when so many authors do make it their business to draw children by cheap passions into their stories [which is why the LMLD Library Project says stay away from the YA shelf—Auntie Leila].
>
> However I would argue that looking at *Quo Vadis* this way would be like mistaking *The Last Judgment* of Michelangelo for pornography

because it has naked bodies in it. We need to be a culture that knows art better: visual art, musical art, and literary art.

An objector might say, "Reading must put no evil thing before the eyes." Reading certainly is about worldly education and being versed in culture. However, it is more deeply a study of the human character in relationship to the world. St. Thomas More, a layman concerned with education, thought that the study of literature was important for these reasons, but more importantly because it allowed our minds to be trained to understand the best, highest, and most perfect literature: Sacred Scripture.

Literature must not be looked upon merely as a worldly trap where there is little to gain to offset the risk of "putting evil before our eyes" for the sake of some fleeting moments of entertainment.

My suggestion to a concerned parent is to read the story himself (not just skim it), beforehand. The father of the family is uniquely suited to make a judgment as to its suitability for his particular children. After this first reading, conversations in the family can take place.

Some of the best discussions about morality that I've had with my parents sprang from reading *With Fire and Sword* as a family when I was still quite young.

I then recounted this exchange to my husband. His response: "Yes, I just read *Quo Vadis*! It's really well done, presenting Roman decadence in a negative way, making it unappealing. I didn't want to go to an orgy for about three weeks after reading it."

(I'm not trying to belittle the issue, believe me. However, mark well, the devil hates laughter!)

Truly, once a child leaves the latency phase of development, during which sexuality does not figure in his consciousness, he becomes aware of things he never noticed before (and this goes for girls as well). Even if our age had any sense of protecting children's innocence, we would, on reflection, realize that struggles with sexuality are part of our fallen world. It's part of growing up to hear things, to see things, and to think about things. Our own reading testifies to the truth of this reality, even in other, less overtly profligate, eras, because it's a universal experience.

Our own healthy realism and solid moral grounding go a long way toward keeping children on the right track to understanding the moral order. We must acknowledge the existence of mature themes and be willing to talk about them, appropriate to the age of the child and our knowledge of his character.

We have to let a good cultural formation—a wide familiarity with time-tested literature—take place in his development, letting others help us. And I do want to emphasize the point that a work such as this one has stood the test of time, of millions of readers formed in more conservative times passing it along to their own children. Artists (in this case, storytellers grounded in morality) help us get the child to the other side (the other side here being a robust, moral, well formed adulthood)—without having experienced all the things he ought to avoid.

Note well that not every book treating intense themes is worthy, nor can prurience be admitted under the guise of culture or the excuse that defects can be remedied with discussion. But discussion is important to solidifying further what we have previously ascertained as the moral context of the author.

I would add my own thought here to my son-in-law's (based on meeting his father, who is keenly interested in reading with his sons): a boy will be safely guided by his father. My recommendation is to share the burden of all the reading; get your husband to delve into some Sienkiewicz with his boys!

My Family and Other Animals

What is reading, teaching, and learning about literature but *enjoying well written books?*

Oh yes, you will have to analyze, scrutinize, and otherwise investigate all the serious matter as it relates to books—great fun, but still, reading and enjoying. If you want to be affirmed in this conclusion, so central to the success of educating children at home, do read Gerald Durrell's book *My Family and Other Animals.*

Gerald Durrell was a British-born naturalist who set out to write about the island in Greece onto which his family decamped and where his love of all things flora and fauna found ample scope. His reminiscences of those things, however, couldn't keep his family from taking over the narrative, for they are by far the most interesting and comical specimens to observe!

For the homeschooling family, *My Family and Other Animals* represents confirmation and consolation for that child or children of yours who simply don't fit the mold. When we recall that the author, a world-famous naturalist, was an apparently incorrigible student who simply could not be made to sit still and learn his "math facts" yet went on to produce *this* delightful work (an instant hit, by the way, at the book stalls), we take heart.

Personally, I wonder if Gerald's novelist brother Lawrence didn't have a hand in the telling, for the naturalist's other books are not as good as this one. However, that does not *seem* to be the case. And while the events are not strictly told according to chronology and absolute adherence to fact, they are more than entertaining enough to make up for any liberties.

Read this book and try your hand—ask your children to try theirs—at recounting events in your own life in an amusing way. It takes skill, but practice and a good example help.

The book was made into a BBC series that was then condensed into a ninety-minute movie. I highly recommend it (but not *The Durrells in Corfu,* the newer series that completely subverts the Wodehousian joy of the original) for anyone who has read the book already.

PART 13

On Foundational Books for You

In this section you will find a miscellany of book thoughts as they occurred to me, either in response to readers or when I observed some serious gap in current knowledge of everyday know-how. My hope is that by offering you "this type of book"—in other words the criteria by which to choose a book in a category—you will benefit not only by that book but in your quest for others. One book leads to another, I always find, once you have a good starting point.

ASK AUNTIE LEILA
Life Syllabus

Dear Auntie Leila,

I recently reread your response to the lady who was feeling guilty for not working. Part of your advice to her was to use her time to learn things, to grow and to read.... However, modern parenting books seem lacking. I can't trust myself to read them, as I know, even if I fundamentally disagree with what they say, that I will feel morally compelled to live up to their expectations.... Could you perhaps recommend some better titles?

Chantelle

Dear Chantelle,

I completely agree with your suspicion of modern parenting books, and I'll tell you why. They are mostly politically driven, and the specific politics that drive them are of the gender-neutral variety that make it impossible to suggest even remotely that a woman—a mother—has something unique to offer a baby, despite the overwhelming, indeed unanimous, research, not to mention common experience throughout history, to the contrary.

Even books written from a putatively Christian perspective—the ones for the popular market—seem to me to suffer from a faulty anthropology. I haven't found any that are based on solid research and that take into account fallen human nature or common sense. To paraphrase from Gilbert and Sullivan's *Ruddigore*, the arguments sound very well, but if reduced to their syllogistical form, they would not hold water.

The Gesell Institute of Child Development is in New Haven, Connecticut, where I lived in my childhood. I don't remember now how I happened to be in the front offices—what could I have been doing there? I picked up and read as quickly as I could what, at the time, must have been pamphlets produced prior to the writing of the books I recommend here. I couldn't have been older than sixteen.

The material was divided by the child's age, and I seem to have stored away certain facts, because they came back to mind when I had little ones of my own. I may have taken the book out of the library at some point and chuckled over its accuracy (since, by the time it was published, I had a five-year-old, a three-year-old, and a one-year-old). It is uncanny how the books predict seemingly random markers such as resting upside down or tummy aches.

Thanks to the Gesell information, many behaviors in children that strike others as faults that need to be corrected are identifiable as developmental issues that need to be guided properly. Knowing about how children act as they grow is just tremendously helpful to prevent excess anxiety on parents' part.

I am happy to see that the institute (at this writing) seems to oppose Common Core and continues to fulfill its original mission to protect the actual development of children from overzealous educators of all stripes. And the books are written in a very positive way. However, I haven't looked into their views enough to recommend the institute itself.

Reading these books, simply take note of the descriptions of the stages. Make your own determination about what to do about them, based on your convictions, your family style, and your knowledge of your child. Perhaps stick with older editions of the Gesell Institute's *Child Behavior: From Birth to Ten* and *Child Behavior: The Classic Child Care Manual from the Gesell Institute of Human Development*, by Frances L. Ilg, Louise Bates Ames, and Sidney M. Baker. You don't have to do what they say about things, in other words, but just appreciate that someone is affirming that what your child is doing is what all children do, pretty much.

Another book I recommend is by an author who has gone completely to the dark side, Penelope Leach. This woman has abandoned all scientific objectivity to promote state-run and gender-neutral child rearing, so do not buy her new books!

Nevertheless, the book I specifically recommend is Leach's *Your Baby and Child: From Birth to Age Five* (the 1989 edition), which should be available secondhand. It systematically goes over everything that you need to know about taking care of a baby and child—with the child's interest at heart, rather than the busy parent's.

I'm sure there is some information in it that is outdated, but then, I think that a lot of today's advice will be outdated soon enough. As I have said before, babies have been babies for a long time! If you like to be told exactly how to do all the little tasks—with nicely drawn pictures—this is the book for you. In terms of the collective memory, there are quite valuable nuggets in here about taking care of sick children and understanding how babies are reacting to their environment. Leach is very practical about tantrums and other kiddo strategies for undermining your sanity. I'm sure you can mentally update things such as diapers and sleep positions (which I take with a grain of salt anyway) as you read.

If you have a child who must be bottle-fed (an adopted child, for instance), she explains it all. I remember Leach's breastfeeding advice as fairly reasonable.

The defects in the Leach book (especially regarding breastfeeding and maternal bonding) are ably remedied by Sheila Kippley in *Breastfeeding and Natural Child Spacing*. But Kippley goes beyond mechanics to explain how the bond between mother and child is for the proper development of each, in every possible way.

The first means of communication that you have with your child are all about holding, cuddling, and feeding him—all of which I call "nursing" in the breastfeeding but also the old-fashioned sense. Communication builds on communication, so I do count a breastfeeding book (well, Kippley's) as in this category of foundational reading.

Lewis and the Hierarchical Vision of Life

As far as I am concerned, I owe C. S. Lewis my interior life. Not my interior spiritual life (for that, I credit Jean-Baptiste Chautard's *Soul of the Apostolate*), but the formation of my imagination along hierarchical lines. So don't expect me to be less than exuberantly enthusiastic about Narnia.

Please give your children the gift of imagination, adventure, wit, and wisdom. Here you will find ample scope for practicing your voices and enjoying the grown-up jokes as well as the simple pleasures, because the writing itself (apart from the deep subject matter) is of the highest quality and eminently read-aloud-able. I personally judge all read-alouds against Lewis's mellifluous prose.

But I will mention, if only to give you a hint of the riches that the Chronicles of Narnia contain, that of all the books to avoid "teaching," they are foremost.

I am afraid (and I hope I don't sound harsh) that those who seek to reduce the Chronicles to lame retellings of Gospel narratives on the level of some sort of one-to-one correspondence are doomed to expose their own ignorance. Perhaps because the centerpiece of the stories is indeed an imaginative (and successful, insofar as success can be achieved in this endeavor) depiction of the Passion and Resurrection of Jesus Christ, we can be misled into thinking that Lewis's intention was to present, somewhat didactically, Christian truths in fictional form.

One *might* find confirmation of this reductive idea in one of his letters:

> I did not say to myself "Let us represent Jesus as He really is in our world by a Lion in Narnia": I said "Let us suppose that there were a land like Narnia and that the Son of God, as He became a Man in our world, became a Lion there, and then imagine what would have happened."

Unless we read and ponder the next line:

> If you think about it, you will see that it is quite a different thing.

The difference is located precisely where an idea becomes art.

This is not to say that I'd be against investigation into meaning—far from it. The symbolism of Lewis's writings is so rich that you'll be rewarded with many insights. I'm just saying: know that until you've studied theology, philosophy (especially Plato and Augustine, but also certainly Aquinas), medieval cosmology, courtly love, all poetry and all prose (epic and otherwise), and all non-Asian ancient languages, you'll be misled by what you think you do know if what you seek to do is tell children what the stories "are about."[26]

Such was the breadth and depth of Lewis's knowledge. Such is the shallowness of thought of those who reduce him, forcing his writings into their narrow categories (seven books? seven sacraments? seven biblical truths?—very pat, very Procrustean), that they miss the point. It's a mysterious process by which the artist synthesizes his learning and makes it art.

---

[26] If you want to teach your children something so that they will appreciate the Narnia stories (and life) more, teach the medieval view of the universe, Ptolemy, *The Faerie Queene*, and all the enduring works and cosmology that Lewis's vision encompasses and depends on.

I certainly make no claim to having a grip on any of the above, but neither am I convinced that Lewis's packagers do. I get the enthusiasm. I deplore the flatness.

You see, Lewis loved the hierarchical view of the universe and of Heaven. His mind was medieval in its tone. That is to say, he immersed himself in that age of the flowering of Christian thought and art and, in the process, patterned his own mind on it.

At this point, I hear the restless murmurings of those who think they understand. "Yes, yes, medieval—that means allegorical. His art was allegorical, and allegory is ... the lesser of the literary modes."

Well.

The fashion today is to take Tolkien at his impatient word, and it's Tolkien who foisted that epithet of "allegorical" on him. Now, Tolkien, another of my loves, was a man completely enamored of what Lewis called "Pure Northernness." Lewis shared that love (for perhaps unknowable reasons, but among them that the early medieval mind emerged from that realm), which is one reason that Lewis had a great friendship with Tolkien and a deep sympathy for Tolkien's work—more than sympathy, in fact; you could call it the admiration of disinterested love (and he was also chief encourager of Tolkien's writing).

Tolkien's tone of mind was "saga," and he wrote a work that surely takes its place in the strictly limited canon of what we might call "the epic"—the handful of truly great sweeping tales that mankind has to offer. (And I would argue that *The Lord of the Rings* uses the device of allegory on occasion, so there.)

But Tolkien had not much reciprocal sympathy for Lewis's interest in and resonance with later medieval cosmology and its texture. He was, possibly, even a bit grouchy about the whole thing. Thus, without a great deal of careful discussion or even close reading, he dismissed Lewis's work as allegorical, and today's critics, I'm sorry to say, lack the perspective to weigh his judgment. They accept it and try to shoehorn Lewis's work into that narrow span. (By the way, most people don't really understand what allegory is, reducing it further to symbolism.)

To be sure, Lewis appreciated allegory—and why not? The term is now (in our decidedly flat age) used as a sneer, but a man who first read *The*

Faerie Queene at the age of eight surely knew the subtle uses of this tool. But to leave it at that is to betray that one simply hasn't *enjoyed* his work as one might, for its own sake. There is symbolism in his work, to be sure—but symbolism per se isn't allegory, nor can a true work of art be reduced to its devices. The sneer is not obligatory.

But Lewis gives us narrative depictions of philosophical and theological arguments, in which characters, rising above the emblematic, with lives of their own, enact the clash of ideas just as deftly as in the hands of a master novelist such as Austen or Tolstoy, although, of course, in a different mode.

Most of all, Lewis breathes life into his hierarchical (and thus, at once profoundly Christian, classical, and realistic) view of things specific and general. In our modernist age of equality as the highest thing, it's hard to understand a view of reality that sees each thing in its place, enhancing the whole, undiminished simply by relative location.

Depicting just this vision, however incomprehensible (including to many Christians) it may be today, was Lewis's gift. Many people do resonate with his imagination, without quite knowing why.

For insight (and a grad-school-level crash course on the subject of ancient and medieval cosmology) into Lewis's vision, I highly recommend *Planet Narnia: The Seven Heavens in the Imagination of C. S. Lewis*, by Michael Ward.[27] If nothing else, you will emerge convinced that you will subtract from your understanding of Narnia only by subjecting it to a conventional study of mere symbolism as correspondence: Aslan stands for Jesus, the table stands for the Cross, and so forth. You will be, among other things, astonished to learn the virtuosity of Lewis's use of words themselves and amazed at his ability to create a complex image in the reader's mind, even if he was unaware of the treatment.

Even this insightful book handles only one aspect of Lewis's work, restricting itself in the main to his love of the image of planetary spheres. I've no doubt that the author could have a go at similar investigations in philosophy and theology and linguistics in Lewis's mind. On the other

---

[27] To understand *Planet Narnia* better, I also recommend first reading Lewis's *The Discarded Image* and *That Hideous Strength*.

hand, such was the vast horizon of Lewis's knowledge that it may take a few other authors to do it all justice.

What's remarkable about Lewis's achievement in the Chronicles of Narnia (and what he himself would value in a story) is the accessibility of his wisdom on the level of "literature enjoyed." A tale well told—that is the highest praise of all.

The Abolition of Man

A s I get older, I sometimes reread (or dip into at random) books that were formative when I was young. In those moments, I encounter the ideas contained therein as my own, given to me by the author at a time opportune for the gift, when my mind was searching and I had the time to absorb them.

The books of my first awakening are indispensable to what I have become, such as it is; to my reactions, my determinations, my choices, my discernment. Whatever those have been (conditioned by all my faults, of course), it's due largely to ideas I've come across in great works, to the extent that I sometimes think, "What if I hadn't found this book at just that moment when my mind reached for answers? What would my intellect be without the clarity they gave me?"

Some of these are the books that come up in conversation (and blog posts and this book) often, although some are on the bookshelf, and it's only when I'm dusting them that I remember with gratitude what I learned.

They are markers when I meet someone who becomes a kindred spirit, when it turns out that she has read one of these books or he exclaims when he sees it on the shelf; then we—my husband and I—know that we can safely allude to the contents in passing, leaping over the necessity for explanation, confident that our intellectual, moral, and spiritual shorthand will be understood. That in itself is a great gift for friendship—the delight and joy of sharing a body of reading with others, with, of course, the ancillary joy of discovering those books they love that we haven't seen yet.

But sometimes I think, "What if a young person today doesn't know about these books and doesn't realize the vital necessity of reading them now, when the mind is fresh?"—although I do think one can clarify one's ideas at any point. But I have that feeling of having avoided a cliff, narrowly and in the mist, when I realize the advantage of having read certain things at the *beginning* of my adult life.

The Abolition of Man, by C.S. Lewis, is one such book. It lays out, in laymen's language, the effects of relativism on the young spirit, the evils of twisting language to one's own ends, and the confused thinking that leads to the complacent separation of faith and knowledge. In it you will find the refutation of the materialist fallacy (what Lewis calls, confusingly for us in twenty-first-century America, "Naturalism") that drives scientism in our age (not science but its antithesis, a religious belief in science). *Abolition* is a prophetic book, accurately predicting the consequences of rejecting objective truth and using doubt (what Lewis calls "debunking") as one's only approach to reality.

Of course, I find all Lewis's work formative. My conversion, you might say, began at the age of six when my mother bought me the seven Narnia books, and I spent the next ten years searching for that land.

Mere Christianity opened the door to the concept of objective truth, so necessary in the search for God and, incidentally, mental and spiritual health. But as a mother striving to guide her children's education, I'd say that *The Abolition of Man* is the one to read. Many times in my writing and in personal e-mails to readers, I urge the study of education—the philosophy behind it—as much as possible when the children are young. This is how one develops the discernment necessary as the deluge of possibilities (for instance, what to buy for curriculum) hits. Start here with *Abolition*.

By the way, it would make a perfect book to read with your crafting/play/nursing/young moms/dinner group—one chapter every month or so.

Cookbooks in the Library Project

continuing my answer to the young woman who asked *what* she could read in the early years to get ready for the hard work ahead—I offer some cookbooks for your perusal. Full disclosure: I spent a lot of time in my younger days just *reading* cookbooks, as opposed to dipping in merely for recipes. I learned a lot this way!

After all, being prepared gives you mental toughness. And as the announcers of a Boston Marathon we listened to on the radio one year on the way home from the race kept pointing out, *you just can't measure mental toughness.* But you'll need it for your family's gustatory requirements.

There are two kinds of cookbooks. There are the lush, photo-rich ones that are all "garnish your charred eggplant with pomegranate seeds," "make peppercorn carrot cake in eighteen steps," and "stroll down to the farmers' market to pick up some organic goat burrata for your basil reduction." (And as anyone who reads *Like Mother, Like Daughter* knows, I, like you, love photos, especially of food.)

And then there are cookbooks that will teach you to cook systematically and provide you with basic recipes that you can modify to your heart's content, including ethnically (so don't lightly dismiss these even if your culture is different from the mostly American one these books admittedly represent).

It used to be that a bride got a small stack of useful, informative books upon her marriage—and they were the ones she had grown up with in her mom's kitchen anyway—and she was all set. She didn't know what a pomegranate is, perhaps, but she could make a pie and a stew and a roast.

With the Internet, I'm afraid that we're just filing away recipes and wondering why our crockpot chicken is tasteless; and then buying the trending cookbooks, which, granted, are irresistible, and in general getting overwhelmed by the stark necessity of *meals*.

I'm sometimes a little surprised, honestly, that when I say to my readers something like "use any sweet dinner roll recipe" or "look up pot-roasting techniques in a comprehensive cookbook," they don't always know what I mean. Hence, a meditation on foundational cookbooks, for the floundering sort of homemaker, the one who thinks in terms of recipes and not cooking with the confidence of one who grasps the process—and in general just having trouble with meals. These are books to *read*.

The Joy of Cooking (1975 edition), by Irma Rombauer, combines recipes, solid analytical information, and a chatty style that can just warm a young woman's heart. You feel as if you're learning from a friend—but really learning *every single thing* you need to know about eggs and butter and sugar and cuts of meat at the butcher. And if you should need to know what to do with a haunch of boar or a leg of venison, perchance, you are in luck. There are menu suggestions that can spark a helpful train of thinking for you.

Julia Child, in *The Way to Cook*, if you don't want to commit to *Mastering the Art of French Cooking* (two volumes), will explain techniques to you. Her *Mastering the Art of French Cooking* is a correspondence course in technique. It may seem counterproductive to have six embedded recipes for making a spinach dish unless you understand what she's trying to do; she's teaching you to fish, not giving you a fish—er, spinach.

In my early days, I made just about everything in *Mastering*, working my way through, meticulously following Julia Child's directions. Had there been blogging in those days, Amy Adams would have been playing me in

Julie and Julia, because I totally did that (and was a lot nicer to my husband than that awful Julie was to hers). (I mean, I was no great shakes, but I was nicer than she.)

And I learned to bone and cook a chicken breast to a fare-thee-well. I can enrich a sauce. I can laminate a dough. I'm so glad I delved into Child's books, because later, it would have been harder to find and spend the time. I literally read all my cookbooks—these and others (for instance, *Larousse Gastronomique*—from cover to cover, multiple times). I know a tremendous amount of French vocabulary for food due to this effort. And yes, I should have been cleaning the house instead of doing this! I suppose . . .

The All New Good Housekeeping Cookbook, edited by Susan Westmoreland, pre-2001, is an inside joke at my house. With my loyalty to *Joy* and Julia fairly rock-solid, I admit I looked with a certain scorn upon this one. I'd taste something delicious that Suki had made but turn up my nose when she said it was from this cookbook. It's more of a straightforward compendium of recipes, without the overtly systematic approach that I appreciate in the others—so I kept referring to it as "that bad cookbook."

When I found one for a dollar at a library sale (a library-bound version, very helpful in a cookbook, with the plastic cover), I made one or two things out of it just to see. Well, it has the virtue of having tasty, tested recipes (yes, like the ones Suki made)! We all like the recipes we use from this book. So we do recommend it. (Similar books would be *The Fannie Farmer Cookbook* and the *Betty Crocker Cookbook*, but I didn't learn with them, and I don't know about various editions. Yet, if you see them at a yard sale, snatch them up. After all, they are time-tested.)

On a lower tier, but very helpful, is *Elegant Meals with Inexpensive Meats*, by Cynthia Scheer. It's quite small and possibly screams eighties. But for thirty years, I have made the things in it—it's in tatters. Why? Because it's methodical and gives you the *whys* and *wherefores* about meat, not just the recipes. And if you are committed to figuring out how to live simply, you need instruction in how to save money on meats. With this book you can figure out all the various cuts you are presented with at the supermarket—most importantly, how to cook them well. Could you recognize a cut of meat if it were presented to you crosswise rather than lengthwise?

Would you still know what kind of heat to use on it? Could you remove the tendon from a piece of otherwise tender chuck steak? Can you tell what a cut is, even if it is given a regional name at the store, just by looking at it? Scheer's book really helps with all that.

This is my organizing principle for a cookbook: that it teach you something about methods and have *time-tested* recipes.

Patterns, Architectural and Otherwise

A *Pattern Language: Towns, Buildings, Construction*, by Christopher Alexander, Sara Ishikawa, and Murray Silverstein, raises "thinking about things" and "ways of doing" to an entirely new level. The authors set about organizing the world—with no irony. To me, it's delightful—the thought that there is some set of principles that can be applied to cities and to closets. To you, it might be madness.

The subject of patterns in life—manifestations of order that somehow relate to other kinds of order and make human life deeper, richer, more possible—instantly grabs my attention. I knew I had to read this book.

The question of why buildings today (but also streets and towns) are ugly begs an answer, because how can it be that we have vast stores of knowledge and mountains of technology, yet millions of people are doomed to live in homes whose mere proportions are an affront? How is it that a lone man with an ax (Pa Ingalls, e.g.) can build a house that, while humble and undeniably small, has charm; but there are whole square miles of land in our country that are devoured by monstrosities of energy-gobbling, Palladio-mocking, plywood palaces that won't last the span of a lifetime?

A *Pattern Language* encompasses more than homebuilding, as I say, but isn't it interesting that, despite the professionalization and industrialization of this activity, our new homes lack a certain something of those of the past? Our constructions might look classical (if that's what they are trying for), but they aren't classical. They can't do it even when they try.[28]

Bathrooms apart,[29] there is nothing superior about most present-day construction. But if you are thinking about remodeling or building or even arranging furniture, you need to take a look at this book. If you are involved, as Mr. Lawler has been, with planning in your town or city, then you must read it, as many of our bylaws and codes make it impossible to have humane communities. Christopher Alexander explains why.[30] The fact is, I wrote these volumes because my mind works this way; I try to discover patterns and apply them to everything.

I have so many thoughts about *A Pattern Language*. Ultimately, it falls short by failing to understand that the order Alexander extols relates to the objective order of beauty in the cosmos and in God's mind. This failing

---

[28] I also recommend *Get Your House Right: Architectural Elements to Use and Avoid*, by Marianne Cusato. It has clear drawings of good and bad examples to help you achieve the design you are seeking.

[29] Another good book on the subject: *The Geography of Nowhere: The Rise and Decline of America's Man-Made Landscape*, which makes this point about bathrooms. There's no arguing with a nice bathroom. The rest of the book is one long, sustained rant against the modern way of building home and cities. Author James Howard Kunstler has some funky progressive ideas, and he contradicts himself occasionally. All that aside, the book is thought provoking as criticism. I especially appreciated the insight that when life was less regulated, rich and poor lived much closer together than they can today, even if they want to. That apartment over the garage or the neighborhood business goes a long way toward creating a just society, bringing together as it does those who otherwise would live on opposite sides of the city, never encountering each other apart from their economic transactions.

[30] Alexander's, and by extension Kunstler's, ideas need to be kept distinct from what is called "new urbanism." In theory, this movement incorporates their (and others') ideas, but in practice, it's often just another exercise in lame and even mocking reference to cherished forms. Until we, as a society, can overcome our desire to regulate everything, we probably won't have organic and lively communities, architecturally speaking.

means that at times there is an odd spirituality that creeps into his think-ing. The one pattern of the past that Alexander is blind to is the literal, physical centrality of the church to a thriving community; to be sure, he mentions the church, but not as the locus.

I must also mention that although I understand the pitiful explanation for the truly inadequate visuals in the book, I deplore it. Obviously, the book would be enhanced by really good illustrations. Those little scribblings are so frustrating. But these criticisms aside, I recommend A *Pattern Language* highly as one of those very few books in life that makes all the little men in your brain run around setting off fireworks!

It's not the kind of book that I can imagine reading on an e-reader, by the way. You dive into a section, go back, go forward, take a peek at what interests you (porches? benches? alleys? bedrooms for children? kitchen cupboards? street frontage? daylight? windowsills?), reread. Finally, you will begin to understand why that step up to her kitchen from the dining room is a feature of Grandma's house, not a problem; and why that balcony at the resort wasn't actually appealing. You may not even have known that it's better for a town to have benches in the park where someone can lie down than to set things up so no one can stop moving.

This book put me in mind of the truth elaborated by Michael Oake-shott in *Rationalism in Politics*, that the things in life that make it beautiful, doable, and enjoyable cannot be reduced to a rational list or be broken into managerial steps. In the past, people built up a body of knowledge that is now hard to recover—a decisive and intentional break having been implemented under the profoundly mistaken notion that going forward, there was nothing we couldn't figure out on our own.

We see the result all around us in the ugliness and, ironically, consider-ing the emphasis placed on function by those who did the dismantling, the inefficiency of our lives. Alexander offers us a way to think about how we can recover some of those old patterns and apply them in our own day.

The Way of Beauty

avid Clayton's *The Way of Beauty*[31] could provide the pattern missing in Christopher Alexander's book (discussed in the previous chapter).

As you may know, David Clayton and I coauthored *The Little Oratory: A Beginner's Guide to Praying in the Home.* Our primary focus there was living the faith in the home, but the reader also gets little hints of his thesis for *The Way of Beauty*, which is the fruit of David's contemplation of beauty and how to inspire its pursuit in the educational setting. If you visit Thomas More College, you will encounter his ideas in action there. The college is a tiny place where the formerly dreary chapel has been made beautiful and great books are studied and *lived*, thanks to David's vision.

The Way of Beauty offers the *principles* needed to make good choices; not so much a laundry list of a curriculum but that elusive overarching framework that we're always searching for. Above all, he gives us objective criteria for beauty by examining mathematical proportions that give rise to harmonious structures (churches and other buildings). Without this

---

[31] David Clayton, *The Way of Beauty: Liturgy, Education, and Inspiration for Family, School, and College* (Brooklyn: Angelico Press, 2015).

objectivity, we are always floundering around, trying to make cultural headway by preference alone. At most, we will find ourselves simply *asserting* something about beauty, and ultimately that will not satisfy; it will seem to be a matter of control or power. We need to connect beauty to transcendent qualities.

David practically and concisely renders lofty philosophical ideas about beauty and its objectivity into understandable prose, making it possible for the family and anyone involved in building an educational institution to know how to go about applying them. These days, with so many homeschoolers starting co-ops and homeschool-support programs, it's vital to have good solid principles to work with.

Especially enjoyable and inspiring is David's recounting of his Oxford days and what characteristics made his time there, ultimately, amount to a real education, even though he wasn't (by his own account) a greatly motivated student. You will be consoled if you happen to know anyone who meets that description; anyone in your home, let's say, even perhaps related to you! David explains that more depends on the culture of a community than on any one particular thing that's done there, and demonstrates that the culture arises from beauty in worship.

To Educate Children, You
Need Books on the Shelves

I have been working on the Library Project for so long, just so our readers can put something on their shelves (and relieve themselves, as one wit commented, of the need to "style" them). We are discussing homeschooling and how to go about it, and unlike cleaning your cast-iron pans, you can't just purchase two things and be all set. (Although, modern life being in thwart mode, one of those things, the strong, *flexible* metal spatula, is incredibly hard to source. I know, because after I posted on the subject, mine died. I had it for only thirty-six years, although I concede that it had been my husband's before we married. More on all this in volume 3.)

But there is a way to relieve the burden on yourself to be providing the all-too-elusive "complete education" for your children at every moment. And it's the same solution to the opposite problem, which is resting too much confidence in that school you are sending them to, the one that you may be paying a lot for, but that simply can't give them the depth of *experience with a life lived with books* that they need.

For it's the home itself that is the learning environment; the medium (as well as the message) of their intellectual formation. (A good school would complement this environment and even expand on it, but there is a shortage of good schools.)

Specifically, the family simply must have actual books on the bookshelves! An article about e-books in a *New York Times* article makes this point:

> Amazon Kindle's Family Library enables two adults in a household to share content with each other and up to four children. But parents must explicitly select which of their books their kids can read. So much for the "casual atmosphere of living in a bookish world."

Leaving aside the "up to four children" curve ball for large families, and also the very real question of *where those books are and whom they belong to*, let's think about how much pressure it puts on you, especially if you are homeschooling (but again, even if you are not, because you're still not only responsible for educating your children, but undeniably you are meant to be their most influential role model), in a sense to come up with an ongoing, relentless "curriculum" in which you somehow give your child the right book at the right time, all the time.

It's not possible. It's not desirable. It's not normal.

Yet somehow, between the disappearance of bookstores, perhaps, and maybe even the ubiquity of that sort of new home that doesn't have many walls—open-concept living doesn't have much scope for bookcases, I think—but most of all because of the socially engineered gap in the collective memory, I see a lot of parents attempting what I consider to be impossible: raising children without books.

Sometimes I'm in a home where there is plenty of new furniture and everything is neat and tidy, but there are no books! And I truly wonder, "How is it that you are homeschooling? How do you do it?"

Think of it this way. If you have all sorts of books, you are outsourcing your task of teaching the children everything. What a relief! A home library leaves you free to pursue your own interests. In turn, pursuing your own interests leads to a richer environment in the home, which furthers the education of the children.

It is possible to learn a lot in a serendipitous way online. There's no question that you can search for the answer to one question and end up in many possible different enchanting places. You can also (and especially if you are young) end up in a lot of desperately awful places, in a way that you simply can't in the home library (and couldn't back in the day in the public library, but that's another issue).

For a good fundamental education, one actually doesn't need a vast library, but one does need the habit of picking up a book. Reading doesn't necessarily come easily. The physical book has an allure that rewards the beginnings of the habit; there is a pleasure in the materials that the book is made of, its illustrations, its binding, that will be lost if everything is leveled to bytes, no matter how useful the virtual product can sometimes be.

I know that the difficulty is in having the confidence to commit. Hence, my attempt on the blog that I call the Like Mother, Like Daughter Library Project. I discuss how to discern which books you ought to be acquiring, as well as which ones to avoid. We even go through the steps of a day spent hopping from used-book sale to used-book sale.

It's true—you may end up with some awfully random volumes, such as the one I recently found on a shelf in a remote bedroom: *Professional Piano Tuning*. And after a decade or two, things might not be in the right categories. But consider the advantage. At any given moment, your child can be reading about, well, any good thing. Anything at all.

A Last Word about Family Culture, Education, and the World

When the weight of ordinary life, special circumstances, or current events feels crushing, remember one thing that shouldn't surprise you, if you are familiar with the Gospels: the antidote to what is huge, overpowering, and violent is that which is small, meek, and humble.

Paradoxically, the remedy for what ails the world is found in the heart of your home. The family forms children in so many ways, not all of them academic, and not all of them (or even most) becoming immediately apparent. Your efforts, especially in striving for virtue and prayer—the prayer of your family, the life you live in union with the Church—joined with the faithful lives of other families, build up the Kingdom.

The home is where we can speak openly about what we really think, whether it is to family members only or with trusted friends as well. We can encourage one another in the task of raising children and following God. This openness is the means by which the goodness of the home becomes available to the larger community and becomes a real force for vigorous life in society. The less welcome we feel to express our true thoughts in the larger arena, the more important it becomes to cultivate open and free conversations in person. Your home is the basis of a real community of people who enjoy each other, find friends for their kids, and help each other in times of need. My friend William Edmund Fahey, president of Thomas More College, writes, on the topic of how great books alone are not enough to make an education: "In [Aristotle's] view, a good education must find the balance between the theoretical, the useful, and that which will form student in virtue. Aristotle admitted to being puzzled as to how one finds the balance. Would that Aristotle had encountered Christ."[32] Life in Christ is life in all its modes and manifestations, providing the balance among all the criteria, even in the midst of our fallen condition. In the sanctuary of the home, we can teach the child the way he should go, with all the love, affection, and firm authority that suit the task perfectly. Have hope and be of good cheer in the beautiful enterprise of educating your children.

---

[32] Beverly Stevens, "Restoring a Radical Tradition," *Regina Magazine*, October 1, 2015, https://www.reginamag.com/restoring-a-radical-tradition/.

Appendices

Appendices

APPENDIX A

Book Lists

n my blog *Like Mother, Like Daughter*, I have many book recommendations in the categories of books, read-alouds, and the Library Project.

In his important work *The Death of Christian Culture*, John Senior appends an excellent book list. That list is reprinted at the end of the delightful essay by William Fahey, "Will Rascals Defend Our Civilization ... and What Books Will They Read?"[33]

For a reading list inspired by the curriculum advocated by Charlotte Mason, see the Ambleside Online site; it has a multitude of suggestions, organized by academic level. The suggestions for additional books for free reading are particularly helpful.

Michael O'Brien has a good book list at the end of his book *A Landscape with Dragons*.

---

[33] William Edmund Fahey, "Will Rascals Defend Our Civilization ... and What Books Will They Read?" *Crisis Magazine*, February 24, 2012, https://www.crisismagazine.com/2012/naughty-boys-and-the-defense-of-civilization-must-we-choose-between-great-or-good-books.

The Mater Amabilis website (MaterAmabilis.org) has many good rec-ommendations, including mentioning problematic editions and updates.

On her blog *Wildflowers and Marbles* Jennifer Mackintosh has helpful booklists embedded in her curriculum suggestions.

Theresa Fagan's *A Mother's List of Books* is invaluable.[34] Theresa is a good friend who alerted me to the need to snatch up books from public-library purges back when I was starting out in my journey of motherhood.

---

[34] The book is available at https://www.amotherslistofbooks.com/.

APPENDIX B

Family Albums for Listening

Fred Penner, *The Cat Came Back*
Raffi, *The Singable Songs Collection*
Sharon, Lois, and Bram, *Great Big Hits*
Elizabeth Mitchell, *You Are My Sunshine*
Nancy Cassidy's albums. She has a voice in a lower pitch which, for us altos, can be a nice change.
Wee Sing America
Bonnie Rideout, *Gi'me Elbow Room* (Scottish favorites)
Emma and Cecilia Black, *Singsong Pennywhistle, Barnyard Dance*
Pa's Fiddle: Charles Ingalls, American Fiddler (the fiddle music of the Little House books)
The Laura Ingalls Wilder Songbook
Burl Ives, *A Collection of Ballads and Folk Songs*
Smithsonian American Folkways recordings

APPENDIX C

Favorite Audiobooks

on't let the professionalism of audiobooks deter you from reading aloud to your children. They love *you*! Reading to them is *so different* from listening to a recording.

Do you have that one child who rarely lets you give him a hug? Do you know that you have to work on making sure you physically touch your children more? In this rushed, busy, hectic life of ours, we need a good excuse to build cuddles into our lives. Reading together is all that and more.

Audiobooks have their own merits, but when you read aloud to your children, you have the chance to stop and talk about things, to laugh and enjoy and savor something you really love, to reread a particularly relished section, to shed a tear together. Bridget and I practically sobbed through the ending of C. S. Lewis's *The Last Battle*, just the two of us on the sofa; for both of us, the vision of Heaven was so beautiful and moving, and for me, I was conscious that this would be the last time I'd read it to one of my children, making the tears extra bittersweet.

All that said, there are times when a recording of a book supplies a need. So, without further ado, here is a list of our favorites—and that means that we *love* the narrator as well as the story.

For Littles

The Tale of Peter Rabbit, by Beatrix Potter. When I was little, I had a (vinyl) record of this whimsical and adorable tale, narrated by Vivien Leigh. Somehow, when I had children of my own, I found a copy in a record store! I really did shed tears when I heard it again, with its delightful songs. You can now purchase a digital recording.

A Bear Called Paddington, by Michael Bond, narrated by Stephen Fry

Frog and Toad, by Arnold Lobel, narrated by the author

Mouse Tales, by Arnold Lobel, narrated by the author

Little Bear books, by Else Holmelund Minarik, narrated by Sigourney Weaver

Little House in the Big Woods, by Laura Ingalls Wilder, narrated by Cherry Jones

Henry Huggins, by Beverly Cleary, narrated by Neil Patrick Harris

Beezus and Henry, by Beverly Cleary, narrated by William Roberts

Vivaldi's Ring of Mystery. As Deirdre says: "It will never get old. I say that having grown up on it myself and now listening to it at a rate that would make me want to smash and burn a lesser recording—but I still love it to pieces." By the same company, *Mr. Bach Comes to Call* is nice—not as stellar as the Vivaldi but still well done.

Winnie-the-Pooh, by A.A. Milne. Deirdre prefers the Jim Broadbent narration to the others, even the Stephen Fry one.

For Those Middle Years

The Melendy Quartet, by Elizabeth Enright, narrated by Pamela Dillman

The Railway Children, by E. Nesbit, narrated by Alice Marti

Centerburg Tales, by John McCloskey, narrated by John McDonough

Great and Good Books for Older Children and Adults

Narrated by the great Martin Jarvis:

David Copperfield, by Charles Dickens

Hard Times, by Charles Dickens

Cranford, by Elizabeth Gaskell

The Canterbury Tales, by Chaucer. This one is narrated by Jarvis and others; if you go to the listing on Audible and look at the reviews, you will find a very helpful one in which the reviewer has offered an"index" of the places in the recording at which to find each tale.

Orgueil et préjugés, by Jane Austen. Do you have someone who is learning French? How about *Pride and Prejudice* in French! My thinking is that if you already know a work backward and forward, listening to it in another language helps with facility. Great narration by Évelyne Lecucq. The translation has come under criticism from some reviewers on Amazon, but it sounded fine to me.

The Abolition of Man and *The Great Divorce*, by C. S. Lewis. The former work must be read carefully and absorbed slowly, but hearing it can be a good supplement!

Uneasy Money, by P. G. Wodehouse. I also like Simon Vance's narration (he did the one above as well). His relaxed voice is easy to listen to!

Dombey and Son, by Charles Dickens, narrated by Frederick Davidson (not Jarvis but pretty good!)

Sir Gawain and the Green Knight, narrated by Bill Wallace. For the advanced student who really wants to hear the Middle English.

Father Sergius and Other Short Stories, by Tolstoy, narrated by Simon Vance

Middlemarch, by George Eliot, narrated by Juliet Stevenson, another favorite narrator of mine

Lord of the Rings, by J. R. R. Tolkien, narrated by Rob Inglis

Bonus: A Couple of Fun Audiobooks for You

What Alice Forgot, by Liane Moriarty. I love the narrator of this book: her accent is perfect for the Australian setting. I will say that it's a book that is only for adults. It's a delightful read that makes you look at life differently, and overall the message is a good, even excellent, one, well delivered. However, there are moral issues that are dealt with in a less than upright way: IVF is taken for granted as a good thing, and even abortion is passed over lightly. In a lesser story, these things would be dealbreakers; in this story, I think the mature person has enough to consider, and the main message is so cleverly delivered that it's worth simply having one's own mental reservations and moving on. I don't think a teen should be subjected to that, though.

The Hundred and One Dalmatians, by Dodie Smith, narrated by Martin Jarvis

APPENDIX D

A Word on "Youth Ministry"

Youth ministry should consist in family life lived in the context of the liturgical year (as I describe, along with David Clayton, in *The Little Oratory: A Beginner's Guide to Praying in the Home*), Bible study, and studies in the *Catechism of the Catholic Church*. Families who enjoy being together and parishes that encourage family life will take part in activities that are perfectly normal and uncontrived: bonfires, dances (contra dances, swing-dance competitions, formal waltzes, square dances —whatever they enjoy), feast-day barbecues, and so on.

Most, but not all, of these activities will include all ages, although some will naturally center on one age group. In his *Crisis Magazine* article "How to Identify a Healthy Culture," Anthony Esolen asks:

> When we get together with all of our neighbors, what do we do? Do we build a house, raise a barn, glean the corn, bale the hay, march in parade, listen to patriotic speeches, play music, compete in games of skill or speed or strength, sing songs, honor the dead, or fall to our knees in prayer? Do we in fact do anything with our neighbors?

I want to gently encourage you to resist the idea that you must rely on experts to bring your children into adulthood in their Faith. The family, together with the community and the Church, is uniquely constituted to make this transition.

For years, I've been saying, to high criticism from the gatekeepers of the youth-ministry industry (for that is what it is), that in the Church we need fewer programs and more family life and good liturgy (with beauty and peace). To many, my assertion seems crazy. I've had mothers look at me with tears in their eyes at the panicked thought of not sending their children to youth conferences, even though they know that the form and content of these events goes against their principles.

The conviction we can't shake is that we have to instruct people consciously on what they need to know at every moment. A little instruction is always necessary. But more than that, we need community life, family life, and worship of God.

An elderly lady in our parish (she has since passed away) told me about Vespers, held every Wednesday evening, during the Depression. The people were poor, of course, so for the youth, it was a way to get out and do something. They loved it, although you can be sure it wasn't aimed at them.

Do you not think that by going to Vespers the faithful became more moral (by being closer to Christ, who is goodness itself), more able to discern their paths, even though that's not the "point" of Vespers and Vespers isn't a morality program?

In *The Red Horse* (a book I highly recommend), an officer on the Russian front who comes from a little town in Italy, dismayed by the depravity of his men, muses that it's "the Rosaries of our parents" that kept him and his fellow officers, all of whom come from the same small city, from succumbing to pornography and other evils at the front.

Eugenio Corti, the author, shows how the people attended Vespers every evening (of course, the church was right there in the village; they could walk). He connects this worship with their ability to discern the truth in their everyday life.

We are starving for worship and authentic community life. Not lectures, not apologetics. All the doctrine we need is contained in the Liturgy. Of course we should study. Study is beautiful. But wisdom and understanding are *gifts* of the Holy Spirit, and they are *given* when we come close to and receive Jesus Christ. The amount of actual study required for a young person is quite small (yet they do not get what they need in youth ministry!).

The St. Gregory Pockets (discussed at length in volume 1) will help you realize this vision for youth down the road; do familiarize yourself with this blueprint for getting started on building the community that has been lost.

All the programs in the world will not teach a thing and, *in fact, will convince people of the opposite of what we are trying to tell them*, if we do not have life in Christ: worship, family life, really restful Sundays, the liturgical year. And if we have those things, the programs will be seen to be unnecessary.

INDEX

repetition, 164, 199, 299
The Republic (Plato), 36
The Restoration of Christian Culture (Senior), 25, 239
retellings, 116–117
rewards, reading and, 282
Rhetoric (Aristotle), 74
rhythm, 121
Richard Scarry's Best Mother Goose Ever (Scarry), 300
Rideout, Bonnie, 359
Roberts, William, 361
Robinson, Arthur, 29, 166, 185, 189
Robinson, Jackie, 285
Robinson Curriculum, 29
Rombauer, Irma, 341
Rosary, 87, 365
rotation, 164
rote learning, 166
Rowling, J. K., 278, 309
rules
    "Christian's Rule of Life," 240
    in libraries, 296, 298

sacred music, 204–205
sadness
    in childhood, 218–219
    external causes of, 219–220
    inner life and, 215–216
    moral sadness, 220–221
    pretending and, 217
    spiritual desolation, 220–222
Saint-Saëns, Camille, 207
Salve Regina, 203
same-sex relationships, 256, 262–263
Saxon Math, 164, 165

Sayers, Dorothy, 22–23, 36, 131, 166, 194
The Scarlet Pimpernel (Orczy), 310
Scarry, Richard, 300
scary news, talking to children about, 252–255
Schall, James, 26
Scheer, Cynthia, 342–343
School of Athens (painting) (Raphael), 32–33
science
    about, 184
    anxiety over teaching, 193–195
    calculus and, 166, 167
    fostering love of, 185–186
    nature journals, 188–189
    observation, 187
    stereomicroscopes, 190–192
The Scotch Twins (Perkins), 157
Scottish games, 8–9
Scripture. *See* Bible
    Catechism and, 243
    hymns and, 202
    reading, 239
    St. Joseph Baltimore Catechism and, 229
    study of literature and, 322
    virtue and, 221
Scruton, Roger, 15
Searching for and Maintaining Peace (Philippe), 14
Second Coming, 229
second graders, 31, 77, 141
secondary school. *See also* upper grades
    mathematics, 164–167
Seeger, Pete, 206
Selected Letters of James Thurber (Thurber), 147n11

Sophia Institute

Sophia Institute is a nonprofit institution that seeks to nurture the spiritual, moral, and cultural life of souls and to spread the gospel of Christ in conformity with the authentic teachings of the Roman Catholic Church.

Sophia Institute Press fulfills this mission by offering translations, reprints, and new publications that afford readers a rich source of the enduring wisdom of mankind.

Sophia Institute also operates the popular online resource Catholic-Exchange.com. *Catholic Exchange* provides world news from a Catholic perspective as well as daily devotionals and articles that will help readers to grow in holiness and live a life consistent with the teachings of the Church.

In 2013, Sophia Institute launched Sophia Institute for Teachers to renew and rebuild Catholic culture through service to Catholic education. With the goal of nurturing the spiritual, moral, and cultural life of souls, and an abiding respect for the role and work of teachers, we strive to provide materials and programs that are at once enlightening to the mind and ennobling to the heart; faithful and complete, as well as useful and practical.

Sophia Institute gratefully recognizes the Solidarity Association for preserving and encouraging the growth of our apostolate over the course of many years. Without their generous and timely support, this book would not be in your hands.

www.SophiaInstitute.com
www.CatholicExchange.com
www.SophiaInstituteforTeachers.org

Sophia Institute Press® is a registered trademark of Sophia Institute.
Sophia Institute is a tax-exempt institution as defined by the
Internal Revenue Code, Section 501(c)(3). Tax ID 22-2548708.